DATE DUE

PRINTED IN U.S.A.

CRIMINAL PROCEDURE
Law and Practice

Second Edition

About the Author

Rolando V. del Carmen is currently Professor of Criminal Justice in the College of Criminal Justice, Sam Houston State University. He holds a Master of Comparative Law from Southern Methodist University, a Master of Laws from the University of California at Berkeley, and a Doctor of the Science of Law degree from the University of Illinois at Champaign-Urbana.

He was Assistant Dean and Associate Professor of the College of Law, Silliman University, in the Philippines and has held administrative and academic positions in the United States. He has taught in various universities and has written extensively. His publications include articles in law journals and several books, the latest being *Civil Liabilities in American Policing* (Prentice-Hall, forthcoming).

In 1986, Dr. del Carmen won the Faculty Excellence in Research award at Sam Houston State University, the first such award ever to be given in the then 108-year history of that university. He has been appointed by Governor Bill Clements to a six-year term in the Texas Commission on Jail Standards and currently serves as vice chairman. He has been named the 1990 Academy Fellow by the Academy of Criminal Justice Sciences.

CRIMINAL PROCEDURE
Law and Practice

Second Edition

Rolando V. del Carmen
Sam Houston State University

Brooks/Cole Publishing Company
Pacific Grove, California

To my wife, Josie, and my daughter, Jocelyn,
and to my colleagues and students
at the Criminal Justice Center

Brooks/Cole Publishing Company
A Division of Wadsworth, Inc.

Printed in the United States of America

10 9 8 7 6 5 4 3 2 1

Library of Congress Cataloging-in-Publication Data

Del Carmen, Rolando V.
   Criminal procedure: law and practice / Rolando V. del Carmen.—
2nd ed.
      p.   cm.
   Rev. ed. of: Criminal procedure for law enforcement personnel.
   © 1987
   Includes bibliographical references and index.
   ISBN 0-534-15552-9
   1. Criminal procedure—United States.   2. Criminal procedure—
United States—Cases.   I. Del Carmen, Rolando V.   Criminal
procedure for law enforcement personnel.   II. Title.
KF9619.D45   1991
345.73′05—dc20
[347.3055]   90-49935
                                                          CIP

Sponsoring Editor: Cynthia C. Stormer
Marketing Representative: Ragu Raghavan
Editorial Assistant: Cathleen S. Collins
Production Coordinator: Fiorella Ljunggren
Production: Rosaleen Bertolino, Bookman Productions
Manuscript Editor: Linda Purrington
Permissions Editor: Carline Haga
Interior Design: Judith Levinson
Cover Design: Roy R. Neuhaus
Art Coordinator: Bookman Productions
Typesetting: Graphic Typesetting Service
Cover Printing: Lehigh Press Lithographers/Autoscreen
Printing and Binding: Arcata Graphics/Fairfield

PREFACE

Law enforcement is essentially what the term literally means—the enforcement of law by duly authorized agents of the state. The term implies that knowledge of the law is central and essential to law enforcement work. Without it, an officer loses sight of the framework for proper job performance; with it, the officer becomes a worthy agent of the immense power of the state. It is important that law enforcement officers know the law; otherwise, public confidence is diminished, if not betrayed.

This text acquaints the reader with the various aspects of criminal procedure. Laws that govern police work have their basis primarily in the U.S. Constitution, the decisions of the U.S. Supreme Court, and statutes passed by state legislatures. This text focuses on these sources but cautions that other court decisions and agency policies must be given equal attention, particularly if they further limit what an officer can do.

The book covers a variety of topics relevant to law enforcement work, from court systems (Chapter One) to sentencing (Chapter Fourteen). Chapter Fifteen discusses a relatively new but growing concern in law enforcement: legal liabilities. Court decisions, in some cases leading to huge damage awards, have had a direct impact on the daily operation of law enforcement agencies and are perhaps currently the single most influential determinant of police agency procedures. That will continue to be a reality in the foreseeable future, hence legal liabilities must be studied and understood.

The study of law can be complex and tedious, as law students have long discovered. It can also be confusing and frustrating, particularly when no specific guidelines are given by statute or court decisions. These imperfections must be recognized and accepted as inherent in any social organization. Judges, prosecutors, defense lawyers, and court personnel have developed terms and concepts that are part of criminal justice usage and that law enforcement officers must learn and understand. Any law-oriented text written primarily for students and in-service personnel faces the challenge of presenting legal terms and concepts in a less obscure and understandable manner without unduly losing substance or content. That is a task this text undertakes. The text presents criminal procedure in a format and language that, we hope, meet the needs and interests of nonlawyers and yet preserve the substance and content of the law.

The text has several features that aid in the understanding and retention of legal material. These are:

- frequent use of examples and illustrations
- analysis and comparison of leading court cases
- a chapter outline at the beginning of each chapter
- a listing of key terms at the beginning of each chapter, in the order they appear in the text

- the presentation of topics in outline form, and use of the narrative style to discuss the topics
- highlighted sections
- samples of police forms
- a summary of the principles of cases at the end of each chapter
- definitions of legal terms used in each chapter
- case briefs of some leading cases at the end of each chapter
- a summary and review questions at the end of each chapter

There are various paths to learning, none of which works equally well with everybody. Legal material, however, is perhaps best learned and retained through mastery of concepts reinforced by examples. As frequently as possible, the text defines a concept and then further clarifies it with an example when appropriate. Situations in law enforcement can never be exactly alike, hence students must learn to apply legal principles, enunciated in court-decided cases, to actual field situations that sometimes involve high risk. If legal concepts are understood well, their applications to similar situations become easier. Memorizing a definition is much less important than understanding and applying it.

The text is so arranged that the sequence of topics is easy to follow. The definition of terms and the summary of case principles at the end of each chapter should reduce the need for notetaking from the text and make it easier to review the chapter. The summaries are useful in retaining the material in compact form; the discussion questions help identify the important topics in the book; and the highlights focus on statements or information worthy of special note.

Although the United States comprises fifty-one different jurisdictions (the fifty states and the federal government), criminal procedure largely transcends jurisdictional boundaries and is applied nationwide. The rules governing law enforcement have, by and large, been "nationalized" through U.S. Supreme Court decisions interpreting specific constitutional provisions, particularly the Bill of Rights. Nonetheless, variations in state procedures abound, particularly where such variations involve no violations of constitutional rights. The legal doctrines and principles discussed in the text apply nationwide except where state law, local ordinance, or agency policy declare otherwise and such are not inconsistent with court decisions or the Constitution. This text is not written for one state or jurisdiction; therefore knowledge of the content of the text should not be a substitute for familiarity with state law or agency policy.

Acknowledgments

The author would like to thank the following colleagues for their various contributions to the book: David Carter of Michigan State University, Tim Oettmeier of the Houston Police Department, Tom Hickey of the University of Oregon Law School, Jack Enter of the Georgia Criminal Justice Coordinating Council, William Pelfrey of Western Carolina University, Richard Christian of the Montgomery County Sheriff Department, and Emory Plitt, General Counsel of the Maryland Department of Public Safety and Correctional Services. My faculty colleagues, administrators, and students at the Criminal Justice Center, Sam Houston State University, gave me full support and encouragement in the writing of this book. They also served as knowledgeable sounding boards for the interpretation of legal concepts, particularly Jerry Dowling, who teaches the criminal procedure course. Special thanks are due to Jamie Tillerson and Kay Billingsley, who spent countless hours typing and proofreading the original manuscript for the first edition, and to Cheryl Williams, who typed portions of the manuscript for the second edition.

Thanks are also owed to the reviewers of this second edition for their helpful comments: Robert W. Drowns of Metropolitan State University, Robert L. Hardgrave, Jr., of the University of Texas at Austin, Louis Holscher of San Jose State University, Pamela J. Moore of the University of Texas at Arlington, Robert Pagnani of Columbia-Greene Community College, Ray Richards of San Jacinto College, and Alvin J. T. Zumbrun of Catonsville Community College.

The strength of the book flows from many sources, not the least of which are the book's editors; its weaknesses, however, should be attributed mainly to the author.

Rolando V. del Carmen

BRIEF CONTENTS

CONTENTS

CHAPTER TWO
OVERVIEW OF THE CRIMINAL JUSTICE PROCESS   23

CHAPTER SIX

ARREST

121

CHAPTER SEVEN

SEARCHES AND SEIZURES   **160**

CHAPTER FIFTEEN

LEGAL LIABILITIES OF LAW ENFORCEMENT PERSONNEL 429

THE COURT SYSTEM AND SOURCES OF RIGHTS

☐ KEY TERMS

dual court system	Bill of Rights
federal court system	case law
en banc	incorporation controversy
per curiam	selective incorporation
state court system	total incorporation
jurisdiction	total incorporation plus
venue	case-by-case approach

We open with a discussion of the structure of the federal and state court systems in the United States. Court decisions are the cornerstone of many police policies and practices; hence the effect of judicial decisions must be properly understood. Criminal cases may be tried in federal and state courts if the act constitutes a violation of the laws of both jurisdictions. Next we distinguish the legal concepts of jurisdiction and venue and enumerate the various sources of individual rights. The chapter ends with a discussion of the incorporation controversy—how it developed and its role in determining which constitutional rights extend to an accused in state prosecutions.

I. STRUCTURE OF THE COURT SYSTEM

The United States has a dual court system, meaning that there is one system for federal cases and another for state cases. The term *dual court system* is, however, misleading because what the United States has is fifty-two separate judicial systems representing the court systems in the fifty states, the federal system, and the courts of Washington, DC. But because these systems have much in common they justify a general grouping into two: federal and state.

A. The Federal Court System

The highest court in the *federal court system* is the U.S. Supreme Court. It is composed of a Chief Justice and eight associate justices, all of whom are appointed for life by the president of the United States with the "advice and consent" of the Senate. Supreme Court justices enjoy life tenure and may be removed only by impeachment, which very rarely occurs. The Court is located in Washington, DC, and always decides cases as one body *(en banc)* and never in small groups or panels (in division). Six justices constitute a quorum, but the votes of five justices are needed to win a case. The "Rule of Four" requires the votes of at least four justices for the Court* to consider a case on its merits. Thousands of cases reach the Supreme Court each year from various federal and state courts, but only a few hundred cases are considered by the Court on their merits. The rest are dismissed *per curiam,* meaning that the decision of the immediate lower court in which the case originated (whether it be a state supreme court, a federal court of appeals, or any other court) is left undisturbed. This action does not imply that the Supreme Court agrees with the decision of the lower court. It simply means that the case could not get the votes of at least four justices in order for it to receive further attention and be considered on its merits.

---

*Whenever the word *Court* is used with a capital *C* in this text, the reference is to the U.S. Supreme Court. The word *court* with a lowercase *c* refers to all other courts on the federal or state levels.

Next to the Supreme Court in the federal judicial hierarchy are the U.S. courts of appeals, also referred to as circuit courts. These courts have a total of 132 judgeships and are located in thirteen judicial "circuits" (including the federal circuit) in different regions of the country, each covering three or more states, except the District of Columbia, which has a whole circuit unto itself. Judges of the courts of appeals are appointed by the president of the United States for life with the "advice and consent" of the Senate and can be removed only by impeachment. Unlike the Supreme Court, courts of appeals may hear cases as one body or in groups of three or five judges.

Occupying the lowest level in the hierarchy of federal courts are the district courts. The federal government has 760 federal judgeships located in 94 judicial districts in the United States, Guam, Puerto Rico, and the Virgin Islands. Judges are appointed by the president of the United States for life with the "advice and consent" of the Senate and can be removed only by impeachment. In practice, a recommendation for appointment is made by the senior U.S. senator from that state if he or she belongs to the president's political party.

Also under the federal system are the U.S. magistrate courts, established primarily to relieve district court judges of heavy caseloads. They are presided over by U.S. magistrates (formerly called U.S. commissioners) and have limited authority, such as trying minor offenses and misdemeanor cases in which the possible penalty is incarceration of one year or less. They are also empowered to hold bail hearings, issue warrants, review habeas corpus petitions, and hold pretrial conferences in civil and criminal cases. Magistrates are appointed by district court judges and must be lawyers.

B. The State Court System

The structure of the *state court system* varies from state to state. In general, however, state courts follow the federal pattern. This means that states have a state supreme court that makes final decisions on cases involving state laws and provisions of the state constitution. Some states have different names for their state supreme court, such names as Court of Appeals, Supreme Court of Errors, Supreme Judicial Court, or Supreme Court of Appeals. Texas and Oklahoma have two highest courts—one for civil and the other for criminal cases.

Underneath the state supreme court in the state judicial hierarchy are the intermediate appellate courts. Only thirty-five of the fifty states have intermediate appellate courts. Where they do not exist, appealed cases from the trial courts go directly to the state supreme court.

HIGHLIGHT 1.1

Article III, Section 1, Constitution of the United States

"The judicial Power of the United States, shall be vested in one supreme Court and in such inferior Courts as the Congress may from time to time ordain and establish. The Judges, both of the supreme and inferior Courts, shall hold their Offices during good Behaviour, and shall, at stated times, receive for their Services, a Compensation, which shall not be diminished during their Continuance in office."

Each state has trial courts with general jurisdiction, meaning that they try civil and criminal cases. They go by various names, such as Circuit Court, District Court, or Court of Common Pleas. New York's court of general jurisdiction is called Supreme Court. Although these courts are of general jurisdiction, some states divide them according to specialty areas such as probate, juvenile, and domestic relations.

At the base of the state judicial hierarchy are lower courts such as county courts, justice of the peace courts, and municipal courts. They have limited jurisdiction in both civil and criminal cases and also deal with laws passed by county or city governments.

II. THE EFFECT OF JUDICIAL DECISIONS

The jurisdiction of every U.S. court is limited in some way. One type of limitation is territorial or geographic. In a strict sense, each judicial decision is authoritative and has value as precedent for future cases only within the geographic limits of the area in which the deciding court has jurisdiction. Consequently, U.S. Supreme Court decisions on questions of federal law and the Constitution are binding on all U.S. courts because the whole country is under its jurisdiction. Federal court of appeals decisions are the last word within the circuit if there is no Supreme Court action. The First Circuit Court of Appeals, for example, settles federal issues for Maine, Massachusetts, New Hampshire, Rhode Island, and Puerto Rico, the areas to which its jurisdiction is limited. When a district court encompasses an entire state, as is the case in Maine, its decision on a federal law produces a uniform rule within the state. In a

---

HIGHLIGHT 1.2

The Dual Court System: Simplified Flow Chart

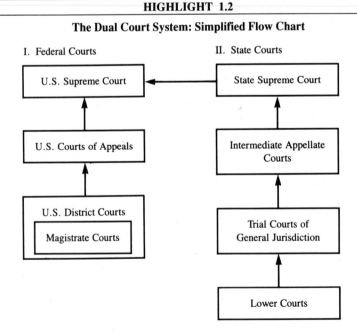

state such as Wisconsin, however, where there are multiple districts, there can be divergent and even conflicting decisions.

The same process operates in the state court systems. There is one regard, however, in which state supreme court decisions are recognized as extending beyond state borders. Since the Constitution declares the sovereignty of the states within the area reserved for state control, the court of last resort of each state is the final arbiter of issues of purely local law. For example, the meaning that the Supreme Court of California gives to a state statute will be respected as authoritative even by the U.S. Supreme Court.

The existence of a dual court system and the limited jurisdictional reach of the vast majority of courts make it highly probable that conflicting decisions on a single point of law will be rendered by the courts. An important function of the appellate process is to provide a forum for resolving these conflicts if the cases are appealed. If no appeal is taken, the conflict remains. For example, a federal district court in the Southern District of Ohio may rule that jail detainees are entitled to contact visits, whereas another federal district court in the Northern District of that state, on a different case, may rule otherwise. The inconsistency will be resolved only if the federal appellate court for Ohio decides the issue in an appealed case.

Despite the territorial or geographic limitations of court decisions, there are important reasons why decisions from other jurisdictions should not be ignored. First, there may be no settled law on an issue in a given area. When the issue is initially presented to a local court (known as a case of first impression), the local federal or state court will probably decide it on the basis of the dominant or "better" rule that is being applied elsewhere. The second reason is that law is evolving, not stagnant. Over a period of time, trends develop in the law. When a particular court senses that its prior decisions on a point are no longer in the mainstream, it may give consideration to revising its holdings, especially if the issue has not been settled by the U.S. Supreme

---

HIGHLIGHT 1.3

Salaries of Court Personnel

Court personnel (1986 and 1987)

State court administrator	$59,257
State general jurisdiction trial court judge	$60,697
State intermediate appellate court justice	$67,172
State associate supreme court justice	$67,434
State supreme court justice	$70,161
U.S. Magistrate	$72,500
U.S. Bankruptcy Court Judge	$72,500
U.S. Court of Claims Judge	$82,500
U.S. Court of International Trade Judge	$89,500
U.S. District (trial) Court Judge	$89,500
U.S. Circuit (appellate) Court Judge	$95,000
U.S. Supreme Court Associate Justice	$110,000
U.S. Supreme Court Chief Justice	$115,000

Source: Bureau of Justice Statistics, *Report to the Nation on Crime and Justice,* 2d ed. (Washington, DC: U.S. Government Printing Office, 1988), at 126.

HIGHLIGHT 1.4

The U.S. Court System

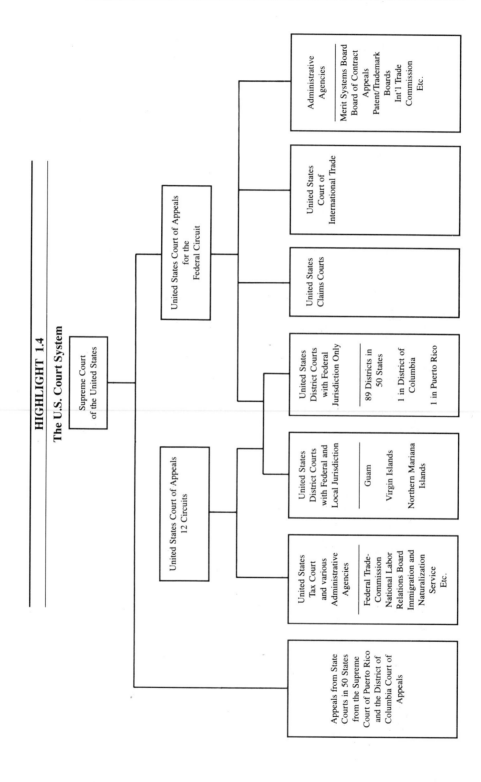

Supreme Court of the United States

United States Court of Appeals 12 Circuits

United States Court of Appeals for the Federal Circuit

Appeals from State Courts in 50 States from the Supreme Court of Puerto Rico and the District of Columbia Court of Appeals

United States Tax Court and various Administrative Agencies
Federal Trade-Commission
National Labor Relations Board
Immigration and Naturalization Service
Etc.

United States District Courts with Federal and Local Jurisdiction
Guam
Virgin Islands
Northern Mariana Islands

United States District Courts with Federal Jurisdiction Only
89 Districts in 50 States
1 in District of Columbia
1 in Puerto Rico

United States Claims Courts

United States Court of International Trade

Administrative Agencies
Merit Systems Board
Board of Contract Appeals
Patent/Trademark Boards
Int'l Trade Commission
Etc.

Court. The decisions in other jurisdictions may enable lawyers to spot a trend and anticipate what local courts may be doing in the future.

III. FEDERAL VERSUS STATE JURISDICTION

The basic rule that determines whether a criminal case should be filed and tried in federal or state court is simple. Generally, if an act is a violation of federal law, the trial will be held in a federal court; if the act is a violation of state law, the trial will be held in a state court. A crime that violates both federal and state laws (such as kidnapping, transportation of narcotics, counterfeiting, or robbery of a federally insured bank) may be tried in both federal and state courts if the prosecutors so desire. If X robs the Miami National Bank, X can be prosecuted for the crime of robbery under Florida law and for robbery of a federally insured bank under federal law. The prosecutions are for the same act but involve two different laws. There is no double jeopardy, because of the concept of *dual sovereignty*. The federal and state governments are considered sovereign in their own right; the rule of double jeopardy (the rule that no person may be convicted of the same offense more than once) applies only to successive prosecutions by the same sovereign jurisdiction.

In the preceding example, the sovereign that first obtains custody of the suspect is usually allowed to try him or her first. In most cases, this will be the state. Although the federal government can try X for the same offense, it will probably refrain from doing so if X has been convicted and sufficiently punished under state law. The state would do likewise if the sequence were reversed. Some states have laws against state prosecution for a criminal act that has been prosecuted by the federal government. In sum, although successive prosecutions are not unconstitutional, they may be prohibited by state law or administrative policy.

IV. JURISDICTION VERSUS VENUE

The terms *jurisdiction* and *venue* can be confusing. Sometimes used interchangeably, they nevertheless represent very different concepts. The term *jurisdiction* refers to the power of a court to try a case. A court's jurisdiction is defined by the totality of the law that creates the court and limits its powers; the parties to litigation cannot vest the court with jurisdiction it does not possess. Defects in the subject matter jurisdiction of a court (as, for example, when a civil case is tried in a criminal court, which does not have the authority to try it) cannot be waived by the parties and can be raised at any stage of the litigation, including on appeal. The court can also raise the question of its jurisdiction on its own motion, without waiting for either party to raise the issue. In order to render a valid judgment against a person, a court must also have jurisdiction over that person. The fact that a defendant has been brought to court against his or her wishes and by the use of questionable methods does not invalidate the jurisdiction of the court. In Frisbie v. Collins, 342 U.S. 519 (1952), the Court said that an invalid arrest is not a defense to being convicted of the offense charged. In that case, the accused, while living in Chicago, was forcibly seized, handcuffed, blackjacked, and then taken back to Michigan by law enforcement officers. The Court ruled that the power of a court to try a person for a crime is not impaired by the fact that the person

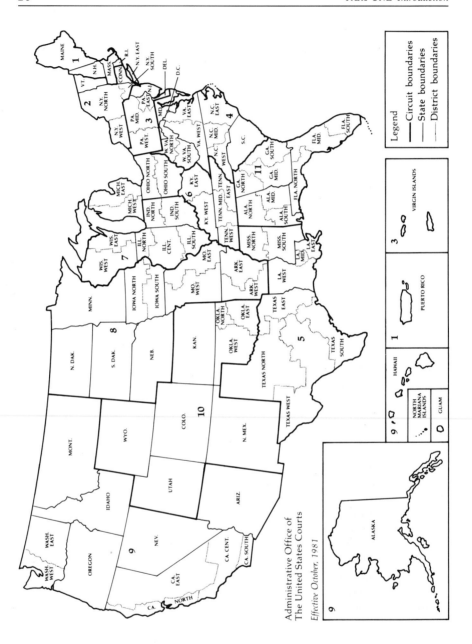

FIGURE 1.1   Geographical boundaries of U.S. Courts of Appeals and District Courts. (*Source*: D. Neubauer, *America's Courts and the Criminal Justice System*, 3d ed., Pacific Grove, CA: Brooks/Cole, 1988, at 47.)

has been brought within the court's jurisdiction through forcible abduction. Defects in obtaining personal jurisdiction can be waived by the defendant's voluntary act or by operation of law, such as when the defendant fails to assert his or her rights in a timely or proper manner.

The concept of *venue is place-oriented.* It flows from the policy of the law to have cases tried in the place where the crime was committed, where a party resides, or where another consideration makes trial in that place justifiable. Legislation establishes mandatory venue for some types of cases and preferred venue for others. In criminal cases, the trial is usually held in the place where the crime was committed. Venue may be changed and the trial held in another place, for causes specified by law. The change is made to assure the accused of a fair and impartial trial in cases that have had such massive pretrial publicity or strong community prejudice as to make it difficult to select an impartial jury. The motion for a change of venue is usually filed by the defendant. The decision of the trial judge to grant or deny the motion is seldom reversed on appeal.

V. SOURCES OF RIGHTS

The rules governing criminal proceedings in the United States come from four basic sources: constitutions, statutes, case law, and court rules.

1. Constitutions

Constitutions are the first and most authoritative sources of rights. The U.S. Constitution contains the most important rights available to an accused in a criminal prosecution. These safeguards are enumerated in the *Bill of Rights*, which are the first ten amendments to the U.S. Constitution. The constitutions of the various states also contain provisions designed to protect the rights of individuals in state criminal proceedings. These rights are basically similar to those enumerated in the Bill of Rights, but apply only to a particular state. For example, most state constitutions guarantee the right to counsel and cross-examination and prohibit self-incrimination.

The following are the federal constitutional provisions most often used in law enforcement cases and the rights they guarantee:

Amendment I

"Congress shall make no law respecting an establishment of religion, or prohibiting the free exercise thereof; or abridging the freedom of speech, or of the press; or the right of the people peaceably to assemble, and to petition the Government for a redress of grievances."

HIGHLIGHT 1.5

Jurisdiction versus *Venue*

The terms *jurisdiction* and *venue* are sometimes used interchangeably. However, the concepts are very different. *Jurisdiction* refers to the power of a court to try a case, whereas *venue* refers to the place or territory where the case is tried.

- Freedom of religion
- Freedom of speech
- Freedom of the press
- Freedom of assembly
- Freedom to petition the government for redress of grievances

Amendment II

"A well regulated Militia, being necessary to the security of a free State, the right of the people to keep and bear Arms, shall not be infringed."

- The right to keep and bear arms

Amendment IV

"The right of the people to be secure in their persons, houses, papers, and effects, against unreasonable searches and seizures, shall not be violated, and no Warrants shall issue, but upon probable cause, supported by Oath or affirmation, and particularly describing the place to be searched, and the persons or things to be seized."

- The right against unreasonable search and seizure (including arrest)

Amendment V

"No person shall be held to answer for a capital, or otherwise infamous crime, unless on a presentment or indictment of a Grand Jury, except in cases arising in the land or naval forces, or in the Militia, where in actual service in time of War or public danger, nor shall any person be subject for the same offense to be twice put in jeopardy of life or limb, nor shall be compelled in any criminal case to be a witness against himself, nor be deprived of life, liberty, or property, without due process of law; nor shall private property be taken for public use, without just compensation."

- Right to a grand jury indictment for capital or otherwise infamous crime
- Right against double jeopardy
- Right against self-incrimination
- Prohibition against the taking of life, liberty, or property without due process of law

Amendment VI

"In all criminal prosecutions, the accused shall enjoy the right to a speedy and public trial, by an impartial jury of the State and district wherein the crime shall have been committed, which district shall have been previously ascertained by law, and to be informed of the nature and cause of the accusation; to be confronted with the witnesses against him; to have the compulsory process for obtaining witnesses in his favor, and to have the Assistance of Counsel for his defence."

- Right to a speedy and public trial
- Right to an impartial jury
- Right to be informed of the nature and cause of the accusation
- Right to be confronted with the witnesses
- Right to have compulsory process for obtaining witnesses
- Right to have assistance of counsel

Amendment VIII

"Excessive bail shall not be required, nor excessive fines imposed, nor cruel and unusual punishments inflicted."

- Right against excessive bail
- Right against cruel and unusual punishment

Amendment XIV

"All persons born or naturalized in the United States and subject to the jurisdiction thereof, are citizens of the United States and of the State wherein they reside. No State shall make or enforce any law which shall abridge the privileges or immunities of citizens of the United States; nor shall any State deprive any person of life, liberty, or property, without due process of law; nor deny to any person within its jurisdiction the equal protection of the laws."

- Right to due process
- Right to equal protection

Note: The right to privacy is a well-established constitutional right, but is not expressly provided for in the Constitution. The Court says it is derived from Amendments I, IV, V, VI, VIII, IX, and XIV.

2. Federal and State Statutes

Federal and state *statutes* frequently cover the same rights mentioned in the U.S. Constitution, but in more detail. For example, an accused's right to counsel during trial is guaranteed by the federal Constitution, but it may also be given by federal or state law and is just as binding in court proceedings. Moreover, the right to counsel given by law in a state may exceed that guaranteed in the federal Constitution. The right to a lawyer during probation revocation, for instance, is not constitutionally required, but many state laws give probationers the right to counsel during probation revocation hearings. The right to jury trial is not constitutionally required in juvenile cases, but it may be given by state law.

3. Case Law

Case law is the law as enunciated in cases decided by the courts. The courts, when deciding cases, gradually evolve legal principles that become law. This law is called *unwritten law* or *judge-made law,* as distinguished from laws passed by legislative bodies. Written laws often represent the codification of case law that has become accepted and is practiced in a particular state. Case law is sometimes confused with *common law,* a term that originated and developed primarily in England. The terms are similar in that neither kind of law is a product of legislative enactment but has evolved primarily through judicial decisions.

4. Court Rules

Various *rules* have developed as a result of the courts' supervisory power over the administration of criminal justice. Federal courts have supervisory power over federal criminal cases, and state courts have similar power over state criminal cases. The rules promulgated by supervisory agencies (such as some states' supreme courts) have the force and effect of law and therefore require compliance. For example, the highest court of some states may promulgate regulations that supplement the provisions of those states' law on pleading and procedure. They cover details that may not be included in the states' codes of criminal procedure.

VI. THE INCORPORATION CONTROVERSY

Over the years since the mid-1920s, one issue affecting individual rights has repeatedly been litigated in federal courts. That issue is *whether or not the Bill of Rights in the U.S. Constitution (referring to Amendments I–X) protects against violations of rights by the federal government only, or whether it also limits what state and local government officials can do*. For example, the Fourth Amendment says: "The right of the people to be secure in their persons, houses, papers, and effects, against unreasonable searches and seizures, shall not be violated. . . ." Does this limitation apply only to federal officials (such as FBI agents), or does it also extend to the conduct of state and local officials (such as police officers)?

The background of the *incorporation controversy* deserves a brief discussion. We know that the most important safeguards available to an accused person are found in the Bill of Rights of the U.S. Constitution. These rights, along with the Ninth and Tenth Amendments, were ratified as a group and made part of the U.S. Constitution in 1791, two years after the Constitution itself was ratified by the thirteen states. Originally the Bill of Rights was viewed as limiting only the acts of federal officers because the Constitution itself limited only the powers of the national government, not the states. State and local officers were regulated only by provisions of their own state constitutions, state laws, or local ordinances.

Nearly eight decades later, in 1868, the Fourteenth Amendment was passed. Section 1 of that amendment states in part: "No State shall make or enforce any law which shall abridge the privileges or immunities of citizens of the United States; nor shall any State deprive any person of life, liberty, or property, without due process of law; nor deny to any person within its jurisdiction the equal protection of the laws." The "due process" clause of the Fourteenth Amendment has been interpreted over the years by the U.S. Supreme Court as "incorporating" most of the provisions of the Bill of Rights, giving rise to the incorporation controversy. Therefore, while the fundamental rights granted by the Bill of Rights (the first eight amendments) were guaranteed only against violations by federal officers, the wording of the Fourteenth Amendment, specifically the "due process" clause, has been interpreted to guarantee against violations of rights by either federal or state officers. In other words, those rights that are incorporated under the Fourteenth Amendment apply to state as well as to federal criminal proceedings. The process that emerges is illustrated in Highlight 1.6.

A. Approaches to Incorporation

Over the years, various justices in the U.S. Supreme Court have taken differing approaches to the incorporation controversy. These approaches, each with proponents in the Court, may be classified into four "positions," namely, selective incorporation (or the "honor roll" approach), total incorporation, total incorporation plus, and the case-by-case approach. (For a leading case on how the Supreme Court incorporates a right, read the Duncan v. Louisiana case brief at the end of this chapter.)

Most U.S. Supreme Court justices since the mid-1920s have taken the *selective incorporation* approach. This selectiveness in the choice of rights to be incorporated has earned for this approach another name —the "honor roll" position. This approach asserts that only those rights considered "fundamental" should be incorporated under the "due process" clause of the Fourteenth Amendment so as to apply to state criminal proceedings. Other criteria used by the Court in making the judgment whether or not to incorporate a right are whether a right is among those "fundamental principles of liberty and justice which lie at the base of our civil and political institutions," whether it is "basic in our system of jurisprudence," and whether it is a "fundamental right essential to a fair trial." Regardless of the phrase used, selective incorporationists say that the "due process" clause of the Fourteenth Amendment requires only fundamental fairness in state proceedings and not the automatic "lock, stock, and barrel" application of all provisions of the Bill of Rights. Selective incorporation has been the predominant approach used by the Court since it started to decide incorporation cases. (For the leading case on selective incorporation, read the Palko v. Connecticut brief at the end of this chapter.)

Justices who have taken the *total incorporation* approach argue that the Fourteenth Amendment's "due process" clause should be interpreted to incorporate all the rights given in Amendments I–VIII of the U.S. Constitution. This position was enunciated by Justice Hugo Black, who, in a concurring opinion in 1968, said, "I believe as strongly as ever that the Fourteenth Amendment was intended to make the Bill of Rights applicable to the states" (Duncan v. Louisiana, 391 U.S. 145 [1968]). His is a blanket and uncomplicated approach in that it proposes to incorporate, "lock, stock, and barrel," all the provisions in the Bill of Rights.

The *total incorporation plus* approach is an extension of total incorporation. It proposes that in addition to extending all the provisions of the Bill of Rights to the

---

HIGHLIGHT 1.6

The Incorporation Process

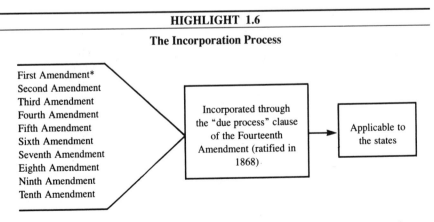

First Amendment*
Second Amendment
Third Amendment
Fourth Amendment
Fifth Amendment
Sixth Amendment
Seventh Amendment
Eighth Amendment
Ninth Amendment
Tenth Amendment

Incorporated through the "due process" clause of the Fourteenth Amendment (ratified in 1868)

Applicable to the states

*These first ten amendments were ratified together in 1791 and were originally meant to apply to only the federal government, not the states. By contrast, the Fourteenth Amendment (which contains the "due process" clause) is applicable to the states.

states, other rights ought to be added (hence the "plus"), such as the right to clean air, clean water, and a clean environment. Justice William O. Douglas was the main advocate of this approach, but over the years it has failed to gain converts in the Court.

In the *case-by-case* incorporation approach, advocates look at the facts of a specific case to determine if the facts are so bad as to justify extending the provisions of the Bill of Rights to that state case. It is otherwise known as the "fair trial" approach because the standard used is whether or not the accused obtained a fair trial. The problem with this approach is that the application of the Bill of Rights becomes subjective and unpredictable. It would be extended to a particular state criminal case only if nonapplication would lead to an unfair trial. But what that means is not clear. Moreover, if applied, the Bill of Rights would extend only to that particular state case, not to every case where a violation of a similar right is alleged or involved.

B. Definition of Fundamental Rights

As the Palko case shows, the Court has defined *fundamental* rights as those "of the very essence of a scheme of ordered liberty" and "principles of justice so rooted in the traditions and conscience of our people as to be ranked as fundamental." These rather vague, though high-sounding, phrases really mean that the Court will determine on a case-by-case basis whether or not a particular right should be incorporated.

C. Rights Held to Be Fundamental and Incorporated

The Court in specific cases (using the selective incorporation approach) has held that the following provisions of the Bill of Rights apply in both federal and state proceedings:

1. First Amendment provisions for freedom of religion, speech, assembly, and petition for redress of grievances (Fiske v. Kansas, 274 U.S. 380 [1927])
2. Fourth Amendment provisions with respect to unreasonable arrest, search, and seizure and to the exclusion from trial of evidence illegally seized (Mapp v. Ohio, 367 U.S. 643 [1961])
3. Fifth Amendment protection against self-incrimination and prohibition against double jeopardy (Mallory v. Hagan, 378 U.S. 1 [1964])
4. Sixth Amendment right to counsel (Gideon v. Wainwright, 372 U.S. 335 [1963])
5. Sixth Amendment right to a speedy trial (Klopfer v. North Carolina, 386 U.S. 213 [1967])
6. Sixth Amendment right to public trial (In re Oliver, 333 U.S. 257 [1948])

HIGHLIGHT 1.7

Total Incorporation versus Selective Incorporation

Total incorporationists advocate that the Fourteenth Amendment's "due process" clause be interpreted to incorporate all the rights given in Amendments I–VIII of the Constitution; selective incorporationists believe that it should incorporate only those rights in Amendments I–VIII of the Constitution that are considered fundamental. Over the years, the selective incorporationists' approach has prevailed.

---

7. Sixth Amendment right to confrontation of opposing witnesses (Pointer v. Texas, 380 U.S. 400 [1965])
8. Sixth Amendment right to compulsory process for obtaining witnesses (Washington v. Texas, 388 U.S. 14 [1967])
9. Eighth Amendment prohibition against cruel and unusual punishment (Robinson v. California, 370 U.S. 660 [1962])

In incorporating a right, the Supreme Court expressly says that a fundamental right in the Bill of Rights is made applicable to the states through the "due process" clause of the Fourteenth Amendment. For example, in Duncan v. Louisiana, 391 U.S. 145 (1968), the Supreme Court said that the right to trial by jury guaranteed to defendants in federal trials under the Sixth Amendment must also be given to defendants in state courts because of the "due process" clause of the Fourteenth Amendment.

D. Rights Not Incorporated

Although they are required in federal proceedings, the states do not have to give an accused the following rights unless they are required by the state constitution or state law:

1. Fifth Amendment guarantee of grand jury indictment
2. Eighth Amendment prohibition against excessive bail and fines

E. Result of Selective Incorporation—A Nationalization of the Bill of Rights

Through a process of selective incorporation, using the Fourteenth Amendment's "due process" clause, persons facing federal or state criminal charges now enjoy the same rights, except those pertaining to grand jury indictment and excessive bail and fines. In effect, the Bill of Rights is now applicable throughout the United States; hence it has become "nationalized." It makes no difference whether an accused is tried in New York, Illinois, California, or any other state—the accused's basic rights are the same because of incorporation.

❑ SUMMARY

The United States has a dual court system, meaning that it has one system of courts on the federal level and another on the state level. In general, a court decision is binding only within the limits of that court's territory and nowhere else. Only the decisions of the U.S. Supreme Court are applicable nationwide. Sometimes this system leads to inconsistent lower court decisions; such inconsistency remains until resolved by an appellate court.

If an act violates a federal law, it is tried in a federal court; if it violates state law, it is tried in a state court. There are acts, however, that are punishable by both federal and state law. In such cases, the offender may be prosecuted and convicted twice, if the prosecutors so desire, without violating the constitutional prohibition against double jeopardy. Some states have laws prohibiting state prosecution after the same offense has been tried in a federal court.

Originally, the Bill of Rights of the Constitution was applied to federal criminal prosecutions only. Its guarantees, except for the right to grand jury indictment and the right against excessive bail, are now extended to state criminal cases. "Selective incorporation" is the process by which those rights considered fundamental have been incorporated into state criminal proceedings through the "due process" clause of the Fourteenth Amendment. In effect, the provisions of the Bill of Rights have been nationalized.

☐ REVIEW QUESTIONS

1. "The United States has a dual court system." Discuss what that means.
2. "A court decision is effective only within a limited jurisdiction." What does that mean?
3. A criminal act is usually prosecuted under state law. In what instance may the same act also be prosecuted under federal law? Give an example.
4. What did the U.S. Supreme Court say in Duncan v. Louisiana?
5. What is the incorporation controversy? How did it originate?
6. Distinguish between "total incorporation" and "selective incorporation."
7. Name five rights that have been made applicable to the states by means of the "due process" clause.

☐ DEFINITIONS

Bill of Rights: The first ten amendments to the U.S. Constitution.

Case-by-Case Incorporation: An approach that looks at the facts of a specific case to determine if the facts are so bad as to justify extending the provisions of the Bill of Rights to that state case.

Case Law: The law as enunciated in cases decided by the courts.

Dual Court System: The two court systems of the United States, one for federal cases and the other for state cases.

"Due Process" Clause: A provision in the Fourteenth Amendment of the Constitution stating that no state shall deprive any person of life, liberty, or property, without due process of law.

Incorporation Controversy: The issue of whether the Bill of Rights in the U.S. Constitution protects against violations of rights by the federal government only, or whether it also limits what state government officials can do.

Jurisdiction: The power of a court to try a case.

Rule of Four: Rule providing that the Supreme Court needs the votes of at least four justices to consider a case on its merits.

Selective Incorporation: An approach to incorporation stating that the Fourteenth Amendment's "due process" clause should be interpreted to incorporate only those rights granted in Amendments I–VIII of the Constitution that are considered fundamental; position advocated by most Supreme Court justices.

Total Incorporation: An approach to incorporation stating that the Fourteenth Amendment's "due process" clause should be interpreted to incorporate all the rights granted in Amendments I–VIII of the Constitution; position advocated by some Supreme Court justices.

Total Incorporation Plus: An approach that proposes that in addition to extending all the provisions of the Bill of Rights to the states, other rights ought to be added, such as the right to clean air, clean water, and a clean environment.

Venue: The place or territory in which a case is tried.

☐   PRINCIPLES OF CASES

DUNCAN V. LOUISIANA, 391 U.S. 145 (1968)   A crime punishable by two years in prison, although classified under Louisiana law as a misdemeanor, is a serious crime, and therefore the defendant is entitled to a jury trial.

PALKO V. CONNECTICUT, 302 U.S. 319 (1937)   The "due process" clause of the Fourteenth Amendment applies to the states and therefore incorporates those provisions of the Bill of Rights that are "of the very essence of the scheme of ordered liberty." The provisions to be incorporated are those that involve "principles of justice so rooted in the traditions and conscience of our people as to be ranked as fundamental." The double jeopardy provision of the Fifth Amendment does not come under this category and therefore does not apply to the states. (The double jeopardy provision of the Fifth Amendment has since been incorporated and held applicable to the states; hence this part of the Palko decision is no longer valid.)

☐   CASE BRIEF—LEADING CASE ON SELECTIVE INCORPORATION

PALKO V. CONNECTICUT, 302 U.S. 319 (1937)

FACTS: Palko was charged with first-degree murder in the state of Connecticut. He was found guilty of murder in the second degree and sentenced to life imprisonment. The prosecution appealed the verdict, and the Supreme Court of Connecticut ordered a new trial on the grounds that an error of law in the lower court had prejudiced the state. At the second trial, additional evidence was admitted and additional instructions given to the jury. A conviction for first-degree murder was returned, and Palko was sentenced to death. He questioned the legality of the second conviction, claiming double jeopardy under the constitutional right guaranteed by the Fifth Amendment as made applicable to the states by the "due process" clause of the Fourteenth Amendment.

ISSUE: *Is the double jeopardy provision of the Fifth Amendment applicable in state criminal prosecutions by way of the "due process" clause of the Fourteenth Amendment? Yes.*

SUPREME COURT DECISION: The "due process" clause of the Fourteenth Amendment applies to the states and therefore incorporates those provisions of the Bill of Rights that are "of the very essence of a scheme of ordered liberty." The provisions deemed incorporated are those that involve "principles of justice so rooted in the traditions and conscience of our people as to be ranked as fundamental." The double jeopardy provision of the Fifth Amendment does not come under this category and therefore does not apply to the states. The second conviction was upheld.

CASE SIGNIFICANCE: The Palko case illustrates the standards used by the Court, under the selective incorporation approach, to determine if a constitutional right should be held applicable to the states under the "due process" clause of the Fourteenth Amendment. The standards used were "of the very essence of a scheme of ordered liberty" and "principles of justice so rooted in the traditions and conscience of our people as to be ranked as fundamental." By 1937, when the Palko case was decided, only the First Amendment and the right to counsel had been found to fit the above tests. Since then, most provisions of the Constitution have been incorporated by the Fourteenth Amendment, including the prohibition against double jeopardy. If the Palko case were decided today, the decision would be different.

EXCERPTS FROM THE DECISION: We have said that in appellant's view the Fourteenth Amendment is to be taken as embodying the prohibitions of the Fifth. His thesis is even broader. Whatever would be a violation of the original Bill of Rights (Amendments I to VIII) if done by the federal government is now equally unlawful by force of the Fourteenth Amendment if done by a state. There is no such general rule.

The Fifth Amendment provides, among other things, that no person shall be held to answer for a capital or otherwise infamous crime unless on presentment or indictment of a grand jury. This court has held that, in prosecutions by a state, presentment or indictment by a grand jury may give way to informations at the instance of a public officer. . . . The Fifth Amendment provides also that no person shall be compelled in any criminal case to be a witness against himself. This court has said that, in prosecutions by a state, the exemption will fail if the state elects to end it. The Sixth Amendment calls for a jury trial in criminal cases and the Seventh for a jury trial in civil cases at common law where the value in controversy shall exceed twenty dollars. This court has ruled that consistently with those amendments trial by jury may be modified by a state or abolished altogether. . . .

The Due Process Clause of the Fourteenth Amendment may make it unlawful for a state to abridge by its statutes the freedom of speech which the First Amendment safeguards against encroachment by the Congress . . . or the like freedom of the press . . . or the free exercise of religion . . . or the right of peaceable assembly, without which speech would be unduly trammeled . . . or the right of one accused of crime to the benefit of counsel. . . . In these and other situations immunities that are valid as against the federal government by force of the specific pledges of particular amendments have been found to be implicit in the concept of ordered liberty, and thus, through the Fourteenth Amendment, become valid as against the states.

The line of division may seem to be wavering and broken if there is a hasty catalogue of the cases on the one side and the other. Reflection and analysis will induce a different view. There emerges the perception of a rationalizing principle which gives to discrete instances a proper order and coherence. The right to trial by jury and the immunity from prosecution except as the result of an indictment may have value and importance. Even so, they are not of the very essence of a scheme of ordered liberty. To abolish them is not to violate a "principle of justice so rooted in the traditions and conscience of our people as to be ranked as fundamental." Few would be so narrow or provincial as to maintain that a fair and enlightened system of justice would be impossible without them. What is true of jury trials and indictments is true also, as the cases show, of the immunity from compulsory self-incrimination. This too might be lost, and justice still be done. Indeed, today as in the past there are students of our penal system who look upon the immunity as a mischief rather than a benefit, and who would limit its scope, or destroy it altogether. No doubt there would remain the need to give protection against torture, physical or mental. . . . Justice, however, would not perish if the accused were subject to a duty to respond to orderly inquiry. The exclusion of these immunities and privileges from the privileges and immunities protected against the action of the states has not been arbitrary or casual. It has been dictated by a study and appreciation of the meaning, the essential implications of liberty itself.

☐ CASE BRIEF—LEADING CASE ON HOW THE SUPREME COURT INCORPORATES A RIGHT

DUNCAN V. LOUISIANA, 391 U.S. 145 (1968)

FACTS: Duncan was convicted in a Louisiana court of simple battery (a misdemeanor punishable under Louisiana law by a maximum sentence of two years in prison and a $300 fine). Duncan requested a jury trial, but the request was denied because under Louisiana law jury trials were allowed only when hard labor or capital punishment could be imposed. Duncan was convicted and given sixty days in jail and fined $150. He appealed to the U.S. Supreme Court, claiming that the state's refusal to give him a jury trial for a crime punishable by two or more years of imprisonment violated his constitutional right.

ISSUE: *Was the state's refusal to give the defendant a jury trial for a crime that carried a two-year imprisonment as maximum sentence a violation of the constitutional right to a jury trial in the Sixth Amendment as incorporated through the "due process" clause of the Fourteenth? Yes.*

SUPREME COURT DECISION: A crime punishable by two years in prison, although classified under Louisiana law as a misdemeanor, is a serious crime, and therefore the defendant is entitled to a jury trial.

CASE SIGNIFICANCE: The Duncan case made the right to trial by jury applicable to the states in cases in which the maximum penalty is two years' imprisonment, regardless of how state law classifies the offense. Although Duncan did not clearly state the minimum, a subsequent case (Baldwin v. New York, 399 U.S. 6 [1970]) later held that any offense that carries a potential sentence of more than six months is a serious offense, so a trial must be afforded on demand. This requirement applies even if the sentence actually imposed is less than six months.

EXCERPTS FROM THE DECISION: The Fourteenth Amendment denies the States the power to "deprive any person of life, liberty, or property, without due process of law." In resolving conflicting claims concerning the meaning of this spacious language, the Court has looked increasingly to the Bill of Rights for guidance; many of the rights guaranteed by the first eight Amendments to the Constitution have been held to be protected against state action by the Due Process Clause of the Fourteenth Amendment. That clause now protects the right to compensation for property taken by the State; the rights of speech, press, and religion covered by the First Amendment; the Fourth Amendment rights to be free from unreasonable searches and seizures and to have excluded from criminal trials any evidence illegally seized; the right guaranteed by the Fifth Amendment to be free of compelled self-incrimination; and the Sixth Amendment rights to counsel, to a speedy and public trial, to confrontation of opposing witnesses, and the compulsory process for obtaining witnesses.

The test for determining whether a right extended by the Fifth and Sixth Amendments with respect to federal criminal proceedings is also protected against state action by the Fourteenth Amendment has been phrased in a variety of ways in the opinions of this Court. The question has been asked whether a right is among those " 'fundamental principles of liberty and justice which lie at the base of all our civil and political institutions,' " Powell v. Alabama, 287 U.S. 45, 67 (1932); whether it is "basic in our system of jurisprudence," In re Oliver, 333 U.S. 257, 273 (1948); and whether it is "a fundamental right, essential to a fair trial," Gideon v. Wainwright, 372 U.S. 335, 343–344 (1963); Malloy v. Hogan, 378 U.S. 1, 6 (1964); Pointer v. Texas, 380 U.S. 400, 403 (1965). The claim before us is that the right to trial by jury guaranteed by the Sixth Amendment meets these tests. The position of Louisiana, on the other hand, is that the Constitution imposes upon the States no duty to give a jury trial in any criminal case, regardless of the seriousness of the crime or the size of the punishment which may be imposed. Because we believe that trial by jury in criminal cases is fundamental to the American scheme of justice, we hold that the Fourteenth Amendment guarantees a right of jury trial in all criminal cases which—were they to be tried in a federal court—would come within the Sixth Amendment's guarantee. Since we consider the appeal before us to be such a case, we hold that the Constitution was violated when appellant's demand for jury trial was refused.

CHAPTER TWO

OVERVIEW OF THE CRIMINAL JUSTICE PROCESS

I. PROCEDURE BEFORE TRIAL
   A. Filing of Complaint
   B. Arrest
   C. Booking at Police Station
   D. Appearance before Magistrate after Arrest
   E. Preliminary Examination
   F. The Decision to Charge
   G. Grand Jury Proceeding or Filing of Information
   H. Arraignment
   I. Plea by Defendant

II. PROCEDURE DURING TRIAL
   A. Selection of Jurors
   B. Opening Statements
   C. Presentation of Case for the Prosecution
   D. Presentation of Case for the Defense
   E. Rebuttal Evidence
   F. Closing Arguments
   G. Judge's Instructions to Jury
   H. Deliberation of the Jury
   I. Verdict

III. PROCEDURE AFTER TRIAL
   A. Sentencing
   B. Appeal

IV. CAUTIONS
   A. Application to Felony Cases
   B. Variation among States
   C. Variation within a State
   D. Theory versus Reality

Summary
Review Questions
Definitions
Principles of Cases
Case Briefs
    SANTOBELLO V. NEW YORK
    APODACA V. OREGON

☐ KEY TERMS

complaint	bill of indictment
arrest	arraignment
citation	plea
summons	nolo contendere plea
booking	motion to suppress
initial appearance	motion for a change of venue
release on recognizance (ROR)	plea bargaining
bail	*voir dire*
preventive detention	peremptory challenge
preliminary examination	motion for directed verdict of
discovery	acquittal
bind over	motion for mistrial
indictment	sentencing
information	

We now present an overview of the criminal process from a legal perspective. The procedure is divided into three time frames: before trial, during trial, and after trial. In the great majority of cases, an arrest triggers the criminal process against the accused. In some cases, however, the procedure is initiated through the filing of a complaint that leads to the issuance of a warrant. Procedure during trial starts with the selection of jurors and ends with a court or jury verdict. If the accused is found guilty, the sentencing phase follows, after which the defendant may appeal the conviction and sentence. The chapter concludes with words of caution concerning the difference between theory and practice in criminal procedure.

I. PROCEDURE BEFORE TRIAL

A. Filing of Complaint

A *complaint* is a charge made before a proper officer alleging the commission of a criminal offense. It may be filed by the offended party or by a police officer who has obtained information about or witnessed the criminal act. The complaint serves as a basis for issuing an arrest warrant. If the accused has been arrested without a warrant, the complaint is prepared and filed at the defendant's initial appearance before the magistrate, usually by the arresting officer.

B. Arrest

There are two kinds of *arrest:* (1) arrest with a warrant and (2) arrest without a warrant. In *arrest with a warrant,* a complaint has been filed and presented to a magistrate, who has read it and found probable cause to justify the issuance of an arrest warrant. In contrast, *arrest without a warrant* usually happens when a crime is committed in the presence of a police officer or, in some jurisdictions, by virtue of a citizen's arrest for specified offenses. As many as 95 percent of all arrests are made without a warrant. This rate is significant because it implies that the officer must be convinced of the presence of probable cause prior to making the arrest. Such belief is later established in a sworn complaint or testimony.

Statutes in many states authorize the use of a citation or summons rather than an arrest for less serious offenses. A *citation* is an order issued by a court or law enforcement officer commanding the person to whom the citation is issued to appear in court at a specified date to answer certain charges. A *summons* is a writ directed to the sheriff or other proper officer requiring that officer to notify the person named that he or she is required to appear in court on a day named and to answer the complaint stated in the summons. In either case, if the person fails or refuses to appear in court as scheduled, an arrest warrant is then issued. Citations and summonses have the advantage of keeping a person out of jail pending the hearing. They also save the police officer time and the paperwork that goes with arrest and booking.

C. Booking at Police Station

Booking involves making an entry in the police blotter or arrest book indicating the suspect's name, the time of arrest, and the offense involved. If the offense is serious, the suspect may also be photographed or fingerprinted. Before or after booking, the suspect is usually placed in a "lockup," which is a place of detention run by the police department.

D. Appearance before Magistrate after Arrest

In some states, this step is known as the *initial appearance,* "presentment," or "arraignment on the warrant." Most states require that an arrested person be brought before a judge, magistrate, or commissioner "without unnecessary delay." What that means varies from state to state, depending on state law or court decisions. In federal and most state proceedings, a delay of more than six hours in bringing the suspect before the magistrate for initial appearance is one factor to be considered in determining the voluntariness of any incriminating statements made by the accused. Other jurisdictions do not specify the number of hours but look at the surrounding circumstances and decide on a case-by-case basis whether the delay was unnecessary.

Once before a magistrate, the arrestee is made aware of his or her rights. This procedure usually includes giving the Miranda warnings.

> To summarize, we hold that when an individual is taken into custody or otherwise deprived of his freedom by the authorities in any significant way and is subjected to questioning, the privilege against self-incrimination is jeopardized. Procedural safeguards must be employed to protect the privilege, and unless other fully effective means are adopted to notify the person of his right of silence and to assure that the exercise of the right will be scrupulously honored, the following measures are required. He must be warned prior to any questioning that he has the right to remain silent, that anything he says can be used against him in a court of law, that he has the right to the presence of an attorney, and that if he cannot afford an attorney one will be appointed for him prior to any questioning if he so desires. Opportunity to exercise these rights must be afforded to him throughout the interrogation. After such warnings have been given, and such opportunity afforded him, the individual may knowingly and intelligently waive these rights and agree to answer questions or make a statement. But unless and until such warnings and waiver are demonstrated by the prosecution at trial, no evidence obtained as a result of interrogation can be used against him. (Miranda v. Arizona, 384 U.S. 436 [1966])

The suspect is also informed of other rights as may be given by statute. These vary from state to state but may include such rights as the right to preliminary hearing, confrontation, and speedy trial, the right not to incriminate oneself, and the exclusion in court of illegally obtained evidence (the exclusionary rule).

Although many jurisdictions require magistrates to give the Miranda warnings when the suspect is brought in, the Miranda warnings must also be given by the arresting officer if the officer questions the suspect prior to the appearance before a magistrate. Failure to issue the warnings makes the suspect's statements inadmissible in court. Conversely, if the officer does not need to ask the suspect any questions (as would usually be the case in arrests with a warrant), the Miranda warnings need not be given by the police.

If the charge is a misdemeanor, the arrestee may be arraigned while before the magistrate and required to plead to the pending charge. Many misdemeanor cases are disposed of at this stage through either a guilty plea or some type of diversionary procedure. If the charge is a felony, the arrestee ordinarily is not required to plead to the charge at this time. Rather, he or she is held for preliminary examination on the felony charge.

If the case is not finally disposed of at this time, the arrestee is either sent back to jail, released on his or her *own recognizance (ROR),* or allowed to post bail in an amount determined by the magistrate. In some cases, bail may be denied.

Bail is defined as the security required by the court and given by the accused to ensure that the accused appears before the proper court at the scheduled time and place to answer the charges brought against him or her. In theory, the only function of bail is to ensure the appearance of the defendant at the time set for trial. In practice, however, bail has also been used to prevent the release of an accused who might otherwise be dangerous to society or whom the judges might not want to release. This latter practice is known as *preventive detention.* The Court has upheld as constitutional a provision of the Federal Bail Reform Act of 1984, which permits federal judges to deny pretrial release to those charged with certain serious felonies, based on a finding that no combination of release conditions can reasonably assure the community of safety from such individuals (U.S. v. Salerno, 41 CrL 3207 [1987]).

When the charge is merely a misdemeanor, most courts have bail schedules pursuant to which the arrested person can post bail with the police or clerk of court in an amount designated in the schedule, without having to see the magistrate. If there is enough evidence to justify charging the accused with a felony, and if the offense is bailable and no bail has been set, the magistrate will fix the amount.

The amount of bail in misdemeanor or felony cases is usually determined in light of the facts then known to the magistrate. They include the nature and seriousness of the crime, previous criminal record of the accused, likelihood of flight from the state, and so forth. Bail is not an absolute right. It may be denied in capital punishment cases in which evidence of guilt is strong.

By statute in a number of states, the magistrate or judge before whom the proceedings are pending may release any accused on his or her own recognizance, meaning without monetary bail. This usually happens when the accused has strong ties in the community and will most likely appear for trial. If he or she fails to do so, however, an arrest warrant may be issued.

E. Preliminary Examination

An accused charged with a felony is usually entitled to a *preliminary examination* (called a "preliminary hearing" or "examining trial" in some states) held before a magistrate within a reasonably short time after arrest. Preliminary examinations closely resemble trials, except that their purpose is more limited and the hearing magistrate is generally not the judge who will preside over the actual trial in the case. Representation by counsel and cross-examination of witnesses are allowed.

Preliminary examinations are usually held for three main purposes:

1. *Determination of probable cause.* The primary purpose of the preliminary hearing is to ascertain whether there is probable cause to support the charges against the accused. If not, the charges are dismissed. This process prevents unsupported charges of grave offenses from coming to trial, and thereby protects people from harassment, expense, and damage to reputation.

2. *Discovery.* Discovery is a procedure used by either party to obtain information that is in the hands of the other party and is necessary or helpful in the case. The scope of discovery in a criminal case is usually limited to materials or evidence

---

HIGHLIGHT 2.1

The Criminal Justice Process

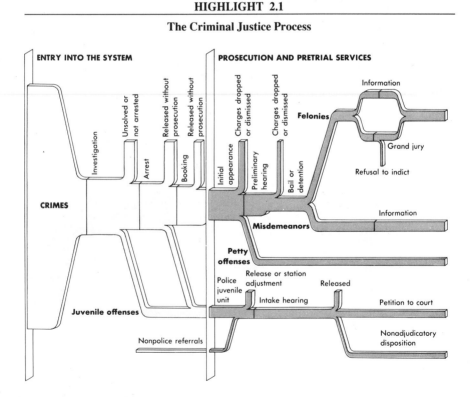

Source: Todd R. Clear and George F. Cole, *American Corrections,* 2d ed., Pacific Grove, CA: Brooks/Cole, 1990, at 34–35.

specified by law to be discoverable. Discovery procedures in criminal cases are usually one-sided in favor of the defense because the accused can usually invoke the guarantee against self-incrimination and refuse to turn over relevant evidence to the prosecution.

3. *Decision on "binding over."* Some states use the preliminary examination to determine if the accused shall be "bound over" for a grand jury hearing. In these states, there must be a finding of cause at the preliminary examination before a grand jury hearing will be held. Other states use the preliminary examination to determine if the accused should be bound over for trial, bypassing grand jury proceedings altogether.

There are cases in which preliminary examination is not required:

1. *In indictments handed down prior to preliminary examination.* When the grand jury has previously returned an indictment (usually because the case was referred to it before arrest), a preliminary examination is not required. The grand jury proceedings constitute a determination that there is probable cause and thus that the accused should stand trial.

HIGHLIGHT 2.1 *(continued)*

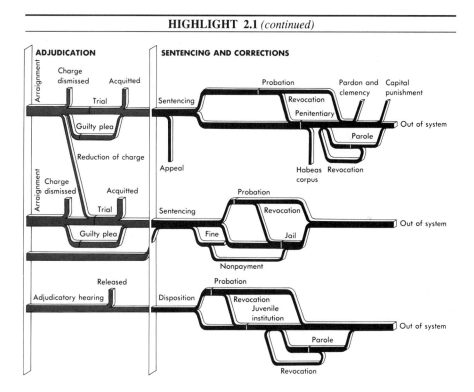

2. *In misdemeanors.* In most jurisdictions, preliminary examinations are not required in misdemeanor cases because only lesser penalties are involved. The accused goes directly to trial on the complaint or information filed by the district attorney.

3. *When there is a waiver of preliminary examination.* The accused may voluntarily give up the right to a preliminary examination. For example, a plea of guilty to the charge generally operates as a waiver of the preliminary examination. The accused is thereupon bound over for sentencing to the court having jurisdiction over the crime involved.

After the preliminary hearing, the magistrate may do any of the following:

1. *"Hold defendant to answer."* If the magistrate finds probable cause, naming facts that would lead a person of ordinary caution or prudence to entertain a strong suspicion of the guilt of the accused, the accused is "held to answer" and bound over for trial in a court having jurisdiction over the offense charged.

2. *Discharge the accused.* If the magistrate does not find probable cause, the accused is discharged.

3. *Reduce the charge.* Most states allow the magistrate to reduce a felony charge to a misdemeanor on the basis of the results of the preliminary hearing. This option serves to avoid cluttering grand juries and higher courts with cases that really belong in the lower courts.

HIGHLIGHT 2.2

Financial Bond and Alternative Release Options

Financial bond	*Alternative release options*

Fully secured bail—The defendant posts the full amount of bail with the court.

Privately secured bail—A bondsman signs a promissory note to the court for the bail amount and charges the defendant a fee for the service (usually 10% of the bail amount). If the defendant fails to appear, the bondsman must pay the court the full amount. Frequently, the bondsman requires the defendant to post collateral in addition to the fee.

Deposit bail—The courts allow the defendant to deposit a percentage (usually 10%) of the full bail with the court. The full amount of the bail is required if the defendant fails to appear. The percentage bail is returned after disposition of the case, but the court often retains 1% for administrative costs.

Unsecured bail—The defendant pays no money to the court but is liable for the full amount of bail should he or she fail to appear.

Release on recognizance (ROR)—The court releases the defendant on the promise that he or she will appear in court as required.

Conditional release—The court releases the defendant subject to his or her following specific conditions set by the court, such as attendance at drug treatment therapy or staying away from the complaining witness.

Third-party custody—The defendant is released into the custody of an individual or agency that promises to assure his or her appearance in court. No monetary transactions are involved in this type of release.

Citation release—Arrestees are released pending their first court appearance on a written order issued by law enforcement personnel.

Source: Bureau of Justice Statistics, *Report to the Nation on Crime and Justice,* 2d ed. (Washington, DC: U.S. Government Printing Office, 1988), at 76.

STATE OF MISSOURI   )
) ss.
COUNTY OF CLINTON)

     IN THE ASSOCIATE CIRCUIT COURT OF CLINTON COUNTY, MISSOURI

STATE OF MISSOURI,   )
                Plaintiff   )
)
  -vs-   )   Case No.
)
                  ,   )
                Defendant   )

                    C O M P L A I N T

_____, being duly sworn, deposes and states that in

the County of Clinton, State of Missouri, heretofore, to-wit: on or about

_____, one _____, in violation

of Section 570.120, RSMo, committed the Class A misdemeanor of passing bad checks

punishable upon conviction under Sections 558.011.1(5) and 560.016, RSMo, in that the

defendant, with purpose to defraud, issued a check in the amount of $_____,

drawn upon the _____, dated _____,

payable to _____, knowing that such check would not

be paid.

    Affiant further states that he has actual personal knowledge of the facts, matters and
things above set out and is a competent witness thereto.

                                _____
                                Plaintiff

Subscribed and sworn to before me this _____ day of _____, 19 ____.

                                _____
                              Clerk of the Associate Circuit Court

F. The Decision to Charge

Discretion abounds in all areas of criminal justice, but particularly in policing and
prosecution. After a suspect is taken into custody, or even before that, the police
usually have the discretion to charge or not to charge the suspect with an offense. As
the seriousness of the offense goes up, the discretion of the police diminishes. For

District Court
Form No. 332
Citation

STATE OF VERMONT
District Court of Vermont
C I T A T I O N

County

TO:

BY THE AUTHORITY OF THE STATE OF VERMONT, you are hereby ordered to appear before a Judicial Officer at the District Court of Vermont, at the following time and place:

Date	Time	Unit	Circuit

Town/City	County	
		to answer to the charge of

Offense

An information charging you with this offense will be presented at the time of your appearance.

IF YOU DO NOT APPEAR AT THE TIME AND PLACE ORDERED, A WARRANT WILL BE ISSUED FOR YOUR ARREST AND YOU MAY BE SUBJECT TO ADDITIONAL CHARGES AND PENALTIES.

Date issued:	Town/City	County

Signature - Issuing Officer	Title

I received this Citation on:	Date	Signature - Defendant
20M 02/84 VT I.I.		

White - Court's Copy   Yellow - Officer's Copy   Pink - Defendant's Copy

example, the police hardly have any discretion to charge or not to charge the suspect with an offense in homicide cases. Minor traffic offenses, however, may be disposed of by the police "on the spot."

The prosecutor also exercises immense discretion. This is most evident in the prosecutor's decision to charge or not to charge. In most cases, the prosecutor has the final say on whether or not a suspect should be prosecuted. Should the prosecutor decide to charge even if the evidence is weak, there is nothing much a suspect can do but go to trial and hope for an acquittal. Conversely, even if the evidence is strong, but the prosecutor refuses to charge, there is not much anybody can do legally to persuade the prosecutor to charge. Even after a suspect has been charged, the prosecutor may file a nolle prosequi motion, which seeks a dismissal of the charges. Such a motion is almost always granted by the court.

G. Grand Jury Proceeding or Filing of Information

A criminal prosecution is initiated by the filing of an accusatory pleading in the court having jurisdiction over the offense. Prior to the filing, the accused will have made an initial appearance before a magistrate to be informed of his or her rights and the posting of bail, and the accused will have had a preliminary examination to determine whether there is probable cause for him or her to be bound over for trial. However, the prosecution formally commences when the government files an indictment or information. An *indictment* is filed by the grand jury and signed by the grand jury foreman, whereas an *information* is filed directly by the prosecutor. In states using the grand jury system, an indictment is usually required in felony offenses, but an information is sufficient in misdemeanors.

Missouri Form 11-85	**SUMMONS IN CRIMINAL CASE**	CASE NUMBER

IN THE CIRCUIT COURT OF   **COUNTY,**   **DIVISION**

The State of Missouri	DEFENDANT SUMMONED
VS.	CHARGE
	DATE AND TIME OF HEARING
	LOCATION OF HEARING
Defendant(s)	

The State of Missouri to Defendant Summoned:

Because you have been charged in this court with the above offense, you are summoned to appear at the above location and time to plead and answer to the charge.

(Seal of Circuit Court)

_____
CLERK

_____   By: _____
DATE ISSUED   DEPUTY CLERK

SHERIFF'S RETURN ON SERVICE OF SUMMONS

I hereby certify that I have served the above summons by: (check one)
☐ delivering a copy of the summons and a copy of the petition to the defendant.
☐ leaving a copy of the summons and a copy of the petition at the dwelling place or usual abode of the defendant with _____, a person of the defendant's family over the age of 15 years.
☐ (for service on a corporation) delivering a copy of the summons and a copy of the petition to (name) _____, (title) _____, at (address) _____
☐ (other) _____

Served in _____ County, MO on this _____ day of _____, 19 _____ .

SHERIFF'S FEES

Summons	$ _____	
Non est	$ _____	_____
		SHERIFF
Mileage	$ _____	By: _____
TOTAL	$ _____	DEPUTY SHERIFF

A grand jury hearing is not a right guaranteed under the U.S. Constitution in all criminal prosecutions; however, most states today use it, some on an optional basis. It is required in all federal felony prosecutions.

The grand jury proceedings start when a *bill of indictment,* defined as a written accusation of the crime, is submitted to the grand jury by the prosecutor. Hearings are then held before the grand jury, and evidence is presented by the prosecutor to prove the accusation. Traditionally the hearings are secret, the reason being that the charges may not be proved and hence it would be unfair to allow their publication. For the same reason, unauthorized persons are excluded, and disclosure of the proceedings is generally prohibited. The accused has no right to present evidence in a grand jury proceeding. However, the accused may be given an opportunity to do so at the discretion of the jury. A person appearing before the grand jury does not have a right to counsel, even if he or she is also the suspect. The reason is that the grand jury proceeding is merely an investigation, not a trial.

If the required number of grand jurors (usually twelve) believes that the evidence warrants conviction for the crime charged, the bill of indictment is endorsed as a "true bill" and filed with the court having jurisdiction over the offense. The bill itself constitutes the formal accusation. If the jury does not find probable cause, the bill of indictment is ignored and a "no bill" results.

An *information* is a written accusation of a crime prepared by the prosecuting attorney in the name of the state. The information is not presented to a grand jury. To safeguard against possible abuse, most states provide that a prosecution by information may be commenced only after a preliminary examination and commitment by a magistrate, or waiver thereof by the accused. The "probable cause" needed in every grand jury indictment is thus assured by the reviewing magistrate.

The information filed by the prosecutor must reasonably inform the accused of the charges against him or her, giving the accused an opportunity to prepare and present a defense. The essential nature of the offense must be stated, although the charges may follow the language of the penal code that defines the offense.

H. Arraignment

At a scheduled time and after prior notice, the accused is called into court, informed of the charges against him or her, and asked how he or she pleads. This step is known as the *arraignment*. The accused's presence during arraignment is generally required, except in minor offenses. If the accused has not been arrested, or if he or she is on bail and does not appear, a bench warrant or capias (warrant issued by the judge) will

---

HIGHLIGHT 2.3

Grand Jury Distinguished from Trial (Petit) Jury

Grand jury	*Trial jury*
1. Usually composed of 16 to 23 members, with 12 votes required for an indictment.	1. Usually consists of 12 members, with unanimous vote required for conviction.
2. Does not determine guilt or innocence. Function is to return indictments or conduct investigations of reported criminality.	2. Decides guilt or innocence and, in some states, determines punishment.
3. Retains same membership for a month, six months, or one year. May return several indictments during that period.	3. Different jury for every case.
4. Hands down indictment based on probable cause.	4. Convicts on the basis of evidence of guilt beyond reasonable doubt.
5. May initiate investigations of misconduct.	5. Cannot initiate investigations of misconduct.

IN THE CIRCUIT COURT OF CLINTON COUNTY, MISSOURI,

.... Term, 19......

State of Missouri
    against

...., Defendant

INDICTMENT

STATE OF MISSOURI, }
County of Clinton.   } ss.

    The Grand Jurors for the State of Missouri, sumoned from the body of the County of Clinton, duly impanelled, charged and sworn to inquire, within and for said County and State, upon their oaths present and charge, that ...., on or about the .... day of ...., 19......, at the County of Clinton in the State of Missouri, did then and there

contrary to the form of the statute in such case made and provided, and against the peace and dignity of the State.

....
Prosecuting Attorney of Clinton County, Missouri

A true Bill.

....
Foreman of the Grand Jury

be issued to compel his or her appearance. An exception in many states provides that an accused charged with a misdemeanor may appear through a lawyer at the arraignment.

I. Plea by Defendant

A *plea* is an accused's response in court to the indictment or information that is read to the accused in court. There are generally three kinds of pleas in modern criminal practice: nolo contendere, not guilty, and guilty. Some states add a fourth plea—not guilty by reason of insanity.

1. Nolo Contendere Plea

A *nolo contendere plea* literally means "no contest." In essence, the defendant accepts the penalty without admitting guilt. The effect of this plea is the same as that of a guilty plea; however, the defendant may benefit in that the plea cannot be used as an admission in any subsequent civil proceeding arising out of the same offense. For example, X pleads nolo contendere to a criminal charge of driving while intoxicated. This plea cannot be used as an admission of guilt in a subsequent civil case brought against X by the injured party to recover damages. The injured party must indepen-

---

HIGHLIGHT 2.4

To Use or Not to Use a Grand Jury

Some states do not require a grand jury indictment to initiate prosecutions

---

Grand jury indictment required	*Grand jury indictment optional*
All crimes	Arizona
New Jersey	Arkansas
South Carolina	California
Tennessee	Colorado
Virginia	Idaho
All felonies	Illinois
Alabama	Indiana
Alaska	Iowa
Delaware	Kansas
District of Columbia	Maryland
Georgia	Michigan
Hawaii	Missouri
Kentucky	Montana
Maine	Nebraska
Mississippi	Nevada
New Hampshire	New Mexico
New York	North Dakota
North Carolina	Oklahoma
Ohio	Oregon
Texas	South Dakota
West Virginia	Utah
Capital crimes only	Vermont
Connecticut	Washington
Florida	Wisconsin
Louisiana	Wyoming
Massachusetts	**Grand jury lacks authority to indict**
Minnesota	Pennsylvania
Rhode Island	

Note: With the exception of capital cases a defendant can always waive the right to an indictment. Thus, the requirement for an indictment to initiate prosecution exists only in the absence of a waiver.

Source: Bureau of Justice Statistics, *Report to the Nation on Crime and Justice*, 2d ed. (Washington, DC: U.S. Government Printing Office, 1988), at 72.

STATE OF MISSOURI   )
) ss.
COUNTY OF CLINTON   )

IN THE ASSOCIATE CIRCUIT COURT OF CLINTON COUNTY, MISSOURI

STATE OF MISSOURI,   )
                     Plaintiff   )
     -vs-   )   Case No.
)
)
                     Defendant   )

I N F O R M A T I O N

GEORGE A. PICKETT, Prosecuting Attorney within and for the County of Clinton, State

of Missouri, charges that the defendant, in violation of Section 577.010, RSMo, committed

the Class _____ of driving while intoxicated, punishable upon

conviction under Section(s) _____, RSMo, in that on

or about _____ at _____

in the County of Clinton, State of Missouri, the defendant, _____,

operated a motor vehicle while under the influence of alcohol.

```
                                   _____
                                   George A. Pickett
```

GEORGE A. PICKETT, Prosecuting Attorney of the County of Clinton, State of Missouri,
being duly sworn, upon his oath says that the facts stated in the above Information are true,
according to his best information, knowledge and belief.

```
                                   _____
                                   George A. Pickett
```

Subscribed and sworn to before me this _____ day of _____, 19 ___.

```
                                   _____
                                   Clerk of the Associate Circuit Court
```

dently prove the liability of X and not simply rely on the nolo contendere plea. In contrast, had X pleaded guilty to the charge of driving while intoxicated, the plea could have been used by the injured party in a civil case. The guilty plea automatically establishes X's civil liability, relieving the plaintiff of having to prove it.

Nolo contendere pleas are permitted in federal courts and in the courts of about half the states, usually in nonserious offenses and at the discretion of the judge. Even where such pleas are permitted, the accused generally does not have an absolute right to make the plea; rather, it can be made only with the consent of the prosecution or with the approval of the court. It is also generally used only for misdemeanor offenses.

2. Plea of Not Guilty

If the defendant pleads not guilty, the trial is usually scheduled to take place within two or three weeks. The delay is designed to give both the prosecution and the defense time to prepare their cases. When the defendant refuses to plead, or when the court is not sure of the defendant's plea, the court will enter a not guilty plea.

Between the not guilty plea and the start of the trial, the defense lawyer often files a number of written motions with the court. One of the most common is a *motion to suppress* evidence that allegedly was illegally seized. The motion requires a hearing at which the police officer who made the search testifies to the facts surrounding seizure of the evidence and the court determines whether the evidence was in fact illegally obtained. Another common motion is a *motion for a change of venue,* which is often made when there has been prejudicial pretrial publicity against the accused.

3. The Guilty Plea

When a defendant pleads guilty, the record must affirmatively show that the plea was voluntary and that the accused had a full understanding of its consequences. Otherwise

---

HIGHLIGHT 2.5

The Use of Discretion in Criminal Justice

Who Exercises Discretion?

These criminal justice officials . . .	. . . must often decide whether or not or how to—
Police	Enforce specific laws Investigate specific crimes Search people, vicinities, buildings Arrest or detain people
Prosecutors	File charges or petitions for adjudication Seek indictments Drop cases Reduce charges
Judges or magistrates	Set bail or conditions for release Accept pleas Determine delinquency Dismiss charges Impose sentence Revoke probation
Correctional officials	Assign to type of correctional facility Award privileges Punish for disciplinary infractions
Paroling authority	Determine date and conditions of parole Revoke parole

Source: Bureau of Justice Statistics, *Report to the Nation on Crime and Justice,* 2d ed. (Washington, DC: U.S. Government Printing Office, 1988), at 59.

the plea is invalid (Boykin v. Alabama, 395 U.S. 238 [1968]). A plea of guilty has the effect of the defendant waiving several important constitutional rights (such as the right to trial by jury, the right to confront witnesses, and protection against self-incrimination); hence, it is necessary to make sure the accused knew exactly what he or she was doing and was not coerced into making the plea.

A plea of guilty that represents an intelligent and informed choice among alternatives available to the defendant is voluntary even if it is entered in the hope of avoiding the death penalty (Brady v. U.S., 397 U.S. 472 [1970]). Likewise, a plea is valid even if the defendant does not admit guilt or even continues to assert his or her innocence, provided that there is some basis in the record for the plea. All that is required for a valid guilty plea is a knowing waiver of the rights involved, not an admission of guilt (North Carolina v. Alford, 400 U.S. 25 [1971]).

Frequently, a defendant is induced to plead guilty to a lesser charge in order to save the time, expense, and uncertainty of a trial. In these cases, the plea must be voluntary and the accused must have a full understanding of its consequences. This process is called *plea bargaining.*

Not all guilty pleas are the result of plea bargaining. Many people plead guilty for other reasons without bargaining with the prosecutor. Conversely, not all plea bargains result in a guilty plea; the terms may be unacceptable to either side or to the judge. Some forms of "inducement" may be inherently unfair or coercive; a plea obtained by such means is involuntary and therefore invalid. For example, a threat to prosecute the accused's spouse as a codefendant (despite lack of evidence) would invalidate the plea because of improper pressure.

If a plea is based to any significant degree upon the prosecutor's promise, that promise must be fulfilled. If not, either the agreement or promise is specifically enforced or the plea may be withdrawn (Santobello v. New York, 404 U.S. 257 [1971]). (Read the Santobello v. New York case brief at the end of this chapter.)

To avoid the awkward result of the Santobello case, most prosecutors tell the accused what they will recommend or not recommend for a possible sentence in exchange for a guilty plea, but they stipulate that the judge is not legally obligated to honor that recommendation. In many states, the judge is required to ask the parties in open court about the terms of the plea bargain. If the terms are unacceptable, the judge enters a not guilty plea for the defendant and then proceeds to try the case. One study found that about 30 percent of the time, judges asked the defendant if promises other than the plea-bargaining agreement had been made. The same study showed that in 65 percent of the cases, judges asked defendants if any threats or pressures had caused them to plead guilty. Judges rejected only 2 percent of the guilty pleas encountered in the study.[1]

Since an involuntary plea violates a defendant's constitutional rights, it may be withdrawn at any time. What constitutes an involuntary plea is a difficult issue and must be determined by the court on the circumstances of each case. Federal procedure permits a voluntary guilty plea to be withdrawn only before sentence is imposed—except that the court may permit a withdrawal after sentencing—"to correct manifest injustice." Some states follow the federal procedure, and others simply do not allow the withdrawal of voluntary pleas.

Plea bargaining is controversial; nonetheless only a few jurisdictions have abolished it. Among them are Alaska and some counties in Louisiana, Texas, Iowa,

Arizona, Michigan, and Oregon. Plea bargains may be prohibited by state law or by agency policy prescribed by chief prosecutors or judges. The predominant view is that, because they reduce the number of cases that come to trial, plea bargains are an essential and necessary part of the criminal justice process.

II. PROCEDURE DURING TRIAL

A. Selection of Jurors

A panel of jurors is assembled according to an established procedure. Twenty-three of the fifty states use the voter registration list as the sole source of names for jury duty. Ten states and the District of Columbia use a merged list of voters and driver's license holders.[2] The jury commissioner then sends letters of notification to the prospective jurors with instructions to report at a specific time and place for possible jury duty. Most states have various statutory exemptions for jury duty, the most common of which are undue hardship, personal bad health, and serving as an officer of the court. Many states by law exempt people in specific occupations, such as doctors, dentists, members of the clergy, elected officials, police officers, fire fighters, teachers, and sole proprietors of businesses.[3]

Prospective jurors may be questioned to determine whether there are grounds for challenge. This process is known as *voir dire,* meaning "to tell the truth." In federal courts, the trial judge usually asks the questions, although the judge may permit counsel to conduct the examination or submit questions for the judge to ask the jury. In most state courts, lawyers themselves often ask the questions.

There are two types of challenges to prospective jury members: (1) challenge for cause and (2) peremptory challenge.

1. Challenge for Cause

Jurors can be dismissed *for causes specified by law,* including actual bias, implied bias, and other factors that would prevent the juror from making a fair and impartial decision. Not residing within the jurisdiction, previous conviction, and insanity are also recognized challenges for cause.

2. Peremptory Challenge

Peremptory challenges are those for which no reason need be stated, meaning that they are made entirely at the discretion of each party. The number of peremptory challenges allowed varies from one state to another and may also depend upon the seriousness of the offense. The more serious the offense, the more peremptory challenges may be allowed. Peremptory challenges have been identified as a reason for minority underrepresentation in trial juries.

B. Opening Statements

1. By the Prosecution

The prosecutor's opening statement acquaints the jury with the nature of the charge against the accused and gives some description of the evidence that will be offered to sustain the charge. Opinions, conclusions, references to the character of the accused, argumentative statements, and references to matters on which evidence will not be offered are out of place, and the defense may object to them.

2. By the Defense

There is a difference of opinion as to the tactical value of an opening statement by the defense. Some argue that the defense should not risk assuming the burden of proving something in the mind of the jury, as it would if such a statement were made. Others note that failure to make a statement may imply a weak or hopeless defense. It is generally considered best for the defense to make its opening statement after the prosecution has presented its entire case; in some jurisdictions, it can be made only at that time.

C. Presentation of Case for the Prosecution

After opening the case, the prosecutor offers evidence in support of the charge. Although physical evidence may be introduced, most evidence takes the form of testimony of witnesses. Witnesses are examined in the following order:

1. Direct examination (by the prosecutor)
2. Cross-examination (by the defense lawyer)
3. Redirect examination (by the prosecutor)
4. Recross examination (by the defense lawyer)

This procedure theoretically can continue on and on, but the judge usually puts a stop to the examination of witnesses at this stage. After presenting all its evidence, the government rests its case.

D. Presentation of Case for the Defense

When the prosecution has rested, the defendant or the defendant's lawyer opens the defense and offers supporting evidence. Witnesses are examined in the order noted above, with the defense lawyer conducting the direct examination and the prosecutor cross-examining the witness. After presenting all the evidence, the defense rests its case.

Motions Prior to Verdict

Defendants can avail themselves of various motions prior to jury deliberations and a verdict. These are the most common:

1. *Motion for acquittal.* In most cases the defense moves for a judgment of acquittal at the close of the prosecution's case on grounds of failure to establish a *prima facie* case (a case established by sufficient evidence; it can be overthrown by evidence presented by the other side). This motion alleges that the prosecution has failed to introduce sufficient evidence on a necessary element of the offense charged, such as intent in robbery or death in homicide. If the motion is denied by the judge (as it usually is), the defendant may renew the motion to acquit at the close of the case.

2. *Motion for directed verdict of acquittal.* At the close of the presentation of evidence in a jury trial, the defendant may ask the court for a directed verdict of

acquittal—again on the ground that the prosecution has failed to introduce sufficient evidence concerning the offense charged. A few states do not permit a motion for directed verdict, on the theory that the right to a jury trial belongs to the prosecution as well as to the accused and hence that the judge cannot take the case away from the jury. Most states, however, allow the judge to direct a verdict of acquittal as part of the court's inherent power to prevent a miscarriage of justice through conviction on insufficient evidence.

Motions for acquittal or for a directed verdict of acquittal are based on the legal tenet that in a criminal case all elements of the offense must be proved by the prosecution beyond reasonable doubt. If the prosecution fails to do this, the defense does not have to present its own evidence in order to win an acquittal.

3. *Motion for a mistrial.* Improper conduct at trial constitutes grounds for a mistrial, and a motion on these grounds may be made prior to jury deliberations. Examples of grounds for a mistrial include the introduction of inflammatory evidence and prejudicial remarks by the judge or prosecution.

E. Rebuttal Evidence

After both sides have presented their main case, an opportunity is afforded to both parties to present evidence in rebuttal. This means that the prosecution may present evidence to destroy the credibility of witnesses or any evidence relied on by the defense, and vice versa. Cross-examination seeks to destroy the credibility of witnesses, but often direct contrary evidence is more effective. It is particularly so when the defense is an alibi, meaning that the accused maintains that he or she was somewhere else and not at the scene of the crime at the time it was committed.

F. Closing Arguments

In most jurisdictions, the prosecution presents its closing argument first; the defense replies; and the prosecution then offers a final argument to rebut the defense. The prosecution is given two presentations because it bears the heavy burden of proving guilt "beyond reasonable doubt."

1. Prosecution's Argument

The prosecution summarizes the evidence and presents theories on how the evidence should be considered to establish the defendant's guilt. The prosecutor's summation may sometimes include improper remarks, to which the defense may object and which (if serious enough) may even secure a mistrial, new trial, or reversal on appeal.

2. Defense's Argument

The closing argument by the defense is an important matter of tactic and strategy. Generally, the defense emphasizes the heavy burden of proof placed on the prosecution—namely, proof of defendant's guilt beyond a reasonable doubt on all elements of the crime charged. The defense then stresses that that obligation has not been met, and hence the defendant must be acquitted. Neither prosecutor nor defense counsel is permitted to express a personal opinion about the defendant's innocence or guilt. It is improper, for example, for a defense lawyer to tell the jury, "I am personally convinced that my client did not commit the crime." The facts as presented must speak for themselves without the lawyer's interjecting his or her own belief.

G. Judge's Instructions to Jury

The trial judge must instruct the jury properly on all general principles of law relevant to the charge and the issues raised by the evidence. Most states empower the trial judge to comment on the evidence. Some states, however, forbid such comment. In most criminal cases, the parties—especially defense counsel—will request of the court that certain instructions be used. The court must decide whether to give, refuse, or modify the instructions proposed by the parties; decide which additional instructions it will give; and advise counsel of its decision. Often an informal conference on instructions is held among the judge, prosecutor, and defense counsel, but the decision on what instructions to give rests with the judge. Any errors in the instructions can be challenged on appeal.

H. Deliberation of the Jury

The foreperson of the jury is usually elected immediately after the jury has been instructed by the judge and has retired from the courtroom to start its deliberations. The foreperson presides over the deliberations and gives the verdict to the court once a decision has been reached.

Jury deliberations are conducted in secret, and jurors are not subject to subsequent legal inquiry regardless of conviction or acquittal. Nothing prevents a juror, however, from later voluntarily discussing the details of the deliberation. There is a conflict among the various jurisdictions as to whether members of a jury—during the trial and/or during its deliberations—should be kept together (sequestered) or allowed to return to their respective homes at night or during weekends. Sequestration is usually an issue in sensational cases. Most states permit the trial judge to order sequestration at his or her discretion.

I. Verdict

A jury or judge's verdict of guilty results in conviction of the accused. In federal and most state trials, the jury vote for conviction or acquittal must be unanimous. Failure to reach a unanimous vote either way results in a hung jury and a mistrial. The length of time a jury must deliberate before a hung jury will be declared is determined by the judge. If the jury is dismissed by the judge because it cannot agree on the result, the case may be tried again before another jury. There is no double jeopardy because the jury did not agree on a verdict.

The U.S. Supreme Court has held that state laws providing for a less-than-unanimous vote for conviction are constitutional and will be upheld—at least in the case of a required 10-to-2 vote (Apodaca v. Oregon, 406 U.S. 404 [1972]). (Read the Apodaca v. Oregon case brief at the end of this chapter.) A law providing for a 9-to-3 jury vote for conviction is also constitutional (Johnson v. Louisiana, 406 U.S. 356 [1972]).

The U.S. Supreme Court has decided that a state law providing for a six-member jury in all criminal cases, except those involving the death penalty, is valid. Most states, however, provide for twelve-member juries in felony trials (Williams v. Florida, 399 U.S. 78 [1970]). Unlike those of twelve-member juries, the verdicts of six-member juries must be unanimous (Burch v. Louisiana, 441 U.S. 130 [1979]).

The Court has also decided that five-person juries are unconstitutional because they would not provide effective group discussion, would diminish the chances of drawing from a fair section of the community, and might impair the accuracy of fact finding (Ballew v. Georgia, 435 U.S. 223 [1978]).

After the jury has announced its verdict, the defendant has a right to have the jury polled. The jury must then express its vote in open court, either as a group or individually.

III. PROCEDURE AFTER TRIAL

A. Sentencing

Sentencing is defined as the formal pronouncing of judgment by the court or judge on the defendant after conviction in a criminal prosecution imposing the punishment to be inflicted.[4] In most states, sentences are imposed by the judge only; however, in a small number of states the defendant may choose to be sentenced by a judge or jury after a jury trial. In capital offenses, states generally require that no death sentence be imposed unless the penalty is imposed by the jury of twelve members after a jury trial.

The imposition of sentence usually does not immediately follow a guilty verdict, particularly in serious offenses. This is because in many states there is a requirement that a presentence investigation report (PSIR) be prepared to help determine the proper sentence to be imposed. The PSIR is either required by law or ordered by the judge and is usually prepared by a probation officer or the probation department. The last part of a PSIR often contains a recommendation by the probation officer as to what sentence might properly be imposed in view of all the circumstances surrounding the case and the defendant.

In plea-bargained cases, the sentence is imposed by the judge, but most judges merely follow the sentence agreed on by the prosecutor and the defense lawyer or the accused. Although the sentencing power is associated with and assigned to the judge, the actual sentence imposed is in fact the result of several influences. First there is the legislature that determines the fixed or maximum and minimum penalty to be imposed. The prosecutor and defense lawyer usually determine the sentence to be given in plea-bargained cases. In serious offenses, the probation officer is ordered by law or the judge to conduct a presentence investigation report (PSIR), which usually contains the sentence recommended by the probation officer. Finally, whatever prison term is set by the judge is subject to the provisions of the parole law in states that use determinate sentencing. Parole boards, therefore, have the final say as to how long an inmate stays in prison.

HIGHLIGHT 2.6

Conviction versus Acquittal Rates

"Whether a criminal case is tried to the bench or to a jury, the odds favor conviction over acquittal. The acquittal rate for felonies typically does not exceed one-third. At the misdemeanor level, the rate of acquittals usually is even lower."

Source: Yale Kamisar, Wayne R. LaFave, and Jerald H. Israel, *Modern Criminal Procedure: Cases—Comments—Questions,* 7th ed. (St. Paul, MN: West, 1990), at 19.

In states where juries may impose the sentence at the option of the accused, juries usually determine guilt or innocence and, for a verdict of guilty, decide on the sentence at the same time. Some states, however, have a bifurcated procedure, meaning that the guilt–innocence stage and the sentencing stage are separate. In those states, after a defendant is found guilty, the jury then receives evidence from the prosecution and the defense concerning the penalty to be imposed. The rules of evidence are relaxed at this stage; hence, evidence not heard during the trial (such as the previous record of the accused and his or her inclination to violence) may be brought out. The jury deliberates a second time to determine the penalty.

Most states give the sentencing power to the judge, even when the case is tried before a jury. After receiving a guilty verdict from the jury, the judge usually postpones the sentencing for a couple of weeks. The delay enables him or her to hear posttrial motions (such as a motion for new trial or a directed verdict) and to order a probation officer to conduct a presentence investigation. The judge has the option to use the presentence investigation report in any manner, meaning that he or she may accept any recommendation made by the probation officer or disregard it completely. Despite controversy, most states now allow the defense lawyer or the accused to see the PSIR, thus affording them an opportunity to rebut any false or unfair information contained in the PSIR.

B. Appeal

After the sentence is imposed, a period of time is usually provided during which the defendant may appeal the conviction and sentence to a higher court. There is no constitutional right to appeal, but all states afford defendants that right by law or court procedure. Theoretically, any criminal case may go as high as the U.S. Supreme Court on appeal as long as either federal law or constitutional issues are involved. In reality, however, the right is curtailed by the refusal of appellate courts, particularly the U.S. Supreme Court, to decide appealed cases on their merits. In cases that do not involve any federal question—when an appeal is based solely on a state constitutional provision or a state law, with no reference at all to any federal law or constitutional right—decisions by state supreme courts are final and unappealable.

IV. CAUTIONS

A. Application to Felony Cases

The procedure just outlined applies mainly to felony cases. Misdemeanors and petty offenses are usually processed in a simpler way. Whether a crime is a felony or a misdemeanor depends on the law of the state and may therefore vary from one state to another. Generally, a felony is a crime punishable by death or imprisonment in a state prison (as opposed to imprisonment in a local jail), or is a crime for which the punishment is imprisonment for more than one year. All other criminal offenses are considered misdemeanors.

B. Variation among States

The procedure just discussed applies in federal court and in most state courts. There are variations, however, from state to state. For example, some states use the grand jury for charging a person with a serious crime, and others do not use the grand jury at all. Some states allow jury trial for all offenses, whereas others impose restrictions. As long as a particular procedure is not required by the U.S. Constitution, the states do not have to use it.

C. Variation within a State

Likewise, there may be variations in procedure among different courts within a given state, even though all are governed by a single state code of criminal procedure. The procedure used in the courts of San Francisco to process felony or misdemeanor offenses may not be exactly the same as the procedure used in Los Angeles. Differences exist because of the preferences of judicial personnel or long-standing practices peculiar to a jurisdiction. For example, some jurisdictions hold preliminary hearings in all cases, and others hardly ever hold preliminary hearings. Variations in procedure are tolerated by the courts as long as they are not violations of the law or basic constitutional rights.

D. Theory versus Reality

The procedures just outlined, as well as those found in codes and textbooks, are the prescribed procedures. There may be differences, however, between the ideal (prescribed) procedure and the procedures actually used by local criminal justice agencies. Many such agencies have their own "convenient" and "traditional" ways of doing things, which are not always in keeping with procedures prescribed by law. Nevertheless, they continue to be used either because they have not been challenged or because they do not grossly prejudice the constitutional and statutory rights of the accused.

☐ SUMMARY

The criminal process in our criminal justice system involves proceedings before trial, during trial, and after trial. Procedure before trial covers the time from the filing of the complaint to the time of the defendant's plea. Procedure during trial begins with the selection of jurors and ends with a verdict of conviction or acquittal (or a mistrial). Procedure after trial involves sentencing and appeal.

The federal courts and practically all states follow a code of criminal procedure that details the procedure to be used in processing offenders in their respective jurisdictions. It is important for a law enforcement officer to know exactly what is prescribed by law for his or her jurisdiction, because the officer will be held accountable for that procedure as prescribed by the legislature and interpreted by the courts of the state.

☐ REVIEW QUESTIONS

1. What are the two kinds of arrests? Discuss how each is initiated.
2. Distinguish between a grand jury and a trial jury.
3. What is the advantage of a nolo contendere plea over a guilty plea?

4. Distinguish between challenge for cause and peremptory challenge in jury trials.
5. What is a motion to suppress evidence?
6. Suppose a state passed a law saying that a nonunanimous jury vote can result in conviction. Would the law be constitutional? Discuss.

❑ DEFINITIONS

Arraignment: A procedure by which, at a scheduled time and after prior notice, the accused is called into court, informed of the charges against him or her, and asked how he or she pleads.

Bail: The security required by the court and given by the accused to ensure that the accused appears before the proper court at the scheduled time and place to answer the charges brought against him or her.

Bifurcated Trial: Trial in which the stages of determining guilt or innocence and of sentencing are separate.

Bill of Indictment: A document submitted to the grand jury by the prosecutor accusing a person of a crime.

Booking: The making of an entry in the police blotter or arrest book indicating the suspect's name, the time of arrest, and the offense involved. If the crime is serious, the suspect may also be photographed or fingerprinted.

Challenge for Cause: Challenging the fitness of a person for jury membership on the basis of causes specified by law.

Citation: An order issued by a court or law enforcement officer commanding the person to whom the citation is issued to appear in court at a specified time to answer certain charges.

Complaint: A charge made before a proper officer alleging the commission of a criminal offense.

Exclusionary Rule: The exclusion in court of evidence illegally obtained.

Felony: A criminal offense punishable by death or imprisonment of more than one year.

Grand Jury: A jury, usually composed of from twelve to twenty-three members, that determines whether or not a suspect should be charged with an offense. A grand jury indictment is required in some states only for serious offenses.

Indictment: A written accusation filed against the defendant by a grand jury, usually signed by the jury foreperson.

Information: A written accusation of a crime prepared by the prosecuting attorney without referring the case to a grand jury.

Miranda Warnings: Warnings informing suspects of their right to remain silent, the fact that anything they say can be used against them in a court of law, their right to counsel, and that, if they are indigent, counsel will be provided by the state.

Misdemeanor: A crime punishable by a fine or imprisonment for less than one year; not as serious as a felony.

Motion for Directed Verdict of Acquittal: A motion by the defendant at the close of the presentation of evidence in a jury trial, asking the court for an acquittal on the ground that the prosecution failed to introduce sufficient evidence concerning the offense charged.

Motion for Mistrial: A motion filed by the defense seeking dismissal of the charges because of improper conduct on the part of the prosecution, judge, jury, or witnesses during the trial.

Nolo Contendere Plea: Literally means "no contest." A plea made when the defendant does not contest the charges. The effects are the same as that of a guilty plea, except that the plea cannot be used against the defendant as an admission in any subsequent civil proceeding arising out of the same offense.

Peremptory Challenge: Challenge to a prospective juror without stating a reason; the challenge is made entirely at the discretion of the challenging party. This is the opposite of "challenge for cause," whereby a reason for the challenge, usually specified by law, must be stated.

Plea Bargaining: A process whereby a defendant is induced to plead guilty to save the time, expense, and uncertainty of a trial.

Preliminary Examination (or Hearing):   A hearing held before a magistrate to determine if there is probable cause to support the charges against the accused. This takes place before the grand jury hearing.

Preventive Detention: The detention of an accused person not for purposes of ensuring his or her appearance in court but to prevent possible harm to society resulting from the accused's dangerousness.

Prima Facie Case: A case established by sufficient evidence; it can be overthrown by contrary evidence presented by the other side.

Rebuttal Evidence: Evidence introduced by one party in the case to discredit the evidence given by the other side.

Release on Recognizance (ROR):   An arrangement whereby the court, on the basis of the defendant's promise to appear in court as required, releases the defendant without requiring him or her to post money or securities.

Sentencing: The formal pronouncement of judgment by the court or judge on the defendant after conviction in a criminal prosecution, imposing the punishment to be inflicted.

Sequestration: Keeping members of the jury together and in isolation during a jury trial to prevent their decision from being influenced by outside factors.

Summons: A writ directed to the sheriff or other proper officer requiring the officer to notify the person named that he or she is required to appear in court on a day named and answer the complaint stated in the summons.

Verdict: A jury or judge's pronouncement of guilt or innocence.

Voir Dire: Literally means "to tell the truth." A process whereby prospective jurors may be questioned by the judge or lawyers to determine whether there are grounds for challenge.

☐ PRINCIPLES OF CASES

APODACA V. OREGON, 406 U.S. 404 (1972)   State laws providing for a less-than-unanimous vote for conviction are constitutional, at least in the case of a required 10-to-2 vote.

BALLEW V. GEORGIA, 435 U.S. 223 (1978)   Five-person juries are unconstitutional because they would not provide effective group discussion, would diminish the chances of drawing from a fair section of the community, and might impair the accuracy of fact finding.

BOYKIN V. ALABAMA, 395 U.S. 238 (1968)   When defendant pleads guilty, the record must affirmatively show that the plea was voluntary and that the accused had a full understanding of its consequences. Otherwise, the plea is invalid.

BRADY V. UNITED STATES, 397 U.S. 472 (1970)   A plea of guilty that represents an intelligent choice among alternatives available to the defendant—especially when represented by competent counsel—is not involuntary simply because it is entered in the hope of avoiding the death penalty. If otherwise voluntary and informed, the plea is valid.

BURCH V. LOUISIANA, 441 U.S. 130 (1979)   Unlike those of twelve-member juries, the verdicts of six-member juries must be unanimous.

JOHNSON V. LOUISIANA, 406 U.S. 356 (1972)   A law providing for a 9-to-3 jury vote for conviction is constitutional.

NORTH CAROLINA V. ALFORD, 400 U.S. 25 (1971)   A guilty plea is not invalid simply because the defendant does not admit guilt, or even continues to assert innocence, provided that there is some basis in the record for the plea. All that is required for a valid guilty plea is a knowing waiver of the rights involved, not an admission of guilt.

SANTOBELLO V. NEW YORK, 404 U.S. 257 (1971)   Once the court has accepted a guilty plea entered in accordance with a plea bargain, the defendant has a right to have the bargain enforced. If the prosecution does not keep the bargain, the court should decide whether the circumstances require enforcement of the plea bargain or whether the defendant should be granted an opportunity to withdraw the guilty plea.

WILLIAMS V. FLORIDA, 399 U.S. 78 (1970)   A state law providing for a six-member jury in all criminal cases, except those involving the death penalty, is valid.

☐ CASE BRIEF—LEADING CASE ON PLEA BARGAINING
SANTOBELLO V. NEW YORK, 404 U.S. 257 (1971)

FACTS: The state of New York indicted Santobello on two felony counts. After negotiations, the assistant district attorney in charge of the case agreed to permit

Santobello to plead guilty to a lesser offense and agreed not to make any recommendation as to the sentence. Santobello then pleaded guilty, but during sentencing a few months later a new assistant district attorney asked for the maximum sentence to be imposed. The judge imposed the maximum, but later maintained that the request was not the reason the maximum was imposed and that he was not influenced by it. The defendant moved to withdraw his guilty plea, but the request was denied.

ISSUE: *May a plea be withdrawn if the prosecution fails to fulfill all its promises, even if the result would have been the same had the prosecution kept its promise? Yes.*

SUPREME COURT DECISION: Once the court has accepted a guilty plea entered in accordance with a plea bargain, the defendant has a right to have the bargain enforced. If the prosecution does not keep the bargain, a court should decide whether the circumstances require enforcement of the plea bargain or whether the defendant should be granted an opportunity to withdraw the guilty plea. In this case, the broken promise (although not maliciously broken) by the original prosecutor to make no sentencing recommendation pursuant to a guilty plea is sufficient to vacate the judgment and remand the case back to the trial court.

CASE SIGNIFICANCE: Santobello gives reliability to the bargaining process in that the defendant can now rely on the promise of the prosecutor. If the defendant relied on that promise as an incentive for pleading guilty and the promise is not kept, the guilty plea can be withdrawn.

EXCERPTS FROM THE DECISION: The plea must, of course, be voluntary and knowing and if it was induced by promises, the essence of those promises must in some way be made known. There is, of course, no absolute right to have a guilty plea accepted. A court may reject a plea in exercise of sound judicial discretion.

This phase of the process of criminal justice, and the adjudicative element inherent in accepting a plea of guilty, must be attended by safeguards to ensure the defendant what is reasonably due in the circumstances. Those circumstances will vary, but a constant factor is that when a plea rests in any significant degree on a promise or agreement of the prosecutor, so that it can be said to be part of the inducement or consideration, such promise must be fulfilled.

On this record, petitioner "bargained" and negotiated for a particular plea in order to secure dismissal of more serious charges, but also on condition that no sentence recommendation would be made by the prosecutor. It is now conceded that the promise to abstain from a recommendation was made, and at this stage the prosecution is not in a good position to argue that its inadvertent breach of agreement is immaterial. The staff lawyers in a prosecutor's office have the burden of "letting the left hand know what the right hand is doing" or has done. That the breach of agreement was inadvertent does not lessen its impact.

We need not reach the question whether the sentencing judge would or would not have been influenced had he known all the details of the negotiations for the plea. He stated that the prosecutor's recommendation did not influence him and we have no reason to doubt that. Nevertheless, we conclude that the interests of justice and appropriate recognition of the duties of the prosecution in relation to promises made in the negotiation of pleas of guilty will be best served by remanding the case to the state courts for further consideration. The ultimate relief for which petitioner is entitled we leave to the discretion of the state court, which is in a better position to decide whether the circumstances of this case require only that there be specific performance of the agreement on the plea, in which case petitioner should be resentenced by a different judge, or whether, in the view of the state court, the circumstances require granting the relief sought by petitioner, i.e., the opportunity to withdraw his plea of guilty. We emphasize that this is in no sense to question the fairness of the sentencing judge; the fault here rests on the prosecutor, not on the sentencing judge.

Vacated and remanded.

❑ CASE BRIEF—LEADING CASE ON NONUNANIMOUS JURIES

APODACA V. OREGON, 406 U.S. 404 (1972)

FACTS: Apodaca, Cooper, and Madden were convicted respectively of assault with a deadly weapon, burglary on a dwelling, and general larceny before separate Oregon juries. None of the convictions was unanimous. The vote in the cases of Apodaca and Madden was 11 to 1, and the vote in Cooper was 10 to 2. Oregon law provided that a defendant could be convicted even if the vote was 10 to 2 for conviction. All three defendants appealed, alleging that a less-than-unanimous jury violates the right to trial by jury in criminal cases specified by the Sixth and the Fourteenth Amendments.

ISSUE: *Does a state law that provides for conviction on a less-than-unanimous vote for conviction violate the Sixth Amendment provision on the right to jury trial? No.*

SUPREME COURT DECISION: Although the right to a jury trial has been incorporated and held applicable to the states through the Fourteenth Amendment, the unanimous-verdict aspect of this right is not so fundamental as to be required by due process; hence although the states must give the defendant a jury trial, they do not have to provide for a unanimous verdict.

CASE SIGNIFICANCE: This decision held, by a 5-to-4 vote, that there is nothing in the Constitution that requires states to convict defendants only by unanimous vote of the jury. The Court rejected the argument that a unanimous jury is required to give substance to the "reasonable doubt" standard required by the "due process" clause, saying that the "reasonable doubt" standard developed separately from both the jury trial and the unanimous verdict. Note that the nonunanimous decision in Oregon was allowable by virtue of statute. Although not many states have passed nonunanimous jury statutes, the message in Apodaca is clear—that the Constitution does not require unanimous juries. In the case of Oregon, the law provided for a minimum vote of 10 to 2 for conviction. Whether a 9-to-3, 8-to-4, or 7-to-5 vote would also be constitutional was not decided by the Court. The result of the decision is that defendants may receive lesser jury protection in state than in federal courts, if the state legislature so wishes.

EXCERPTS FROM THE DECISION: Our inquiry must focus upon the function served by the jury in contemporary society. As we said in Duncan, the purpose of trial by jury is to prevent oppression by the Government by providing a "safeguard against the corrupt or overzealous prosecutor and against the compliant, biased, or eccentric judge." Duncan v. Louisiana, 391 U.S., at 156. "Given this purpose, the essential feature of a jury obviously lies in the interposition between the accused and his accuser of the commonsense judgment of a group of laymen. . . ." Williams v. Florida, supra, at 100. A requirement of unanimity, however, does not materially contribute to the exercise of this commonsense judgment. As we said in Williams, a jury will come to such a judgment as long as it consists of a group of laymen representative of a cross section of the community who have the duty and the opportunity to deliberate, free from outside attempts at intimidation, on the question of a defendant's guilt. In terms of this function we perceive no difference between juries required to act unanimously and those permitted to convict or acquit by votes of 10 to two or 11 to one. Requiring unanimity would obviously produce hung juries in some situations where nonunanimous juries will convict or acquit. But in either case, the interest of the defendant in having the judgment of his peers interposed between himself and the officers of the State who prosecute and judge him is equally well served.

Petitioners nevertheless argue that unanimity serves other purposes constitutionally essential to the continued operation of the jury system. Their principal contention is that a Sixth Amendment "jury trial" made mandatory on the States by virtue of the Due Process Clause of the Fourteenth Amendment, Duncan v. Louisiana, supra, should be held to require a unanimous jury verdict in order to give substance to the reasonable doubt standard otherwise mandated by the Due Process Clause.

We are quite sure, however, that the Sixth Amendment itself has never been held to require proof beyond a reasonable doubt in criminal cases. The reasonable doubt standard developed separately from both the jury trial and the unanimous verdict. As the Court noted in the Winship case, the rule requiring proof of crime beyond a reasonable doubt did not crystallize in this country until after the Constitution was adopted. And in that case, which held such a burden of proof to be constitutionally required, the Court purported to draw no support from the Sixth Amendment.

☐ NOTES

1. Bureau of Justice Statistics, *Report to the Nation on Crime and Justice* (Washington, DC: U.S. Government Printing Office, 1983), at 65.
2. Ibid., at 67.
3. Ibid.
4. *Black's Law Dictionary* (St. Paul, MN: West, 1968), at 1528.

PART TWO

THE EXCLUSIONARY RULE AND PROBABLE CAUSE

THE EXCLUSIONARY RULE

□ KEY TERMS

exclusionary rule
silver platter doctrine
harmless error
illegally seized evidence
fruit of the poisonous tree

"purged taint" exception
"inevitable discovery" exception
"independent untainted source"
  exception
"good faith" exception

The exclusionary rule is one of the most controversial rules in criminal evidence and has generated heated debate among criminal justice professionals at all levels. The rule is applied by the judiciary but has direct impact on law enforcement and police task performance. It is also a rule of evidence on which law enforcement officers have strong opinions and on which a high degree of consensus exists. The rule continues to undergo scrutiny and modification in Supreme Court decisions. How far the changes will go remains to be seen. Regardless of its future direction, every law enforcement officer should be familiar with the exclusionary rule because the success or failure of criminal prosecutions may depend on it.

I. GENERAL CONSIDERATIONS

A. Definition

The *exclusionary rule* provides that *any evidence obtained by the government in violation of the Fourth Amendment guarantee against unreasonable search or seizure is not admissible in a criminal prosecution to prove guilt.* This definition limits the exclusionary rule to search and seizure cases under the Fourth Amendment and not to violations of other constitutional rights. What happens if the right violated is a Fifth, Sixth, or Fourteenth Amendment right? May the exclusionary rule be used to exclude such evidence? For example, X is charged with an offense and retains a lawyer to represent him. Nonetheless, the police interrogate X in the absence of his lawyer—a violation of his Sixth Amendment right to counsel. Or suppose that X is interrogated by the police while in custody without having been given the Miranda warnings, in violation of his Fifth Amendment right not to incriminate himself. In both instances, the evidence obtained is inadmissible, but will it be suppressed under the exclusionary rule?

Any time evidence is obtained in violation of a constitutional right, the evidence is not admissible in court during the trial and therefore must be suppressed. Strictly speaking, however, only suppression based on a violation of the Fourth Amendment guarantee against unreasonable search and seizure and any evidence derived from it come under the exclusionary rule. In United States v. Leon, 35 CrL 3273 (1984), the Court said that the exclusionary rule is a "judicially created remedy designed to safeguard Fourth Amendment rights . . ."; therefore, not every violation of a constitutional right comes under the exclusionary rule. It must be added that evidence obtained in violation of any of the other constitutional rights is also excludable in criminal trial; not, however, under the exclusionary rule. An example is a confession obtained without giving the suspect the Miranda warnings. Such confession is not admissible in court but not, strictly speaking, under the exclusionary rule. Miranda is primarily a Fifth Amendment right against self-incrimination cases, hence what is violated is a suspect's Fifth Amendment right. The evidence is excludable anyway, but not under the exclusionary rule, which applies only to Fourth Amendment violations.

B. Purpose

The Court has stated in a number of cases that the primary purpose of the exclusionary rule is to *deter police misconduct.* The assumption is that if the evidence obtained illegally is not admitted in court, police misconduct in search and seizure cases will cease or at least be minimized. The rule now applies to federal and state cases. This means that evidence illegally seized by state or federal officers cannot now be used in any state or federal prosecution.

C. Source

Is the exclusionary rule a constitutional or judge-made rule? If the rule is mandated by the Constitution, then the Supreme Court cannot eliminate it, and neither may it be changed by Congress. If it is judge-made, however, then the Court may eliminate it at any time, or it can perhaps be modified by Congress. Some writers maintain that this rule of evidence is man-made, not God-given, and that it is not in the Constitution. Its proponents disagree, saying that the rule is of constitutional origin and therefore beyond the reach of Congress, should Congress want to limit it. The proponents point to a statement of the Court, in Mapp v. Ohio, 367 U.S. 643 (1961), saying that "the exclusionary rule is an essential part of both the Fourth and Fourteenth Amendment. . . ." The Court, however, has again spoken in favor of the concept that the exclusionary rule is in fact a judge-made rule of evidence. In United States v. Leon, 35 CrL 3273 (1984), the Court said,

> The Fourth Amendment contains no provision expressly precluding the use of evidence obtained in violation of its commands, and an examination of its origin and purposes makes clear that the use of fruits of a past unlawful search or seizure works no new Fourth Amendment wrong. . . . This rule thus operates as a "judicially created remedy designed to safeguard Fourth Amendment rights generally through its deterrent effect, rather than a personal constitutional right of the person aggrieved."

Whether or not the Court will adhere to that position in the future is speculative. At present the issue appears settled in favor of the "judge-made" approach.

The exclusionary rule is used only in criminal proceedings, not in civil cases. This is because it is meant to control the conduct of public officers and not of private individuals, the usual parties in civil proceedings. It is a remedy and not a source of an additional right, meaning that it is an avenue of redress for those whose Fourth Amendment rights have been violated.

D. Historical Development

1. Federal Courts

The exclusionary rule is of U.S. origin. The first exclusionary rule case was decided by the Court in 1886 when it held that the forced disclosure of papers amounting to evidence of crime violated the constitutional right of the suspect against unreasonable search and seizure and therefore that such items were inadmissible in court proceedings (Boyd v. U.S., 116 U.S. 616 [1886]). It was not until 1914, however, that evidence illegally obtained by federal officers was held excluded in all federal criminal prosecutions (Weeks v. U.S., 232 U.S. 383 [1914]). In the Weeks case, the Court said: "To sustain the unlawful invasion of the sanctity of his home by officers of the law would be to affirm by judicial decision a manifest neglect, if not an open defiance, of the prohibitions of the Constitution, intended for the protection of the people against such unauthorized action."

From 1914 to 1960, federal courts would admit evidence of a federal crime if the evidence had been illegally obtained by state officers, as long as it had not been obtained in connivance with federal officers. This questionable practice was known as the *silver platter doctrine*. Under the silver platter doctrine (the term came from the practice of virtually handing over illegally seized evidence on a silver platter), such evidence was admissible because the illegality was not committed by federal officers. In 1960, the Court rejected the silver platter doctrine, holding that the Fourth Amendment prohibited the use of illegally obtained evidence in federal prosecutions, whether obtained by federal or state officers (Elkins v. U.S., 364 U.S. 206 [1960]).

2. State Courts

In 1949, the Court held that state courts were not constitutionally required to exclude illegally obtained evidence; hence the exclusionary rule did not apply to the states (Wolf v. Colorado, 388 U.S. 25 [1949]). In 1952, the Court modified that position, finding that some searches were so "shocking" as to require exclusion of the evidence seized; however, these were limited to cases involving coercion, violence, or brutality (Rochin v. California, 342 U.S. 165 [1952]). Finally, in Mapp v. Ohio, the Court overruled the Wolf case and held that the Fourth Amendment required the state courts to exclude evidence obtained by unlawful searches and seizures.

II. MAPP V. OHIO: THE EXCLUSIONARY RULE APPLIED TO THE STATES

In Mapp v. Ohio, 467 U.S. 643 (1961), defendant Dollree Mapp was convicted of knowingly possessing certain lewd and lascivious books, pictures, and photographs, in violation of Ohio law. Three Cleveland police officers went to Mapp's residence. Upon arrival at the house, the officers knocked on the door and demanded entrance, but Mapp, after telephoning her attorney, refused to admit them without a search warrant. The officers again sought entrance three hours later when four or more additional officers had arrived on the scene. When Mapp did not come to the door

---

HIGHLIGHT 3.1

Justification for the Exclusionary Rule

"The exclusionary rule has rested primarily on the judgment that the importance of deterring police conduct that may violate the constitutional rights of individuals throughout the community outweighs the importance of securing the conviction of the specific defendant on trial" (U.S. v. Caceres, 440 U.S. 741 [1979]).

immediately, the police forcibly opened one of the doors and gained entry. Meanwhile, Mapp's attorney arrived, but the officers would not permit him to see his client or to enter the house. Mapp demanded to see the search warrant, which the officers by then claimed to have.

A paper, claimed to be a warrant, was held up by one of the officers. Mapp grabbed the "warrant" and placed it in her bosom. A struggle ensued in which the officers handcuffed Mapp because she was belligerent. An officer grabbed her and twisted her hand, and she yelled and pleaded with him because "it was hurting." In handcuffs, Mapp was forcibly taken upstairs to her bedroom, where the officers searched a dresser, a chest of drawers, a closet, and some suitcases. They also looked into a photo album and through personal papers belonging to Mapp. The search spread to the rest of the second floor, including the child's bedroom, the living room, the kitchen, and a dinette. The basement of the building and a trunk found in it were also searched. The obscene materials, for possession of which Mapp was ultimately convicted, were discovered in the course of that widespread search. At the trial no search warrant was produced by the prosecution, and neither was the absence of a warrant explained. The seized materials were admitted into evidence by the trial court, and the defendant was convicted. On appeal, the Court excluded the evidence, holding that the exclusionary rule prohibiting the use of evidence in federal courts if illegally obtained is now applicable to state criminal proceedings.

Mapp is significant in that since 1961 the exclusionary rule has been applied with equal vigor in federal and state proceedings. Before Mapp, the use of the exclusionary rule was optional in state proceedings. It is perhaps the second most important law enforcement case ever to be decided by the Court, the first being Miranda v. Arizona, discussed in Chapter Eleven. (Read the Mapp v. Ohio case brief at the end of this chapter.)

III. PROCEDURE FOR INVOKING THE EXCLUSIONARY RULE

In both federal and state courts, the basic procedure for excluding evidence on a claim of illegal search and seizure is a pretrial motion to suppress the evidence. If the accused loses at this pretrial hearing, he or she can object again at the time it is offered into evidence during the trial. If the accused loses at the trial, he or she can raise the issue again in a postconviction proceeding, such as in a writ of habeas corpus. There are therefore many opportunities to invoke the exclusionary rule.

The burden of proof in a motion to suppress depends upon whether the search or seizure in question was made with or without a warrant. If the search or seizure was pursuant to a warrant, there is a presumption of validity. The burden is therefore on the accused to show that the warrant was issued without probable cause. This is a heavy burden for the accused to bear. It usually takes clear and convincing evidence to prove that probable cause did not in fact exist. If the search was made without a warrant, however, the prosecution has the burden of establishing the existence of probable cause or, in its absence, the fact that the search was valid because of consent or because it came under any of the exceptions to the warrant requirement. Establishing validity usually means that the police officer must testify during the hearing on the motion to suppress. Validity can be established through a mere preponderance of the evidence. The validity of warrants may also be attacked on grounds other than the lack of probable cause.

If the evidence in question is admitted by the trial judge, the trial then goes on, with the prosecution using the evidence. Should the accused be convicted, the defense may appeal to the appellate court the allegedly erroneous decision to admit the evidence. If the trial judge decides to exclude the evidence, most jurisdictions allow the prosecution to appeal that decision immediately because otherwise the effect of the allegedly wrongful decision might be the acquittal of the defendant. If the defendant is acquitted, there can be no appeal at all, hence depriving the prosecution of the opportunity to challenge the judge's decision to suppress.

If a motion to exclude was made in a timely manner, it is an error for the court to receive evidence obtained by illegal search or seizure. Such mistakes require reversal on appeal of any conviction unless admission of the evidence is found to be a *harmless error.* To prove harmless error, the prosecution must show beyond a reasonable doubt that the evidence erroneously admitted did not contribute to the conviction. Also, in attempting to demonstrate harmless error, it is not enough for the prosecution simply to show that there was other evidence sufficient to support the verdict. Rather, it must show that there is no reasonable possibility that a different result would have been reached without the tainted evidence (Chapman v. California, 386 U.S. 18 [1967]).

IV. WHAT IS NOT ADMISSIBLE

1. Illegally Seized Evidence

Illegally seized evidence includes contraband, fruits of the crime (for example, stolen goods), instruments of the crime (such as burglar tools), or "mere evidence" (shoes, shirt, or the like connecting a person to the crime), which, if seized illegally, may not be admitted at a trial to show the defendant's guilt.

2. "Fruit of the Poisonous Tree"

Any evidence (verbal or physical) that is the direct or indirect result of the initial illegally obtained evidence is known as *fruit of the poisonous tree* and must also be excluded. The "fruit of the poisonous tree" doctrine states that once the primary source (the "tree") is shown to have been unlawfully obtained, any secondary evidence (the "fruit") derived from it is also inadmissible (Silverthorne Lumber Co. v. U.S., 251 U.S. 385 [1920]).

The doctrine may be illustrated as follows:

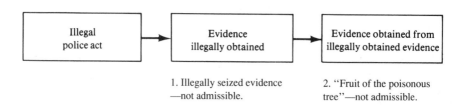

| Illegal police act | → | Evidence illegally obtained | → | Evidence obtained from illegally obtained evidence |

1. Illegally seized evidence —not admissible.

2. "Fruit of the poisonous tree"—not admissible.

This rule is based on the principle that evidence illegally obtained should not be used to gain other evidence because the original illegally obtained evidence "taints" all evidence subsequently obtained. The tainted secondary or derivative evidence can take various forms.

> Example 1: The police conduct an illegal search of a house and find a map that shows the location of the stolen goods. Using the map, the police recover the goods in an abandoned warehouse. Both the map and the goods are inadmissible as evidence, but for different reasons. The map is not admissible because it is illegally seized evidence, whereas the goods (physical evidence) are not admissible because they are a "fruit of the poisonous tree."

> Example 2: Police officers make an illegal search of D's house and find heroin. They confront D with the evidence and she confesses to possession of an illicit drug. D's confession is likewise the "fruit" of the illegal search (verbal evidence) and must be excluded.

> Example 3: The police obtain a confession from X without giving him the Miranda warnings. X tells the police the location of the murder weapon, which the police subsequently recover. X's confession is inadmissible because it is illegally obtained evidence; the murder weapon is inadmissible because it is "fruit of the poisonous tree."

In summary, these two types of inadmissible evidence may be distinguished as follows: Illegally seized evidence is obtained as a direct result of the illegal act, whereas the "fruit of the poisonous tree" is the indirect result of the same illegal act. The "fruit of the poisonous tree" is therefore at least once removed from the illegally seized evidence, and is also inadmissible.

V. EXCEPTIONS TO THE EXCLUSIONARY RULE

Recent Court decisions have identified instances in which the evidence obtained is admissible in court although something may have been wrong initially with either the conduct of the police or the court that issued the warrant. These exceptions fall into four categories.

HIGHLIGHT 3.2

The Origin of the Exclusionary Rule

Under the exclusionary rule, evidence obtained in violation of the Fourth Amendment cannot be used in a criminal trial against the victim of the illegal search and seizure. The Constitution does not require this remedy; it is a doctrine of judicial design. Excluded evidence is oftentimes quite reliable and the "most probative information bearing on the guilt or innocence of the defendant." Nonetheless, the rule's prohibition applies to such direct evidence, as well as to the "fruit of the poisonous tree"—secondary evidence derived from the illegally seized evidence itself (U.S. v. Houltin, 566 F.2d 1027 [5th Cir. 1978]).

---

1. The "Purged Taint" Exception

The term *purged taint* refers specifically to the "fruit of the poisonous tree" doctrine and applies when the defendant's subsequent voluntary act dissipates the taint of the initial illegality. A defendant's intervening act of free will is sufficient to break the causal chain between the tainted evidence and the illegal police conduct; hence the evidence becomes admissible. For example, the police broke into a suspect's house illegally and obtained a confession from him, but the suspect refused to sign it. The suspect was released on his own recognizance. A few days later he went back to the police station and signed the confession. The Court said that the suspect's act manifested free will and therefore cleaned the tainted evidence of illegality (Wong Sun v. U.S., 371 U.S. 471 [1963]). Note, however, that to break the causal connection between an illegal arrest and a confession that is the fruit of the illegal arrest, the intervening event must be meaningful. For example, after an unlawful arrest, a suspect confessed to the commission of a robbery. Even though the suspect received three sets of Miranda warnings, and met briefly at the police station with friends before confession, the Court said that these events were not meaningful and that the evidence obtained was therefore not admissible during the trial (Taylor v. Alabama, 102 S.Ct. 2664 [1982]).

2. The "Inevitable Discovery" Exception

The *"inevitable discovery" exception* also refers to the "fruit of the poisonous tree" doctrine and is usually limited to instances where the evidence obtained is a weapon or a body. In a number of cases, the Court has said that evidence is admissible if the police can prove that they *would inevitably have discovered the evidence anyway by lawful means regardless of their illegal action*. For example, while the police were taking a suspect back to Des Moines from Davenport, Iowa, where he surrendered, they induced the suspect to tell them the location of the body of the murdered girl by appealing to the suspect (whom the police addressed as "Reverend"), saying that it would be nice to give the deceased a Christian burial. The police did not directly question the suspect, but instead asked him to "think it over." The police did this despite repeated requests by the suspect's lawyer before departure from Davenport that no questioning take place during that drive. The suspect led the police to the body of the murdered girl. While conceding that the police violated the defendant's right to counsel by encouraging him to discuss the location of the body, the Court nevertheless admitted the evidence on the ground that the police would have discovered it anyway. At the time that the police were being led by the suspect to the body, the searchers were approaching the actual location, and therefore the body inevitably would have been found (Nix v. Williams, 35 CrL 3119 [1984]).

3. The "Independent Untainted Source" Exception

The *"independent untainted source" exception* too has reference to the "fruit of the poisonous tree" doctrine. The evidence obtained is admissible *if the police can prove that it was obtained from an independent source not connected with the illegal search or seizure* (U.S. v. Crews, 445 U.S. 463 [1980]). In the Crews case, the Court said that the initial illegality (the illegal detention of the suspect) could not deprive the prosecutors of the opportunity to prove the defendant's guilt through the introduction of evidence wholly untainted by police misconduct. For example, a 14-year-old girl was found in the defendant's apartment during an illegal search. The girl's testimony that the defendant had had carnal knowledge of her was admissible because she was an independent source that predated the search of the apartment. Prior to the search, the girl's parents had reported her missing, and a police informant had already located her in the defendant's apartment (State v. O'Bremski, 70 Wash. 2d 425 [1967]).

In another case, the Court said that when an illegal search enables the police to locate a witness, that witness's statements will less readily be excluded as the "fruit of the poisonous tree" than other types of evidence. A direct link will be required before the testimony will be excluded. The factors a court will consider include the extent to which the witness is willing to testify and the extent to which disallowing the witness from testifying would deter future police misconduct (U.S. v. Ceccolini, 425 U.S. 268 [1978]).

4. The "Good Faith" Exception: The Sheppard and Leon Cases

In the most significant exception carved out thus far to the exclusionary rule, the Court recently held that *evidence obtained by the police acting in good faith on a search warrant that was issued by a neutral and detached magistrate, but that is ultimately found to be invalid, may be admitted and used at the trial* (Massachusetts v. Sheppard, 35 CrL 3296 [1984]).

In Massachusetts v. Sheppard, a police detective executed an affidavit for an arrest and search warrant authorizing the search of Sheppard's residence. The affidavit stated that the police wished to search for certain described items, including clothing of the victim and a blunt instrument that might have been used on the victim. The affidavit was reviewed and approved by the district attorney. Because it was Sunday, the local court was closed, and the police had a difficult time finding a warrant application form. The detective finally found a warrant form previously used in another district in the Boston area to search for controlled substances. After making some changes in the form, the detective presented it and the affidavit to the judge at his residence, informing him that the warrant form might need to be further changed. Concluding that the affidavit established probable cause to search the residence and telling the detective that the necessary changes in the warrant form would be made, the judge made some changes, but did not change the substantive portion, which continued to authorize a search for controlled substances; neither did he alter the form so as to incorporate the affidavit. The judge then signed the warrant and returned it and the affidavit to the detective, informing him that the warrant was of sufficient authority in form and content to authorize the search. The ensuing search of Sheppard's residence was limited to the items listed in the affidavit, and several incriminating pieces of evidence were discovered. The defendant was convicted of first-degree murder in a trial at which the evidence obtained under the warrant was used. On appeal, the Court said that evidence obtained was admissible in court because the officer conducting the search had acted in objectively good-faith reliance on a search warrant that had been issued by a magistrate but that was subsequently declared to be invalid.

In a companion case decided that same day, United States v. Leon, 35 CrL 3273 (1984), the Court made the same decision on a different set of facts. Acting on information from a confidential informant, officers of the Burbank, California, police department had initiated a drug-trafficking investigation involving a surveillance of Leon's activities. On the basis of an affidavit summarizing the officer's observations, the police prepared an application for a warrant to search three residences and Leon's automobiles for an extensive list of items. The application was reviewed by several deputy district attorneys, and a facially valid warrant was issued by a state court judge. Leon was later indicted for federal drug offenses and filed motions to suppress the evidence seized. The trial court excluded the evidence on the ground that no probable cause had existed for the issuance of the warrant because the reliability of the informant had not been established and the information obtained from the informant was "stale." This decision was affirmed by the Court of Appeals. The government then took the case to the Supreme Court solely on the question of whether a "good faith" exception to the exclusionary rule should be recognized. The Court ruled that the Fourth Amendment's exclusionary rule should not be applied to bar the use in the prosecution's case of evidence that has been obtained by officers acting in reasonable reliance on a search warrant issued by a detached and neutral magistrate, but that is ultimately found to be invalid because it lacks probable cause.

The Sheppard and Leon cases are arguably the most important cases decided on the exclusionary rule since Mapp v. Ohio. They represent a significant, although still narrow, exception to the exclusionary rule, and thus a breakthrough that police proponents have long been advocating. In these cases, the Court said that there were objectively reasonable grounds for the police's mistaken belief that the warrants authorized the searches. The officers took every step that could reasonably have been taken to ensure that the warrants were valid. *The difference between these two cases is that in Sheppard the issue is the improper use of a form, a technical error, by the judge; whereas in Leon it is the use of a questionable informant and stale information by the judge to determine probable cause. The cases are similar, however, in that the mistakes were made by the judges, not the police.* When the warrants were given to the officers, anyone would have concluded that the warrant authorized a valid search. In the Sheppard case, the Court said:

> An error of constitutional dimension may have been committed with respect to the issuance of the warrant in this case, but it was the judge, not the police officer, who made the crucial mistake. Suppressing evidence because the judge failed to make all the necessary clerical corrections despite his assurance that such changes would be made will not serve the deterrent function that the exclusionary rule was designed to achieve.

HIGHLIGHT 3.3

The Independent Source Exception

An unlawful search taints all evidence obtained at the search or through leads uncovered by the search. The rule, however, extends only to facts that were actually discovered by a procedure initiated by the unlawful act. If information that could have emerged from an unlawful search in fact stems from an independent source, the evidence is admissible (U.S. v. Paroutian, 299 F.2d 488 [2d Cir. 1962]).

And in the Leon case, the Court said:

> The exclusionary rule is designed to deter police misconduct rather than to punish the errors of judges and magistrates. Admitting evidence obtained pursuant to a warrant while at the same time declaring that the warrant was somehow defective will not reduce judicial officers' professional incentives to comply with the Fourth Amendment, encourage them to repeat their mistakes, or lead to the granting of all colorable warrant requests.

In sum, the Court reasoned that the evidence was admissible because the judge erred, not the police, and the exclusionary rule is designed to control the conduct of the police, not of judges.

The *"good faith" exception* carved out by the Court in the Sheppard and Leon cases was extended three years later to instances when the police act in reliance on a statute that is later declared to be unconstitutional (Illinois v. Krull, 480 U.S. 340 [1987]). In the Krull case, police officers entered the wrecking yard of Krull without a warrant and found evidence of stolen vehicles. Such warrantless entry was authorized by state statute. The next day, however, a federal court declared the statute unconstitutional, saying that it permitted police officers too much discretion and hence violated the Fourth Amendment. On appeal, the Court did not dispute the constitutionality of the statute; the Court said instead that the evidence obtained was admissible under the "good faith" exception to the exclusionary rule. The Court concluded that suppression is inappropriate where the fault is not with the police, but—in this case—with the legislature.

Some legal scholars predict that the Sheppard and Leon cases "bring the exclusionary rule one step closer to its ultimate demise and take a good-sized bite out of the rule in its central application." Others believe, however, that the decision should be interpreted and applied very narrowly—that is, applied only to cases in which the police are not at fault and the fault lies solely with the judge who issues the warrants. The Krull case indicates that the Court is inclined to extend the "good faith" exception to instances other than a magistrate's mistake. Nonetheless, there has been no indiscriminate application of the exception to all instances when the police are not at fault. The more logical view appears to be that the "good faith" exception will be applied cautiously by the Court. In another case decided in 1990, the Court reaffirmed the exclusionary rule when it decided that the prosecutor's use of illegally obtained statements to impeach a defense witness's testimony required a reversal of the defendant's conviction (James v. Illinois, 493 U.S. _____ [1990]).

VI. PROCEEDINGS TO WHICH THE RULE DOES NOT APPLY

1. Private Searches

Since the Fourth Amendment's prohibition against unreasonable searches and seizures prohibits only the action of governmental officials, prosecutors may use evidence illegally obtained by private individuals (by methods such as illegal wiretap or trespass) as long as the police did not encourage or participate in the illegal private search. In one case the Court said that the Fourth Amendment's "origin and history clearly show that it was intended as a restraint upon the activities of sovereign authority, and was not intended to be a limitation upon other than governmental agencies" (Burdeau v. McDowell, 256 U.S. 465 [1921]).

2. Grand Jury Investigations

A person being questioned by the grand jury cannot refuse to answer questions on the ground that the questions are based on illegally obtained evidence (such as information from an illegal wiretap). The reason is that the application of the exclusionary rule in such proceedings would unduly interfere with the grand jury's investigative function (U.S. v. Calandra, 414 U.S. 338 [1974]).

3. Postconviction Sentencing

Some lower courts have likewise permitted the trial judge to consider illegally obtained evidence in fixing sentence after conviction, even when the same evidence had been excluded during the trial because it was illegally obtained. During sentencing, they reason, a trial judge should consider any reliable evidence. The fact that it was obtained illegally does not necessarily affect its reliability. The practice is not permitted if state law provides that the evidence is not admissible even in these proceedings.

4. Cases in Which Only an Agency Rule Is Violated

The evidence is admissible if the search violates only an agency rule, but not the Constitution. Such violation does not offend fundamental fairness under the Constitution. For example, police department rules provide that a person suspected of driving while intoxicated who refuses to take a blood-alcohol test must be informed that the refusal may be used as evidence against him or her in court. Failure by the police to give this warning does not exclude the evidence (South Dakota v. Neville, 459 U.S. 553 [1983]). Exception is made if state law provides that the evidence is not admissible even in these proceedings.

5. Cases Where Arrest Was Illegal

The jurisdiction of a court to try a person for a crime is not affected by how the custody of the accused is obtained. This is so because the exclusionary rule is an evidentiary rule, not a rule of jurisdictional limitation (Frisbie v. Collins, 342 U.S. 519 [1952]). Collins brought a habeas corpus case in federal court seeking release from a Michigan state prison, alleging that while he was living in Chicago, Michigan officers forcibly seized, handcuffed, blackjacked, and then forcibly abducted him so that he could face murder charges in Michigan. The Court said that an unlawful arrest has no impact on a subsequent criminal prosecution and that an invalid arrest does not deprive the court of jurisdiction to try a criminal case. The Court added: "There is nothing in the Constitution that requires a court to permit a guilty person rightfully convicted to escape justice because he was brought to trial against his will." (Read the Frisbie v. Collins case brief at the end of this chapter.)

6. Noncriminal Proceedings

The exclusionary rule applies only to criminal proceedings and not to other types of proceedings, such as civil or administrative hearings. Illegally obtained evidence may be admissible against another party in a civil suit. It may also be admissible in administrative proceedings, such as if an employee is being disciplined. For example, illegally obtained evidence may be admissible in cases where a police officer is being investigated by the internal affairs division of the police department for violation of departmental rules. It may also be admissible in probation or parole revocation cases, these being administrative in nature. Court decisions have established, however, that even in administrative cases there are instances when illegally obtained evidence may not be admitted. One is if state law or agency policy prohibits the admission of such evidence. The second is if such evidence was obtained in bad faith, as when evidence against a police officer under investigation is obtained illegally and for the purpose of establishing grounds for disciplinary action.

VII. ARGUMENTS IN SUPPORT OF THE EXCLUSIONARY RULE

Among the arguments in support of the exclusionary rule by its proponents are these:[1]

1. It definitely deters violations of constitutional rights by police and prosecutor. A number of studies and testimonies by police officers support this contention.
2. It manifests society's refusal to convict lawbreakers by relying on official lawlessness, a clear demonstration of our commitment to the rule of law that states that no person, not even a law enforcement official, is above and beyond the law.
3. It results in the freeing of the guilty in a relatively small proportion of cases. A 1978 study by the General Auditing Office found that of 2,804 cases in which defendants were likely to file a motion to suppress evidence, exclusion succeeded in only 1.3 percent. Moreover, the same study reported that of the cases presented to federal prosecutors for prosecution, only 0.4 percent were declined by the prosecutors because of Fourth Amendment search and seizure problems.[2]
4. It has led to more professionalism among the police and increased attention to training programs. Fear of exclusion of evidence has forced the police to develop greater expertise in their work.
5. It preserves the integrity of the judicial system. The admission of illegally seized evidence makes the court a party to violations of constitutional rights.
6. It prevents the government, whose agents have violated the Constitution, from profiting from its wrongdoing. Somebody has to pay for the mistake. Let the government absorb it, not the suspect who has already been wronged.
7. It protects the right to privacy.

VIII. ARGUMENTS AGAINST THE EXCLUSIONARY RULE

Opponents, including justices in the Supreme Court, have argued strongly in rejection of the exclusionary rule. Among their arguments are these:

1. The criminal goes free because the constable has blundered. It is wrong to make society pay for an officer's mistake. Punish the officer, not society.

2. It excludes the most credible, probative kinds of evidence—fingerprints, guns, narcotics, or dead bodies—and thereby impedes the truth-finding function of the courts.[3]

3. It discourages internal disciplinary efforts by law enforcement agencies. Why discipline when the evidence will be excluded anyway? The police would suffer a double setback.

4. It encourages perjury by the police in an effort to admit the evidence, particularly in major cases, in which the police might feel that the end justifies the means. It is better to lie than to let a presumably guilty person go free.

5. It diminishes respect for the judicial process and generates disrespect for the law and the administration of justice.[4]

6. There is no proof that the exclusionary rule deters police misconduct. In the words of former Chief Justice Burger, "There is no empirical evidence to support the claim that the rule actually deters illegal conduct of law enforcement officials."

7. Only the United States uses the exclusionary rule. No other civilized country does.

8. It has no effect on those large areas of police activity that do not result in criminal prosecutions. If the police make an arrest or search without any thought of subsequent prosecution (such as when they simply want to remove a person from the streets overnight or when they confiscate contraband so as to eliminate the supply), they do not have to worry about the exclusionary rule because that is effective only if the case gets to trial and the evidence is used.

9. The rule is not based on the Constitution and is only an invention of the Court.[5]

10. It does not punish the individual police officer whose illegal conduct led to the exclusion of the evidence.

IX. ALTERNATIVES TO THE EXCLUSIONARY RULE

The continuing and often heated debate on the exclusionary rule has produced several proposals to admit the evidence obtained and then to deal with the wrongdoing of the police. Among the proposals are these:

1. *An independent review board in the executive branch.* This proposal envisions a review board composed of nonpolice personnel to review allegations of violations of constitutional rights by the police. The problem with this alternative is that it is opposed by the police because it singles them out as public officials for differential treatment. Moreover, outsiders are viewed by the police as unlikely to be able to understand the difficulties and dangers inherent in police work.

2. *A civil tort action against the government.* This measure means filing an action seeking damages from the government for acts of its officers. It poses real difficulty for the plaintiff who has to shoulder the financial cost of the litigation. Most defendants do not have the resources to finance a civil case, particularly after a criminal

trial. Low damages awards against police officers usually discourage the filing of civil tort actions, except in gross cases.

3. *A hearing separate from the main criminal trial but before the same judge or jury.* The purpose of the hearing is to determine if in fact the officer behaved illegally in obtaining the evidence used during the trial and, if so, to impose the necessary sanctions on the officer. Although this is the least expensive and most expedient alternative, its effectiveness is questionable. If the violation is slight, the judge or jury will not look with favor on what may be considered an unnecessary extension of the original trial. Furthermore, if the criminal trial ends in a conviction, the chances of the officer's being punished for what he or she did become understandably remote.

4. *Adoption of an expanded "good faith" exception.* The final report of the Attorney General's Task Force on Violent Crime has proposed a "good faith" exception different from and broader than that allowed by the Court in the Sheppard and Leon cases. The proposed "good faith" exception covers all cases in which the police would claim and can prove that they acted in good faith (not just when the magistrate issues an invalid warrant). It is based on two conditions: (1) the officer must allege that he or she had probable cause for the action in question and (2) the officer's apparent belief that he or she was acting legally must be a reasonable one. These are questions of fact that will be determined by the judge or jury. Opponents fear that this proposal would lead to more violations of rights using good faith as a convenient excuse. Good faith is a vague concept that is best determined on a case-by-case basis and may therefore vary from one judge or jury to another. It is also maintained that this exception discourages training and rewards lack of knowledge, the theory being that the more untrained and uninformed the police officer, the greater the claim to good faith his or her ignorance would permit.

5. *Adoption of the British system.* Under the British system, the illegally obtained evidence is admitted in court, but the erring officer is subject to internal departmental sanctions. The objection is that this system is not effective even in England, where the police system is highly centralized and generally has attained a higher level of professionalization. Internal discipline by peers has been and is a problem in U.S. policing and will most likely be viewed with disfavor by the public as an ineffective means of control.

HIGHLIGHT 3.4

A Justification for the Exclusionary Rule

There are those who say, as did Justice Cardozo, that under our constitutional exclusionary doctrine "the criminal is to go free because the constable has blundered." In some cases this result will undoubtedly occur. But there is another consideration—the imperative of judicial integrity. The criminal goes free—he or she must—but it is the law that sets the criminal free. Nothing can destroy a government more quickly than its failure to observe its own laws, or worse, its disregard of the charter of its own existence (Mapp v. Ohio, 367 U.S. 643 [1961]).

X. THE FUTURE OF THE EXCLUSIONARY RULE

The debate on the exclusionary rule continues. The Sheppard and Leon cases may simply have sharpened the controversy, each side claiming a measure of victory but neither side being quite satisfied with the results. Proponents and opponents of the exclusionary rule are at polar opposites. Those who are for it want the rule to remain intact and be applied strictly, the way it has been applied in the two decades since Mapp v. Ohio. Any concession is interpreted as widening the door that eventually leads to the doctrine's demise. Yet opponents of the rule are not satisfied with such victories as Sheppard and Leon. Some want to scrap the rule completely, admit the evidence, and impose the sanctions later. If opponents agree on anything, it is the elimination of the rule. Beyond that, there is no consensus on alternatives; no single proposal has gained general support of those who oppose the rule.

What, then, of the future? It is certain that the recent Court decisions have not settled the controversy. During his time in the Court, former Chief Justice Burger of the U.S. Supreme Court called for the rule's abolition, terming it "conceptually sterile and practically ineffective." Other justices have publicly expressed dissatisfaction with the rule and wish its abolition or modification. They have made some inroads, but that may not be enough for them and other opponents. If the Court becomes more conservative in composition, further modification of the exclusionary rule becomes a possibility, although not a certainty. Whether that means its ultimate eradication is an entirely different matter. To paraphrase Mark Twain, it just might be that the reports concerning the demise of the exclusionary rule are greatly exaggerated.

☐ SUMMARY

The exclusionary rule is a rule of evidence that provides that evidence obtained by the government in violation of the Fourth Amendment's guarantee against unreasonable search or seizure is not admissible in a criminal prosecution to prove guilt. Its main purpose is to deter police misconduct, the assumption being that if the evidence obtained illegally is not admitted in court, police misconduct in search and seizure cases will cease or at least be minimized.

HIGHLIGHT 3.5

Perspective on the Exclusionary Rule

The fate of the exclusionary rule over the long run is difficult to predict. It has endured for seventy turbulent years. Do the Leon and Sheppard decisions portend further modifications and exceptions to the rule by our highest Court? To two of the dissenters in those cases, "it now appears that the Court's victory over the Fourth Amendment is complete." Undoubtedly, to several of the justices in the majority, the decisions were a blow struck for criminal justice and against a rule that Chief Justice Burger has called "conceptually sterile and practically ineffective."

Source: Bradford P. Wilson, "Exclusionary Rule," *Crime File Study Guide* (National Institute of Justice, Rockville, MD), at 3.

Since 1914, the exclusionary rule has been applied to federal criminal prosecutions. It was not until 1961, however, that the application of the rule was required in state prosecutions. Illegally seized evidence is excluded under the rule; so are "fruits of the poisonous tree," meaning evidence obtained as an indirect result of police misconduct. There are several exceptions to the exclusionary rule, the most notable being the "good faith" exception enunciated by the Court in Massachusetts v. Sheppard and United States v. Leon. In these cases, the Court said that evidence obtained is admissible in court when the officer conducting the search acted in good-faith reliance on a search warrant that is subsequently declared to be invalid.

There are proceedings in which the exclusionary rule does not apply. Among them are private searches, grand jury investigations, postconviction sentencing, cases in which only an agency rule is violated, and cases in which court jurisdiction is at issue. There are various arguments for and against the exclusionary rule. The debate over the rule has been brisk and intense, but it has probably produced more heat than light. Of several proposed alternatives to the exclusionary rule, none has gained general endorsement by those who decry the rule. Despite the Court decisions in Sheppard and Leon, which were victories for the rule's opponents, the controversy over the exclusionary rule is bound to continue within the court and among criminal justice personnel. Although the rule has suffered erosion, it is premature to consider it seriously weakened or damaged.

❑ REVIEW QUESTIONS

1. What is the exclusionary rule? Does it apply only to violations of Fourth Amendment rights or to violations of any constitutional right?
2. Is the exclusionary rule a constitutional or a judge-made rule? May it be modified by the U.S. Congress through legislation?
3. What did the Court hold in Mapp v. Ohio? Why is that case significant?
4. Distinguish between illegally seized evidence and the "fruit of the poisonous tree."
5. What is the "good faith" exception to the exclusionary rule as approved by the Court in Massachusetts v. Sheppard? Will "good faith" be applied to cases not involving errors by magistrates in the issuance of warrants?
6. Name at least four types of proceedings to which the exclusionary rule does not apply. Discuss each.
7. Give four arguments in support of the exclusionary rule and discuss each.
8. Give four arguments against the exclusionary rule and discuss each.
9. Give four alternatives to the exclusionary rule and discuss each.
10. Discuss the future of the exclusionary rule.

❑ DEFINITIONS

Exclusionary Rule: Rule of evidence that provides that any evidence obtained by the government in violation of the Fourth Amendment's guarantee against unreasonable search or seizure is not admissible in a criminal prosecution to establish defendant's guilt.

"Fruit of the Poisonous Tree" Doctrine: Once the primary evidence (the "tree") is shown to have been unlawfully obtained, any secondary evidence (the "fruit") derived from it is also inadmissible.

"Good Faith" Exception: An exception to the exclusionary rule pertaining to evidence obtained by the police acting in good faith on a search warrant issued by a neutral and detached magistrate. Even if the warrant is ultimately found to be invalid, the evidence may be admitted and used at the trial.

Harmless Error Doctrine: If a motion to exclude illegally seized evidence is made on time, it is an error for the court to receive the evidence. This mistake requires a reversal on appeal of any conviction unless admission of the evidence is found to be a harmless error.

"Independent Untainted Source" Exception: An exception to the "fruit of the poisonous tree" doctrine that provides that the evidence obtained is admissible, despite its initial illegality, if the police can prove that it was obtained from an independent source not connected to the illegal search or seizure.

"Inevitable Discovery" Exception: An exception to the "fruit of the poisonous tree" doctrine that provides that the evidence is admissible, despite its initial illegality, if the police can prove that they would inevitably have discovered the evidence by lawful means, regardless of their illegal action.

"Purged Taint" Exception: An exception to the "fruit of the poisonous tree" doctrine that applies when the defendant's subsequent voluntary act dissipates the taint of the initial illegality. A defendant's intervening act of free will is sufficient to break the causal chain between the tainted evidence and the illegal police conduct; hence the evidence becomes admissible.

Silver Platter Doctrine: A doctrine in federal courts from 1914 to 1960 under which evidence of a federal crime that had been illegally obtained by state officers was admissible in federal courts although it would not have been admissible if it had been obtained by federal officers.

❏   PRINCIPLES OF CASES

BOYD V. UNITED STATES, 116 U.S. 616 (1886)   The forced disclosure of papers amounting to evidence of crime violated the constitutional right of the suspect against unreasonable search and seizure and therefore the papers were inadmissible in court proceedings.

BURDEAU V. MCDOWELL, 256 U.S. 465 (1921)   The Fourth Amendment's origin and history clearly show that it was intended as a restraint upon the activities of sovereign authority and not a limitation upon other than governmental agencies.

CHAPMAN V. CALIFORNIA, 386 U.S. 18 (1967)   In attempting to demonstrate mere "harmless error," it is not enough for the prosecution simply to show that there was other evidence sufficient to support the verdict. Rather, it must show that there was no reasonable possibility that a different result would have been reached without the tainted evidence.

ELKINS V. UNITED STATES, 364 U.S. 206 (1960)   The Fourth Amendment prohibits the use of illegally obtained evidence in federal prosecutions, whether the evidence be obtained by federal or state officers. This case did away with the "silver platter" doctrine.

FRISBIE V. COLLINS, 342 U.S. 519 (1952)   An unlawful arrest has no impact on a subsequent criminal prosecution. An invalid arrest therefore does not deprive the court of jurisdiction to try a criminal case.

ILLINOIS V. KRULL, 480 U.S. 340 (1987)   Evidence obtained by the police in accordance with a state law that is later declared by the court to be unconstitutional is admissible in court as part of the good-faith exception to the exclusionary rule.

JAMES V. ILLINOIS, 493 U.S. ____ (1990)   The prosecutor's use of illegally obtained statements to impeach a defense witness's testimony requires a reversal of the defendant's conviction.

MAPP V. OHIO, 367 U.S. 643 (1961)   The exclusionary rule, which prohibits the use of evidence obtained as a result of unreasonable search and seizure, is applicable to state criminal proceedings.

MASSACHUSETTS V. SHEPPARD, 35 CrL 3296 (1984)   Evidence obtained by search is admissible in court when the officer conducting the search acted in objectively reasonable reliance on a search warrant that is subsequently declared to be invalid.

NIX V. WILLIAMS, 35 CrL 3119 (1984)   Evidence discovered because of a violation of the Sixth Amendment is admissible if the evidence would have been discovered anyway by lawful means. The prosecution must show "inevitable discovery" by a preponderance of evidence and need not prove absence of bad faith by the government officer responsible for the violation of the Sixth Amendment.

ROCHIN V. CALIFORNIA, 342 U.S. 165 (1952)   Even before the exclusionary rule was applied to the states, the Court held that some searches were so "shocking" as to require exclusion of the evidence seized. These cases were limited to acts of coercion, violence, or brutality.

SILVERTHORNE LUMBER CO. V. UNITED STATES, 251 U.S. 385 (1920)   Once the primary evidence (the "tree") is shown to have been unlawfully obtained, any secondary evidence (the "fruit") derived from it is also inadmissible. This case enunciated the "fruit of the poisonous tree" doctrine.

SOUTH DAKOTA V. NEVILLE, 459 U.S. 553 (1983)   Evidence obtained is admissible if the search does not violate the Constitution, but only violates an agency rule.

STATE V. O'BREMSKI, 70 Wash. 2d 425 (1967)   Testimony that the defendant had had carnal knowledge of her was admissible because it had an independent source that predated the search of the apartment. Prior to the search, the girl's parents had reported her missing, and a police informant had already located her in the defendant's apartment.

TAYLOR V. ALABAMA, 102 S.Ct. 2664 (1982)   To break the causal connection between an illegal arrest and a confession that is the fruit of the illegal arrest, and therefore make the evidence admissible, the intervening event must be meaningful.

UNITED STATES V. CACERES, 440 U.S. 741 (1979)   The exclusionary rule has rested primarily on the judgment that the importance of deterring police conduct that may violate the constitutional rights of individuals throughout the community outweighs the importance of securing the conviction of the specific defendant on trial.

UNITED STATES V. CALANDRA, 414 U.S. 338 (1974)   A person being questioned by the grand jury cannot refuse to answer questions on the ground that the questions asked are based on illegally obtained evidence.

UNITED STATES V. CECCOLINI, 425 U.S. 268 (1978)   If an illegal search enables the police to locate a witness, that witness's statements will less readily be excluded as the "fruit of the poisonous tree" than other types of evidence. A direct link will be required before the testimony will be excluded.

UNITED STATES V. CREWS, 445 U.S. 463 (1980)   Illegally obtained evidence is admissible if the police can prove that it was obtained from an independent source not connected to the illegal search or seizure.

UNITED STATES V. HOULTIN, 566 F.2d 1027 (5th Cir. 1978)   Under the exclusionary rule, evidence obtained in violation of the Fourth Amendment cannot be used in a criminal trial against the victim of the illegal search or seizure. The Constitution does not require this remedy; it is a doctrine of judicial design.

UNITED STATES V. LEON, 35 CrL 3273 (1984)   The Fourth Amendment's exclusionary rule should not be applied to bar the use in the prosecution's case of evidence that has been obtained by officers acting in reasonable reliance on a search warrant issued by a detached and neutral magistrate, but that is ultimately found to be invalid because it lacks probable cause.

UNITED STATES V. PAROUTIAN, 299 F.2d 488 (2nd Cir. 1962)   An unlawful search taints all evidence obtained at the search or through leads uncovered by the search. The rule, however, extends only to facts that were actually discovered by a procedure initiated by the unlawful act. If information that could have emerged from an unlawful search in fact stems from an independent source, the evidence is admissible.

WEEKS V. UNITED STATES, 232 U.S. 383 (1914)   Evidence illegally obtained by federal officers is inadmissible in federal criminal prosecutions.

WOLF V. COLORADO, 388 U.S. 25 (1949)   State courts were not constitutionally required to exclude illegally obtained evidence; hence the exclusionary rule did not apply to the states. This decision was overturned in 1961 in Mapp v. Ohio.

WONG SUN V. UNITED STATES, 371 U.S. 471 (1963)   A defendant's intervening act of free will is sufficient to break the causal chain between the tainted evidence and the illegal police conduct; thus the evidence otherwise illegally obtained becomes admissible.

☐   CASE BRIEF—LEADING CASE ON THE EXTENSION OF EXCLUSIONARY RULE TO THE STATES

MAPP V. OHIO, 367 U.S. 643 (1961)

FACTS: Defendant Mapp was convicted of knowingly having had in her possession and under her control certain lewd and lascivious books, pictures, and photographs in violation of Ohio law. The records show that three Cleveland police officers went to Mapp's residence pursuant to information that a person was hiding out in her home who was wanted for questioning in connection with a recent bombing, and that there was a large amount of gambling paraphernalia hidden in her home. Mapp and her daughter by a former marriage lived on the top floor of a two-family dwelling. Upon arrival at the house, the officers knocked on the door and demanded entrance, but Mapp, after telephoning her attorney, refused to admit them without a search warrant. The police advised their headquarters of the situation and undertook a surveillance of the house. The officers again sought entrance three hours later when four or more additional officers had arrived on the scene. When Mapp did not come to the door immediately, the police forcibly opened one of the doors and gained admittance. Meanwhile, Mapp's attorney arrived, but the officers would not permit him to see his client or to enter the house. Mapp demanded to see the search warrant. A paper, claimed to be a warrant, was held up by one of the officers. She grabbed the "warrant" and placed it in her bosom. A struggle ensued in which the officers recovered the piece of paper and as a result of which they handcuffed Mapp because she had been "belligerent." An officer grabbed her and twisted her hand, and she yelled and pleaded with him because "it was hurting." In handcuffs, Mapp was forcibly taken upstairs to her bedroom, where the officers searched a dresser, a chest of drawers, a closet, and some suitcases. They also looked into a photo album and through personal papers belonging to Mapp. The search spread to the rest of the second floor, including the child's bedroom, the living room, the kitchen, and a dinette. The basement of the building and a trunk found in it were also searched. The obscene materials, for possession of which Mapp was ultimately convicted, were discovered in the course of that widespread search. The materials were admitted into evidence by the trial court and the defendant was convicted. The Supreme Court of Ohio upheld the conviction.

ISSUE: *Is evidence obtained in violation of the Fourth Amendment guarantee against unreasonable search and seizure admissible in state court? No.*

SUPREME COURT DECISION: The exclusionary rule that prohibits the use of evidence obtained as a result of unreasonable search and seizure is applicable to state criminal proceedings.

CASE SIGNIFICANCE: The Mapp case is significant because here the Court held that the exclusionary rule was thenceforth to be applied nationally, thus forbidding both state and federal courts to accept evidence obtained illegally in violation of constitutional protection against unreasonable search and seizure. The facts in the Mapp case are given above, as detailed in the Court decision, to show why it was relatively "easy" for the Court to decide to exclude the evidence. In the minds of the Court, the facts in Mapp illustrate what can happen if police conduct is not restricted. Mapp was therefore an ideal case for the Court to use in settling an issue that had to be addressed: whether the exclusionary rule should now be applicable to state criminal proceedings. The facts in Mapp made it easier for the Court to answer that question in the affirmative.

EXCERPTS FROM THE DECISION: Since the Fourth Amendment's right of privacy has been declared enforceable against the States through the Due Process Clause of the Fourteenth, it is enforceable against them by the same sanction of exclusion as is used against the Federal Government. Were it otherwise, then just as without the Weeks rule the assurance against unreasonable federal searches and seizures would be "a form of words," valueless and undeserving of mention in a perpetual charter of inestimable human liberties, so too, without that rule the freedom from state invasions of privacy would be so ephemeral and so neatly severed from its conceptual nexus with the freedom from all brutish means of coercing evidence as not to merit this Court's high regard as a freedom "implicit in the concept of ordered liberty." At the time that the Court held in Wolf that the Amendment was applicable to the States through the Due Process Clause, the cases of this Court, as we have seen, had steadfastly held that as to federal officers the Fourth Amendment included the exclusion of the evidence seized in violation of its provisions. Even Wolf "stoutly adhered" to that proposition. The right to privacy, when conceded operatively enforceable against the States, was not susceptible of destruction by avulsion of the sanction upon which its protection and enjoyment had always been deemed dependent under the Boyd, Weeks and Silverthorne cases. Therefore, in extending the substantive protections of due process to all constitutionally unreasonable searches—state or federal—it was logically and constitutionally necessary that the exclusion doctrine— an essential part of the right to privacy—be also insisted upon as an essential ingredient of the right newly recognized by the Wolf case. In short, the admission of the constitutional right by Wolf could not consistently tolerate denial of its most important constitutional privilege, namely, the exclusion of the evidence which an accused had been forced to give by reason of the unlawful seizure. To hold otherwise is to grant the right but in reality to withhold its privilege and enjoyment. Only last year the Court itself recognized that the purpose of the exclusionary rule "is to deter—to compel respect for the constitutional guaranty in the only effectively available way— by removing the incentive to disregard it."

Moreover, our holding that the exclusionary rule is an essential part of both the Fourth and Fourteenth Amendments is not only the logical dictate of prior cases, but it also makes very good sense. There is no war between the Constitution and common sense. Presently, a federal prosecutor may make no use of evidence illegally seized, but a State's attorney across the street may, although he supposedly is operating under the enforceable prohibitions of the same Amendment. Thus the State, by admitting evidence unlawfully seized, serves to encourage disobedience to the Federal Constitution which it is bound to uphold. Moreover, as was said in Elkins, "[t]he very essence of a healthy federalism depends upon the avoidance of needless conflict between state and federal courts." . . . Yet the double standard recognized until today hardly put such a thesis into practice. In non-exclusionary States, federal officers, being human, were by it invited to and did, as our cases indicate, step across the street to the State's attorney with their unconstitutionally seized evidence. Prosecution on the basis of that evidence was then had in a state court in utter disregard of the enforceable Fourth Amendment. If the fruits of an unconstitutional search had been inadmissible in both state and federal courts, this inducement to evasion would have been sooner eliminated.

The ignoble shortcut to conviction left open to the State tends to destroy the entire system of constitutional restraints on which the liberties of the people rest. Having once recognized that the right to privacy embodied in the Fourth Amendment is enforceable against the States, and that the right to be secure against rude invasions of privacy by state officers is, therefore, constitutional in origin, we can no longer permit that right to remain an empty promise. Because it is enforceable in the same manner and to like effect as other basic rights secured by the Due Process Clause, we can no longer permit it to be revocable at the whim of any police officer who, in the name of law enforcement itself, chooses to suspend its enjoyment. Our decision, founded on reason and truth, gives to the individual no more than that which the Constitution guarantees him, to the police officer no less than that to which honest law enforcement is entitled, and, to the courts, that judicial integrity so necessary in the true administration of justice.

The judgment of the Supreme Court of Ohio is reversed and the case remanded for further proceedings not inconsistent with this opinion.

Reversed and remanded.

☐ CASE BRIEF—LEADING CASE ON VALIDITY OF COURT JURISDICTION

FRISBIE V. COLLINS, 342 U.S. 519 (1952)

FACTS: Acting as his own lawyer, Collins brought a habeas corpus case in federal court seeking release from a Michigan state prison where he was serving a life sentence for murder. He alleged that while he was living in Chicago, Michigan officers forcibly seized, handcuffed, blackjacked, and then forcibly abducted him back to Michigan. He claimed that the trial and subsequent conviction under such circumstances violated his "due process" rights under the Fourteenth Amendment and also under the Federal Kidnaping Act and were therefore void.

ISSUE: *Does the unlawful arrest of a defendant affect the legality of the court's jurisdiction in a criminal proceeding? No.*

SUPREME COURT DECISION: An unlawful arrest has no impact on a subsequent criminal prosecution. An invalid arrest therefore does not deprive the court of jurisdiction to try a criminal case.

CASE SIGNIFICANCE: The Collins decision constitutes what to some might be a surprising exception to the type of proceedings in which the exclusionary rule applies. It would seem logical to think that if items subject to illegal search and seizure are not admissible in evidence, then defendants illegally arrested ought not to be subjected to court jurisdiction either. The Court disagrees, stating that "the power of a court to try a person for crime is not impaired by the fact that he has been brought within the court's jurisdiction by reason of a 'forcible abduction.' " It then added that "there is nothing in the Constitution that requires a court to permit a guilty person rightfully convicted to escape justice because he was brought to trial against his will." It must be noted that the Collins case was decided in 1952, before the exclusionary rule was applied to the states in Mapp v. Ohio. Nonetheless, the validity of the above ruling holds even now.

EXCERPTS FROM THE DECISION: This Court has never departed from the rule announced in Ker v. Illinois, 119 U.S. 436, that the power of a court to try a person for crime is not impaired by the fact that he had been brought within the court's jurisdiction by reason of a "forcible abduction." No persuasive reasons are now presented to justify overruling this line of cases. They rest on the sound basis that due process of law is satisfied when one present in court is convicted of crime after having been fairly apprized of the charges against him and after a fair trial in accordance with constitutional procedural safeguards. There is nothing in the Constitution that requires a court to permit a guilty person rightfully convicted to escape justice because he was brought to trial against his will.

Despite our prior decisions, the Court of Appeals, relying on the Federal Kidnaping Act, held that respondent was entitled to the writ if he could prove the facts he alleged. The Court thought that to hold otherwise after the passage of the Kidnaping Act "would in practical effect lend encouragement to the commission of criminal acts by those sworn to enforce the law." In considering whether the law of our prior cases has been changed by the Federal Kidnaping Act, we assume, without intimating that it is so, that the Michigan officers would have violated it if the facts are as alleged. This Act prescribes in some detail the severe sanctions Congress wanted it to have. Persons who have violated it can be imprisoned for a term of years or for life; under some circumstances violators can be given the death sentence. We think the Act cannot fairly be construed so as to add to the list of sanctions detailed a sanction barring a state from prosecuting persons wrongfully brought to it by its officers. It may be that Congress could add such a sanction. We cannot.

The judgment of the Court of Appeals is reversed and that of the District Court is affirmed.

It is so ordered.

Judgment of Court of Appeals reversed.

☐ NOTES

1. For an excellent discussion of the arguments for and against the exclusionary rule, see "Symposium on the Exclusionary Rule," by Yale Kamisar, Stephen H. Sach, Malcolm R. Wilkey, and Frank G. Carrington, in *Criminal Justice Ethics* 1 (1982), at 4ff. Some arguments for and against the exclusionary rule in this list are taken from that article.
2. *The Houston Chronicle,* July 8, 1979, Section 4, at 2.
3. Kamisar et al., op. cit., at 18.
4. Steven Schlesinger, "Criminal Procedure in the Courtroom," in *Crime and Public Policy,* ed. James Q. Wilson (San Francisco: ICS Press, 1983), at 195.
5. Bradford P. Wilson, "Exclusionary Rule," *Crime File Study Guide* (National Institute of Justice, Rockville, MD), at 1.

PROBABLE CAUSE

☐ KEY TERMS

probable cause	old interpretation of Aguilar
"man of reasonable caution"	new interpretation of Aguilar
reliability of informant	stale information
reliability of informant's information	level of proof

If there is one legal term with which police officers must be thoroughly familiar, it is *probable cause*. That term is used extensively in police work and often determines whether the police acted lawfully or not. If the police acted lawfully, the arrest is valid and the evidence obtained is admissible in court. Without probable cause, the evidence will be thrown out of court. In one case the Court said: "The general rule is that every arrest, and every seizure having the essential attributes of a formal arrest, is unreasonable unless it is supported by probable cause" (Michigan v. Summers, 452 U.S. 692 [1981]).

The "probable cause" requirement in police work is based on the Fourth Amendment of the U.S. Constitution, which states:

> The right of the people to be secure in their persons, houses, papers, and effects, against unreasonable searches and seizures, shall not be violated, and no Warrants shall issue, but upon probable cause. . . .

I. WHAT CONSTITUTES PROBABLE CAUSE

Probable cause is defined as more than bare suspicion; it exists when "the facts and circumstances within the officers' knowledge and of which they had reasonably trustworthy information are sufficient in themselves to warrant a man of reasonable caution in the belief that an offense has been or is being committed" (Brinegar v. U.S., 338 U.S. 160 [1949]).

In the Brinegar case, the Court added: "The substance of all the definitions of probable cause is a reasonable ground for belief of guilt. . . . And this means less than evidence which would justify condemnation or conviction. . . ." A practical, nontechnical probability that incriminating evidence is involved is all that is required. The terms *probable cause* and *reasonable ground* are used interchangeably in many jurisdictions.

The term *"man of reasonable caution"* (some jurisdictions use the term *"ordinarily prudent and cautious man"*) does not refer to a person with training in the law,

---
HIGHLIGHT 4.1

Probable Cause Defined

Probable cause is defined as more than bare suspicion; it exists when "the facts and circumstances within the officers' knowledge and of which they had reasonably trustworthy information are sufficient in themselves to warrant a man of reasonable caution in the belief that an offense has been or is being committed" (Brinegar v. U.S., 338 U.S. 160 [1949]).

such as a magistrate or lawyer. Instead, it refers to the average "man in the street" (for instance, mechanic, butcher, baker, or teacher) who, under the same circumstances, would believe that the person being arrested had committed the offense or that things to be seized would be found in a particular place. Despite this, however, the *experience of the police officer must be considered in determining whether probable cause existed in a specific situation.* In United States v. Ortiz, 422 U.S. 891 (1975), the Court said that "officers are entitled to draw reasonable inferences from these facts in light of their knowledge of the area and their prior experience with aliens and smugglers." In view of his or her work experience, training, and background, the police officer may be better qualified than the average person in the street to evaluate certain facts and circumstances. Thus, what may not amount to probable cause to an untrained person may be sufficient for probable cause in the estimation of a police officer because of his or her training and background. This is particularly true in property or drug cases, in which what may look like an innocent activity to an untrained person may indicate to a police officer that a criminal activity is taking place.

For practical purposes, probable cause exists when the police have trustworthy evidence sufficient to make "a reasonable man" think it more likely than not that the proposed arrest or search is justified. In mathematical terms, this means that the police officer (in cases of arrest or search without a warrant) or the magistrate (in cases of arrest or search with a warrant) is *more than 50 percent* certain that the suspect has committed the offense or that the items can be found in a certain place. It is important to note, however, that the "more than 50 percent" certainty standard is a very safe estimate of the degree of certainty for probable cause. Most courts would perhaps be satisfied with something less than a 50-percent certainty. For instance, in Illinois v. Gates, 103 S.Ct. 2317 (1983), the Court said this:

> Probable cause is a fluid concept—turning on the assessment of probabilities in particular factual contexts—not readily, or even usefully, reduced to a neat set of legal rules. . . . While an effort to fix some general, numerically precise degree of certainty corresponding to "probable cause" may not be helpful, it is clear that "only the probability, and not a prima facie showing, of criminal activity is the standard of probable cause."

Since probable cause, if later challenged in court, must be established by police testimony in warrantless arrests or searches, it is important that the police officer observe keenly and take careful notes of the facts and circumstances establishing that probable cause existed at the time he or she acted. For example, if an officer arrests a person who is seen coming out of a building at midnight, the officer must be able to articulate (if asked to do so later in court) what factors led him or her to make the arrest. These can be such factors as the furtive behavior of the suspect, nervousness when questioned, possession of what appear to be stolen items, and the prior criminal record of the suspect.

If no probable cause existed at the time the officer took action, the fact that probable cause is later established does not make the act legal; the evidence obtained cannot be used in court. For example, an officer arrests a suspicious-looking person. After arrest, a body search reveals that the person had several vials of cocaine in her pocket. The evidence obtained cannot be used in court because there was no probable cause to make the arrest. *Probable cause is never established by what turns out after the initial illegal act. Suspicion alone is never sufficient for an arrest.* Note, however, that what starts off as mere suspicion can later develop into probable cause sufficient to make an arrest. For example, a police officer asks questions of the owner of a car that failed to stop at a stop sign. The police suspects that the driver may be drunk. If the initial inquiries in fact show that the driver is drunk, then the officer may make a valid arrest. Any evidence obtained as a result of the arrest is admissible in court.

An officer may have probable cause to arrest without having personally observed the commission of the crime. For example, while out on patrol, an officer is told by a motorist that a robbery is taking place in a store down the block. The officer proceeds to the store and sees a man running toward a car with goods in his hands. The man sees the police car, drops the items, gets into the car, and hastily drives away. In this case, probable cause is present.

The Supreme Court recognizes that affidavits or complaints are often prepared hastily in the midst of a criminal investigation. Therefore, the policy is to interpret the allegations in a common-sense rather than in an overly technical manner and to uphold the sufficiency of the affidavit in close cases (U.S. v. Ventresca, 300 U.S. 102 [1965]).

In establishing probable cause, the officer may use any trustworthy information even if the rules of evidence prohibit its admission during the trial. For example, hearsay information and a prior criminal record (both inadmissible in a trial) may be taken into consideration when determining probable cause. In cases of hearsay information, trustworthiness depends upon the reliability of the source and the information given, whereas prior criminal record needs other types of evidence. The point is that in determining whether probable cause exists, the magistrate may consider any evidence, regardless of source.

Because probable cause is based on a variety and totality of circumstances, police officers must report accurately and exhaustively the facts that led them to believe that probable cause existed. As one publication notes,[1]

> Probable cause can be obtained from police radio bulletins, tips from "good citizen" informers who have happened by chance to see criminal activity, reports from victims, anonymous tips, and tips from "habitual" informers who mingle with people in the underworld and who themselves may be criminals. Probable cause can be based on various combinations of these sources.

In case of doubt, it is better to overinclude than to underinclude information, provided such information is true.

Probable cause, if originally present, is not erased by a subsequent finding of unconstitutionality. If the police, for example, act in accordance with an ordinance that is later declared by the courts to be unconstitutional, the subsequent declaration of unconstitutionality does not affect the finding of probable cause. In the case of Michigan v. DeFillippo, 443 U.S. 31 (1979), defendant DeFillippo was arrested for violating a city ordinance that made it unlawful for a person stopped by a police officer to refuse to identify him- or herself if the officer had reasonable cause to believe that the person's behavior warrants further investigation. During trial, the ordinance was declared invalid by the court because of its vagueness. Although the conviction itself had to be reversed because the law was unconstitutional, probable cause was nonetheless considered as having been present. The Court said that the police are charged with the obligation of enforcing laws unless they are declared unconstitutional. The Court added that "society itself would be ill served if its police officers took it upon themselves to determine which laws are and which are not constitutionally entitled to enforcement." Laws and ordinances enjoy a presumption of constitutionality and may therefore be enforced by the police, unless declared otherwise by a court of law.

II. WHEN PROBABLE CAUSE IS REQUIRED

Probable cause is required in four basic areas of police work: (1) in arrests with warrant, (2) in arrests without warrant, (3) in searches and seizures with warrant, and (4) in searches and seizures without warrant.

    Although the definition of probable cause is the same in all four instances, certain differences must be noted.

A. Arrest versus Search and Seizure

In cases of *arrest* the probable cause concern is twofold: (1) whether an offense has been committed, and (2) whether the suspect did in fact commit the offense. In contrast, in cases of *search and seizure,* the concerns are (1) whether the item or property to be seized is connected with criminal activity, and (2) whether it can be found in the place to be searched. It follows, therefore, that what constitutes probable cause for arrest may not constitute probable cause for search and seizure—not because of different definitions but because the officer is looking at different concerns. For example, a suspect is being arrested in her apartment for robbery, but the police have reason to believe that the stolen goods are in her getaway car parked in the driveway. There is probable cause for arrest in this case but not for a search of the apartment, except only such search as is incidental to the arrest.

B. With Warrant versus Without Warrant

In *arrests and seizures with a warrant,* the determination of probable cause is made by the magistrate to whom the complaint or affidavit is presented by the police or victim. The officer therefore does not have to worry about establishing probable cause. Such finding of probable cause by the magistrate, however, is not final. It may be reviewed during the trial and if probable cause in fact did not exist, the evidence obtained is not admissible in court. In some jurisdictions, the absence of probable cause in a warrant must be established by the defendant through clear and convincing evidence—a difficult quantum of evidence for the defendant to establish.

    In contrast, in *arrests and searches and seizures without warrant* it is the police officer who makes the determination, usually on the spot and with very limited time. This determination is subject to review by the court if challenged at a later time, usually in a motion to suppress prior to or during the trial.

    If probable cause for the arrest or search and seizure did not exist, the consequences are twofold. First, the evidence obtained cannot be admitted in court during the trial, and its inadmissibility may endanger the success of the prosecution; and second, the police officer may be subject to a civil action for damages or, in extreme cases, to criminal sanctions.

The U.S. Supreme Court has expressed a strong preference for the use of a warrant in police work. Because the affidavit has been reviewed by a neutral and detached magistrate, the issuance of a warrant assures a more orderly procedure and is a better guarantee that probable cause is in fact present. In reality, however, most arrests and searches are made without a warrant under the numerous exceptions to the warrant requirement.

Police officers are advised to obtain a warrant whenever possible because the practice has two advantages. First, a warrant means that a presumption of probable cause exists because the affidavit or complaint has been reviewed by the magistrate who found probable cause to justify issuance of the warrant. The arrest or search and seizure is therefore presumed valid unless the accused proves otherwise in court by clear and convincing evidence. It is difficult for the accused to overcome the presumption of validity of the warrant. If the finding of probable cause is reviewed during the trial, the court's remaining task is simply to determine if there was a substantial basis for the issuing magistrate's finding of probable cause, not to look at specific factual allegations (Illinois v. Gates, 103 S.Ct. 2317 [1983]).

A second advantage is that having a warrant is likewise a valid defense in civil cases for damages brought against the police officer for alleged violation of a defendant's constitutional rights. The only exception to a warrant being a valid defense in civil cases for damages is the serving of a warrant that is clearly invalid due to obvious mistakes that the officer should have discovered, such as absence of a signature or failure to specify the place or person subject to the warrant. For example, a police officer is sued for damages by a person who alleges that she was arrested without probable cause. If the arrest was made by virtue of a warrant, the officer is not held liable even if in fact it is later determined in court that the magistrate erred in thinking that probable cause existed. But the officer will be liable if the warrant contains mistakes that should have been obvious to the officer, such as the absence of a signature or an improper address.

III. HOW PROBABLE CAUSE IS ESTABLISHED

Probable cause may be established in three general ways, namely (1) the officer's own knowledge of particular facts and circumstances, (2) information given by a reliable third person (informant), and (3) information plus corroboration. In all these cases, the officer must be able to establish probable cause, although in different ways. If the officer seeks the issuance of an arrest or a search and seizure warrant, probable cause is established through an affidavit (although some states allow what is in writing to be supplemented by oral testimony). If the officer acts without a warrant, probable cause is established by oral testimony in court during the trial. It is therefore important for the officer to be able to state clearly, whether in an affidavit or in court later, why he or she felt probable cause was present.

In some cases, in addition to the evidence contained in the affidavit, the police officer presents oral evidence to the judge. Courts are divided on whether such oral evidence should be considered in determining probable cause; some courts consider it, others do not.

A. Officer's Own Knowledge of Facts and Circumstances

The officer's own knowledge is knowledge obtained personally by the officer, using any of his or her five senses (in contrast to knowledge supplied by another person). Factors that a police officer may take into account in establishing his or her belief that probable cause exists include the following:

1. prior criminal record of the suspect
2. suspect's flight from the scene of the crime when approached by the officer
3. highly suspicious conduct on the part of the suspect
4. admissions by the suspect
5. presence of incriminating evidence
6. unusual hour
7. resemblance of the suspect to the description of the perpetrator
8. failure to answer questions satisfactorily
9. physical clues, such as footprints or fingerprints, linked to a particular person
10. suspect's presence in a high-crime area

It is hard to say to what extent some or any of the preceding factors contribute to establishing probable cause. That would depend on the type of event, the strength of the relationship, and the intensity of the suspicion. One factor may be sufficient to establish probable cause in some instances, whereas in others several factors may be required. The preceding list is not exhaustive. Courts have also taken other factors into account.

(For a leading case on the sufficiency of allegation in any affidavit to constitute probable cause, read the Spinelli v. U.S. case brief at the end of this chapter.)

B. Information Given by an Informant Engaged in Criminal Activity

In Aguilar v. Texas, 378 U.S. 108 (1964), the Court established a two-pronged test for determining probable cause on the basis of information obtained from an informant engaged in criminal activity and who therefore has low credibility with the court.

Prong 1. Reliability of Informant

The affidavit must describe the underlying circumstances from which a neutral and detached magistrate may find that the informant is reliable; for example, "Affiant (a person who makes or subscribes to an affidavit) received information this morning from a trustworthy informant who has supplied information to the police during the past five years and whose information has proved reliable, resulting in numerous drug convictions."

Prong 2. Reliability of Informant's Information

The affidavit must also describe the underlying circumstances from which the magistrate can find that the informant's information is itself reliable and not the result of mere rumor or suspicion; for example, "My informant told me that he personally saw

Henry Banks, a former convict, sell heroin worth $500 to a buyer named Skippy Smith, at ten o'clock last night in Banks's apartment located at 1300 Shady Lane, Apt. 10, and that Banks has been selling and continues to sell drugs from this location."

a. Old interpretation of Aguilar.

Court decisions interpreted the two prongs in Aguilar as separate and independent of each other. This meant that the reliability of each—informant and information—had to stand on its own and be established separately before probable cause could be established. For example, the fact that the informant is absolutely reliable (Prong 1) could not make up for the lack of a description of how the informant obtained his information (Prong 2).

b. New interpretation of Aguilar.

The "separate and independent" interpretation of the two prongs in Aguilar was overruled by the Supreme Court in Illinois v. Gates, 103 S.Ct. 2317 (1983). (Read the Illinois v. Gates case brief at the end of this chapter.) In Gates, the Court abandoned the requirement of two independent tests as being too rigid, holding instead that the two prongs should be treated merely as relevant considerations in the totality of circumstances. Therefore, *"totality of circumstances"* has replaced *"separate and independent"* as the standard for probable cause in the Aguilar test.

Said the Court:

> . . . we conclude that it is wiser to abandon the "two-pronged test" established by our decisions in Aguilar and Spinelli. In its place we reaffirm the totality of the circumstances analysis that traditionally has informed probable cause determinations. The task of the issuing magistrate is simply to make a practical, common-sense decision whether, given all the circumstances set forth in the affidavit before him, including the "veracity" and "basis of knowledge" of persons supplying hearsay information, there is a fair probability that contraband or evidence of a crime will be found in a particular place. And the duty of a reviewing court is simply to ensure that the magistrate had a "substantial basis for . . . concluding" that probable cause existed.

The new test, therefore, is thus: *if a neutral and detached magistrate determines that, based on informant's information and all other available facts, there is probable cause to believe that an arrest or a search is justified, then the warrant may be issued.*

Under the Gates ruling, if an informer has been very reliable in the past, his or her tip may say little about how he or she obtained the information. Conversely, if the informant gives a lot of detail and says that he or she personally observed the event, then doubts about the informant's reliability may be overlooked. Corroboration by the police of the informant's story and/or all other available facts may be taken into account in determining probable cause based on the "totality of circumstances."

c. Identity of informant.

The Constitution does not require an officer to reveal the identity of an informant either to the magistrate when seeking the issuance of a warrant or during the trial. As long as the magistrate is convinced that the police officer is truthfully describing what the informant told him or her, the informant need not be produced nor his or her identity revealed. For example, a defendant was arrested by the police without a warrant and was searched in conjunction with the arrest.

Heroin was found on his person. During the trial the police officer refused to reveal the name of the informant, claiming instead that the informant was reliable because the information he had given in the past had led to arrests. The defendant was convicted and appealed. The court held that a warrantless arrest, search, and seizure may be valid even if the police officer does not reveal the identity of the informant because other evidence at the trial proved that the officer did rely on credible information supplied by a reliable informant. The court added that the issue in this case was whether probable cause existed, not the defendant's guilt or innocence (McCray v. Illinois, 386 U.S. 300 [1967]).

An exception to the preceding rule is that when the informant's identity is material to the issue of guilt or innocence, the identity must be revealed. Refusal by the state to reveal the identity of the informant requires dismissal of the case. The circumstances in which the informant's identity is material to the issue of guilt or innocence is a matter to be determined by the judge. In McCray, the Court said that the determination of whether the informant's name should be revealed "rests entirely with the judge who hears the motion to suppress to decide whether he needs such disclosure as to the informant in order to decide whether the officer is a believable witness." If the judge decides that the informant's name should be disclosed because such disclosure is material (nobody knows what that really means) to the issue of guilt or innocence, then the police must make a decision to drop the case in order to preserve the anonymity of the informant, or to disclose the name and therefore blow the informant's cover. An alternative to the disclosure of the informant's name in court is to hold an in camera (in private) hearing, producing the informant before the judge only so that the informant may be examined by the judge in private.

d. Information from noncriminal sources. The preceding discussions refer to informants who are themselves engaged in criminal activity and who therefore suffer from low credibility. If the information comes from noncriminal sources, the courts tend to be more lenient in determining the informant's reliability.

1. *If given by an ordinary citizen.* Most courts have ruled that the ordinary citizen who is either a victim of crime or an eyewitness to crime is a reliable informant, even though his or her reliability has not been established by previous incidents. For example, a woman tells an officer that she has personally seen a particular individual selling narcotics in the adjoining apartment. She gives a detailed description of the

---

HIGHLIGHT 4.2

Gates Modifies Aguilar

The "separate and independent" interpretation of the two prongs in Aguilar was overruled by the Supreme Court in Illinois v. Gates. In Gates, the Court abandoned the requirement of two independent tests as being too rigid, holding instead that the two prongs should be treated merely as relevant considerations in the totality of circumstances. Therefore, "totality of circumstances" has replaced "separate and independent" as the standard for probable cause in the Aguilar test.

alleged seller and describes the way sales are made. There is probable cause to obtain a warrant or (in exigent circumstances) make a warrantless arrest.

2. *If given by another police officer.* Information given by a police officer is considered reliable by the courts. In one case the court said, "Observations of fellow officers of the government engaged in a common investigation are plainly a reliable basis for a warrant applied for by one of their number" (U.S. v. Ventresca, 401 U.S. 560 [1971]).

Sometimes the police officer makes an affidavit in response to statements made by other police officers, as in cases of inside information from a detective, or to orders from a superior. The court has implied that under these circumstances, the arrest or search is valid only if the officer who passed on the information acted with probable cause.

e. Stale information. In search and seizure cases, problems may arise concerning whether the information provided has become "stale" after a period of time. The problem is peculiar to search and seizure cases because in these cases the question always is whether or not evidence of crime may be found at that time in a certain place. In one case, the Court held that there was no probable cause to search for illegal drinks in a hotel where the affidavit alleged a purchase of beer had occurred more than three weeks earlier (Sgro v. U.S., 287 U.S. 206 [1932]). A more recent case involved an informant's information that he had witnessed a sale of drugs at the suspect's residence approximately five months earlier and had observed, at that time, a shoebox containing a large amount of cash that belonged to the suspect. The Court said that this was "stale" information that could not establish probable cause (U.S. v. Leon, 35 CrL 3273 [1984]). The Court, however, has not specified how much time may elapse between the informant's observation and the warrant's issuance, stating instead that the issue "must be determined by the circumstances of each case."

C. Information plus Corroboration

If probable cause cannot be established by using information gathered from the informant alone (despite the now more liberal Gates test for determining probable cause), the police officer can remedy the deficiency by conducting his or her own investigation to corroborate the information given by the informant. Together, the two may establish probable cause even if the informant's information or the corroborative findings alone would not have been sufficient. For example, an informant tells a police officer that she has heard that X is selling drugs and that the sale is usually made at night in the apartment of X's girlfriend. That information alone would not establish probable cause. However, if the officer, acting on the information, places the apartment under surveillance, sees people going in and out, and in fact is told by a buyer that he has just purchased drugs from X inside the apartment, there is strong basis for probable cause either to arrest X without a warrant (if exigent circumstances exist) or to obtain a warrant from a magistrate.

A leading case on information plus corroboration is Draper v. United States, 358 U.S. 307 (1959). In that case, a narcotics agent received information from an informant that the petitioner had gone to Chicago to bring three ounces of heroin back to Denver by train. The informant also gave a detailed description of Draper. Given this information, police officers set up surveillance of trains coming from Chicago on the mornings of September 8 and 9, the dates the informant had indicated. On seeing a man that fitted the informant's description, the police moved in and made the arrest. Heroin and a syringe were seized in a search incident to the arrest. During trial, Draper sought exclusion of the evidence, claiming that the information given to the police failed to establish probable cause. The Court disagreed, saying that information received from an informant that is corroborated by an officer may be sufficient to provide probable cause for an arrest even though such information was hearsay and would not otherwise have been admissible in a criminal trial.

IV. PROBABLE CAUSE COMPARED WITH OTHER LEVELS OF PROOF

Probable cause is only one *level of proof* under the rules of evidence. There are other degrees of certainty, which may be categorized in descending order as shown in the table below.

Level of proof	Degree of certainty	Required in proceedings
Absolute certainty	100%	Not required in any legal proceeding.
Guilt beyond reasonable doubt	95%	To convict an accused; to prove every element of a criminal act.
Clear and convincing evidence	80%	Denial of bail in some states and insanity defense in some states.
Probable cause*	More than 50%	Issuance of warrant; search, seizure, and arrest without warrant; filing of an indictment or information; citizen's arrest.
Preponderance of the evidence*	More than 50%	Winning a civil case; affirmative criminal defense.
Reasonable suspicion	20%	Stop and frisk by police.
Suspicion	10%	To start a police or grand jury investigation.
Reasonable doubt	5%	To acquit an accused.
Hunch	0%	Not sufficient in any legal proceeding.
No information	0%	Not sufficient in any legal proceeding.

*Probable cause and preponderance of the evidence have the same level of certainty—more than 50 percent. This means that anything from 50.01 percent up will suffice. The difference is that "probable cause" is used in criminal proceedings, whereas "preponderance of the evidence" is usually used in civil proceedings, although aspects of a criminal proceeding use this term as well.

Despite attempts at quantification in order to establish certainty, the officer must realize that all the terms, including "probable cause," are subjective; what may be probable cause to one may not be probable cause to another. Nonetheless, the levels and percentages should afford the officer a good working knowledge of the meaning of various terms that are often used in law enforcement work.

□ SUMMARY

The term *probable cause* comes from the Fourth Amendment of the Constitution and applies to arrests, searches, and seizures. Probable cause exists when the facts and circumstances within the police officer's knowledge and of which he or she has trustworthy information are sufficient in themselves to warrant a "man of reasonable caution" in the belief that an offense has been or is being committed or that property subject to seizure can be found in a particular place or on a particular person. For practical purposes, there is probable cause when the police have trustworthy evidence sufficient to make a reasonable person think it more likely than not that the proposed arrest or search is justified. Mathematically speaking, this means that the officer must be more than 50 percent certain of the person's guilt or of finding the item sought.

When an arrest or search warrant is issued, probable cause has been determined by a magistrate through a filed complaint or affidavit. In other cases, the officer makes the determination, and it is subject to challenge and review by the accused in court.

The existence of probable cause is required in all arrests and searches, with or without a warrant. Although the standard for probable cause is the same in all situations, the person making the determination and the matters of concern may differ. A police officer is advised to obtain a warrant from a magistrate whenever possible, since this is a strong protection against civil liability and creates a presumption of the legality of the arrest or search. Probable cause may be established through personal knowledge of the facts by the police officer, through information given by other persons, or by a combination of both sources.

□ REVIEW QUESTIONS

1. What is the Supreme Court's definition of probable cause? For practical purposes, when does probable cause exist?
2. What are the advantages of obtaining a warrant whenever possible in arrest and search and seizure cases?
3. What are the three general ways whereby probable cause may be established? Discuss each.
4. How has the recent case of Gates v. Illinois changed the interpretation of the two-pronged test established earlier in Aguilar v. Texas?
5. What did the U.S. Supreme Court say in Spinelli v. United States?
6. What are the various levels of proof in evidence and the degree of certainty of each?

□ DEFINITIONS

"Man of Reasonable Caution":   Does not refer to a person with training in the law; instead it refers to the average "man on the street" who, under the same circumstances, would believe that the person being arrested had committed the offense or that things to be seized would be found in a particular place.

Probable Cause: Probable cause is defined as more than bare suspicion; it exists when the facts and circumstances within the officers' knowledge and of which they have reasonably trustworthy information are sufficient in themselves to warrant "a man of reasonable caution" in the belief that an offense has been or is being committed.

"Totality of Circumstances Test" (on information given by an informant): If a neutral and detached magistrate determines that, based on informant's information and all other available facts, there is probable cause to believe that an arrest or a search is justified, then the warrant may be issued. This replaces the "separate and independent" two-pronged test in the Aguilar case.

☐ PRINCIPLES OF CASES

AGUILAR V. TEXAS, 378 U.S. 108 (1964)   The Supreme Court established a two-pronged test for determining probable cause on the basis of information obtained from an informant: (1) reliability of informant and (2) reliability of informant's information. Both conditions of the test must be satisfied before probable cause can be established on information obtained from an informant. (*Note:* The independent two-pronged Aguilar test was replaced in 1983 by the "totality of circumstances" test in the Illinois v. Gates case.)

BRINEGAR V. UNITED STATES, 338 U.S. 160 (1949)   Defined probable cause as more than bare suspicion; it exists when the facts and circumstances within the officers' knowledge and of which they had reasonably trustworthy information are sufficient in themselves to warrant "a man of reasonable caution" in the belief that an offense has been or is being committed. The substance of all the definitions of probable cause is a reasonable ground for belief of guilt. This means less than evidence that would justify condemnation or conviction.

DRAPER V. UNITED STATES, 358 U.S. 307 (1959)   Information received from an informant that is corroborated by an officer may be sufficient to provide probable cause for an arrest even though such information was hearsay and would not otherwise have been admissible in a criminal trial.

ILLINOIS V. GATES, 103 S.Ct. 2317 (1983)   A warrant may be issued on the basis of affidavits that are entirely hearsay (such as when a police officer swears to facts reported to him or her by the crime victim, witnesses, or police informants). However, the affidavit must show by a *totality of the circumstances* that there is a fair probability that contraband or evidence of crime will be found in a particular place. Among the considerations are whether the affidavit shows that (1) the informant is reliable and (2) the informant's information is reliable. (*Note:* The Gates case still preserves the two-pronged test established under Aguilar, but it does not treat the two aspects separately and independently. Instead, the "totality of circumstances" approach is used, meaning that whatever deficiencies there may be in one can be supplemented or overcome by the other.)

McCRAY V. ILLINOIS, 386 U.S. 300 (1967)   A warrantless arrest, search, and seizure may be valid even when the police officer does not reveal the identity of the informant, if other evidence at the trial proves that the officer did rely on credible information supplied by a reliable informant. The issue in this case was whether probable cause existed, not defendant's guilt or innocence.

MICHIGAN V. SUMMERS, 452 U.S. 692 (1981)   The general rule is that every arrest and every seizure having the essential attribute of a formal arrest is unreasonable unless it is supported by probable cause.

SGRO V. UNITED STATES, 287 U.S. 206 (1932)   There was no probable cause to search for illegal drinks in a hotel where the affidavit alleged a purchase of beer had taken place more than three weeks earlier. The grounds for probable cause had become "stale."

SPINELLI V. UNITED STATES, 393 U.S. 410 (1969)   "Innocent-seeming activity and data" and a "bald and unilluminating assertion of suspicion" in an affidavit are not to be given weight in a magistrate's determination of probable cause. An officer may use credible hearsay to establish probable cause; however, an affidavit based on an informant's tip must satisfy the two-pronged Aguilar test.

UNITED STATES V. LEON, 35 CrL 3273 (1984)   Informant supplied information that he had witnessed a sale of drugs at suspect's residence approximately five months earlier and had at that time observed a shoebox containing a large amount of cash that belonged to the suspect; the information was judged "stale" and could not establish probable cause.

UNITED STATES V. ORTIZ, 422 U.S. 891 (1975)   In determining probable cause, "officers are entitled to draw reasonable inferences from . . . facts in light of their knowledge of the area and their prior experience with aliens and smugglers."

UNITED STATES V. VENTRESCA, 300 U.S. 102 (1965)   The Supreme Court recognizes that affidavits or complaints are often prepared hastily in the midst of a criminal investigation. Therefore, the policy is to interpret the allegations in a common-sense rather than in an overly technical manner and to uphold the sufficiency of the affidavit in close cases.

☐   CASE BRIEF—LEADING CASE ON SUFFICIENCY OF ALLEGATION FOR PROBABLE CAUSE

SPINELLI V. UNITED STATES, 393 U.S. 410 (1969)

FACTS: Spinelli was convicted by a federal court of interstate travel in aid of racketeering. The evidence used against Spinelli was obtained by use of a search warrant issued by a magistrate authorizing the search of the apartment. The warrant was issued on the basis of an affidavit from an FBI agent that stated the following:

1. That the FBI had kept track of Spinelli's movements on five days during the month of August 1965. On four of those five occasions, Spinelli was seen crossing one of two bridges leading from Illinois into St. Louis, Missouri, between 11 A.M. and 12:15 P.M.
2. That an FBI check with the telephone company revealed that an apartment house near a parking lot that Spinelli frequented had two telephones listed under the name of Grace P. Hagen.
3. That Spinelli was known to the affiant and to federal law enforcement agents and local police "as a bookmaker, an associate of bookmakers, a gambler, and an associate of gamblers."

4. That the FBI "has been informed by a confidential reliable informant that William Spinelli is operating a handbook and accepting wagers and disseminating wagering information by means of the telephones" listed under the name of Grace P. Hagen.

ISSUE: *Did the above affidavit contain probable cause sufficient for the issuance of a search warrant? No.*

SUPREME COURT DECISION: Allegations 1 and 2 in the affidavit reflect only innocent-seeming activity and data: "Spinelli's travels to and from the apartment building and his entry into a particular apartment on one occasion could hardly be taken as bespeaking gambling activity; and there is nothing unusual about an apartment containing two separate telephones." Allegation 3 is "but a bald and unilluminating assertion of suspicion that is entitled to no weight in appraising the magistrate's decision." Allegation 4 must be measured against the two-pronged Aguilar test. Here the reliability of the informant was not established; neither did the affidavit prove the reliability of informant's information. The affidavit therefore failed to establish probable cause; hence the conviction was reversed and remanded.

CASE SIGNIFICANCE: The Spinelli case illustrates the types of allegations that are insufficient to establish probable cause. It restates the two-pronged Aguilar test for probable cause if the information comes from an informant. Note, however, that the Aguilar test, though still valid, has been modified by Illinois v. Gates.

EXCERPTS FROM THE DECISION: Applying these principles to the present we first consider the weight to be given the informer's tip when it is considered apart from the rest of the affidavit. It is clear that a Commissioner could not credit it without abdicating his constitutional function. Though the affiant swore that his confidant was "reliable," he offered the magistrate no reason in support of this conclusion. Perhaps even more important is the fact that Aguilar's other test has not been satisfied. The tip does not contain a sufficient statement of the underlying circumstances from which the informer concluded that Spinelli was running a bookmaking operation. We are not told how the FBI's source received his information—it is not alleged that the informant personally observed Spinelli at work or that he had ever placed a bet with him. Moreover, if the informant came by the information indirectly, he did not explain why his sources were reliable. . . . In the absence of a statement detailing the manner in which the information was gathered, it is especially important that the tip describe the accused's criminal activity in sufficient detail that the magistrate may know that he is relying on something more substantial than a casual rumor circulating in the underworld or an accusation based merely on an individual's general reputation.

We conclude, then, that in the present case the informant's tip—even when corroborated to the extent indicated—was not sufficient to provide the basis for a finding of probable cause. This is not to say that the tip was so insubstantial that it could not properly have counted in the magistrate's determination. Rather, it needed some further support. When we look to the other parts of the application, however, we find nothing alleged which would permit the suspicions engendered by the informant's report to ripen into a judgment that a crime was probably being committed. As we have already seen, the allegations detailing the FBI's surveillance of Spinelli and its investigation of the telephone company records contain no suggestion of criminal conduct when taken by themselves—and they are now endowed with an aura of suspicion by virtue of the informer's tip. Nor do we find that the FBI's reports take on a sinister color when read in light of common knowledge that bookmaking is often carried on over the telephone and from premises ostensibly used by others for perfectly normal purposes. Such an argument would carry weight in a situation in which the premises contain an unusual number of telephones or abnormal activity is observed . . . but it does not fit this case where neither of these factors is present. All that remains to be considered is the flat statement that Spinelli was "known" to the FBI and others as a gambler. But just as a simple assertion of police suspicion is not itself a sufficient basis for a magistrate's finding of probable cause, we do not believe it may be used to give additional weight to allegations that would otherwise be insufficient.

☐ CASE BRIEF—LEADING CASE ON PROBABLE CAUSE BASED ON INFORMANT'S INFORMATION

ILLINOIS V. GATES, 103 S.Ct. 2317 (1983)

FACTS: On May 3, 1978, the police department of Bloomingdale, Illinois, received an anonymous letter that included statements that the Gateses were engaged in selling drugs; that the wife would drive their car to Florida on May 3 to be loaded with drugs, and the husband would fly down in a few days to drive the car back; that the car's trunk would be loaded with drugs; and that the Gateses then had more than $100,000 worth of drugs in their basement. Acting on the tip, a police officer determined the Gateses' address and learned that he had made a reservation on a May 5 flight to Florida. Arrangements for surveillance for the flight were made with an agent of the Drug Enforcement Administration (DEA), and the surveillance disclosed that Gates took the flight, stayed overnight in a motel room registered in his wife's name, and left the following morning with a woman in a car bearing an Illinois license plate, heading north to the Bloomingdale area. A search warrant for the Gateses' residence and automobile was then obtained from an Illinois state court judge on the basis of the Bloomingdale police officer's affidavit setting forth the foregoing facts and a copy of the anonymous letter. When the Gateses arrived at their home, the police were waiting. In a search of the house and car, the police discovered marijuana and other contraband.

ISSUE: *Did the affidavit and the anonymous letter provide sufficient facts to establish probable cause for the issuance of the warrant? Yes.*

SUPREME COURT DECISION: Yes, probable cause was established. The rigid two-pronged test under Aguilar and Spinelli for determining whether an informant's tip establishes probable cause for issuance of a warrant is abandoned, and the "totality of circumstances" approach is substituted in its place. The task of an issuing magistrate is simply to make a practical, common-sense decision whether, given all the circumstances set forth in the affidavit before him, there is a fair probability that contraband or evidence of a crime will be found in a particular place. Here the judge issuing the warrant had a substantial basis for concluding that probable cause to search the Gateses' home and car existed. Under the "totality of circumstances" test, corroboration of details of an informant's tip by independent police work is of significant value. Even standing alone, the facts obtained through the independent investigation of the Bloomingdale police officer and the DEA at least suggested that the Gates couple was involved in drug trafficking. In addition, the judge could rely on the anonymous letter, which had been corroborated in major part by the police officer's efforts. Conviction is affirmed.

CASE SIGNIFICANCE: The two-pronged independent test for establishing probable cause under Aguilar, in cases in which information is given by an informant, is now replaced by the "totality of circumstances" test, making it easier for police officers to establish probable cause for the issuance of a warrant.

EXCERPTS FROM THE DECISION: This totality-of-the-circumstances approach is far more consistent with our prior treatment of probable cause than is any rigid demand that specific "tests" be satisfied by every informant's tip. Perhaps the central teaching of our decisions bearing on the probable cause standard is that it is a "practical, nontechnical conception." Brinegar v. United States, 338 U.S. 160, 176 (1949). "In dealing with probable cause, . . . as the very name implies, we deal with probabilities. These are not technical; they are the factual and practical considerations of everyday life on which reasonable and prudent men, not legal technicians, act." Id., at 175. Our observation in United States v. Cortez, 449 U.S. 411, 418 (1981), regarding "particularized suspicion," is also applicable to the probable cause standard:

> The process does not deal with hard certainties, but with probabilities. Long before the law of probabilities was articulated as such, practical people formulated certain common-sense conclusions about human behavior; jurors as factfinders are permitted to do the same—and so are law enforcement officers. Finally, the evidence thus collected must be seen and weighed not in terms of library analysis by scholars, but as understood by those versed in the field of law enforcement.

As these comments illustrate, probable cause is a fluid concept—turning on the assessment of probabilities in particular factual contexts—not readily, or even usefully, reduced to a neat set of legal rules. Informants' tips doubtless come in many shapes and sizes from many different types of persons. As we said in Adams v. Williams, 407 U.S. 143, 147 (1972): "Informants' tips, like all other clues and evidence coming to a policeman on the scene, may vary greatly in their value and reliability." Rigid legal rules are ill-suited to an area of such diversity. "One simple rule will not cover every situation."

Moreover, the "two-pronged test" directs analysis into two largely independent channels—the informant's "veracity" or "reliability" and his "basis of knowledge." . . . There are persuasive arguments against according these two elements such independent status. Instead, they are better understood as relevant considerations in the totality-of-the-circumstances analysis that traditionally has guided probable cause determinations: a deficiency in one may be compensated for, in determining the overall reliability of a tip, by a strong showing as to the other, or by some other indicia of reliability. . . .

If, for example, a particular informant is known for the unusual reliability of his predictions of certain types of criminal activities in a locality, his failure, in a particular case, to thoroughly set forth the basis of his knowledge surely should not serve as an absolute bar to a finding of probable cause based on his tip. . . . Likewise, if an unquestionably honest citizen comes forward with a report of criminal activity— we have found rigorous scrutiny of the basis of his knowledge unnecessary. . . . Conversely, even if we entertain some doubt as to an informant's motives, his explicit and detailed description of alleged wrongdoing, along with a statement that the event was observed first-hand, entitles his tip to greater weight than might otherwise be the case. Unlike a totality-of-the-circumstances analysis, which permits a balanced assessment of the relative weights of all the various indicia of reliability (and unreliability) attending an informant's tip, the "two-pronged test" has encouraged an excessively technical dissection of informants' tips, with undue attention being focused on isolated issues that cannot sensibly be divorced from the other facts presented to the magistrate.

☐ CASE BRIEF—LEADING CASE ON INFORMANT'S INFORMATION PLUS POLICE CORROBORATION

DRAPER V. UNITED STATES, 358 U.S. 307 (1959)

FACTS: A narcotics agent received information, from an informant who had proven himself reliable, that petitioner had gone to Chicago to bring three ounces of heroin back to Denver by train either the morning of September 8 or 9. The informant also gave a detailed physical description of petitioner, the clothes he would be wearing, and that he habitually "walked real fast." Based on this information, police officers set up surveillance of all trains coming from Chicago. The morning of September 8 produced no one fitting the informant's description. On the morning of September 9, officers observed an individual matching the exact description the informant had supplied get off of a train from Chicago and begin to walk quickly toward the exit. Officers overtook the suspect and arrested him. Heroin and a syringe were seized in a search incident to the arrest. The informant died before the trial and was unable to testify. Draper was convicted of knowingly concealing and transporting drugs.

ISSUE: *Can information provided by an informant, which is subsequently corroborated by an officer, provide probable cause for an arrest without a warrant? Yes.*

SUPREME COURT DECISION: Information received from an informant that is corroborated by an officer may be sufficient to provide probable cause for an arrest even though such information was hearsay and would not otherwise have been admissible in a criminal trial.

CASE SIGNIFICANCE: The evidence from the informant in this case could be considered hearsay—ordinarily inadmissible in a criminal trial. The Court said, however, that it could be used to show probable cause for purposes of a search; thus, evidence that may not be admissible in a trial may be used by the police to establish probable cause. This is important because all information from an informant is considered hearsay as the basis for police action, but the police can act on such information as long as it is good enough to establish probable cause. The Court held that there was probable cause here because the information came from "one employed for that purpose and whose information had always been found accurate and reliable." The Court added that "it is clear that [the police officer] would have been derelict in his duties had he not pursued it."

EXCERPTS FROM THE DECISION: In dealing with probable cause, . . . as the very name implies, we deal with probabilities. These are not technical; they are the factual and practical considerations of everyday life on which reasonable and prudent men, not legal technicians, act. Probable cause exists where "the facts and circumstances within the arresting officers'" knowledge and of which they had reasonably trustworthy information are sufficient in themselves to warrant a man of reasonable caution in the belief that an offense has been or is being committed.

We believe that, under the facts and circumstances here, Marsh had probable cause and reasonable grounds to believe that petitioner was committing a violation of the laws of the United States relating to narcotic drugs at the time he arrested him. The arrest was therefore lawful, and the subsequent search and seizure, having been made incident to that lawful arrest, were likewise valid.

☐ NOTE

1. John G. Miles, Jr., David B. Richardson, and Anthony E. Scudellari, *The Law Officer's Pocket Manual* (Washington, DC: Bureau of National Affairs, 1988–89), at 6:4.

PART THREE

ARRESTS, SEARCHES, AND SEIZURES

CHAPTER FIVE

STOP AND FRISK, IMMIGRATION AND BORDER SEIZURES, AND STATIONHOUSE DETENTION

☐   KEY TERMS

"stop and frisk"	frisk
stop	fishing expedition
reasonable suspicion	factory surveys
"drug courier profile"	stationhouse detention

This chapter deals with *"stop and frisk"* and other forms of intrusion into a person's freedom. In these cases no arrest can be undertaken because probable cause has not been established. Note, however, that what starts off as a form of intrusion, as described in this chapter, can easily turn into an arrest if subsequent developments lead the police to conclude that probable cause has been established. The forms of intrusion discussed here are "stop and frisk," stationhouse detention, and immigration and border seizures. Motor vehicle stops and searches, an important part of police work, are discussed in Chapter Eight.

I. STOP AND FRISK—TERRY V. OHIO IS THE LEADING CASE

A legal issue in policing is whether a police officer may stop a person in a public place (or in an automobile), question the person about his or her identity and activities at the time, and frisk the person for dangerous (and perhaps illegally possessed) weapons. "Stop and frisk" is a form of search and seizure and therefore comes under the Fourth Amendment, but because it is less intrusive than an arrest it may be carried out based on reasonable suspicion instead of probable cause.

Therefore, several states have passed "stop and frisk" laws that allow an officer to stop a person in a public place if the officer has "reasonable suspicion" that the person has committed or is about to commit a felony and to demand the person's name and address and an explanation of his or her actions. Other states, and some federal courts, have upheld such practices in judicial decisions even without statutory authorization. Underlying both statutory and judicial approval of "stop and frisk" is the notion that this practice does not constitute an arrest (although it comes under the Fourth Amendment) and hence can be justified on less than probable cause for an arrest.

One of the most important cases in law enforcement, and the landmark case that declared "stop and frisk" based on reasonable suspicion constitutional, is Terry v. Ohio, 392 U.S. 1 (1968). (Read the Terry v. Ohio case brief at the end of this chapter.) The last paragraph of the majority opinion in that case says:

> We . . . hold today that where a police officer observes unusual conduct which leads him reasonably to conclude in light of his experience that criminal activity may be afoot and that the person with whom he is dealing may be armed and presently dangerous, where in the course of investigating this behavior he identifies himself as a policeman and makes reasonable inquiries, and where nothing in the initial stages of the encounter serves to dispel his reasonable fear for his own or others' safety, he is entitled for the protection of himself and others in the area to conduct a carefully limited search of the outer clothing of such persons in an attempt to discover weapons which might be used

to assault him. Such a search is a reasonable search under the Fourth Amendment, and any weapons seized may properly be introduced in evidence against the person from whom they are taken.

Terry v. Ohio set the following guidelines to determine whether a stop and frisk is valid:

1. *Circumstances.* The police officer must observe unusual conduct that leads him or her reasonably to conclude, in the light of his or her experience, that
   a. criminal activity may be afoot, and
   b. the person with whom he or she is dealing may be armed and presently dangerous.
2. *What police officer must initially do.* In the course of investigating such behavior, the officer must
   a. identify himself or herself as a police officer, and
   b. make reasonable inquiries.
3. *Extent of what an officer may do.* If these first two requirements are satisfied, the officer, for the protection of himself or herself and others in the area, may conduct a carefully limited search of the outer clothing of the person in an attempt to discover weapons that might be used to assault him or her.

The preceding legal guidelines in Terry v. Ohio are usually translated into instructions in police manuals as the steps officers are to follow in "stop and frisk" cases. These are:

- observe
- approach and identify
- ask questions

If answers do not dispel police concern for safety:

- conduct pat-down of outer clothing
- if weapon is felt, may confiscate weapon and effect arrest
- may conduct full body search after arrest

If in the course of a frisk under the above circumstances the officer finds a dangerous weapon, he or she may seize it, and the weapon may be introduced in evidence against the party from whom it was taken. An example, taken from the *Law Officer's Pocket Manual,* goes like this: an officer observes two men loitering outside a bank in broad daylight. The men confer several times in front of the bank, looking through the bank's windows. Each wears a topcoat, although it is a warm day. One of the suspects goes to a car parked directly across from the bank and sits behind the wheel. As the bank guard leaves the bank, the second suspect starts to head into the bank. The officer can then stop the suspect, identify himself or herself, ask for an explanation of the suspect's conduct, and then frisk the suspect if the answers do not relieve the officer of his or her suspicions. There is reason, based on the officer's experience, to believe that criminal activity is about to take place, that the suspects are likely to be armed, and that they pose a threat to safety.[1]

Although the term *"stop and frisk"* is often used as though one continuous act were involved, there are actually two separate acts in the process, each having its own requirements for legality.

A. Stop

A stop is justified only if the police officer has reasonable suspicion, in light of his or her experience, that criminal activity is about to take place. Therefore, the purpose of a stop is to prevent criminal activity. A stop for anything else is illegal unless it meets the standard of "probable cause" (thus making the act an arrest). For example, an officer stopped a suspect on the grounds that (1) he was walking in an area that had a high incidence of drug traffic, (2) he "looked suspicious," and (3) he had not been seen in that area previously by the officer. The Court held that these circumstances, although amounting to vague suspicion, did not meet the "reasonable suspicion based on objective facts" test and therefore the stop was unconstitutional (Brown v. Texas, 443 U.S. 47 [1979]). Clearly, then, vague suspicion is not enough.

1. What Constitutes Reasonable Suspicion?

The term *reasonable suspicion* is hard to define with precision and has not been authoritatively defined by the Court. In one case, however, the Court said, "Reasonable suspicion is a less demanding standard than probable cause not only in the sense that reasonable suspicion can be established with information that is different in quantity or content than that required to establish probable cause, but also in the sense that reasonable suspicion can arise from information that is less reliable than that required to show probable cause" (Alabama v. White, 58 L.W. 4747 [1990]). To justify a stop, reasonable suspicion must be anchored on specific objective facts and logical conclusions based on the officer's experience. Such general considerations as the high-crime nature of the area are no substitute for specific facts about the suspect or the suspect's conduct.[2] On a scale of certainty, therefore, reasonable suspicion is higher than vague suspicion but lower than probable cause.

2. What Constitutes a Stop?

A person has been *"seized" within the meaning of the Fourth Amendment only if, in view of all of the circumstances surrounding the incident, a reasonable person would have believed that he or she was not free to leave.* These are some circumstances that might indicate a seizure, even if the person detained did not attempt to leave: (1) the threatening presence of several officers, (2) the display of a weapon by an officer, (3) some physical touching of the person, and (4) the use of language or tone of voice indicating that compliance with the officer's request might be compelled (U.S. v. Mendenhall, 446 U.S. 544 [1980]).

3. Are Stops Based on Hearsay Information Valid?—Yes

An investigative stop based on second-hand or hearsay information is valid. For example, a police officer on patrol in a high-crime area received a tip from a person known to the officer that a suspect was carrying narcotics and had a gun. The officer approached the suspect's parked automobile and ordered him to step out. When the suspect responded by rolling down his window, the officer reached into the car and removed a loaded pistol from the suspect's waistband. The suspect was then arrested, and subsequent search of the car led to recovery of additional weapons and a substantial quantity of heroin. The Court rejected the defense's contention that a stop and frisk cannot be based on second-hand information, saying that the information from the known informant "carried enough indicia of reliability to justify" the forcible stop of the suspect (Adams v. Williams, 407 U.S. 143 [1972]).

The preceding case involved information obtained by the police from a known informant. What if the tip is anonymous? The Court has said that an anonymous tip, corroborated by independent police work, may provide reasonable suspicion to make an investigatory stop if it provides a sufficient indicia of reliability (Alabama v. White, 58 L.W. 4747 [1990]). In this case, the police received an anonymous tip through the telephone that a certain White would leave a certain apartment at 3 P.M. in a brown Plymouth station wagon with a broken taillight, that she would be going to Dobey's Motel, and that she would have cocaine in a brown attache case. The police immediately proceeded to the apartment building, where they saw a vehicle matching the anonymous caller's description. They then observed White leaving the building and driving a vehicle. The police followed her to Dobey's Motel and stopped her vehicle before reaching the motel. She consented to a search of her vehicle, which revealed marijuana. White was then arrested; a subsequent search found cocaine in her purse. She was tried and convicted. On appeal, she sought suppression of the evidence alleging that the search was illegal because the stop was not based on reasonable suspicion. The Court disagreed, saying that "standing alone, the tip here is completely lacking in the necessary indicia of reliability, since it provides virtually nothing from which one might conclude that the caller is honest or his information reliable and gave no indication of the basis for his predictions regarding White's criminal activities." The Court added, however, that "although it is a close question, the totality of the circumstances demonstrates that significant aspects of the informant's story were *sufficiently corroborated by the police* to furnish reasonable suspicion."

4. Is Information from Another Jurisdiction Sufficient for a Stop?—Yes

The Court has decided that the police may stop a suspect on the basis of reasonable suspicion that the person is wanted for investigation in another jurisdiction (U.S. v. Hensley, 53 L.W. 4053 [1985]). In this case, Hensley was wanted for questioning about an armed robbery in St. Bernard, Ohio. The police circulated a "wanted" flyer to neighboring police departments. The police in nearby Covington, Kentucky, saw Hensley's car a week later and, knowing that he had been wanted for questioning, stopped him and discovered firearms in the car. He was later charged in federal court with and convicted of illegal possession of firearms. He appealed the conviction, claiming that the stop was illegal because there was no probable cause and therefore the evidence obtained should have been excluded. In a unanimous opinion, the Court said that the police may act without a warrant to stop and briefly detain a person they know is wanted for investigation by a police department in another city. If the police have a reasonable suspicion, grounded in specific and articulable facts, that a person they encounter is involved in or is wanted for questioning in connection with a completed felony, then a "Terry-type" stop may be made to investigate that suspicion. Any evidence legally obtained as a result of that stop is admissible in court. In the Hensley case, the Court publicly recognized the need among law enforcement agencies for rapid communication and cooperation, saying:

> In an era when criminal suspects are increasingly mobile and increasingly likely to flee across jurisdictional boundaries, this rule is a matter of common sense: it minimizes the

volume of information concerning suspects that must be transmitted to other jurisdictions and enables police in one jurisdiction to act promptly in reliance on information from another jurisdiction.

5. Are Stops Based on "Drug Courier Profile" Valid?

May a person who fits a "drug courier profile" be stopped by the police? The Court has said that profiles are helpful in identifying people who are likely to commit crimes, but failed to indicate that fitting a "drug courier profile" alone justifies a Terry-type stop. What is needed is that the facts, taken together, must amount to a reasonable suspicion (U.S. v. Sokolow, 109 S.Ct. 1581 [1989]). In this case, Sokolow purchased two round-trip tickets for a flight from Honolulu to Miami. The facts surrounding that purchase, and known to the Drug Enforcement Administration agents, were that (1) Sokolow paid $2,100 for two round-trip tickets from a roll of $20 bills; (2) he traveled under an assumed name that did not match his listed telephone number; (3) his original destination was Miami, a place known for illicit drugs; (4) he stayed in Miami for only 48 hours, although the flight from Honolulu to Miami and back took 20 hours; (5) he appeared nervous during his trip; and (6) he had luggage, but none was checked. Because of these facts, which fit a "drug courier profile" developed by the Drug Enforcement Agency, Sokolow and his companion were stopped and taken to the DEA office at the airport where their luggage was examined by a drug dog. Cocaine was found, and Sokolow was convicted of possession with intent to distribute cocaine. On appeal, the Court said there was nothing wrong with the use of a "drug courier profile" in this case because the facts, taken together, amounted to reasonable suspicion that criminal conduct was taking place. The Court indicated, however, that whether or not the facts in this case fit a "drug courier profile" was less important than that taken together the facts established a reasonable suspicion sufficient to warrant a Terry-type stop. (Read the U.S. v. Sokolow case brief at the end of this chapter.)

6. Scope and Duration of a Stop

An investigatory stop must be temporary and no longer than necessary under the circumstances to achieve its purpose. Officers cannot detain a person for as much time as is convenient. This has been decided by the Court in a number of cases.

In one case, the Court held that a ninety-minute detention of an air traveler's luggage was excessive. In that case, the suspect's luggage was detained long enough to enable a trained dog to sniff for marijuana. The Court decided that such initial seizure was justified under Terry v. Ohio but that the ninety-minute delay exceeded the permissible limits of an investigative stop. The Court added: "Although we decline to adopt any outside time limitation for a permissible Terry stop, we have never approved a seizure of the person for the prolonged 90-minute period involved here and cannot do so on the facts presented by this case" (U.S. v. Place, 462 U.S. 696 [1983]).

In another case, the Court held that the removal of a detainee without his consent from the public area in an airport to the police room in the airport converted the stop to an arrest. In this case, airport narcotics police stopped the suspect because he fit the "drug courier profile" used to identify people who are likely to be drug couriers.

After stopping the suspect, the agents asked for and examined his ticket and driver's license. They discovered that he was traveling under an assumed name. The police then identified themselves as narcotics agents and told the suspect that he was suspected of being a drug courier. Without his consent, they took him to a separate police room about forty feet away from the main concourse. One officer sat with the suspect in the room while another officer retrieved the suspect's luggage from the airline and brought it back to the room. The agents then asked the suspect if he would consent to a search of the suitcases. The suspect took out a key and unlocked one of the bags, which contained drugs. The Court concluded that although the initial stop and questioning was valid, the subsequent conduct of the officers was "more intrusive than necessary" to carry out the limited investigation permitted under "stop and frisk"; hence it constituted an arrest. Since the police were interested mainly in gaining consent to search the suspect's luggage, there was no need to remove him to the small room forty feet away in order to gain that consent (Florida v. Royer, 460 U.S. 491 [1983]).

In a third case, a certain Luckett was stopped for jaywalking. He was detained for longer than was necessary to write out a ticket because the police wanted to radio headquarters on a completely unsubstantiated hunch that there was a warrant for Luckett's arrest. The Court of Appeals held that the duration of the stop was unreasonable and that it therefore turned the stop into an arrest (U.S. v. Luckett, 484 F.2d 89 [1973]).

7. Degree of Intrusiveness

The investigative method used must be that which is *least intrusive and reasonably available to verify or dispel the officer's suspicion.* Anything more intrusive makes the act invalid. Therefore, the greater the degree of police control over a detainee, the greater the likelihood that reviewing courts will impose the higher standard of probable cause. In the absence of some justification, the display of weapons by the police when making an investigative stop can turn a stop into an arrest. But the display of weapons in itself does not automatically convert a stop into an arrest. Lower courts tend to look at display of weapons on a case-by-case basis to determine if the stop has been converted into an arrest.

A 1985 case shows that the concept of "least intrusive means" can be modified by a "reasonableness" approach. In United States v. Sharpe, 105 S.Ct. 1568 (1985), the Court found it reasonable for the police to detain a truck driver for twenty minutes. The driver was suspected of carrying marijuana in a truck camper. The length of the stop was due in part to the fact that the driver attempted to evade the stop, causing the two officers pursuing him to be separated. The officer who performed the stop therefore had to wait fifteen minutes for his more experienced partner to arrive before making the search. Marijuana was found in the camper, and the driver was arrested. The Court held that to determine whether a detention is reasonable in length, the Court *must look at the purpose to be served by the stop and the time reasonably needed to carry it out.* It added that courts should refrain from second-guessing police officers' choices, especially when the police are acting in a swiftly developing situation, as in this case. This case indicates that the reasonableness of a stop must take into account not just the length of time involved but the needs of law enforcement as well.

B. Frisk

1. Does a Frisk Automatically Follow a Stop?—No

A frisk should follow only if there is nothing in the initial stages of the encounter (after the stop) that would dispel reasonable fear about the safety of the police officer or of others. The purpose of a frisk is *protection;* frisking should take place only if justified after the stop. For example, X is stopped by a police officer late one night in a dimly lighted street on reasonable suspicion that X is about to commit an offense. The officer asks X questions to which X gives evasive answers, appearing uneasy and nervous. The officer may go ahead and frisk because nothing in the initial encounter has dispelled reasonable fear about the safety of the officer or of others. In contrast, suppose that after the stop and initial questioning the officer is convinced that X in fact resides in one of the nearby apartments and that he is returning home from a trip to a nearby grocery store to buy cigarettes. The officer has no justification to go ahead and frisk.

The Court has stated that the *totality of circumstances,* meaning the whole picture, must be taken into account when determining the legality of a frisk. The detaining officers must have a particularized objective basis for suspecting the stopped person of criminal activity (U.S. v. Cortez, 449 U.S. 411 [1981]).

2. Extent of Frisk—Pat-down of Outer Clothing

A frisk must be limited initially to a pat-down of a person's outer clothing, and only an object that feels like a weapon may properly be seized. The object may not turn out to be a weapon, but if it feels like one the frisk is justified. Conversely, if the object does not feel like a weapon, it cannot be seized. For example, after a valid stop based on reasonable suspicion, a police officer has reasonable fear that the suspect may be armed. She then frisks the suspect and in the process feels something soft that cannot possibly be considered a weapon. She cannot legitimately seize the object in question.

Possible confusion has arisen over the extent of the frisk after a stop because of the decision in United States v. Robinson, 414 U.S. 218 (1973). In the Robinson case, the Supreme Court held that a *body search after an authorized arrest for driving without a permit is valid even when the officer admits there was no possible danger to him and therefore no reason to look for a weapon.* However, the Robinson case involved an arrest, not a stop and frisk; hence arrest laws applied. Once the stop and frisk turns into an arrest, based on probable cause, then the Robinson case applies, meaning that a body search may now be conducted.

C. Distinctions Between "Stop and Frisk" and Arrest

The concepts of stop and frisk and of arrest can be confusing because both involve a restriction of an individual's freedom by the police, and both can lead to a similar result—the individual being charged with a crime. The confusion can be avoided, however, if the distinctions between these two concepts are clearly understood. These distinctions are shown in the table below.

	"Stop and frisk"	*Arrest*
1. Degree of certainty	"Reasonable suspicion" (about 20% certainty)	"Probable cause" (more than 50% certainty)
2. Scope	Very limited—only pat-down for weapons	Full body search
3. Purpose	Stop—to prevent criminal activity Frisk—to protect officer and others	To take person into custody
4. Warrant	Not needed	May or may not need warrant

D. Other Considerations in "Stop and Frisk" Cases

1. No "Fishing Expeditions" Allowed

The frisk cannot be used to see if some type of evidence can be found on the suspect. Its only purpose is to protect the police officer and others in the area from possible harm. A frisk for any other reason is illegal and leads to the exclusion of any evidence obtained, regardless of how incriminating the evidence may be. The purpose of a frisk is police protection; therefore, anything felt in the course of the frisk that does not feel like a weapon cannot be seized. For example, police officers frisk a person because they suspect, after a valid stop, that he is dangerous. In the course of the pat-down, they feel a soft object in the person's pocket that they think is a pound of cocaine. If confiscated based on that suspicion alone, the evidence is not admissible in court because the police did not think that what they felt was a weapon. Suppose, however, that in the course of that frisk the police also come across something that feels like a weapon. That weapon can be confiscated, the suspect arrested, and then searched. If the pound of cocaine is found in his pocket in the course of that search, such evidence is admissible.

2. Stop and Frisk Can Lead to Immediate Arrest

Although stop and frisk is not an arrest, what the officer discovers while stopping or frisking the suspect may give cause to make an immediate arrest. For example, an officer stops a suspect and subsequently frisks him. In the course of the pat-down, the officer touches something that feels like a weapon. If it is in fact a prohibited weapon, the officer may confiscate it and immediately place the suspect under arrest. Once placed under arrest, the suspect may be then searched in full (as authorized in the Robinson case), and any contraband found on the suspect may also be confiscated.

3. Suspect Cannot Be Forced to Answer Questions

A suspect who is stopped cannot be forced by the officer to reply to questions, but such refusal may give the officer sufficient justification to frisk on account of the suspect's failure to dispel suspicions of danger.

4. Stop and Frisk Applies to Motor Vehicles

Motorists are subject to stop and frisk under the same circumstances as pedestrians. Moreover, a police officer may order the driver to step out of the car after a routine stop for issuance of a traffic ticket even if the officer has no reasonable suspicion that the driver poses a threat to the officer's safety (Pennsylvania v. Mimms, 434 U.S. 106 [1977]). In that case, two police officers, while on routine patrol, observed Mimms driving an automobile with an expired license plate. The officers stopped the vehicle for the purpose of issuing a traffic summons. One of the officers approached and asked Mimms to step out of the car and produce his owner's card and operator license. Mimms alighted, whereupon the officers noticed a large bulge under his sports jacket. Fearing it might be a weapon, the officer frisked Mimms and discovered in his waistband a .38-caliber revolver loaded with five rounds of ammunition. Mimms sought to exclude the evidence during trial, saying it was obtained illegally. On appeal, the Court rejected Mimms's contention, saying that once a police officer has lawfully stopped a vehicle for a traffic violation, he or she may order the driver to get out even without suspecting any other criminal activity or danger to the officer's safety. After the driver has stepped out, if the officer then reasonably believes that the driver may be armed and dangerous, the officer may conduct a frisk.

The police may also conduct a brief search of the vehicle after a stop, if the officer has reasonable suspicion that the motorist is dangerous and that there might be a weapon in the vehicle to which the motorist may have quick access.[3]

II. STOP AND FRISK AS APPLIED TO IMMIGRATION AND BORDER SEIZURES

1. General Rule—Forced Temporary Detention Allowed

The rule is that Fourth Amendment standards govern the stopping, interrogating, and arrest of suspected illegal aliens. The Court has said that, for the purpose of questioning, an immigration officer may detain against his or her will an individual reasonably believed to be an alien. The Court added:

> We hold that immigration officers, in accordance with the Congressional grant of authority found in Section 287(a)(1) of the Immigration and Nationality Act, may make forcible detentions of a temporary nature for the purposes of interrogation under circumstances created by reasonable suspicion, not arising to the level of probable cause to arrest, that the individual so detained is illegally in this country. (Au Yi Lau v. U.S. INS, 445 F.2d 217 at 223 [9th Cir.], cert. denied, 404 U.S. 864 [1971])

2. Stopping Vehicles Allowed

It is permissible for border officials to stop vehicles at reasonably located, fixed checkpoints to question occupants of vehicles, even without reasonable suspicion that the vehicles contain illegal aliens. However, border officials must have probable cause or consent before conducting a search (U.S. v. Martinez-Fuerte, 428 U.S. 543 [1976]).

3. Detention for Questioning Allowed

A roving patrol cannot detain persons for questioning in an area near the border solely because the occupants of the vehicle "looked Mexican." The patrol must have a *reasonable suspicion* in order to detain and question the car's occupants (U.S. v. Brignoni-Ponce, 422 U.S. 873 [1975]).

4. Factory Surveys of Aliens Allowed

Immigration officials sometimes conduct "factory surveys" in which they pay surprise visits to factories and ask employees questions to determine if they are illegal aliens or not. These may be such questions as "What is your nationality?" "Where were you born?" and so on. The Court has said that this type of brief questioning does not constitute a Fourth Amendment "seizure" and therefore no "particularized and objective basis" for suspecting the worker of being an illegal alien need be shown before conducting the survey (Immigration and Naturalization Service v. Delgado, 104 S.Ct. 1758 [1984]).

5. Alimentary Canal Smugglers May Be Detained

In a case involving the "alimentary canal smuggling" of narcotics across the nation's borders, the Court said that "reasonable suspicion" (instead of probable cause) is sufficient to permit customs agents at the border to detain a traveler suspected of engaging in this offense. The Court also concluded that agents were justified in the detention of a traveler (who was suspected of having swallowed balloons containing drugs) for twenty-seven hours before they found drugs in her rectum and arrested her.

The facts showed that the suspect had arrived at the Los Angeles International Airport on a flight from Colombia. Agents suspected that the suspect was a "balloon swallower." The suspicion was based on a number of facts, among which were that her flight had originated in Colombia, a well-known source for narcotics; that she carried $5,000 in U.S. currency; that she had made many recent short trips to the United States; that she had no hotel reservations; that she planned to spend the $5,000 on taxi rides to visit retail stores to buy goods for her husband's store in Colombia; and that she spoke no English. All these did not constitute probable cause. She was detained anyway on the basis of reasonable suspicion. After twenty-four hours the officers finally obtained a court order authorizing an involuntary x-raying and rectal examination (which she had earlier refused). The rectal examination disclosed a balloon containing a foreign substance; only then (nearly twenty-seven hours after her initial detention) was the suspect placed under arrest. The Court said that such detention prior to arrest, although lengthy, was reasonable, primarily because of the hard-to-detect nature of alimentary canal smuggling and the fact that the detention occurred at the international border, where the Fourth Amendment balance of interests between individual rights and governmental concerns weighs heavily in favor of the government (U.S. v. Hernandez, 37 CrL 3175 [1985]).

The Hernandez case involved a twenty-seven-hour detention of the suspected smuggler, yet the Court considered such detention reasonable. The Court emphasized, though, that such detention was necessary because of "the hard-to-detect nature of alimentary canal smuggling and the fact that the detention occurred at the international border." The Court took into account the needs of law enforcement under those circumstances and concluded that what the customs agents did was reasonable. Had Hernandez not been an immigration and border seizure case, the Court would doubtless have considered the length of time involved to be unreasonable.

III. STATIONHOUSE DETENTION

Stationhouse detention is short of arrest but a greater limitation of freedom than the on-the-street detention in a stop and frisk. It is used in many jurisdictions for obtaining fingerprints or photographs, ordering police line-ups, administering polygraph examinations, or securing other identification or nontestimonial evidence.

A. For Fingerprinting—Need for Probable Cause

The Supreme Court excluded the evidence obtained from fingerprints in a rape case (involving twenty-five youths who were detained for questioning and fingerprinting when the only leads were a general description and a set of fingerprints), but nonetheless implied that detention for fingerprinting might be made even without probable cause to arrest. However, the Court made it clear that "narrowly circumscribed procedures" were required, including at least some objective basis for suspecting the person of a crime, a legitimate investigatory purpose for the detention (such as fingerprinting), scheduling of the detention at a time not inconvenient for the subject, and a court order that adequate evidence existed to justify the detention (Davis v. Mississippi, 394 U.S. 721 [1969]).

In a more recent case, however, the Court held that mere "reasonable suspicion" alone does not permit the police to detain a suspect at the police station to obtain fingerprints. Therefore, when the police transported a suspect to a stationhouse for fingerprinting without his consent, probable cause, or prior judicial authorization, the detention violated the Fourth Amendment. Said the Court:

> Our view continues to be that the line is crossed when the police, without probable cause or a warrant, forcibly remove a person from his home or other place in which he is entitled to be and transport him to the police station, where he is detained, although briefly, for investigative purposes. We adhere to the view that such seizures, at least where not under judicial supervision, are sufficiently like arrests to invoke the traditional rule that arrests may constitutionally be made only on probable cause. (Hayes v. Florida, 36 CrL 3216 [1985])

In the same case, however, the Court said that field detention (as opposed to a stationhouse detention) for purposes of fingerprinting a suspect does not require probable cause as long as the following are present: (1) there is reasonable suspicion that the suspect has committed a criminal act; (2) there is reasonable belief that the fingerprinting will either negate or establish suspect's guilt; and (3) the procedure is promptly effectuated.

B. For Interrogation—Need for Probable Cause

The Court has held that probable cause is necessary for a stationhouse detention accompanied by interrogation (as opposed to just fingerprinting), even if no formal arrest is made. In one case, the defendant was asked to come to police headquarters, where he received his Miranda warnings, was questioned, and ultimately confessed. There was no probable cause to arrest him, but there was some reason for the police to suspect him in connection with a crime being investigated. The Court held that the defendant was taken into custody and not simply stopped on the street and therefore that probable cause was required to take him to the police station. Since that was absent, the confession obtained could not be admissible in court (Dunaway v. New York, 442 U.S. 200 [1979]). The Court added that the detention of Dunaway in this case was indistinguishable from a traditional arrest because he was not questioned briefly where he was found but instead was transported to a police station and would have been physically restrained if he had refused to accompany the officers or had tried to escape from their custody.

C. Stop and Frisk versus Stationhouse Detention

The obvious difference between stop and frisk and stationhouse detentions is that *one takes place on the street, whereas the other occurs in a police facility.* This difference is so significant that, in contrast to its position in Terry, the Court decided that the full Fourth Amendment protections come into play "when the police, without probable cause or a warrant, forcibly remove a person from his home or other place in which he is entitled to be and transport him to the police station where he is detained, although briefly, for investigative purposes." This means, for one thing, that at this stage the person detained is entitled to his or her constitutional rights, including freedom from self-incrimination and the right to counsel.

☐ SUMMARY

This chapter discusses some forms of limitation of a person's freedom other than arrest. Stop and frisk is a police practice based on reasonable suspicion instead of probable cause, whereby a person is stopped in public and questioned about his or her identity and activities. If the officer senses that the person may be dangerous, then a frisk follows for the purpose of removing the weapon. Although *"stop and frisk"* is often used as a single term, *"stop"* and *"frisk"* in fact represent two separate acts. A stop is justified only if the officer has reasonable suspicion that criminal activity is about to take place. A frisk follows and is justified only if there is nothing in the initial stages of the encounter that would dispel reasonable fear about the safety of the police officer or of others. The purpose of a frisk is the protection of the officer. What happens during the stop and frisk can easily lead to an arrest if the officer subsequently finds that there is probable cause to believe that the suspect has committed a crime.

Fourth Amendment standards also govern the stopping, interrogation, and arrest of suspected illegal aliens. It is permissible for border officials to stop vehicles at reasonably located, fixed checkpoints to question occupants of vehicles, even without reasonable suspicion that the vehicles contain illegal aliens. However, they must have probable cause or consent before conducting a search. "Factory surveys" do not constitute a Fourth Amendment seizure; hence no particularized and objective basis for suspecting the worker of being an illegal alien need be shown before conducting them.

Stationhouse detention is short of an arrest but constitutes a greater limitation of freedom than the on-the-street detention in a stop and frisk. The Court has decided that reasonable suspicion alone does not permit the police to detain a suspect at the police station to obtain fingerprints; there must be probable cause or prior judicial authorization. Stationhouse detention accompanied by interrogation also needs probable cause, even if no formal arrest is made.

☐ REVIEW QUESTIONS

    1. Although often used as one phrase, "stop" and "frisk" constitute two separate acts. When may an officer stop and when may an officer frisk?

2. What did the Court say in the case of Terry v. Ohio? That case used the phrase "reasonable suspicion" to justify stop and frisk. What does that phrase mean?
3. Is there any definite length of time after which a stop becomes an arrest? Explain. Are stops based on "drug courier profiles" valid?
4. Distinguish between "stop and frisk" and arrest.
5. What are stationhouse detentions? Are they valid if based on reasonable suspicion? Discuss.
6. May border officials, on the basis of suspicion, stop vehicles at checkpoints to ask if they contain illegal aliens? May they conduct a search?
7. Distinguish between "stop and frisk" and stationhouse detention.
8. "Stop and frisk applies to motor vehicles." What does this statement mean?
9. What are "factory surveys"? Are they valid?

❑ DEFINITIONS

Drug Courier Profile: Identifiers developed by law enforcement agencies that indicate the types of individuals who are likely to transport drugs.

Factory Surveys: A practice whereby immigration officials pay surprise visits to factories and ask employees questions to determine if they are illegal aliens or not.

Fishing Expedition: A search conducted by law enforcement officers with no definite seizable contraband or items in mind, the search being conducted in hopes that any type of usable evidence will turn up.

Frisk: The pat-down of a person's outer clothing after a stop to see if the suspect has a weapon or something that feels like a weapon, which can then be seized by the officer; frisk is performed for the officer's own protection.

Reasonable Suspicion: Degree of proof that is less than probable cause, but more than vague suspicion. It is sufficient to enable a police officer to conduct a stop and frisk. Reasonable suspicion must be anchored on specific objective facts and logical conclusions based on officer's experience. It represents a degree of certainty (around 20 percent) that a crime has been or will be committed and that the suspect is involved in it.

Stationhouse Detention: A form of detention, usually in a police facility, that is short of arrest but greater than the on-the-street detention of stop and frisk. It is used in many jurisdictions for obtaining fingerprints or photographs, ordering police line-ups, administering polygraph examinations, or securing other identification or non-testimonial evidence.

Stop: The brief detention of a person when the police officer has reasonable suspicion, in light of his or her experience, that criminal activity is about to take place.

Stop and Frisk: A police practice, based on reasonable suspicion instead of probable cause, whereby an officer stops and frisks a person in a public place (or in an automobile), questions the person about his or her identity and activities at the time, and frisks the person for dangerous (and perhaps illegally possessed) weapons.

☐ PRINCIPLES OF CASES

ADAMS V. WILLIAMS, 407 U.S. 143 (1972)   The Fourth Amendment does not require a police officer who lacks the precise level of information necessary for probable cause to arrest simply to shrug his or her shoulders and allow a crime to occur or a criminal to escape. A brief stop of a suspicious individual, in order to determine his or her identity or to maintain the status quo momentarily while obtaining more information, may be most reasonable in light of the facts known to the officer at the time. The basis for stop and frisk need not be the officer's personal observations. The information may be given by a reliable informant.

ALABAMA V. WHITE, 58 L.W. 4747 (1990)   Reasonable suspicion is a less demanding standard than probable cause not only because it can be established with information different in quantity or content from that required to establish probable cause, but also because reasonable suspicion can arise from information that is less reliable than that required to show probable cause.

AU YI LAU V. UNITED STATES IMMIGRATION & NATURALIZATION SERVICE, 445 F.2d 217 (9th Cir.), cert. denied, 404 U.S. 864 (1971)   An immigration officer may, for purposes of questioning, detain against his or her will an individual reasonably believed to be an alien. Detention may be based on reasonable suspicion that the individual so detained is illegally in this country; probable cause is not required.

DAVIS V. MISSISSIPPI, 394 U.S. 721 (1969)   Implied that fingerprinting a suspect may be made even without probable cause to arrest. For it to be valid, however, narrowly circumscribed procedures are required—including at least some objective basis for suspecting the person of a crime, a legitimate investigatory purpose for the detention, scheduling of the detention at a time not inconvenient for the subject, and a court order that adequate evidence existed to justify the detention.

DUNAWAY V. NEW YORK, 442 U.S. 200 (1979)   Probable cause is necessary for a stationhouse detention of a suspect when accompanied by interrogation (as opposed to just fingerprinting), even if no formal arrest is made. Here there was no probable cause to arrest the suspect, but there was some reason for the police to suspect him in connection with a crime being investigated. The suspect was therefore asked to come to police headquarters, where he received his Miranda warnings, was questioned, and ultimately confessed. The Court held that the suspect was in fact taken into custody by the police and not simply stopped on the street, and therefore probable cause was required to take him to the police station.

FLORIDA V. ROYER, 460 U.S. 491 (1983)   Although the initial stopping and questioning of a suspect who fell within the "drug courier profile" was valid, the subsequent conduct of the police in taking the suspect forty feet away from the main concourse and keeping him there while his luggage was retrieved was more intrusive than necessary to carry out the limited investigation permitted under stop and frisk.

HAYES V. FLORIDA, 36 CrL 3216 (1985)   Mere "reasonable suspicion" alone does not permit the police to detain a suspect at the police station to obtain fingerprints. Therefore, when the police transported a suspect to a stationhouse for fingerprinting without his consent, probable cause, or prior judicial authorization, the detention violated the Fourth Amendment. Reasonable suspicion, however, is sufficient for field detention for fingerprinting.

IMMIGRATION AND NATURALIZATION SERVICE (INS) V. DELGADO, 104 S.Ct. 1758 (1984) "Factory surveys" in which INS officials pay surprise visits to factories and ask employees questions to determine if they are in this country legally or not does not constitute a Fourth Amendment "seizure," and therefore no particularized and objective basis for suspecting the worker of being an illegal alien need be shown.

PENNSYLVANIA V. MIMMS, 434 U.S. 106 (1977) A police officer may order the driver of a vehicle to step out of the vehicle after a routine stop for issuance of a traffic ticket even if the officer has no reasonable suspicion that the driver poses a threat to the safety of the officer.

TERRY V. OHIO, 392 U.S. 1 (1968) The police have the authority to detain a person briefly for questioning even without probable cause to believe that the person has committed a crime. Such an investigatory stop does not constitute an arrest. It is permissible when prompted by the observation of unusual conduct leading to a reasonable suspicion that criminal activity may be afoot and when the officer can point to specific and articulable facts to justify that suspicion. Subsequently, an officer may frisk a person if the officer reasonably suspects that he or she is in danger.

UNITED STATES V. BRIGNONI-PONCE, 422 U.S. 873 (1975) The foreign appearance of passengers in a car is not by itself sufficient to allow even a brief stop for questioning. Reasonable suspicion must be present.

UNITED STATES V. HENSLEY, 53 L.W. 4053 (1985) The police may act without a warrant to stop and briefly detain a person they know is wanted for investigation by a police department in another city. If the police have a reasonable suspicion, grounded in specific and articulable facts, that a person they encounter was involved in or is wanted for questioning in connection with a completed felony, then a "Terry-type stop" may be made to investigate that suspicion. Any evidence legally obtained as a result of that stop is admissible in court.

UNITED STATES V. HERNANDEZ, 37 CrL 3175 (1985) Detention for twenty-seven hours of a suspect for alimentary canal drug smuggling was reasonable because of the hard-to-detect nature of that type of smuggling and the fact that the detention occurred at the international border, where the Fourth Amendment balance of interests weighs heavily in favor of the government.

UNITED STATES V. LUCKETT, 484 F.2d 89 (1973) Detaining a person (who was stopped for jaywalking) for longer than was necessary to write out a ticket—because the police wanted to radio headquarters on a completely unsubstantiated hunch that there was a warrant for his arrest—constitutes detention of unreasonable length. The detention had therefore turned into an arrest.

UNITED STATES V. PLACE, 462 U.S. 696 (1983) The detention of an air traveler's luggage for ninety minutes so a trained dog could sniff it for marijuana constituted an excessive investigative stop and therefore made it an arrest.

UNITED STATES V. ROBINSON, 414 U.S. 218 (1973) A body search, after an authorized arrest for driving without a permit, is valid even when the officer admits that there was no possible danger to him or her and therefore had no reason to search for a weapon.

UNITED STATES V. SHARPE, 105 S.Ct. 1568 (1985)   The detention of a truck driver, who was suspected of carrying marijuana in a truck camper, for twenty minutes was reasonable because the truck driver attempted to evade the stop, causing the two officers pursuing him to be separated. The Court said that courts should refrain from second-guessing police officers' choices in a stop, especially when the police are acting in a swiftly developing situation.

UNITED STATES V. SOKOLOW, 109 S.Ct. 1581 (1989)   Taken together, the circumstances in this case (which included the use of a "drug courier profile") established a reasonable suspicion that the suspect was transporting illegal drugs and therefore the investigative stop without warrant was valid under the Fourth Amendment. Although the use of a "drug courier profile" was helpful, the totality of the circumstances was more important in establishing reasonable suspicion.

☐ CASE BRIEF—LEADING CASE ON STOP AND FRISK
TERRY V. OHIO, 392 U.S. 1 (1968)

FACTS: Police detective McFadden observed two men on a street in downtown Cleveland at approximately 2:30 P.M. on October 31, 1963. It appeared to Detective McFadden that the two men (one of whom was petitioner Terry) were "casing" a store because each walked up and down, peering into the store window, and then both returned to the corner to confer. At one point a third man joined them but left quickly. After McFadden observed the two rejoining the same third man a couple of blocks away, he approached them, told them who he was, and asked them for identification. Receiving a mumbled response, the officer frisked all three men. Terry and one of the other men were carrying handguns. Both were tried and convicted of carrying concealed weapons. They appealed.

ISSUE: *Is "stop and frisk" valid under the Fourth Amendment? Yes.*

SUPREME COURT DECISION: The police have the authority to detain a person briefly for questioning even without probable cause to believe that the person has committed a crime. Such an investigatory stop does not constitute an arrest and is permissible when prompted by both the observation of unusual conduct leading to a reasonable suspicion that criminal activity may be afoot and the ability to point to specific and articulable facts to justify that suspicion. Subsequently, an officer may frisk a person if the officer reasonably suspects that he or she is in danger.

CASE SIGNIFICANCE: The Terry case made clear that the practice of stop and frisk is valid. Prior to Terry, police departments regularly used stop and frisk either by law or by judicial authorization, but its validity was doubtful because the practice is based on *reasonable suspicion* instead of *probable cause,* which is necessary in arrest and search cases. The Court held that stop and frisk is constitutionally permissible despite the lack of probable cause for either full arrest or full search, and despite the fact that a brief detention not amounting to full arrest is a "seizure" requiring some degree of protection under the Fourth Amendment.

EXCERPTS FROM THE DECISION: The Fourth Amendment provides that "the right of the people to be secure in their persons, houses, papers, and effects, against unreasonable searches and seizures, shall not be violated. . . ." This inestimable right of personal security belongs as much to the citizen on the streets of our cities as to the homeowner closeted in his study to dispose of his secret affairs. . . . We have recently held that "the Fourth Amendment protects people, not places," Katz v. United States, 389 U.S. 347, 351 (1967), and wherever an individual may harbor a reasonable "expectation of privacy," id., at 361 (Mr. Justice Harlan, concurring), he is entitled to be free from unreasonable governmental intrusion. Of course, the specific content and incidents of this right must be shaped by the context in which it is asserted. For "what the Constitution forbids is not all searches and seizures, but unreasonable searches and seizures." Elkins v. United States, 364 U.S. 206, 222 (1960). Unquestionably petitioner was entitled to the protection of the Fourth Amendment as he walked down the street in Cleveland. . . . The question is whether in all the circumstances of this on-the-street encounter, his right to personal security was violated by an unreasonable search and seizure.

On the one hand, it is frequently argued that in dealing with the rapidly unfolding and often dangerous situations on city streets the police are in need of an escalating set of flexible responses, graduated in relation to the amount of information they possess. For this purpose it is urged that distinctions should be made between a "stop" and an "arrest" (or a "seizure" of a person), and between a "frisk" and a "search." Thus, it is argued, the police should be allowed to "stop" a person and detain him briefly for questioning upon suspicion that he may be connected with criminal activity. Upon suspicion that the person may be armed, the police should have the power to "frisk" him for weapons. If the "stop" and the "frisk" give rise to probable cause to believe that the suspect has committed a crime, then the police should be empowered to make a formal "arrest," and a full incident "search" of the person. This scheme is justified in part upon the notion that a "stop" and a "frisk" amount to a mere "minor inconvenience and petty indignity" which can properly be imposed upon the citizen in the interest of effective law enforcement on the basis of a police officer's suspicion. . . .

Our first task is to establish at what point in this encounter the Fourth Amendment becomes relevant. That is, we must decide whether and when Officer McFadden "seized" Terry and whether and when he conducted a "search." There is some suggestion in the use of such terms as *"stop"* and *"frisk"* that such police conduct is outside the purview of the Fourth Amendment because neither action rises to the level of a "search" or "seizure" within the meaning of the Constitution. We emphatically reject this notion. It is quite plain that the Fourth Amendment governs "seizures" of the person which do not eventuate in a trip to the stationhouse and prosecution for crime—"arrests" in traditional terminology. It must be recognized that whenever a police officer accosts an individual and restrains his freedom to walk away, he has "seized" that person. And it is nothing less than sheer torture of the English language to suggest that a careful exploration of the outer surfaces of a person's clothing all over his or her body in an attempt to find weapons is not a "search." Moreover, it is simply fantastic to urge that such a procedure performed in public by a policeman while the citizen stands helpless, perhaps facing a wall with his hands raised, is a "petty indignity." It is a serious intrusion upon the sanctity of the person, which may inflict great indignity and arouse strong resentment, and it is not to be undertaken lightly.

☐ CASE BRIEF—LEADING CASE ON "DRUG COURIER PROFILE"

UNITED STATES V. SOKOLOW 109 S.Ct. 1581 (1989)

FACTS: Sokolow purchased two round-trip tickets for a flight from Honolulu to Miami under an assumed name. He paid for the tickets from a roll of $20 bills and appeared nervous during the transaction. Neither he nor his companion checked their luggage. Sokolow scheduled a return flight three days later. Using these and other facts, which fit a "drug courier profile" developed by the Drug Enforcement Agency, officers stopped the couple and took them to the DEA office at the airport where their luggage was examined by a drug dog. Narcotics were found; Sokolow was arrested, and a search warrant was obtained for the bag. No narcotics were found in the bag, but documents indicating involvement in drug trafficking were discovered. On a second search with the drug dog, narcotics were detected in another of Sokolow's bags. Sokolow was released until a search warrant could be obtained the next morning. A search of the bag revealed more cocaine. Sokolow was subsequently charged with possession with intent to distribute cocaine, was tried and convicted. He appealed.

ISSUE: *May a "drug courier profile" be used to justify a stop? Yes, if . . .*

SUPREME COURT DECISION: Taken together, the circumstances in this case (which included the use of a "drug courier profile") established a reasonable suspicion that the suspect was transporting illegal drugs and therefore the investigative stop without warrant was valid under the Fourth Amendment.

CASE SIGNIFICANCE: In this case the Court said that there is nothing wrong with the use of "drug courier profiles" if the facts, taken in totality, amounted to reasonable suspicion that criminal conduct was taking place. The court indicated that whether or not the facts in this case fit a "profile" was less significant than the fact that taken together they establish a reasonable suspicion that justified a stop. This case indicates that while a "drug courier profile" is helpful, the totality of the circumstances is more important in establishing reasonable suspicion. In this case, the Court noted that the activities of Sokolow, taken in isolation and individually, were consistent with innocent travel, but taken together they amounted to reasonable suspicion. In sum, there is nothing wrong with using "drug courier profiles" for a stop if the facts in a particular case, taken together, amount to reasonable suspicion.

EXCERPTS FROM THE DECISION: The concept of reasonable suspicion, like probable cause, is not "readily, or even usefully, reduced to a neat set of legal rules." We think the Court of Appeals' effort to refine and elaborate the requirements of "reasonable suspicion" in this case create unnecessary difficulty in dealing with one of the relatively simple concepts embodied in the Fourth Amendment. In evaluating the validity of a stop such as this, we must consider the "totality of the circumstances— the whole picture."

. . . Paying $2,100 in cash for two airplane tickets is out of the ordinary, and it is even more out of the ordinary to pay that sum from a roll of $20 bills containing nearly twice that amount of cash. Most business travelers, we feel confident, purchase airline tickets by credit card or check so as to have a record for tax or business purposes, and few vacationers carry with them thousands of dollars in $20 bills. We also think the agents had reasonable ground to believe that respondent was traveling under an alias; the evidence was by no means conclusive, but it was sufficient to warrant consideration. While a trip from Honolulu to Miami, standing alone, is not a cause for any sort of suspicion, here there were more; surely few residents of Honolulu travel from that city for 20 hours to spend 48 hours in Miami during the month of July.

Any one of these factors is not by itself proof of any illegal conduct and is quite consistent with innocent travel. But we think taken together they amount to reasonable suspicion.

□ NOTES

1. John G. Miles, Jr., David B. Richardson, and Anthony E. Scudellari, *The Law Officer's Pocket Manual* (Washington, DC: Bureau of National Affairs, 1988–89), at 4:1–4:2.
2. Ibid.
3. Ibid., at 4:3.

CHAPTER SIX

ARREST

I. ARREST DEFINED

II. ELEMENTS OF ARREST
A. Intention to Arrest
B. Arrest Authority
C. Seizure and Detention
D. The Individual's Understanding

III. TYPES OF AUTHORIZED ARREST
A. Arrest with Warrant
B. Arrest without Warrant
C. Citizen's Arrest

IV. WHAT THE POLICE MAY DO AFTER AN ARREST
A. Search the Arrested Person
B. Search the Area within Immediate Control of the Arrested Person
C. Use Handcuffs According to Department Policy or at Discretion
D. Monitor the Movements of the Arrested Person
E. Conduct a Warrantless Protective Sweep of the Area in Which the Suspect Is Arrested
F. Search Arrestee at Place of Detention

V. DISPOSITION OF PRISONER AFTER ARREST
A. Booking
B. Appearance before Magistrate

VI. USE OF FORCE DURING ARREST
A. Nondeadly Force
B. Deadly Force
C. What Governs the Police Use of Force?
D. Test to Determine Police Civil Liability in Use of Force Cases—The Graham v. Connor Case
E. Is Tennessee v. Garner Consistent with Graham v. Connor?—Yes

Summary
Review Questions
Definitions
Principles of Cases
Case Briefs
    PAYTON V. NEW YORK
    TENNESSEE V. GARNER

☐ KEY TERMS

arrest	booking
actual seizure	without unnecessary delay
constructive seizure	nondeadly force
summons	reasonable force
citation	punitive force
bench warrant	deadly force
capias	"objective reasonableness"
citizen's arrest	standard
protective sweep	

The Fourth Amendment to the U.S. Constitution provides that "the right of the people to be secure in their persons . . . against unreasonable . . . seizures, shall not be violated. . . ." Arrest constitutes a "seizure" of a person and therefore the restrictions of the Fourth Amendment apply.

Police officers must be well informed about the law of arrest because successful prosecution usually depends upon the legality of the arrest. *If the arrest is legal, then searches of person and the area within the arrestee's control are also legal; conversely, if the arrest is illegal, any evidence obtained thereafter is not admissible in court.*

The validity of an arrest is determined primarily by federal constitutional standards, particularly the requirement of probable cause. An arrest, with or without a warrant, cannot be valid unless there is probable cause—as determined by federal constitutional standards (discussed in Chapter Four). In arrest cases (as distinguished from searches and seizures of items), probable cause "exists if the facts and circumstances known to the officer warrant a prudent man in believing that the offense has been committed" (Henry v. U.S., 361 U.S. 98 [1959]). Any state provisions that are inconsistent with federal standards are invalid and unconstitutional, but state statutes may give more rights to a suspect than are required by the Fourth Amendment.

I. ARREST DEFINED

An arrest is defined as the taking of a person into custody against his or her will for the purpose of criminal prosecution or interrogation (Dunaway v. New York, 442 U.S. 200 [1979]). An arrest deprives a person of liberty by legal authority. Mere words alone do not normally constitute an arrest. There must be some kind of restraint. A person's liberty must be restricted by law enforcement officers to the extent that the person is not free to leave at his or her own volition.

It does not matter whether the act is termed an "arrest" or a mere "stop" or "detention" under state law. *When a person has been taken into custody against his or her will for purposes of criminal prosecution or interrogation, there is an arrest under the Fourth Amendment, regardless of what state law says.* For example, state law provides that a police officer may "detain" a suspect for four hours in the police station for questioning without having "arrested" that person. If the suspect is in fact detained in the police station against his or her will, that person has been "arrested" under the Constitution and is therefore entitled to any rights given to suspects who have been arrested. In one case, the police asked for and examined suspect's ticket and his driver's license, identified themselves as narcotics agents, told the suspect that he was suspected of transporting narcotics, and asked him to accompany them to a room forty feet away; they retained his ticket and driver's license and never indicated to the suspect that he was free to depart. The Court said that there had been an arrest since a reasonable person in the suspect's position would have concluded that he was not free to leave (Florida v. Royer, 460 U.S. 491 [1983]).

On the other hand, *no arrest or seizure occurs when an officer simply approaches a person in a public place and asks if he or she is willing to answer questions—as long as the person is not involuntarily detained.* The question, however, is: How long can the suspect be detained and how intrusive must be the investigation before the "stop" becomes an "arrest" requiring probable cause? The answer depends upon (1) the reasonableness of the detention and (2) the reasonableness of the intrusion. The detention must not be longer than that required by the circumstances and the intrusion must be by the "least intrusive means," meaning that it must not be more than that needed to verify or dispel the officer's suspicions.

II. ELEMENTS OF ARREST

Four essential elements must be present for an arrest to take place: intention to arrest, authority to arrest, seizure and detention, and the understanding of the individual that he or she is being arrested.

A. Intention to Arrest

In the words of one police manual, "You have made an arrest as soon as you indicate by words or action your intention to take the person to the police station or before a

---

HIGHLIGHT 6.1

Crimes Cleared by Arrests

Most crimes are not cleared by arrest

	Reported crimes cleared by arrest
Murder	72%
Aggravated assault	62
Forcible rape	54
Robbery	25
Larceny-theft	20
Motor vehicle theft	15
Burglary	14
All UCR [Uniform Crime Reports] Index Crimes	21%

Source: Bureau of Justice Statistics, *Report to the Nation on Crime and Justice,* 2d ed. (Washington, DC: U.S. Government Printing Office, 1988), at 68.

judicial officer, or otherwise to take him into custody."[1] In this case, the intention to arrest is clear either because it is expressed or clearly implied from the officer's action. Without the requisite intent, there is no arrest even if a person is temporarily stopped or inconvenienced. No arrest is occurring when an officer is stopping a motorist for the issuance of a ticket, asking a motorist to step out of his or her car, stopping a motorist to check his or her driver's license, or stopping a person to warn of possible

---

HIGHLIGHT 6.2

Offenses and Arrests

11.9 million arrests were reported by law enforcement agencies in 1985

Rank	Offense	Estimated number of arrests
1	All other offenses (except traffic)	2,489,200
2	Driving under the influence	1,788,400
*3	Larceny-theft	1,348,400
4	Drunkenness	964,800
5	Drug abuse violations	811,400
6	Disorderly conduct	671,700
7	Simple assaults	637,600
8	Liquor law violations	548,600
*9	Burglary	443,300
10	Fraud	342,600
*11	Aggravated assault	305,390
12	Vandalism	259,600
13	Weapons: carrying, possessing, etc.	180,900
14	Runaway	161,200
*15	Robbery	136,870
*16	Motor vehicle theft	133,900
17	Stolen property: buying, receiving, possessing	127,100
18	Prostitution and commercial vice	113,800
19	Sex offenses (except forcible rape)	100,600
20	Forgery and counterfeiting	87,600
21	Curfew and loitering law violations	81,500
22	Offenses against family and children	58,800
*23	Forcible rape	36,970
24	Vagrancy	33,800
25	Gambling	32,100
*26	Arson	19,500
*27	Murder and nonnegligent manslaughter	18,330
28	Suspicion	12,900
29	Embezzlement	11,400

*UCR [Uniform Crime Reports] Index Crimes.

Source: FBI, *Crime in the United States, 1985.* Reprinted in Bureau of Justice Statistics, *Report to the Nation on Crime and Justice,* 2d ed. (Washington, DC: U.S. Government Printing Office, 1988), at 67.

danger. In these cases, there may be temporary deprivation of liberty or a certain amount of inconvenience, but there is no intent on the part of the police officer to take the person into custody; therefore there is no arrest.

The requirement of intention to arrest is essentially subjective—meaning that it exists in the mind of the police officer. Intention to arrest is always difficult to prove in court, but there have been cases in which the actions of the police officer clearly indicated that he intended to take the person into custody, even though he or she later denied it in court. For example, when an officer places handcuffs on a suspect, the intent to arrest likely exists even if the officer denies such intent later in court. The same may be true if the suspect is taken to the police wagon for interrogation. But if the officer merely blocks the way of a suspect, an intention to arrest is not clear.

When it is not clear from the officer's act whether there was intent to arrest or not, the U.S. Supreme Court has said that "a policeman's unarticulated plan has no bearing on the question whether a suspect was 'in custody' at a particular time" (Berkemer v. McCarty, 35 CrL 3192 [1984]).

In a leading case, the Court said that the appropriate test to determine if a seizure has occurred is "whether a reasonable man, viewing the particular police conduct as a whole and within the setting of all the surrounding circumstances, would have concluded that the police had in some way restrained his liberty so that he was not free to leave" (Michigan v. Chesternut, 43 CrL 3077 [1988]). The Court then added: "No bright-line rule applicable to all investigatory pursuits can be fashioned." In that case, after observing the approach of a police car Chesternut began to run. Officers followed him "to see where he was going." As the officers drove alongside Chesternut, they observed him pull a number of packets from his pocket and throw them down. The officers stopped and seized the packets, concluding that they might be contraband. Chesternut was arrested; a subsequent search revealed more narcotics. Chesternut was charged with felony narcotics possession and convicted. On appeal, he sought exclusion of the evidence, alleging that the officer's investigatory pursuit "to see where he was going" constituted a seizure under the Fourth Amendment. The Court rejected this contention, saying that Chesternut was not "seized" before he discarded the drug packets and that the activity of the officers in following him to see where he was going did not come under the Fourth Amendment.

The general rule, therefore, is that a person has been arrested if, under the totality of the surrounding circumstances, a reasonable person would not believe himself or herself free to go. This is ultimately a question for a judge or jury to decide, if raised during the trial, taking into account such things as "the threatening presence of several officers, the display of a weapon by an officer, some physical touching of

---

HIGHLIGHT 6.3

When Seizure Occurs

"No bright-line rule applicable to all investigatory pursuits can be fashioned. Rather, the appropriate test is whether a reasonable man, viewing the particular police conduct as a whole and within the setting of all the surrounding circumstances, would have concluded that the police had in some way restrained his liberty so that he was not free to leave" (Michigan v. Chesternut, 43 CrL 3077 [1988]).

---

the person or the citizen, or the use of language or tone of voice indicating that compliance with the officer's request might be compelled" (U.S. v. Mendenhall, 446 U.S. 544 [1980]).

B. Arrest Authority

Authority to restrain distinguishes *arrest* from deprivations of liberty (such as kidnapping or illegal detention) committed by private individuals. When there is proper authorization, the arrest is valid; conversely, when proper authorization is lacking, the arrest is invalid. Invalid arrest can arise in the following cases: (1) when the police officer mistakenly thinks he or she has authority to arrest when he or she in fact does not, and (2) when the officer knows that he or she is not authorized to make the arrest, but does so anyway.

Whether or not a police officer has arrest authority when "off duty" varies in practice from state to state. Some states authorize police officers (by law, court decision, or agency policy) to make an arrest any time they witness a criminal act. In these states, the officer is in effect on duty twenty-four hours a day, seven days a week, for purposes of making an arrest, whether in uniform or not. Other states limit the grant of arrest power only to instances when the officer is "on duty." Arrest authority is, therefore, defined by the law or regulations of the state and police agency.

C. Seizure and Detention

Restraint of the subject may be either actual or constructive. *Actual seizure* is accomplished by taking the person into custody with the use of hands or firearms (denoting use of force without touching the individual) or by merely touching the individual

---

HIGHLIGHT 6.4

Salaries of Law Enforcement Personnel

Justice Dollars Pay Personnel Costs

(Average annual salary. There are jurisdictions where the salaries are higher or lower than these averages.)

Law enforcement officers (1985 and 1986)

City police officer (entry level)	$18,913
City police officer (maximum)	$24,243
City police chief	$33,158
County sheriff patrol officer	Not available
State trooper (entry level)	$18,170
State trooper (maximum)	$28,033
Deputy U.S. marshal	$19,585
U.S. border patrol agent	$23,058
U.S. immigration inspector	$24,719
U.S. immigration agent	$34,259
Federal drug agent	$36,973
FBI agent	$40,321

Source: Bureau of Justice Statistics, *Report to the Nation on Crime and Justice,* 2d ed. (Washington, DC: U.S. Government Printing Office, 1988), at 126.

without the use of force. *Constructive seizure* is accomplished without any physical touching, grabbing, holding, or the use of force. It occurs when the individual peacefully submits to the officer's will and control.

Mere words alone do not constitute an arrest. The fact that a police officer tells a person, "You are under arrest," is not sufficient. The required restraint must be accompanied by actual seizure or peaceful submission to the officer's will and control.

D. The Individual's Understanding

The understanding that he or she is being arrested may be conveyed to the arrestee through words or actions. In most cases the police officer says, "You are under arrest," hence conveying intention through words. Similarly, some actions strongly imply that a person is being taken into custody, even though the police officer makes no statement. Examples of actions that strongly imply arrest occur when a suspected burglar is subdued by police and taken to a squad car, or when a person is being handcuffed to be taken to the police station even though no words are spoken. The element of understanding is not required for an arrest in the following instances: (1) if the suspect is drunk or under the influence of drugs and does not understand what is going on, (2) if the suspect is insane, and (3) if the suspect is unconscious.

III. TYPES OF AUTHORIZED ARREST

There are two types of authorized arrest: *arrest with a warrant* and *arrest without a warrant*. The Court has repeatedly expressed preference for arrests with warrants although it is not constitutionally required except when making a routine felony arrest in a residence. In one case it said: "Law enforcement officers may find it wise to seek arrest warrants where practicable to do so, and their judgments about probable cause may be more readily accepted where backed by a warrant issued by a magistrate" (U.S. v. Watson, 423 U.S. 411 [1976]).

A. Arrest with Warrant

Black's Law Dictionary defines an arrest warrant as *"a writ or precept issued by a magistrate, justice, or other competent authority, addressed to a sheriff, constable, or other officer, requiring him to arrest the body of a person therein named, and bring him before the magistrate or court to answer, or to be examined, concerning some offense which he is charged with having committed."* [2]

1. Issuance of Warrant

To secure the issuance of a warrant, a complaint (filed by the offended party or by the police officer) must be filed before a magistrate, showing probable cause for arrest of the accused. It must set forth facts showing that an offense has been committed and that the accused is responsible for it. If it appears to the magistrate from the complaint and accompanying documents or testimony that probable cause exists for the charges made against the accused, the magistrate issues an arrest warrant.

Most states provide that the issuance of arrest warrants is strictly a judicial function and must therefore be performed by a judge or judicial officer. The issuing party must also be "neutral and detached." Some states, however, hold that since the

Supreme Court Form No. 21

WARRANT FOR ARREST

(FOR USE IN ANY COURT IN EITHER MISDEMEANOR OR FELONY CASES)

STATE OF MISSOURI,

County of

⎱ ss.
⎰

IN THE   COURT WITHIN AND FOR SAID COUNTY

THE STATE OF MISSOURI TO ANY PEACE OFFICER IN THE STATE OF MISSOURI:

You are hereby commanded to arrest
who is charged with

alleged to have been committed within the jurisdiction of this court and in violation of the laws of the State of Missouri, and to bring him forthwith before this court to be here dealt with in accordance with law; and you, the officer serving this warrant, shall forthwith make return hereof to this court.

WITNESS THE HONORABLE   , Judge of
the said court and the seal thereof, issued in the county and state aforesaid on this   **day of**   , 19

Judge/Clerk of said Court

RETURN:

Served the within warrant in my County of
and in the State of Missouri on this   day of   , 19
by arresting the within named   and producing him before the said court on the
day of   , 19

----

requirement of probable cause is designed to be applied by laypeople (as when a police officer arrests a suspect without a warrant upon probable cause), a nonjudicial officer—such as a court clerk—may properly issue warrants if empowered to do so by statute and if otherwise "neutral and detached."

The term *neutral and detached* means that the issuing officer is not unalterably aligned with the police or prosecutor's position in the case. Several cases illustrate its meaning.

STATE OF VERMONT
ARREST / CUSTODY REPORT

CAUTION
Y | N

DATE OF ARREST

| | | | | | | |
AGENCY COMPLAINT NO.

MO | DAY | YR

ARRESTING AGENCY _____

IDENTIFICATION:

| LAST NAME | FIRST NAME | MIDDLE NAME | / / DOB | AGE | SEX | RACE* | ETHNIC* |

| EMPLOYED | UNEMPLOYED | STUDENT | REFUSED TO ANSWER |

STREET

PLACE OF BIRTH (CITY/STATE)

CITY/TOWN

EMPLOYER/SCHOOL

STATE | ZIP CODE | SOC. SEC. NO. | ID NUMBER

ADDRESS

ALIAS | LAST NAME | FIRST NAME | MIDDLE NAME

SCARS/MARKS

| 1 | 2 | 3 | 4 | 5 | 6 |
| SING | MAR | SEP | DIV | WID | COHAB |
MARITAL STATUS

HEIGHT | WEIGHT lb.

| 1 | 2 | 3 | 4 | 5 | 6 | 7 |
| BLA | BRO | BLD | RED | GREY | BALD | WHI |
HAIR COLOR

| 1 | 2 | 3 | 4 |
| BRO | BLU | HAZ | OTH |
EYE COLOR | SPECIFY

D.M.V. INFORMATION:

D.M.V. CASE NO. _____

| INJURY | FATAL | PROP. DAMAGE |
ACCIDENT

| REFUSED | NO | YES | RESULT % |
TEST

OPERATOR LICENSE NO. | STATE | / / EXPIRATION DATE

REGISTRATION NO. | STATE | / / EXPIRATION DATE | VEHICLE MAKE | TYPE | YEAR

ARREST DATA:

TIME | PLACE | GRID/COUNTY-TOWN | OFFENSE GRID

V.S.A.

OFFENSE | TITLE | SECTION | SUB-SECTION | / / OFFENSE DATE

| FINGERPRINTS | PHOTOGRAPH |
| Y N | Y N |

| | | | |
OFFENSE CODE | ATTACH TO A/C-3

| RELEASED TO GUARDIAN | ARRAIGNED | CITED | LODGED | BAIL |
IMMEDIATE DISPOSITION

COMMENTS

COMPANION CASE NO.

ARRESTING OFFICER SIGNATURE | ID. NO.

FINGERPRINT OFFICER

PHOTOGRAPH OFFICER | APPROVING OFFICER SIGNATURE | ID. NO.

OFFENSE: (STATE'S ATTORNEY USE)

DOCKET # _____

V.S.A.

COUNT: _____ OF _____

CHARGED | TITLE | SECTION | SUB-SECTION

| NO PROSECUTION | DIVERSION | FORWARDED TO COURT | RETURNED | COMMENT: _____

*RACE CODE: W - WHITE, B - BLACK, I - INDIAN, A - ASIAN, U - UNKNOWN

*ETHNIC CODE: 1 - HISPANIC, 2 - NON HISPANIC   **A/C - 1 AGENCY**

VT 453
7/83

Example 1: A magistrate who receives a fee when issuing a warrant but not when denying one is not neutral and detached (Connally v. Georgia, 429 U.S. 245 [1977]).

Example 2: A magistrate who participates in the search to determine its scope lacks the requisite neutrality and detachment (Lo-Ji Sales, Inc. v. New York, 442 U.S. 319 [1979]).

Example 3: The state's chief investigator and prosecutor (state attorney general) is not neutral and detached; therefore any warrant issued by him is invalid (Coolidge v. New Hampshire, 403 U.S. 443 [1971]).

The warrant requirement assumes that the complaint or affidavit has been reviewed by a magistrate prior to issuance. Therefore presigned warrants used in some jurisdictions are of doubtful validity. Nonetheless, they continue to be used, primarily because of lack of challenge.

2. Contents of Warrant

The warrant must describe the offense charged and contain the name of the accused or, if unknown, some description by which he or she can be identified with reasonable certainty. Thus, a "John Doe" warrant (defined as one in which only the name "John Doe" appears because the real name of the suspect is not known to the police) *is valid only if it contains a particular description of the accused by which he or she can be identified with reasonable certainty.* A "John Doe" warrant without such a description is invalid, since it could be used by the police to arrest almost anyone and therefore lends itself to abuse.

3. Service of Warrant

An arrest warrant is directed to, and may be executed by, any peace officer in the jurisdiction. In some states, a properly designated private person can also serve a warrant.

a. Service within state.   Inside the state of issuance, a warrant issued in one county or judicial district may be served by peace officers of any other county or district in which the accused is found. Some states, such as Texas and California, have statutes giving local peace officers statewide power of arrest—thereby allowing the peace officers of the county or district where the warrant was issued to make the arrest anywhere in the state. Even if statewide power of arrest is given, it is better, whenever possible, to inform local police agencies of service within their jurisdiction as a matter of courtesy and to avoid jurisdictional misunderstanding.

b. Service outside state.   A warrant has no authority beyond the territorial limits of the state in which it is issued. Hence, an arrest in Illinois cannot be made on the basis of a warrant issued in Wisconsin. There is a "hot pursuit" exception: most states today have adopted a uniform act authorizing peace officers from one state who enter another in fresh pursuit to arrest the suspect for a felony committed in the first state.

c. Time of arrest.   In general, felony arrests may be made at any time, day or night, but misdemeanor arrests are usually made during daylight hours. In some states, an arrest for any crime—felony or misdemeanor—can be made at any hour of the day or night.

The arresting officer need not have the arrest warrant in his or her possession at the time of the arrest as long as he or she shows it to the accused after the arrest, if so requested. An arrest warrant should be executed without unreasonable delay, but it usually does not expire until executed or withdrawn.

4. Announcement Requirement

Federal and many state statutes require that an officer making an arrest or executing a search warrant announce his or her purpose and authority before breaking into a dwelling. The idea is to allow voluntary compliance and avoid violence. Breaking into premises without first complying with the announcement requirement may or may not invalidate the entry and any resulting search, depending upon the law or court decisions in the state. Some states invalidate the entry and resulting search; others do not. There is no constitutional requirement that announcement be made before entry.

There are cases in which, because of exigent circumstances, an announcement is not required or necessary. The usual instances are these:

   a. When announcing presents a *strong threat of violence or danger to the officers;* for example, when the police are serving a warrant on a fugitive who is dangerous and armed.
   b. When there is *danger that contraband or other property sought might be destroyed.* Some states permit a magistrate to issue so-called "no knock" searches, particularly in drug cases. They authorize entry without announcement because otherwise the evidence might be destroyed. The constitutionality of such statutes has not been fully tested, although they have been upheld by lower courts.
   c. When officers reasonably believe that *persons within the premises are in imminent peril of bodily harm.*
   d. When people within are reasonably believed to be *engaged in the process of destroying evidence or escaping because they are aware of the presence of the police.*
   e. When the person to be arrested is in the *process of committing the crime.*

Exceptions to the announcement requirement are usually governed by state law, state court decisions, and agency regulations. They therefore vary from state to state.

In the words of one police manual, "As a general rule, an officer may not break into or force entry into private premises without prior self-identification and statement of purpose and after being refused admittance. Forced entry includes not only the use of actual force but also the opening of a locked door with a passkey or the opening of a closed but unlocked door."[3]

5. Need for Search Warrant to Enter Residence of Third Party

In the absence of exigent circumstances, police officers executing an arrest warrant may not search for the person named in the warrant in the home of a third party without first obtaining a separate search warrant to enter the home. For example, federal agents learned from an informer that a federal fugitive could probably be found at a certain address. They procured a warrant for his arrest, but the warrant did not mention the address. With the arrest warrant, the agents went to the address, which was the residence of a third person. The Court held that the arrest warrant could not be used as a legal authority to enter the home of a person other than the person named in the warrant. A search warrant had to be obtained (Steagald v. U.S., 451 U.S. 204 [1981]). Note, however, that the Steagald case involved the residence of a third party. The case does not apply when the place to be entered is the fugitive's residence.

In a subsequent case, the Court said that a warrantless nonconsensual entry of a residence to arrest an overnight guest was not justified by exigent circumstances and therefore violated the Fourth Amendment (Minnesota v. Olson, 58 L.W. 4464 [1990]). In that case, the police suspected a certain Olson of being the driver of a getaway car used in a robbery and murder. The police arrested the suspected murderer and recovered the murder weapon. They then surrounded the home of two women with whom they believed Olson had been staying. Without seeking permission and with weapons drawn, they entered the home and found Olson hiding in a closet. They arrested him, and he implicated himself in the crime. On appeal, Olson sought to exclude his statement, saying that there were no exigent circumstances to justify the warrantless entry. The Court agreed, saying that Olson's status as an overnight guest was in itself sufficient to show that he had an expectation of privacy in the home that society was prepared to recognize as reasonable. The Court further said that there were no exigent circumstances justifying the warrantless entry, hence the statement could not be admitted in court.

6. Other Processes for Arrest

a. Summons or citation. Statutes in many states authorize the use of a citation or summons (written notice to appear) for less serious offenses, such as traffic violations. A summons or citation means the offender does not have to be taken into custody for that offense at that time. In the event of failure to appear at the time and date indicated in the summons or citation, however, a warrant of arrest may then be issued.

b. Bench warrant. Bench warrants are used to bring nonappearing defendants before the court. Failure to appear is an offense against the court itself; hence no complaint need be filed.

c. Capias. *Capias* is a Latin term meaning "you take." This is the general name for several species of writ, the common characteristic of which is that they require the officer to take the body of the defendant into custody; they are writs of attachment or arrest.[4]

B. Arrest without Warrant

Although arrest warrants are preferred by the courts and desirable for purposes of police protection from liability lawsuits, they are in fact seldom used in police work and are not constitutionally required, except in home arrests. About 95 percent of all arrests are made without a warrant. Police officers have a general power to arrest without a warrant. Laws vary from state to state, but the following provisions on warrantless arrests are typical, classified into arrests for felonies or misdemeanors.

1. Arrests by Police for Felonies

a. When a crime is actually committed in the presence of the officer. The authority is based on common-law principles, which have since been enacted into state statutes. For example, while on patrol an officer sees a robbery being committed. She can make the arrest without a warrant. The term *in the presence of* a police officer refers to knowledge gained first-hand by the officer as a result of using any of his or her five senses—*sight, hearing, smell, touch,* or *taste.* Therefore, the police may make a warrantless arrest if probable cause is established by such means as these:

Sight: Officer sees X stab Y, or S breaking into a residence.

Hearing: Officer hears a shot, or a cry for help from inside an apartment.

Smell: Officer smells gasoline, gunpowder, gas fumes, or marijuana.

Touch: Officer examines doors or windows in the dark, or touches car muffler of engine to determine if it has just been used.

Taste: Officer tastes a white substance to identify it as sugar, salt, or something else!

b. Arrests for felonies in public places—no warrant required. The police are not required to obtain an arrest warrant before arresting a person in a public place even if there was time and opportunity to do so as long as the police are duly authorized to do so by statute (U.S. v. Watson, 423 U.S. 411 [1976]). In the Watson case, such authorization was given by federal law. The Court said in Watson, however, that such authorization is given "in almost all of the States in the form of express statutory authorization."

By contrast, the police may not enter a private home to make a routine warrantless arrest in the absence of exigent circumstances or consent (Payton v. New York, 445 U.S. 573 [1980]). In that case, New York detectives, after two days of intensive investigation, assembled evidence sufficient to establish probable cause to believe that Payton had murdered the manager of a gas station. They went to Payton's apartment to arrest him without a warrant, such warrantless search being authorized by New York law. They knocked on the metal door, and when there was no response the police summoned emergency assistance and then used crowbars to open the door and enter the apartment. No one was there, but in plain view was a .30-caliber shell casing that was seized and later admitted into evidence at Payton's murder trial. Payton was convicted; he appealed alleging that the Fourth Amendment requires police officers to obtain a warrant if making a felony arrest in a private residence when there is time to obtain a warrant. The Court agreed, saying that a warrant was needed in these types of cases (routine arrests in the absence of exigent circumstances or consent) and that state laws, such as that of New York, that authorized warrantless arrests in these types of cases, were unconstitutional. (Read the case brief of Payton v. New York at the end of this chapter.)

In a subsequent case, the Court held that a violation of the Fourth Amendment rule forbidding the police from making a warrantless and nonconsensual entry of a suspect's residence so as to make a routine felony arrest does not require the exclusion of a statement made by the suspect after his or her removal from that residence as long as the arrest was supported by probable cause (New York v. Harris, 47 CrL 2024 [1990]). Despite the "fruit of the poisonous tree" doctrine, the Court admitted the evidence (the statement), saying that "the rule in Payton was designed to protect the physical integrity of the home, not to grant criminal suspects protection for statements made outside their premises where the police have probable cause to make an arrest."

c. When a person has committed a felony, even though the felony was not committed in the officer's presence. For example, a woman comes running to an officer to report that her husband has just been shot by a neighbor. The officer can make an arrest without a warrant.

d. When exigent (emergency) circumstances are present that would jeopardize the arrest or seizure of evidence. The term *exigent circumstances* has many meanings, as the following examples illustrate.

Example 1: Possibility of disappearance. An officer is told by a reliable informant that he has just bought cocaine from a stranger in Apartment 141, corner of Main and Commerce Streets, and that the seller was getting ready to leave. Given the possibility of the suspect's disappearance, the officer can make the arrest without a warrant.

Example 2: Hot pursuit. In cases of hot pursuit, when a suspect enters his own or another person's dwelling, an officer can make the arrest without a warrant. In one case, police officers, acting without a search or arrest warrant, entered a house to arrest an armed-robbery suspect who had been seen entering the place just minutes before. The Supreme Court upheld the warrantless entry and search as reasonable because to delay the entry would have allowed the suspect time to escape (Warden v. Hayden, 387 U.S. 294 [1967]). The term *hot pursuit* denotes some kind of chase, but it need not be extended. The fact that the pursuit ended almost as soon as it began does not render it any less a hot pursuit sufficient to justify an entry without warrant into a suspect's house. The following factors are relevant in a fleeing-suspect case: "(1) the gravity of the offense committed, (2) the belief that the suspect was armed, and (3) the likelihood that the suspect would escape in the absence of swift police action" (U.S. v. Williams, 612 F.2d 735 [3rd Cir. 1979]).

e. When there is danger to the arresting officer. In Warden v. Hayden, 387 U.S. 294 (1967), the Court said: "The Fourth Amendment does not require officers to delay in the course of an investigation if to do so would gravely endanger their lives or the lives of others. Speed . . . was essential. . . ." This safety consideration has been extended by lower courts to include the safety of informants or the public.

2. Arrests by Police for Misdemeanors

A warrantless arrest for misdemeanors may be made in the following cases if probable cause is present:

a. If the offense is actually committed or attempted in the officer's presence.
The police cannot make an arrest if the misdemeanor was merely reported to them by a third party. This is one big difference in an officer's power to make an arrest in felony and misdemeanor cases. What the officer does in these cases is to secure an arrest warrant or have the complaining party file a complaint, which can lead to the issuance of a warrant or summons. This rule has its origin in common law. This rule is subject to so many exceptions, however, that it becomes practically meaningless in many states. These are some of the common exceptions:

1. if the misdemeanant will flee if not immediately arrested
2. if the misdemeanant will conceal or destroy evidence if not immediately arrested
3. if the case involves a traffic accident
4. if the officer has probable cause to believe that a misdemeanor is being committed, although not in his or her presence

b. Home entry.   In the case of a minor offense, a warrantless entry into a home to make an arrest will rarely be justified. For example, an officer suspects a person of driving while intoxicated, a nonjailable offense in the state. The officer goes to the suspect's home to make an arrest before the alcohol can dissipate from his body. The officer cannot enter the home without a warrant or consent. Given the state's relatively tolerant view of this offense, an interest in preserving the evidence cannot overcome the strong presumption against warrantless invasion of homes.[5] Thus, in determining whether there are exigent circumstances, a court must consider the seriousness of the offense (Welsh v. Wisconsin, 104 S.Ct. 2091 [1984]). Note, however, that home entry in felony or misdemeanor cases is justified if there is valid consent.

C. Citizen's Arrest

States authorize arrests by citizens without warrant, but these arrests are usually limited to situations in which a *felony has actually been committed and the citizen has probable cause to believe that the person arrested committed the crime.* Some states also allow private citizens to make warrantless arrests for certain types of misdemeanors—usually those involving a "breach of the peace." The problem is that the definition of "breach of the peace" varies from one state to another and is usually ambiguous. The citizen who may not know the difference between a felony and a misdemeanor is taking a risk. Some states provide by law that police officers, when making an arrest, may enlist the aid of citizens and that the citizens are obliged to respond. Arrests by police officers with probable cause outside their territorial jurisdiction are valid, but they are in the category of citizens' arrests and are therefore subject to corresponding limitations.

IV. WHAT THE POLICE MAY DO AFTER AN ARREST

Arrest is a significant part of the criminal justice process, both for the suspect as well as for the police officer. For the suspect, the arrest signifies the start of a deprivation of freedom that can last until after the sentence term has been served, if convicted.

For the police, it sets in motion certain procedures that must be observed or followed if the arrestee is to be processed properly. It is important that the officer become fully aware of what he or she can do, particularly immediately after an arrest is made, otherwise the whole process might be subject to challenge. Some of the things an officer may do after an arrest, according to court decisions, are the following.

A. Search the Arrested Person

After an arrest, the police may search the arrested person regardless of the offense for which the person has been placed under arrest (U.S. v. Robinson, 414 U.S. 218 [1973]). Whether the suspect be arrested for a brutal murder or for shoplifting, that suspect can be searched by the police. The reason for this rule is to protect the police and to prevent the destruction of evidence.

Although a full body search after an arrest is allowed, a departmental policy that orders body cavity searches in all felony arrests has been declared by at least one Federal Circuit Court of Appeals as unconstitutional (Kennedy v. Los Angeles Police Department, 887 F.2d 920 [9th Cir. 1989]). The Los Angeles Police Department policy challenged in that case required the Los Angeles police to body cavity search in all felony arrests, but limited that form of strip search in misdemeanor cases to those involving narcotics arrests or those suspected of concealing weapons. Such policy was justified by the department as necessary for "safety, security and the proper administration of the jail system." The Ninth Circuit Court of Appeals held such searches to be unconstitutional, holding that they are allowed only if the police have "reasonable suspicion that the individual arrested may be likely to conceal a weapon, drugs or other contraband prior to conducting a body cavity search." The reason for the "reasonable suspicion" requirement, as opposed to automatic authorization for a full body search in arrests, is that, according to the court, "strip searches involving the visual exploration of body cavities [are] dehumanizing and humiliating."

B. Search the Area within Immediate Control of the Arrested Person

Once a lawful arrest has been made, the police may search the area within the suspect's *immediate control,* meaning the area from which the suspect may grab a weapon or destroy evidence (Chimel v. California, 395 U.S. 752 [1969]). What is meant by "area within immediate control"? In Chimel, the Court defined the allowable area of search by saying:

> When an arrest is made, it is reasonable for the arresting officer to search the person arrested in order to remove any weapons that the latter might seek to use in order to resist arrest or effect his escape. . . . In addition, it is entirely reasonable for the arresting officer to search for and seize any evidence on the arrestee's person in order to prevent its concealment or destruction. And the area into which an arrestee might reach in order to grab a weapon or evidentiary items must, of course, be governed by a like rule. (Chimel v. California, 395 U.S. 752 [1969])

The most limited (and perhaps more accurate) interpretation of that phrase is that the area is limited to the person's *wingspan*—the area covered by the spread of the suspect's arms and hands. Some lower courts tend to be liberal in defining the area into which there is some possibility that an arrested person might reach for a weapon. In one case an accused was sitting on a bed at the time of her arrest; the area underneath her bed was deemed to be within her "reach." In another case, the fact that the arrestee was handcuffed (and his reach thereby limited) did not mean that the officers could not go ahead and search the area of immediate control. In a third case, the search of a kitchen shelf six feet away from the arrestee was considered by the court as a search incident to an arrest, although an officer stood between the female arrestee (who was being arrested for forgery) and the kitchen shelf while the arrest was being made.[6]

By contrast, the Court has held that a search incident to arrest is valid only if it is "substantially contemporaneous with the arrest and is confined to the immediate vicinity of the arrest." The Court added that "if a search of a house is to be upheld as incident to an arrest, that arrest must take place inside the house, not somewhere outside—whether two blocks away, twenty feet away, or on the sidewalk near the front steps" (Vale v. Louisiana, 399 U.S. 30 [1970]).[7]

If the search goes beyond the area of immediate control, the officer must obtain a search warrant. Some courts, however, have permitted the police to search areas in a residence that are beyond a defendant's "reach" even without a warrant if (1) there is some type of emergency requiring immediate action that cannot await the preparation of a search warrant (such as possible destruction of evidence) and (2) the search is focused on a predetermined target (such as narcotics in a particular dresser drawer), rather than being a general exploratory search.

If the search of the arrested person is valid, then the evidence obtained from the search of the arrested person or of the area within the immediate control of the arrested person is admissible in court. If, however, the arrest is invalid, then any evidence obtained after the arrest will not be admissible because it is considered "fruit of the poisonous tree."

> Example 1: The police arrest X on suspicion (not amounting to probable cause) that he has cocaine in his pockets. Immediately after the arrest, they search him and cocaine is found. Since the arrest is invalid, the cocaine found is "fruit of the poisonous tree" and therefore will not be admitted in evidence.

> Example 2: The police have information (not amounting to probable cause) from an unreliable informant that Y has heroin in his car. The police spot Y driving down the street. They stop him allegedly for speeding (actually a pretext to stop the car), look around the car, and see cocaine on the back seat. Such evidence is not admissible because the car stop was illegal, hence the evidence obtained is "fruit of the poisonous tree."

The basic principle is that an illegal act of the police is never cured by what turns up after the arrest. The evidence obtained can be excluded because of the initial illegal act. There is a strong temptation in these cases for the police to color their story and be "creative" about the facts in an effort to "legitimize" the arrest—justifying such creativity by saying that the ends justify the means. This is a matter of police ethics that can lead, if exposed, to administrative or legal action.

C. Use Handcuffs According to Department Policy or at Discretion

The use of handcuffs in arrests is either governed by department rules or left to the sound discretion of the police. The Court has not addressed the use of handcuffs by the police, and there are no authoritative lower court decisions on the issue. As a general rule, however, handcuffs are required or recommended by police departments in felony offenses but not in misdemeanor cases unless there is some personal danger to the police. Given the presence of a policy or, in the absence thereof, because of discretion, it is difficult to hold a police officer liable for using handcuffs in the process of making an arrest.

D. Monitor the Movements of the Arrested Person

The police may accompany an arrested person into his or her residence after a lawful arrest, if the arrested person is allowed to go there by the police before the police take him or her to the police station. For example, X is arrested by virtue of an arrest warrant. After arrest, X asks the arresting officer permission to go to his apartment to see his wife and pick up things he would need in jail. The officer may allow X to do that, but the movements of the arrestee can be monitored. In one case the Court said: "It is not unreasonable under the Fourth Amendment for a police officer, as a matter of routine, to monitor the movements of an arrested person, as his judgment dictates, following an arrest. The officer's need to ensure his own safety—as well as the integrity of the arrest—is compelling" (Washington v. Chrisman, 455 U.S. 1 [1982]). In this case the Court said that the officer is allowed to remain with the arrestee at all times after the arrest.

E. Conduct a Warrantless Protective Sweep of the Area in Which the Suspect Is Arrested

The practice of warrantless *protective sweeps* has been authorized by the Court in the case of Maryland v. Buie, 58 L.W. 4281 (1990). In that case, police officers obtained and executed arrest warrants for Buie and an accomplice in connection with an armed robbery. On reaching Buie's house, the officers went through the first and second floors. One of the officers observed the basement so no one would surprise the officers. This officer shouted into the basement and ordered anyone there to come out. A voice asked who was there. The officer ordered the person to come out three more times before that person, Buie, emerged from the basement. After placing Buie under arrest, another officer entered the basement to see if there was anyone else there. Once in the basement, the officer noticed in plain view a red running suit similar to the one worn by one of the suspects in the robbery. The running suit was admitted into evidence at Buie's trial over his objection, and he was convicted of robbery with the use of a deadly weapon. Buie raised the legality of the protective sweep (which led to the discovery of the evidence) on appeal. The Court rejected Buie's challenge, saying that "The Fourth Amendment permits a properly limited protective sweep in conjunction with an in-home arrest when the searching officer possesses a reasonable belief based on specific and articulable facts that the area to be swept harbors an individual posing a danger to those on the arrest scene."

The protective sweep allowed in Buie is limited in scope and does not allow a protective sweep by the police every time an arrest is made. The Court said that the following limitations, taken from various parts of the decision, must be present and observed for a valid protective sweep to take place:

1. "There must be specific and articulable facts which . . . would warrant a reasonably prudent officer in believing that the area to be swept harbors an individual posing a danger."
2. "Such a protective sweep is not a full search of the premises, but may extend only to a cursory inspection of those spaces where a person may be found."
3. "The sweep lasts no longer than is necessary to dispel the reasonable suspicion of danger and in any event no longer than it takes to complete the arrest and depart the premises."

F. Search Arrestee at Place of Detention

Once brought to the place of detention (usually either a jail or a police lockup), the arrestee may be subjected to a complete search of his or her person if it was not done during arrest. This procedure is valid even in the absence of probable cause to search. Justification for the search of an arrestee's person on arrival at the station is that of inventory incident to being booked in jail. The inventory, which is a search under the Fourth Amendment, has these legitimate objectives: (1) protecting the arrestee's property while he or she is in jail, (2) protecting the police from groundless claims that they have not adequately safeguarded the defendant's property, (3) safeguarding the detention facility by preventing introduction of weapons or contraband, and (4) ascertaining or verifying the identity of the person arrested.[8]

Such searches may include the individual's wallet or other personal property. This rule that a routine inventory search is lawful applies only when the prisoner is to be jailed. If the suspect is brought in merely to be booked and then released, some other reasons will have to be used to justify a warrantless search by the officers.

V. DISPOSITION OF PRISONER AFTER ARREST

In minor offenses, police usually have the discretion to arrest or not to arrest. The more serious the offense, the less discretion the officer has to release. After a suspect has been arrested, however, the police must follow constitutionally prescribed (often incorporated into departmental policy) procedures for keeping that person in detention.

A. Booking

As discussed in Chapter Two, *booking* involves making an entry in the police blotter or arrest book indicating the suspect's name, the time of arrest, and the offense involved. If the offense is serious, the suspect may also be photographed or fingerprinted. If the offense is minor, the suspect may be released based on "stationhouse bail," which involves the posting of cash and the promise to appear in court for a hearing at a specified date. If the offense is serious, the arrestee will be kept in jail or holding facility (a temporary facility usually maintained by the police department instead of by the county) until bail, as set by the magistrate, is posted. In the process of booking, the officer may, in accordance with departmental procedures, effect without warrant an inventory of the arrestee's personal property.

B. Appearance before Magistrate

Statutes or court rules in most states require that an arrested person be brought before a magistrate *without unnecessary delay.* This is the "initial appearance" stage of the criminal justice process. The term *without unnecessary delay* varies in meaning from one jurisdiction to another and is difficult to express in terms of maximum hours or days because the surrounding circumstances must be taken into account. The Court has not set any maximum limit. In one case, the Second Circuit Court of Appeals held that arrestees may be kept up to seventy-two hours in New York City without arraignment (Williams v. Ward, 845 F.2d 374 [2d Cir. 1988]). In that case, several arrestees filed a class action seeking a declaration that seventy-two hours without arraignment violated their Fourth Amendment right against unreasonable seizure. The court rejected that claim, saying that the enormous problems involved in processing more than 200,000 arrested people each year justified the delay. Other courts, however, will allow no more than twenty-four hours of delay. Police officers must be familiar with the time limit set by law or the courts in their jurisdiction.

The purposes of the initial appearance vary from place to place, but usually they are as follows:

1. to warn the suspect of his or her rights, including being given the Miranda warnings;
2. to determine if there is probable cause to process the suspect further through the system or, in its absence, to set the suspect free; and
3. if the suspect is to be further processed, to set bail for release, except if the offense is nonbailable.

VI. USE OF FORCE DURING ARREST

The law of the use of force during arrest can be confusing unless studied in a proper legal framework. The officer must first realize that generally there are two kinds of force in police work; namely, *nondeadly force* and *deadly force. Nondeadly force is force that when used is not likely to result in or produce serious bodily injury or death. Deadly force is that level of force that would lead a reasonable police officer objectively to conclude that its use poses a high risk of death or serious injury to its human target, regardless of whether or not death, serious injury, or any harm actually occurs.* Firearms are clear examples of instruments of deadly force; so are long knives, daggers, and lead pipes. Nightsticks and chokeholds are considered by some courts to mean deadly force; a lot depends on how they are used.

These two types of force need to be discussed separately because they are governed by completely different rules.

A. Nondeadly Force

The general rule is that *nondeadly force may be used as long as it is reasonable force. Reasonable force* is defined as force that a prudent and cautious person would use if exposed to similar circumstances; it is limited to the amount of force that is necessary to accomplish legitimate and proper results. Anything beyond that becomes unreasonable force. For example, the police arrest a suspect who kicks, uses fists, and refuses to be handcuffed. The police may use as much force as is necessary to bring that person under control. Suppose, however, that after subduing him, the police beat him up. Such use of force is unreasonable because it is unnecessary to place the suspect under control and therefore it becomes punitive.

The problem is that the term *reasonable force* is extremely subjective. It depends on the circumstances in each case and the perception of the judge or jury. The officer therefore needs to remember the circumstances that led him or her to use a certain kind of force so that he or she can articulate the reasons on the witness stand and then hope that the jury will agree. Most states allow the use of nondeadly force under myriad circumstances; these are the most common:

1. to overcome an offender's resistance to a lawful arrest;
2. to prevent escape;
3. to retake a suspect after escape;
4. to protect people and property from harm; and
5. to protect the officer from bodily injury.

The opposite of reasonable force is unreasonable force. This dichotomy, however, does not give the police a clear mental guideline. Given this problem, it is best to think of the opposite of reasonable force as *punitive force,* meaning force that is used to punish rather than to achieve legitimate and proper results. This is easier for the officer to conceptualize because an officer, even in highly emotional situations, generally knows instinctively whether the force he or she is administering is necessary to achieve valid and proper results or is for punishment.

B. Deadly Force

The law on the use of *deadly force* is more precise and much more strict. It is governed by specific rules that are more limiting. The rules on the use of deadly force in felony and misdemeanor cases usually differ. Although they vary widely from state to state, the usual rules can be summarized as follows.

1. In Felony Cases—The Tennessee v. Garner Case

The safest rule is that force may be used only when the life of the officer or another person is in danger and the use of force is immediately necessary to preserve that life. These are essentially the elements of self-defense and defense of third persons. This is the rule used in federal jurisdictions. In all other cases—such as flight from resistance to arrest or escape from custody—the use of deadly force poses great risks for the police officer and must be regarded only as an act of last resort. If authorized, however, by state law or departmental policy, then the use of deadly force in these instances is valid—as long as it is not so disproportionate to the severity of the offense committed as to constitute cruel and unusual punishment. For example, a state law or departmental policy that allows the use of deadly force to prevent the escape of a dangerous murder suspect will likely be constitutional because of the seriousness of the offense. Yet if the crime were theft, even if it were a felony, serious constitutional questions would arise from the use of deadly force because of its possible disproportionality to the nature of the offense.

Until recently, there were no judicial guidelines on the use of deadly force by police officers to arrest a suspect. The limits for such use were set instead by departmental rules or state law. In 1985, the Supreme Court decided Tennessee v. Garner, 53 L.W. 4410 (1985), setting the following guideline for the use of deadly force to prevent escape: *When the officer has probable cause to believe that the suspect poses a threat of serious physical harm, either to the officer or to others, it is not constitutionally unreasonable to prevent escape by using deadly force. Thus, if the suspect threatens the officer with a weapon or there is probable cause to believe that the suspect has committed a crime involving the infliction or threatened infliction of serious physical harm, the officer may use deadly force if necessary to prevent escape and if, when feasible, some warning has been given.* (Read the Tennessee v. Garner case brief at the end of this chapter.)

In Garner, two Memphis police officers one evening answered a "prowler inside call." Upon arriving at the scene, they saw a woman standing on her porch and gesturing toward the adjacent house where, she said, she heard glass shattering and was certain that someone was breaking in. One police officer radioed the dispatcher to say that they were on the scene, while the other officer went behind the neighboring house. The officer heard a door slam and saw someone run across the back yard. The suspect, Edward Garner, stopped at a six-feet-high chain link fence at the edge of the yard. With the aid of a flashlight, the officer saw Garner's face and hands. He saw no sign of a weapon and admitted later that he was reasonably sure that Garner was unarmed. While Garner was crouched at the base of the fence, the officer called out "Police, halt" and took a few steps toward him. Garner then began to climb over the fence. The officer shot him. Garner died; ten dollars and a purse taken from the house were found on his body.

In using deadly force to arrest the suspect, the officer was acting upon the authority of a Tennessee statute and pursuant to police department policy. That statute provided that "if after notice of the intention to arrest the defendant, he either flees or forcibly resists, the officer may use all the necessary means to effect the arrest." The department policy was slightly more restrictive but still allowed the use of deadly force in cases of burglary.

HIGHLIGHT 6.5

Police Shooting Policies

State laws and departmental shooting policies are likely to remain fairly diverse even after Garner, although within narrower bounds. No longer can these provisions leave officers virtually untethered, as in the extreme case of one small American town whose only gun-use guidance to its officers was this homily, "Never take me out in anger, never put me away in disgrace."

Source: "Deadly Force," by W. Geller, *Crime File Study Guide,* National Institute of Justice, at 4.

In deciding that the Tennessee statute was unconstitutional insofar as it authorized the use of deadly force in this particular situation, the Court concluded that the use of deadly force to prevent the escape of an apparently unarmed suspected felon was constitutionally unreasonable. The Court emphasized that "where the suspect poses no immediate threat to the officer and no threat to others, the harm resulting from failing to apprehend him does not justify the use of deadly force," adding that "a police officer may not seize an unarmed nondangerous suspect by shooting him dead."

Tennessee v. Garner sets the following guideline on the use of deadly force to arrest a suspect:[9] *It is constitutionally reasonable for a police officer to use deadly force when the officer has probable cause to believe that the suspect poses a threat of serious physical harm, either to the officer or to others.* But then the Court adds:

> . . . if the suspect threatens the officer with a weapon or there is probable cause to believe that he has committed a crime involving the infliction or threatened infliction of serious physical harm, deadly force may be used if necessary to prevent escape, and if, where feasible, some warning has been given.

In the words of one writer, three elements may be deduced from the preceding quotation that should offer some guidance in assessing situations to determine whether or not the officer's belief that a suspect is dangerous is in fact justified:[10]

1. "The suspect threatens the officer with a weapon; or
2. "The officer has probable cause to believe that the suspect has committed a crime involving the infliction or threatened infliction of serious physical harm; and
3. "The officer has given some warning, if feasible."

The writer goes on to say that either Condition 1 or Condition 2 would satisfy the requirement of dangerousness, but that Condition 3 applied to both 1 and 2, meaning that some warning must be given, if feasible, in either instance.

> Example 1: Officer Y tries to arrest Suspect A, who is sought for murder. Suspect A threatens to shoot the officer so he can escape. Officer Y may then use deadly force to repel that threat and to prevent escape.

> Example 2: Officer Z has probable cause to believe that Suspect B has just killed his wife with a knife. Officer Z tries to arrest Suspect B, but B tries to escape. Officer Z may use deadly force to prevent the escape.

In both examples, the officer must give some warning, if feasible, that deadly force is about to be used. This can take the form of such statements as "Put that knife down or I'll shoot" or "Halt, or I'll shoot." If the suspect heeds the warning, the necessity to use force then ceases.

The Court in Garner also concluded that the use of deadly force to prevent the escape of an apparently unarmed suspected felon was constitutionally unreasonable. The Court emphasized that "where the suspect poses no immediate threat to the officer and no threat to others, the harm resulting from failing to apprehend him does not justify the use of deadly force," adding that "a police officer may not seize an unarmed nondangerous suspect by shooting him dead."

The Garner decision rendered unconstitutional the then existing "fleeing felon" statutes in nearly half of the states insofar as those statutes allowed the use by the police of deadly force to prevent the escape of a fleeing felon regardless of circumstances. "Fleeing felon" statutes are constitutional only if they comport with the requirements set by the Court in Tennessee v. Garner. The Court based its decision on the Fourth Amendment, saying that "there can be no question that apprehension by the use of deadly force is a seizure subject to the reasonable requirement of the Fourth Amendment." It follows that if an arrest of a suspect with the use of nondeadly force is governed by the Fourth Amendment, the use of deadly force to make an arrest should also be so governed.

There are a number of unaddressed issues in Tennessee v. Garner. Some of these issues are as follows.

a. Must the police actually be threatened before deadly force can be used to prevent escape? This was not directly answered in Garner, but the Tenth Circuit Court of Appeals has said that where the suspect has placed the officer in a dangerous, life-threatening situation, there is no requirement that a suspect actually be armed. It is enough that the officer have a *reasonable belief* that it is so. In cases where the suspect is fleeing from the commission of an inherently violent crime, the court also said that there is no requirement that a suspect actually be armed. It is enough that the officer have a *reasonable belief* that the suspect is armed. In cases where the suspect is fleeing from the commission of an inherently violent crime, the court also said that there is no requirement that the officer's life actually be threatened by the suspect. Instead, the officer is allowed to infer that the suspect is inherently dangerous by the violent nature of the crime (Ryder v. City of Topeka, 814 F.2d 1412 [10th Cir. 1987]).

In another case, the police shot and killed an armed suspect who was positioned in front of a residential home with a rifle. The estate of the deceased brought action against the police alleging violation of civil rights. The court rejected plaintiff's claim, stating that since the suspect was armed and the police had a good faith and reasonable belief that such action was necessary, liability did not ensue (Ealey v. City of Detroit, 375 N.W. 2d 435 [MI 1985]).

All the preceding cases indicate that the police need not be "actually threatened" before deadly force can be used to prevent escape. What is needed is an objective reasonable belief on the part of the officer that he or she is in a life-threatening situation.

b. Does Garner allow the use of deadly force by the police to prevent the escape of a felon who committed an offense involving the use or threat of physical violence, but who is not armed and does not pose a present threat to the officer or to others at the time he or she attempts to escape? For example, X shoots and kills a pedestrian, escapes in a car and is being chased by the police. In the course of the chase, the police see X throw the gun away. Will the police be justified in using deadly force to prevent the escape? Although Garner can be interpreted to mean that deadly force should not be used merely to prevent escape by a fleeing felon, the language of the decision is not all that clear. A safe interpretation of Garner would be that deadly force ought not to be used in these instances. It is different, however, if the police reasonably believe that a threat to the officer's life still exists, such as if the suspect might have another gun.

c. Must a police officer fire warning shots before aiming at a fleeing suspect? This question was not addressed in Garner. Although the Court said that the officer must give some warning, if feasible, warning shots were not specified. The current practice is that the firing of warning shots is governed by state law or departmental policy. Some jurisdictions require warning shots; others prohibit them. Garner set no constitutional rule one way or the other, hence state law or local policy prevails.

d. May the police use deadly force to prevent escape in cases where there are multiple felony suspects but only one is armed?[11] For example, A and B rob a 7-Eleven store, but only A carries a gun while B acts as the lookout. Are the police justified in using deadly force to prevent the escape of B, the unarmed suspect? Lower courts have not adequately addressed the issue, but a reasonable interpretation of Garner suggests that deadly force should be used only on the armed suspect.

e. If the use of deadly force is justified, is there a limit to the type or degree of force that is applied?[12] Does it make any difference, for example, that a .22-caliber pistol or a double-barrel shotgun was used? How about the firing of multiple shots at a suspect when a single shot would have sufficed? The assumption behind these questions is that there are varying levels of the use of deadly force and that the level of deadly force to be used should be dictated by circumstances. Most lower courts have refused to accept the concept or address further the issue of the proper level of deadly force to be used. The courts are less concerned about the type or degree of force applied than they are with whether or not such use is justified.

A concluding observation: Tennessee v. Garner is not a criminal case, meaning that the officer who killed the suspect was not being prosecuted for murder or homicide. Instead, it was a civil case where the plaintiffs sought monetary damages from the department and the state of Tennessee. Nonetheless, Tennessee v. Garner is the only case decided by the Court thus far that sets guidelines for the use of *deadly force* by the police. The implications of the Garner case are being addressed by lower courts; these cases may eventually find their way to the U.S. Supreme Court. It is a case of which every police officer must be aware, because the use of deadly force can lead to serious criminal and civil consequences. Police departments need to give police officers training on the meaning of the Garner case and to incorporate the Garner decision in their police manuals.

2. In Misdemeanor Cases

The safest advice for the police officer is *not to use deadly force in misdemeanor cases. The only exception is that it may be used if necessary for self-defense or defense of the life of a third person.* The use of deadly force in misdemeanor cases almost always raises questions of disproportionality because the designation of the offense as a misdemeanor signifies that society does not consider the act serious in that jurisdiction.

C. What Governs the Police Use of Force?

The use of force, nondeadly or deadly, is governed by the following: (1) the Constitution, particularly the "due process" and "cruel and unusual punishment" provisions, (2) state law, usually the Penal Code or Code of Criminal Procedure, which defines when an officer may or may not legally use force, (3) judicial decisions, and (4) departmental or agency rules or guidelines.

Officers must be very familiar with all of the above, but *particularly with departmental rules on the use of force.* Those rules are often more limiting than state law and are binding on the officer. For example, suppose the law of the State of Illinois provides that deadly force may be used to prevent the escape of a jail inmate. If the policy of the Chicago Police Department, however, limits the use of deadly force only to cases of self-defense by the police and therefore precludes the use of deadly force to prevent jail escapes, that departmental policy must be followed. Violation of that policy makes the act punishable even if allowed by state law.

D. Test to Determine Police Civil Liability in Use of Force Cases— The Graham v. Connor Case

Since the police can be held liable for excessive use of force, nondeadly or deadly, what test will the courts use to determine whether or not the use of force amounts to a violation of a constitutional right so that the officer can then be held civilly liable?[13] The Court has answered this by saying that allegations that law enforcement officers used excessive force in arrests, investigative stops, or other forms of seizure, must be analyzed and judged under the Fourth Amendment *"objective reasonableness" standard,* rather than under the "substantive due process" clause of the Fourteenth Amendment (Graham v. Connor, 45 CrL 3033 [1989]).

The facts of the Graham case are as follows: Graham, a diabetic, asked a friend to drive him to a convenience store to buy orange juice to counteract the onset of an insulin reaction. On arrival at the store, Graham saw a lot of people ahead of him, so he asked his friend to drive him to another friend's house. Connor, a police officer, saw Graham enter and leave the store hastily. Suspicious, Connor stopped the car and ordered Graham and his friend to wait while he ascertained what happened in the store. Backup police arrived, handcuffed Graham, and ignored explanations about his diabetic condition. A scuffle ensued, and Graham sustained multiple injuries. Graham was released when the officer learned that nothing had happened in the store. He later sued, alleging excessive use of force by the police.

The Graham case sets the legal standard by which allegations of excessive use of force by police officers are determined for civil liability purposes, that standard being "objective reasonableness" under the Fourth Amendment. In a case decided earlier (Johnson v. Glick, 481 F.2d 1028 [2d Cir. 1973]), the Court of Appeals enumerated four factors that courts are to use in determining constitutional violations in "use of force" cases. Taken together, that test required consideration by the court of whether the officer acted in "good faith" or "maliciously and sadistically for the very purpose of causing harm." This "substantive due process" standard was hard on the police because it allowed the jury or judge, in the comfort of the courtroom and with sufficient time for deliberation, to evaluate the conduct of an officer who had to make split-second field decisions that could mean the life or death of an officer or the suspect. Nonetheless, a vast majority of lower federal courts applied this test to all "excessive force" claims against law enforcement and prison officials filed under Section 1983.

All that has changed. Under the Graham test, the reasonableness of a particular use of force by the police, deadly or nondeadly, "must be judged from the *perspective of a reasonable officer on the scene,* rather than with the 20/20 vision of hindsight." The Court added that whether the conduct of officers is reasonable in an "excessive use of force" case is determined by asking the following question: *Are the officers' actions "objectively reasonable" in light of the facts and circumstances confronting them, without regard to their underlying intent or motivation?"*

The Court did not specify factors that might lead to a finding of "objective reasonableness" by a judge or jury. All it said was this finding should be judged from the "perspective of a reasonable officer on the scene." Although a new standard has thus been set, the standard still leaves room for subjectivity in that even reasonable officers can differ as to what action ought to have been taken under the circumstances.

Under this new test, the officer's motivation, therefore, becomes unimportant. The Court said in Graham: "An officer's evil intentions will not make a Fourth Amendment violation out of an objectively reasonable use of force; nor will an officer's good intentions make an objectively reasonable use of force constitutional." In sum, if the officer's conduct is objectively reasonable (judged from the "perspective of a reasonable officer on the scene, rather than with the 20/20 vision of hindsight"), there is no "excessive use of force" violation even if the officer had bad motives or evil intent. Conversely, if the officer's conduct is objectively unreasonable (judged again from the "perspective of a reasonable officer on the scene, rather than with the 20/20 vision of hindsight"), there is a Fourth Amendment violation even if the officer's motives were good or pure. Motives, under the Graham test, are irrelevant. In short, good motives do not justify the use of unreasonable force; conversely, bad motives do not lead to liability as long as the use of force is objectively reasonable.

Note that the Graham test just discussed applies only to civil rights cases—a required element of which is a violation of a constitutional right. It does not apply to cases brought under state tort law, such cases being governed by the standards set under state law.

HIGHLIGHT 6.6

FBI Reports Sixty-seven Officers Feloniously Killed in 1989

Sixty-seven law enforcement officers were killed feloniously in the line of duty during 1989, according to preliminary national figures released by FBI Director William S. Sessions. Last year's total was the lowest during the decade, except for 1986 when 66 officers were killed.

Firearms continued to be the weapon most used in the slaying of officers in 1989. Handguns were used in 42 of the murders, rifles in 10, and shotguns in six. Five officers were intentionally struck with vehicles, two were stabbed, one was beaten with a blunt object, and one was shoved to his death.

Source: Crime Control Digest, May 14, 1990, at 1.

E. Is Tennessee v. Garner Consistent with Graham v. Connor?—Yes

Is there any relationship between the Garner and Graham cases? Are the two consistent? The answer is that the two cases are consistent and reconcilable. The Garner case applies to the use of deadly force in felony arrest cases, whereas the Graham case applies to all types of "excessive use of force" cases, deadly or nondeadly. The Graham case lays out the test to be used in all "excessive use of force" cases, deadly or nondeadly, and should be considered the general rule. The Garner case has specific application in that it should be used to determine liability only in felony arrest cases.

☐ SUMMARY

Arrest is defined as the taking of a person into custody against his or her will for the purpose of criminal prosecution or interrogation. It constitutes a "seizure" and is therefore subject to the restrictions of the Fourth Amendment. There are four elements of arrest: intention to arrest, authority to arrest, seizure and detention, and the understanding of the individual that he or she is being arrested.

Arrests may be made with or without a warrant. In arrests with warrant, probable cause has been determined by a magistrate; all the officer does is serve the warrant and take the person to the magistrate. In arrests without warrant, the officer makes an on-the-spot determination of probable cause. The Supreme Court has expressed preference for arrests with warrant, but they are not constitutionally required except in routine home arrests for felonies. Police officers are authorized to make warrantless arrests for felonies if committed in or outside their presence as long as there is probable cause. Such is not the case with misdemeanors; the general rule is that a police officer has the power to arrest without a warrant only if the offense is actually committed in his or her presence. Arrests may also be made by citizens, but this practice is limited to cases in which a felony has actually been committed and probable cause is present.

After an arrest, the police may search the arrested person and the area within immediate control. Police officers may also conduct a warrantless protective sweep of the area in which the suspect is arrested, provided there are specific and articulable facts that would warrant a prudent officer in believing that danger is present.

The arrested person is booked and brought before the magistrate "without unnecessary delay." The meaning of that phrase varies from one jurisdiction to another. Detentions of up to seventy hours without an appearance before a magistrate have been approved.

Police officers are authorized to use nondeadly or, sometimes, deadly force when making an arrest. Nondeadly force may be used as long as it is reasonable force, meaning force that is used to accomplish legitimate and proper results instead of force that is used to punish. Tennessee v. Garner, the leading case on the use of deadly force, says that it is constitutionally reasonable for a police officer to use deadly force when the officer has probable cause to believe that the suspect poses a threat of serious physical harm, either to the officer or to others.

Whether or not the police may be held civilly liable in use of force cases is now determined by the "objective reasonableness" standard. This means that the conduct of the officer is determined by asking the following question: Is that conduct objectively reasonable in light of surrounding facts and circumstances, without regard to the officer's underlying intent or motivation? Such reasonableness "must be judged from the perspective of a reasonable officer on the scene, rather than with the 20/20 vision of hindsight."

☐ REVIEW QUESTIONS

1. Define arrest and discuss its four elements.
2. How long can a suspect be detained and how intrusive must be the investigation before a stop becomes an arrest? Explain.
3. Distinguish between felonies and misdemeanors with respect to the warrantless arrest power of police officers.
4. What is meant by a "neutral and detached" magistrate? Give examples.
5. Give four instances in which announcement prior to arrest may not be necessary.
6. Distinguish between the power of the police to arrest (a) in felony and (b) in misdemeanor cases.
7. "A citizen may make an arrest any time he or she sees a crime being committed." Is this statement true or false? Discuss.
8. Discuss the rules governing the use of nondeadly and deadly force when arresting a suspect.
9. Give the Supreme Court decision in the case of Tennessee v. Garner.
10. What is meant by the "immediate area of arrestee's control"?
11. What is meant by the phrase "without unnecessary delay"?
12. What is the "objective reasonableness" standard used by the courts in police liability cases?

☐ DEFINITIONS

Actual Seizure: A seizure accomplished by taking the person into custody with the use of hands or firearms or by merely touching the individual without the use of force.

Arrest: The taking of a person into custody against his or her will for the purpose of criminal prosecution or interrogation.

Arrest Warrant: A writ or precept issued by a magistrate, justice, or other competent authority, addressed to a sheriff, constable, or other officer, requiring him or her to arrest the body of the person it names and bring the person before the magistrate or court to answer, or to be examined, concerning some offense that he or she is charged with having committed.

Bench Warrant: An order issued at the direction of a court or judge for the arrest of an individual, such as in cases of contempt or where an indictment has been issued.

Booking: The making of an entry in the police blotter or arrest book indicating the suspect's name, the time of arrest, and the offense involved. If the crime is serious, the suspect may also be photographed or fingerprinted.

Capias: A Latin term meaning "you take." It is a general name for several species of writ, the common characteristic of which is that they require the officer to take the body of the defendant into custody; they are writs of attachment or arrest.

Citation: An order from a court commanding a person to appear before that court in connection with an action or proceeding; it is usually used instead of an arrest in minor offenses.

Citizen's Arrest: Arrest made by a citizen without a warrant; usually limited to situations in which a felony has actually been committed and the citizen has probable cause to believe that the person arrested committed the offense.

Constructive Seizure: A seizure accomplished without any physical touching, grabbing, holding, or the use of force; occurs when the individual peacefully submits to the officer's will and control.

Deadly Force: Level of force that would lead a reasonable police officer objectively to conclude that its use poses a high risk of death or serious injury to its human target, regardless of whether or not death, serious injury, or any harm actually occurs.

Exigent Circumstances: Emergency circumstances that justify warrantless arrests or entries into homes or premises.

"Hot Pursuit" Exception (to the warrant rule): Peace officers from one state, through a uniform act adopted by most states, are authorized to enter another state in fresh pursuit to arrest a suspect for a felony committed in the first state.

John Doe Warrants: A warrant in which only the name "John Doe" appears because the real name of the suspect is not known to the police. It is valid only if it contains a particular description of the accused by which he or she can be identified with reasonable certainty.

Neutral and Detached Magistrate: A magistrate (issuing a warrant) who is not unalterably aligned with the police or the prosecutor's position in a case.

Nondeadly Force: Force that, when used, is not likely to result in or produce serious bodily injury or death.

Objective Reasonableness Standard: The standard used to determine whether police officers may be held civilly liable in "excessive use of force" cases, that standard being "Are the officers' actions objectively reasonable in light of the facts and circumstances confronting them, without regard to their underlying intent or motivation?"

Protective Sweep: Entry made by the police into places or areas other than where an arrest or seizure is taking place, for purposes of personal protection.

Punitive Force: Force that is used to punish rather than to achieve legitimate and proper results.

Reasonable Force: Force that a prudent and cautious person would use if exposed to similar circumstances; limited to the amount of force that is necessary to achieve valid and proper results.

Summons: A written notice to appear in court; usually used instead of an arrest in less serious offenses.

Without Unnecessary Delay: When used in connection with arrests, it means that the arrestee must be brought before a magistrate as soon as possible. Its meaning, however, varies from one jurisdiction to another, taking surrounding circumstances into account. Maximum limits are set by various jurisdictions.

☐ PRINCIPLES OF CASES

BERKEMER V. MCCARTY, 35 CrL 3192 (1984)   A police officer's unarticulated plan has no bearing on the question of whether a suspect was "in custody" at a particular time; the only relevant inquiry is how a reasonable person in the suspect's position would have understood the situation. Also, the roadside questioning of a motorist pursuant to a routine traffic stop (not an arrest) is not custodial interrogation and therefore does not require the Miranda warnings.

CHIMEL V. CALIFORNIA, 395 U.S. 752 (1969)   After making an arrest, the police may search the area of the arrestee's immediate control to discover and seize any evidence in the possession of the arrested person and to prevent its concealment or destruction.

CONNALLY V. GEORGIA, 429 U.S. 245 (1977)   A magistrate who receives a fee when issuing a warrant but not when denying one is not neutral and detached.

COOLIDGE V. NEW HAMPSHIRE, 403 U.S. 443 (1971)   The state's chief investigator and prosecutor (state attorney general) is not neutral and detached; therefore any warrant issued by him or her is invalid.

DUNAWAY V. NEW YORK, 442 U.S. 200 (1979)   An arrest is defined as the taking of a person into custody against his or her will for the purpose of criminal prosecution or interrogation.

EALEY V. CITY OF DETROIT, 375 N.W. 2d 435 (MI 1985)   Liability does not ensue in cases of use of deadly force by the police in cases where the suspect was armed and the police had good faith and a reasonable belief that such action was necessary.

FLORIDA V. ROYER, 460 U.S. 491 (1983)   The removal of a detainee without his consent from the public area in an airport to the police room in the airport converted the stop to an arrest.

GRAHAM V. CONNOR, 45 CrL 3033 (1989)   Allegations that law enforcement officers used excessive force in arrests, investigative stops, or other forms of seizure, must be analyzed and judged under the Fourth Amendment "objective reasonableness" standard. This means that whether the conduct of an officer is reasonable is determined by asking the following question: Are the officer's actions "objectively reasonable" in light of the facts and circumstances confronting him or her, without regard to his or her underlying intent or motivation?

HENRY V. UNITED STATES, 361 U.S. 98 (1959)   Probable cause exists if the facts and circumstances known to the officer warrant a prudent person in believing that the offense has been committed.

JOHNSON V. GLICK, 481 F.2d 1028 (2d Cir. 1973)   The Court of Appeals enumerated four factors that courts were then using to determine constitutional violations in use of force cases. Taken together, that test required consideration by the court of whether the officer acted in "good faith" or "maliciously and sadistically for the very purpose of causing harm." (This has since been replaced by the "objective reasonableness" standard set by the Court in Graham v. Connor.)

KENNEDY V. LOS ANGELES POLICE DEPARTMENT, 887 F.2d 920 [9th Cir. 1989])   A departmental policy that orders body cavity searches in all felony arrests is unconstitutional. There must be reasonable suspicion, prior to conducting a body cavity search, that the individual arrested may be likely to conceal a weapon, drugs, or other contraband.

Lo-Ji Sales, Inc. v. New York, 442 U.S. 319 (1979)   A magistrate who participates in the search to determine its scope lacks the requisite neutrality and detachment.

Maryland v. Buie, 58 L.W. 4281 (1990)   "The Fourth Amendment permits a properly limited protective sweep in conjunction with an in-home arrest when the searching officer possesses a reasonable belief based on specific and articulable facts that the area to be swept harbors an individual posing a danger to those on the arrest scene."

Michigan v. Chesternut, 43 CrL 3077 (1988)   The appropriate test to determine if a seizure has occurred is "whether a reasonable man, viewing the particular police conduct as a whole and within the setting of all the surrounding circumstances, would have concluded that the police had in some way restrained his liberty so that he was not free to leave."

Minnesota v. Olson, 58 L.W. 4464 (1990)   A warrantless nonconsensual entry by the police of a residence to arrest an overnight guest was not justified by exigent circumstances and therefore violated the Fourth Amendment.

New York v. Harris, 47 CrL 2024 (1990)   A violation of the Fourth Amendment rule forbidding the police from making a warrantless and nonconsensual entry of a suspect's residence so as to make a routine felony arrest does not require the exclusion of a statement made by the suspect after his or her removal from that residence as long as the arrest was supported by probable cause.

Payton v. New York, 445 U.S. 573 (1980)   In the absence of exigent circumstances or consent, the police may not enter a private home to make a routine warrantless arrest.

Ryder v. City of Topeka, 814 F.2d 1412 (10th Cir. 1987)   In use of deadly force cases by the police, the court said that where the suspect is fleeing from the commission of an inherently violent crime, there is no requirement that the officer's life actually be threatened by the suspect. Instead, the officer is allowed to infer that the suspect is inherently dangerous by the violent nature of the crime.

Steagald v. United States, 451 U.S. 204 (1981)   An arrest warrant cannot be used as a legal authority to enter the home of a person other than the person named in the arrest warrant. If the person to be arrested is in the home of another person, a search warrant must be obtained to enter the home in order to make an arrest. The only exception is that exigent circumstances justify a warrantless entry.

Tennessee v. Garner, 53 L.W. 4410 (1985)   Deadly force to prevent an escape may be used only if the suspect threatens the officer with a weapon or there is probable cause to believe that he or she has committed a crime involving the infliction or threatened infliction of serious physical harm. In addition, where feasible, the suspect must first be warned.

United States v. Mendenhall, 446 U.S. 544 (1980)   When determining whether a person has been arrested, the court takes into account the totality of the surrounding circumstances, including such considerations as "the threatening presence of several officers, the display of a weapon by an officer, some physical touching of the person or the citizen, or the use of language or tone of voice indicating that compliance with the officer's request might be compelled.''

UNITED STATES V. ROBINSON, 414 U.S. 218 (1973)   After making an arrest, the police may make a warrantless search of the arrested person.

UNITED STATES V. WATSON, 423 U.S. 411 (1976)   Law enforcement officers may find it wise to seek arrest warrants when practical to do so, and their judgments about probable cause may be more readily accepted when backed by a warrant issued by a magistrate. Also, the police are not required to obtain an arrest warrant before arresting a person in a public place even if there was time and opportunity to do so.

VALE V. LOUISIANA, 399 U.S. 30 (1970)   A search incident to arrest is valid only if it is "substantially contemporaneous with the arrest and is confined to the immediate vicinity of the arrest." The Court added that "if a search of a house is to be upheld as incident to an arrest, that arrest must take place inside the house, not somewhere outside—whether two blocks away, twenty feet away, or on the sidewalk near the front steps."

WARDEN V. HAYDEN, 387 U.S. 294 (1967)   Warrantless entries and searches are reasonable if to delay them would have allowed the suspect time to escape. The Court also said that the Fourth Amendment does not require officers to delay an arrest if to do so would endanger their lives or the lives of others.

WASHINGTON V. CHRISMAN, 455 U.S. 1 (1982)   It is not unreasonable under the Fourth Amendment for a police officer, as a matter of routine, to monitor the movements of an arrested person, as his or her judgment dictates, following an arrest. The officer's need to ensure his or her own safety, as well as the integrity of the arrest, is compelling.

WELSH V. WISCONSIN, 104 S.Ct. 2091 (1984)   In determining whether exigent circumstances exist to justify a home entry without a warrant, the seriousness of the offense must be considered. In case of a minor offense, a warrantless entry into a home will rarely be justified.

WILLIAMS V. WARD, 845 F.2d 374 (2d Cir. 1988)   Arrestees may be held up to seventy-two hours in New York City without arraignment; the court said that the enormous problems involved in processing more than 200,000 arrested people each year justified the delay.

☐ CASE BRIEF—LEADING CASE ON HOME ARREST

PAYTON V. NEW YORK, 445 U.S. 573 (1980)

FACTS: After two days of intensive investigation, New York detectives had assembled evidence sufficient to establish probable cause to believe that Payton had murdered the manager of a gas station. Early the following day, six officers went to Payton's apartment in the Bronx, intending to arrest him. They had not obtained a warrant. Although light and music emanated from the apartment, there was no response to their knock on the metal door. They summoned emergency assistance and, about thirty minutes later, used crowbars to break open the door and enter the apartment. No one was there. In plain view, however, was a .30-caliber shell casing that was seized and later admitted into evidence at Payton's murder trial. Payton was convicted and appealed.

ISSUE: *Does the Fourth Amendment's guarantee against unreasonable search and seizure require police officers to obtain a warrant if making a felony arrest when there is time to obtain a warrant? Yes.*

SUPREME COURT DECISION: In the absence of exigent circumstances or consent, the police may not enter a private home to make a routine warrantless arrest; the entry is invalid and the evidence obtained inadmissible.

CASE SIGNIFICANCE: The Payton case settled the issue of whether or not the police can make a warrantless arrest in a routine felony case. The practice was authorized by the state of New York and twenty-three other states at the time Payton was decided. These authorizations are now unconstitutional and officers must obtain a warrant before making a routine felony arrest.

EXCERPTS FROM THE DECISION: It is familiar history that indiscriminate searches and seizures conducted under the authority of "general warrants" were the immediate evils that motivated the framing and adoption of the Fourth Amendment. Indeed, as originally proposed in the House of Representatives, the draft contained only one clause, which directly imposed limitations on the issuance of warrants, but imposed no express restrictions on warrantless searches or seizures. As it was ultimately adopted, however, the Amendment contained two separate clauses, the first protecting the basic right to be free from unreasonable searches and seizures and the second requiring that warrants be particular and supported by probable cause. . . .

It is thus perfectly clear that the evil the Amendment was designed to prevent was broader than the abuse of a general warrant. Unreasonable searches or seizures conducted without any warrant at all are condemned by the plain language of the first clause of the Amendment. Almost a century ago the Court stated in resounding terms that the principles reflected in the Amendment "reached farther than the concrete form" of the specific cases that gave it birth, and "apply to all invasions on the part of the Government and its employees of the sanctity of a man's home and the privacies of life." Boyd v. United States, 116 U.S. 616, 630. Without pausing to consider whether that broad language may require some qualification, it is sufficient to note that the warrantless arrest of a person is a species of seizure required by the Amendment to be reasonable. . . . Indeed, as Mr. Justice Powell noted in his concurrence in United States v. Watson, the arrest of a person is "quintessentially a seizure." 423 U.S., at 428.

A majority of the States that have taken a position on the question permit warrantless entry into the home to arrest even in the absence of exigent circumstances. At this time, 24 States permit such warrantless entries; 15 States clearly prohibit them, though 3 States do so on federal constitutional grounds alone; and 11 States have apparently taken no position on the question.

But these current figures reflect a significant decline during the last decade in the number of States permitting warrantless entries for arrest. Recent dicta in this Court raising questions about the practice . . . and Federal Courts of Appeals' decisions on point . . . have led state courts to focus on the issue. Virtually all of the state courts that have had to confront the constitutional issue directly have held warrantless entries into the home to arrest to be invalid in the absence of exigent circumstances. ... Three state courts have relied on Fourth Amendment grounds alone, while seven have squarely placed their decisions on both federal and state constitutional grounds. A number of other state courts, though not having had to confront the issue directly, have recognized the serious nature of the constitutional question. Apparently, only the Supreme Court of Florida and the New York Court of Appeals in this case have expressly upheld warrantless entries to arrest in the face of a constitutional challenge.

A longstanding, widespread practice is not immune from constitutional scrutiny. But neither is it to be lightly brushed aside. This is particularly so when the constitutional standard is as amorphous as the word "reasonable," and when custom and contemporary norms necessarily play such a large role in the constitutional analysis. In this case, although the weight of state-law authority is clear, there is by no means the kind of virtual unanimity on this question that was present in United States v. Watson, with regard to warrantless arrests in public places. Only 24 of the 50 States currently sanction warrantless entries into the home to arrest ... and there is an obvious declining trend. Further, the strength of the trend is greater than the numbers alone indicate. Seven state courts have recently held that warrantless home arrests violate their respective State constitutions. ... That is significant because by invoking a state constitutional provision, a state court immunizes its decision from review by this Court. This heightened degree of immutability underscores the depth of the principle underlying the result.

☐ CASE BRIEF—LEADING CASE ON THE USE BY POLICE OF DEADLY FORCE DURING ARREST

TENNESSEE V. GARNER, 53 L.W. 4410 (1985)

FACTS: Memphis police officers Hymon and Wright were dispatched to answer a "prowler inside" call. Upon arriving at the scene, they saw a woman standing on her porch and gesturing toward the adjacent house. She told them she had heard glass breaking and that someone was breaking in next door. While Wright radioed the dispatcher to say that they were on the scene, Hymon went behind the adjacent house. He heard a door slam and saw someone run across the back yard. The fleeing suspect, Edward Garner, stopped at a six-feet-high chain link fence at the edge of the yard. With the aid of a flashlight, Hymon was able to see Garner's face and hands. He saw no sign of a weapon, and, though not certain, was "reasonably sure" that Garner was unarmed. While Garner was crouched at the base of the fence, Hymon called out, "Police, halt," and took a few steps toward him. Garner then began to climb over the fence. Convinced that if Garner made it over the fence he would elude capture, Hymon shot him. Garner was taken by ambulance to a hospital, where he died. Ten dollars and a purse taken from the house were found on his body.

In using deadly force to prevent the escape, Hymon was acting under the authority of a Tennessee statute and pursuant to police department policy. That statute provides that "if after notice of the intention to arrest the defendant, he either flees or forcibly resists, the officer may use all the necessary means to effect the arrest." The department policy was slightly more restrictive than the statute but still allowed the use of deadly force in cases of burglary.

ISSUE: *Is the use of deadly force to prevent the escape of an apparently unarmed suspected felon constitutional? No.*

SUPREME COURT DECISION: The use of deadly force to prevent an escape of all felony suspects, whatever the circumstances, is constitutionally unreasonable. When the suspect poses no immediate threat to the officer and no threat to others, the use of deadly force is unjustified.

CASE SIGNIFICANCE: This case clarifies the extent to which the police can use deadly force to prevent the escape of an unarmed felon. The Court made it clear that deadly force may be used only if the officer has probable cause to believe that the suspect poses a threat of serious physical harm, either to the officer or to others. In addition, when feasible, the suspect must first be warned. The decision renders unconstitutional existing laws in nearly half of the states that impose no restrictions on the use by police officers of deadly force to prevent the escape of a person suspected of a felony.

State laws and departmental rules can set narrower limits on the use of force (as when the rules say that deadly force cannot be used at all except in self-defense, even when a suspected felon attempts to escape from the custody of a police officer), but broader limits are unconstitutional. The Court based its decision on the Fourth Amendment, saying that "there can be no question that apprehension by the use of deadly force is a seizure subject to the reasonableness requirement of the Fourth Amendment."

EXCERPTS FROM THE DECISION: The use of deadly force to prevent the escape of all felony suspects, whatever the circumstances, is constitutionally unreasonable. It is not better that all felony suspects die than that they escape. Where the suspect poses no immediate threat to the officer and no threat to others, the harm resulting from failing to apprehend him does not justify the use of deadly force to do so. It is no doubt unfortunate when a suspect who is in sight escapes, but the fact that the police arrive a little late or are a little slower afoot does not always justify killing the suspect. A police officer may not seize an unarmed, nondangerous suspect by shooting him dead. The Tennessee statute is unconstitutional insofar as it authorizes the use of deadly force against such fleeing suspects.

It is not, however, unconstitutional on its face. Where the officer has probable cause to believe that the suspect poses a threat of serious physical harm, either to the officer or to others, it is not constitutionally unreasonable to prevent escape by using deadly force. Thus, if the suspect threatens the officer with a weapon or there is probable cause to believe that he has committed a crime involving the infliction or threatened infliction of serious physical harm, deadly force may be used if necessary to prevent escape, and if, where feasible, some warning has been given. As applied in such circumstances, the Tennessee statute would pass constitutional muster.

In evaluating the reasonableness of police procedures under the Fourth Amendment, we have also looked to prevailing rules in individual jurisdictions. . . . The rules in the States are varied. . . . Some 19 States have codified the common-law rule, though in two of these the courts have significantly limited the statute. Four States, though without a relevant statute, apparently retain the common-law rule. Two States have adopted the Model Penal Code's provision verbatim. Eighteen others allow, in slightly varying language, the use of deadly force only if the suspect has committed a felony involving the use or threat of physical or deadly force, or is escaping with a deadly weapon, or is likely to endanger life or inflict serious physical injury if not arrested. Louisiana and Vermont, though without statutes or case law on point, do forbid the use of deadly force to prevent any but violent felonies. The remaining States either have no relevant statute or case law, or have positions that are unclear.

It cannot be said that there is a constant or overwhelming trend away from the common-law rule. In recent years, some States have reviewed their laws and expressly rejected abandonment of the common-law rule. Nonetheless, the long-term movement has been away from the rule that deadly force may be used against any fleeing felon, and that remains the rule in less than half the States.

This trend is more evident and impressive when viewed in light of the policies adopted by the police departments themselves. Overwhelmingly, these are more restrictive than the common-law rule. For accreditation by the Commission on Accreditation for Law Enforcement Agencies, a department must restrict the use of deadly force to situations where "the officer reasonably believes that the action is in defense of human life . . . or in defense of any person in immediate danger of serious physical injury." Commission on Accreditation for Law Enforcement Agencies, Inc., Standards for Law Enforcement Agencies 1–2 (1983). A 1974 study reported that the police department regulations in a majority of the large cities of the United States allowed the firing of a weapon only when a felon presented a threat of death or serious bodily harm. . . . Overall, only 7.5% of departmental and municipal policies explicitly permit the use of deadly force against any felon; 86.8% explicitly do not. . . . In light of the rules adopted by those who must actually administer them, the older and fading common-law view is a dubious indicium of the constitutionality of the Tennessee statute now before us.

☐ NOTES

1. John G. Miles, Jr., David B. Richardson, and Anthony E. Scudellari, *The Law Officer's Pocket Manual* (Washington, DC: Bureau of National Affairs, 1988–89), at 6:1.
2. *Black's Law Dictionary* (St. Paul, MN: West, 1968), at 1756.
3. Miles, op. cit., at 6:16.
4. *Black's,* op. cit., at 261.
5. Miles, op. cit., at 6:11–6:12.
6. S. Emmanuel and S. Knowles, *Emmanuel Law Outlines* (Larchmont, NY: Emmanuel Law Outlines, Inc., 1989–1990), at 59.
7. Ibid., at 62.
8. W. LaFave and J. Israel, *Criminal Procedure* (St. Paul, MN: West, 1985), at 147.
9. This discussion of the Tennessee v. Garner case on the police use of deadly force in arrest cases is taken from Chapter 7 of R. V. del Carmen, *Civil Liabilities in American Policing* (Englewood Cliffs, NJ: Prentice-Hall, in press).
10. J. C. Hall, "Police Use of Deadly Force to Arrest: A Constitutional Standard" (Part II), *FBI Law Enforcement Bulletin,* July 1988, at 23.

11. Americans for Effective Law Enforcement, *Legal Defense Manual,* Brief No. 85-4, at 13.
12. Hall, op. cit., at 27–28.
13. This discussion of the Graham v. Connor case is taken from Chapter 7 of R. V. del Carmen, *Civil Liabilities in American Policing* (Englewood Cliffs, NJ: Prentice-Hall, in press).

CHAPTER SEVEN

SEARCHES AND SEIZURES

V. OTHER SEARCH AND SEIZURE ISSUES

A. Drug-Testing Police Officers as a Form of Search and Seizure: Is It Constitutional?—No Authoritative Answer

B. Searches of Employee Office—Generally No Need for Warrant

C. Searches and Seizures by Private Persons—No Need for Warrant

D. Searches by Government Agents of Same Material Searched by Private Parties—No Need for Warrant

E. Search by "Off-Duty" Officer—Considered a Government Search

F. Use of Police Dogs for Detection of Drugs—Not Considered a Search

G. Use of Pen Registers—Not Considered a Search

H. Searches of Nonresident Alien in Foreign Country—Fourth Amendment Does Not Apply

VI. GUIDE TO UNDERSTANDING SEARCH AND SEIZURE CASES

Summary
Review Questions
Definitions
Principles of Cases
Case Briefs
     Coolidge v. New Hampshire
     Maryland v. Garrison

☐ KEY TERMS

search	contemporaneous search
seizure	reasonable expectation of
search warrant	privacy
probable cause	"special needs" exception
"no knock" searches	exigent circumstances
anticipatory search warrant	administrative searches

I. INTRODUCTION

The Fourth Amendment to the U.S. Constitution provides:

> The right of the people to be secure in their persons, houses, papers, and effects, against unreasonable searches and seizures, shall not be violated, and no Warrants shall issue, but upon probable cause, supported by Oath or affirmation, and particularly describing the place to be searched, and the persons or things to be seized.

The general rule is that searches and seizures can be made only by virtue of a warrant; therefore, *warrantless searches and seizures are exceptions to the general rule.* In the words of the Court, "the most basic constitutional rule . . . is that 'searches conducted outside the judicial process, without prior approval by judge or magistrate, are per se unreasonable under the Fourth Amendment—subject only to a few specifically established and well-delineated exceptions' " (Katz v. U.S., 389 U.S. 347 [1967]).

In reality, most searches and seizures are made without a warrant. Nonetheless, police officers must always be aware of the general rule so that warrantless searches are made only if justified under one of the exceptions. In the words of the Court, "The point of the Fourth Amendment, which often is not grasped by zealous officers, is not that it denies law enforcement the support of the usual inferences which reasonable men draw from evidence. Its protection consists in requiring that those inferences be drawn by a neutral and detached magistrate instead of being judged by the officer engaged in the often competitive enterprise of ferreting out crime" (Johnson v. U.S., 333 U.S. 10 [1948]). The term *search and seizure* often conveys the impression that it represents one and the same act. Search and seizure are in fact two separate acts, each with its own meaning.

A. Search Defined

A *search* is defined as any governmental intrusion into a person's reasonable and justifiable expectation of privacy. It is not limited to homes, offices, buildings, or other enclosed places. Rather, it can occur in any place where a person has a *"reasonable and justifiable expectation of privacy,"* even if the place is in a public area (meaning a place to which anyone has access) (Katz v. U.S., 389 U.S. 347 [1967]). For example, police installed a peephole in the ceiling of a public restroom to allow them to observe what occurred in the stalls. Officers observed two people engaging in illegal sexual acts in one of the stalls. What the officers did without a warrant was illegal because the two people involved had a reasonable expectation of privacy, meaning that they could reasonably expect that their acts would not be observed by others even though the restroom was in a public place. The evidence obtained was not admissible in court.

In another case, the Court held that no search occurs when an undercover officer examines the wares offered for sale in an "adult" bookstore, nor is the officer's purchase of some of those wares a seizure; hence no warrant is needed (Maryland v. Macon, 37 CrL 3111 [1985]). The Macon case settled an issue that had featured conflicting decisions in state courts. A police detective entered a bookstore, browsed for a few minutes, and then bought two magazines. He left the store, read the magazines with two other detectives, and concluded that the magazines were obscene. Without a warrant, the trio entered the store and arrested the clerk. At the clerk's trial for obscenity, the state introduced the magazines as evidence. The trial court said that the police needed a warrant to take the magazines and arrest the defendant operator and therefore excluded the evidence. The Supreme Court disagreed, saying that "a search occurs when the expectation of privacy that society is prepared to consider reasonable is infringed." The detective's entry of the bookstore and examination of its publicly displayed wares was held not to constitute a search under this test. The Court added: "The mere expectation that the possibly illegal nature of a product will not come to the attention of the authorities, whether because a customer will not complain or because undercover officers will not transact business with the store, is not one that society is prepared to recognize as reasonable." There was therefore no reasonable expectation of privacy.

B. Seizure Defined

A *seizure* is defined as *the exercise of dominion or control by the government over a person or thing because of a violation of law.* In the Macon case, above, the Court said that "a seizure occurs when there is some meaningful interference with an individual's possessory interests in the property seized." The Court held, however, that there was no interference with possessory interests amounting to a seizure in Macon because the defendant voluntarily transferred to the detective any possessory interest he held in the magazines.

The law on search and seizure is best understood if classified into two categories: *search and seizure with warrant* and *search and seizure without warrant.*

C. Items Subject to Search and Seizure

There are generally four types of items that can be searched and seized:

1. Contraband, such as drugs, counterfeit money, and gambling paraphernalia. With limited exceptions, these items are illegal for anybody to possess.

HIGHLIGHT 7.1

What the Fourth Amendment Protects

"The Fourth Amendment protects people, not places. What a person knowingly exposes to the public, even in his own home or office, is not a subject of Fourth Amendment protection. . . . But what he seeks to preserve as private even in an area accessible to the public, may be constitutionally protected" (Katz v. U.S., 389 U.S. 347 [1967]).

---

2. Fruits of the crime, such as stolen goods and forged checks.
3. Instrumentalities of the crime, such as weapons and burglary tools.
4. "Mere evidence" of the crime, such as a suspect's clothing containing bloodstains of the victim, suspect's mask, shoes, wig, and so on, provided there is probable cause to believe that the item is related to criminal activity.

These are merely general categories of items officers may search and seize. In many states, the law enumerates in detail the items subject to search and seizure. Whatever the listing, the likelihood is that an item listed will fall into one of the four categories just mentioned.

II. SEARCH AND SEIZURE WITH WARRANT

A *search warrant* is defined as *a written order, issued by a magistrate, directing a peace officer to search for property connected with a crime and bring it before the court.* In nearly all states, the police officer seeking a search warrant must state the facts establishing probable cause in a written and signed affidavit. The general rule is that a search or seizure is valid under the Fourth Amendment only if made with a warrant. Searches without warrant may be valid but they are the exception rather than the rule.

A. Requirements

There are four basic requirements for the valid issuance of a search warrant: (1) statement of probable cause, (2) supporting oath or affirmation, (3) particular description of the place to be searched and the things to be seized, and (4) signature of a magistrate.

1. Probable Cause

The conditions required to establish probable cause are discussed more extensively in Chapter Four. For our purposes here, it is sufficient to restate the definition of probable cause used in Chapter Four. *Probable cause is more than bare suspicion; it exists when the facts and circumstances within the officers' knowledge and of which they have reasonably trustworthy information are sufficient in themselves to warrant a person of reasonable caution in the belief that an offense has been or is being committed.* In searches and seizures (as contrasted with arrests), the issue of probable cause focuses on whether the *property* to be seized is connected with criminal activity and whether it can be found in the place to be searched.

2. Supporting Oath or Affirmation

A *search warrant* is issued on the basis of a sworn affidavit presented to the magistrate and establishing grounds for the warrant. The magistrate issues the warrant only if he or she is satisfied upon the affidavit that probable cause for a warrant exists. The contents of the affidavit must be sufficient to allow an independent evaluation of probable cause by the magistrate. To enable the magistrate to make an independent evaluation, the affidavit must contain more than mere conclusions by the police officer. It must allege facts showing that seizable evidence will be found in the place to be

THE STATE OF TEXAS
COUNTY OF _____   AFFIDAVIT FOR THE ISSUANCE OF A SEARCH WARRANT

THE UNDERSIGNED AFFIANT, BEING A PEACE OFFICER UNDER THE LAWS OF TEXAS AND BEING DULY SWORN, ON OATH MAKES THE FOLLOWING STATEMENTS AND ACCUSATIONS.

1. THERE IS IN _____ COUNTY, TEXAS A SUSPECTED PLACE DESCRIBED AND LOCATED AS FOLLOWS:

2. SAID SUSPECTED PLACE IS IN CHARGE OF AND CONTROLLED BY EACH OF THE FOLLOWING NAMED PARTIES (HEREAFTER CALLED "SUSPECTED PARTY" WHETHER ONE OR MORE) TO WIT:

3. IT IS THE BELIEF OF AFFIANT, AND AFFIANT HEREBY CHARGES AND ACCUSES THAT SAID SUSPECTED PARTY HAS POSSESSION OF AND IS CONCEALING AT SAID SUSPECTED PLACE IN VIOLATION OF THE LAWS OF TEXAS THE FOLLOWING DESCRIBED PERSONAL PROPERTY, TO WIT:

4. AFFIANT HAS PROBABLE CAUSE FOR THE SAID BELIEF BY REASON OF THE FOLLOWING FACTS, TO WIT:

WHEREFORE, AFFIANT ASKS FOR ISSUANCE OF A WARRANT THAT WILL AUTHORIZE THE SEARCH OF SAID SUSPECTED PLACE FOR SAID PERSONAL PROPERTY AND SEIZE THE SAME AND TO ARREST EACH SAID SUSPECTED PARTY, AND TO TAKE CUSTODY OF ALL SEIZED PROPERTY AND SAFEKEEP SUCH PROPERTY AS PROVIDED BY STATUTE.

_____
AFFIANT

SUBSCRIBED AND SWORN TO BEFORE ME BY SAID AFFIANT ON THIS THE _____ DAY OF _____, A.D., 19_____.

_____
MAGISTRATE

searched. The affidavit may be filed by the police officer or the offended or injured party. A warrant may be issued on the basis of affidavits containing only hearsay as long as there is probable cause.

There is no constitutional requirement for a warrant application to be in writing. In many jurisdictions, a warrant may be issued based on an oral statement, either in person or by telephone. The oral statement is usually recorded and becomes the basis for a probable cause determination.

To be valid, the warrant must be based on fresh information. If the information is "stale," the warrant lacks probable cause and is invalid (U.S. v. Leon, 468 U.S. 897 [1984]). In the Leon case, the information contained in the affidavit was given

SEARCH WARRANT

SEARCH WARRANT FOR   DRUGS

THE STATE OF TEXAS |

                            | To the Sheriff or Any Peace Officer of _____

COUNTY OF _____ | County, Texas, GREETINGS:

Whereas, complaint in writing, under oath has been made before me by _____

which complaint is hereto attached and expressly made a part hereof alleging that on or about the _____ day of

_____ , A.D. 19 _____ , in the _____ County, Texas,

one _____

_____

did then and there unlawfully possess and does at this time unlawfully possess a controlled substance, to-wit: _____

_____

and further that he has cause to believe that the said controlled substance are now concealed by _____

_____

_____

_____

_____

_____

situated in _____ County, Texas, located _____

_____

_____

which said _____

now possess, occupies, controls and has charge of.

And after examining the said complaint in writing and under oath, I have determined that the said complaint does state

facts and information sufficient to establish probable cause for the issuance of this warrant to search for and seize the said

controlled substance in accordance with the law in such cases provided.

YOU ARE THEREFORE COMMANDED TO FORTHWITH SEARCH THE PLACE ABOVE NAMED AND DESCRIBED WHERE

THE SAID CONTROLLED SUBSTANCE, TO-WIT: _____

are alleged to be concealed, and if you find such controlled substance or any portion thereof, you will seize the same and bring it before

me at my office, situated at_____ County, Texas, on the _____ day of _____ A.D.19 _____.

AND, you are commanded to arrest and bring before me, at said place and time, the said: _____

_____

_____

accused of the possession of the said controlled substance.

HEREIN FAIL NOT, AND DUE RETURN MAKE HEREOF TO ME AT THE TIME AND PLACE ABOVE NAMED.

by the police officer to the magistrate in September 1981. It was based partially on
information the officer obtained from a confidential informant in August 1981. The
Court said that "to the extent that the affidavit set forth facts demonstrating the basis

of the informant's knowledge of criminal activity, the information included was fatally stale." The reason for the "fresh information" rule is that conditions change fast and that an item found in one place may not in fact be there when the warrant is issued. How much time should elapse before an information becomes stale is not known. It is safe to assume, however, that, as one writer states, "the longer the delay, the greater the chance that the information will be 'stale.' "[1]

3. Particular Description of Place to Be Searched and Persons or Things to Be Seized

a. Place. The warrant must remove any doubt or uncertainty about which premises are to be searched. For example, if the premises are an apartment in a multiple-dwelling apartment house, the warrant must specify which apartment is to be searched. The address of the apartment building is not sufficient. An exact address prevents confusion and mistakes that intrude on the privacy of innocent persons.

In one case, however, the Court said that the validity of a warrant must be judged in light of the "information available to the officers at the time they obtained the warrant" (Maryland v. Garrison, 55 L.W. 4190 [1987]). In this case, police officers obtained a warrant to search "the premises known as 2036 Park Avenue, third floor apartment" for drugs and drug paraphernalia that supposedly belonged to a person named McWebb. The police reasonably believed there was only one apartment at that location. In fact, there were two apartments on the third floor, one belonging to McWebb and the other belonging to Garrison. Before the officers became aware that they were in Garrison's apartment instead of McWebb's, they searched the apartment and discovered drugs that provided the basis for Garrison's subsequent conviction. Garrison sought exclusion of the evidence, saying that the search warrant was so unnecessarily broad as to allow the search of the wrong apartment. The Court admitted the evidence, however, saying that the validity of a warrant must be judged in light of the information available to the officers when the warrant is sought. Therefore, a warrant that is overly broad in describing the place to be searched is not in violation of the Fourth Amendment *if it was based on a reasonable but mistaken belief* at the time the warrant was issued. (Read the Maryland v. Garrison case brief at the end of this chapter.)

Relying on the Maryland v. Garrison case, the Fourth Circuit Court of Appeals has said that the execution of a warrant for a different apartment than that named in the warrant was valid because there were only two apartments on the floor, one of which was vacant. Moreover, the correct apartment was readily ascertainable and the mistake (which in this case was a reliance on utility company information) was reasonable and in good faith (U.S. v. Owens, 848 F.2d 462 [4th Cir. 1988]).

b. Things. Items for seizure must also be described with sufficient particularity that the officer will have to exercise little discretion over what may be seized. For example, the warrant cannot simply provide for the seizure of "stolen goods" since this language is too general and can lead to a "fishing expedition." An acceptable identification would be "a 25-inch Zenith television set." Contraband, however, does not have to be described with as much particularity because it is in itself seizable. So the words "cocaine" or "prohibited substances" would be sufficient.

4. Signature of a Magistrate

As in the cases of arrest warrants, search warrants must be issued only by a "neutral and detached" magistrate. The Court has said: "Inferences must be drawn by a neutral and detached magistrate instead of being judged by the officer engaged in the often competitive enterprise of ferreting out crime" (Johnson v. U.S., 333 U.S. 10, at 14 [1948]).

> Example 1: A magistrate who receives a fee when issuing a warrant but not when denying one is not neutral and detached (Connally v. Georgia, 429 U.S. 245 [1977]).

> Example 2: A magistrate who participates in the search to determine its scope lacks the requisite neutrality and detachment (Lo-Ji Sales, Inc. v. New York, 442 U.S. 319 [1979]).

> Example 3: The state's chief investigator and prosecutor (state attorney general) is not neutral and detached; therefore any warrant issued by him or her is invalid (Coolidge v. New Hampshire, 403 U.S. 443 [1971]).

B. Procedure for Service of Warrant

The search warrant is directed to a law enforcement officer and must state the grounds for issuance and the names of those who gave affidavits in support of it. The execution of a warrant is specified in detail by state law, usually in the state's code of criminal procedures.

The warrant usually directs that it be served in the daytime, but if the affidavits are positive that the property is on the person or in the place to be searched, the warrant may direct that it be served at any time. Some states, by law, authorize night searches. The warrant must designate the judge or magistrate to whom the warrant is to be returned. It must be executed and delivered within a specified number of days from the date of issuance. Some states specify ten days; others allow less time. *If the search warrant is not served during that time, it expires and can no longer be served.* Note that *search warrants differ in this respect from arrest warrants, which are usually valid until served.* The officer executing the warrant must give a copy of the warrant and a receipt for any seized property to the person from whom it is taken or must leave a copy and receipt on the premises. A written inventory must be made, and the officer's report, accompanied by the inventory, must be submitted promptly.

HIGHLIGHT 7.2

Determining the Validity of a Warrant

"Just as the discovery of contraband cannot validate a warrant invalid when issued, so it is equally clear that the discovery of facts demonstrating that a valid warrant was unnecessarily broad does not retroactively invalidate the warrant. The validity of the warrant must be assessed on the basis of information that the officers disclosed, or had a duty to discover and to disclose, to the issuing magistrate" (Maryland v. Garrison, 55 L.W. 4190 [1987]).

C. Announcement Requirement

The rule about *announcements* in searches and seizures is the same as the one that pertains to arrests. Federal and many state statutes require that an officer making an arrest or executing a search warrant announce his or her purpose and authority before breaking into a dwelling. The idea is to allow voluntary compliance and avoid violence. Breaking into the premises without first complying with the announcement requirement may or may not invalidate the entry and any resulting search, depending upon the law or court decisions in that state. Some states invalidate the entry and resulting search, others do not. *There is no constitutional requirement that an announcement must be made before entry.*

In some cases, because of exigent circumstances, an announcement is not required. These are the usual instances:

1. When announcing presents a strong threat of violence or danger to the officer.
2. When there is danger that contraband or other property might be destroyed. Some states permit a magistrate to issue so-called *"no knock" searches*, particularly in drug cases. They authorize entry without announcement. The constitutionality of such statutes has not been fully tested, although they have been upheld by the lower courts.
3. When officers reasonably believe that the persons within the premises are in imminent peril of bodily harm.
4. When persons within are reasonably believed to be engaged in the process of destroying evidence or escaping because they are aware of the presence of the police.
5. When the person to be arrested is in the process of committing the crime.

Exceptions to the announcement requirement are usually governed by state law, state court decisions, and agency regulations. They therefore vary from state to state.

D. Scope of Search and Seizure

The scope and manner of the search must be reasonable; that is, the officer's actions must be *reasonable in terms of the object of the search.* A wise legal maxim for officers to remember is: *"It is unreasonable for a police officer to look for an elephant in a matchbox."* For example, a search warrant is issued for the recovery of a stolen 25-inch Zenith TV set. In looking for the TV set, the officer cannot open lockers and drawers—unless, of course, the locker or drawer is big enough to contain the TV set. On the other hand, if the search warrant is for the confiscation of heroin, then the officer is justified in opening lockers and drawers in the course of the search. It therefore follows that the smaller the item sought, the more extensive the scope of allowable search.

While the search is being conducted, the police may detain persons who are in the premises to be searched (Michigan v. Summers, 452 U.S. 692 [1981]). But although the officer may detain persons in the premises to be searched, the search warrant does not authorize the police to search persons found on the premises who are not named in the warrant (Ybarra v. Illinois, 444 U.S. 85 [1979]).

Searches of property belonging to persons not suspected of crime are permissible as long as probable cause exists to believe that evidence of someone's guilt or other items subject to seizure will be found. For example, a demonstration occurs in which police officers are hurt. The police cannot identify their attackers, but they know a newspaper staff photographer took photographs of the demonstration. The police may get a warrant to search the newspaper's offices provided that probable cause exists that evidence of someone's guilt may be found (Zurcher v. Stanford Daily, 436 U.S. 547 [1978]).

E. Amount of Time Allowed for Search

The search cannot last indefinitely even if it is by virtue of a warrant. Once the item mentioned in the warrant has been recovered, the search should cease. Continued search without justification takes the nature of a "fishing expedition" for evidence and is illegal. An illegal search is not justified by what turns up. For example, the police go to an apartment to execute a search for a shotgun allegedly used in a murder. After the shotgun is recovered, the police continue to search for other evidence in connection with the murder. They open a bedroom closet and find a pair of bloodied jeans used by the suspect during the murder. The bloodied jeans, if seized and used in evidence, will not be admissible because they were illegally obtained. Note, however, that items in plain view in the course of executing the warrant can be seized by the police because "plain view" items do not come under the Fourth Amendment protection.

F. Anticipatory Search Warrant

An *anticipatory search warrant* is a warrant obtained based on probable cause and on an expectation that seizable items will be found at a certain place at a certain time. An article in the *FBI Law Enforcement Bulletin* characterizes the warrant in this manner:

> Where officers have probable cause to believe that evidence or contraband will arrive at a certain location within a reasonable period of time, they need not wait until delivery before requesting a warrant. Instead, officers may present this probable cause to a magistrate before the arrival of that evidence, and the magistrate can issue an anticipatory search warrant based on probable cause that the evidence will be found at the location to be searched at the time the warrant is executed.[2]

The same article maintains that although the Supreme Court has not resolved the constitutionality of anticipatory warrants, "the vast majority of State and Federal courts that have considered this question have concluded that anticipatory warrants are constitutional and consistent with the longstanding preference that whenever possible, police obtain judicial approval before searching."[3] There is nothing, however, that requires a magistrate to issue anticipatory warrants, and therefore its issuance

---

HIGHLIGHT 7.3

Search Maxim

A wise legal maxim for officers to remember when making searches is: "It is unreasonable for an officer to look for an elephant in a matchbox."

---

is a matter of a magistrate's discretion. But, should the magistrate decide to issue it, such issuance would most likely be valid.

III. SEARCH AND SEIZURE WITHOUT WARRANT

Although the general rule is that searches and seizures must be made on the authority of a warrant, most searches and seizures, like most arrests, by the police are in fact made without a warrant. Warrantless searches incident to arrest in themselves greatly outnumber searches made with warrant. In searches and seizures without a warrant, the burden is on the police to prove in court, if the legality of the search or seizure is challenged, that probable cause existed at the time the warrantless search or seizure was made. It is therefore essential for the law enforcement officer to be thoroughly familiar with the law on warrantless searches and seizures. Generally, there are six exceptions to the rule that searches and seizures must be made with a warrant:

1. the "searches incident to lawful arrest" exception (discussed in this chapter)
2. the "search with consent" exception (discussed in this chapter)
3. the "special needs beyond law enforcement" exception (discussed in this chapter)
4. the "presence of exigent circumstances" exception (discussed in this chapter)
5. the "stop and frisk" exception (discussed in Chapter Five)
6. the "motor vehicles" exception (discussed in Chapter Eight)

A. The "Searches Incident to Lawful Arrest" Exception

As an exception to the warrant requirement, search incident to lawful arrest is widely used because it is invoked just about every time an officer makes an arrest, with or without a warrant. There are two requirements for this search to be valid:

1. The *arrest itself must be lawful*, meaning that there must be an arrest warrant based on probable cause, or the arresting officer must have had probable cause to make the arrest without a warrant.
2. The *search must be limited in scope*, meaning that the search is reasonably required to protect the arresting officer from a possibly armed suspect or to prevent the destruction of evidence.

1. Arrest of Suspect: Search of Area within Immediate Control Permitted

The leading case on warrantless search incident to arrest in Chimel v. California, 395 U.S. 752 (1969), discussed in the chapter on arrest. In Chimel, the Court said:

> When an arrest is made, it is reasonable for the arresting officer to search the person arrested in order to remove any weapons that the latter might seek to use in order to resist arrest or effect his escape. . . . In addition, it is entirely reasonable for the arresting officer to search for and seize any evidence on the arrestee's person in order to prevent its concealment or destruction.

There are therefore three justifications for warrantless searches incident to arrest: (1) officer safety, (2) to prevent escape, and (3) to prevent concealment or destruction of evidence. The authorization to search incident to arrest is always available to the officer after an arrest, meaning that it can be exercised even if there is no probable cause to believe that it is necessary for officer safety, to prevent escape, or to prevent concealment or destruction of evidence. The authorization is automatic whenever an arrest is made. Therefore, searches incident to arrest constitute an *exception* to the Fourth Amendment that (1) searches must be made by virtue of a warrant, and that (2) searches must be based on probable cause.

2. Chimel Applied to Car Searches

The Chimel principle that a warrantless search incident to arrest must be limited to areas within the suspect's immediate control has been largely abandoned in arrests involving automobile occupants. The Court has held that when the police have made a lawful custodial arrest of the occupant of a car, they may, incident to that arrest, search the car's entire passenger compartment (front and back seats) and open any containers found in the compartment (New York v. Belton, 435 U.S. 454 [1981]).

3. Warrantless Search Must Be Contemporaneous

The search must occur at the same time as, or very close in time and place to, the arrest. A search conducted long after the arrest is illegal. In one case, the police arrested several smugglers and seized the footlocker in which the police thought the marijuana was being transported. One hour after the arrest and after the suspects were in jail, the officers opened and searched the footlocker without a warrant. The Court invalidated the search, saying that it was "remote in time and place from the arrest" (U.S. v. Chadwick, 433 U.S. 1 [1977]). However, the custodial search may be deemed "incident to arrest" even when carried out later than the time of arrest if there was valid reason for the delay. For example, a suspect was arrested and jailed late at night. A clothing search for evidence was not conducted until the following morning. The Court said that the delayed search was justified because substitute clothing was not available for use at the time of the booking (U.S. v. Edwards, 415 U.S. 800 [1974]).

B. The "Searches with Consent" Exception

Warrantless searches with consent are valid, but the consent must be *voluntary* and *intelligent.* Police must show that the accused's consent was not the result of force or coercion and that the accused knew what he or she was doing. Voluntariness and intelligence are determined by looking at the *totality of circumstances.* For example, consent given only after the officer demands entry cannot be deemed to be free and voluntary. "Open the door" will most likely be interpreted by the courts as giving the occupant no choice and therefore making the consent involuntary. The better practice is for the officer to "request" rather than "demand." Words such as "Would you mind if I come in and look around?" are more likely to result in voluntary consent.

Mere silence or failure to object to a search does not necessarily mean consent. The consent must be clear. A shrug of the shoulder may signify indifference or resignation rather than consent. In one case, the Ninth Circuit Court of Appeals said that there was no valid consent where the resident opened his door, stepped into the

VOLUNTARY CONSENT FOR SEARCH AND SEIZURE

Date: _____

I, _____ , having been informed of my con-

stitutional right not to have a search made of the premises hereinafter mentioned without

a search warrant and of my right to refuse to consent to such a search, hereby authorize

_____ and _____ ,

Police Officers of the Houston Police Department, to conduct a complete search of my

residence located at _____. These

officers are authorized by me to take from my residence any letters, papers, materials, or

other property which they may desire. This written permission is being given by me to the

above named officers voluntarily and without threats or promises of any kind and is given

with my full and free consent.

_____
(Signed)

WITNESSES:

_____

_____

Form No. NAR-0009

---

hallway, listened to the officers identify themselves and explain the purpose of their visit, and then retreated wordlessly back into the apartment without closing the door (U.S. v. Shaibu, 43 CrL 1470 [9th Cir. 1990]). The government in this case failed to meet its heavy burden of proving consent, by merely showing that the defendant left his door open.

Consent given by a child will not likely be considered intelligent or voluntary and hence is invalid. For example, the police knock at an apartment door. A ten-year-old boy opens the door. The officers ask if his parents are in. When told that the parents are out, the officers ask if they could "look around"—to which the boy willingly consents. The officers look around and find drugs on the kitchen table. The consent is invalid, the search illegal, and the evidence not admissible in court.

There is no valid consent if permission is given as a result of police misrepresentation or deception, such as saying, "We have a warrant," when in fact none exists (Bumper v. North Carolina, 391 U.S. 543 [1968]). Lower courts are divided on the issue of whether consent is valid if the officer does not have a warrant but threatens to obtain one. The issue has not been resolved by the Supreme Court.

Consent to enter does not necessarily mean consent to search. For example, consent to enter for purposes of asking some questions does not mean consent to search. However, any seizable item in "plain view" after valid entry may be properly seized.

Warning of rights is not required. There is no need for the police to prove that the person who gave consent knew he or she could have refused permission. What is needed is merely that the consent was given voluntarily (meaning that it was given out of free will) and intelligently. There is no need, either, for the police to have the occupant sign a consent form to prove that consent was in fact given. Many police departments do require signing a consent form as a matter of policy, not because they are legally obliged to do so but to make it easier to prove consent if they are later challenged in court.

The scope of allowable search depends upon type of consent given. For example, the statement "You may look around" does not authorize the opening of closets, drawers, trunks, and boxes. Consent given may be revoked at any time, even in the course of a search, by the person giving it. But any evidence obtained before revocation is admissible.

Who May Give Consent to Search?

1. *Landlord—no.* A landlord cannot give valid consent to search property that he or she has rented to another person (Stoner v. California, 376 U.S. 483 [1964]).

2. *Hotel clerk—no.* A hotel clerk cannot give consent to the search of a guest's room (Stoner v. California, 376 U.S. 483 [1964]).

3. *Family members—yes.* A wife or a husband can give effective consent to search the family home. There is no clear rule as to whether or not parents can give consent to search the room of a child who lives with them. Lower court decisions tend to say that parents may give consent to search the room of their minor children, but not if the minor child is paying room and board to the parents. On the other hand, in most states a child cannot validly give consent to a search of his parents' home. Whether or not adult offspring who live with their parents can give consent to search their parents' home has not been clearly addressed by the courts.

4. *College and university administrators—no.* Most lower courts hold that college administrators (dormitory managers, etc.) cannot give consent for the police to search a student's dormitory room. The fact that some resident or dormitory managers may enter a student's room for certain purposes (such as health and safety) does not mean that they can give consent. This issue, however, has not been authoritatively settled by the Supreme Court.

5. *High school administrators—yes.* Most lower courts hold that high school administrators, given proper circumstances, may give consent for the police to search a high school student's locker. This is so because high school students are considered wards of the school; therefore the authority given to high school administrators is greater than that afforded to their college counterparts.

6. *Business employer—no.* If the property is under the exclusive use and control of the employee, the employer cannot give valid consent to search (U.S. v. Bok, 188 F.2d 1019 [DC Cir. 1951]). For example, a department store supervisor cannot give consent to search an employee's desk if only the employee is using it. By the same token, a college dean or department head should not be able to give consent for the police to search a desk given to a faculty member for his or her exclusive use.

7. *Business employee—no.* Unless specifically authorized, a business employee cannot consent to the search of his or her employer's business premises. Although the employee may have access to the property, he or she does not own it.

8. *Roommate—yes.* A roommate may give valid consent to search the room. That consent, however, *cannot extend to areas in which another roommate has a reasonable expectation of privacy* because only he or she uses it. For example, X gives consent for the police to search the room X and Y occupy. That consent is valid with respect to all areas that both X and Y use, such as the bathroom or study table. The consent is not valid for the search of Y's closet, to which only Y has access. If Y lives in another room (as in a multiroom apartment), X cannot give consent to search the room used only by Y.

9. *Former girlfriend whom police reasonably believe to possess common authority over premises but who in fact does not have such authority—yes.* The Court has held that the warrantless entry of private premises by police officers is valid if based on the consent of a third party whom the police, at the time of entry, reasonably believed to possess common authority over the premises, but who in fact did not have such authority (Illinois v. Rodriguez, 58 L.W. 4892 [1990]). In that case, Rodriguez was arrested in his apartment and charged with possession of illegal drugs that the police said were in plain view on entry. The police gained entry into Rodriguez's apartment with the assistance of Gail Fischer, who represented that the apartment was "ours" and that she had clothes and furniture there. She unlocked the door with her key and gave the officers permission to enter. In reality, Fischer had moved out of the apartment and therefore no longer had any common authority over the apartment. The Court nonetheless held the consent given by Fischer to be valid because the police reasonably believed, given the circumstances, that she had the authority to give consent.

C. The "Special Needs beyond Law Enforcement" Exception

The Court has carved out, comparatively recently, a series of exceptions to the warrant requirement based on what it terms the *"special needs* beyond the normal need for law enforcement" situations. In these cases, the Court has consistently held that (1) these types of searches may be made without a warrant, and (2) on less than probable cause. What these cases have in common is that they are not purely police cases, but instead involve other public agencies that perform tasks closely related to law enforcement. Examples are school searches, searches of prisoners, and searches of probationers and parolees.

1. School Searches

In a 1983 decision, the Court resolved an issue that had long bothered students, public school teachers, and administrators. Voting 6 to 3, the Court said that public school teachers and administrators do not need a warrant or probable cause to believe that a student is violating the law or school rule before searching that student. What is needed is *reasonable grounds* for suspecting that the search will turn up evidence that the student has violated or is violating either the law or the rules of the school (New Jersey v. T.L.O., 53 L.W. 4083 [1985]). In this case, a teacher at a New Jersey high school discovered a student and her companion smoking cigarettes in a school lavatory in violation of the school rule. She took them to the principal's office, where they met with the assistant vice principal. When the student denied that she had been smoking, the assistant vice principal demanded to see her purse. On opening the purse, he found a pack of cigarettes and also noticed a package of cigarette-rolling papers, which are commonly associated with the use of marijuana. He then proceeded to search the purse thoroughly and found marijuana, a pipe, plastic bags, a fairly substantial amount of money, and other items that implicated her in marijuana dealing. She moved to suppress the evidence in juvenile court, alleging that the search was illegal for lack of probable cause and a warrant.

The Court rejected her allegation, saying that the Fourth Amendment prohibition against unreasonable searches and seizures applies to searches conducted by public school officials, but the school's legitimate need to maintain a learning environment requires some easing of the Fourth Amendment restrictions. Therefore, public school officials do not need a warrant or probable cause to conduct a search. All they need is *reasonable grounds* to suspect that the search will turn up evidence that the student has violated or is violating either the law or the rules of the school.

The T.L.O. ruling just discussed applies only to public school teachers and administrators. It does not apply to police officers who are bound by the "probable cause and warrant" requirements even in school searches. The only possible exception is if the officers are to perform the search at the request of school authorities. The T.L.O. ruling does not apply to college or university students either because unlike high school or elementary school students for whom school teachers and administrators serve *in loco parentis* (in place of parents), college students are considered adults and therefore entitled to undiminished constitutional rights.

HIGHLIGHT 7.4

The "Special Needs" Exception to Judicial Warrants

"Except in certain well-defined circumstances, a search or seizure in such a case is not reasonable unless it is accomplished pursuant to a judicial warrant issued upon probable cause. We have recognized exceptions to this rule, however, 'when special needs beyond the normal need for law enforcement, make the warrant and probable cause requirement impracticable' " (Skinner v. Railway Labor Executives Association, 109 S.Ct. 1402 [1989]).

---

2. Searches of Prisoners and Detainees

The Fourth Amendment offers an inmate absolutely no protection against unreasonable searches and seizures in his or her cell because the inmate has no reasonable expectation of privacy there. The right to privacy is fundamentally incompatible with the close and continual surveillance of inmates and their cells required to ensure institutional security and internal order. In the words of Justice O'Connor, "All searches and seizures of the contents of an inmate's cell are reasonable" (Hudson v. Palmer, 35 CrL 3230 [1984]). Necessary surveillance does not, however, legitimize harassment tactics by prison guards. Such tactics are subject to redress in state courts.

Strip searches and body cavity searches sometimes occur in prisons or jails. The rule is that they are permissible so long as they are conducted in a reasonable manner and are justified under the circumstances.[4] The Court has said:

> We do not underestimate the degree to which these searches may invade the personal privacy of inmates. The searches must be conducted in a reasonable manner. We deal here with the question of whether visual body-cavity inspections contemplated by prison rules can ever be conducted on less than probable cause. Balancing the significant and legitimate security interest of the institution against the privacy interest of the inmates, we conclude that they can. (Bell v. Wolfish, 441 U.S. 520 at 560 [1979])

3. Searches of Probationers' and Parolees' Homes

In probation cases, the Court has held that a state law or agency rule permitting probation officers to search probationers' homes without warrant and based on reasonable grounds instead of probable cause is a reasonable response to the "special needs" of the probation system and is therefore constitutional (Griffin v. Wisconsin 41 CrL 3424 [1987]). The Court added that the supervision of probationers is a "special need" of the state that justifies a departure from the usual warrant and probable cause requirements. Although the Griffin case involves probationers, there is little doubt that the same principle applies to warrantless searches of parolees' homes.

Some states allow warrantless searches of probationers' homes based on suspicion, a lower degree of certainty than reasonable grounds. Although the Supreme Court has not ruled on this issue, lower courts have upheld the practice based on the twin concepts of "diminished constitutional rights" and "special needs."

4. Border Searches

The magnitude of smuggling and theft problems at international borders, airports, and seaports has led to a relaxation of the probable cause requirement for searches at such locations. Hence, a border patrol or customs officer is entitled to search on the basis of a *reasonable suspicion* (a lower degree of certainty than probable cause) that the person is engaged in illegal activity. This rule applies to both U.S. citizens and aliens.

The person searched need not be entering the country. Anyone found in a "border area" is subject to search on the basis of reasonable suspicion, including visitors, employees, and transportation workers. The area in which a border search may be conducted is not limited to the actual point of entry. It may also be conducted at any place that is the "functional equivalent" of the border, such as an established station or intersection near the border or the place where the plane first lands. For example, the Chicago O'Hare Airport in Illinois is the functional equivalent of a border for international flights landing there. Customs agents may search the baggage of arriving international passengers on the basis of an inherent sovereign authority of the United States to protect its territorial integrity (Torres v. Puerto Rico, 442 U.S. 465 [1979]). Postal officials may open international mail at its place of entry into the country when they have reasonable cause to suspect that the mail contains contraband; however, postal regulations forbid officials from reading any correspondence inside (U.S. v. Ramsey, 431 U.S. 606 [1977]).

5. Airport Searches

A limited search of air travelers is permissible for the purpose of discovering weapons and preventing hijacking. There is no need for probable cause, reasonable suspicion, or even mere suspicion. The search is an administrative measure based on safety needs. In one case, a court said: "The need to prevent airline hijacking is unquestionably grave and urgent. . . . A pre-boarding screening of all passengers and carry-on articles sufficient in scope to detect the presence of weapons or explosives is reasonably necessary to meet . . . the administrative need that justifies it" (U.S. v. Davis, 482 F.2d 893 [9th Cir. 1973]). If an electronic search, using a magnetometer, is used and the reading indicates a possible weapon, a frisk or pat-down of the traveler's clothing is then justified. Evidence discovered is admissible in court. A person who refuses to submit to the limited search may be excluded from entry to the boarding area.

One Court of Appeals decision justifies airport searches in these words:

> When the risk is the jeopardy to hundreds of human lives and millions of dollars of property inherent in the pirating or blowing up of a large airplane, that danger alone meets the test of reasonableness, so long as the search is conducted in good faith for the purpose of preventing hijacking or like damage and with reasonable scope and the passenger has been given advance notice of his liability to such a search so that he can avoid it by choosing not to travel by air. (U.S. v. Edwards, 498 F.2d 496 [2d Cir. 1974])

The use of police dogs to sniff containers and luggage to detect contraband at airports does not constitute a search. No warrant or probable cause is needed as long as the container or luggage is located in a public place. A court has said: "It cannot be considered a search within the protection of the Fourth Amendment for a dog to sniff bags handled by an airline. There can be no reasonable expectation of privacy when any passenger's bags may be subjected to close scrutiny for the protection of public safety" (U.S. v. Sullivan, 625 F.2d 9, at 13 [4th Cir. 1980]).[5]

6. Searches of Goods in Transit

A warrantless search of goods in transit is allowed. There are, however, two requirements for such searches to be valid: (1) there is probable cause to believe that the shipment in transit (such as by air, train, bus, or other form of transportation) contains contraband, and (2) a search warrant cannot be obtained in time to detain the shipment.

D. The "Presence of Exigent Circumstances" Exception

The exception for *exigent circumstances* is a general catch-all category that encompasses a number of diverse situations. What they have in common is some kind of an "emergency" that makes obtaining a search warrant impractical, useless, dangerous, or unnecessary. Among these situations are danger of physical harm to the officer or destruction of evidence, danger to a third person, driving while intoxicated, and searches in hot pursuit.

1. Danger of Physical Harm to the Officer or Destruction of Evidence

The Court has implied that a warrantless search may be justified if there is reasonable ground to believe that delaying the search until the warrant is obtained would endanger the physical safety of the officer or would allow the destruction or removal of the evidence (Vale v. Louisiana, 399 U.S. 30 [1970]). Note, however, that in Vale the Supreme Court did not allow a warrantless search when there was merely a possibility that the evidence would be destroyed, thus giving Vale a narrow interpretation. The threat of danger or destruction must therefore be real or imminent.

2. Danger to a Third Person

An officer may enter a dwelling without a warrant in response to screams for help. In one case the Court said: "The Fourth Amendment does not require police officers to delay in the course of an investigation if to do so would gravely endanger their lives or the lives of others" (Warden v. Hayden, 387 U.S. 294, at 29811 [1967]).

3. Driving While Intoxicated (DWI)

The police may, without a search warrant and by force, if necessary, take a blood sample from a person arrested for drunk driving, as long as the setting and procedures are reasonable (as when the blood is drawn by a medical doctor in a hospital). Exigent circumstance exists because alcohol in the suspect's bloodstream might disappear in the time required to obtain a warrant (Schmerber v. California, 384 U.S. 757 [1966]).

A case decided by the U.S. Supreme Court, however, has placed limits on what the police can do in simple DWI cases. The Court held that the Fourth Amendment prohibits the police from making a warrantless nighttime entry of a suspect's house in order to arrest him or her for drunken driving if the offense is a misdemeanor for which state law does not allow any jail sentence. The fact that the police had an interest in preserving the evidence (because the suspect's blood-alcohol level might diminish while the police procured a warrant) was held insufficient to create the required exigent circumstance (Welsh v. Wisconsin, 35 CrL 3080 [1984]). In Welsh, the defendant had run his car off the road and abandoned it. By the time police officers arrived at the scene and learned from a witness that the defendant was either inebriated or very ill, the defendant had gone home and was sleeping. The officers checked the vehicle's registration and learned that the defendant lived close by. Without obtaining a warrant, they went to the suspect's home and arrested him. The Wisconsin Supreme Court held that the officers' actions were justified by exigent circumstances. The Supreme Court reversed that decision, saying that "an important factor to be considered when determining whether any exigency exists is the gravity of the underlying offense for which the arrest is being made. . . . Application of the exigent circumstances exception in the context of a home entry should rarely be sanctioned when there is probable cause to believe that only a minor offense has been committed." The Court concluded that in this case there was no immediate pursuit of the defendant from the scene; nor was there any need to protect either the public or the defendant, inasmuch as he had abandoned the vehicle and was at home sleeping. Only the need to preserve the evidence remained, and that was not enough, given the type of offense involved and the state's treatment of it as a civil matter, to justify the warrantless intrusion. The Court's decision states that "an important factor to be considered when determining whether any emergency exists is the gravity of the underlying offense for which the arrest is being made." Implicit in this is the assumption that had the offense been serious (such as if the driver had seriously injured somebody before running off the road and abandoning his car), the warrantless search of the driver's home would have been allowed.

4. Searches in "Hot Pursuit" (or "Fresh Pursuit") of Dangerous Suspects

The police may enter a house without warrant to search for a dangerous suspect who is being pursued and whom they have reason to believe is within the premises. For example, the police pursued a robbery suspect to a house (which later turned out to be his own). The suspect's wife opened the door to the police, who asked and received permission to search for a "burglar." The police looked for weapons that might have been concealed and found incriminating clothing in a washing machine. The clothing was confiscated and introduced as evidence in court during the trial. The Court held that the warrantless search was justified by "hot pursuit" (regardless of the validity of the suspect's wife's consent). Because the police were informed that an armed robbery had taken place and that the suspect had entered a certain house less than five minutes before they got there, they acted reasonably when they entered the house and began to search for a man of the description they had obtained and for weapons that he had allegedly used in the robbery (Warden v. Hayden, 387 U.S. 294 [1967]).

IV. SPECIFIC SEARCHES AND SEIZURES

There are other types of special searches and seizures that deserve discussion, among them searches of employees, body searches, surgery to remove a bullet from a suspect's body, mail searches, and administrative searches.

A. Body Searches—May Be Conducted after Lawful Arrest

A body search is valid in any situation in which a full custody arrest of a person occurs. There is no requirement that the officers fear for their safety or believe that they will find evidence of a crime before the body search can be made (U.S. v. Robinson, 414 U.S. 218 [1973]).

Aside from a body search after a lawful arrest, there are other instances of body searches that may be conducted by police officers. The general rule is that exterior intrusions on a person's body (such as swabbing, hand inspections, the taking of hair samples, and retrieval of evidence from the mouth) do not normally require a search warrant. In one case a court held that the clipping by the officer of a few strands of hair from the appellant's head was so minor an imposition that the appellant suffered no true humiliation or affront to his dignity; therefore no search warrant was required to justify the officer's act (U.S. v. D'Amico, 408 F.2d 331, at 333 [2d Cir. 1969]). In contrast, interior intrusions on a person's body (such as blood tests, stomach pumping, and surgery) are permitted by the Fourth Amendment only if they are conducted pursuant to a warrant or if exigent circumstances exist and there is a clear indication that the desired evidence will be found.[6] For example, a blood test performed by a skilled technician is not conduct that shocks the conscience, nor is this method of obtaining evidence offensive to a sense of justice (Breithaupt v. Abram, 352 U.S. 432 [1957]). On the other hand, the action by the police in restraining a suspect while a heroin capsule was removed from his stomach by a stomach pump was such that it shocks the conscience and therefore violated the suspect's right to due process (Rochin v. California, 342 U.S. 165 [1952]).

B. Surgery to Remove Bullet from Suspect's Body—No, Because Too Intrusive

In a recent case, the Court held that proposed surgery, under general anesthetic, to remove a bullet from a suspect's chest for use as evidence would involve such severe intrusion on his interest in privacy and security that it would violate the Fourth Amendment. The surgery could not be constitutionally undertaken despite existence of probable cause and the provision to the suspect of all relevant procedural safeguards (Winston v. Lee, 53 L.W. 4367 [1985]). This decision is significant because in an earlier case (Schmerber v. California, 384 U.S. 757 [1966]) the Court held that a state may, over the suspect's protest, have a physician extract blood from a person suspected of drunken driving without violating the suspect's right secured by the Fourth Amendment not to be subjected to unreasonable searches and seizures. However, according to the Schmerber decision, the holding that the Constitution does not forbid the states minor intrusions into an individual's body under stringently limited conditions in no way indicates that it permits more substantial intrusions or intrusions under other conditions.

In the Lee case, the state of Virginia sought to compel Rudolph Lee, a suspect in an attempted armed robbery who had allegedly been wounded by gunfire in that attempt, to undergo a surgical procedure under a general anesthetic for removal of a bullet lodged in his chest. Prosecutors alleged that the bullet would provide evidence of the suspect's guilt or innocence. The suspect opposed the surgery. The Court concluded that the procedure sought in Lee was an example of a "more substantial intrusion" cautioned against in the Schmerber case, and it therefore held that to permit the procedure to take place would violate the suspect's right to be secure in his person, as guaranteed by the Fourth Amendment.

C. Mail Searches—Warrant Generally Needed

First-class letters and sealed packages are fully protected by the Fourth Amendment and therefore cannot be searched by the police or postal authorities without a search warrant. However, if postal authorities have probable cause to believe that such mail contains contraband or other seizable evidence, they have the right to detain the mail for a reasonable time—long enough to enable them, acting diligently, to obtain a search warrant. After the warrant has been obtained, the mail may be opened but cannot be read (U.S. v. Van Leeuwen, 397 U.S. 249 [1970]).

D. Administrative Searches—Warrant Needed for Private Residences and Commercial Buildings

Administrative searches are those conducted by government investigators to determine if there are violations of governmental rules and regulations. The Court has decided that *government inspectors must have a warrant for searches of private residences and commercial buildings* (Camara v. Municipal Court, 387 U.S. 523 [1967]). However, the "probable cause" standard is not strictly applied. A valid administrative inspection warrant does not require showing specific violations of laws or particular conditions of particular buildings. What is required for the issuance of an administrative inspection warrant is merely a "showing of a general and neutral enforcement plan." Also, probable cause may be based on such factors as the passage of time, the nature of the building, or conditions elsewhere in the same geographic area. Random, periodic area inspections are therefore permitted. The issuance of a warrant serves only as a judicial check against selective enforcement of common health and safety regulations (Marshall v. Barlow's, Inc., 436 U.S. 307 [1978]). A warrant is not required for searching highly regulated industries such as those dealing in liquor, guns, or strip mining. The absence of a warrant is justified by the urgent public interest involved and the implied consent of businesses engaged in such industries. Neither is it required in emergency situations.

V. OTHER SEARCH AND SEIZURE ISSUES

A. Drug-Testing Police Officers as a Form of Search and Seizure: Is It Constitutional?—No Authoritative Answer

Drug-testing public employees, including police officers, has become fashionable and therefore needs to be addressed as a form of Fourth Amendment search and seizure. Two cases were decided by the Court in 1989 on this issue, but the decisions fail to provide definitive answers because they were based on the peculiar facts involved in those cases.

HIGHLIGHT 7.5

Seizures in the Federal Drug Forfeiture Program

"Congressman Bill Hughes (D-N.J.) disclosed on April 25 that the Federal Government expects to seize more than one billion dollars worth of cash and other assets from drug traffickers this year under the Federal Drug Forfeiture Program.

"Hughes said the breaking of the billion-dollar barrier in asset seizures demonstrates that forfeiture has become one of the most dramatic and successful law enforcement tools ever developed to combat drug trafficking.

"He said the U.S. Drug Enforcement Administration (DEA) alone expects to seize an estimated $1 billion worth of drug-related property this year—up from $655 million in 1988 and more than double the agency's entire authorized budget. More than $100 million of this money will be channeled directly to state and local governments to finance additional drug enforcement operations and step up the pressure on the traffickers."

Source: Crime Control Digest, May 8, 1989, p. 4.

In the first case (National Treasury Employees Union v. Von Raab, 109 S.Ct. 1384 [1989]), the Court, in a 5–4 split, held that the Custom Service's suspicionless drug-testing program for employees seeking promotion or transfer to positions (1) involving interdiction of illegal drugs, or (2) requiring the carrying of firearms, constitutes a "search" within the meaning of the Fourth Amendment. But such search was deemed by the Court to be constitutional because of the government's compelling interest in public safety and in safeguarding borders, and because of the diminished privacy interests of employees who seek such positions.

In the second case (Skinner v. Railway Labor Executives Association, 109 S.Ct. 1402 [1989]), the Court, in a 7–2 vote, held that drug testing of employees in accordance with Federal Railroad Administration regulations that require private railroads (under government regulation) to administer blood and urine tests to railroad employees involved in certain train accidents and fatal accidents, and that further authorize railroads to administer breath and urine tests following certain accidents, also constitutes a "search" under the Fourth Amendment. Again, such search was considered by the Court to be constitutional because the safety-sensitive tasks of the employees justified the departure from the search requirements of warrant and probable cause.

The preceding cases say that warrantless and suspicionless testing programs as implemented by the agencies involved (the Customs Service and the railroad company that was under government regulation) are reasonable and do not violate Fourth Amendment rights. Both cases involved mandatory testing, not testing at random. Whether or not completely random mandatory drug testing of public employees is constitutional has not been resolved by the U.S. Supreme Court. Most lower-court decisions hold, however, that mandatory random testing of public employees is unconstitutional. This holds true even in police departments, where the need for drug testing is more compelling than in other public agencies because police officers carry guns and are involved in law enforcement. Yet drug-testing public employees based on reasonable suspicion (as distinguished from suspicionless, mandatory, random testing) has been upheld by most lower courts. Unless the Supreme Court addresses the issue of police drug testing, the safer department policy appears to be testing based on reasonable suspicion, even in police departments.

B. Searches of Employee Office—Generally No Need for Warrant

The Court has decided that the office of a government employee may be searched by the employer without a warrant or probable cause as long as such search is work related (O'Connor v. Ortega, 107 S.Ct. 1492 [1987]). In this case, officials in a public hospital searched the office and seized personal items from the desk and file cabinets

---

HIGHLIGHT 7.6

Urine Tests Are Searches

"Because it is clear that the collection and testing of urine intrudes upon expectations of privacy that society has long recognized as reasonable, the Federal Courts of Appeals have concluded unanimously, and we agree, that these intrusions must be deemed searches under the Fourth Amendment" (Skinner v. Railway Labor Executives Association, 109 S.Ct. 1402 [1989]).

---

of a psychiatrist who was an employee of that state hospital. The items seized were used in an administrative proceeding that resulted in his discharge. The employee appealed his discharge, saying that the search of his office violated the Fourth Amendment. The Court rejected the employee's contention, holding the search constitutional even though such searches come under the Fourth Amendment. Said the Court:

> Requiring an employer to obtain a warrant whenever the employer wishes to enter an employee's office, desk, or file cabinets for work-related purpose would seriously disrupt the routine conduct of business and would be unreasonable. Moreover, requiring a probable cause standard for searches of the type at issue here would impose intolerable burdens on public employers.

The Court did not say, however, that public employers have unlimited authority to search the desks and files of employees at any time. The O'Connor case was decided on the basis of the peculiar facts of that case, the Court concluding that under the circumstances the physician had no reasonable expectation of privacy in his desk and file cabinets. The Court added, however, that "given the great variety of work environments in the public sector, the question whether an employee has a reasonable expectation of privacy must be addressed on a case-by-case basis."

C. Searches and Seizures by Private Persons—No Need for Warrant

Searches and seizures by private persons do not come under the Fourth Amendment protection because the constitutional amendments apply only to acts of governmental agencies and officers. This is true even if the act by private persons is unlawful and illegal.

Evidence obtained by private people is admissible in court as long as the private person acted purely on his or her own and the police did not encourage or participate in the private search and seizure. For example, X breaks into his neighbor's house because he suspects his neighbor of having stolen his TV set. X recovers the set and now brings a case of robbery against his neighbor. The TV set is admissible in evidence because the Fourth Amendment guarantee against unreasonable searches and seizures applies only to acts of government officers. Note, however, that X may be liable for breaking into and entering his neighbor's house in a separate criminal case. Note also that the evidence is not admissible if a police officer participated in, ordered, or encouraged X to effect the search.

If a government official aids in a search or seizure by a private citizen, then the Fourth Amendment protections apply.[7] It is immaterial whether a government officer originated the idea or joined in it while the search was in progress. So long as he or she was in it before the object of the search was completely accomplished, the officer must be considered to have participated in it; the evidence secured is therefore inadmissible.

D. Searches by Government Agents of Same Material Searched by Private Parties—No Need for Warrant

The U.S. Supreme Court has held that if government agents perform a search or seizure of the same material that has already been subjected to a private search or seizure, that government search will be considered to have intruded into the owners' privacy interests *only to the extent that the governmental search or seizure exceeded the scope of the private search.* Moreover, it is valid for government agents to conduct a warrantless "chemical field test" of suspected controlled substances (U.S. v. Jacobsen, 104 S.Ct. 1652 [1984]).

E. Search by "Off-Duty" Officer—Considered a Government Search

Search by an officer who is off duty is usually considered to be a governmental search. Many jurisdictions consider police officers to be law enforcement officers twenty-four hours a day and all days of the week. If this were not the rule, it would be easy for police officers to conduct searches while off duty and therefore subvert the provisions of the Fourth Amendment. Although not litigated in court, the rule would most probably be the same even in jurisdictions where a police officer is not expected to be on duty at all times.

F. Use of Police Dogs for Detection of Drugs—Not Considered a Search

There is *no "search" within the meaning of the Fourth Amendment* if the police use narcotics detection dogs to smell closed containers for drugs, as long as the police are legally in the place. There is therefore no need for a search warrant or for probable cause to conduct dog sniffs (U.S. v. Place, 462 U.S. 696 [1983]). Some of the justifications for this judicial rule are that the use of dogs does not involve any physical intrusion; the intrusion upon an individual's privacy is inoffensive; the intrusion is restricted because the dog is discriminate; the intrusion is not aimed at persons but rather at an inanimate object, and the use of dogs is not the same as using a sophisticated electronic device.[8]

G. Use of Pen Registers—Not Considered a Search

The use of pen registers to record the numbers dialed from a telephone *does not constitute search or seizure* and therefore does not require prior judicial authorization (Smith v. Maryland, 442 U.S. 735 [1979]). Moreover, no judicial approval is required under Title III of the 1968 Omnibus Crime Control and Safe Streets Act. In fact, the police may obtain a court order to require the telephone company to assist in installing pen registers.

H. Searches of Nonresident Alien in Foreign Country—Fourth Amendment Does Not Apply

The Court has held that a nonresident alien may not invoke the protections of the Fourth Amendment to challenge the seizure without warrant of items from a residence located in a foreign country (U.S. v. Verdugo-Urquidez, 46 CrL 2136 [1990]). In this case, Verdugo-Urquidez, a citizen and resident of Mexico, was arrested by the Mexican police in Mexico in accordance with a warrant issued in the United States. He was turned over to U.S. officials at the border and was placed in a detention center in San Diego, California. Believing that Verdugo-Urquidez was involved not only in drug smuggling, but also in the torture and murder of DEA Special Agent Enrique Camarena, U.S. agents decided to search two of the suspect's residences in Mexico. They obtained the cooperation of Mexican officials and, working with them, executed warrantless searches. He was later tried and convicted in California. The Ninth Circuit

Court of Appeals affirmed the trial judge's suppression of the evidence, saying that U.S. investigators are required to obtain a warrant in the United States even if the warrant is not required under Mexican law and would have no effect on Mexican soil. On appeal, the Court held the evidence admissible, saying that the Fourth Amendment has "no application" to search of an alien's residence located in a foreign country, even if that resident is later tried by and the evidence seized is used in a U.S. court.

VI. GUIDE TO UNDERSTANDING SEARCH AND SEIZURE CASES

The following questions will help students understand search and seizure cases and determine their legality. Ask the questions and analyze the answers in the following sequence:

1. Is the police activity in question a search and seizure, or is it something else (such as stop and frisk or arrest)?
2. If the police activity in question is search and seizure, was there a search warrant? If a search warrant exists, the search is presumably valid (although the validity may be challenged later in court).
3. If there is no search warrant, does the search and seizure come under any of the exceptions (of which there are many, as discussed in this chapter)? If it comes under one of the exceptions, then the warrantless search and seizure is valid and the evidence is admissible in court.
4. If the search is valid (because there was a warrant or because the search is a valid exception), was the scope of police search within allowable limits (remember the "elephant in a matchbox" and Chimel limitations)? If it is, then the search is valid and the evidence admissible in court.

Remember that any evidence obtained after an illegal act by the police cannot be admitted in court. Nothing that turns up later in the course of the search will cure the initial illegality.

❑ SUMMARY

Although often used as one, the terms *search* and *seizure* represent two separate acts. A search is any governmental intrusion into a person's reasonable and justifiable expectation of privacy, whereas a seizure is the exercise of dominion or control by the government over a person or thing because of a violation of law.

Searches are generally classified by presence or lack of warrant. The general rule is that to be valid, searches must be made by authority of a warrant. The basic requirements for the issuance of a warrant are probable cause, supported by oath or affirmation, particular description of the place to be searched and persons or things to be seized, and signature of a magistrate. The search warrant is directed to a law enforcement officer and must state the grounds for issuance and the names of those who gave affidavits in its support. Federal and many state statutes require an officer to announce his or her purpose and authority before breaking into a dwelling to serve a warrant; this, however, is not a constitutional rule and is subject to numerous exceptions.

Searches without warrant are the exception rather than the rule, but they are more often undertaken by the police. There are various conditions under which searches can be made without a warrant, four of which are discussed in this chapter. The first exception is searches incident to a lawful arrest. The rule is that once a lawful arrest is made, the police may search any area within the suspect's "immediate control," meaning the area into which the suspect may reach to grab a weapon or destroy evidence. The second exception is searches with consent. Some individuals may validly give consent; others cannot. The third exception is special needs beyond law enforcement. These are instances where public officials other than police officers are involved in particular searches and seizures. The fourth exception is the presence of exigent circumstances, such as when there is danger to the officer's physical safety or risk of the destruction of evidence, danger to a third person, driving while intoxicated, and hot pursuit.

Special rules govern certain types of searches. For example, a full body search may be made of an arrested person, but surgery to remove a bullet from suspect's body for evidence has been declared too intrusive. Government inspectors must have a warrant for searches of private residences and commercial buildings for administrative purposes, but the "probable cause" standard is not strictly applied.

Searches and seizures by private persons do not come under the Fourth Amendment; hence evidence obtained in such searches is admissible in court. If, however, a government official aids in such search, then the Fourth Amendment applies. The use of police dogs to sniff closed containers for drugs is not considered a search and therefore no warrant is needed, as long as the police are legally in the place. Pen registers do not constitute a search or seizure and therefore do not need prior judicial authorization.

◻ REVIEW QUESTIONS

1. Distinguish between a search and a seizure.
2. What are the four requirements for the valid issuance of a search warrant? Discuss each.
3. "The announcement requirement is not a constitutional rule." Discuss what that means. Then give at least three exceptions to the announcement requirement.
4. Identify the four exceptions to the search warrant requirement that were discussed in this chapter.
5. Chimel v. California gives the constitutional rule on searches incident to a lawful arrest. What is that rule?
6. Identify three individuals who may validly give consent and three individuals who may not validly give consent.
7. What is meant by the "special needs beyond law enforcement" exception to the warrant and probable cause requirements? Give three examples.
8. What is meant by the "presence of exigent circumstances" exception? Give two examples.
9. Discuss the constitutionality of drug-testing police officers.
10. What is the rule concerning searches of students by public school teachers and administrators?

11. Is evidence illegally seized by private persons admissible in court? How about evidence illegally seized by an "off-duty" officer?
12. In general, what items are subject to search and seizure?

□ DEFINITIONS

Administrative Searches: Searches conducted by government inspectors to determine if there are violations of governmental rules and regulations.

Anticipatory Search Warrant: A warrant obtained based on probable cause and an expectation that seizable items will be found at a certain place at a certain time.

Area of Immediate Control: The area from within which an arrested person may gain possession of a weapon or destructible evidence.

Contemporaneous Search: Search made at the same time as or very close in time and place to the arrest.

Exigent Circumstances: Emergency circumstances that make obtaining a warrant impractical, useless, dangerous, or unnecessary.

"No Knock" Searches: Searches without announcement, authorized by state statutes, particularly in drug cases.

Probable Cause: More than bare suspicion; it exists when the facts and circumstances within the officers' knowledge and of which they have reasonably trustworthy information are sufficient in themselves to warrant a person of reasonable caution in the belief that an offense has been or is being committed. In searches and seizures (as contrasted with arrests), the issue of probable cause focuses on whether the property to be seized is connected with criminal activity and whether it can be found in the place to be searched.

Reasonable Expectation of Privacy: Degree of privacy that entitles a person's constitutional rights to be protected from governmental intrusion in private or public places.

Search: Any governmental intrusion into a person's reasonable and justifiable expectation of privacy.

Search Warrant: A written order issued by a magistrate, directing a peace officer to search for property connected with a crime and bring it before the court.

Seizure: The exercise of dominion or control by the government over a person or thing because of a violation of law.

"Special Needs" Exception: This is an exception to the warrant and probable cause requirements under the Fourth Amendment; it allows warrantless searches and searches on less than probable cause in cases where there are needs to be met other than those of law enforcement, such as the supervision of high school students, prisoners, probationers, and parolees.

□ PRINCIPLES OF CASES

BELL V. WOLFISH, 441 U.S. 520 (1979)   Strip searches and body cavity searches in prisons or jails are permissible as long as they are conducted in a reasonable manner and are justified under the circumstances.

BREITHAUPT V. ABRAM, 352 U.S. 432 (1957)   A blood test performed by a skilled technician is not such conduct that shocks the conscience, nor is this method of obtaining evidence such that it offends a sense of justice.

BUMPER V. NORTH CAROLINA, 391 U.S. 543 (1968)   There is no valid consent to search if permission is given as a result of police misrepresentation or deception.

CAMARA V. MUNICIPAL COURT, 387 U.S. 523 (1967)   Government inspectors must have a warrant for searches of private residences and commercial buildings.

CHIMEL V. CALIFORNIA, 395 U.S. 752 (1969)   Once a lawful arrest has been made, the police may search any area within the suspect's "immediate control," meaning the area from which the suspect may grab a weapon or destroy evidence.

CONNALLY V. GEORGIA, 429 U.S. 245 (1977)   A magistrate who receives a fee when issuing a warrant but not when denying one is not neutral and detached.

COOLIDGE V. NEW HAMPSHIRE, 403 U.S. 443 (1971)   A state's chief investigator and prosecutor (state attorney general) is not neutral and detached; therefore any warrant issued by him or her is invalid.

GRIFFIN V. WISCONSIN, 41 CrL 3424 (1987)   A state law or agency rule permitting probation officers to search probationers' homes without warrant and based on reasonable grounds instead of probable cause is a reasonable response to the "special needs" of the probation system and is therefore constitutional.

HUDSON V. PALMER, 35 CrL 3230 (1984)   The Fourth Amendment offers an inmate absolutely no protection against unreasonable searches and seizures in his or her cell because the inmate has no reasonable expectation of privacy there.

ILLINOIS V. RODRIGUEZ, 58 L.W. 4892 (1990)   The warrantless entry of private premises by police officers is valid if based on the consent of a third party whom the police, at the time of entry, reasonably believed to possess common authority over the premises, but who in fact did not have such authority.

JOHNSON V. UNITED STATES, 333 U.S. 10 (1948)   Inferences leading to the issuance of a search warrant must be drawn by a neutral and detached magistrate instead of being judged by the officer engaged in the often competitive enterprise of ferreting out crime.

KATZ V. UNITED STATES, 389 U.S. 347 (1967)   The prohibition against unreasonable search and seizure is not limited to homes, offices, buildings, or other enclosed places. It can occur in any place where a person has a "reasonable and justifiable expectation of privacy," even if the place is in a public area.

LO-JI SALES, INC. V. NEW YORK, 442 U.S. 319 (1979)   A magistrate who participates in the search to determine its scope lacks the requisite neutrality and detachment.

LUSTIG V. UNITED STATES, 388 U.S. 74 (1949)   If a government official aids in a search or seizure by a private citizen, the Fourth Amendment applies. It is immaterial whether a government official originated the idea or joined in the search while it was in progress. So long as the officer was in it before the object of the search was completely accomplished, he or she must be considered to have participated in it.

MARSHALL V. BARLOW'S, INC., 436 U.S. 307 (1978)   What is required for the issuance of an administrative inspection warrant is merely a showing of a general enforcement plan. Probable cause may be based on such factors as the passage of time, the nature of the building, and conditions elsewhere in the same geographic area.

MARYLAND V. GARRISON, 55 L.W. 4190 (1987) The validity of a warrant must be judged in light of the information available to the officers at the time they obtained the warrant. A warrant that is overbroad in describing the place to be searched is valid if based on a reasonable but mistaken belief at the time the warrant was issued.

MARYLAND V. MACON, 37 CrL 3111 (1985) No search occurs when an undercover officer examines the wares offered for sale in an "adult" bookstore, nor is the officer's purchase of some of those wares a "seizure"; hence no warrant is needed.

MICHIGAN V. SUMMERS, 452 U.S. 692 (1981) While the search is being conducted, the police may detain persons found in the premises that are to be searched.

NATIONAL TREASURY EMPLOYEES UNION V. VON RAAB, 109 S.Ct. 1384 (1989) The Custom Service's suspicionless drug-testing program for employees seeking promotion or transfer to positions (1) involving interdiction of illegal drugs, or (2) requiring the carrying of firearms, is constitutional because of the government's compelling interest in public safety and in safeguarding borders, and because of the diminished privacy interests of employees who seek such positions.

NEW JERSEY V. T.L.O., 53 L.W. 4083 (1985) Public school teachers and administrators do not need a warrant or probable cause before searching a student. What is needed is merely reasonable ground for suspecting that the search will turn up evidence that the student has violated or is violating either the law or the rules of the school.

NEW YORK V. BELTON, 435 U.S. 454 (1981) When the police have made a lawful custodial arrest of the occupant of a car, they may, incident to that arrest, search the car's entire passenger compartment (front and back seats) and open any containers found in the compartment.

O'CONNOR V. ORTEGA, 107 S.Ct. 1492 (1987) The office of a government employee may be searched by the employer without a warrant or probable cause as long as such search is related to work.

ROCHIN V. CALIFORNIA, 342 U.S. 165 (1952) The action by the police in restraining a suspect while a heroin capsule was removed from his stomach by a stomach pump was such that it shocks the conscience and therefore violated the suspect's right to due process.

SCHMERBER V. CALIFORNIA, 384 U.S. 757 (1966) The police may, without a search warrant and by force, if necessary, take a blood sample from a person arrested for drunk driving, as long as the setting and procedures are reasonable (as when the blood is drawn by a medical doctor in a hospital). Exigent circumstance exists because alcohol in the suspect's bloodstream might disappear in the time required to obtain a warrant.

SKINNER V. RAILWAY LABOR EXECUTIVES ASSOCIATION, 109 S.Ct. 1402 (1989) Drug testing of employees in accordance with Federal Railroad Administration regulations that require private railroads to administer blood and urine tests to railroad employees involved in certain train accidents and fatal accidents and that further authorize railroads to administer breath and urine tests following certain accidents is constitutional because the safety-sensitive tasks of the employees justified the departure from the search requirements of warrant and probable cause.

SMITH V. MARYLAND, 442 U.S. 735 (1979)   The use of pen registers to record the numbers dialed from a telephone does not constitute search or seizure and therefore does not require prior judicial authorization.

STONER V. CALIFORNIA, 376 U.S. 483 (1964)   A landlord cannot give valid consent to search property that he or she has rented to another person. Neither can a hotel clerk give valid consent to the search of a guest's room.

TORRES V. PUERTO RICO, 442 U.S. 465 (1979)   Customs agents may search the baggage of arriving international travelers on the basis of the inherent sovereign authority of the United States to protect its territorial integrity.

UNITED STATES V. BOK, 188 F.2d 1019 (DC Cir. 1951)   The employer cannot give valid consent to search if the property is under the exclusive use and control of the employee.

UNITED STATES V. CHADWICK, 433 U.S. 1 (1977)   A search that is remote in time and place from the arrest is not contemporaneous and therefore invalid. In this case, the officers opened and searched a footlocker without a warrant one hour after the arrest.

UNITED STATES V. D'AMICO, 408 F.2d 331 (2d Cir. 1969)   The clipping by the officer of a few strands of hair from a suspect's head was so minor an imposition that the suspect suffered no true humiliation or affront to his dignity; therefore a search warrant was not required to justify the officer's act.

UNITED STATES V. DAVIS, 482 F.2d 893 (9th Cir. 1973)   A preboarding screening of all passengers and carry-on articles, sufficient in scope to detect the presence of weapons or explosives, is reasonable to meet the administrative needs (of discovering weapons and preventing hijacking) that justify it.

UNITED STATES V. EDWARDS, 415 U.S. 800 (1974)   A suspect was arrested and jailed late at night. A clothing search for evidence was not conducted until the following morning. The Court said that the delayed search was justified because substitute clothing was not available for use at the time of booking.

UNITED STATES V. EDWARDS, 498 F.2d 496 (2d Cir. 1974)   When the risk is the jeopardy to hundreds of human lives and millions of dollars of property inherent in the pirating or blowing up of a large airplane, that danger alone meets the test of reasonableness, so long as the search is conducted in good faith for the purpose of preventing hijacking or like damage and with reasonable scope and the passenger has been given advance notice of his or her liability to such a search so that he or she can avoid it by choosing not to travel by air.

UNITED STATES V. JACOBSEN, 104 S.Ct. 1652 (1984)   If government agents perform a search or seizure of the same material that has already been subjected to a private search or seizure, that government search will be considered to have intruded into the owner's privacy only to the extent that the governmental search or seizure exceeded the scope of the private search.

UNITED STATES V. LEON, 468 U.S. 897 (1984)   To be valid, the warrant must be based on fresh information. If the information is "stale," the warrant lacks probable cause and is invalid.

UNITED STATES V. OWENS, 848 F.2d 462 (4th Cir. 1988)   The execution of a warrant for a different apartment than that named in the warrant was valid because there were only two apartments on the floor, one of which was vacant. Moreover, the correct apartment was readily ascertainable and the mistake was made in good faith.

UNITED STATES V. PLACE, 462 U.S. 696 (1983)   There is no search within the meaning of the Fourth Amendment if the police use narcotics detection dogs to smell closed containers for drugs, as long as the police are legally in the place. There is no need for a search warrant or for probable cause to conduct dog sniffs.

UNITED STATES V. RAMSEY, 431 U.S. 606 (1977)   Postal officials may open international mail at its place of entry into the country when they have reasonable cause to suspect that the mail contains contraband; however, postal regulations forbid officials from reading any correspondence inside.

UNITED STATES V. ROBINSON, 414 U.S. 218 (1973)   The police may conduct a body search of the arrestee after a full custodial arrest even if the officers do not fear for their safety or believe that they will find evidence of crime.

UNITED STATES V. SHAIBU, 43 CrL 1470 (9th Cir. 1990)   There is no valid consent where the resident opened his door, stepped into the hallway, listened to the officers identify themselves and explain the purpose of their visit, and then retreated wordlessly back into the apartment without closing the door. The government in this case failed to meet its heavy burden of proving consent, by merely showing that the defendant left his door open.

UNITED STATES V. SULLIVAN, 625 F.2d 9 (4th Cir. 1980)   It is not a search within the protection of the Fourth Amendment for a dog to sniff bags handled by an airline. There can be no reasonable expectation of privacy when any passenger's bags may be subjected to close scrutiny for the protection of public safety.

UNITED STATES V. VERDUGO-URQUIDEZ, 46 CrL 2136 (1990)   Nonresident aliens may not invoke the protections of the Fourth Amendment to challenge the seizure without warrant of items from a residence located in a foreign country.

VALE V. LOUISIANA, 399 U.S. 30 (1970)   The Court has implied that a warrantless search may be justified if there is reasonable ground to believe that delaying the search until the warrant is obtained would endanger the physical safety of the officer or would allow the destruction or removal of the evidence.

WARDEN V. HAYDEN, 387 U.S. 294 (1967)   The police may make a warrantless search and seizure when they are in "hot pursuit" of a dangerous suspect. The scope of such a search may be as extensive as reasonably necessary to prevent the suspect from resisting or escaping.

WELSH V. WISCONSIN, 35 CrL 3080 (1984)   The Fourth Amendment prohibits the police from making a warrantless nighttime entry of a suspect's house in order to arrest him or her for drunken driving if the offense is a misdemeanor for which state law does not allow any jail sentence.

WINSTON V. LEE, 53 L.W. 4367 (1985)   Surgery, under general anesthetic, to remove a bullet from a suspect's chest for use as evidence could involve such severe intrusion of the suspect's interest in privacy and security that it would violate the Fourth Amendment.

YBARRA V. ILLINOIS, 444 U.S. 85 (1979)   Although the officer may detain persons in the premises to be searched, the search warrant does not authorize the police to search persons found on the premises who are not named in the warrant.

ZURCHER V. STANFORD DAILY, 436 U.S. 547 (1978)   Searches of property belonging to persons not suspected of crime are permissible as long as probable cause exists to believe that evidence of someone's guilt or other items subject to seizure will be found.

☐   CASE BRIEF—LEADING CASE ON VALIDITY OF SEARCH WARRANT AND ADMISSIBILITY OF EVIDENCE SEIZED

COOLIDGE V. NEW HAMPSHIRE, 403 U.S. 443 (1971)

FACTS: A 14-year-old girl left her home in response to a man's request for a babysitter. Thirteen days later her body was found by the side of a major highway. On January 28, the police questioned Coolidge in his home concerning the ownership of guns, and asked if he would take a lie detector test concerning his whereabouts on the night of the girl's disappearance. He produced three guns voluntarily and agreed to the lie detector test. The following Sunday, Coolidge was called to the police station to take the lie detector test and for further questioning. While he was being questioned, two officers (not those who had questioned him earlier) went to his house and questioned his wife. During the course of the questioning, she voluntarily produced four of Coolidge's guns and the clothes he was believed to have been wearing on the night of the girl's disappearance. After a meeting involving the officers working on the case and the attorney general, the attorney general signed an arrest warrant for Coolidge and search warrants for his house and car. Pursuant to those warrants, Coolidge was arrested and his cars impounded. The car was searched two days later and twice after that. Evidence presented over Coolidge's objection included gunpowder residue, microscopic particles taken from the car and from the clothes provided by Coolidge's wife, and a .22-caliber rifle also provided by her. Coolidge was charged with and convicted of murder.

ISSUES:

1. *Was the warrant authorizing the search of Coolidge's house and car valid? No.*
2. *If the warrant was not valid, could the seizure of the evidence in Coolidge's house and car be justified as an exception to the warrant requirement? No.*
3. *Were the guns and clothes given to the officers by Coolidge's wife prior to the issuance of the warrant admissible as evidence? Yes.*

SUPREME COURT DECISION:

1. The warrant issued by the state's chief investigator and prosecutor (the state attorney general) was not issued by a neutral and detached magistrate; hence, the warrant was invalid.
2. The evidence seized from Coolidge's house (vacuum sweepings of the clothes taken from the house) and from the car (particles of gunpowder) could not be admissible as exceptions to the warrant requirement.
3. The guns and clothes given by Coolidge's wife to the police were given voluntarily; hence they were admissible.

CASE SIGNIFICANCE: The Coolidge case is best known for the principle that a warrant is valid only if issued by a *neutral and detached magistrate*. If issued by any person who has an interest in the outcome of the case (such as the state attorney general who was also the state's chief investigator and prosecutor in the case), the warrant is invalid. In this case, since the warrant was invalid, the state sought to justify the admission of the evidence under the various exceptions to the warrant requirement. The Court said that the evidence here did not come under such exceptions as "search incident to an arrest," "automobile exception," or the "instrumentality of the crime." The evidence (guns and clothes) given by Coolidge's wife, however, were admissible because they were given not as the result of improper conduct on the part of the police, but because she wanted to help clear her husband of the crime.

EXCERPTS FROM THE DECISION:

1. "When the right of privacy must reasonably yield to the right of search is, as a rule, to be decided by a judicial officer, not by a policeman or government enforcement agency." A warrant must, therefore, be issued by a neutral and detached magistrate.
2. "Since the police knew of the presence of the automobile and planned all along to seize it, there was no 'exigent circumstance' to justify their failure to obtain a warrant." Such warrantless seizures could not be justified under any of the exceptions to the warrant requirement.
3. "[T]he policemen were surely acting normally and properly when they asked her [Coolidge's wife], as they had asked those questioned erlier in the investigation, including Coolidge himself, about any guns there might be in the house. The question concerning the clothes Coolidge had been wearing the night of the disapperance was logical and in no way coercive. Indeed, one might doubt the competence of the officers involved had they not asked exactly the questions they did ask. And surely when Mrs. Coolidge of her own accord produced the guns and clothes for inspection, rather than simply describing them, it was not incumbent on the police to stop her or avert their eyes."

❏ CASE BRIEF—LEADING CASE ON PARTICULAR DESCRIPTION OF PLACE TO BE SEARCHED

MARYLAND V. GARRISON, 55 L.W. 4190 (1987)

FACTS: Police officers obtained a warrant to search "the premises known as 2036 Park Avenue, third-floor apartment," for drugs and drug paraphernalia that supposedly belonged to a person named McWebb. The police reasonably believed that there was only one apartment at the location when, in fact, there were actually two apartments on the third floor, one belonging to McWebb and one belonging to Garrison. Before the officers became aware that they were in Garrison's apartment instead of McWebb's, they discovered contraband that provided the basis for Garrison's conviction for violating Maryland's Controlled Substance Act.

ISSUE: *Is a search in the wrong apartment conducted pursuant to a search warrant in which the officers had a reasonable but mistaken belief that the address was correct valid? Yes.*

SUPREME COURT DECISION: The validity of a warrant must be judged in light of the information available to officers when the warrant is sought; thus, a warrant that is overbroad in describing the place to be searched based on a reasonable but mistaken belief of the officer is not in violation of the Fourth Amendment. In this case, the search warrant was valid even though the warrant proved to be too broad to authorize the search of both apartments. Evidence obtained from the search may be used in a criminal trial.

CASE SIGNIFICANCE: One of the elements of a valid search is that the warrant must contain a "particular description of the place to be searched." This means that the warrant must remove any doubt or uncertainty about which premises are to be searched. The Garrison case appears to soften the demands of that requirement. Here was a case of mistaken place description, leading to a mistake in the execution of the warrant. Despite this mistake, which stemmed from a warrant that was characterized as "ambiguous in scope," the Courts said that the "validity of the warrant must be judged in light of the information available to the officers at the time they obtained the warrant." The fact that later discovery found the warrant to be unnecessarily broad did not invalidate the warrant nor affect the admissibility of evidence obtained. It is important to note here that the Court found the warrant to be valid on its face although its broad scope led to an error in the place of execution. There was reasonable effort on the part of the officers to ascertain and identify the place that was the target of the search, nonetheless a mistake took place. This case should not be interpreted as validating all search warrants where there is a mistake made in the description of the place to be searched. The test as to the validity of search warrants that are "ambiguous in scope" appears to be "whether the officers' failure to realize the overbreadth of the warrant was objectively understandable and reasonable. . . ."

EXCERPTS FROM THE DECISION: In this case there is no claim that the "persons or things to be seized" were inadequately described or that there was no probable cause to believe that those things might be found in "the place to be searched" as it was described in the warrant. With the benefit of hindsight, however, we now know that the description of that place was broader than appropriate because it was based on the mistaken belief that there was only one apartment on the third floor of the building at 2036 Park Avenue. The question is whether that factual mistake invalidated a warrant that undoubtedly would have been valid if it had reflected a completely accurate understanding of the building's floor plan.

Plainly, if the officers had known, or even if they should have known, that there were two separate dwelling units on the third floor of 2036 Park Avenue, they would have been obligated to exclude respondent's apartment from the scope of the requested warrant. But we must judge the constitutionality of their conduct in light of the information available to them at the time they acted. Those items of evidence that emerge after the warrant is issued have no bearing on whether or not a warrant was validly issued. Just as the discovery of contraband cannot validate a warrant invalid when issued, so it is equally clear that the discovery of facts demonstrating that a valid warrant was unnecessarily broad does not retroactively invalidate the warrant. The validity of the warrant must be assessed on the basis of the information that the officers disclosed, or had a duty to discover and to disclose, to the issuing magistrate. On the basis of that information, we agree with the conclusion of all three Maryland courts that the warrant, insofar as it authorized a search that turned out to be ambiguous in scope, was valid when it was issued.

◻ NOTES

1. John G. Miles, Jr., David B. Richardson, and Anthony E. Scudellari, *The Law Officer's Pocket Manual* (Washington, DC: Bureau of National Affairs, 1988–89), at 9:27.
2. A. L. Dipietro, "Anticipatory Search Warrants," *FBI Law Enforcement Bulletin*, July 1990, at 27.
3. Ibid. at 28.
4. M. Hermann, *Search and Seizure Checklists*, 3d ed. (New York: Clark Boardman, 1983), at 197.
5. Ibid. at 166.
6. Ibid. at 192–193.
7. Ibid. at 204.
8. Note, "Constitutional Limitations on the Use of Canines to Detect Evidence of Crime," *Fordham Law Review*, at 973.

CHAPTER EIGHT

VEHICLE STOPS AND SEARCHES

☐ KEY TERMS

roadblock	vehicle impoundment
sobriety checkpoint	beeper
vehicle inventory	

Stops and searches of motor vehicles are an important and highly visible part of daily police patrol work, and have been so for decades. They will continue to command attention in the coming years as the number of motor vehicles continues to increase and vehicle gadgets become more sophisticated. The Court first addressed the issue of motor vehicles and the Fourth Amendment several decades ago, but questions as to what the police can do and cannot do in motor vehicle cases continue to reach the Court each year and will invite the attention of the Court in years to come. It is therefore important that the police become familiar with the laws on motor vehicle stops and searches, because a large percentage of arrests and searches are either made in or related to motor vehicles.

I. THE RULE—NO NEED FOR A WARRANT: THE CASE OF CARROLL V. UNITED STATES

The rule is that the search of an automobile does not need a warrant and is therefore an exception to the warrant requirement of the Fourth Amendment. The original case on automobile stops and searches is Carroll v. United States, 267 U.S. 132 (1925). In that case, a certain George Carroll and John Kiro were indicted and convicted for transporting "intoxicating spirituous liquor" (68 quarts of bonded whiskey and gin, in violation of the National Prohibition Act). They appealed their conviction, saying that it was wrong for the trial court to admit two of the sixty-eight bottles, one of whiskey and one of gin, because they were seized by the agents without a warrant. The agents had probable cause to believe that the automobile contained bootleg liquor, but said that had they tried to obtain a warrant, the car, which they had stopped while traveling on a highway, would have been gone. The Court said that the warrantless search of the automobile was reasonable because it would have been gone if the agents tried to obtain a warrant. After a discussion of various laws, the Court said:

> We have made a somewhat extended reference to these statutes to show that the guaranty of freedom from unreasonable searches and seizures by the Fourth Amendment has been construed, practically since the beginning of the government, as recognizing a necessary difference between a search of a store, dwelling house, or other structure in respect of which a proper official warrant readily may be obtained and a search of a ship, motor boat, wagon, or automobile for contraband goods, *where it is not practicable to secure a warrant, because the vehicle can be quickly moved out of the locality or jurisdiction in which the warrant must be sought* [italics added].

Although the Carroll case says that there is no need for a warrant to search vehicles "where it is not practicable to secure a warrant," subsequent court decisions, with limited exceptions (as in the case of vehicles at home and not in use at the time of search) have generally held that warrantless vehicle searches are constitutional.

The "automobile exception" to the warrant requirement is justified by the following considerations: (1) the mobility of motor vehicles often produces exigent circumstances,[1] (2) a diminished expectation of privacy surrounds the automobile, (3) a car is used for transportation and not as a residence or a repository of personal effects, (4) the car's occupants and contents travel in plain view, and (5) automobiles are necessarily highly regulated by the government (Robbins v. California, 453 U.S. 420 [1981]).

As in all search and seizure cases, a distinction must be made in automobile exceptions between *search* and *seizure*. Stopping a vehicle constitutes seizure and will be discussed first. Vehicle searches after the car is stopped or immobilized will then be addressed. Vehicle stops usually lead to some type of search; hence seizures and searches of motor vehicles may sometimes be difficult to separate.

II. VEHICLE STOPS

A seizure occurs every time a motor vehicle is stopped; the provisions of the Fourth Amendment against unreasonable searches and seizures therefore apply. In one case the Court said: "The Fourth and Fourteenth Amendments are implicated in this case because stopping an automobile and detaining its occupants constitute a 'seizure' within the meaning of those Amendments, even though the purpose of the stop is limited and the resulting detention quite brief" (Delaware v. Prouse, 440 U.S. 648 at 653 [1979]). Nonetheless, there is no need for a warrant because the movable nature of a motor vehicle makes it impractical to obtain a warrant.

A. Types of Vehicle Stops

Vehicle stops are of several types, depending on the intrusiveness and purpose of the stop. What they have in common is that they are all investigatory stops conducted in law enforcement work. The more significant motor vehicle stops are discussed as follows.

1. Suspicion of Involvement in Criminal Activity

In one case, the Court said that there must be at least a reasonable suspicion to justify an investigatory stop of a motor vehicle in connection with possible involvement in criminal activity (U.S. v. Cortez, 449 U.S. 411 [1981]). In that case, the Court said:

> Based upon that whole picture, the detaining officers must have a particularized and objective basis for suspecting the particular person stopped of criminal activity. First, the assessment must be based upon all of the circumstances. The analysis proceeds with various objective observations, information from police reports, if such are available, and considerations of the modes or patterns of operation and certain kinds of law-breakers. . . . The second element contained in the idea that an assessment of the whole picture must yield a particularized suspicion is the concept that the process just described must raise a suspicion that the particular individual being stopped is engaged in wrongdoing.

A lower court has also said: "The police do not have an unrestricted right to stop people, either pedestrians or drivers. The 'good faith' of the police is not enough,

nor is an inarticulate hunch. They must have an articulable suspicion of wrongdoing, done or in prospect" (U.S. v. Montgomery, 561 F.2d 875 [1977]).[2]

The preceding cases say that the warrantless exception in motor vehicle stop cases does not give the police unlimited authority to stop vehicles.

2. Roadblocks—Brower v. County of Inyo

A *roadblock* is a form of seizure under the Fourth Amendment (Brower v. County of Inyo, 57 L.W. 4321 [1989]). In this case, the police, in an effort to stop Brower, who had stolen a car and eluded the police in a chase of over 20 miles, placed an 18-inch-wheel truck across both lanes of a highway beyond a curve, with a police car's headlights pointed in a manner as to blind Brower. Brower was killed in the crash as a result of the roadblock. In a civil rights case for damages against the police, the Court said that a seizure occurs when there is a "governmental termination of freedom of movement through means intentionally implied."

Roadblocks are used by the police for a variety of purposes, including spot checks of drivers' licenses, car registrations, and violations of motor vehicle laws and apprehension of fleeing criminals and suspects. Roadblocks may be set up for inspection purposes, provided the officer stops every car passing the checkpoint or has an articulable, neutral principle (such as stopping every fifth car) for justifying the stop (Delaware v. Prouse, 440 U.S. 648 [1979]). In some circumstances near the border, immigration officers may check the identification papers of everyone in the car. And if a driver reaches below the seat or makes a quick gesture, the officer has the right to order him out of the car to submit to a search for weapons. Whereas roadblocks are legitimate, a "roving and random" stop of motor vehicles without prior suspicion of criminal activity violates the Fourth Amendment.

Although roadblocks can be imposed without probable cause, searches of a motor vehicle during a roadblock can be undertaken only with probable cause. For example, officers set up a roadblock to apprehend intoxicated drivers. The officers can ask the drivers questions and observe their behavior, but they cannot search the cars. However, once the officers have probable cause to believe that a driver is intoxicated, they may then search the arrested person and car for possible evidence. Roadblocks are constitutional, but they may in fact be prohibited by the state constitution, state law, or state regulation.

3. Sobriety Checkpoints—Michigan Department of State Police v. Sitz

A *sobriety checkpoint* is a form of roadblock, but deserves further discussion because of its growing use in police work as a result of an important Supreme Court decision. In a 1990 case, the Court said that sobriety checkpoints in which the police stop every vehicle do not violate the Fourth Amendment protections against unreasonable searches and seizures and are therefore constitutional (Michigan Department of State Police v. Sitz, 58 L.W. 4781 [1990]).

In the Sitz case, the Michigan State Police Department established a highway checkpoint program pursuant to established guidelines. Under these guidelines, checkpoints would be set up at selected sites along state roads and all vehicles passing through the checkpoint would be stopped and the drivers checked for signs of intoxication. If intoxication was suspected, the vehicle would be pulled to the side of the road for further tests; all other drivers would be permitted to resume their journey.

During the only operation of the checkpoint, which lasted about an hour and fifteen minutes, 126 vehicles were checked with an average delay of twenty-five seconds. Two individuals were arrested for DWI. These guidelines and the Michigan sobriety checkpoint practice were challenged in courts as violating the Fourth Amendment. The Court rejected such challenge, saying that sobriety checkpoints are a form of seizure, but such seizure is reasonable because the "measure of intrusion on motorists stopped briefly at sobriety checkpoints is slight."

The Sitz case is significant because for a long time lower courts made conflicting decisions about the constitutionality of sobriety checkpoints. Courts in twenty-one states had upheld them, while courts in twelve states declared them unconstitutional. By a 6-to-3 vote, the Court has now declared that the police may establish highway checkpoints in an effort to catch drunken drivers.

It is important to note that the Sitz case does not allow the police to make random stops; what it does authorize are well-conceived and carefully structured sobriety checkpoints such as that of Michigan. Also, although sobriety checkpoints are constitutional, they may be prohibited by departmental policy or state law. (Read the Michigan Department of State Police v. Sitz case brief at the end of this chapter.)

In a case decided less than a week after Sitz, the Court further strengthened the authority of the police in drunk-driving cases when the Court ruled that the police may ask routine questions of suspected drunken drivers and videotape answers without giving them the Miranda warnings (Pennsylvania v. Muniz, 58 L.W. 4817 [1990]). Ruling 8 to 1, the Court said that the videotaped slurred answers in response to questions about height, weight, and age are admissible in court to convict drivers despite the absence of the Miranda warnings.

4. Stops for Brief Questioning

Stops for *brief questioning* that are routinely conducted at permanent checkpoints are consistent with the Fourth Amendment, and so obtaining a warrant before setting up a checkpoint is not necessary (U.S. v. Martinez-Fuerte, 428 U.S. 543 [1976]). However, the foreign appearance of the passengers in a car is not by itself sufficient to allow even a brief stop for questioning. Some other cause must be present (U.S. v. Brignoni-Ponce, 422 U.S. 873 [1975]).

5. Stops to Check Driver's License and Registration

Establishing a roadblock to check drivers' licenses and car registrations is legitimate. If in the process the officers see evidence of other crimes, they have the right to take reasonable investigative steps and are not required to close their eyes (U.S. v. Prichard, 645 F.2d 854 [1981]). However, police officers may not stop a single vehicle for the sole purpose of checking the driver's license and the vehicle registration. To do that,

---

HIGHLIGHT 8.1

Need to Control DWI

"No one can seriously dispute the magnitude of the drunken driving problem or the State's interest in eradicating it. Media reports of alcohol-related death and mutilation on the Nation's roads are legion" (Michigan Department of State Police v. Sitz, 58 L.W. 4781 [1990]).

TABLE 8.1 DWI Penalties

In 42 states imprisonment is mandatory for driving while intoxicated

State	Is imprisonment mandatory?	After which offense does imprisonment become mandatory?	Length of imprisonment
Alabama	Yes	2nd offense	2 days
Alaska	Yes	1st	3
Arizona	Yes	1st	1
Arkansas	No		
California	Yes	2nd	2
Colorado	Yes	2nd	7
Connecticut	Yes	1st	2
Delaware	Yes	2nd	60
DC	No		
Florida	Yes	2nd	10
Georgia	Yes	2nd	2
Hawaii	Yes	1st	2
Idaho	Yes	2nd	10
Illinois	Yes	2nd	2
Indiana	Yes	2nd	5
Iowa	Yes	2nd	7
Kansas	Yes	1st	2
Kentucky	Yes	2nd	7
Louisiana	Yes	1st	2
Maine	Yes	1st	2
Maryland	Yes	2nd	2
Massachusetts	Yes	2nd	14
Michigan	No		
Minnesota	No		
Mississippi	No		

the officers must reasonably believe that the stopped car's driver has violated a traffic law. Mere suspicion is not enough (Delaware v. Prouse, 440 U.S. 648 [1979]).

B. What an Officer May Do after a Vehicle Stop

What an officer may or may not do after stopping a vehicle has been addressed in a number of cases. Stopping the vehicle is not an end in itself; it is only a means to determine if a criminal activity has occurred or is about to occur. What follows after a stop is important for officer protection as well as for the admissibility of any seized evidence. There are a number of things an officer can do after a valid stop, the most significant of which are as follows.

1. Ask Driver to Get out of Vehicle—Pennsylvania v. Mimms

Once a vehicle is lawfully stopped for a traffic violation, the officer may order the driver to get out even without suspecting criminal activity. If the officer then reasonably believes that the driver may be armed and dangerous, the officer may conduct a limited protective frisk for a weapon that might endanger his or her personal safety (Pennsylvania v. Mimms, 434 U.S. 106 [1977]). For example, X is stopped by the police for running a red light. X may be asked to get out of the car. If, after X complies, the officer reasonably believes that X may be armed and dangerous, then X may be frisked. If during the frisk an illegal weapon is found, then X may be arrested.

TABLE 8.1 *(continued)*

State	Is imprisonment mandatory?	After which offense does imprisonment become mandatory?	Length of imprisonment
Missouri	Yes	2nd	2
Montana	Yes	1st	1
Nebraska	Yes	2nd	2
Nevada	Yes	1st	2
New Hampshire	Yes	2nd	7
New Jersey	Yes	2nd	2
New Mexico	Yes	2nd	2
New York	No		
North Carolina	Yes	2nd	7
North Dakota	Yes	2nd	4
Ohio	Yes	1st	3
Oklahoma	No		
Oregon	Yes	1st	2
Pennsylvania	Yes	2nd	30
Rhode Island	Yes	2nd	2
South Carolina	Yes	1st	2
South Dakota	No		
Tennessee	Yes	1st	2
Texas	Yes	2nd	3
Utah	Yes	1st	2
Vermont	Yes	2nd	2
Virginia	Yes	2nd	2
Washington	Yes	1st	1
West Virginia	Yes	1st	1
Wisconsin	No		
Wyoming	Yes	2nd	7

Source: A digest of state alcohol-highway safety related legislation, 5th ed., National Highway Traffic Safety Administration, U.S. Department of Transportation, as reprinted in *Report to the Nation on Crime and Justice* (Bureau of Justice Statistics, 1988), at 94.

Conversely, if the officer does not believe that the driver may be armed and dangerous, all the officer can do is ask the driver to get out of the car. A subsequent frisk, in the absence of the belief that the driver is armed and dangerous, is illegal even if the initial traffic stop was legal.

HIGHLIGHT 8.2

The Police and Motor Vehicle Drivers

"We think this additional intrusion [referring to the officer's order for the driver to get out of the car] can only be described as *de minimis*. The driver is being asked to expose to view very little more of his person than is already exposed. The police have already lawfully decided that the driver shall be briefly detained; the only question is whether he shall spend that period sitting in the driver's seat of his car or standing alongside of it. Not only is the insistence of the police on the latter choice not a 'serious intrusion upon the sanctity of the person,' but it hardly rises to the level of 'petty indignity' . . . what is at most a mere inconvenience cannot prevail when balanced against legitimate concerns for the officer's safety" (Pennsylvania v. Mimms, 434 U.S. 106, at 111 [1977]).

---

2. Ask Driver to Produce Driver's License and Other Documents Required by State Law

An officer has the authority, after a valid stop, to ask the driver to show a driver's license and other documents that state laws require to be produced. A number of states require that the driver produce the vehicle registration and proof of insurance in addition to a driver's license. The justification for this automatic authorization is that operating a motor vehicle on public highways is considered a privilege rather than a right. Practically all states consider the refusal to produce the required documents a criminal offense, hence the driver can be sanctioned accordingly.[3]

3. Ask Questions of Driver and Occupants

Once a valid stop has been made, the officer may ask questions of the occupants without giving the Miranda warnings. The Court has said that the roadside questioning of a motorist pursuant to a routine traffic stop (provided it is not an arrest) is not custodial interrogation and therefore does not require the Miranda warnings. But while the officer may ask questions, the driver and occupants have a constitutional right not to respond. Such a refusal to respond, however, may be taken into consideration by the officer to determine whether there is probable cause to arrest or search.[4]

4. Locate and Examine the Vehicle Identification Number (VIN)

Federal rules require that vehicles sold in the United States have a vehicle identifying number. This must be displayed on the dashboard of recently manufactured cars so the number can be read from outside the car through the windshield.[5] The Court has decided that motorists have no reasonable expectation of privacy with respect to the VIN located on the vehicle's dashboard, even if objects on the dashboard prevent the VIN from being observed from outside the car (New York v. Class, 54 L.W. 4178 [1986]). In this case, the officer reached into the car (which he had stopped after observing the motorist commit traffic offenses) in order to remove papers that prevented the officer from viewing the VIN. The driver said that this act was illegal in the absence of a warrant. The Court rejected the challenge, saying that such warrantless search was reasonable in view of its minimal intrusiveness, its furtherance of legitimate concerns for public safety, the motorist's lack of reasonable expectation of privacy in the VIN, and the offenses the officer had observed the motorist commit.

5. Search Vehicle

As long as the vehicle stop was lawful, what officers observe can evolve into probable cause to believe that the car contains the fruits and instrumentalities of crime or contraband, hence establishing a justification for a full warrantless search of the vehicle. In Colorado v. Bannister, 499 U.S. 1 (1980), the police stopped Bannister's automobile to issue him a speeding ticket. While writing out the citation, the officer observed the following: (1) Bannister and his companion fit a broadcast description of persons involved in theft of auto parts, and (2) there were wrenches and other materials in the back seat, suggesting tools for theft of parts. The Court held that what the officer observed established probable cause to justify a warrantless search because if a magistrate had been present while Bannister's car was stopped, the police could have obtained a warrant on the information the officer possessed. The warrantless search was therefore proper under the automobile exception.

Even in the absence of probable cause or reasonable suspicion, the officer may search the car if a valid consent is given. The Court has said that an officer, after validly stopping a car, may request the person in control of the car for permission to search (Schneckloth v. Bustamonte, 412 U.S. 218 [1973]). Such consent must be intelligent and voluntary, although it does not have to be in writing. The burden is on the officer to prove, if challenged, that the consent was in fact valid.

If the officer has reasonable suspicion that the motorist who has been stopped is dangerous and may be able to gain control of a weapon in the car, the officer may conduct a brief search of the passenger compartment even if the motorist is no longer inside the car (Michigan v. Long, 463 U.S. 1032 [1983]). Such search should be limited to areas in the passenger compartment where a weapon might be found or hidden. Note that this authorization for a brief search for a weapon is an extension of a stop and frisk rather than of an arrest situation.

6. Seize Items in Plain View

After a valid stop, the officer may seize illegal items in *plain view*. The seizure then establishes probable cause, which justifies an arrest. For example, officers lawfully stop a car to issue the driver a citation for driving through a red light. While writing out the citation, the officers see contraband in the passenger compartment. The officers may then seize the contraband and place the driver under arrest.

7. Arrest if Probable Cause Is Established

A stop may immediately turn into an arrest *if probable cause is established.* For example, a driver is stopped by an officer for speeding. She is ordered to get out of the car. The officer senses danger to himself and so frisks the driver. The frisk produces an illegal weapon. The officer may then arrest the driver and search the whole car. He may also conduct a full body search of the arrested driver.

III. WARRANTLESS VEHICLE SEARCHES

Warrantless searches of automobiles have been upheld as reasonable and therefore valid. This is because of the inherent mobility of vehicles (making it difficult to obtain a warrant) and the fact that a person's "reasonable expectation of privacy" in an automobile is significantly less than that in a home or office. The warrantless search, however, *must be based on probable cause that seizable items are contained in the vehicle.* It is important to remember, therefore, that vehicle searches may be made without a warrant, but they must be based on probable cause. Probable cause must be established by the officer through testimony if the search is later challenged in court. Again, a "fishing expedition" is not allowed.

A. Search of Passenger Compartment—Yes

Once a driver has been arrested, the police may conduct a warrantless search of the passenger compartment of the automobile. The police may examine the contents of any container found within the passenger compartment, as long as it may reasonably contain something that might pose a danger to the officer or hold evidence in support of the offense for which the suspect has been arrested (New York v. Belton, 453 U.S. 454 [1981]). (Read the New York v. Belton case brief at the end of this chapter.)

In Belton, a New York State officer noticed an automobile traveling at an excessive rate of speed. The officer gave chase and ordered the car to pull over to the side of the road. The officer asked to see the driver's license and in the process smelled burnt marijuana and saw an envelope on the floor of the car marked "Supergold." The officer placed the four occupants under arrest, picked up the envelope, and found marijuana. He then searched the passenger compartment and, on the back seat, found a black leather jacket belonging to Belton. The police unzipped one of the pockets of the jacket and discovered cocaine. During the trial, Belton moved to suppress the introduction of the cocaine as evidence, claiming that it had not been within the area of his immediate control and thus that its seizure had been illegal. The Court rejected this contention, saying that the police may conduct a warrantless search of the passenger compartment of a car incident to a lawful arrest.

Belton is significant in that it defines the extent of allowable search inside the automobile after a lawful arrest. Prior to Belton, there was confusion as to whether the police may search parts of the automobile outside the driver's "wingspan." The Court expanded the area of allowable search to the whole compartment, including the back seat; it also authorized the opening of containers found in the passenger compartment that might contain the object sought.

The term *container* denotes any object capable of holding another object. It thus includes closed or open glove compartments, consoles, or other receptacles located anywhere within the passenger compartment, as well as luggage, boxes, bags, clothing, and the like. In a footnote to Belton, the Court said: "Our holding encompasses only the interior of the passenger compartment of an automobile and does not encompass the trunk." The issue of whether or not the trunk may be opened was decided later in United States v. Ross, discussed below.

The Belton rule for passenger compartment searches applies only when there is custodial arrest. It therefore does not change the preexisting rule that a search of an automobile incident to arrest is not allowed when the person merely receives a citation at the scene. However, items in plain view during the issuance of a citation may be seized. Belton also requires that the arrest and search be contemporaneous; therefore the search of the vehicle must occur at the place of arrest and not at the station.[6] Note, however, that a later search at the station may be valid, but under the impoundment rationale, not as a search incident to arrest.

A lawful warrantless search of the vehicle does not automatically extend to a search of the person of an occupant. This rule is similar to the one stating that officers cannot search guests of a house for which a warrant has been issued. It has been argued, however, that if the objects sought are not found in the car and they are of such a size that they could be concealed on the person, then the occupants of the

---

HIGHLIGHT 8.3

Vehicle Searches and Search Warrants

Vehicle searches may be made without a warrant, but they must be based on probable cause. Probable cause must be established by the officer through testimony if the search is later challenged in court (New York v. Belton, 453 U.S. 454 [1981]).

vehicle should be subject to search if the officer has reason to suspect that one of them has the objects concealed on his or her person. For example, X is driving a car in which Y is a passenger. The car is stopped because of information amounting to probable cause that it contains stolen items. The car may be searched for stolen items and X, the driver, may be searched if the officer believes that X may be armed and dangerous. Y, the passenger, may not be searched—unless the officer has reason to suspect that Y has the stolen object concealed on his or her person.

B. Search of Trunks and Closed Packages Found in Trunks—Yes

If the police legitimately stop a car and have probable cause to believe that it contains contraband, they may conduct a warrantless search of the car. The search can be as thorough as a search authorized by a warrant issued by a magistrate. Therefore, every part of the vehicle in which the contraband might be stored may be inspected, including the trunk and all receptacles and packages that could possibly contain the object of the search (U.S. v. Ross, 31 CrL 3051 [1982]). (Read the United States v. Ross case brief at the end of this chapter.)

In the Ross case, after effecting a valid stop and arrest for narcotics sale, one of the officers opened the car's trunk and found a closed brown paper bag. Inside the bag were glassine bags containing white powder, which was later determined to be heroin. The officer then drove the car to police headquarters, where another warrantless search of the trunk revealed a zippered leather pouch containing cash. During trial, the suspect argued that the police officers should not have opened either the paper bag or the leather pouch found in the trunk without first obtaining a warrant. The Court disagreed and allowed the evidence to be admitted.

The Ross case is important because it further defines the scope of police authority in searches of vehicles. The Court in the Belton case had specifically refused to address the issue of whether or not the police could open the trunk of a car in connection with a warrantless search incident to a valid arrest. Ross addressed that issue and authorized such action; but it went beyond that and said that any packages or luggage found in the trunk that could reasonably contain the items for which the officers have probable cause to search could also be opened without a warrant. Ross has therefore greatly expanded the scope of allowable warrantless search incident to a valid arrest, *limited only by what is reasonable—considering the item or items searched.*

In the Ross case, the search focused on the whole automobile as the possible source of evidence. There was no need to obtain a search warrant to search the car or open containers found in the car that might reasonably conceal any evidence sought.

HIGHLIGHT 8.4

Extent of Automobile Searches

"We hold that the scope of the warrantless search authorized by that [automobile] exception is no broader and no narrower than a magistrate could legitimately authorize by warrant. If probable cause justifies the search of a lawfully stopped vehicle, it justifies the search of every part of the vehicle and its contents that may conceal the object of the search" (U.S. v. Ross, 31 CrL 3051, at 3058 [1982]).

Opening the brown paper bag and the pouch were legitimate by extension of police authority to conduct a warrantless search of the car.

It is an entirely different situation, however, if the object of the police's suspicion is a particular container in the car rather than the car itself (see discussion of the Chadwick case, below). The above examples indicate that car searches are usually conducted *contemporaneously* with (together with or immediately after) the arrest. There are instances, however, in which the officer may not be able to conduct a search contemporaneously. In these cases, the rule is that if the police have probable cause to stop and search an automobile on the highway, they may take the automobile to the police station and search it there without warrant—even if there was time for the police to obtain a warrant. The Court has said:

> For constitutional purposes, we see no difference between on the one hand seizing and holding a car before presenting the probable cause issue to a magistrate and on the other hand carrying out an immediate search without a warrant. Given probable cause to search, either course is reasonable under the Fourth Amendment. (Chambers v. Maroney, 399 U.S. 42 [1970])

For example, the police, having probable cause, stopped X's car on the highway and arrested him for robbery. There was probable cause to search the car, but the police towed the car instead to the police station and searched it there. During the trial, X objected to the introduction of the seized evidence, saying that the search was illegal because the police had had time to obtain a warrant: they already had the car at the police station and so no exigent circumstances existed. The Court said that the warrantless search was proper because the *police had probable cause to search when the vehicle was first stopped on the highway.* That probable cause justified a later search without a warrant (Chambers v. Maroney, 399 U.S. 42 [1970]).

A subsequent case reiterated this decision by saying that a vehicle may be searched under the automobile exception to the Fourth Amendment even if it has been immobilized and released to the custody of the police (Florida v. Meyers, 35 CrL 4022 [1984]). In sum, if the police could have conducted a warrantless search of the car when it was first stopped, then the car may be towed to the police station and searched without a warrant at a later time even if the police had time to obtain a warrant.

The ruling in the Ross case was later used to justify a warrantless search of a container even if there is a significant delay between the time the police stop the vehicle and the time they perform the search of the container. In a 1985 case, customs officers stopped two trucks suspected of carrying marijuana. Officers removed several sealed packages believed to contain marijuana and placed them in a government warehouse. Three days later, officials opened them without a warrant and found marijuana. Justice O'Connor, writing for the majority, said that neither Ross nor any other case establishes a requirement that a vehicle search occur immediately as part of the vehicle inspection or soon thereafter; hence a three-day delay before making the search was permissible (U.S. v. Johns, 36 CrL 3134 [1985]).

C. Search of Movable Containers Found in a Public Place—No

Although searches of trunks and closed packages found in trunks are valid, the same rule cannot apply to the search of a movable container found in a public place—even if the container was originally taken from a car. The case of United States v. Chadwick, 433 U.S. 1 (1977), involved the warrantless search of a 200-pound footlocker secured by two padlocks. Federal railroad officials in San Diego became suspicious when they noticed that a footlocker loaded into a train bound for Boston was unusually heavy and leaking talcum powder, a substance often used to mask the odor of marijuana. Narcotics agents met the train upon arrival in Boston and a trained police dog signaled the presence of a controlled substance inside the footlocker. The agents did not seize the footlocker at that time. Instead they waited until Chadwick arrived and the footlocker was placed in the trunk of Chadwick's automobile. Before the engine was started, the officers arrested Chadwick and his two companions. The agents took the footlocker to a secured place, opened it without a warrant, and discovered a large quantity of marijuana. The Court, on appeal, held the evidence to have been illegally seized, rejecting the argument that the warrantless search was reasonable because a footlocker has some of the mobile characteristics that support warrantless searches of automobiles. In ruling that the *warrantless search of the footlocker was unjustified*, the Court reaffirmed the general principle that *closed packages and containers may not be searched without a warrant.* The Court said: "Unlike an automobile, whose primary function is transportation, luggage is intended as a repository of personal effects. In sum, a person's expectations of privacy in personal luggage are substantially greater than in an automobile." Therefore, the Court in Chadwick declined to extend the automobile exception to permit a warrantless search of any movable container found in a public place.

The difference between the Chadwick (1977) and Ross (1982) cases appears to be that Chadwick involved a footlocker, which was *luggage* and only incidentally loaded in a car when the seizure was made, whereas Ross involved a *paper bag and a leather pouch*, both of which were found in the trunk of the car. The issue in Chadwick was whether the automobile exception should be applied to movable containers such as a footlocker that had traveled from San Diego and that had incidentally been taken from the trunk of a car. In contrast, the issue in Ross was whether or not officers can make a warrantless search of a closed container found in the trunk of a motor vehicle. Apparently, a piece of luggage has an identity of its own separate from an automobile, whereas a paper bag or a leather pouch does not.

In a 1985 case, an evenly divided Court affirmed without any extended discussion a decision by the Oklahoma Court of Criminal Appeals that police officers were constitutionally required to obtain a warrant before they could remove from an auto-

---

HIGHLIGHT 8.5

Automobiles v. Luggage

"The factors which diminish the privacy aspects of an automobile do not apply to . . . [a] footlocker. Luggage contents are not open to public view, except as a condition to a border entry or common carrier travel; nor is luggage subject to regular inspections and official scrutiny on a continuing basis. Unlike an automobile, whose primary function is transportation, luggage is intended as a repository of personal effects. In sum, a person's expectations of privacy in personal luggage are substantially greater than in an automobile" (U.S. v. Chadwick, 433 U.S. 1 [1977]).

mobile trunk and subsequently open a suitcase in which they suspected drugs were located (Oklahoma v. Castleberry, 37 CrL 3001 [1985]).

D. Search of Car on Private Property and Not in Use at Time of Search—No

The rule allowing warrantless searches of cars probably does not extend to cars that are not "mobile," meaning those that are not being driven at the time of the search, located on private property, and there is time to obtain a warrant. In one case, after months of investigation, police arrested a man for murder and at the same time seized his car, which was parked in the driveway, and later searched it because it was believed to have been used in the commission of a crime. The Court held the warrantless search to be unlawful, saying (1) that the objects sought were neither stolen nor contraband nor dangerous, and (2) that the car was not stopped on the open highway but was an unoccupied vehicle on private property (Coolidge v. New Hampshire, 403 U.S. 443 [1971]).[7] In that case, warrants were issued for Coolidge's arrest and for a search of his house and car in connection with the murder of a 14-year-old girl. The warrants were signed by the state attorney general, who was also the state's chief investigator and prosecutor. Coolidge was convicted and appealed, alleging, among other things, that the gunpowder residue and microscopic particles taken from the car should have been excluded from evidence because the search warrant was not issued by a "neutral and detached magistrate." The Court agreed and ruled the warrant to be invalid. The state argued in the alternative, however, that even if the warrant was not valid, the search of the car was valid because car searches do not need a search warrant. The Court disagreed, saying that a warrant was needed in this case because the car was not stopped on the open highway, it was an unoccupied vehicle on private property, and there was time for the officers to obtain a warrant. If the vehicle had been located in a public place and there had been no time to obtain a warrant, the Court would most likely have decided differently.

E. Vehicle Inventory Searches Immediately after an Arrest—Yes

Two cases have been decided by the Court addressing the validity and scope of inventory searches immediately after an arrest. In the first case, the Court said that inventory searches without a warrant of the person and possession of arrested individuals are permissible under the Fourth Amendment (Colorado v. Bertine, 479 U.S. 367 [1987]). In this case, Bertine was arrested for driving under the influence of alcohol. After he was taken into custody and before the arrival of a tow truck to impound the van, another officer inventoried the van in accordance with departmental procedures. During the inventory search, the officer opened a backpack and found various contents: controlled substances, drug paraphernalia, and money. Bertine challenged the admissibility of the evidence, saying that a warrant was needed to open the closed backpack. The Court rejected his challenge, saying that the police must be allowed to conduct warrantless inventory searches to secure an arrestee's property from loss or damage and to protect the police from false claims. Since closed containers may hold items that need to be secured, the police must be allowed to open them without a warrant. The Bertine case specified two requisites for the valid inventory search of a motor vehicle: (1) that the police follow standardized procedures so as to eliminate uncontrolled discretion to determine the scope of the search; and (2) that there be no bad faith on the part of the police, meaning that the inventory search is not used as an excuse for a warrantless search.

In a subsequent case reiterating Bertine, the Court said that a police department's "utter lack of any standard policy regarding the opening of closed containers encountered during inventory searches requires the suppression of contraband found in a locked suitcase removed from the trunk of an impounded vehicle and pried open by police after the driver's arrest on drunken driving charges" (Florida v. Wells, 47 CrL 2021 [1990]). In this case, Wells gave the Florida Highway Patrol permission to open the trunk of his car following his arrest for DWI. An inventory search turned up two marijuana cigarette butts in an ashtray and a locked suitcase in the trunk. The suitcase was opened and marijuana was found. Wells sought to reverse his conviction on appeal, saying that the marijuana found in his locked suitcase should not have been admitted as evidence. The Court agreed to suppress the evidence, saying that "absent any Highway Patrol policy with the opening of closed containers . . . the instant search was insufficiently regulated to satisfy the Fourth Amendment."

The message for the police from the Bertine and Wells cases is clear: a standardized policy is a must in vehicle inventory cases, meaning in cases where the police list the personal effects and properties found in the vehicle after impoundment. Such policy, said the Court, "prevents individual police officers from having so much latitude that inventory searches are turned into a ruse for a general rummaging in order to discover incriminating evidence." It is also clear from the preceding cases that the opening of a closed container or a locked suitcase is allowable in a vehicle inventory search.

F. Inventory Search of Vehicles Impounded by Police—Yes

The police have authority to seize and impound motor vehicles for various reasons, such as when the vehicle has been used for the commission of an offense or when it should be removed from the streets because it impedes traffic or threatens public safety. This type of search is distinguished from searches immediately after an arrest where the vehicle is not necessarily impounded.

When the police lawfully impound a vehicle, they may conduct a routine inventory search without warrant or probable cause to believe that the car contains seizable evidence. The leading case on impoundment search is South Dakota v. Opperman, 428 U.S. 364 (1976). In that case, the defendant's illegally parked car was taken to the city impound lot, where an officer, observing articles of personal property in the car, proceeded to inventory it. In the process, he found a bag of marijuana in the unlocked glove compartment. The Court concluded that "in following standard police procedures, prevailing throughout the country and approved by the overwhelming majority of courts, the conduct of the police was not 'unreasonable' under the Fourth Amendment." The case clearly legitimizes car inventories.

Although it is true that when a vehicle is abandoned or illegally parked, or when the owner is arrested, the courts permit vehicles to be impounded and inventoried, that rule should not apply when the driver has been arrested for a minor traffic violation, primarily because the police are expected to give the suspect a reasonable opportunity to post bail and obtain his or her prompt release. In Dyke v. Taylor

Implement Manufacturing Company, 391 U.S. 216 (1968), a driver who was arrested for reckless driving was at the courthouse to make bail when his vehicle was being searched. The Court concluded that the search of the vehicle could not be deemed incident to impoundment because the police seemed to have parked the car near the courthouse merely as a convenience to the owner who, if he were soon to be released from custody, could then have driven it away.[8]

Another issue in car impoundment is whether other alternatives to impoundment should be explored before placing the vehicle under police control (at least in cases in which the vehicle itself has not been involved in the crime). One writer notes:

> There is a growing body of authority that when the arrestee specifically requests that his car be lawfully parked in the vicinity of the arrest or that it be turned over to a friend, the police must honor his request. Indeed more and more courts are moving to the sound conclusion that the police must take the initiative with respect to apparent alternatives, such as permitting a licensed passenger to take custody of the car. . . .[9]

G. Search of Motor Homes—Yes

The Court has held that motor homes are automobiles for purposes of the Fourth Amendment and are therefore subject to the automobile exception, meaning that they can be searched without a warrant. The application of this decision is limited, however, to a motor home capable of being used on the road and located in a place not regularly used for residential purposes. Note that the decision specifically states that the case does not resolve whether the automobile exception would apply to a motor home "situated in a way or place that objectively indicates that it is being used as a residence" (California v. Carney, 37 CrL 3033 [1985]).

In the Carney case, above, federal narcotics agents had reason to believe that the defendant was exchanging marijuana for sex with a boy in a motor home parked on a public lot in downtown San Diego. The vehicle was outfitted to serve as a residence. The agents waited until the youth emerged and convinced him to return and ask the defendant to come out. When the defendant came out, an agent entered the motor home without a warrant and found marijuana lying on a table. During the trial, the defendant sought to suppress the evidence, saying that it was obtained without a warrant and hence excludible. The Court disagreed, saying that the evidence was admissible, adding that the vehicle in question was readily mobile and that there was a reduced expectation of privacy stemming from its use as a licensed motor vehicle. Also, the vehicle was so situated as to suggest that it was being used as a vehicle, not a residence. The Court refused to distinguish motor homes from ordinary automobiles simply because motor homes are capable of functioning as dwellings, saying that motor homes lend themselves easily to use as instruments of illicit drug traffic and other illegal activity.

H. Use of Beepers to Detect Cars—It Depends

A person traveling in a car on a public road has *no reasonable expectation of privacy*, and therefore a visual surveillance by the police does not constitute a search. Moreover, the Fourth Amendment does not prohibit the police from supplementing their sensory faculties with technological aids to help the police identify the car's location (U.S. v. Knotts, 459 U.S. 817 [1983]). The facts in Knotts are as follows: With the cooperation of a chemical supply company, state narcotics agents installed an electronic beeper in a container of chloroform. When a man the agents suspected of manufacturing controlled substances turned up at the chemical company to purchase chloroform, the bugged can was sold to him. The agents used both the beeper signal and visual means to follow the suspect to a house where the container was placed in another car. The second car then proceeded into another state, where the agents lost both visual and beeper contact. The beeper signal was picked up again, however, by a monitoring device aboard a helicopter. By this means, the agents learned that the container was locked in or near a secluded cabin owned by defendant Knotts. Armed with this and other information, the agents obtained a warrant that, upon execution, uncovered a secret drug laboratory. The Court held the police act to be valid and the evidence admissible, saying that by using the public roadways the driver of the car voluntarily conveyed to anyone that he was traveling over particular roads and in a particular direction. Moreover, no expectation of privacy extended to the visual observation of the automobile arriving on private premises after leaving the public highway, nor to movements of objects such as the drum of chloroform outside the cabin in the "open fields."

The Knotts case did not address the question of monitoring in private places; neither did it examine the legality of the original installation and transfer of the beeper. That issue was addressed in United States v. Karo, decided a year later (35 CrL 3246 [1984]).

In United States v. Karo, government agents, upon learning that the defendants had ordered a quantity of ether from a government informant to use in extracting cocaine, obtained a court order authorizing the installation and monitoring of a beeper in one of the cans. The agents installed the beeper with the informant's consent, and the can was subsequently delivered to the defendants. Over a period of months, the beeper enabled the agents to monitor the can's movements to a variety of locations, including several private residences and two commercial storage facilities. The agents obtained a search warrant for one of the homes. When the evidence obtained from that warrant was introduced in court, the defendant promptly objected. The Court first explained that neither the initial installation of the beeper nor the container's subsequent transfer to defendant Karo infringed any constitutional right of privacy of the defendant, and they did not constitute search or seizure under the Fourth Amendment. The monitoring of the beeper, however, was an entirely different matter. The Court said that the monitoring of a beeper in a private dwelling, a location not open to visual surveillance, violates the rights of individuals to privacy in their own homes. Although the monitoring here was less intrusive than a full search, it revealed facts that the government was interested in knowing and that it could not otherwise have obtained legally without a warrant. The Court considered the use of the beeper to have been violative of Karo's Fourth Amendment right, but decided anyway that the evidence obtained ought not to be suppressed because ample evidence other than that obtained through use of the beeper existed to establish probable cause for the issuance of the warrant.

Karo is different from Knotts in that in Knotts the agents learned nothing from the beeper that they could not have visually observed; hence there was no Fourth Amendment intrusion. Moreover, the monitoring in Knotts occurred in a public place, whereas the beeper in Karo intruded on the privacy of a home.

I. Other Car Searches

There are other miscellaneous circumstances under which warrantless car searches
may be allowed, among them:

1. *Accident cases.* If because of an accident or other circumstances a car is to
   remain in a location where it is vulnerable to intrusion by vandals, the police,
   if they have probable cause to believe that the vehicle contains a weapon or
   a similar device that would constitute a danger if it fell into the wrong hands,
   may make a warrantless search for the particular item (Cady v. Dombrowski,
   413 U.S. 433 [1973]).
2. *Cases in which the vehicle itself has been the subject of crime.* If an officer
   has probable cause to believe that a car has been the subject of burglary,
   tampering, or theft, he may make a limited warrantless entry and investigation of those areas that he reasonably believes might contain evidence of
   ownership.
3. *Cases in which the vehicle is believed abandoned.* A limited search of an
   automobile in an effort to ascertain ownership is allowable when the car has
   apparently been abandoned or when the arrested driver is possibly not the
   owner and does not otherwise establish the matter of ownership.

TABLE 8.2   Warrantless Vehicle Searches—A Summary of Cases

Case	Factual situation	Valid?
New York v. Class (1986)	Search of vehicle identification number.	Yes
New York v. Belton (1981)	Search of passenger compartment	Yes
U.S. v. Ross (1982)	Search of trunks and closed packages found in trunks	Yes
U.S. v. Chadwick (1977)	Search of movable containers found in a public place	No
Coolidge v. New Hampshire (1971)	Search of car on private property and not in use at time of search	No
Colorado v. Bertine (1987)	Inventory search of closed backpack	Yes
Florida v. Wells (1990)	Inventory search of locked suitcase in absence of standard procedure	No
South Dakota v. Opperman (1976)	Search of vehicles impounded by police	Yes
California v. Carney (1985)	Search of motor homes	Yes
U.S. v. Knotts (1983) & U.S. v. Karo (1984)	Use of beepers to detect cars	Yes, in public place; no, in private place

IV. CAUTION

The rules discussed here on automobile searches are based primarily on U.S. Supreme
Court decisions. They are not reflective of state law or policies and regulations in
particular police departments. State law and departmental policies and regulations
may limit, and frequently do limit, what the police can do. In case of conflict, follow
state law and departmental policies and regulations because they are binding on the
police officer, regardless of what the U.S. Supreme Court says. For example, the
Court has decided that if the police have probable cause to stop and search an

automobile on the highway, they may take it to the police station and search it there without a warrant—even if there was time for the police to obtain a warrant. Assume, however, that state law and departmental policies say that once the car is brought to the police station and the driver incarcerated, the police must obtain a warrant before conducting a search of the car. In that case, a warrant must be obtained, otherwise the search is illegal and the evidence obtained is inadmissible.

☐ SUMMARY

A seizure occurs every time a motor vehicle is stopped. Searches and seizures of motor vehicles, however, generally do not need a warrant and are therefore an exception to the warrant requirement of the Fourth Amendment.

There are various types of vehicle stops, among them stops for suspicion of involvement in criminal activity, roadblocks, sobriety checkpoints, stops for brief questioning, and stops to check driver's license and registration. All these vehicular stops may be made without a warrant and on less than probable cause.

After the vehicle is validly stopped, the officer can do a number of things. These include asking the driver to get out of the vehicle, asking the driver to produce a driver's license and other documents required by state law, asking questions of the driver and occupants, locating and examining the vehicle identification number, searching the vehicle, seizing items in plain view, and making an arrest if probable cause is established.

Vehicle searches must be conducted based on probable cause, with some exceptions. Based on probable cause, the officer may search the passenger compartment, search the trunk and closed packages found in the trunk, conduct a vehicle inventory search immediately after an arrest, and search motor homes.

The law on motor vehicle searches is complex and made more difficult because constitutional rules are often superseded by state law or agency rules. For example, what the Constitution allows on vehicle stops may be prohibited by state law or agency policy. In addition to knowing the constitutional rules discussed in this chapter, police officers must know by heart their state law or agency rules on vehicle searches.

☐ REVIEW QUESTIONS

1. What is the automobile exception to the search and seizure rule? Give reasons for this exception.
2. What did the Supreme Court say in the case of Michigan Department of State Police v. Muniz?
3. "Under certain circumstances, a stop for a traffic violation can lead to a search of the entire vehicle." When can this take place?
4. Assume that a police officer has made a valid arrest of a car driver for possession of drugs. To what extent may the police search the vehicle incident to that arrest?
5. What did the Supreme Court say in the case of United States v. Ross?
6. Contrast the Supreme Court decisions in the United States v. Ross and the United States v. Chadwick cases on items and containers found in a car.

7. May a car that is not in use at the time of search be searched without a warrant? Explain.
8. Taken together, what do the Bertine and Wells cases say about vehicle inventory searches immediately after an arrest?
9. Give the rule concerning searches of motor homes.
10. Discuss the distinction between the Knotts and the Karo cases on the use of beepers.

☐ DEFINITIONS

Beeper: An electronic device sometimes used by the police to monitor the movement and location of a motor vehicle.

Roadblock: A law enforcement practice for halting traffic; it is not strictly a form of detention, but it limits a person's freedom of movement by blocking vehicular movement. It is used by the police for a variety of purposes, including spot checks of drivers' licenses, car registrations, and violations of motor vehicle laws and apprehension of fleeing criminals and suspects.

Sobriety Checkpoint: Checkpoint set up by the police at selected sites along public roads wherein all vehicles passing through the checkpoint are stopped and the drivers checked for signs of intoxication.

Vehicle Impoundment: The taking by the police into custody of vehicles for such reasons as use in a crime, impeding of traffic, and threat to public safety.

Vehicle Inventory: The listing by the police of personal effects and properties found in the vehicle after impoundment.

☐ PRINCIPLES OF CASES

BROWER V. COUNTY OF INYO, 57 L.W. 4321 (1989) Roadblocks are a form of seizure under the Fourth Amendment.

CADY V. DOMBROWSKI, 413 U.S. 433 (1973) If because of an accident or other circumstances a car is to remain in a location where it is vulnerable to intrusion by vandals, the police, if they have probable cause to believe that the vehicle contains a weapon or a similar device that would constitute a danger if it fell into the wrong hands, may make a warrantless search for the particular item.

CALIFORNIA V. CARNEY, 37 CrL 3033 (1985) Motor homes are automobiles for purposes of the Fourth Amendment and are therefore subject to the automobile exception, meaning that they can be searched without warrant.

CARROLL V. UNITED STATES, 267 U.S. 132 (1925) The search of an automobile does not need a warrant, where it is not practicable to do so, because the vehicle can be quickly moved out of the locality or jurisdiction in which the warrant must be sought.

CHAMBERS V. MARONEY, 399 U.S. 42 (1970) For constitutional purposes, there is no difference between seizing and holding a car before presenting the probable cause issue to a magistrate and carrying out an immediate search without a warrant. Given probable cause to search, either course is reasonable under the Fourth Amendment.

COLORADO V. BANNISTER, 499 U.S. 1 (1980)   As long as the stopping of the vehicle was lawful, what officers observe can evolve into probable cause to believe that the car contains the fruits and instrumentalities of crime or contraband, hence establishing a justification for a full warrantless search of the vehicle.

COLORADO V. BERTINE, 479 U.S. 367 (1987)   Inventory searches without a warrant of the person and possession of arrested individuals are permissible under the Fourth Amendment.

COOLIDGE V. NEW HAMPSHIRE, 403 U.S. 443 (1971)   The automobile exception does not apply to cars that are not "mobile," meaning those that are not in use at the time of search. This is so because (1) the objects sought were neither stolen nor contraband nor dangerous and (2) the car was not stopped on the open highway but was an unoccupied vehicle on private property.

DELAWARE V. PROUSE, 440 U.S. 648 (1979)   Stopping an automobile and detaining its occupants constitute a "seizure" within the meaning of the Fourth and Fourteenth Amendments, even though the purpose of the stop is limited and the resulting detention quite brief. Roadblocks may be set up for inspection purposes, provided the officer stops every car passing the checkpoint or has an articulable, neutral principle (such as stopping every fifth car) for justifying the stop.

DYKE V. TAYLOR IMPLEMENT MANUFACTURING COMPANY, 391 U.S. 216 (1968)   The search of the vehicle in this case could not be deemed incident to impoundment because the police seemed to have parked the car near the courthouse merely as a convenience to the owner who, if he were soon to be released from custody, could then have driven it away.

FLORIDA V. MEYERS, 35 CrL 4022 (1984)   A vehicle may be searched under the automobile exception to the Fourth Amendment even if it has been immobilized and released to the custody of the police.

FLORIDA V. WELLS, 47 CrL 2021 (1990)   A police department's utter lack of any standard policy regarding the opening of closed containers encountered during inventory searches requires the suppression of contraband found in a locked suitcase removed from the trunk of an impounded vehicle and pried open by the police after the driver's arrest on drunken driving.

MICHIGAN DEPARTMENT OF STATE POLICE V. SITZ, 58 L.W. 4781 (1990)   Sobriety checkpoints in which the police stop every vehicle do not violate the Fourth Amendment protections against unreasonable searches and seizures and are therefore constitutional.

MICHIGAN V. LONG, 463 U.S. 1032 (1983)   If the officer has reasonable suspicion that the motorist who has been stopped is dangerous and may be able to gain control of a weapon in the car, the officer may conduct a brief search of the passenger compartment even if the motorist is no longer inside the car. Such search should be limited to areas in the passenger compartment where a weapon might be found or hidden.

NEW YORK V. BELTON, 453 U.S. 454 (1981)   Once a driver has been arrested, the police may conduct a warrantless search of the passenger compartment of the automobile. The police may examine the contents of any container found within the passenger compartment, as long as it may reasonably contain something that might pose a danger to the officer or hold evidence in support of the offense for which the suspect has been arrested.

NEW YORK V. CLASS, 54 L.W. 4178 (1986)   Motorists have no reasonable expectation of privacy with respect to the vehicle identification number (VIN) located on the car's dashboard, even if objects on the dashboard prevent the vehicle identification number from being observed from outside the car.

PENNSYLVANIA V. MIMMS, 434 U.S. 106 (1977)   Once a vehicle has been lawfully stopped for a traffic violation, the officer may order the driver to get out even without suspecting criminal activity. If the officer then reasonably believes that the driver may be armed and dangerous, the officer may conduct a limited protective frisk for a weapon that might endanger his or her personal safety.

PENNSYLVANIA V. MUNIZ, 58 L.W. 4817 (1990)   Videotaped slurred answers in response to questions about height, weight, and age are admissible in court to convict drivers despite the absence of the Miranda warnings.

ROBBINS V. CALIFORNIA, 453 U.S. 420 (1981)   The automobile exception to the warrant requirement is justified by the following considerations: (1) the mobility of motor vehicles, (2) the diminished expectation of privacy, (3) the fact that the car is used for transportation and not as a residence or a repository of personal effects, (4) the fact that the car's occupants and contents travel in plain view, and (5) the necessarily high degree of regulation of automobiles by the government.

SCHNECKLOTH V. BUSTAMONTE, 412 U.S. 218 (1973)   After validly stopping a car, an officer may ask the person in control of the car for permission to search.

SOUTH DAKOTA V. OPPERMAN, 428 U.S. 364 (1976)   When the police lawfully impound a vehicle, they may conduct a routine inventory search without a warrant or probable cause to believe that the car contains seizable evidence. This procedure is reasonable to protect the owner's property, to protect the police against a claim that the owner's property was stolen while the car was impounded, and to protect the police from potential danger.

UNITED STATES V. BRIGNONI-PONCE, 422 U.S. 873 (1975)   The foreign appearance of the passengers in a car is not by itself sufficient to allow even a brief stop for questioning. Some other cause must be present.

UNITED STATES V. CHADWICK, 433 U.S. 1 (1977)   The warrantless search of a movable container (in this case a 200-pound footlocker secured by padlocks) found in a public place is invalid because the container does not come under the automobile exception even if it happens to have been removed from a car.

UNITED STATES V. CORTEZ, 449 U.S. 411 (1981)   There must be at least a reasonable suspicion to justify an investigatory stop of a motor vehicle.

UNITED STATES V. JOHNS, 36 CrL 3134 (1985)   The warrantless search of containers found in a car is valid even if there is a significant delay (three days in this case) between the time the police stop the vehicle and the time they perform the search.

UNITED STATES V. KARO, 35 CrL 3246 (1984)   The monitoring by a beeper in a private dwelling, a location not open to visual surveillance, violates the rights of individuals to privacy in their own homes. It therefore cannot be conducted without a warrant.

UNITED STATES V. KNOTTS, 459 U.S. 817 (1983)   The use by the police of beepers in a car on a public road does not constitute a search because there is no reasonable expectation of privacy. Moreover, the Fourth Amendment does not prohibit the police from supplementing their sensory faculties with technological aids to help the police identify the car's location.

UNITED STATES V. MARTINEZ-FUERTE, 428 U.S. 543 (1976)   Stops for brief questioning that are routinely conducted at permanent checkpoints are consistent with the Fourth Amendment, and so obtaining a warrant before setting up a checkpoint is not necessary.

UNITED STATES V. PRICHARD, 645 F.2d 854 (1981)   Establishing a roadblock to check drivers' licenses and car registrations is legitimate. If in the process of doing so the officers see evidence of other crimes, they have the right to take reasonable investigative steps and are not required to close their eyes.

UNITED STATES V. ROSS, 102 S.Ct. 2157 (1982)   If the police legitimately stop a car and have probable cause to believe that it contains contraband, they can conduct a warrantless search of the car. The search can be as thorough as a search authorized by a warrant issued by a magistrate. Therefore, every part of the vehicle in which the contraband might be stored may be inspected, including the trunk and all receptacles and packages that could possibly contain the object of the search.

☐ CASE BRIEF—LEADING CASE ON SEARCH OF CAR TRUNK AND CLOSED PACKAGE IN TRUNK

UNITED STATES V. ROSS, 102 S.Ct. 2157 (1982)

FACTS: Washington, DC, police received information from an informant that Ross was selling narcotics kept in the trunk of his car, which was parked at a specified location. The police drove to the location, spotted the person and car that matched the description given by the informant, and made a warrantless arrest. The officers opened the car's trunk and found a closed brown paper bag containing glassine bags of a substance that turned out to be heroin. The officers then drove the car to police headquarters, where another warrantless search of the trunk revealed a zippered leather pouch containing cash. Ross was charged with possession of heroin with intent to distribute. He sought to suppress the heroin and cash as evidence, alleging that both were obtained in violation of his constitutional rights because both were found in the absence of exigent circumstances that would justify a warrantless search.

ISSUE   *After a valid arrest, may the police open the trunk of the car and containers found therein without a warrant and in the absence of exigent circumstances? Yes.*

SUPREME COURT DECISION: When the police have probable cause to justify a warrantless search of a car, they may search the entire car and open the trunk and any packages or luggage found therein that could reasonably contain the items for which they have probable cause to search.

CASE SIGNIFICANCE: The Ross case is important in that it further defines the scope of police authority in vehicle searches. The Belton case specifically refused to address the issue of whether or not the police could open the trunk of a car in connection with a search incident to a valid arrest. Ross addressed that issue and authorized such action. It went beyond that and said that any packages or luggage found in the car that could reasonably contain the items for which they have probable cause to search could also be opened without a warrant. Ross has therefore greatly expanded the scope of allowable warrantless search, limited only by what is reasonable. Note, however, that this authorization is not without limit. The police may not open big items taken from a car (such as a footlocker) without a warrant if there is time to obtain one. This is because those items have identities of their own separate and apart from the car. Also, although the police may constitutionally open smaller items without a warrant, that action may be prohibited by state law or departmental policy, which prevails over constitutional license.

EXCERPTS FROM THE DECISION: A lawful search of fixed premises generally extends to the entire area in which the object of the search may be found and is not limited by the possibility that separate acts of entry or opening may be required to complete the search. Thus, a warrant that authorizes an officer to search a home for illegal weapons also provides authority to open closets, chests, drawers, and containers in which the weapon might be found. A warrant to open a footlocker to search for marijuana would also authorize the opening of packages found inside. A warrant to search a vehicle would support a search of every part of the vehicle that might contain the object of the search. When a legitimate search is under way, and when its purpose and its limits have been precisely defined, nice distinctions between closets, drawers, and containers, in the case of a home, or between glove compartments, upholstered seats, trunks, and wrapped packages, in the case of a vehicle, must give way to the interest in the prompt and efficient completion of the task at hand.

This rule applies equally to all containers, as indeed we believe it must. One point on which the Court was in virtually unanimous agreement in Robbins was that a constitutional distinction between "worthy" and "unworthy" containers would be improper. Even though such a distinction perhaps could evolve in a series of cases in which paper bags, locked trunks, lunch buckets, and orange crates were placed on one side of the line or the other, the central purpose of the Fourth Amendment forecloses such a distinction. For just as the most frail cottage in the kingdom is absolutely entitled to the same guarantees of privacy as the most majestic mansion, so also may a traveler who carries a toothbrush and a few articles of clothing in a paper bag or knotted scarf claim an equal right to conceal his possessions from official inspection as the sophisticated executive with the locked attache case.

□   **CASE BRIEF—LEADING CASE ON CONSTITUTIONALITY OF SOBRIETY CHECKPOINTS**

MICHIGAN DEPARTMENT OF STATE POLICE V. SITZ 58 L.W. 4781 (1990)

FACTS: The Michigan State Police Department established a highway checkpoint program pursuant to guidelines established by a Checkpoint Advisory Committee that governed checkpoint operations, site selection, and publicity. Under these guidelines, checkpoints would be set up at selected sites along state roads and all vehicles passing through the checkpoint would be stopped and the drivers checked for signs of intoxication. If intoxication was indicated, the vehicle would be pulled to the side of the road for further tests; all other drivers would be permitted to resume their journey.

During the only operation of the checkpoint, which lasted approximately 1 hour and 15 minutes, 126 vehicles were checked with an average delay of 25 seconds. Two individuals were arrested for driving while intoxicated. On the day before the checkpoint was established, both respondents filed a suit in the county court seeking relief from potential subjection to the checkpoints.

ISSUE: *Is the use of a sobriety checkpoint that stops all vehicles a violation of the Fourth and Fourteenth Amendments? No.*

SUPREME COURT DECISION: Sobriety checkpoints in which the police stop every vehicle do not violate the Fourth and Fourteenth Amendment protections against unreasonable searches and seizures and are therefore constitutional.

CASE SIGNIFICANCE: For a long time, lower courts had conflicting opinions about the constitutionality of sobriety checkpoints. Courts in twenty-one states had upheld sobriety checkpoints, while courts in twelve states had declared them unconstitutional. By a 6-to-3 vote, the Court has now declared that the police may establish highway checkpoints in an effort to catch drunk drivers.

Although the Court admits that sobriety checkpoints constitute a form of seizure and therefore come under the Fourth Amendment, the intrusion on the driver is minimal and therefore considered reasonable, particularly in light of the state interest involved. The Court quoted media accounts of the seriousness of drunk drivers, saying: "drunk drivers cause an annual death toll of over 25,000 and in the same time span cause nearly one million personal injuries and more than five billion dollars in property damage." Balancing the state interest involved and the individual constitutional rights invoked, the Court came down on the side of the state, hence giving the police an added weapon in the fight against drunk drivers.

Police departments should note that the sobriety checkpoint procedures declared constitutional by the Court in Sitz were a product of careful study and thinking. According to the Court, the following were the main features of the Michigan procedure:

> . . . checkpoints would be set up at selected sites along state roads. All vehicles passing through a checkpoint would be stopped and their drivers briefly examined for signs of intoxication. In cases where a checkpoint officer detected signs of intoxication, the motorist would be directed to a location out of the traffic flow where an officer would check the motorist's driver's license and car registration and, if warranted, conduct further sobriety tests. Should the field tests and the officer's observations suggest that the driver was intoxicated, an arrest would be made. All other drivers would be permitted to resume their journey immediately.

The Sitz case does not allow police to make random stops; what it does authorize are well-conceived and carefully structured sobriety checkpoints such as that of Michigan.

Although sobriety checkpoints are constitutional, such may be prohibited by departmental policy or state law.

EXCERPTS FROM THE DECISION: No one can seriously dispute the magnitude of the drunken problem or the States' interest in eradicating it. Media reports of alcohol-related death and mutilation on the Nation's roads are legion. The anecdotal is confirmed by the statistical. "Drunk drivers cause an annual death toll of over 25,000 and in the same time span cause nearly one million personal injuries and more than five billion dollars in property damage." For decades, this Court has "repeatedly lamented the tragedy." "The increasing slaughter on our highways . . . now reaches the astounding figures only heard of on the battlefield."

Conversely, the weight bearing on the other scale—the measure of the intrusion on motorists stopped briefly at sobriety checkpoints—is slight. We reached a similar conclusion as to the intrusion on motorists subjected to a brief stop at a highway checkpoint for detecting illegal aliens. We see virtually no difference between the levels of intrusion on law-abiding motorists from the brief stops necessary to the effectuation of these two types of checkpoints, which to the average motorist would seem identical save for the nature of the questions the checkpoint officers might ask.

◻ NOTES

1. M. Hermann, *Search and Seizure Checklists*, 3d ed. (New York: Clark Boardman, 1983), at 78.
2. Ibid., at 71.
3. See "Traffic Stops: Police Powers under the Fourth Amendment," by J. Gales Sauls, *FBI Law Enforcement Bulletin*, September 1989, at 29.
4. Ibid.
5. Ibid., at 30.
6. W. LaFave and J. Israel, *Criminal Procedure* (St. Paul, MN: West, 1985), at 164.
7. Ibid., at 166.
8. LaFave and Israel, op. cit., at 170.
9. Ibid.

Chapter Nine

PLAIN VIEW, OPEN FIELDS, ABANDONMENT, AND ELECTRONIC SURVEILLANCE

Summary
Review Questions
Definitions
Principles of Cases
Case Briefs
    HORTON V. CALIFORNIA
    KATZ V. UNITED STATES

□ KEY TERMS

"plain view" doctrine
officer's sight
immediately apparent
inadvertence
open view
"open fields" doctrine
curtilage
abandonment

electronic surveillance
old concept of electronic surveillance
new concept of electronic surveillance
Title III of the Omnibus Crime Control
    and Safe Streets Act of 1968
Electronic Communications and
    Privacy Act of 1986 (ECPA)
pen register

This chapter discusses four topics relating to searches and seizures that justify separate consideration because of their importance in law enforcement work. What plain view, open fields, abandonment, and electronic surveillance have in common is some form of "taking" by the government of something that belongs to or used to belong to somebody. They do differ enough in concept, legal rules, and practice to deserve individual discussion. Plain view, open fields, and abandonment justify warrantless seizures because they do not come under the Fourth Amendment, whereas electronic surveillance is governed rigidly by the Fourth Amendment and federal law.

I. THE "PLAIN VIEW" DOCTRINE
A. Definition

The *"plain view" doctrine* states that items that are within the sight of an officer who is legally in a place from which the view is made may properly be seized without a warrant—as long as such items are immediately recognizable as subject to seizure. In the words of the Court: "It has long been settled that objects falling in the plain view of an officer who has a right to be in a position to have that view are subject to seizure and may be introduced in evidence" (Harris v. U.S., 390 U.S. 234 [1968]).

Although considered by most writers as an exception to the search warrant requirement, plain view is really not a "search" within the terms of the Fourth Amendment because no search for that specific item has been or is being undertaken. No warrant or probable cause is necessary because the officer simply seizes what he or she sees, not something for which he or she has searched. Seeing the item is accidental and unplanned.

B. Requirements

The above definition indicates that there are three basic elements of the "plain view" doctrine:

1. Item's Position within the Officer's Sight

Awareness of the items must be gained solely through the officer's sight, not through the other senses—hearing, smelling, tasting, or touching. This means that the item must be *plainly visible* to the officer for plain view to apply. For example, while executing a search warrant for a stolen typewriter, the officer sees marijuana on the suspect's nightstand. Seizure may be made because through the sense of sight the officer knows that the items are contraband and therefore seizable. But if the officer senses that there is marijuana in the apartment because of the smell, as might occur if the item were hidden in a closet or drawer, its seizure in the course of a search cannot be justified under the "plain view" doctrine because it was not discovered through the officer's sense of sight. (Of course, it may be validly seized without warrant if the officer can establish probable cause and the presence of exigent circumstances when justifying a warrantless seizure.)

Some writers maintain that the "plain view" doctrine also applies to "plain odor," citing the case of United States v. Johns, 469 U.S. 478 (1985), in which the Court said that "whether defendant ever had a privacy interest in the packages reeking of marijuana is debatable."[1] This issue has not been directly addressed by the Court because most, if not all, "plain view" cases involve the sense of sight. In the absence of definite pronouncement from the Court, the better view seems to be that plain view, as the term itself implies, should be limited to the sense of sight.

2. Officer's Legal Presence in the Place from which Item Is Seen

The officer must have done nothing illegal to get to the spot from which he or she sees the items in question. An officer comes to be in a place properly in a number of ways; for instance, when serving a search warrant, while in hot pursuit of a suspect, having made entry through valid consent, and when making a valid arrest with or without a warrant. For example, while executing a search warrant for a stolen TV set, an officer sees gambling slips on a table. She may properly seize them even though they were not included in the warrant, as long as her presence in the premises is legal. By contrast, a police officer who forces himself into a house and then sees drugs on the table cannot properly seize the drugs because he entered the house illegally. What the officer sees subsequent to entry can never offset the initial illegality.

3. "Immediately Apparent" That the Item Is Subject to Seizure

Recognition of the items in plain view must be immediate and not the result of further prying or examination. In other words, the items must be out in the open and immediately recognizable as seizable. For example, Officer P sees something that he immediately recognizes as gambling paraphernalia. It is seizable under plain view. By contrast, suppose that after a valid entry the officer sees a typewriter that he suspects to be stolen. He calls the police station to ask for the serial number of a

---

HIGHLIGHT 9.1

The "Plain View" Doctrine v. Privacy

"The plain view doctrine is grounded on the proposition that once police are lawfully in a position to observe an item first-hand, its owner's privacy interest in that item is lost; the owner may retain the incidents of title and possession but not privacy" (Illinois v. Andreas, 103 S.Ct. 3319 [1983]).

---

typewriter earlier reported stolen and, after verification of the number, seizes the typewriter. This seizure cannot be justified under the "plain view" doctrine because the item was not immediately recognizable as subject to seizure. The evidence may be seized, but the action would have to be based on consent or exigent circumstance.

The *"immediately apparent"* requirement must be based on *probable cause* and not on any lower degree of certainty, such as reasonable suspicion (Arizona v. Hicks, 480 U.S. 321 [1987]). In this case, a bullet fired through the floor of Hicks's apartment, injuring a man below, prompted the police to enter Hicks' apartment to search for the suspect, weapons, and other victims. The officer discovered three weapons and a stocking cap mask. He also noticed several pieces of stereo equipment, which seemed out of place in the ill-appointed apartment. The officer therefore read and recorded the serial numbers of the equipment, moving some of the pieces in the process. A call to the police headquarters confirmed that one of the pieces of equipment was stolen; a later check revealed that the other pieces of equipment were also stolen. Hicks was charged with and convicted of robbery. On appeal, he sought suppression of the evidence saying that the "plain view" search was illegal. The Court agreed, saying that probable cause to believe that items being searched are in fact contraband or evidence of criminal activity is required for the items to be searched under plain view. A lower degree of certainty, such as reasonable suspicion, as in this case, would not suffice. The evidence was excluded.

Although the item must be immediately recognizable as subject to seizure, *"certain knowledge"* that incriminating evidence is involved is not necessary. All that is needed is *probable cause*. For example, an officer stops a car at night to check the driver's license. He shines his flashlight into the car's interior and sees the driver holding an opaque green party balloon, knotted about one-half inch from the tip. The officer also sees white powder in the open glove compartment. In court the officer testifies that he has learned from experience that inflated, tied-off balloons are often used to transport narcotics. The Court concludes that the officer had probable cause to believe that the balloon contained narcotics and that therefore a warrantless seizure was justified under plain view (Texas v. Brown, 103 S.Ct. 1535 [1983]).

It must be emphasized that the "plain view" doctrine is simply one of the legal justifications for admitting evidence obtained by the police. It is used as a legal justification for seizure only if all of the above three elements are present. The absence of one of the elements means that the evidence is not admissible under plain view, but the evidence may still be admissible under another legal doctrine. For example, an officer arrests a suspect at home by authority of an arrest warrant. While there, the officer sees in the living room several TV sets that the officer suspects may be stolen. He telephones the police department to give the serial numbers and is informed that those sets have been reported stolen. At this stage, the officer has probable cause to seize the items. The officer cannot seize them under plain view because the items were not "immediately recognizable as subject to seizure." Ordinarily, the officer would need a warrant to seize the sets, but warrantless seizures may be justified if the officer can establish exigent circumstances (such as that the sets would most likely be hauled away by the other occupants should the officer leave the house). The sets are then admissible in court on the basis of probable cause and exigent circumstances.

C. Issues Raised by the "Plain View" Doctrine

To better understand the "plain view" doctrine, several related issues need to be addressed and clarified, among them inadvertence, access to object, mechanical devices, and open view.

1. "Plain View" and Inadvertence—The Horton v. California Case

The traditional view has been that *"inadvertence"* is one of the plain view requirements. This means that the officer must have no prior knowledge that the evidence was present in the place and therefore the discovery must be purely accidental. In the words of one court: "The plain view doctrine is properly applied to situations in which a police officer is not searching for evidence against the accused but nevertheless inadvertently comes across an incriminating object" (U.S. v. Sedillo, 496 F.2d 151 [9th Cir. 1974]).

That is no longer true, at least while in the process of executing a search warrant. In a 1990 case, the Court said: "The Fourth Amendment does not prohibit the warrantless seizure of evidence in plain view *even though the discovery of the evidence was not inadvertent.* Although inadvertence is a characteristic of most legitimate plain view seizures, it is not a necessary condition" (Horton v. California, 47 CrL 2135 [1990]). In that case, a police officer determined that there was probable cause to search Horton's home for the proceeds of a robbery and for weapons used in the robbery. The affidavit filed by the officer referred to police reports that described both the weapons and the proceeds, but for some reason the warrant issued by the magistrate only authorized a search for the proceeds. When the officer went to Horton's home to execute the warrant, he did not find the stolen property (proceeds), but found the weapons (an Uzi machine gun, a .38-caliber revolver, and two stun guns) in plain view and seized them. At trial, the officer testified that while he was searching Horton's home for the proceeds, he was also interested in finding "other evidence" related to the robbery. Tried and convicted, Horton argued on appeal that the weapons should have been suppressed because their discovery was not "inadvertent." The Court rejected this contention, saying that "although inadvertence is a characteristic of most legitimate plain view seizures, it is not a necessary condition." The Court expressly rejected the inadvertence requirement, saying that (1) evenhanded law enforcement is best achieved by the application of objective standards of conduct, rather than by standards that depend on the officer's subjective state of mind; and (2) the suggestion that the inadvertence requirement is necessary to prevent the police from conducting general search, or from converting specific warrants into general warrants, is not persuasive. In this case, "the scope of the search was not enlarged in the slightest by the omission of any reference to the weapons in the warrant." The evidence was held admissible. (Read the Horton v. California case brief at the end of the chapter.)

It is important to note that while the Horton case rejects the inadvertence requirement, the facts in the case justified the decision to admit the evidence. A warrant had been issued based on an affidavit that mentioned the presence of a weapon. For reasons not made clear in the case, the magistrate only authorized the search and seizure of the "proceeds." Nonetheless, the warrant was executed by the officer, in the process of which the weapons were observed in plain view. There was no bad faith on the part of the officer; neither was the warrant used as a pretext to seize evidence that the officer expected to find. This is different from a situation where the officer uses plain view as a pretext for seizing without warrant items that he or she already knows are in a certain location. For example, Officer P knows from a reliable informant that a murder weapon may be found in the suspect's apartment. He asks for and is given valid permission by X to enter and look around. Officer P then goes to the bedroom where, his informant says, the murder weapon can be found. Even under Horton, the evidence will likely not be admissible because in this case the officer should have obtained a warrant.

Two important facts in the Horton case must be noted because without them the case would most likely have been decided differently. First, although the officer knew there were weapons in the place to be searched before he went there (his affidavit for a search warrant referred to police reports that described the proceeds as well as the weapons), they were seized while serving a valid search warrant and therefore this was not a case of a warrantless search. Second, the officer did not act in bad faith in executing the warrant. These facts are stressed because the Court said: "The fact that an officer is interested in an item of evidence and fully expects to find it in the course of a search should not invalidate its seizure *if the search is confined in area and duration by the terms of a warrant* or if it is a valid exception to the warrant requirement" (italics added).

It is hard to say whether the failure of the magistrate in Horton to include the weapons in the warrant as seizable items was an oversight or was because of the absence of probable cause. Whatever the reason, the officer did not intend to use the search warrant as a pretext to obtain the weapons without a warrant. The Horton decision may cause confusion in the lower courts for some time. For now, a safe interpretation is that Horton does away with the inadvertence requirement in the process of serving a search warrant and in cases where no bad faith is involved. This means that most "plain view" cases will still be the result of inadvertence (meaning that the officer sees a seizable item which he or she did not expect to see), but that in the process of serving a warrant an officer may also seize items he or she knew beforehand would be there even if such item is not listed in the warrant as one of those to be seized.

2. "Plain View" in Open Spaces

Although the "plain view" doctrine usually applies when the officer is within an enclosed space (such as a house, an apartment, or an office—hence the concept used by some courts of a "prior valid intrusion into a constitutionally protected area"), it also applies when the officer is out in the open, such as out on the street when on patrol. In open spaces, there is a need to distinguish between *seeing* and *seizing*. For example, while walking around an apartment complex, an officer sees illegal weapons through a window. This also is plain view. The difference between this situation and when the officer is "within an enclosed space" is that here the officer cannot make an entry to seize the items without a warrant, unless there is consent or exigent circumstance. When the officer is in an enclosed space (such as a house or apartment), *seizing follows seeing* almost as a matter of course. By contrast, when an entry is needed, *seeing* and *seizing* become two separate acts because of the need for a legal entry. In the absence of consent or exigent circumstance, therefore, a warrant is needed.

An exigent circumstance would exist, for example, if the officer could establish that the evidence would most likely no longer be available unless immediate action were taken.

Plain view also applies to items seen from outside fences or enclosures. For example, an officer on patrol sees pots of marijuana grown inside a fenced yard. This falls under plain view, but a warrant is needed for entry.

3. "Plain View" and Motor Vehicles

Plain view applies to motor vehicles. For example, while out on patrol one day, an officer sees a car parked on the street. He or she looks at the front seat and sees drugs. This occurrence falls under plain view. But the officer cannot seize the drugs without a warrant unless there is consent or exigent circumstances because the officer must first enter the vehicle to effect a seizure. Such entry ordinarily needs a warrant to be valid.

4. "Plain View" and Mechanical Devices

The use of mechanical devices by the police does not affect the applicability of the "plain view" doctrine. For example, the use of a flashlight by an officer during an evening to look into the inside of a car does not constitute a search under the Fourth Amendment. Evidence that would not have been discovered and seized without the use of a flashlight is admissible in court (Texas v. Brown, 103 S.Ct. 1535 [1983]). The same is true with the use of binoculars. In another case, the use by the police of a beeper to monitor the whereabouts of a person traveling in a car on public highways did not turn the surveillance into a search. Such monitoring on a public highway was considered by the Court as falling under the "plain view" doctrine (U.S. v. Knotts, 459 U.S. 817 [1983]).

The officer need not be standing upright for plain view to apply. For example, in the preceding Texas v. Brown case, the police officer who legally stopped the automobile changed his position and bent down at an angle so he could see what was inside the car. The Court said that the fact that the officer got into an unusual position in order to see the contents did not prevent the "plain view" doctrine from applying.

5. "Plain View" versus "Open View"

Some lower courts distinguish between "plain view" and "open view." They apply plain view to cases in which the officer has made a "prior valid intrusion into a constitutionally protected area" (meaning when the officer is inside an enclosed space, such as a house or an apartment) and apply the term *open view* to instances when the

---

HIGHLIGHT 9.2

Inadvertence No Longer Necessary in "Plain View" Searches

"The fact that an officer is interested in an item of evidence and fully expects to find it in the course of a search should not invalidate its seizure if the search is confined in area and duration by the terms of a warrant or a valid exception to the warrant requirement" (Horton v. California, 47 CrL 2135 [1990]).

officer is out in open space (such as the street) but sees an item within an enclosed area (Hawaii v. Stachler, 570 P.2d 1329 [1977]). The Supreme Court, however, has not made this distinction; hence the use of "plain view" in this text includes the concept of "open view."

D. When Does "Plain View" Apply?

There are many situations in police work when the "plain view" doctrine applies. Among these are the following:

1. When the police have a warrant to search a given place for named objects, and in the process come across other incriminating articles
2. When the police are in "hot pursuit" of a fleeing suspect
3. When making a search incident to a valid arrest
4. When making an arrest with or without warrant
5. When making searches without warrant
6. When officers are out on patrol
7. When making a car inventory search subsequent to impoundment
8. When conducting an investigation in a residence
9. When making an entry into a home as a result of a valid consent

This list is illustrative, not comprehensive. In sum, the "plain view" doctrine applies to every aspect of police work as long as all of the three requirements are present.

II. THE "OPEN FIELDS" DOCTRINE

A. Definition

The *"open fields" doctrine* states that items in *open fields are not protected* by the Fourth Amendment's guarantee against unreasonable searches and seizures and therefore can properly be taken by an officer without warrant or probable cause. The Fourth Amendment protects only "houses, papers, and effects" against unreasonable searches and seizures. Open fields do not come under "houses, papers, and effects"; therefore the constitutional protection does not apply. In the words of Justice Holmes: "The special protection accorded by the Fourth Amendment to the people in their persons, houses, papers, and effects is not extended to the open fields" (Hester v. U.S., 265 U.S. 57 [1924]).

B. Areas Not Included in "Open Fields"

Certain areas come under the protection of the Fourth Amendment and therefore cannot be classified as "open fields":

1. Houses

The courts have interpreted the term *houses* under the Fourth Amendment rather broadly, applying it to homes (owned, rented, or leased), apartments, hotel or motel rooms, hospital rooms, and even sections not generally open to the public in places of business.

2. Curtilage

Curtilage means the grounds and buildings immediately surrounding a dwelling and associated with it. In general, "curtilage has been held to include all buildings in close proximity to a dwelling, which are continually used for carrying on domestic employment; or such place as is necessary and convenient to a dwelling and is habitually used for family purposes" (U.S. v. Potts, 297 F.2d 68 [6th Cir. 1961]). Curtilage is not considered an open field and hence is protected against unreasonable searches and seizures. Items seized in the curtilage need a warrant. Curtilage may encompass a variety of places, including the following:

- *Residential yards.* Courts disagree on whether yards are part of the curtilage. If members of the public have access to the yard at any time, it is probably not curtilage. But if only members of the family have access to it, it may be part of the curtilage.
- *Fenced areas.* A fence around a house makes the immediate environs within that fence a part of the curtilage because the owner clearly intended for that area to be private and not open to the general public.
- *Apartment houses.* Areas of an apartment building that are used in common by all tenants are not considered part of any tenant's curtilage. However, if the apartment building is of limited size (such as a four-unit building) and each apartment has its own back yard or front yard, which is not accessible to the general public, such areas would be part of the curtilage.
- *Barns and other outbuildings.* Outbuildings are usually considered part of the curtilage if they are used extensively by the family, are enclosed by a fence, or are close to the house. The farther such buildings are from the house, the less likely it is that they will be considered part of the curtilage.
- *Garages.* Garages are usually considered part of the curtilage, unless far from the house and very seldom used.

C. Tests to Determine Curtilage—The United States v. Dunn Case

How is curtilage to be determined? The Court has answered that question, saying that whether or not an area is considered a part of the curtilage and therefore covered by Fourth Amendment protections rests on four factors:

1. The proximity of the area to the home
2. Whether the area is in an enclosure surrounding the home
3. The nature and uses of the area
4. The steps taken to conceal the area from public view

HIGHLIGHT 9.3

Fourth Amendment Does Not Apply to "Open Fields"

"Inasmuch as the protection of the Fourth Amendment against unreasonable searches and seizures does not extend to 'open fields,' there is no unreasonable search. . . . Moreover, even if the officers were trespassing on private property, a trespass does not itself constitute an illegal search" (Atwell v. United States, 414 F.2d 136 [1969]).

Applying these factors, the Court concluded that the barn in this case could not be considered part of the curtilage (United States v. Dunn, 480 U.S. 294 [1987]). In Dunn, after learning that a codefendant purchased large quantities of chemicals and equipment used in the manufacture of controlled substances, drug agents obtained a warrant to place an electronic tracking beeper in some of the equipment. The beeper ultimately led agents to Dunn's farm. The farm was encircled by a perimeter fence with several interior fences of the type used to hold livestock. Without a warrant, officers entered the premises over the perimeter fence, interior fences, and a wooden fence that encircled a barn, approximately 50 yards from respondent's home. Without entering the barn, the officers stood at a locked gate and shone a flashlight into the barn where they observed what appeared to be a drug laboratory. Officers returned twice the following day to confirm the presence of the laboratory, each time without entering the barn. Based on information gained from these observations, officers obtained a search warrant and seized incriminating evidence therefrom. Dunn was charged with and convicted of conspiracy to manufacture controlled substances. On appeal he sought exclusion of the evidence, saying that a barn located 50 yards from a house and surrounded by a fence is part of the curtilage and therefore could not be searched without a warrant.

The Court disagreed, saying that judged in terms of the four tests (enumerated above), this particular barn could not be considered a part of the curtilage.

The good news about the Dunn case is that for the first time the Court has laid out the tests lower courts should use to determine whether or not a barn, building, garage, or so forth is part of the curtilage. The bad news is that these factors are subjective and therefore lend themselves to imprecise application. Nonetheless, they are an improvement over the complete absence of guidance under which the lower court decided cases prior to Dunn.

D. Aerial Surveillance of Curtilage Is Valid

The fact that a space is part of a home curtilage, however, does not mean it is automatically entitled to constitutional protection against any and all intrusions. In a 1986 case, the Court decided that the constitutional protection against unreasonable search and seizure is not violated by the naked-eye aerial observation by the police of a suspect's back yard (admittedly a part of the curtilage) (California v. Ciraolo, 54 L.W. 4471 [1986]). In this case, the Santa Clara, California, police received an anonymous tip over the telephone that marijuana was being grown in suspect Ciraolo's back yard. The back yard was shielded from public view by a six-foot outer fence and a ten-foot inner fence completely enclosing the yard. On the basis of the tip, officers trained in marijuana identification obtained a private airplane and flew over the suspect's house at an altitude of 1,000 feet. They readily identified the plants growing in the yard as marijuana. A search warrant was later obtained on the basis of the naked-eye observation of one of the officers, supported by a photograph of the surrounding area taken from the airplane. The warrant was executed and the marijuana plants were seized. In a motion to suppress the evidence, the defendant alleged that the warrantless aerial observation of the yard violated the Fourth Amendment.

The Court rejected the suspect's contention, saying that no Fourth Amendment right was violated. The Court admitted that here the suspect "took normal precautions to maintain his privacy" by erecting the fence, but added:

The area is within the curtilage and does not itself bar all police observation. The Fourth Amendment protection of the home has never been extended to require law enforcement officers to shield their eyes when passing by a home on public thoroughfares. Nor does the mere fact that an individual has taken measures to restrict some views of his activities preclude an officer's observations from a public vantage point where he has a right to be and which renders the activities clearly visible. . . . The observations by Officers Shutz and Rodriguez in this case took place within public navigable airspace, in a physically nonintrusive manner; from this point they were able to observe plants readily discernible to the naked eye as marijuana. . . . On this record, we readily conclude that respondent's expectation that his garden was protected from such observation is unreasonable and is not an expectation that society is prepared to honor.

In the Ciraolo case, the private airplane flew over the suspect's house at an altitude of 1,000 feet to make the observations. Suppose the flight were made by the police in a helicopter and at a height of 400 feet, would the evidence still be admissible? The Court answered yes, saying that as long as the police are flying at an altitude where Federal Aviation Administration regulations allow members of the public to fly (the FAA sets no minimum for helicopters), such aerial observation is valid because in the absence of FAA prohibitions, the homeowner would have no reasonable expectation of privacy from such flights (Florida v. Riley, 109 S.Ct. 693 [1989]).

E. The "Open Fields" Doctrine Is Alive and Well

In a 1984 decision, the Supreme Court gave the "open fields" doctrine a broader meaning. In that case, the Court said that it is legal for the police to enter and search unoccupied or underdeveloped areas outside the curtilage without either a warrant or probable cause as long as the place comes under the category of "fields," even if the police had to walk past a locked gate and a "No Trespassing" sign. The "field" in this case was secluded and not visible from any point of public access. The Court defined the term *open fields* to include "any unoccupied or underdeveloped area outside the curtilage," a definition sufficiently broad to include the heavily wooded area where the defendant's illicit marijuana crop was discovered by the police (Oliver v. U.S., 35 CrL 3001 [1984]). (Read the Oliver v. U.S. case brief at the end of this chapter.)

The significance of the Oliver case is that it reiterates the doctrine that the "reasonable expectation of privacy" standard does not apply when the property involved is an open field. The Court stressed that steps taken to protect privacy, such as planting the marijuana on secluded land and erecting a locked gate (but with a footpath along one side) and posting "No Trespassing" signs around the property, do not necessarily establish any reasonable expectation of privacy. The test, according to the Court, is not whether the individual chooses to conceal assertedly "private activity, but whether the government's intrusion infringes upon the personal and societal values protected by the Fourth Amendment." The fact that the government's intrusion upon an open field (as in this case) is a trespass at common law does not make it a "search" in the constitutional sense; hence the Fourth Amendment does not apply.

The Oliver case involved a warrantless observation of a marijuana patch located more than a mile from Oliver's house. The Dunn case, also discussed above, involved the warrantless observation of a barn located just 50 yards from a house and surrounded by a wooden fence that, in turn, was within a bigger perimeter fence. In both cases, the Court concluded that neither property could be considered a part of the curtilage and therefore became open field. It is clear from these decisions that the concept of curtilage has become severely restricted and that of open field significantly broadened by the Court, hence giving law enforcement officials much greater leeway in search and seizure cases.

F. Comparison of "Open Fields" and "Plain View"

1. Similarities

In both situations, there is no need for a search warrant to seize items because both are not considered searches or seizures under the Fourth Amendment.

2. Differences

The doctrines differ in these respects: (1) under the "open fields" doctrine, the seizable property is not in a "house" or other place to which that term applies (apartments, hotel or motel rooms, hospital rooms, places of business not open to the public, or curtilage), whereas items under plain view are found in those places; (2) under the "open fields" doctrine, items hidden from view may be seized—something not permitted under plain view, which limits seizure to items within sight of the officer.

III. ABANDONMENT

A. Definition

Abandonment is defined as *the giving up of a thing or item absolutely, without limitation as to any particular person or purpose.* Abandonment implies the giving up of possession or ownership or of any reasonable expectation of privacy. Abandoned property is not protected by the Fourth Amendment guarantee against unreasonable searches and seizures, and thus it may be seized without warrant or probable cause. For example, if a car is left in a public parking lot for so long that it is reasonable to assume that the car has been abandoned, the police may seize the car without a warrant.

Abandoned property does not belong to anyone because the owner has given it up—in some cases involuntarily (such as when items are thrown out of a house or car for fear of discovery by the police). Persons who find such property, including the police, may therefore keep it and introduce it as evidence in a criminal proceeding. For example, the police approach a group of juveniles in an apartment parking lot to quiet them down because of complaints from nearby residents. One of the juveniles throws away an envelope, which is retrieved by the police and later ascertained to contain drugs. The recovery is legal and the evidence usable in court.

B. Factors Determining When Items Are Considered Abandoned

Abandonment is frequently difficult to determine; however, the two basic guidelines are (1) the place where the property is left and (2) intent to abandon.

1. Where the Property Is Left

a. Property left in open field or public place—abandoned.   Property discarded or thrown away in an open field or public place is considered abandoned. For example, drugs discarded by a suspect at an airport restroom when she realizes she is under surveillance, or drugs thrown by the suspect from a speeding car when he realizes that the police are closing in, would be considered abandoned.

b. Property left in private premises—it depends.   Property may sometimes be considered abandoned in private premises if circumstances indicate that the occupant has left the premises. For example, if a suspect pays his bills and checks out of a hotel room, items left behind that are of no apparent value but that the police can use as evidence—such as photographs or clippings—are considered abandoned property and may be seized by the police.

If the occupant has not left the premises, there is no abandonment. For example, while "looking around" the house after receiving a valid consent, the police see the wife grab a package containing marijuana from the kitchen table and throw it into the bedroom. That package might be seized by the police, but not under the abandonment doctrine, because the property is still in the house and the occupant has not left the premises. The seizure might be justified, however, under probable cause and exigent circumstance.

c. What about trash or garbage at curbside?—abandoned.   The Court has decided that garbage left outside the curtilage of a home for regular collection is considered abandoned and therefore may be seized by the police without a warrant (California v. Greenwood, 56 L.W. 4409 [1988]). In this case, the Court said that "having deposited their garbage in an area particularly suited for public inspection . . . [owners] could have no reasonable expectation of privacy in the inculpatory items that they discarded (in the Greenwood case, items indicating narcotics use).

By contrast, if the trash were left in the curtilage of a home (but where trash collectors are allowed to enter) or on one's own property, this would not be considered an abandonment and therefore Fourth Amendment protections would apply.

2. Intent to Abandon

Intent to abandon is generally determined objectively, meaning by what a person does. Throwing items away in a public place shows an intent to abandon; denial of ownership when questioned also constitutes abandonment. For example, when questioned by the police, a suspect denies that the confiscated wallet belongs to him. If in fact the suspect owns that wallet, the wallet may now be considered abandoned. Failure to claim something over a long period of time also indicates abandonment—and the longer the period, the clearer the intent. The prosecution must prove that there was in fact an intent to abandon the item.

Note, however, that the activities of the police that led to the abandonment must be legal, otherwise the evidence obtained cannot be admissible. For example, the police, for no reason, decide to search a pedestrian one evening. Terrified, the pedestrian throws something away. It turns out to be a bag of cocaine. It cannot be used in evidence because the abandonment was caused by illegal conduct on the part of the police.

C. Comparison of Abandonment and "Plain View"

1. Similarities

In both cases, there is no need for a search warrant because both are outside the protection of the Fourth Amendment.

2. Differences

Abandonment means that the former owner of the item has given up ownership prior to its being seized by the police. The giving up of ownership may have taken place some time earlier (as in the case of abandoned barns) or just seconds before the evidence is obtained by the police (as when contraband is thrown out of a car during a chase). When the "plain view" theory applies, ownership or possession has not been given up prior to seizure.

IV. ELECTRONIC SURVEILLANCE

Electronic surveillance is the use of electronic devices to monitor a person's activities or whereabouts. It is a type of search and seizure and can take various forms, such as *wiretapping* or *bugging*. This form of surveillance is regulated strictly by the U.S. Constitution, federal law, and state statutes. The Fourth Amendment limitation against "unreasonable searches and seizures" protects a person's conversation from unreasonable intrusion. Federal and state laws further limit what the police can do.

A. Old Concept: Olmstead v. United States

The first major case in electronic surveillance, decided in 1928, was Olmstead v. United States, 277 U.S. 438 (1928). Olmstead involved a bootlegging operation against which evidence was gathered through the use of wiretaps on telephone conversations. The Court held that wiretapping did not violate the Fourth Amendment unless there was *"some trespass into a constitutionally protected area."* Under this concept, evidence obtained through a bugging device placed against a wall to overhear conversation in an adjoining office was admissible because there was *no actual trespass.* Said the Court: "The Amendment does not forbid what was done here. There was no searching. There was no seizure. The evidence was secured by the use of the sense of hearing and that only. There was no entry of the houses or offices of the defendants. . . ." This *old concept of electronic surveillance* lasted from 1928 to 1967.

In 1934, Congress passed the Federal Communications Act, which provided that "no person not being authorized by the sender shall intercept any communication and divulge or publish the existence, contents, substance, purport, effect or meaning of such intercepted communication to any person." In 1937, the Court interpreted this provision as forbidding federal agents, as well as other persons, *from intercepting and disclosing telephone messages by the use of wiretaps* (Nardone v. U.S., 302 U.S. 379 [1937]). In 1942, the Court held that wiretap evidence could be used against persons other than those whose conversations had been overheard and whose Fourth Amendment rights were therefore violated (Goldstein v. U.S., 316 U.S. 114 [1942]). That same year, the Court also held that the use of a "bug" (an electronic device but not a wiretap on telephone lines) was not in violation of the Communications Act because the act applied only to actual interference with communication wires and telephone lines.

In 1961, the Court took a tougher view on electronic surveillance in the case of Silverman v. United States, 365 U.S. 505 (1961). In Silverman, the Court held that the Fourth Amendment was violated by the use of a "spike-mike" driven into a building wall without warrant to allow police to overhear conversations within the building. The fact that the device, although tiny, *actually penetrated the building wall* was held by the Court to be sufficient to constitute physical intrusion in violation of the Fourth Amendment. In 1964, the Court further decided that evidence obtained by the police using an electronic device attached to the exterior wall of a building was illegally obtained (Clinton v. Virginia, 377 U.S. 158 [1964]). These decisions eroded the impact of the Olmstead case.

B. New Concept: Katz v. United States

The old concept of "some trespass into a constitutionally protected area" was rejected in 1967 in the Katz case (Katz v. U.S., 389 U.S. 347 [1967]). (Read the Katz v. U.S. brief at the end of this chapter.) The *new concept of electronic surveillance* enunciated in Katz, states that a search occurs whenever there is police activity that *violates a "reasonable expectation of privacy."* Such activity includes any form of electronic surveillance, with or without actual physical trespass or wiretap. In the Katz case, the police attached an electronic listening device to the outside of a public telephone booth that the defendant was using. Although there was no tapping of the line, the Court held that the listening device still violated the defendant's reasonable expectation that his conversations were private. The Court said that what Katz "sought to exclude when he entered the booth was not the intruding eye—it was the uninvited ear." He did not shed his right to do so simply because he made his calls from a place where he might be seen. The key phrase, therefore, to determine intrusion is "reasonable expectation of privacy." This, in effect, makes the Fourth Amendment protection *"portable,"* meaning that it *follows the individual wherever that individual goes.* In the words of the Court, the Fourth Amendment *"protects people, not places."*

There is no reasonable expectation of privacy, however, if there is no attempt, while in a public place, to keep the communication private. For example, X uses a telephone in the lobby of a hotel to transmit gambling information to a client. If X talks in a loud voice and does not care if people hear what is said then there is no reasonable expectation of privacy. In contrast, even if the setting is the lobby of a hotel, if the suspect takes precautions by conversing in low tones and cupping the telephone receiver, chances are that the individual would be considered to have a reasonable expectation of privacy.

What about cordless telephones? Do they enjoy a "reasonable expectation of privacy," and therefore are they protected by the Fourth Amendment? Although the Supreme Court has not resolved the issue, lower courts have said no. The legal rationale appears to be that cordless telephones "unlike standard wire phones and sophisticated cellular devices—transmit radio signals between a handset and a base unit that occasionally can be intercepted by other cordless telephones or even by short-wave radio sets."[2] This is bad news for the 21 million American households that have cordless telephones.[3] In the words of one observer, "Those who seek privacy protection for their conversations on cordless telephones should remember that the airwaves are public."[4]

C. Federal Law: Title III of the Omnibus Crime Control and Safe Streets Act of 1968

1. Main Provision

At present, the use of wiretapping and electronic surveillance and bugging devices is largely governed by the provisions of Title III of the Omnibus Crime Control and Safe Streets Act of 1968. That law is long and complicated, but its provisions may be summarized as follows: Law enforcement officers nationwide, federal and state, cannot tap or intercept wire communications or use electronic devices to intercept private conversations, except under one of two conditions:

- If there is a court order authorizing the wiretap
- If consent is given by one of the parties

Any violation of the above rule by federal or state officers is a federal crime punishable by five years' imprisonment or a fine of $10,000, or both. Furthermore, the evidence obtained is inadmissible in any state or federal proceeding. These two exceptions need further discussion.

Exception 1: If there is a court order authorizing the wiretap. A judge may issue a court order for a wiretap only if all the following are present:

a. There is probable cause to believe that a specific individual has committed one of the crimes enumerated under the act.
b. There is probable cause to believe that the interception will furnish evidence about the crime.
c. Normal investigative procedures have been tried and have failed or reasonably appear likely to fail or to be dangerous.
d. There is probable cause to believe that the facilities or the place from which or where the interception is to be made are used in connection with the offense or are linked to the individual under suspicion.

HIGHLIGHT 9.4

Justification for Reasonable Expectation of Privacy

". . . what he sought to exclude when he entered the booth was not the intruding eye — it was the uninvited ear. He did not shed his right to do so simply because he made his calls from a place where he might be seen. No less than an individual in a business office, in a friend's apartment, or in a taxicab, a person in a telephone booth may rely upon the protection of the Fourth Amendment. One who occupies it, shuts the door behind him, and pays the toll that permits him to place a call is surely entitled to assume that the words he utters into the mouthpiece will not be broadcast to the world. To read the Constitution more narrowly is to ignore the vital role that the public telephone has come to play in private communication" (Katz v. U.S., 389 U.S. 347 [1967]).

Note: Once law enforcement officials have obtained judicial authorization to intercept wire or oral communications, they do not have to obtain another judicial authorization to enable them to enter the premises to install the listening device. Such authorization comes with the court order.

Exception 2: If consent is given by one of the parties. Consent is one of the exceptions to the court order requirements under Title III and has also been exempted from the warrant requirement by several court decisions. Note, however, that some states, by law, expressly prohibit electronic eavesdropping or wiretapping even if consent is given by one of the parties.[5] Such statutes, if they exist, take precedence over any consent given by one of the parties and must therefore be followed.

The Court has concluded that the Constitution does not prohibit a government agent from using an electronic device to record a telephone conversation between two parties with the consent of one party to the conversation (U.S. v. White, 401 U.S. 745 [1970]). The Court has also said that the Fourth Amendment does not protect persons against supposed friends who turn out to be police informers. Thus, a person assumes the risk that whatever he says to others may be reported by them to the police, there being no police "search" in such cases. It follows that if the supposed "friend" allows the police to listen in on a telephone conversation with the suspect, there is no violation of the suspect's Fourth Amendment rights. The evidence obtained is admissible because of the consent given by one party to the conversation (On Lee v. U.S., 343 U.S. 747 [1952]).

Neither is the Fourth Amendment violated when a police informer carries into the suspect's home an electronic device that transmits the conversation to the police outside, but the evidence obtained is not admissible if the defendant has been charged and has obtained a lawyer. In one case, the Court said that the evidence was inadmissible, not because there was a violation of the right against unreasonable search and seizure under the Fourth Amendment but because the right to counsel under the Sixth Amendment had been violated (Massiah v. United States, 377 U.S. 201 [1964]). Therefore, if the suspect does not yet have a lawyer, the evidence obtained from this procedure is admissible because the right to counsel in these types of questioning applies only after a lawyer has been obtained.

2. Other Provisions

Aside from those discussed above, there are other provisions of Title III of the Omnibus Crime Control and Safe Streets Act of 1968 of which law enforcement officers must be keenly aware. These provisions are summarized as follows:

a. Title III provides that electronic surveillance authorized by a state or local judge is illegal under federal law unless the state has passed legislation authorizing the judge to issue such an order. In other words, Title III has preempted the field on electronic surveillance, but it allows the states to authorize surveillance by court order based on state law. If the state has not passed an enabling statute, no electronic surveillance can be allowed, even by virtue of judicial order by a state judge.

b. Title III provides that only the attorney general of the United States or a specially designated assistant attorney general may authorize an application for a federal interception order and that only a federal investigative or law enforcement officer or an attorney authorized to prosecute Title III offenses may make an application for a federal interception order.

c. Federal court may issue an interception order only for specified crimes, including espionage, treason, labor racketeering, murder, kidnapping, robbery, extortion, bribery of public officials, gambling, trafficking, and counterfeiting.

d. The federal law also exempts from restriction the constitutional authority of the president of the United States to protect the country against certain foreign threats. In these cases, surveillance may be conducted without a court order. But the Court has held that this power does not allow the president to authorize interceptions in domestic security cases (U.S. vs. U.S. District Court, 407 U.S. 297 [1972]).

e. On the state level, Title III authorizes a state prosecutor to seek a warrant when evidence of certain felonies is to be gathered. The judicial order authorizing interception may be granted only for the purpose of gathering evidence for the following offenses: "murder, kidnapping, gambling, robbery, bribery, extortion, or dealing in narcotic drugs, marijuana or other dangerous drugs, or other crimes dangerous to life, limb, or property, and punishable by imprisonment for more than one year, or any conspiracy to commit any of the foregoing offenses." Note again that such authorization is allowed only in states that have passed legislation providing for such procedure.

f. The director of the administrative office of the U.S. Courts is required, under Title III, to transmit to Congress an annual report regarding applications for orders authorizing or approving the interception of wire or oral communications. Every state that has passed an enabling law and every federal judge are required to retain information on the grants and denials of application, name of applicant, offense involved, and duration of authorized interception.

3. Constitutionality of Title III

The constitutionality of Title III has not been directly tested in the Supreme Court; however, lower courts have held it to be constitutional. Also in 1972, the Court unanimously rejected the contention of the Nixon administration that the provisions of Title III did not require judicial approval of warrants for wiretaps or surveillance in national security cases (U.S. v. U.S. District Court, 407 U.S. 297 [1972]). In 1974, the Court in effect nullified hundreds of criminal prosecutions based on evidence obtained by surveillance when it held that then-Attorney General John N. Mitchell had not himself signed the applications for the warrant authorizing the surveillance and had allowed an aide other than the designated assistant attorney general to approve the application (U.S. v. Giordano, 416 U.S. 505 [1974]). In 1979, the Court held that because Congress must have recognized that most electronic bugs can only be installed by agents who secretly enter the premises, warrants authorizing such surveillance need not explicitly authorize entry.

4. State Laws and Title III

As noted earlier, under Title III of the Omnibus Crime Control and Safe Streets Act of 1968 an electronic surveillance is illegal even if authorized by state or local judge *if there is no law passed by the state legislature authorizing the judge to issue the order.* Such enabling legislation has been passed in more than half of the states. It is therefore important that police officers ascertain whether or not electronic surveillance is specifically authorized in their state, and, if so, what procedures are to be followed. Without an enabling state statute, a police officer faces possible criminal prosecution for unauthorized electronic surveillance.

States may pass laws *further limiting,* but *not broadening,* the restrictions imposed by Title III. For example, although Title III allows the use of evidence obtained with the consent of one party to the conversation, a state statute may prohibit such use without the consent of both parties. In states having that prohibition, the evidence is not admissible in state court for criminal prosecution.

If the language of a state law authorizing eavesdropping is too broad in scope, it intrudes into a constitutionally protected area and is therefore violative of the Fourth Amendment. An example of such a statute was a New York law that the Court declared unconstitutional because it was too broad and did not contain sufficient safeguards against unwarranted invasion of constitutional rights (Berger v. New York, 388 U.S. 41 [1967]).

Berger is significant in that it specified several requirements for a warrant authorizing any form of electronic surveillance to be valid. These are the requirements:

a. The warrant must describe with *particularity* the conversations that are to be overheard.
b. There must be a showing of *probable cause* to believe that a specific crime has been or is being committed.
c. The wiretap must be for a *limited period*, although extensions may be obtained upon adequate showing.
d. The *suspects* whose conversations are to be overheard must be *named* in the judicial order.
e. A *return* must be made to the court, showing what conversations were intercepted.
f. The wiretapping must *terminate* when the desired information has been obtained.

The Berger case was decided in 1967, one year prior to the enactment of Title III of the Omnibus Crime Control and Safe Streets Act. Since then, these six requirements have been enacted into law by Title III, along with the other provisions discussed above. Berger is important because it tells us that overly broad eavesdropping statutes are unconstitutional and also lays out what state statutes need if they are to be declared valid.

D. Federal Law: The Electronic Communications and Privacy Act of 1986 (ECPA)

Title III of the Omnibus Crime Control and Safe Streets Act of 1968 continues to be the main federal law on electronic surveillance. In 1986, however, the U.S. Congress passed the *Electronic Communications and Privacy Act (ECPA),* which amends and supplements the provisions of Title III. A series of excellent law-oriented articles by Robert A. Fiatal in the *FBI Law Enforcement Bulletin* features the main provision of that law and is the main source of the discussion in this section.[6]

According to this series of articles, ECPA contains three provisions that relate to federal, state, and local law enforcement work (italics added):

- "It amends the law of *nonconsensual interception of wire communications* (wiretaps) and oral communications by a concealed microphone or electronic device (bugs)."
- "It sets forth specific procedures for *obtaining authorization to use pen registers* (telephone decoders), which record the numbers dialed from a telephone, and trap and trace devices, which ascertain the origin of a telephone call."
- "It prescribes the *procedure law enforcement officers must follow to obtain stored communications and records* relating to communications services, such as telephone toll records and unlisted telephone subscriber information."[7]

1. Interception of Electronic Communications

The *FBI Law Enforcement Bulletin* series of articles states that this new law has "significantly expanded the traditional wiretapping and bugging law by also affording the same protections previously supplied to wire and oral communications to electronic communications." The core of the amendment is that "in order to intercept an electronic communication during the course of its transmission, without the consent of one of the parties to that communication, *the police officer must obtain an extraordinary order,* just as if he were intercepting a wire communication or an oral communication involving a reasonable expectation of privacy" (italics added).[8] The following types of electronic communication, however, are not covered by this section of the ECPA: publicly accessible radio communications, tracking devices, radio portion of cordless telephones, tone-only paging devices, surreptitious video surveillance, and pen registers and trap and trace devices.[9]

Congress passed the ECPA on October 2, 1986, but state and local law enforcement officers were given until October 2, 1988, to comply with the preceding sections of the law.[10] The various states could enact laws that are more restrictive than the preceding sections and state and local law enforcement officials would be bound by them.

2. Pen Registers and Trap and Trace Devices

A *pen register* records the number dialed from a particular telephone; it is installed on the property of the telephone company rather than at the place where the suspect has access to the telephone. Such registers are helpful in police investigations, particularly in such crimes as kidnappings, extortions, and obscene telephone calls. ECPA specifically provides that "law enforcement officers are not required to obtain wiretap-type orders to use these devices."[11] Despite this, telephone companies, in the absence of emergency, often require court authorization before cooperating with law enforcement agencies. Under the 1986 Electronic Communication Privacy Act, 18 U.S.C. Section 312, et. seq., however, the law enforcement agency must apply for and get a court order (instead of a wiretap-type order) before installing the pen register. ECPA specifies the procedures that law enforcement officers are to follow in obtaining court authorization to use these investigative electronic devices.[12]

3. Stored Communications and Transactional Records

Under ECPA, law enforcement officers are required to adhere to certain procedures when seeking to obtain information from agencies providing services to the public, such agencies as telephone and computerized message companies. This portion of the ECPA applies to federal, state, and local investigative activities since January 20, 1987.[13]

E. Electronic Devices That Do Not Intercept Communication

There are some electronic devices that gather information (such as a suspect's location) but do not necessarily intercept communication. These devices do not come under Title III coverage; neither are they governed strictly by the concept of reasonable expectation of privacy under the Fourth Amendment. Pen registers and beepers are two examples.

1. Pen Registers

The Fourth Amendment does not require that the police obtain judicial authorization before using pen registers (Smith v. Maryland, 442 U.S. 735 [1979]). The Smith case says that not every use of an electronic device to gather information is governed by the Constitution. Pen registers gather information but do not necessarily intercept communication; hence they do not come under Fourth Amendment protection. The Court gave two reasons for this decision. First, it is doubtful that telephone users in general have any expectation of privacy regarding the numbers they dial, since they typically know that they must convey phone numbers to the telephone company and that the company has facilities for recording this information and in fact records it routinely for various legitimate business purposes. Second, even if the petitioner did harbor some subjective expectation of privacy, this expectation was not one that society is prepared to recognize as reasonable. When the petitioner voluntarily conveyed numerical information to the phone company and "exposed" that information to its equipment in the normal course of business, he assumed the risk that the company would reveal the information to the police.

The Court has also held that the police may obtain a court order to require the telephone company to assist in installing the pen register (U.S. v. New York Telephone Company, 434 U.S. 159 [1977]).

HIGHLIGHT 9.5

Significance of ECPA

"The Electronic Communications Privacy Act of 1986 (the ECPA) significantly alters the procedure that Federal, State, and local law enforcement officers must follow to intercept communications during the course of their transmission and to acquire transactional information of those communications, such as telephone toll records. For these reasons, law enforcement officers must understand the impact of the ECPA in their investigative efforts in the communications area."

Source: Robert A. Fiatal, "The Electronic Communications Privacy Act: Assessing Today's Technology (Part 1)," *FBI Law Enforcement Bulletin,* February 1988, at 25.

---

2. Electronic Beepers

The use of a *beeper* to keep track of a person traveling on the public road does not constitute a search because a person has no reasonable expectation of privacy when traveling on a public thoroughfare (U.S. v. Knotts, 459 U.S. 817 [1983]). In a subsequent case that same year, the Court said that the warrantless monitoring of a beeper (which was installed by the police in an ether can and later delivered to the defendants) after the device had been unwittingly taken into a private residence violated the Fourth Amendment rights of the residents and others. Nonetheless, the Court concluded that the evidence obtained could not be excluded because, in the Court's view, ample probable cause existed aside from the information that had been obtained as a result of the beeper to justify the issuance of a warrant. In sum, beepers can be used legally to monitor the movements of a suspect in a public place but not in a private residence (U.S. v. Karo, 35 CrL 3246 [1984]).

☐ SUMMARY

This chapter discussed the "plain view" doctrine, the "open fields" doctrine, abandonment, and electronic surveillance. These topics have in common some form of "taking" by the government of something that belongs to, or used to belong to, somebody. They do differ, however, in concept, legal rules, and practice.

The "plain view" doctrine states that items within the sight of an officer who is legally in a place from which the view is made, may properly be seized without a warrant—as long as such items are immediately apparent as subject to seizure. The requirements for the "plain view" doctrine are that the item's position must be within the officer's sight, the officer's legal presence in the place from which the item is seen, and the item must be immediately apparent as subject to seizure. Inadvertence, once considered a requirement for plain view, has recently been rejected by the Court.

The "open fields" doctrine holds that items in open fields may be legally taken by an officer without warrant or probable cause because they are not protected by the Fourth Amendment. A curtilage is considered part of a house and is therefore protected by the warrant and "probable cause" requirement. Of late, however, the Court has restricted the concept of curtilage and expanded the extent of open fields.

Abandonment means the giving up of a thing or item absolutely. Abandoned property may be seized without warrant because it no longer belongs to anyone and therefore does not enjoy a reasonable expectation of privacy.

Electronic surveillance is governed by the Constitution, federal law, and state statutes. The Fourth Amendment to the Constitution protects communication if the person has a reasonable expectation of privacy. Two federal laws govern the use by federal, state, or local law enforcement agencies of electronic surveillance: Title III of the Omnibus Crime Control and Safe Streets Act of 1968, and the Electronic Communications and Privacy Act of 1986 (ECPA).

☐ REVIEW QUESTIONS

1. Define the "plain view" doctrine and discuss its three basic requirements.
2. Explain what is meant by something being "immediately apparent" as a "plain view" requirement.

3. What is "inadvertence"? Is it a "plain view" requirement?
4. Is there any distinction to be made between "plain view" and "open view"?
5. What is the "open fields" doctrine?
6. What is a curtilage? How is the extent of curtilage determined?
7. Is trash or garbage considered abandoned? Discuss.
8. Distinguish between the old and the new concepts of electronic surveillance.
9. What did the U.S. Supreme Court say in the Katz case? Why is Katz important to our understanding of when a warrant is needed in search and seizure cases?
10. Compare and contrast "abandonment" and "plain view."
11. Give the main provisions of Title III of the Omnibus Crime Control and Safe Streets Act of 1968.
12. Give the main provisions of the Electronic Communications and Privacy Act of 1986 (ECPA).

☐ DEFINITIONS

Abandonment: The giving up of a thing or item absolutely, without limitation as to any particular person or purpose. It implies the giving up of possession or ownership or of any reasonable expectation of privacy.

Beepers: Electronic devices that track a person's or item's location or whereabouts.

Curtilage: The grounds and buildings immediately surrounding a dwelling.

Electronic Communications and Privacy Act of 1986 (ECPA):   An act passed by Congress modifying and supplementing Title III of the Omnibus Crime Control and Safe Streets Act of 1968. Its main provisions, for purposes of law enforcement, are requiring a judicial order for the nonconsensual interception of wire communications, specifying the procedure law enforcement officers must follow to obtain authorization to use pen registers, and prescribing the procedure for officers to obtain stored communications and records relating to communications services.

Electronic Surveillance: The use of electronic devices to monitor a person's activities or whereabouts.

Inadvertence: To come under the "plain view" doctrine, the evidence must be discovered by the officer accidentally; the officer must have had no prior knowledge that the evidence was present in the place. No longer required in "plain view" doctrine.

New Concept of Electronic Surveillance: Electronic surveillance constitutes a search under the Fourth Amendment if the police activity violates a person's "reasonable expectation of privacy."

Old Concept of Electronic Surveillance: Electronic surveillance did not violate the Fourth Amendment unless there was "some trespass into a constitutionally protected area."

"Open Fields" Doctrine: Items in open fields are not protected by the Fourth Amendment guarantee against unreasonable searches and seizures, and therefore they can properly be taken by an officer without warrant or probable cause.

"Open View":   Used to describe the circumstances of an officer who is out in open space (such as out on the streets) but sees an item within an enclosed area.

Pen Register: An electronic device that records the number dialed from a particular telephone; installed on the property of the telephone company rather than at the place where a suspect has access to the telephone.

"Plain View" Doctrine: Items that are within the sight of an officer who is legally in the place from which the view is made, and who had no prior knowledge that the items were present, may properly be seized without a warrant—as long as the items are immediately recognizable as subject to seizure.

Title III of the Omnibus Crime Control and Safe Streets Act of 1968:   The federal law that provides that law enforcement officers nationwide, federal and state, cannot tap or intercept wire communications or use electronic devices to intercept private conversations, except (1) if there is a court order authorizing the wiretap or (2) if consent is given by one of the parties. Any violation of the law is punishable by five years' imprisonment or a fine of $10,000, or both.

□ PRINCIPLES OF CASES

ARIZONA V. HICKS, 480 U.S. 321 (1987)   The "immediately apparent" requirement of the "plain view" doctrine must be based on probable cause and not on any lower degree of certainty, such as reasonable suspicion.

ATWELL V. UNITED STATES, 414 F.2d 136 (1969)   Inasmuch as the protection of the Fourth Amendment against unreasonable searches and seizures does not extend to "open fields," there is no unreasonable search. Moreover, even if the officers were trespassing on private property, a trespass does not itself constitute an illegal search.

BERGER V. NEW YORK, 388 U.S. 41 (1967)   A valid warrant authorizing any form of electronic surveillance, including wiretapping, must satisfy certain stringent requirements.

CALIFORNIA V. CIRAOLO, 54 L.W. 4471 (1986)   The constitutional protection against unreasonable search and seizure is not violated by the naked-eye aerial observation by the police of a suspect's back yard, which is admittedly a part of the curtilage.

CALIFORNIA V. GREENWOOD, 56 L.W. 4409 (1988)   Garbage left outside the curtilage of a home for regular collection is considered abandoned and therefore may be seized by the police without a warrant.

CLINTON V. VIRGINIA, 377 U.S. 158 (1964)   Evidence obtained by the police using an electronic device attached to the exterior wall of a building was illegally obtained.

FLORIDA V. RILEY, 109 S.Ct. 693 (1989)   Evidence obtained by the police in a helicopter flight at 400 feet altitude is admissible because in the absence of FAA prohibition the homeowner would have no reasonable expectation of privacy from such flights.

GOLDSTEIN V. UNITED STATES, 316 U.S. 114 (1942)   Wiretap evidence could be used against persons other than those whose conversations had been overheard and whose Fourth Amendment rights were therefore violated.

HARRIS V. UNITED STATES, 390 U.S. 234 (1968)   Objects falling within the plain view of an officer who has a right to be in a position to have that view are subject to seizure and may be introduced in evidence.

HAWAII V. STACHLER, 570 P.2d 1329 (1977)   The "plain view" doctrine can be applied to cases in which the officer has made "a prior valid intrusion into a constitutionally protected area" (meaning when the officer is inside an enclosed space, such as a house or an apartment); the term *open view* applies to instances when the officer is out in open space (such as on the streets) but sees an item within an enclosed area.

HESTER V. UNITED STATES, 265 U.S. 57 (1924)   The special protection accorded by the Fourth Amendment to the people in their persons, houses, papers, and effects is not extended to the open fields.

HORTON V. CALIFORNIA, 47 CrL 2135 (1990)   The Fourth Amendment does not prohibit the warrantless seizure of evidence in plain view even though the discovery of the evidence was not inadvertent.

ILLINOIS V. ANDREAS, 103 S.Ct. 3319 (1983)   The "plain view" doctrine is grounded on the proposition that once police are lawfully in a position to observe an item first-hand, its owner's privacy interest in that item is lost; the owner may retain the incidents of title and possession but not privacy.

KATZ V. UNITED STATES, 389 U.S. 347 (1967)   Any form of electronic surveillance, including wiretapping, that violates a reasonable expectation of privacy constitutes a search. No actual physical trespass is required.

MASSIAH V. UNITED STATES, 377 U.S. 201 (1964)   When a police informer carries into the suspect's home an electronic device that transmits the conversation to the police outside, the evidence obtained is not admissible if the defendant was questioned without a lawyer by police agents after the defendant has been charged and has obtained a lawyer. The evidence is inadmissible not because there was a violation of the right against unreasonable search and seizure but because the right to counsel under the Sixth Amendment has been violated.

NARDONE V. UNITED STATES, 302 U.S. 379 (1937)   The Court interpreted the 1934 Federal Communications Act as forbidding federal agents, as well as other persons, from intercepting and disclosing telephone messages by the use of wiretaps.

OLIVER V. UNITED STATES, 35 CrL 3001 (1984)   It is legal for the police to enter and search unoccupied or underdeveloped areas outside the curtilage without either a warrant or probable cause as long as the place comes under the category of "fields," even if the police had to walk past a locked gate and a "No Trespassing" sign.

OLMSTEAD V. UNITED STATES, 277 U.S. 438 (1928)   Wiretapping does not violate the Fourth Amendment unless there is some trespass into a "constitutionally protected area." Under this concept, evidence obtained through a bugging device placed against a wall to overhear conversation in an adjoining office is admissible because there is no actual trespass. (*Note:* This doctrine was expressly overruled by the Court in the Katz case.)

ON LEE V. UNITED STATES, 343 U.S. 747 (1952)   There is no violation of a suspect's Fourth Amendment rights if his or her supposed "friend" allows the police to listen in on a telephone conversation; hence the evidence obtained is admissible in court.

SILVERMAN V. UNITED STATES, 365 U.S. 505 (1961)   The Court held that the Fourth Amendment was violated by the use of a "spike-mike" driven into a building wall without warrant to allow police to overhear conversations within the building. This was physical intrusion in violation of the Fourth Amendment.

SMITH V. MARYLAND, 442 U.S. 735 (1979)   Pen registers (devices that record the number dialed from a particular telephone and installed on the property of the telephone company) do not come under the Fourth Amendment and therefore the police do not have to obtain judicial authorization before using them.

TEXAS V. BROWN, 103 S.Ct. 1535 (1983)   Although items must be immediately recognizable as subject to seizure if they are to fall under the "plain view" doctrine, "certain knowledge" that incriminating evidence is involved is not necessary. Probable cause is sufficient to justify seizure. Also, the use of a flashlight by an officer during the evening to look into the inside of a car does not constitute a search under the Fourth Amendment. The items discovered still fall under plain view.

UNITED STATES V. DUNN, 480 U.S. 294 (1987)   Whether or not an area is considered a part of the curtilage and therefore covered by the Fourth Amendment rests on four factors: (1) the proximity of the area to the home; (2) whether the area is in an enclosure surrounding the home; (3) the nature and uses of the area; and (4) the steps taken to conceal the area from public view.

UNITED STATES V. GIORDANO, 416 U.S. 505 (1974)   The Court nullified hundreds of criminal prosecutions based on evidence obtained by surveillance when it held that then-Attorney General John N. Mitchell had not himself signed the applications for the warrant authorizing the surveillance and had allowed an aide other than the designated assistant attorney general to approve the applications.

UNITED STATES V. JACKSON, 544 F.2d 407 (9th Cir. 1976)   Abandonment is not meant in the strict property-right sense, but rests instead on whether the person so relinquishes his or her interest in the property that he or she no longer retains a reasonable expectation of privacy in it at the time of the search.

UNITED STATES V. JOHNS, 469 U.S. 478 (1985)   Implies that the "plain view" doctrine might not be limited to plain sight, but might also include "plain odor" by saying that "whether defendant ever had a privacy interest in packages reeking of marijuana is debatable."

UNITED STATES V. KARO, 35 CrL 3246 (1984)   The warrantless monitoring of a beeper after the device had been unwittingly taken into a private residence violated the Fourth Amendment rights of the residents and others.

UNITED STATES V. KNOTTS, 459 U.S. 817 (1983)   The use by the police of a beeper to monitor the whereabouts of a person traveling in a car on public highways does not turn the surveillance into a search. Such monitoring falls under the "plain view" doctrine and therefore does not need a warrant.

UNITED STATES V. NEW YORK TELEPHONE COMPANY, 434 U.S. 159 (1977)   The police may obtain a court order to require the telephone company to assist in installing a pen register device.

UNITED STATES V. POTTS, 297 F.2d 68 (6th Cir. 1961)   In general, the term *curtilage* has been held to include all buildings that are in close proximity to a dwelling and are continually used for carrying on domestic employment; or places that are necessary and convenient to a dwelling and habitually used for family purposes.

UNITED STATES V. SEDILLO, 496 F.2d 151 (9th Cir. 1974)   The "plain view" doctrine is properly applied to situations in which the police officer is not searching for evidence against the accused but nevertheless inadvertently comes across an incriminating object.

UNITED STATES V. U.S. DISTRICT COURT, 407 U.S. 297 (1972)   The Court rejected the contention of the Nixon administration that the provisions of Title III of the Omnibus Crime Control and Safe Streets Act did not require judicial approval of warrants for wiretaps or surveillance in national security cases.

UNITED STATES V. WHITE, 401 U.S. 745 (1970)   The Constitution does not prohibit a government agent from using an electronic device to record a telephone conversation between two parties with the consent of one party to the conversation.

☐ CASE BRIEF—LEADING CASE ON PLAIN VIEW AND INADVERTENCE

HORTON V. CALIFORNIA 47 CrL 2135 (1990)

FACTS: A police officer determined that there was probable cause to search suspect Horton's home for the proceeds of a robbery and weapons used in the robbery. The affidavit filed by the officer referred to police reports that described both the weapons and the proceeds, but the warrant that was issued only authorized a search for the proceeds. When the officer went to Horton's home to execute the warrant, he did not find the stolen property (proceeds), but found the weapons in plain view and seized them. At the trial, the officer testified that while he was searching Horton's home for the proceeds, he was also interested in finding other evidence related to the robbery. Tried and convicted, Horton argued on appeal that the weapons should have been suppressed during the trial because their discovery was not "inadvertent."

ISSUE: *Is inadvertence a necessary element of the "plain view" doctrine? No.*

SUPREME COURT DECISION: "The Fourth Amendment does not prohibit the warrantless seizure of evidence in plain view even though the discovery of the evidence was not inadvertent. Although inadvertence is a characteristic of most legitimate plain view seizures, it is not a necessary condition."

CASE SIGNIFICANCE: This case does away with the requirement that for plain view to apply, the discovery of the evidence must be purely accidental. The police officer in this case knew that the evidence was there because it was in fact described in the officer's affidavit, but for some reason the warrant issued by the magistrate only authorized a search for the proceeds. Nonetheless, the officer saw the weapons in plain view during the search and seized them. Expressly rejecting the inadvertence requirement, the Court said that the seizure was valid because

1. "The items seized from petitioner's home were discovered during a lawful search authorized by a valid warrant."
2. When they were discovered, it was immediately apparent to the officer that they constituted incriminating evidence."

3. "The officer had probable cause, not only to obtain a warrant to search for the stolen property, but also to believe that the weapons and handguns had been used in the crime he was investigating."
4. "The search was authorized by the warrant."

EXCERPTS FROM THE DECISION: Justice Stewart [in Coolidge v. New Hampshire, 403 U.S. 443 (1979)] concluded that the inadvertence requirement was necessary to avoid a violation of the express constitutional requirement that a valid warrant must particularly describe the things to be seized. He explained:

> The rationale of the exception to the warrant requirement, as just stated, is that a plain view seizure will not turn an initially valid (and therefore limited) search into a "general" one, while the inconvenience of procuring a warrant to cover an inadvertent discovery is great. But where the discovery is anticipated, where the police know in advance the location of the evidence and intend to seize it, the situation is altogether different. The requirement of a warrant to seize imposes no inconvenience whatever, or at least none which is constitutionally cognizable in a legal system that regards warrantless searches as "per se unreasonable" in the absence of "exigent circumstances."

We find two flaws in this reasoning. First, evenhanded law enforcement is best achieved by the application of objective standards of conduct, rather than standards that depend upon the subjective state of mind of the officer. The fact that an officer is interested in an item of evidence and fully expects to find it in the course of a search should not invalidate its seizure if the search is confined in area and duration by the terms of a warrant or a valid exception to the warrant requirement. If the officer has knowledge approaching certainty that the item will be found, we see no reason why he or she would deliberately omit a particular description of the items to be seized from the application of a search warrant.

Specification of the additional item could only permit the officer to expand the scope of the search. On the other hand, if he or she has a valid warrant to search for one item and merely a suspicion concerning the second, whether or not it amounts to probable cause, we fail to see why that suspicion should immunize the second item from seizure if it is found during a lawful search for the first.

Second, the suggestion that the inadvertence requirement is necessary to prevent the police from conducting general searches, or from converting specific warrants into general warrants, is not persuasive because that interest is already served by the requirements that no warrant issue unless it "particularly describes the place to be searched and the persons or things to be seized," and that a warrantless search be circumscribed by the exigencies which justify its initiation.

☐ CASE BRIEF—LEADING CASE ON THE RIGHT TO PRIVACY

KATZ V. UNITED STATES, 389 U.S. 347 (1967)

FACTS: Katz was convicted in federal court of transmitting wagering information by telephone across state lines. Evidence of Katz's end of the conversation, overheard by FBI agents who had attached an electronic listening and recording device to the outside of the telephone booth from which the calls were made, was introduced at the trial. Katz sought to suppress the evidence, but the trial court admitted it. The Court of Appeals affirmed the conviction, finding that there was no Fourth Amendment violation since there was "no physical entrance into the area occupied" by Katz.

ISSUE: *Is a public telephone booth a constitutionally protected area such that evidence obtained by attaching an electronic listening/recording device to the top of it is obtained in violation of the right to privacy of the user of the booth? Yes.*

SUPREME COURT DECISION: Any form of electronic surveillance, including wiretapping, that violates a reasonable expectation of privacy constitutes a search. No actual physical trespass is required.

CASE SIGNIFICANCE: The Katz decision expressly overruled the ruling 39 years earlier in Olmstead v. United States, 277 U.S. 438 (1928), which held that wiretapping did not violate the Fourth Amendment unless there was some trespass into a "constitutionally protected area." In Katz, the Court said that the coverage of the Fourth Amendment does not depend on the presence or absence of a physical intrusion into a given enclosure. The current test is that a search exists and therefore comes under the Fourth Amendment protection whenever there is a "reasonable expectation of privacy." The concept that the Constitution "protects people rather than places" is very significant because it makes the protection of the Fourth Amendment "portable," meaning that it is carried by persons wherever they go as long as their behavior and circumstances are such that they are entitled to a reasonable expectation of privacy. This was made clear by the Court when it said that "an individual in a business office, in a friend's apartment, or in a taxicab, a person in a telephone booth may rely upon the protection of the Fourth Amendment. One who occupies it, shuts the door behind him, and pays the toll that permits him to place a call is surely entitled to assume that the words he utters into the mouthpiece will not be broadcast to the world." Katz has therefore made a significant change in the concept of the right to privacy and has greatly expanded the coverage of that right, particularly as applied to Fourth Amendment cases. It is the current standard by which the legality of search and seizure cases is tested.

EXCERPTS FROM THE DECISION: The Government stresses the fact that the telephone booth from which the petitioner made his calls was constructed partly of glass, so that he was as visible after he entered it as he would have been if he had remained outside. But what he sought to exclude when he entered the booth was not the intruding eye—it was the uninvited ear. He did not shed his right to do so simply because he made his calls from a place where he might be seen. No less than an individual in a business office, in a friend's apartment, or in a taxicab, a person in a telephone booth may rely upon the protection of the Fourth Amendment. One who occupies it, shuts the door behind him, and pays the toll that permits him to place a call is surely entitled to assume that the words he utters into the mouthpiece will not be broadcast to the world. To read the Constitution more narrowly is to ignore the vital role that the public telephone has come to play in private communication. . . .

We conclude that the underpinnings of Olmstead and Goldman have been so eroded by our subsequent decisions that the "trespass" doctrine there enunciated can no longer be regarded as controlling. The Government's activities in electronically listening to and recording the petitioner's words violated the privacy upon which he justifiably relied while using the telephone booth and thus constituted a "search and seizure" within the meaning of the Fourth Amendment. The fact that the electronic device employed to achieve that end did not happen to penetrate the wall of the booth can have no constitutional significance.

The question remaining for decision, then, is whether the search and seizure conducted in this case complied with constitutional standards. In that regard, the Government's position is that its agents acted in an entirely defensible manner: They did not begin their electronic surveillance until investigation of the petitioner's activities had established a strong probability that he was using the telephone in question to transmit gambling information to persons in other States, in violation of federal law. Moreover, the surveillance was limited, both in scope and in duration, to the specific purposes of establishing the contents of the petitioner's unlawful telephonic communications. The agents confined their surveillance to the brief periods during which he used the telephone booth, and they took great care to overhear only the conversations of the petitioner himself.

Accepting this account of the Government's actions as accurate, it is clear that this surveillance was so narrowly circumscribed that a duly authorized magistrate, properly notified of the need for such investigation, specifically informed of the basis on which it was to proceed, and clearly apprised of the precise intrusion it would entail, could constitutionally have authorized, with appropriate safeguards, the very limited search and seizure that the Government asserts in fact took place.

□ NOTES

1. S. Emmanuel and S. Knowles, *Criminal Procedure* (Larchmont, NY: Emmanuel Law Outlines, 1989–90), at 19.
2. *Time Magazine,* January 1, 1990, at 55.
3. Ibid.
4. *Time Magazine,* February 12, 1990, at 8.
5. John G. Miles, Jr., David B. Richardson, and Anthony E. Scudellari, *The Law Officer's Pocket Manual* (Washington, DC: Bureau of National Affairs, 1988–89), at 10:5.
6. See R. A. Fiatal, "The Electronic Communications Privacy Act: Addressing Today's Technology" (Part 1), *FBI Law Enforcement Bulletin,* February 1988, at 25–30; R. A. Fiatal, "The Electronic Communications Privacy Act: Addressing Today's Technology" (Part II), *FBI Law Enforcement Bulletin,* March 1988, at 26–30; R. A. Fiatal, "The Electronic Communications Privacy Act: Addressing Today's Technology" (Part III), *FBI Law Enforcement Bulletin,* April 1988, at 24–30.
7. Ibid., Part I, at 25.
8. Ibid., Part II, at 27.
9. Ibid., Part II, at 28–30.
10. Ibid., Part II, at 27.
11. Ibid., Part II, at 24.
12. Ibid., Part III, at 25.
13. Ibid., Part III, at 26.

PART FOUR

IDENTIFICATION AND INTERROGATION

CHAPTER TEN
LINE-UPS AND OTHER PRETRIAL IDENTIFICATION PROCEDURES

CHAPTER ELEVEN
CONFESSIONS AND ADMISSIONS: THE MIRANDA CASE

LINE-UPS AND OTHER PRETRIAL IDENTIFICATION PROCEDURES

☐ KEY TERMS

line-ups
show-ups
photographic identifications
physical (or real) self-
      incrimination
testimonial (or communicative)
      self-incrimination

formally charged with an offense
Wade-Gilbert rule
Kirby rule
Frye doctrine
DNA "fingerprinting"

The police use a variety of procedures to verify whether a suspect who has been taken into custody is in fact guilty of an offense. These identification procedures serve the dual function of solving crimes and providing evidence at the trial. Three general procedures are often used by the police to identify suspects who have been taken into custody:

1. *Line-ups,* at which a victim or witness to a crime is shown several possible suspects at the police station for purpose of identification
2. *Show-ups,* at which only one suspect is shown to the witness or victim, usually at the scene of the crime and immediately following a quick arrest of the suspect
3. *Photographic identifications* (rogue's galleries), which entail showing photographs of possible suspects to the victim or witness

Four constitutional rights are often invoked by suspects during the pretrial identification stage: (1) the right not to incriminate oneself under the Fifth Amendment; (2) the right to counsel under the Sixth Amendment; (3) the right to due process under the Fifth and Fourteenth Amendments; and (4) protection against unreasonable search and seizure under the Fourth Amendment. The discussion in this chapter will look into how these rights apply in pretrial identification procedures.

I. PRIVILEGE AGAINST SELF-INCRIMINATION— DOES NOT APPLY

Suspects often claim that they cannot be required to appear in a line-up or show-up because it forces them to incriminate themselves. That claim appears logical because, indeed, it is incriminating to be fingered as the culprit in a line-up or to be identified in a show-up. The Court, however, has resolved this issue authoritatively against the suspect. The rule is that a suspect *may be compelled* to appear in a police line-up before or after being charged with an offense. The reason is that protection against compulsory self-incrimination refers only to evidence that is *"testimonial or communicative"* in nature. It does not extend to *"real or physical" evidence.* Therefore, the government can force a suspect to do the following things because they involve only the giving of physical evidence:

1. Appear in a police line-up before or after formal charge
2. Give a blood sample, even unwillingly, as long as proper conditions are present; moreover, even if state law allows a suspect to refuse to take a blood alcohol test, a refusal may be constitutionally introduced as evidence of guilt in court

3. Submit to a photograph
4. Give handwriting samples
5. Submit to fingerprinting
6. Repeat certain words or gestures, or give voice exemplars (the voice here is used as an identifying physical characteristic, not to give testimony)

The rule that the Fifth Amendment right not to incriminate oneself protects only against "testimonial or communicative" rather than "real or physical" self-incrimination was enunciated by the Court in Schmerber v. California, 384 U.S. 757 (1966). In that case, the suspect was arrested for drunk driving and a blood sample was extracted from him, over his objection, by a medical doctor who was acting under police direction. The suspect objected to the use of the incriminating evidence during the trial, claiming that it was obtained in violation of his right to protection against self-incrimination. The Court disagreed, saying that the seizure of "real or physical" evidence does not involve Fifth Amendment guarantees because that amendment applies only to "testimonial or communicative" rather than "real or physical" evidence. *"Testimonial or communicative" incrimination occurs when a suspect is required to "speak his guilt."*

Following the Schmerber decision, the Court later ruled that appearance in a police line-up was a form of *physical self-incrimination* that was not protected by the Constitution. There is no self-incrimination even if the suspect is required to "speak up" for identification, by repeating words such as "Put the money in the bag." The objective of having the suspect "speak up" is not to evaluate what is said, which would be testimonial, but to measure the level, tone, and quality of voice, which are physical properties (U.S. v. Wade, 388 U.S. 218 [1967]).

It follows from the Schmerber ruling that a suspect does not have a constitutional right to refuse to appear or participate in a line-up. If a suspect refuses, he or she may be held in contempt of court, unless the refusal to participate is allowed by state law or departmental policy. Moreover, the suspect's refusal to cooperate in the identification procedure may be commented on by the prosecution during the trial. Another possibility for the police, in the event that the suspect refuses to cooperate, is to conduct the investigation over the suspect's objection. However, the use of force to compel the suspect to mount the stage and remain there might make the proceeding unduly suggestive and thus violate the suspect's "due process" rights. It has also been suggested that refusal to participate in a line-up might justify the use by the police of a show-up in which the suspect alone is viewed by a witness.[1]

II. THE RIGHT TO COUNSEL

A. Line-ups

The right to counsel in line-ups must be considered in terms of two stages: prior to the filing of a formal charge and after the filing of a formal charge.

1. Prior to the Filing of a Formal Charge—No Right to Counsel

A suspect in a line-up has no right to a lawyer if he or she *has not been formally charged with an offense. "Formally charged with an offense" means after an indictment, information, preliminary hearing, or arraignment* (Kirby v. Illinois, 406 U.S.

SUPPLEMENTARY OFFENSE REPORT   **SERIAL NO.**

Name of Complainant

Address

Date of Offense   19

HOUSTON POLICE DEPARTMENT
SHOWUP PROCEDURE

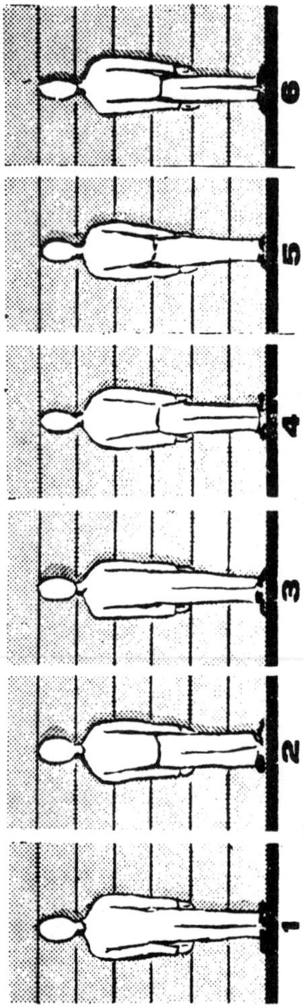

Column labels (rows):
Name
Race & Age
Height
Weight
Color Shirt
Color Pants
Color Shoes

WITNESS PRESENT AT SHOWUP:
Name   Address   Phone

LIST SUSPECTS NUMBER IN SHOWUP
Positive I.D.   Tentative I.D.   Negative I.D.   Time Viewed

1.
2.
3.
4.
5.
6.
7.
8.

CASE BE DECLARED   INACTIVE (NOT CLEARED) ☐
                    CLEARED BY ARREST   ☐   CASE DECLARED
                    UNFOUNDED   ☐
_____BADGE NO. _____   SIGNED _____

CASE DECLARED   INACTIVE (NOT CLEARED) ☐
                 UNFOUNDED   ☐
                 CLEARED BY ARREST   ☐

682 [1972]). In the Kirby case, a robbery suspect was identified by the victim in a pretrial identification process at the police station. No lawyer was present in the room during the identification; neither was the suspect advised by the police of any right to the presence of counsel. Kirby was convicted of robbery and appealed his conviction. The Court held that Kirby was not entitled to the presence and advice of a lawyer because he had not been formally charged with an offense. The identification process in which he participated was a matter of routine police investigation and hence not considered a "critical stage of the prosecution." Only when the proceeding is considered a "critical stage of the prosecution" is a suspect entitled to the presence and advice of counsel. (Read the Kirby v. Illinois case brief at the end of this chapter.)

Most lower courts have held that taking the accused into custody under an arrest warrant is equivalent to filing a formal charge. But if the line-up is conducted after a warrantless arrest, formal charges have not yet been filed; the suspect therefore has no right to the presence of counsel. In these cases, though, the officer must be careful not to violate the suspect's right to due process (discussed below). Some states, however, require counsel for the suspect at all line-ups, whether before or after the formal charge. State law or local policy prevails. The stage at which "formal charges" are considered filed varies from state to state, or even from one court to another, so it is best to know the law in a particular jurisdiction.

2. After the Filing of a Formal Charge—Right to Counsel Applies

In contrast, a line-up or other "face-to-face" confrontation *after the accused has been formally charged with an offense* is considered a "critical stage of the proceedings," and therefore the accused has a right to have counsel present (U.S. v. Wade, 388 U.S. 218 [1967]). (Read the U.S. v. Wade case brief at the end of this chapter.)

In the Wade case, the suspect was arrested for bank robbery and later indicted. He was subsequently assigned a lawyer to represent him. Fifteen days after the lawyer was assigned, an FBI agent, without notice to Wade's lawyer, arranged to have two bank employees observe a line-up of Wade and five or six other prisoners in a courtroom of the local county courthouse. Each person in the line wore strips of tape like those allegedly worn by the robber during the bank robbery, and upon direction each said something like "Put the money in the bag," the words allegedly uttered by the robber. Wade was tried for the offense and convicted. He appealed, claiming that the bank employees' courtroom identifications were unconstitutional because the line-up violated his rights to protection against self-incrimination and to have the assistance

---

HIGHLIGHT 10.1

Withdrawing Blood Does Not Violate Privilege Against Self-Incrimination

"We therefore must now decide whether the withdrawal of the blood and admission in evidence of the analysis involved in this case violated petitioner's privilege [to avoid self-incrimination]. We hold that the privilege protects an accused only from being compelled to testify against himself, or otherwise provide the State with evidence of a testimonial or communicative nature, and that the withdrawal of blood and use of the analysis in question in this case did not involve compulsion to these ends" (Schmerber v. California, 384 U.S. 757 [1966]).

of counsel. The Court rejected the first claim but upheld the second. The Court said that there is grave potential for prejudice, intentional or not, in the pretrial line-up, which may not be capable of reconstruction at the trial. Since the presence of counsel itself can often avert prejudice and assure a meaningful confrontation at trial, the line-up is a "critical stage of the prosecution" at which the accused is as much entitled to the aid of counsel as at the trial itself.

Is the filing of a formal charge a logical dividing line by which to determine if an accused should have a right to counsel in cases involving pretrial identification? The Supreme Court certainly believes so. In the Kirby case, the Court said that "the initiation of judicial criminal proceedings is far from a mere formalism," adding that "it is only then that the adverse positions of government and defendant have solidified . . . a defendant finds himself faced with the prosecutorial forces of organized society and immersed in the intricacies of substantive and procedural criminal law." Critics of the Court maintain that the boundary between "prior to" and "after" filing is artificial in that any identification made against the suspect at any stage is important in establishing guilt or innocence.

In a companion case to Wade, the Court held that requiring a suspect to give a handwriting sample without a lawyer present does not violate the suspect's right to avoid compulsory self-incrimination or the right to counsel (Gilbert v. California, 388 U.S. 263 [1967]). In the Gilbert case, the line-up was conducted in an auditorium in which were gathered about a hundred witnesses to alleged offenses by the suspect. They made wholesale identification of the suspect in one another's presence. Aside from the procedure's being legally deficient because of absence of counsel, the Court also said that this procedure was "fraught with dangers of suggestion." Taken together, the decisions in United States v. Wade and Gilbert v. California are known in legal circles as the *Wade-Gilbert rule*, as distinguished from the *Kirby rule* (taken from the Kirby v. Illinois case) discussed earlier.

Failure to provide a lawyer at a line-up after a formal charge has been filed against the suspect makes the evidence inadmissible; however, it does not automatically exclude the testimony of the witness if the witness can identify the accused in court without having to rely on the earlier line-up identification (Gilbert v. California, 388 U.S. 263 [1967]). To determine if this in-court testimony is admissible, the judge must conclude that the testimony is "purged of the primary taint" caused at the line-

---

HIGHLIGHT 10.2

Right to Counsel Applies When Defendant Is Formally Charged

"The initiation of judicial criminal proceedings is far from a mere formalism. It is the starting point of our whole system of adversary criminal justice. For it is only then that the government has committed itself to prosecute, and only then that the adverse positions of government and defendant have solidified. It is then that a defendant finds himself faced with the prosecutorial forces of organized society, and immersed in the intricacies of substantive and procedural criminal law. It is this point, therefore, that marks the commencement of the 'criminal prosecutions' to which alone the explicit guarantees of the Sixth Amendment [right to counsel] are applicable" (Kirby v. Illinois, 406 U.S. 682 [1972]).

up. For example, X, a suspect, is made by the police to appear in a line-up without a lawyer after he has been indicted by a grand jury. The witness identifies X as the person who raped her. This identification is invalid because X was not afforded a lawyer. However, if it can be established in court that the victim would have identified X in court anyway without the line-up (if, for instance, it is established that she in fact saw X a couple of times before the line-up, or had a good view of the suspect at the time of the crime), then the identification may be admissible because it may be considered purged of the illegality associated with the line-up.

Note that although a suspect is entitled to a lawyer during a line-up after formal charge, the suspect cannot refuse to participate in the line-up even if advised by the lawyer against appearing. The lawyer is present primarily to observe the proceedings. If the suspect cannot afford a lawyer, one must be appointed for him or her by the state. A lawyer may be appointed temporarily just for the purposes of the line-up.

a. Right to counsel versus Miranda warnings. Why is a suspect not entitled to a lawyer during a line-up prior to the filing of formal charges and yet is entitled to the Miranda warnings (which state that the suspect has a right to a lawyer and that if the suspect cannot afford a lawyer, the state will provide one) immediately upon arrest even if he or she is still out in the streets? The answer is that the Miranda warnings must be given any time the police officer interrogates a suspect who is under custody. This rule protects the suspect's right not to incriminate himself or herself. In contrast, line-ups do not involve any form of interrogation and the danger of self-incrimination is merely physical, not testimonial or communicative. The issue of Miranda v. Arizona is primarily the right not to incriminate oneself rather than the right to counsel.

b. Role of lawyer during line-up. The main role of a lawyer is to *make sure that the procedure is fair.* Therefore the lawyer's function is that of a "watchman" who makes sure that things are done right so as not to violate the suspect's "due process" rights. The Supreme Court has not given any guidelines on the role of a lawyer during line-ups. Most commentators believe that the lawyer should, at the very least, *observe the proceedings*—including taking notes or making a recording—and be able to state any objection to the proceedings. Others have suggested that the line-

---

HIGHLIGHT 10.3

Physical Self-Incrimination Not Prohibited by the Fifth Amendment

"We have no doubt that compelling the accused merely to exhibit his person for observation by a prosecution witness prior to trial involves no compulsion of the accused to give evidence having testimonial significance. It is compulsion of the accused to exhibit his physical characteristic, not compulsion to disclose any knowledge he might have. It is no different from compelling Schmerber to provide a blood sample or Holt to wear the blouse, and as in those instances, is not within the cover of the privilege. Similarly, compelling Wade to speak within hearing distances of the witnesses, even to utter words purportedly uttered by the robber, was not compulsion to utter statements of a 'testimonial' nature; he was required to use his voice as an identifying physical characteristic, not to speak his guilt . . ." (U.S. v. Wade, 388 U.S. 218 [1967]).

up procedure should be treated as an adversary proceeding in which the lawyer may question the witnesses, make objections, and have reasonable recommendations respected by the police. Since no guidelines have been set by the Supreme Court, the officer should follow the practice in the local jurisdiction. Most jurisdictions follow the "observe the proceeding" rule.

Lawyers should be *accorded all professional courtesies but must not be allowed to control the proceedings; neither should an attorney's disruptive presence be tolerated.* In case the lawyer acts improperly, it is best to invite the judge or the district attorney to witness the proceedings. Counsel should not be allowed to question the witness before, during, or after the line-up, although if an attorney asks to speak to his or her client prior to or after the line-up, he or she should be allowed to do so. If the suspect has an attorney (that is, after the suspect has been formally charged with the offense), the attorney must be notified of the line-up in advance. If the main role of a lawyer during line-up is as an observer, unless local practice provides otherwise, how is the defendant benefited by a lawyer's presence? The Court has answered this saying: "Attuned to the possibilities of suggestive influences, a lawyer could see any unfairness at a lineup, question the witnesses about it at trial, and effectively reconstruct what had gone on for the benefit of the jury or trial judge" (U.S. v. Ash, 413 U.S. 300 [1973]).

c. What if the lawyer does not appear?   The officer has a number of options if the lawyer, after having been duly informed of the line-up, fails to show up:

1. Ask the suspect if he or she is willing to waive the right to counsel; such a waiver is valid as long as it is voluntary and intelligent. The waiver is best obtained in writing.
2. Postpone the line-up to another time when counsel can be present.
3. Get a substitute counsel only for the line-up.
4. In case the preceding options are not available, or are impossible or impractical, conduct a "photo line-up." This is a form of line-up where those appearing are photographed or videotaped in one room and the witness is kept isolated in a different room. The photograph or tape is then shown to the witness. The theory is that "because there is no constitutional right to have counsel present when a suspect's photograph is shown to witnesses for identification, the Sixth Amendment is not implicated."[2]

B. Show-ups

The rule in show-ups is the same as in line-ups:

1. *Prior to the Filing of a Formal Charge—No Right to Counsel*   In most cases, the police bring a suspect to the scene immediately after the commission of a crime for the purpose of identification by the victim or other eyewitnesses. Since the suspect has not been charged with a crime, there is no right to counsel. For example, minutes after a purse is snatched, a suspect fitting the description given by the victim is apprehended several blocks away and is brought back to the scene of the crime for identification by the victim. There is no right to counsel even if the suspect asks for one.

2. *After the Filing of a Formal Charge—Right to Counsel Applies*   The rule is different once the adversary judicial criminal proceedings are initiated. In one case, for example, a rape suspect appeared with a police officer in the courtroom for a preliminary hearing to determine whether his case was to be sent to the grand jury and to set bail. After the suspect's appearance before the judge, the rape victim was asked by the prosecutor if she saw the suspect in the courtroom. She then pointed to the suspect. Such identification was admitted in court during trial over defendant's objections. On appeal, the Court held that this violated defendant's right to counsel, saying that since the adversary criminal proceedings at that time had been initiated, the defendant was entitled to a lawyer at that form of show-up (Moore v. Illinois, 434 U.S. 220 [1977]).

C. Photographic Identifications—No Right to Counsel

There is *no right to counsel* when the prosecution seeks to identify the accused by displaying photographs to witnesses prior to trial (a process otherwise known as mug shot identification) (U.S. v. Ash, 413 U.S. 300 [1973]). This is true even if the suspect has already been formally charged with the crime.

In the Ash case, Charles Ash was charged with five counts of bank robbery. In preparing for trial, the prosecutor decided to use a photographic display to determine whether the witnesses he planned to call would be able to make in-court identifications of the accused. Shortly before the trial, an FBI agent and the prosecutor showed five color photographs to the four witnesses who previously had tentatively identified the black-and-white photograph of Ash. Three of the witnesses selected the picture of Ash, but one was unable to make any selection. The postindictment identification provided the basis for Ash's claim on appeal that he was denied the right to counsel at a "critical stage" of the prosecution. The Court disagreed, holding that photographic identification is not like a line-up: the suspect is not present when the witnesses view the photographs. Since the main reason for lawyers' presence at line-ups is to prevent suspects from being disadvantaged by their ignorance and failure to ascertain and object to biased conditions, there is therefore no need for lawyers when the suspects themselves are absent.

III. THE RIGHT TO DUE PROCESS OF LAW—APPLIES
A. When Is the Right Violated?

A suspect has a right to due process of law, meaning that the identification procedure must not be unfair. In the words of the Court: "The influence of improper suggestion upon identifying witnesses probably accounts for more miscarriages of justice than any other single factor—perhaps it is responsible for more such errors than all other factors combined" (U.S. v. Wade, 388 U.S. 218 [1967]).[3]

In determining what is fair or unfair in identification procedures, courts generally consider all the circumstances leading up to the identification. Unfairness will be found only when, in light of all such circumstances (otherwise known as the "totality of circumstances"), the identification procedure is so *impermissibly suggestive* as to give rise to a real and substantial likelihood of irreparable misidentification (Neil v. Biggers, 409 U.S. 188 [1973]). In the Biggers case, the rape victim could

HOUSTON POLICE DEPARTMENT — OFFENSE REPORT SUPPLEMENT   INCIDENT NO._____

OFFENSE.. LOCATION...
COMPLAINANT(S).. DATE OF OFFENSE...
.... DATE SUPPLEMENT MADE.......................................

	SHORT FORM SUPPLEMENT INFORMATION	
☐ CONTACTED COMPLAINANT NO ADDITIONAL INFORMATION	☐ CONTACTED WITNESS/S LISTED NO ADDITIONAL INFORMATION	☐ UNABLE TO CONTACT COMPLAINANT AND/OR WITNESS/S LISTED
DATE & TIME:	DATE & TIME	DATE & TIME

RECOVERED STOLEN VEHICLE: YEAR......... MAKE................. MODEL................. LIC.YR.STATE&NO. ....
CONDITION OF VEHICLE: ☐ DAMAGED ☐ WRECKED ☐ BURNED   AMOUNT OF DAMAGE $_____
☐ STRIPPED (LIST ITEMS STRIPPED AND THEIR VALUE AT START OF NARRATIVE BELOW)
VEH. RELEASED TO: TOWED TO: BY:
PROGRESS OF INVESTIGATION, ADDITIONAL INFORMATION, ETC.:...

WAIVER OF RIGHT TO HAVE AN ATTORNEY PRESENT AT A SHOW UP

I, _____ , have been notified

that I will be placed in a lineup (showup) at _____
                                               (time)   (Date)

_____ , in Harris County, Texas.
        (Building)

The purpose of this showup is to let witnesses view me to see whether or not
they can identify me as a person who has committed crime or crimes. I have
been informed that I have a right to have my lawyer present at said showup
and to have a lawyer appointed free of charge for such purpose if I cannot afford
to hire one, and I here and now state that I do not now have a lawyer and I do not
want one for this showup. No threats or promises have been made to me in
connection with this waiver which I now sign of my own free will.

_____

WITNESSES:

_____

_____

                            ☐ SUPPLEMENT COMPLETE   ☐ CONTINUED
OFFICER(S) MAKING REPORT: STATUS: ☐ OPEN ☐ CLEARED ☐ INACTIVE ☐ UNFOUNDED
.... EMP. NO. .... UCR DISPOSITION: ....
.... EMP. NO. .... S.R.OFFICER .... EMP. NO. ....

Form No. ROB-0005

give no description of her attacker other than that he was a black man wearing an
orange-colored shirt and that he had a high-pitched voice. The victim went through
several photographs and was shown several line-ups but could not make any identification. The police arrested the defendant seven months later on information supplied
by an informer. The defendant was brought before the suspect alone. The police
showed the victim the defendant's orange-colored shirt and asked her if she could
identify the defendant's voice (from an adjoining room). No other voices were provided for comparison. The Court held that, taking into account the "totality of circumstances," the identification process was nonetheless lawful.

On the other hand, in the Gilbert v. California case, discussed above, the Court
held that a line-up conducted in an auditorium where the defendant was identified by

about a hundred witnesses violated the suspect's "due process" rights because the procedure was "fraught with dangers of suggestion."

In Foster v. California, 394 U.S. 440 (1969), the Court also found the confrontation to be violative of due process. The following circumstances attended the line-up in the Foster case: the suspect was lined up with men several inches shorter than he; only the suspect wore a jacket similar to that of the robber; when the line-up produced no positive identification, the police used a one-man show-up of the suspect; and because even the show-up was tentative, the police later used a second line-up in which only the suspect was a repeater from the earlier line-up. The Court said that the suspect's "due process" rights were violated because under those conditions the identification of the suspect was inevitable.

In photographic identifications, a number of photographs must be shown so as to avoid charges of impermissive suggestions. Moreover, there should be nothing in the photographs that focuses attention on a single person. For example, if the suspect is Hispanic, the photographs should feature several Hispanic-looking individuals. To do otherwise would be fundamentally unfair to the suspect and would violate due process.

B. Factors Courts Will Take into Account

The courts will most likely take the following factors into account to determine whether, considering all the circumstances, the suspect's "due process" rights have been violated during a line-up (Manson v. Brathwaite, 432 U.S. 98 [1977]):

1. The witness's opportunity to view the criminal at the time of the crime
2. The witness's degree of attention at that time
3. The accuracy of any prior description given by the witness
4. The level of certainty demonstrated by the witness at the identification
5. The length of time between the crime and the identification

C. Line-up Composition and Procedure

To ensure that "due process" rights are observed, the International Association of Chiefs of Police Legal Center recommends the following guidelines for every line-up held:[4]

1. All line-ups should consist of at least five or preferably six people, including the suspect.
2. All prisoners and suspects placed in the line-up must execute the line-up waiver form, unless an attorney is present.
3. All persons in the line-up must be of the same sex, race, and nearly the same age. The participants should also be of the same height, weight, coloring of skin and hair, and physical build as the accused. If this cannot be done with reasonable proximity, the line-up should be postponed.
4. All participants should wear the same type clothing; for example, the suspect must not appear in prison garb if others are clothed in civilian attire. Detectives dressed in suits should not appear with a suspect who is clothed in slacks and a wrinkled shirt.

5. The accused should be placed in the line-up at random, so as not to suggest identity by position.
6. Persons who may be known to the witness must not be placed in the line-up with the suspect.
7. If private citizens are recruited to participate in a line-up due to a lack of sufficient prisoners in custody matching a suspect's general appearance, they should execute a written consent form indicating: that they are aware that there are no charges against them, have not been arrested, are under no compulsion to participate, are legally free to leave at any time, and, if minors, have consulted with and received permission from their parent or guardian to participate in the line-up.

In addition to the above, the International Association of Chiefs of Police Legal Center also recommends that the following practices be observed every time a line-up is conducted:[5]

1. Each witness should view the line-up separately; this avoids the situation where one witness identifies the suspect out loud. If multiple line-ups cannot be held, the witnesses should be separated in the room.
2. Each participant in the line-up must be given the same instructions given others. For example, if it is desirable for the suspect to repeat the phrase, "This is a stick-up," each participant from left to right should repeat the phrase. If it is desirable to have the suspect try on a mask, each participant should put it on, in the order of their position in the line-up.
3. Witnesses should be instructed not to make any statement or comment *during* the line-up, which pertains to an identification. Witnesses should be given a sheet of paper and pen, and told to write the position number of any person he or she recognizes on this sheet.
4. Two photographs should be taken of the line-up. One should be a frontal view, the other a profile. All persons in the line-up should be included in a single photograph. Whenever possible, color Polaroid film should be used. This photograph is admissible in court, if it is later claimed the line-up was visually suggestive.
5. A single officer, usually the detective assigned to the case, should (a) advise the participants of their rights and obtain the waivers, (b) conduct the actual line-up, (c) take the photographs, and (d) afterward question the witnesses. This is important because it will reduce the number of officers who may have to appear in court, and preserve the "chain of evidence."

IV. THE RIGHT TO BE FREE FROM UNREASONABLE SEARCH AND SEIZURE—USUALLY DOES NOT APPLY

Violation of the guarantee against unreasonable search and seizure during pretrial identification was claimed by the plaintiff in Schmerber v. California, discussed above. In Schmerber, blood was withdrawn from a suspect by a doctor in a hospital upon request of a police officer for use as evidence in a drunk-driving case. The defendant raised the issue on appeal, claiming that the police should have obtained a warrant before extracting blood from him. The Court rejected this claim, saying that the officer might reasonably have believed that he was confronted with an emergency in which the delay necessary to obtain a warrant, under the circumstances, would have led to the destruction of the evidence. The Court added: "Particularly in a case such as this, where time had to be taken to bring the accused to a hospital and to investigate the scene of the accident, there was no time to seek out a magistrate and secure a warrant. Given these special facts, we conclude that the attempt to secure evidence of blood-alcohol content in this case was an appropriate incident to petitioner's arrest."

Claims of unreasonable search and seizure in pretrial identification procedures are few and, when raised, do not succeed. They fail because they basically allege, as in Schmerber, that the police ought to have obtained a warrant before conducting the identification procedure. Compelling a suspect to appear in a line-up or show-up is a form of seizure, but it is usually easily justified under the numerous exceptions to the warrant rule, such as the "exigent circumstances" justification invoked by the police in Schmerber. Moreover, many line-ups occur after a warrant has been issued or the suspect brought before a magistrate. In these cases, the search and seizure challenge becomes moot.

V. OTHER MEANS OF PRETRIAL IDENTIFICATION

In addition to line-ups, show-ups, and photographic arrays, the police sometimes use indirect forms of identification such as *polygraph examinations, hypnosis,* or *DNA "fingerprinting."* These are forms of scientific evidence whose admissibility in court varies. Constitutional rights may also be involved in each procedure.

A. Polygraph Examinations—Not Admissible in Most Courts

Most courts refuse to admit the results of polygraph (lie detector) tests in either civil or criminal proceedings unless admissibility is agreed to by both parties. The reliability of polygraphs is under question, particularly when the tests are administered by unqualified operators. Use of polygraphs therefore fails to conform to the *Frye doctrine.* This doctrine, enunciated in Frye v. United States, 293 F.2d 1013 (DC Cir. 1923), states that before the results of scientific tests will be admissible as evidence

---

HIGHLIGHT 10.4

Justifiable Search without Warrant

"The officer in the present case . . . might reasonably have believed that he was confronted with an emergency, in which the delay necessary to obtain a warrant, under the circumstances, threatened the 'destruction of evidence.' . . . We are told that the percentage of alcohol in the blood begins to diminish shortly after drinking stops, as the body functions to eliminate it from the system. Particularly in a case such as this, where time had to be taken to bring the accused to a hospital and to investigate the scene of the accident, there is no time to seek out a magistrate and secure a warrant. Given these special facts, we conclude that the attempt to secure evidence of blood-alcohol content in this case was an appropriate incident to petitioner's arrest" (Schmerber v. California, 384 U.S. 757 [1966]).

in a trial, the procedures used must be sufficiently established to have gained general acceptance in the particular field to which they belong.[6] In a 1983 report, the Office of Technology Assessment reported that "there is at present only limited scientific evidence for establishing the validity of polygraph testing." That report also stated that its review of twenty-four relevant studies meeting minimal acceptable scientific criteria found that correct detections ranged from about 35 to 100 percent.[7] The mathematical chance of misidentification is highest when the polygraph is used for screening purposes.

In the words of one writer:[8]

> Departmental policy should recognize that polygraph is not a perfect investigative process and that polygraph results, both examiner opinions following chart evaluation and (even) confessions and admissions obtained from examinees, are subject to error. Therefore, results should be considered in the context of a complete investigation. They should not be relied upon to the exclusion of other evidence or used as the sole means of resolving questions of verity.

Even if reliability were to be greatly enhanced, polygraphs might still find limited use in criminal proceedings because of possible objections on grounds of self-incrimination. It can be argued, with a great deal of justification, that forcing a person to take a polygraph examination and using the results against the person would be violative of the right to protection against compulsory self-incrimination because the nature of the examination is testimonial or communicative instead of real or physical. Questions of right to counsel and due process might also arise, although chances of a successful challenge would most likely be minimal.

B. Hypnosis—Not Admissible in Most Courts

The use of hypnotically induced identification and testimony is gaining popularity among police agencies, but their usefulness and reliability are also under question; hence the Frye doctrine again applies. There is also disagreement about who should perform the hypnosis and whether a witness whose memory has been hypnotically enhanced helps or harms a case when it gets to court.

Under hypnosis, a witness may be able to give a physical description of a suspect that can then be sketched by an artist and used as the basis of a search or investigation. A number of states allow the use of hypnosis-induced identification and testimony in court, but other states prohibit it because of unreliability. Although the procedure does not trigger any challenges relating to self-incrimination or right to counsel (primarily because the suspect is not present during the hypnotic session), questions about due process might arise, particularly if suggestiveness were injected into the procedure. There has been no Supreme Court decision on the admissibility of this type of testimony. What the Court has decided is that a rule adopted by the trial court that automatically bars hypnotically refreshed favorable testimony of criminal defendants violates the constitutional right to testify in one's own behalf (Rock v. Arkansas, 41 CrL 3329 [1987]). The Rock case, however, involved a defendant who wanted to take the witness stand to present a hypnotically induced testimony favorable to her defense in a manslaughter case, but was barred from doing so by the trial judge. It was not a case where a witness produces in incriminating testimony against a suspect while under hypnosis. This type of testimony for purposes of suspect identification is therefore generally governed by state law.

C. DNA "Fingerprinting"—The Jury Is Still Out

Some police departments have started to use *DNA "fingerprinting"* not only to prove their cases in court, but also to screen out or identify possible suspects. This procedure matches the suspect's DNA with DNA found in the semen or blood recovered from the scene of the crime. It first gained prominence in the mid-1980s and quickly caught the fancy of the law enforcement community and prosecutors as an infallible means of suspect identification.[9] It has been used in many trials in the United States, some of which have led to convictions. Most courts have accepted this type of evidence, assuming that its reliability is as good as claimed.

But in what is perhaps its first major setback, a federal judge in a highly publicized case in New York has ruled that DNA fingerprinting is not scientifically reliable enough to be admissible into evidence (People v. Castro, 545 N.Y.S. 2d 985 [N.Y. Sup. Ct., Bronx County, 1989]). After an exhaustive look at DNA fingerprinting through the testimony of various experts, the judge urged all lawyers in previous DNA cases to study their trial records to determine if appeals were warranted on the basis of his conclusion.[10]

The initial euphoria over DNA fingerprinting has markedly declined primarily because experts now have second thoughts, not as much about the technology itself, but about the competence of those administering it.[11] Most experts now believe that DNA fingerprinting is not as yet sufficiently scientifically reliable as to be accepted into evidence. One problem is the absence of industry regulation and adequate standards. Moreover, the test is not as remarkably accurate as originally claimed, that claim being that the chance of a match occurring at random was 1 in 100 million and that therefore the test was virtually infallible.[12] Despite these objections, the acceptance of DNA fingerprinting may be suffering merely from a temporary setback. As technology and the competence of laboratory personnel improve, in the near future DNA may yet live up to its promise as a powerful tool in law enforcement.

☐ SUMMARY

The police use a variety of procedures to identify criminal suspects, the most common of which are line-ups, show-ups, and photographic identification. Four constitutional rights are often invoked by defendants during the pretrial identification stage: the right not to incriminate oneself, the right to counsel, the right to due process, and the right to freedom from unreasonable search and seizure.

Suspects may be compelled to appear in a line-up before or after they have been charged with an offense; protection against self-incrimination refers only to evidence that is testimonial or communicative in nature, not real or physical evidence. In addition to being required to appear in a line-up, the accused may also be compelled to give a blood sample (as long as proper conditions are present), submit to photographing, give handwriting samples, submit to fingerprinting, repeat certain words or gestures, or give voice exemplars.

A suspect in a line-up has no right to a lawyer if he or she has not been formally charged with an offense, meaning that there has been no indictment, information, preliminary hearing, or arraignment. A suspect in a line-up or other "face-to-face" confrontation is entitled to a lawyer after he or she has been formally charged. The test used by the Court is whether or not the identification procedure is considered a "critical stage of the proceedings." Failure to provide a lawyer at a line-up after filing a formal charge makes the evidence inadmissible in court; however, it does not automatically exclude the testimony of the witness if the witness can identify the accused in court without having to rely on the earlier line-up identification. The main role of a lawyer during a line-up is to make sure that the procedure is fair—that things are done right so as not to violate the suspect's "due process" rights. A suspect has no right to counsel during either show-ups or photographic identification proceedings.

Line-ups must be fair, otherwise the suspect's right to due process of law is violated. In determining what is fair or unfair, the court considers all the circumstances (totality of circumstances) leading up to the identification. Unfairness will be found only when, in the light of all such circumstances, the identification is so impermissibly suggestive as to lead to misidentification.

Claims of unreasonable search and seizure in pretrial identification procedures are few and do not succeed. Compelling a suspect to appear in a line-up or show-up constitutes a seizure but is usually justified under the numerous exceptions to the warrant rule, such as the presence of exigent circumstances. Polygraph examinations have also been used, although indirectly, to identify suspects. Most courts refuse to admit the results of lie detector tests in either civil or criminal proceedings unless admissibility is agreed to by both parties. Similarly, the use of hypnotically induced identification and testimony is suspect because of its unreliability. There has been no Supreme Court decision on the use of polygraph examinations and hypnotically induced evidence; hence their usage in court is governed by state law or lower court decisions. DNA "fingerprinting" is still in limbo as a means of identifying suspects, although its status might improve in the near future.

☐ REVIEW QUESTIONS

1. What four constitutional rights are often invoked by suspects during the pretrial identification stage? Briefly discuss how they apply to line-ups, show-ups, and photographic displays.
2. "Compelling a suspect to appear in a police line-up is not violative of the suspect's right to avoid self-incrimination." Is that statement true or false? Support your answer.
3. What can the police do if a suspect refuses to appear in a line-up?
4. Does a suspect have a right to counsel during a police line-up? Distinguish between the Wade-Gilbert and the Kirby rules.
5. What does the phrase "formally charged with an offense" mean? Has a person on preliminary examination been formally charged with an offense?
6. What would deprive a suspect of the right to due process of law during a line-up? Give an example.
7. Discuss the role of a lawyer during a police line-up.
8. Discuss the admissibility in court of the results of lie detector tests.

9. What is the Frye doctrine?

10. Are hypnotically induced identifications admissible in court? Discuss.

❑ DEFINITIONS

DNA "Fingerprinting":   A procedure that matches the suspect's DNA with the DNA found in the semen or blood recovered from the scene of the crime.

Formally Charged with an Offense: Indictment, information, preliminary hearing, or arraignment of the suspect.

Frye Doctrine: Before the results of scientific tests will be admissible as evidence in a trial, the procedures used must be sufficiently established to have gained general acceptance in the particular field to which they belong. Enunciated in Frye v. United States, 293 F.2d 1013 (DC Cir. 1923).

Kirby Rule: A suspect in a line-up or other "face-to-face" confrontation before being formally charged with a crime is not entitled to have a lawyer present.

Line-up: A procedure in which a victim or witness to a crime is shown several possible suspects at the police station for purposes of identification.

Photographic Identification (Rogue's Gallery):   Procedures in which photographs of possible suspects are shown to the victim or witness.

Physical (or Real) Self-Incrimination: Incrimination that involves the physical body or objects, not protected by the Fifth Amendment.

Show-up: A procedure in which only one suspect is shown to the witness or victim, usually at the scene of the crime and immediately following a quick arrest of the suspect.

Testimonial (or Communicative) Self-Incrimination: Self-incrimination through oral testimony or communication, prohibited by the Fifth Amendment. It occurs when the suspect is required to "speak his guilt."

Wade-Gilbert Rule: A suspect in a line-up or other "face-to-face" confrontation after being formally charged with a crime is entitled to have a lawyer present.

❑ PRINCIPLES OF CASES

FOSTER V. CALIFORNIA, 394 U.S. 440 (1969)   The suspect's right to due process was deemed violated during a line-up in which the circumstances were such that identification of the suspect by the witness was inevitable.

FRYE V. UNITED STATES, 293 F.2d 1013 (DC Cir. 1923)   Before the results of scientific tests will be admissible as evidence in a trial, the procedures used must be sufficiently established to have gained general acceptance in the particular field to which they belong.

GILBERT V. CALIFORNIA, 388 U.S. 263 (1967)   Police identification procedures that are "fraught with dangers of suggestion" are invalid as violative of the accused's right to due process.

KIRBY V. ILLINOIS, 406 U.S. 682 (1972)   There is no right to counsel at police line-ups or identification procedures prior to the time the suspect is formally charged with a crime.

MANSON V. BRATHWAITE, 432 U.S. 98 (1977)   The courts will most likely take the following factors into account to determine whether, considering all the circumstances, the suspect's "due process" rights have been violated during a line-up: (1) the witness's opportunity to view the criminal at the time of the crime; (2) the witness's degree of attention at that time; (3) the accuracy of any prior description given by the witness; (4) the level of certainty demonstrated by the witness at the identification; and (5) the length of time between the crime and the identification.

MOORE V. ILLINOIS, 434 U.S. 220 (1977)   A defendant is entitled to a lawyer during a form of show-up during the preliminary hearing because at that time the criminal proceedings are considered to have been initiated.

NEIL V. BIGGERS, 409 U.S. 188 (1973)   Identification procedures must not be unfair. In determining what is fair or unfair, courts consider all the circumstances leading up to the identification. Unfairness will be found only when, in the light of all such circumstances, the identification procedure is so suggestive as to give rise to a real and substantial likelihood of irreparable misidentification.

PEOPLE V. CASTRO, 545 N.Y.S. 2d 985 (N.Y. Sup. Ct., Bronx County [1989])   DNA fingerprinting is not sufficiently scientifically reliable to be admissible into evidence.

ROCK V. ARKANSAS, 41 CrL 3329 (1987)   A rule adopted by the trial court that automatically bars hypnotically refreshed favorable testimony of criminal defendants violates the constitutional right to testify in one's own behalf.

SCHMERBER V. CALIFORNIA, 384 U.S. 757 (1966)   The removal of blood from a suspect without his or her consent to obtain evidence is not a violation of any constitutional rights as long as the removal is done by medical personnel using accepted medical methods.

UNITED STATES V. ASH, 413 U.S. 300 (1973)   There is no right to counsel when the prosecution seeks to identify the accused by displaying photographs to witnesses prior to trial.

UNITED STATES V. WADE, 388 U.S. 218 (1967)   A police line-up or other "face-to-face" confrontation after the accused has been formally charged with a crime is considered a "critical stage of the proceedings," and therefore the accused has a right to have counsel present. The absence of counsel during such proceeding renders the evidence obtained inadmissible. Also, requiring the suspect to "speak up" for identification is not a violation of the safeguard against self-incrimination because it is physical instead of testimonial self-incrimination.

☐ CASE BRIEF—LEADING CASE ON RIGHT TO COUNSEL DURING LINE-UP BEFORE FORMAL CHARGE

KIRBY V. ILLINOIS, 406 U.S. 682 (1972)

FACTS: A man named Willie Shard reported to the Chicago police that the previous day on a Chicago street two men had robbed him of a wallet containing traveler's checks and a Social Security card. The following day, two police officers stopped Kirby and a companion named Bean. When asked for identification, Kirby produced a wallet that contained three traveler's checks and a Social Security card, all bearing the name of Willie Shard. Papers with Shard's name on them were also found in Bean's possession. The officers took Kirby and his companion to a police station. Only after arriving at the police station and checking the records there did the arresting officers learn of the Shard robbery. A police car was dispatched to Shard's place of employment and brought him to the police station. Immediately upon entering the room in the police station where Kirby and companion were seated at a table, Shard positively identified them as the men who had robbed him two days earlier. No lawyer was present in the room, and neither Kirby nor his companion asked for legal assistance or were advised by the police of any right to the presence of counsel. Kirby was convicted of robbery and appealed his conviction, alleging that his identification should have been excluded because it was extracted unconstitutionally.

ISSUE: *Was Kirby entitled to the presence and advice of a lawyer during this pretrial identification stage? No.*

SUPREME COURT DECISION: There is no right to counsel at police line-ups or identification procedures prior to the time the suspect is formally charged with the crime.

CASE SIGNIFICANCE: Kirby was decided five years after United States v. Wade. It clarified an issue that was not directly resolved in Wade: whether the ruling in Wade applies to cases in which the line-up or pretrial identification takes place prior to the filing of a formal charge. The Court answered this question in the negative, saying that what happened in Kirby was a matter of routine police investigation, hence not considered a "critical stage of the prosecution." The Court reasoned that a post-indictment line-up is a "critical stage" whereas a preindictment line-up is not. The dissenters disagreed with this distinction, but the majority of the Court apparently felt that it was a good standard to use in determining when a suspect's right to counsel applies in pretrial identification procedure.

EXCERPTS FROM THE DECISION: The initiation of judicial criminal proceedings is far from a mere formalism. It is the starting point of our whole system of adversary criminal justice. For it is only then that the government has committed itself to prosecute, and only then that the adverse positions of government and defendant have solidified. It is then that a defendant finds himself faced with the prosecutorial forces of organized society, and immersed in the intricacies of substantive and procedural criminal law. It is this point, therefore, that marks the commencement of the "criminal prosecutions" to which alone the explicit guarantees of the Sixth Amendment are applicable.

In this case we are asked to import into a routine police investigation an absolute constitutional guarantee historically and rationally applicable only after the onset of formal prosecutorial proceedings. We decline to do so. Less than a year after Wade and Gilbert were decided, the Court explained the rule of those decisions as follows: "The rationale of those cases was that an accused is entitled to counsel at any 'critical stage of the prosecution,' and that a postindictment lineup is such a 'critical stage.'" We decline to depart from that rationale today by imposing a *per se* exclusionary rule upon testimony concerning an identification that took place long before the commencement of any prosecution whatever.

☐ CASE BRIEF—LEADING CASE ON RIGHT TO COUNSEL DURING LINE-UP AFTER FORMAL CHARGE

UNITED STATES V. WADE, 388 U.S. 218 (1967)

FACTS: A federally insured bank in Eustace, Texas, was robbed on September 21, 1964. A man with a small strip of tape on each side of his face entered the bank, pointed a pistol at the female cashier and the vice president, the only persons in the bank at the time, and forced them to fill a pillowcase with the bank's money. The man then drove away with an accomplice who had been waiting in a stolen car outside the bank. On March 23, 1965, an indictment was returned against Wade and two others for conspiring to rob the bank, and against Wade and the accomplice for the robbery itself. Wade was arrested on April 2, and counsel was appointed to represent him on April 26. Fifteen days later an FBI agent, without notice to Wade's lawyer, arranged to have the two bank employees observe a line-up made of Wade and five or six other prisoners and conducted in a courtroom of the local county courthouse. Each person in the line wore strips of tape such as those allegedly worn by the robber and upon direction each said something like "Put the money in the bag," the words allegedly uttered by the robber. Both bank employees identified Wade in the line-up as the bank robber.

At trial, the two employees, when asked on direct examination if the robber was in the courtroom, pointed to Wade. The prior line-up identification was then elicited from both employees on cross-examination. At the close of testimony, Wade's counsel moved for a judgment of acquittal or, alternatively, to strike the bank employees' courtroom identifications on the ground that conduct of the line-up, without notice to and in the absence of his appointed counsel, violated his Fifth Amendment right not to incriminate himself and his Sixth Amendment right to the assistance of counsel. The motion was denied, and Wade was convicted.

ISSUE: *Should the courtroom identification of an accused at trial be excluded as evidence because the accused was exhibited to the witnesses before trial at a post-indictment line-up conducted for identification purposes without notice to and in the absence of accused's appointed lawyer? Yes.*

SUPREME COURT DECISION: A police line-up or other "face-to-face" confrontation after the accused has been formally charged with a crime is considered a "critical stage of the proceedings"; therefore the accused has a right to have counsel present. The absence of counsel during such proceeding renders the evidence obtained inadmissible.

CASE SIGNIFICANCE: The Wade case settled the issue of whether or not an accused has a right to counsel after the filing of a formal charge. The standard used by the Court was whether or not the identification was part of the "critical stage of the proceedings." The Court, however, did not clarify exactly what this phrase meant; hence lower courts did not know where to draw the line. In a subsequent case, Kirby v. Illinois, the Court said that any pretrial identification prior to the filing of a formal charge was not part of the "critical stage of the proceeding," and therefore no counsel was required. The Wade case also did not authoritatively state what is meant by "formal charge," so that phrase has been subject to varying interpretations, depending upon state law or practice.

EXCERPTS FROM THE DECISION: We have no doubt that compelling the accused merely to exhibit his person for observation by a prosecution witness prior to trial involves no compulsion of the accused to give evidence having testimonial significance. It is compulsion of the accused to exhibit his physical characteristics, not compulsion to disclose any knowledge he might have. It is no different from compelling Schmerber to provide a blood sample or Holt to wear the blouse, and as in those instances, is not within the cover of the privilege. Similarly, compelling Wade to speak within hearing distance of the witnesses, even to utter words purportedly uttered by the robber, was not compulsion to utter statements of a "testimonial" nature; he was required to use his voice as an identifying physical characteristic, not to speak his guilt. . . .

Moreover, it deserves emphasis that this case presents no question of the admissibility in evidence of anything Wade said or did at the lineup which implicates his privilege. The Government offered no such evidence as part of its case, and what came out about the lineup proceedings on Wade's cross-examination of the bank employees involved no violation of Wade's privilege.

The Government characterizes the lineup as a mere preparatory step in the gathering of the prosecution's evidence, not different—for Sixth Amendment purposes—from various other preparatory steps, such as systemized or scientific analyzing of the accused's fingerprints, blood sample, clothing, hair, and the like. We think there are differences which preclude such stages being characterized as critical stages at which the accused has the right to the presence of his counsel. Knowledge of the techniques of science and technology is sufficiently available, and the variables in techniques few enough, that the accused has the opportunity for a meaningful confrontation of the Government's case at trial through the ordinary processes of cross-examination of the Government's expert witnesses and the presentation of the evidence of his own experts. The denial of a right to have his counsel present at such analyses does not therefore violate the Sixth Amendment; they are not critical stages since there is minimal risk that his counsel's absence at such stages might derogate from his right to a fair trial.

☐ NOTES

1. W. LaFave and J. Israel, *Criminal Procedure* (St. Paul, MN: West, 1985), at 325.
2. See L. Rissler, "The Role of Defense Counsel at Lineups," *FBI Law Enforcement Bulletin,* February 1980, at 24.
3. As quoted in ibid., at 23.
4. "Eyewitness Identification," *Legal Points* (Gaithersburg, MD: IACP Police Legal Center, 1975), at 1. This material is used with the permission of the International Association of Chiefs of Police, Thirteen Firstfield Road, P.O. Box 6010, Gaithersburg, MD 20878.
5. Ibid., at 1–2.

6. P. Lewis and K. Peoples, *The Supreme Court and the Criminal Process—Cases and Comments* (Philadelphia: Saunders, 1978), at 496.

7. *Houston Chronicle*, November 23, 1985, Sec. 3, at 1.

8. R. Furgerson, "Polygraph Policy Model for Law Enforcement," *FBI Law Enforcement Bulletin,* June 1987, at 7.

9. *Time Magazine,* "A Trial of High-Tech Detectives," June 5, 1989, at 63.

10. *New York Times,* "Some Scientists Doubt the Value of 'Genetic Fingerprint' Evidence, June 15, 1989, at 24.

11. Ibid., see Note 8 above.

12. Ibid.

CONFESSIONS AND ADMISSIONS: THE MIRANDA CASE

IX. IS MIRANDA HERE TO STAY?—YES

Summary
Review Questions
Definitions
Principles of Cases
Case Briefs
    Berkemer v. McCarty
    New York v. Quarles

☐ KEY TERMS

confession	"deprived of freedom in a significant
admission	way"
voluntary statement	interrogation
Miranda rule	"functional equivalent" of
waiver	interrogation
intelligent waiver	"public safety" exception
voluntary waiver	general on-the-scene questioning
custodial interrogation	volunteered statement

The terms *confession* and *admission* are often used as though they are one and interchangeable. They are not. In criminal justice, a confession means that a person says he or she committed the act; while an admission means that the person owns up to something related to the act but may not have committed it. A confession is therefore more incriminating than an admission. Here are two examples:

Confession: "Yes, I shot him."

Admission: "Yes, I was there, but I did not shoot him."

The Fifth Amendment to the U.S. Constitution provides that "No person shall . . . be compelled in any criminal case to be a witness against himself, nor be deprived of life, liberty, or property, without due process of law." The guarantee against compulsory self-incrimination in the Bill of Rights was incorporated under the Fourteenth Amendment of the Constitution and held applicable to state criminal proceedings in 1964 (Malloy v. Hogan, 378 U.S. 1 [1964]). This right has been a source of controversy and confusion and has generated a host of litigated issues, some of which are still unanswered. The main question is: When are confessions and admissions admissible as evidence in a criminal trial and when are they excludible? The answers are not simple, but this chapter's discussion should provide some insights. One case stands out above all other cases in this chapter—the case of Miranda v. Arizona. The Miranda rule says that evidence obtained by the police during custodial interrogations of a suspect cannot be used in court during trial, unless the suspect was first informed of the right not to incriminate oneself and of the right to counsel.

I. OLD STANDARD FOR ADMISSIBILITY—WAS THE ADMISSION OR CONFESSION VOLUNTARY?

Prior to Miranda, the Supreme Court decided confessions and admissions issues on a case-by-case basis. The practice was confusing to the lower courts because in those cases *the Court failed to set any definitive standard by which the admissibility of confessions could be judged.* In general, the Court held that confessions obtained by force or coercion could not be used in court. Conversely, confessions were admissible if they were voluntary. *Voluntariness,* therefore, was the basic standard used. But the meaning of the term *voluntary statement* was imprecise and changed over the years.

Originally, only confessions or statements obtained by physical force (such as beating, whipping, or maiming) were considered inadmissible. Later, however, it was recognized that coercion could be *mental* as well as *physical.* Even at that, the hard question always was: At what point did physical or mental (psychological) coercion become so excessive as to render the confession involuntary? It was clear that physical torture was prohibited, but how about a push, a shove, a slap, or a mere threat? As for mental coercion, suppose the police did not physically abuse the suspect, but simply detained him "until he talks"? Was this coercion? If so, how long must the detention last before the confession could be considered coerced? A few hours, a day, a week?

The following cases, all decided prior to Miranda, give a glimpse into the evolution of the Court's rulings and are illustrative of the difficulty the Court faced in prescribing a workable criterion for admissibility of the confession or statements prior to Miranda. Each case was decided on circumstances that could hardly be replicated in other cases. This variability led to a spate of confusing and conflicting decisions in the lower courts, a confusion that has largely been cleared by the Miranda decision. These are the leading pre-Miranda cases:

1. Brown v. Mississippi, 297 U.S. 278 (1936)—Coercion and Brutality

A deputy sheriff, accompanied by other persons, took one of the defendants to the crime scene, where he was questioned about a murder. The defendant denied guilt and was hanged by a rope from the limb of a tree for a period of time. He was then let down, after which he again denied his guilt. He was next tied to the tree and whipped. He still refused to confess and was allowed to go home. Later he was seized again and whipped until he confessed. The Court reversed the conviction and held that the confession was a product of utter *coercion and brutality* and thus violative of the Fourteenth Amendment right to due process. (At that time the Fifth Amendment protection against compulsory self-incrimination had not been applied to state prosecutions; hence the Court had to use the "due process" clause of the Fourteenth Amendment to reverse the conviction.)

2. Chambers v. Florida, 309 U.S. 227 (1940)—Coercion

Four youths were convicted of murder, primarily on the basis of their confessions. No physical coercion was used by the police, but pressure was exerted through prolonged questioning while the defendants were held in jail without contact with the outside world. The Court reversed the convictions on the ground that the confessions had been *coerced* and that the defendants had therefore been deprived of their Fourteenth Amendment right to due process of law.

3. Ashcraft v. Tennessee, 322 U.S. 143 (1944)—Involuntary

Ashcraft was suspected of murdering his wife. He was taken to the police station and questioned continuously for two days. At the end of that time, Ashcraft confessed his involvement in a plot to have his wife killed. During the trial the officers admitted that Ashcraft had had to be questioned in relays because the officers doing the questioning became tired and needed rest. Ashcraft, however, was not permitted to sleep or rest during the questioning until after he had given the confession. The Court held that the prolonged questioning of the defendant was sufficiently coercive to make the confession *involuntary* and therefore inadmissible.

4. Spano v. New York, 360 U.S. 315 (1959)—Deception

The defendant was suspected of murder in New York. About ten days after the alleged incident, Spano telephoned a close friend who was a rookie police officer in the New York police. Spano told his friend that he (Spano) had taken a terrific beating from the murder victim and since he was dazed he did not know what he was doing when he shot the victim. The officer relayed this information to his superiors. Spano was brought in to answer questions, but his attorney advised him not to answer. Spano's rookie friend was called and told to inform Spano that the telephone call from Spano had caused the officer a lot of trouble. The officer was instructed to win sympathy from Spano for the sake of his wife and children. Spano refused to cooperate, but on the fourth try by the officer, Spano finally agreed to tell the police about the shooting. Spano was convicted and appealed. The Court said that the use of *deception* as a means of psychological pressure to induce a confession was a violation of the defendant's constitutional rights and therefore excluded the evidence.

5. Rogers v. Richmond, 365 U.S. 534 (1961)—Involuntary

Defendant Rogers was charged with murder and found guilty by a jury. While in jail pending trial, Rogers was questioned concerning the killing. The interrogation started in the afternoon of the day of arrest and continued through the evening. During the interrogation, Rogers was allowed to smoke and was given a sandwich and some coffee. At no time was he ever subjected to violence or threat of violence by the police. Six hours after the start of the interview, Rogers still refused to give any information. The police then indicated that they were about to have Rogers's wife taken into custody, whereupon Rogers indicated his willingness to confess. The confession was introduced as evidence during the trial and Rogers was convicted. The Court held that the confession by Rogers was *involuntary* and therefore not admissible on the ground that there was no complete freedom of the mind on the part of the accused when making his confession.

6. Escobedo v. Illinois, 378 U.S. 748 (1964)—Denied Counsel at Police Station

Escobedo was arrested for murder and interrogated for several hours at the police station, during which time he was persuaded to confess. During the interrogation, Escobedo made repeated requests to see his lawyer, who was also at the police station at that time and who demanded to see him. The police refused both requests and proceeded to interrogate Escobedo. Escobedo eventually confessed, was tried, and was convicted. On appeal, the Court held that Escobedo was *denied his right to counsel* and therefore no statement taken during the interrogation could be admitted against him at the trial. The Court said that "where, as here, the investigation is no longer a general inquiry into the unsolved crime but has begun to focus on a particular suspect . . . no statement elicited by the police during the investigation may be used against him at a criminal trial."

The facts in Escobedo add up to a blatant violation of a right in that Escobedo was accused of a serious offense, was being questioned at the police station, and repeatedly asked for his lawyer, his lawyer was at the station and had demanded to see Escobedo, and yet the police refused contact between client and lawyer. It was therefore an easy case for the Court to decide because the police had indeed grossly violated Escobedo's right to counsel. Escobedo, however, left two issues unsettled: (1) Was the right to counsel available only when the suspect was accused of a serious offense, was being questioned at the police station, had asked to see his lawyer, and when the lawyer was there and demanded to confer with the client? and (2) What did the Court mean when it said in the decision that the right to counsel could be invoked when the investigation had "begun to focus" on a particular suspect? Because of its peculiar facts, the Escobedo case raised more questions than it answered. Lower court decisions disagreed on the meaning of Escobedo, leading to conflicting interpretations. Further guidance from the Court became necessary. Escobedo therefore set the stage for Miranda and in fact made the Miranda decision necessary because of the two unsettled issues.

II. NEW STANDARD FOR ADMISSIBILITY—DID POLICE COMPLY WITH MIRANDA V. ARIZONA?

Miranda v. Arizona, 384 U.S. 436 (1966), is the best-known and perhaps the most significant law enforcement case ever to be decided by the U.S. Supreme Court. Because of its importance, the case deserves a detailed and analytical discussion.

The facts.   Ernesto Miranda was arrested at his home in Phoenix, Arizona, and taken to a police station for questioning in connection with a rape and kidnapping. Miranda was then twenty-three years old, was poor, and had completed only half the ninth grade. The officers interrogated him for two hours, after which they emerged from the interrogation room with a written confession signed by Miranda. The confession was admitted during the trial. Miranda was convicted of rape and kidnapping and was sentenced to twenty to thirty years' imprisonment on each count. The Arizona Supreme Court affirmed the conviction; Miranda appealed to the U.S. Supreme Court.

The legal issue.   Must the police inform a suspect who is subject to a custodial interrogation of his or her constitutional rights involving self-incrimination and coun-

---

HIGHLIGHT 11.1

Standard for Right to Counsel Used in Escobedo Case

"We hold . . . that where, as here, the investigation is no longer a general inquiry into an unsolved crime but *has begun to focus* on a particular suspect, the suspect has been taken into police custody, the police carry out a process of interrogations that lends itself to eliciting incriminating statements, the suspect has requested and been denied an opportunity to consult with his lawyer, and the police have not effectively warned him of his constitutional rights to remain silent, the accused has been denied 'the Assistance of Counsel' in violation of the Sixth Amendment to the Constitution as made obligatory upon the States by the Fourteenth Amendment . . . and that no statement elicited by the police during the investigation may be used against him at a criminal trial" (Escobedo v. Illinois, 378 U.S. 748 [1964]). (Italics added.)

sel prior to questioning in order for the evidence to be admissible in court during the trial?

The Court's decision. Evidence obtained by the police during custodial interrogation of a suspect cannot be used in court during the trial unless the suspect was first informed of the right not to incriminate oneself and of the right to counsel. The Court said:

> We hold that when an individual is taken into custody or otherwise deprived of his freedom by the authorities and is subject to questioning, the privilege against self-incrimination is jeopardized. Procedural safeguards must be employed. . . . He must be warned prior to any questioning that he has a right to remain silent, that anything he says can be used against him in a court of law, that he has a right to the presence of an attorney, and that if he cannot afford an attorney one will be appointed for him prior to any questioning if he so desires. Opportunity to exercise these rights must be afforded to him throughout the interrogation.

Case significance—a "bright line" rule. Miranda v. Arizona has had the deepest impact on the day-to-day crime investigation phase of police work. It has drawn a "bright line" rule specifying what police should do and has led to changes that have since become an accepted part of routine police work. No other law enforcement case has generated more controversy within and outside police circles. Supporters of the Miranda decision hail it as properly protective of individual rights, whereas critics have accused the Court of being soft on crime and coddling the criminal. The 5-to-4 split among the justices served to fan the flames of the controversy in its early stages, opponents of the ruling hoping that a change in Court composition would hasten its demise. That has not happened, and neither is it likely to happen in the immediate future.

Miranda is significant in that seldom does the Court tell the police exactly what ought to be done. The Court literally told the police what warnings ought to be given if the evidence attained from the interrogation were to be admitted in court. Miranda also clarified some of the ambiguous terms used in Escobedo. "By custodial interrogation," said the Court, "we mean questioning initiated by law enforcement officers after a person has been taken into custody or otherwise deprived of his freedom of action in any significant way." It then added in a footnote: "This is what we meant in Esobedo when we spoke of an investigation which had focused on an accused."

HIGHLIGHT 11.2·

What Happened to Miranda?

Postscript to Miranda. Ernesto Miranda was later retried (under an assumed name to avoid publicity) for the same offenses of rape and kidnapping. His original confession was not used, but he was reconvicted on the basis of other evidence gathered by the police. After serving time in prison, Miranda was released on parole, but was killed in 1972 in a skid row card game in Phoenix, Arizona. The police gave his alleged assailant, an illegal alien, the proper Miranda warnings.

Statement of Miranda Rights

FORM USED BY SOME POLICE DEPARTMENTS

1. You have the right to remain silent.

2. Anything you say can and will be used against you in a court of law.

3. You have the right to talk to a lawyer and have him present with you while you are being questioned.

4. If you cannot afford to hire a lawyer, one will be appointed to represent you before any questioning, if you wish.

5. You can decide at any time to use these rights and not answer questions or make a statement.

Waiver of Rights

I have read the above statement of my rights and I understand each of those rights, and having these rights in mind I waive them and willingly make a statement.

SIGNED: _____ Age _____

Address_____

Date _____ Time _____ Location_____

Witnessed by _____ Department _____

Witnessed by _____ Department _____

Witnessed by _____ Department _____

Remarks:

GO-WRITE FORM: 710/75/MF

Yet the "focus" test was abandoned by the Court in later cases, preferring instead to use the "custodial interrogation" test to determine if the Miranda warnings needed to be given. The Escobedo case brought the right to counsel to the *police station prior to trial;* the Miranda case went beyond the police station and brought the right to counsel *out into the street* if an interrogation is to take place.

A. The Miranda Warnings

The basic Miranda warnings that must be given to a suspect or accused prior to custodial interrogation are as follows:

1. You have a right to remain silent.
2. Anything you say can be used against you in a court of law.
3. You have a right to the presence of an attorney.
4. If you cannot afford an attorney, one will be appointed for you prior to questioning.

Most jurisdictions add a *fifth warning,* saying: "You have the right to terminate this interview at any time." This additional statement, however, is not constitutionally required under the Miranda decision. Most police departments direct officers to issue the warnings as given above (taken directly from the Miranda decision); however, in some cases warnings that are not worded exactly as above may still comply with Miranda provided the defendant is given adequate information concerning the right to remain silent and to have an attorney present.

In one case, the police gave the following warnings:

- "You have a right to talk to a lawyer for advice before we ask you any questions, and to have him with you during questioning.
- "You have the right to the advice and presence of a lawyer even if you cannot afford to hire one.
- "We have no way of giving you a lawyer, but one will be appointed for you, if you wish, if and when you go to court."

The last part of that warning, "if you wish, if and when you go to court," was challenged as ambiguous and therefore inadequate. In a 5-to-4 vote, the Court disagreed, saying that the warning, although ambiguous, was sufficient to inform the suspect of his rights (Duckworth v. Eagan, 109 S.Ct. 2875 [1989]). The Court further said that Miranda does not require that lawyers be producible on call. It is enough that the suspect be informed of his or her right to an attorney and to appointed counsel, and that if the police cannot provide appointed counsel, they will not question the suspect until and unless there is a valid waiver.

B. For What Offenses Must the Miranda Warnings Be Given?

A source of confusion has been the type of offense that requires the Miranda warnings. Obviously, the Miranda warnings must be given in felonies and serious offenses. But how about misdemeanors, petty offenses, or traffic violations? In Berkemer v. McCarty, 35 CrL 3192 (1984), the Court answered this question as follows:

1. A person subjected to custodial interrogation must be given the Miranda warnings *regardless of the nature or severity of the offense* of which the person is suspected or for which he or she was arrested; but
2. The *roadside questioning* of a motorist detained pursuant to a routine traffic stop does not constitute "custodial interrogation," and therefore there is no

need to give the Miranda warnings. However, if a motorist who has been merely detained for questioning is subjected to treatment that renders him or her "in custody" for practical purposes, the motorist is entitled at that stage to be given the Miranda warnings.

(Read the Berkemer v. McCarty case brief at the end of this chapter.) In sum, *the Miranda warnings must be given when the suspect is interrogated for any type of offense (felonies, misdemeanors, or petty offenses). The only exception: roadside questioning of a motorist detained pursuant to a routine traffic stop.*

C. Is Miranda a "Right against Self-Incrimination" or a "Right to Counsel" Case?

Miranda is primarily a Fifth Amendment (privilege against self-incrimination) case. Miranda warnings 1 and 2, as listed above, protect the right not to incriminate oneself. Warnings 3 and 4 are right-to-counsel warnings, but they are there primarily to protect suspects against compulsory self-incrimination. In other words, a suspect is entitled to a lawyer during interrogation so that his or her right to avoid self-incrimination may be protected properly. Even if the proper Miranda warnings are given, however, the evidence is not admissible if the right to counsel under the Sixth Amendment has been violated. It is clear, therefore, that in confessions and admissions cases, the Fifth Amendment guarantee against compulsory self-incrimination and the Sixth Amendment right to counsel are closely intertwined. Moreover, it is not enough that the accused be afforded an opportunity to consult a lawyer prior to questioning. The right refers to having a lawyer present while the suspect is being questioned.

D. Miranda Rights May Be Waived

In Miranda, the Court said, "After . . . warnings have been given, and such opportunity [to exercise these rights] afforded him, the individual may knowingly and intelligently waive these rights and agree to answer questions or make a statement." A *waiver* is defined as an intentional relinquishment of a known right or remedy. The rights under Miranda may therefore be waived, expressly or implicitly, but the Court also said that "a heavy burden rests on the government to demonstrate that the defendant knowingly and intelligently waived his privilege against self-incrimination and his right to retained or appointed counsel." Certain aspects of a valid waiver need further discussion.

1. Waiver Must Be Intelligent and Voluntary

The waiver must be intelligent and voluntary. The Miranda decision specifically states that the prosecution must prove that the defendant intelligently and voluntarily waived his or her right to silence and his or her right to retained or court-appointed counsel. An *intelligent waiver* means one given by a suspect who knows what he or she is doing and is sufficiently competent to waive his or her rights. In cases involving a suspect who is drunk, under the influence of drugs, in a state of trauma or shock, has been seriously injured, is senile, or is too young, intelligent waiver is difficult for the prosecution to prove. There is no definite guidance from the courts on these cases, but the best policy is for the police either to wait until the suspect's competency is

D-316 S/O (REV.) WARNING OF RIGHTS   WALRAVEN-DALLAS

FORM USED BY SOME MAGISTRATES

State of Texas

County of_____

Before me, the undersigned magistrate of the State of Texas on this day personally appeared_____

_____in the custody of_____, a peace
officer, and said person was given the following warning by me:

☐ (1) You are charged with the offense of_____.
An affidavit charging you with this offense *(has) *(has not) been filed in this Court.

☐ (2) You have a right to hire a lawyer and have him present prior to and during any interview and questioning by peace officers or attorneys representing the State. If you are too poor to afford a lawyer, you have the right to request the appointment of a lawyer to be present prior to and during any such interview and questioning. You may have reasonable time and opportunity to consult your lawyer if you desire.

☐ (3) You have the right to remain silent.

☐ (4) You are not required to make a statement, and any statement you make can and may be used against you in Court.

☐ (5) You have the right to stop any interview or questioning at any time.

☐ (6) You have the right to have an examining trial.

*Your bail is set at $_____.

*Bail not determined.

*Bail is denied

☑ Check while reading

Place of Warning:_____   Person Warned _____

_____   Magistrate _____

_____   Title _____

TIME:_____M.

DATE:_____19____   WITNESSES:

REMARKS:_____   Name _____

_____   Address _____

_____   City _____

_____   Name _____

_____   Address _____

_____   City _____

*Delete what is not applicable.

ORIGINAL

restored (even if temporarily) or to be certain that the suspect understands the warnings sufficiently. A *voluntary waiver* means that the waiver is not the result of any threat, force, or coercion, and is made of the suspect's own free will.

2. Waiver "Following the Advice of God" May Be Valid Depending on State Rules

The admissibility of statements made when the mental state of the suspect interferes with his or her "rational intellect" and "free will" is governed by state rules of evidence rather than by Supreme Court decisions on coerced confessions. Such statements are therefore not automatically excluded; admissibility instead depends on state rules (Colorado v. Connelly, 479 U.S. 157 [1986]). In that case, Connelly approached a uniformed Denver police officer and confessed that he had murdered someone in Denver in 1982 and wanted to talk to the officer about it. The officer advised Connelly of his Miranda rights. Connelly indicated that he understood his rights and wanted to talk about the murder. After a homicide detective arrived, Connelly was again advised of his Miranda rights and again indicated that he wanted to speak with the police. Connelly was then taken to the police station where he told officers that he had come from Boston to confess to the murder. When he became visibly disoriented, he was sent to a state hospital where, in an interview with a psychiatrist, Connelly revealed that he was "following the advice of God" in confessing to the murder. He sought exclusion of the evidence during trial, saying that the confession was in effect coerced. The Court rejected the challenge, saying that confessions and admissions are involuntary and invalid under the Constitution *only if the coercion is exerted by the police* and not if it was exerted by somebody else. In this case, the police did not act improperly or illegally and therefore admissibility is not excluded by the Constitution. It may, however, be excluded by state law.

3. Express Waiver Is Not Required

An express waiver is not required. The failure to make an explicit statement regarding the waiver does not determine whether the evidence is admissible or not. Instead, the trial court must look at all the circumstances to determine if a valid waiver has in fact been made. Therefore, an express waiver, although easier to establish in court, is not required (North Carolina v. Butler, 441 U.S. 369 [1979]). The court will most likely take into account a variety of considerations, such as the age of the suspect, whether the suspect was alone with the officers at the time of interrogation or was in the presence of other people, the time of day, and the suspect's mental condition at the time of questioning.

4. No Presumption of Waiver from Silence

A waiver *cannot be presumed from silence* after the defendant has been warned of his or her rights. The trial court cannot presume waiver from the failure of the accused to complain after the giving of warning or from the fact that the accused spoke with the police after the warnings were given (Tague v. Louisiana, 444 U.S. 469 [1980]). It has not been decided authoritatively by the court whether a nod or a shrug constitutes a valid waiver.

5. A Signed Waiver Not Required

A signed waiver is not required. Refusal by the suspect to sign the waiver form (used by most police departments) does not necessarily mean that there is no valid waiver.

The Court has said that "the question is not one of form, but rather whether the defendant in fact knowingly and voluntarily waived the rights delineated in Miranda." A written waiver, however, makes it easier to prove a valid waiver in court.

6. Request for Someone Other Than Lawyer Is Waiver

The request by the suspect for somebody other than a lawyer means a valid waiver of the right to counsel. For example, the request of a juvenile on probation to see his probation officer instead of a lawyer (after having been given the Miranda warnings by the police and asked if he wanted to see a lawyer) was considered by the Court to be a waiver of the juvenile's right to a lawyer because a probation officer and a lawyer perform two different functions (Fare v. Michael C., 442 U.S. 707 [1979]).

7. Lawyer Already Retained—Waiver May Be Valid

Waiver of right by a suspect who already has a lawyer may be valid. A suspect who already has a lawyer may waive the right to a lawyer in the absence of that lawyer as long as the waiver is intelligent and voluntary. If the retained lawyer, however, wishes to see the client, even though the client has not requested to see his lawyer, the police are best advised at least to tell the defendant that his or her lawyer wants to speak to him or her.

8. Suspect May Withdraw Waiver

Suspect may withdraw a waiver once given. If the waiver is withdrawn, the interrogation must stop immediately. However, evidence obtained before the waiver is withdrawn is admissible in court.

E. Proof of Voluntary Waiver

Although a written waiver is not constitutionally required, most police departments have a written waiver form that suspects are asked to sign. The written waiver may be a part of the written confession, either before or after the statement by the accused, or be attached to it. If witnesses to the waiver are available (such as police officers, other police personnel, or private persons), they should be asked to sign the waiver to strengthen the showing of voluntariness. If the confession is typewritten, it is good practice to have the defendant read it and correct any errors in his own handwriting. This procedure reinforces the claim of a valid waiver. In the absence of a written waiver, the issue boils down to the testimony of the suspect against the testimony of the police officer that the waiver was in fact voluntary. A written waiver makes the claim of voluntariness by the police more credible. A simple waiver-of-rights form is as follows:

Date _____   Time _____

This is to certify that I have been given my Miranda warnings by Officer _____ and I fully understand them.

Signed _____

Location where warning was given _____

In juvenile cases, the waiver form is usually governed by state law concerning waivers by juveniles. In many states, there is a minimum age below which a juvenile cannot waive his or her rights. In other states, the waiver is valid only if signed by a parent or guardian, and/or signed in the presence of a lawyer.

F. The Effect of Miranda on the Old Voluntariness Rule

In Miranda, the Court rejected "voluntariness" (used in previous cases) as the sole test to determine whether or not statements from suspects are admissible in evidence. Under Miranda, voluntariness is now only one element in a three-pronged test. The current test asks three questions:

1. Is the statement *voluntary?*
2. Were the Miranda *warnings given?*
3. If there was a *waiver,* was the waiver intelligent and voluntary?

These three questions must all be answered in the affirmative for the suspect's statement to be admissible. One negative answer means that the evidence cannot be admitted for prosecution purposes. For example, if the statement is not voluntary, the statement cannot be used by the police for anything, even if the Miranda warnings were given. Likewise, even if the statement is voluntary but the Miranda warnings were not given when they should have been given, then the evidence has limited use—such as for impeachment purposes. Finally, if the statement is voluntary and the Miranda warnings were given, but there is no voluntary and intelligent waiver, the evidence obtained is not admissible in court.

> Example 1:　The police give X her Miranda warnings, but then force her to confess by questioning her continuously for 36 hours. X's confession would be excluded at trial because it was involuntary and made in the absence of a valid waiver.
>
> Example 2:　After arrest and in response to questions without the Miranda warnings Y gives the police a confession that is clearly voluntary. The evidence cannot be used in court, except for impeachment should Y take the witness stand, because Y was not given her Miranda warnings.
>
> Example 3:　Z gave a voluntary statement to the police after having been given the Miranda warnings. During the trial, however, the police cannot prove that Z's waiver was intelligent and voluntary. The evidence is not admissible.

III. WHEN MUST THE MIRANDA WARNINGS BE GIVEN?—WHENEVER THERE IS "CUSTODIAL INTERROGATION"

An important question for law enforcement officers is: When must the Miranda warnings be given? The simple but sometimes difficult-to-determine answer is: *Whenever there is custodial interrogation.* That does not tell us much, however, so the next question is: *When is there custodial interrogation?* In Escobedo v. Illinois, discussed earlier, the Court stated that the warnings must be given when the investigation has "focused" on the individual as a suspect. Since then, the Court has abandoned the "focus of the investigation" test and has used instead the "custodial interrogation" standard under Miranda.

The term *custodial interrogation* means that the individual must be "in custody" and under "interrogation." These are two distinct terms that must be viewed *separately* and not as a single term. The absence of one of the terms means that there is no custodial interrogation. For example, when a suspect is "in custody" but no questions are being asked, there is obviously no need for the Miranda warnings. Conversely, even if an individual is being interrogated but he or she is not "in custody," there is no need to give the Miranda warnings.

A. When Is a Suspect in Custody?

A suspect is in custody in two general situations: (1) when the suspect is under arrest and (2) when the suspect is not under arrest, but is *"deprived of freedom in a significant way."* According to the Court, the ultimate determinant of whether or not a person is "in custody" for Miranda purposes is "whether the suspect has been subjected to a formal arrest or to equivalent restraints on his freedom of movement" (California v. Bakeler, 33 CrL 4108 [1983]). Each of these situations deserves an extended discussion.

1. When the Suspect Is under Arrest

The rule is clear that when a person is under arrest the Miranda warnings must be given prior to interrogation. It makes no difference whatsoever whether the arrest be for a felony or a misdemeanor; once a person has been arrested, he or she must be given the Miranda warnings if interrogated. A troublesome question, however, is: When is a suspect under arrest? Answer: If the four elements of arrest are present; namely, intent, authority, custody, and understanding (as discussed in Chapter Six).

> Example 1:   A suspect has been arrested by virtue of a warrant. En route to the police station, the officer questions the suspect about the crime. The suspect must be given the Miranda warnings.

> Example 2:   A suspect has been arrested without a warrant because the police had probable cause to make a warrantless arrest (as when a crime is committed in the presence of the police). If the suspect is questioned at any time by the police, the suspect must first be given the Miranda warnings.

Note that brief questioning of a person by the police is not an arrest if the police officer intends to let the person go after the brief detention. Also, stopping a motor vehicle for the purpose of issuing the driver a ticket or citation is not an arrest; hence the Miranda warnings are not needed even if the police ask questions.

2. When the Suspect Is Not under Arrest but Is Deprived of Freedom in a Significant Way

This is the more difficult situation. The problem is: When is a person deprived of his or her freedom in a significant way? The answer is: *If the person's freedom of movement has been limited by the police.* Therefore, even if the investigation has focused on a person, the Miranda warnings need not be given unless the defendant will not be allowed to leave after the questioning. Whose perception determines whether a suspect has been deprived of freedom—that of the police or of the suspect? The Court has said that a "policeman's unarticulated plan has no bearing on the question whether a suspect was 'in custody' at a particular time; the only relevant inquiry is how a *reasonable man in the suspect's position would have understood his position*" (Berkemer v. McCarty, 35 CrL 3192 [1984]). In the words of one writer: "To trigger the Miranda safeguards, it is not sufficient that the suspect have a subjective belief that he is not free to go, nor that unknown to him, the officers intend to restrain him if he tries to leave. The test is whether a reasonable person in the suspect's position would conclude that he is not free to go."[1] This is based on a "totality of the circumstances" and is therefore determined on a case-by-case basis. Some factors to be considered are the location of the encounter and the nature and tone of the officer's questions.[2] It is hard, however, to establish a definite test to cover all contingencies. The question is best answered instead in the context of specific situations such as those discussed below.

3. Questioning at Police Station—Requires Miranda

Questioning at the police station requires that the Miranda warnings be given.

> Example 1:   The police invite a suspect to come to the police station "to answer a few questions." This type of interrogation requires the Miranda warnings because a police station lends a "coercive atmosphere" to the interrogation. But a suspect who voluntarily goes to the police station in response to a police request is not in custody and therefore is not entitled to the Miranda warnings.

> Example 2:   The police suspected a parolee of involvement in a burglary. The suspect came to the police station in response to an officer's message that the officer would "like to discuss something with you." It was made clear to the suspect that he was not under arrest, but that the police believed he was involved in the burglary. The suspect confessed, but later sought to exclude the evidence. The Court said that the Miranda warnings are necessary only if the suspect is in custody "or otherwise deprived of freedom in a significant way." Since those things had not occurred, the confession was admissible (Oregon v. Mathiason, 429 U.S. 492 [1977]).

4. Questioning in Police Cars—Requires Miranda

Questioning in police cars generally *requires* the Miranda warnings because of its custodial nature. The warnings must be given even if the suspect has not been placed under arrest. The reason is that questionings in police cars tend to be inherently coercive.

5. Questioning When the Suspect Is Not Free to Leave— Requires Miranda

When the police would not allow the suspect to leave their presence, or when the police will not leave the suspect alone, or if the police would not leave if asked by the suspect, then the Miranda warnings *must be given*. If the police would consider the suspect's attempt to leave or the suspect's refusal to answer questions as reasons enough to stop the suspect from leaving or to arrest him or her formally, then the Miranda warnings must be given. It is clear that under these conditions the suspect is being deprived of freedom in a significant way.

6. Questioning in Homes—It Depends

Whether or not the Miranda warnings must precede questioning in a suspect's home *depends upon the circumstances of the case.* The Court has held that the questioning of a suspect in his bedroom by four police officers at four o'clock in the morning needed the Miranda warnings (Orozco v. Texas, 394 U.S. 324 [1969]). In a later case, however, the Court held that statements obtained by Internal Revenue Service agents during a noncustodial, noncoercive interview with a taxpayer under criminal tax investigation, conducted in a private home where the taxpayer occasionally stayed, did not need the Miranda warnings as long as the taxpayer had been told that he was free to leave (Beckwith v. U.S., 425 U.S. 341 [1976]).

Note that in both the Orozco and Beckwith cases above, the investigation had already "focused" on the suspect. Under the old Escobedo standard, therefore, the warnings ought to have been given in both cases. The key consideration under Miranda, however, is whether the suspect's freedom of movement has been limited in a significant way, meaning whether the suspect is truly free to leave after the questioning. In Orozco, aside from the coercive nature of the questioning, the suspect was not free to leave after the questioning, whereas in Beckwith the suspect was free to go. It is clear, therefore, that the test to determine whether the Miranda warnings need to be given is not whether the investigation has "focused" on the individual but whether the suspect is under arrest or has been deprived of freedom in a significant way and therefore there is custodial interrogation.

7. Questioning Defendant Who Is in Custody for Another Offense—Requires Miranda

Any time the suspect being questioned for another offense is in jail or prison, the Miranda warnings *must be given* because the suspect is in custody. For example, D, in prison and serving a state sentence, is questioned by federal agents regarding a completely separate offense. D is entitled to the Miranda warnings even though no federal criminal charges are contemplated at the time of questioning. Failure to give the Miranda warnings when the suspect is in jail or prison means that the evidence obtained cannot be used in a criminal trial. There is no need for jail or prison officials, however, to give the Miranda warnings in prison disciplinary cases, such being administrative proceedings.

Note: A safe policy in situations involving the criterion "deprived of freedom in a significant way" is: When in doubt, give the Miranda warnings so that the admissibility of the evidence obtained is not jeopardized.

B. When Is a Suspect under Interrogation?—The Concept of "Functional Equivalent"

Ordinarily, interrogation means the asking of questions by the police. For purposes of the Miranda rule, however, interrogation refers not only to express questioning by the police; it also takes place when the officer does something that or acts in a way he or she knows or should have known is "reasonably likely to elicit an incriminating response" from the suspect. Most interrogation situations are obvious, such as when the police ask: "Did you kill him?" or "Where is the gun?" or "Why did you do it?" There are instances, however, when no questions are actually asked by the police but the circumstances are so conducive to making a statement or giving a confession that the courts consider them to be the *"functional equivalent"* of interrogation. In one case, the Court said:

> A practice that the police should know is reasonably likely to evoke an incriminating response from a suspect thus amounts to interrogation. But since the police surely cannot be held accountable for the unforeseeable results of their words or actions, the definition of interrogation can extend only to words or actions on the part of the police officers that they would have known were reasonably likely to elicit an incriminating response. Rhode Island v. Innis, 446 U.S. 291 (1980).

In specific cases, the Court has said the following:

1. *An appeal to the defendant's religious interests constitutes interrogation.* In one case, the suspect in a murder case turned himself in to the police. His lawyer told him he would not be interrogated or mistreated. On the drive from Davenport, Iowa (where he had turned himself in), to Des Moines, Iowa (where he was facing the charge), the officer gave the suspect the now-famous "Christian burial" speech, in which the officer called the suspect "Reverend" and indicated that the parents of the missing girl should be entitled to give a Christian burial to the poor child who had been snatched away from them on Christmas Eve. The defendant then showed the officers where the body was to be found. The Court said that the evidence obtained was not admissible because of a violation of the suspect's right to counsel. The defendant had clearly asserted this right, and there was no evidence of knowing and voluntary waiver. Moreover, although there was no actual interrogation, the Court held that interrogation nonetheless occurs when the police, knowing of the defendant's religious interest, make remarks designed to appeal to that interest and thus induce the defendant to confess (Brewer v. Williams, 430 U.S. 387 [1977]).

2. *The conversing of officers between themselves does not constitute interrogation.* Compare the Brewer case with the case of Rhode Island v. Innis. In Innis, the officers were conversing between themselves while they had the suspect in the back of the car. The suspect had been arrested in connection with the shotgun robbery of a taxicab driver. The officers talked about the fact that "it would be a terrible thing if

---

HIGHLIGHT 11.3

What Interrogation Means under Miranda

"The Miranda safeguards come into play whenever a person in custody is subjected to either express questioning or its functional equivalent. That is to say, the term 'interrogation' under Miranda refers not only to express questioning, but also to any words or actions on the part of the police . . . that the police should know are reasonably likely to elicit an incriminating response from the suspect. The latter portion of this definition focuses primarily upon the perceptions of the suspect, rather than the intent of the police" (Rhode Island v. Innis, 446 U.S. 291 [1980]).

one of the handicapped in the area from the school for the handicapped nearby where the crime took place would find a loaded shotgun and get hurt." The conversation, although addressed to a fellow officer, was within the hearing of the suspect. The suspect then interrupted the police and told them the location of the shotgun. The Court held that this did not constitute interrogation and therefore the volunteered evidence was admissible (Rhode Island v. Innis, 446 U.S. 291 [1980]).

3. *A conversation between a suspect and his wife that is recorded by an officer does not constitute an interrogation.* In one case, the police received a call that a man had just entered a store claiming that he had killed his son. When police officers reached the store, the man admitted to committing the act and directed officers to the body. He was then arrested and advised of his Miranda rights. He was taken to the police station where he was again given the Miranda warnings. The suspect then told the officers that he did not wish to make any more statements until a lawyer was present. At that time the police stopped questioning him. The suspect's wife was in another room, and the police questioned her. She insisted on speaking with the suspect. The police allowed the meeting on condition that an officer be present to tape the conversation. The tape was later used to impeach the suspect's contention that he was insane at the time of the murder. During trial, the suspect sought the exclusion of the recording, saying that he should have been given the Miranda warnings prior to the recording. The Court disagreed, saying that a conversation between a suspect and his or her spouse that is recorded by and in the presence of an officer does not constitute the functional equivalent of an interrogation under Miranda and therefore the evidence was admissible (Arizona v. Mauro, 481 U.S. 520 [1987]). The Court added that what the police did was to merely "arrange a situation" wherein there was likelihood that the suspect would say something incriminating.

IV. WHEN ARE THE MIRANDA WARNINGS NOT REQUIRED?

Given what we know from Section III (preceding), the easy answer to the question "When are the Miranda warnings not required?" would be: "Whenever there is no 'custodial interrogation.' " The Miranda decision and subsequent cases have further clarified the instances when there is no need to give the Miranda warnings. These instances are:

1. Roadside Questioning of a Motorist Detained Pursuant to a Routine Traffic Stop

The Miranda warnings must be given whether the custodial interrogation of a suspect be for a felony or a misdemeanor. The Court has said, however, that there is no need to give the Miranda warnings prior to routine questioning of a motorist detained pursuant to a routine traffic stop. This is because a routine traffic stop is usually brief, and the motorist expects that, although he or she may be given a citation, in the end he or she most likely will be allowed to continue; hence there is no deprivation of freedom in a significant way (Berkemer v. McCarty, 35 CrL 3192 [1984]). The Court further said that the typical traffic stop is public; such exposure to public view reduces the ability of unscrupulous police officers to use illegitimate means to solicit self-incriminating statements and diminishes the motorist's fear of being subjected to abuse unless he or she cooperates.

In a subsequent case, the Court reiterated this principle, saying that the curbside stop of a motorist for a traffic violation, although representing a Fourth Amendment seizure of the person, is not sufficiently custodial as to require the Miranda warnings (Pennsylvania v. Bruder, 109 S.Ct. 205 [1988]).

2. When Asking Routine Questions of Drunk-Driving Suspects and Videotaping the Proceeding

The Court has said that the police may ask people suspected of driving while intoxicated routine questions and videotape their responses without giving the Miranda warnings (Pennsylvania v. Muniz, 58 L.W. 4817 [1990]). In this case, an officer stopped Muniz's vehicle and directed him to perform three standard field sobriety tests. Muniz performed poorly and informed the officer that he failed the tests because he had been drinking. The officer then arrested Muniz and took him into custody. After being informed that his actions and voice would be videotaped, Muniz was processed through procedures for receiving people suspected of driving while intoxicated. Without being given his Miranda warnings, Muniz was asked seven questions regarding his name, address, height, weight, eye color, date of birth, and age. He was also asked but was unable to give the exact date of his sixth birthday. The evidence obtained by the police in the form of Muniz's responses and the videotape of his performance during booking was submitted into evidence over his objections. Muniz was convicted of DWI and appealed, alleging that the evidence should have been excluded because he was not given the Miranda warnings.

The Court disagreed, saying that the Miranda warnings were not needed because the police were merely asking routine questions and videotaping the proceeding. The seven questions asked were not intended to obtain information for investigatory purposes. As for the self-incrimination aspect of Muniz's responses, the Court said that videotaping the suspect and taking his slurred responses into consideration when determining his guilt constituted physical, not mental or testimonial, self-incrimination and therefore did not come under the Fifth Amendment umbrella. Significantly, however, the Court held that Muniz's answer to the question about the exact date of his sixth birthday was not admissible because "the content of his answer supported the inference that his mental state was confused," meaning that such evidence was *mental* instead of *physical*.

3. When There Is a Threat to Public Safety

The Court has carved out a *"public safety" exception* to the Miranda rule, saying that when questions asked by police officers are reasonably prompted by concern for public safety, the responses are admissible in court even though the suspect was in police custody and not given the Miranda warnings (New York v. Quarles, 104 S.Ct. 2626 [1984]). In the Quarles case, a woman approached two police officers who were on patrol, told them that she had just been raped, described her assailant, and said that the man had just entered a nearby supermarket and was carrying a gun. One officer entered the store and spotted Quarles, who matched the description given by the woman. Quarles ran toward the rear of the store, but was finally subdued. The officer noticed that Quarles was wearing an empty shoulder holster. After handcuffing the suspect, the police asked where the gun was; Quarles nodded toward some empty cartons where the gun was found. The suspect was given the Miranda warnings only after the gun was recovered. The Court said that the gun was admissible as evidence under the "public safety" exception.

4. When No Questions Are Asked

The Miranda warnings are unnecessary when the police do not ask questions of the suspect. Miranda applies only if the police question the suspect; therefore, if the police do not ask questions, no warnings need be given. For example, X is arrested by the police by virtue of an arrest warrant. If the police do not question X during the time he is in police custody, the Miranda warnings need not be given. In many states, the magistrate gives the Miranda warnings when the arrested person is brought before him or her for initial appearance or presentment.

5. General On-the-Scene Questioning

Miranda warnings do not have to be given prior to *general on-the-scene questioning*, at the scene of the crime. In the words of the Court in Miranda:

> General on-the-scene questioning as to facts surrounding a crime is not affected by our holding. It is an act of responsible citizenship for individuals to give whatever information they may have to aid in law enforcement. In such situations the compelling atmosphere inherent in the process of in-custody interrogation is not necessarily present.

A distinction must be made, however, between general on-the-scene questioning and questioning at the scene of the crime after the police officer has "focused" on an individual, which requires the Miranda warnings.

> Example 1: Z has been stabbed fatally in a crowded bar. A police officer arrives and questions people at the scene of the crime to determine if anyone saw the actual stabbing. This is considered "general on-the-scene questioning" for which there is no need to give the Miranda warnings.

> Example 2: Assume instead that upon arrival at the bar, the officer sees X with a bloody knife in his hands. The suspicion of the officer will doubtless be focused on X; therefore, any questioning of X requires the Miranda warnings even though such questioning is at the scene of the crime.

6. When Asking Identification or Routine Booking Questions

Identification and routine booking questions are such questions as: What is your name, where do you live, do you have a driver's license, what is your Social Security number, and so on. Such questions are not considered self-incriminatory and not unduly intrusive. Note, however, that while the asking of these questions does not require the Miranda warnings, their answers cannot be coerced. Should the suspect refuse to respond, state or departmental rules about what to do next should be followed. In some jurisdictions, failure to respond to preliminary questions may be introduced as evidence later in court; in others, it may be the basis for a criminal charge.

7. During Line-ups, Show-ups, or Photographic Identifications

There is no need to give the Miranda warnings in line-ups, show-ups, or photographic pretrial identifications because they are not protected by the Fifth Amendment right against self-incrimination. The evidence obtained is physical in nature and does not constitute oral or testimonial self-incrimination.

8. When Questioning Witnesses

When the person being interrogated is merely a witness to a crime, not a suspect, the warnings are not needed. In the course of the questioning, however, if the officer suspects that the witness might be involved in the offense, then the Miranda warnings must be given at that stage.

9. When Statement Is Volunteered

A person who volunteers a statement does not have to receive Miranda warnings before speaking. A statement is volunteered if made by a suspect without interrogation. For example, X enters the police station and announces: "I just killed my wife." The statement is admissible in court because it was volunteered. A *volunteered statement* is different from a *voluntary statement*, which is a statement given without coercion and of the suspect's own free will. A volunteered statement is one given to the police apart from and not in response to any interrogation. Both are generally admissible in evidence.

10. When Statement Is Made to a Private Person

Miranda does not apply to statements or confessions made to private persons. Protection against compulsory self-incrimination applies only to interrogations initiated by law enforcement officers. Therefore, incriminating statements made by the accused to friends or cellmates while in custody are admissible even if made without the Miranda warnings. This is so unless government agents arranged the situation.

11. When Questioning Is in an Office or Place of Business

The Court has not addressed this issue, but lower courts have said that the Miranda warnings need not be given as long as the person is free to leave at any time.

12. In "Stop and Frisk" Cases

There is no need to give the Miranda warnings if a person is stopped by the police and asked questions to determine if a criminal activity is about to take place. In this brief encounter, which is preceded by a casual type of questioning, the suspect is not deprived of freedom in a significant way. The purpose of a stop is to determine whether a criminal activity is about to take place, and the purpose of a frisk is to protect the officer. In neither case is custodial interrogation involved. Note, however, that once a "stop and frisk" situation turns into an arrest, the Miranda warnings must be given.

13. When Appearing before a Grand Jury

Interrogation of a potential criminal defendant before a grand jury does not require the Miranda warnings, even if the prosecutor intends to charge the witness with an offense. This is because grand jury questioning does not constitute custodial interrogation. The theory is that such interrogation does not present the same opportunities for abuse as custodial interrogation by the police. Questioning in a grand jury room is different from custodial police interrogation (U.S. v. Mandujano, 425 U.S. 564 [1976]).

14. In Noncustodial Interrogations by a Probation Officer

The Miranda warnings need not be given in cases of noncustodial interrogation of a probationer by a probation officer. For example, an interview situation between a probationer and a probation officer for purposes of supervision is noncustodial in nature. Custodial interrogation by a probation officer does require the Miranda warnings if the evidence obtained is to be used for trial. However, if the evidence obtained is to be used not for trial but for revocation proceedings, its admissibility is governed by state law. Some states require that the Miranda warnings must be given in custodial interrogation even if the evidence is to be used in revocation proceedings, whereas other states admit the evidence in a revocation proceeding even without the Miranda warnings (Minnesota v. Murphy, 465 U.S. 420 [1984]).

V. OTHER CASES AFFIRMING THE MIRANDA DOCTRINE

Leading post-Miranda decisions may be classified into two general categories: those *affirming Miranda* and those *eroding Miranda*. The four cases discussed below hold that the evidence obtained was not admissible, thus affirming Miranda.

1. Questioning of Defendant without a Lawyer after Indictment—Not Admissible

When the defendant is questioned without a lawyer by police agents after an adversary judicial proceeding (such as an indictment) has been started, the evidence is not admissible. The Court has ruled that incriminating statements made to a government informant sharing a suspect's cell (who was not planted by the FBI, but was told by an FBI agent to listen for any statements the accused made) were not admissible in evidence because they violated the suspect's right to a lawyer (U.S. v. Henry, 447 U.S. 264 [1979]). In the Henry case, the defendant was indicted for armed robbery of a bank. While the defendant was in jail pending trial, government agents contacted an informant who was confined in the same cell block as Henry. An FBI agent instructed the informant to be alert to any statements Henry made but not to initiate conversations with Henry or question him regarding the charges against him. After the informant was released from jail, he reported to the FBI agent that he and Henry had engaged in conversation and that Henry had made incriminating statements about the robbery. The informant was paid for furnishing the information. The Court excluded the evidence, saying that the government had violated the defendant's Sixth Amendment right to a lawyer by intentionally creating a situation likely to induce the accused to make incriminating statements without the presence of a lawyer. The right was violated even if the defendant was not explicitly questioned, as long as the incriminating information was secured in the absence of a lawyer and after the defendant had been indicted.

2. Further Questioning after Suspect Invokes Right to Counsel— Not Admissible

A suspect was charged with robbery, burglary, and murder. At his first interrogation, the suspect asked for a lawyer. Interrogation was stopped. The next day, the suspect still had not seen a lawyer, but talked to two detectives and implicated himself in the crimes. The admittedly voluntary confession was held inadmissible in court because it had not been established that the suspect waived his right to counsel "intelligently and knowingly." The Court said that once a suspect invokes his right to remain silent until he consults a lawyer, the suspect cannot be questioned again for the same offense *unless he himself initiates further communication, exchanges, or conversations with the police.* In this case, the suspect did not initiate further communication. Instead, the police came back the next morning and gave the suspect his Miranda warnings a second time. Since at that time the suspect had learned that he had already been implicated by another suspect in the crime, he gave an incriminating statement. The Court held the evidence obtained to be inadmissible (Edwards v. Arizona, 451 U.S. 477 [1981]).

In a subsequent case, the Court reiterated the Edwards ruling, saying that *invoking the Miranda rights to one offense also invokes the Miranda rights to an unrelated offense* (Arizona v. Roberson, 108 S.Ct. 2093 [1988]). In that case, Roberson, after having been given his Miranda warnings, advised the police that he wanted an attorney. The police stopped questioning him. Three days later, however, while still in custody, another police officer who did not know that Roberson had previously invoked his right to an attorney, again advised Roberson of his Miranda rights and then interrogated him about an unrelated burglary. Roberson incriminated himself. During trial, he sought exclusion of the evidence, relying on the Edwards rule. The Court agreed, saying that this case came under the "bright-line rule" enunciated in Edwards and therefore the evidence could not be admitted. The rule is now clear: once the Miranda rights are invoked by a suspect in one offense, that suspect cannot be interrogated further even for an unrelated offense.

3. After Invocation of Right to Counsel during Questioning— Not Admissible

Once a suspect has clearly invoked his or her right to counsel during questioning, nothing the suspect says in response to further interrogation may be used to cast doubt on that invocation. An invocation of rights may be made very early in the process— even during the interrogator's reading of the suspect's Miranda rights. Therefore, the questioning of an in-custody suspect may have to end even before it starts (Smith v. Illinois, 36 CrL 4126 [1985]). In the Smith case, the defendant was interrogated by the police. They informed him that they wanted to talk about a particular robbery and then began to advise him of his rights. As they read the suspect each right, they asked if he understood. Warnings on the right to silence and the state's right to use what the suspect might say were given. Then the right-to-counsel warning was given as follows: "You have a right to consult a lawyer and to have a lawyer present with you when you're being questioned. Do you understand that?" The suspect responded, saying, "Uh, yeah. I'd like to do that." The officer continued with the rest of the Miranda warnings. When the suspect was asked whether he wanted to talk without a lawyer, he replied, "Yeah and no, uh. I don't know what's that, really." The officer replied, "Well, you either have to talk to me this time without a lawyer being present and if you do agree to talk with me without a lawyer being present you can stop at any time you want to." The suspect agreed to talk and made some incriminating statements before cutting off the questioning with a request for counsel. The Court held that the evidence obtained could not be admitted in court because the suspect had invoked the right to counsel.

4. Right to Counsel Invoked at Arraignment—Cannot Be Interrogated Further

The Court has said that if the police initiate an interrogation after a defendant's assertion of his or her right to counsel at an arraignment or similar proceeding, any waiver of that right for that police-initiated interrogation is invalid (Michigan v. Jackson, 54 L.W. 4329 [1986]). This means that once the defendant has asked for a lawyer during arraignment, the Sixth Amendment right to counsel prohibits the police from initiating interrogation of the accused until counsel has been made available. In the Jackson case, the defendants each requested appointment of counsel at separate arraignments. But before the defendants had had an opportunity to consult with counsel, police officers, after advising the defendants of their Miranda rights, questioned them and obtained confessions. Both defendants were convicted despite their objections to the admission of their confessions. The Court held that the confessions obtained were not admissible because of a violation of the right to counsel.

This does not mean that the confession is worthless, however, because in a subsequent case, the Court held that statements obtained in violation of the rule in Michigan v. Jackson may be used to impeach a defendant's false or inconsistent testimony should the defendant decide to take the witness stand in the case (Michigan v. Harvey, 46 CrL 2158 [1990]).

The Michigan v. Jackson case involved a defendant who during arraignment asserted his right to counsel. In a subsequent case, the Court said that a criminal defendant who has been indicted but has not asked for a lawyer may be questioned by police and prosecutors (Patterson v. Illinois, 108 S.Ct. 2389 [1988]). Note, however, that the Patterson case, although involving an interrogation, was decided by the Court under the constitutional right to counsel rather than under self-incrimination and therefore is not really a Miranda case.

HIGHLIGHT 11.4

No Further Interrogation after Suspect Asks for Lawyer

"An accused . . . having expressed his desire to deal with the police only through counsel, is not subject to further interrogation by the authorities until counsel has been made available to him, unless the accused himself initiates further communication, exchanges or conversations with the police. . . . It is inconsistent with Miranda and its progeny for the authorities, at their instance, to reinterrogate an accused in custody if he has clearly asserted his right to counsel" (Edwards v. Arizona, 451 U.S. 477 [1981]).

VI. OTHER CASES ERODING THE MIRANDA DOCTRINE

In the cases discussed below, the Court held that the evidence obtained was admissible despite the absence of the Miranda warnings, hence eroding the Miranda doctrine.

1. Evidence May Be Used to Impeach Defendant's Credibility

Trustworthy statements taken in violation of Miranda may be used to impeach the credibility of a defendant who takes the witness stand. The jury is to be instructed that the confession may not be considered as evidence of guilt but may only be considered to determine whether the defendant is telling the truth or not (Harris v. New York, 401 U.S. 222 [1971]).

Note, however, that the admission or confession cannot be used in court for any purpose whatsoever if it was obtained involuntarily. For example, D gives a confession to the police even though she was not given the full Miranda warnings (she may have been warned that she has a right to remain silent but not of her right to a lawyer). The evidence is not admissible in court to prove the guilt of the defendant. Suppose, however, that D takes the witness stand during the trial and testifies that she knew nothing at all about the crime. The confession may be used by the prosecutor to challenge D's credibility as a witness. In this case, the confession is voluntary. On the other hand, if the confession is involuntary (obtained, for example, through threats by the police), the confession cannot be used for any purpose, not even for impeachment.

2. Evidence May Be Used to Obtain Collateral Derivative Evidence

Trustworthy statements obtained in violation of Miranda may be used to obtain collateral derivative evidence (evidence of a secondary nature that is related to the cases but not directly a part of it) (Michigan v. Tucker, 417 U.S. 433 [1974]). In this case, the police interrogated a suspect without the Miranda warnings (the interrogation had actually taken place before Miranda was decided in 1966, but the trial was conducted after the Miranda decision came out) and in the process obtained from the suspect the name of a person who eventually became a prosecution witness. The Court held that although the defendant's own statements could not be used against him because they were obtained in violation of Miranda, the prosecution witness's testimony had been purged of its original taint and hence was admissible.

3. When Confession Is Obtained after Warnings Given Following Earlier Voluntary But Unwarned Admission—Confession Admissible

When an earlier voluntary but unwarned admission from defendant has been obtained, the evidence is still admissible. The Fifth Amendment guarantee against compulsory self-incrimination does not require suppression of a confession made after proper Miranda warnings were given and a valid waiver of rights, even if the police had earlier obtained a voluntary but unwarned admission from the defendant (Oregon v. Elstad, 53 L.W. 4244 [1985]). In Elstad, officers from the sheriff's office picked up Elstad in his home as a suspect in a burglary. He made an incriminating statement without having been given the Miranda warnings. After he was taken to the station-house and after he had been advised of and waived his Miranda rights, Elstad executed a written confession. In a subsequent prosecution for burglary, the state trial court excluded from evidence Elstad's first statement because he had not been given the Miranda warnings but admitted the written confession, which was obtained after the warnings were given. The issue was whether the confession made after the Miranda warnings were properly given, but made close in time to an incriminating statement given by the suspect before the Miranda warnings were given, was admissible in court as evidence. The Court said that the self-incrimination clause of the Fifth Amendment did not require the suppression of the written confession solely on account of the earlier voluntary but unwarned admission. Here the Court carved out another narrow exception to Miranda in that it excluded the initial statement obtained before the warnings were given, but held that the initial illegality did not extend to the confession obtained after the warnings were given.

4. Undercover Officer Posing as Fellow Inmate Need Not Give Miranda Warnings before Asking Questions

The Court has decided that an undercover law enforcement officer posing as a fellow inmate need not give the Miranda warnings to a suspect in jail before asking questions that may produce an incriminating response (Illinois v. Perkins, 47 CrL 2131 [1990]). In this case, the police placed undercover agent Parisi in a jail cellblock with suspect Perkins, who was detained on charges unrelated to the murder that Parisi was investigating. When Parisi asked him if he had ever killed anybody, Perkins made statements incriminating himself in the murder. He was subsequently charged, tried, and was convicted. On appeal, he sought to exclude the evidence, claiming that he should have been given the Miranda warnings before being asked the incriminating question by the agent. The Court disagreed, saying that "the Miranda doctrine must be enforced strictly, but only in situations where the concerns underlying that decision are present." These concerns were not present here because the essential ingredients of a "police-dominated atmosphere" and "compulsion" were absent. Said the Court: "That coercive atmosphere is not present when an incarcerated person speaks freely to someone whom he believes to be a fellow inmate and whom he assumes is not an officer having official power over him." The Court then added that "in such circumstances, Miranda does not forbid mere strategic deception by taking advantage of a suspect's misplaced trust."

5. Suspect Need Not Be Informed of All Crimes before Interrogation

A suspect's waiver of Miranda rights is valid even if he or she believes the interrogation will merely focus on minor crimes but is shifted by the police to cover a different and more serious crime (Colorado v. Spring, 479 U.S. 564 [1987]). In that case, Spring and a companion shot a man during a hunting trip in Denver. An informant told federal agents that Spring was engaged in interstate trafficking in stolen firearms and that he had participated in the murder. Spring was arrested in Kansas City and advised of his Miranda rights. He signed a statement that he understood and waived his rights. He was asked about the firearms transaction (that led to his arrest), but was also asked if he had ever shot a man. Spring answered yes, but denied the shooting in question. He confessed to the murder later, however, after having been given the Miranda warnings. Tried and convicted, he appealed, saying that he needed to be informed of all crimes of which he was to be questioned before there could be a valid waiver of his Miranda rights. The Court rejected his challenge, saying that the Constitution does not require that a suspect know and understand every possible consequence of a waiver of a Fifth Amendment privilege. There was no allegation here that Spring failed to understand that privilege or that he did not understand the consequence of speaking freely.

6. Statement Need Not Be Written—Oral Statement Admissible

An oral confession is admissible even if the suspect tells the police he would talk with them but would not make a *written statement* without a lawyer present (Connecticut v. Barrett, 479 U.S. 523 [1987]). In that case, Barrett was arrested in connection with a sexual assault. On arrival at the police station, he was advised of his Miranda rights and signed a statement saying he understood his rights. Barrett then stated that he would not give a written statement in the absence of counsel, but would talk to the police about the incident. In two subsequent interrogations, Barrett was again advised of his rights and signed a statement of understanding. On both occasions he gave an oral statement admitting his involvement in the sexual assault but refused to make or sign a written statement. Charged with and convicted of sexual assault, he appealed, alleging that his oral statements should not be admissible in court. The Court rejected his challenge, saying that refusal by a suspect to put his statement in writing does not make an admission or confession inadmissible, as long as the police can establish that the Miranda warnings were given and the waiver was intelligent and voluntary.

7. Failure of Police to Inform Suspect of Attorney Retained for Him—Confession Admissible

The failure of police officers to inform a suspect that the attorney retained for him by his sister was attempting to reach him did not make evidence inadmissible. The Court has held that a suspect's waiver of the Fifth Amendment right to remain silent and to have counsel present during custodial interrogation is not nullified either by the failure of police officers to inform the suspect that the attorney retained on his or her behalf by a third party is attempting to reach the suspect or by misleading information given to the attorney by the police regarding their intention to interrogate the suspect at that time (Moran v. Burbine, 54 L.W. 4265 [1986]).

VII. A SUMMARY OF SIGNIFICANT POST-MIRANDA CASES

A summary of cases *affirming* the Miranda doctrine is shown in Table 11.1 and a summary of cases *eroding* the Miranda doctrine is shown in Table 11.2.

VIII. UNRESOLVED QUESTIONS ON THE MIRANDA RULE

A number of questions related to Miranda have not as yet been addressed by the Supreme Court. These are the more significant ones.

1. Follow-up Questions

If a confession is volunteered, must the police give the suspect the Miranda warnings before asking follow-up questions? For example, X goes to the police station and

TABLE 11.1   Cases Affirming Miranda

	Factual situation	Evidence admissible?
1. U.S. v. Henry (1979)	Questioning of defendant without a lawyer after indictment	No
2. Edwards v. Arizona (1981)	No valid waiver of right to counsel	No
3. Smith v. Illinois (1985)	After invocation of right to counsel during questioning	No
4. Michigan v. Jackson (1986)	Right to counsel invoked at arraignment	No
5. Arizona v. Roberson (1988)	Invoking Miranda for one offense, admissible for second offense?	No

TABLE 11.2   Cases Eroding Miranda

	Factual situation	Evidence admissible?
1. Harris v. New York (1971)	Impeachment of credibility	Yes
2. Michigan v. Tucker (1974)	Collateral derivative evidence	Yes
3. Michigan v. Mosley (1975)	Questioning on an unrelated offense	Yes
4. New York v. Quarles (1984)	Threat to public safety	Yes
5. Berkemer v. McCarty (1984)	Roadside questioning of a motorist pursuant to routine traffic stop	Yes
6. Oregon v. Elstad (1985)	Confession obtained after warnings given following earlier voluntary but unwarned admission	Yes
7. Moran v. Burbine (1986)	Failure of police to inform suspect of attorney retained for him	Yes
8. Colorado v. Connelly (1986)	Confession following advice of God	Yes
9. Connecticut v. Barrett (1987)	Oral confession	Yes
10. Colorado v. Spring (1987)	Shift to another crime	Yes
11. Arizona v. Mauro (1987)	Officer recorded conversation with defendant's wife	Yes
12. Pennsylvania v. Bruder (1988)	Curbside stop for traffic violation	Yes
13. Duckworth v. Eagan (1989)	Variation in warning	Yes
14. Michigan v. Harvey (1990)	Impeach testimony	Yes
15. Illinois v. Perkins (1990)	Officer posing as inmate	Yes
16. Pennsylvania v. Muniz (1990)	Routine questions and videotaping DWI	Yes

says, "I just killed my wife." Obviously, the police would want further details. The Court has not decided whether the Miranda warnings must be given before asking follow-up questions. Some lower courts have held that the warnings are not necessary if the suspect is only asked "clarifying" questions. What "clarifying questions" means is unclear!

2. Delayed Questioning

Must the Miranda warnings be repeated after a significant delay in the questioning? The Supreme Court has not decided this issue, but the better practice is for the police to repeat the warnings. For example, Z is given the Miranda warnings; she waives her rights and answers questions. It is getting late in the evening and so the police stop questioning Z. If questioning is resumed the following day, it is best for the police to give her the Miranda warnings again if they want to make sure that the statements given the second day are admissible.

3. Juvenile Suspects

Must the Miranda warnings be given if the suspect is a juvenile? This has not been addressed by the Supreme Court, but practically all state courts require that the warnings be given. If the warnings must be given to adults, there is no justification not to give them to juveniles, who need even greater protection against coercive questioning. It must be noted that most states have specific rules, which are more restrictive than those for adults, governing the interrogation of juveniles. For example, many states require that a waiver of rights by a juvenile cannot be valid unless the juvenile's parent, guardian, or lawyer is present. State law, if it is more restrictive, must be followed.

IX. IS MIRANDA HERE TO STAY?—YES

Miranda has survived the test of time and, although some decisions have weakened it, a complete overruling of Miranda even by a conservative Court is remote and unlikely. When first announced, the Miranda rule was seen by some critics as the precursor of doom for law enforcement. Predictions were that it would shackle the police and make it difficult for prosecutors to convict. In his dissent in Miranda, Justice Byron White warned:

> The rule announced today will measurably weaken the ability of the criminal law to perform these [law enforcement] tasks. It is a deliberate calculus to prevent interrogations, to reduce the incidence of confessions and pleas of guilty and to increase the number of trials.

This dire prediction has not materialized. In the words of one chief prosecutor of a major city: ". . . I don't think it is the terrible thing we thought it was. We still get as many confessions as we ever did, and we still get as much evidence."[3] However, Miranda and the exclusionary rule "are widely credited with improving professionalism among policemen—and as a result the reforms enjoy growing support among even the most hard-bitten cops."[4] Studies show that the warnings rarely stop people from confessing and that less than 1 percent of cases are thrown out because of illegal confessions.[5]

Nonetheless, the clamor for a reversal of Miranda has not completely faded away. In the words of one former attorney general: "The interesting question is not whether Miranda should go, but how we should facilitate its demise, and what we should replace it with. We regard a challenge to Miranda as essential."[6]

Such concern, however, is more the exception rather than the rule. There is realization that Miranda has hastened reforms rather than impeded law enforcement. There is also the feeling that it has made the police more aware of their responsibilities as agents of the state in a "free society." In the words of a former police director: "Officers want respect. We have gotten away from force and coercion. Nor do we want to be accused of that."[7] More than two decades after the decision, it can be said that on the balance Miranda has done more good than harm to U.S. society and that it has led to better law enforcement. There will always be those who would wish its demise and soon. In the end, the debate over Miranda is more philosophical than legal, hence the disagreement will linger. But despite erosion, we now know that Miranda will continue to be a part of law enforcement for years and years to come. It is here to stay.

☐ SUMMARY

The Fifth Amendment to the U.S. Constitution provides that no person may be compelled to be a witness against him- or herself. This means that involuntary admissions or confessions cannot be admitted as evidence in a criminal prosecution. Originally, "involuntariness" referred only to the use of physical force or coercion. This interpretation was later extended to include mental coercion. Voluntariness, however, was difficult for the courts to determine, hence decisions were made on a case-by-case basis and became subjective.

The Miranda decision now governs the admissibility of confessions and incriminating statements. Miranda requires that the warnings be given in cases of custodial interrogation; that is, when a suspect is questioned while under arrest or deprived of freedom in a significant way. Failure to give the warnings means that the evidence will not be admitted in court even if voluntary. In addition to voluntariness and the giving of the Miranda warnings, courts require that there be an intelligent and voluntary waiver if a suspect's statement is to be admissible.

The Miranda rule has many exceptions. In these cases, the Miranda warnings need not be given. These exceptions fall under two headings: when the questioning is not custodial and where there is in fact no interrogation. The most important of these exceptions are: the roadside questioning of a motorist detained pursuant to a routine traffic stop, when asking routine questions of drunk-driving suspects, and when there is a threat to public safety.

Miranda continues to be refined by the Court in subsequent decisions. These cases can generally be classified into those affirming Miranda and those eroding it. The controversy over Miranda has subsided and chances are that although the controversy will linger, the Miranda rule is here to stay.

☐ REVIEW QUESTIONS

1. Distinguish between a confession and an admission. As a police officer, which would you rather have and why?
2. What was the old standard for the admissibility of confessions and admissions? Discuss what that standard meant and why it was difficult to determine.
3. What is the new standard for admissibility as laid out in Miranda v. Arizona?
4. State four principles a police officer ought to know about the waiver of Miranda rights.
5. In general, when must the Miranda warnings be given? Explain.
6. Describe at least six instances when the Miranda warnings need not be given.
7. Distinguish between "volunteered" and "voluntary" statements.

8. What is the "functional equivalent" concept in interrogation? Give an example.
9. Give four Court decisions that have affirmed the Miranda doctrine.
10. Give four Court decisions that have eroded the Miranda doctrine.
11. "If the Miranda warnings are not given by the officer, the confession or admission obtained might as well be thrown away because it is useless." Is that statement true or false? Explain.
12. Give two unresolved questions on the Miranda rule.

☐ DEFINITIONS

Admission: A person owns up to something related to the act but may not have committed it.

Confession: A person says that he or she committed the act.

Custodial Interrogation: Interrogation that takes place (1) when the suspect is under arrest or (2) when the suspect is not under arrest but is "deprived of his freedom in a significant way."

"Deprived of Freedom in a Significant Way":   Describes a person whose freedom of movement has been limited by the police.

"Functional Equivalent" of Interrogation: Instances when no questions are actually asked by the police, but the circumstances are so conducive to making a statement or confession that the courts consider them to be the equivalent of interrogation.

General On-the-Scene Questioning: Questioning at the scene of the crime for the purpose of gathering information that might enable the police to identify the criminal. Miranda warnings not needed.

Intelligent Waiver: A waiver by a suspect who knows what he or she is doing and is sufficiently competent to waive his or her rights.

Interrogation: The asking of questions by the police. For purposes of the Miranda rule, however, "interrogation" refers not only to express questioning but also to words or actions on the part of the police (other than those attendant to arrest and custody) that the police should have known are reasonably likely to elicit an incriminating response from the suspect.

Miranda Rule: Evidence obtained by the police during custodial interrogation of a suspect cannot be used in court during the trial, unless the suspect was first informed of the right not to incriminate oneself and of the right to counsel.

"Public Safety" Exception: Responses to questions asked by police officers, which questions are reasonably prompted by concern for public safety, are admissible in court even though the suspect was in police custody and not given the Miranda warnings.

Voluntary Statement: A statement given without threat, force, or coercion and of the suspect's own free will.

Voluntary Waiver: A waiver that is not the result of any threat, force, or coercion and is of the suspect's own free will.

Volunteered Statement: A statement made by a suspect without interrogation. Miranda warnings not needed.

Waiver: The intentional relinquishment of a known right or remedy. The waiver of Miranda rights must be intelligent and voluntary.

☐ PRINCIPLES OF CASES

ARIZONA V. MAURO, 481 U.S. 520 (1987)   A conversation between a suspect and his or her spouse that is recorded by and in the presence of an officer does not constitute the functional equivalent of an interrogation under Miranda and therefore the evidence obtained is admissible.

ARIZONA V. ROBERSON, 108 S.Ct. 2093 (1988)   Invoking the Miranda rights to one offense also invokes the Miranda rights to an unrelated offense.

ASHCRAFT V. TENNESSEE, 322 U.S. 143 (1944)   The protracted questioning of a defendant, during which he was questioned in relays and continuously for two days, was so coercive as to make the confession involuntary and therefore inadmissible in a state criminal proceeding.

BECKWITH V. UNITED STATES, 425 U.S. 341 (1976)   Statements obtained by Internal Revenue Service agents during a noncustodial, noncoercive interview with a taxpayer under criminal tax investigation, conducted in a private home where the taxpayer occasionally stayed, did not need the Miranda warnings as long as the taxpayer had been told he was free to leave at any time.

BERKEMER V. McCARTY, 35 CrL 3192 (1984)   The Court decided:

1. A person subjected to custodial interrogation must be given the Miranda warnings regardless of the nature or severity of the offense of which the person is suspected or for which he or she was arrested; but
2. The roadside questioning of a motorist detained pursuant to a routine traffic stop does not constitute "custodial interrogation," so there is no need to give the Miranda warnings.

BREWER V. WILLIAMS, 430 U.S. 387 (1977)   Interrogation takes place when the police officers, knowing of the defendant's religious interest, make remarks designed to appeal to that interest and thus induce a confession. Moreover, the courts look carefully at confessions obtained from defendants who have retained lawyers when police do not allow the lawyer to assist in interrogation. When the police have promised the attorney that no questioning will take place, any confession obtained after questioning, without clear waiver of the right to counsel, is inadmissible.

BROWN V. MISSISSIPPI, 297 U.S. 278 (1936)   Confession obtained as a result of utter coercion and brutality by law enforcement officers was held violative of the "due process" clause of the Fourteenth Amendment and therefore inadmissible in a state criminal proceeding.

CALIFORNIA V. BAKELER, 33 CrL 4108 (1983)   The ultimate determinant of whether or not a person is "in custody" for Miranda purposes is whether the suspect has been subjected to a formal arrest or to equivalent restraints on freedom of movement.

CHAMBERS V. FLORIDA, 309 U.S. 227 (1940) Evidence obtained as a result of pressure brought about through protracted questioning while defendants were held in jail without contact with the outside world was violative of the defendants' right to due process of law under the Fourteenth Amendment and therefore inadmissible in a state criminal trial.

COLORADO V. CONNELLY, 479 U.S. 157 (1986) The admissibility of statements made when the mental state of the suspect interfered with his "rational intellect" and "free will" is governed by state rules of evidence rather than by Supreme Court decisions on coerced confessions. Confessions and admissions are involuntary and invalid under the Constitution only if the coercion is exerted by the police, not if the suspect was "following the advice of God."

COLORADO V. SPRING, 479 U.S. 564 (1987) A suspect's waiver of Miranda rights is valid even if the suspect believes the interrogation will merely focus on minor crimes but is shifted by the police to cover a different and more serious crime.

CONNECTICUT V. BARRETT, 479 U.S. 523 (1987) An oral confession is admissible even if the suspect tells the police he or she would talk with them but would not make a written statement without a lawyer present.

DUCKWORTH V. EAGAN, 109 S.Ct. 2875 (1989) The Miranda warnings need not be given exactly as worded in the Miranda case. What is required is that the wording reasonably convey to a suspect his or her rights. Informing a suspect that an attorney will be appointed "if and when you go to court" does not render the Miranda warnings inadequate. Miranda does not require that lawyers be producible on call. It is enough that the suspect be informed of his or her right to an attorney and to appointed counsel, and that if the police cannot provide appointed counsel, the police will not question the suspect until and unless there is valid waiver.

EDWARDS V. ARIZONA, 451 U.S. 477 (1981) Once the suspect has invoked the right to remain silent until he or she has consulted a lawyer, the suspect cannot be questioned again for the same offense unless the suspect himself or herself initiates further communication, exchanges, or conversations with the police.

ESCOBEDO V. ILLINOIS, 378 U.S. 748 (1964) A confession obtained from a defendant was inadmissible under these circumstances, even though adversarial judicial proceeding had not yet been started: the investigation had focused on the suspect, he had been taken into custody, he had requested and been denied an opportunity to consult with his lawyer, and the lawyer was present and available to consult with him.

FARE V. MICHAEL C., 442 U.S. 707 (1979) The request of a juvenile on probation to see his probation officer instead of a lawyer (after having been given the Miranda warnings by the police and asked if he wanted to see a lawyer) was considered to be a waiver of the juvenile's right to a lawyer because a probation officer and a lawyer perform two different functions.

HARRIS V. NEW YORK, 401 U.S. 222 (1971) Trustworthy statements taken in violation of Miranda may be used to impeach the credibility of a defendant who takes the witness stand, as long as the statements are voluntary.

ILLINOIS V. PERKINS, 47 CrL 2131 (1990) An undercover law enforcement officer posing as a fellow inmate need not give the Miranda warnings to a suspect in jail before asking questions that may produce an incriminating response.

MALLOY V. HOGAN, 378 U.S. 1 (1964) The Fifth Amendment guarantee against compulsory self-incrimination in the Bill of Rights was incorporated under the Fourteenth Amendment of the Constitution and held applicable to state criminal proceedings.

MICHIGAN V. HARVEY, 46 CrL 2158 (1990) Statements obtained in violation of the rule in Michigan v. Jackson (stating that when the right to counsel is invoked at arraignment, the suspect cannot be interrogated further) may be used to impeach a defendant's false or inconsistent testimony should the defendant decide to take the witness stand in the case.

MICHIGAN V. JACKSON, 54 L.W. 4329 (1986) If the police initiate an interrogation after the defendant's assertion of his or her right to counsel at an arraignment or similar proceeding, any waiver of that right for that police-initiated interrogation is invalid.

MICHIGAN V. TUCKER, 417 U.S. 433 (1974) Trustworthy statements obtained in violation of Miranda may be used to obtain collateral derivative evidence.

MINNESOTA V. MURPHY, 465 U.S. 420 (1984) The Miranda warnings need not be given in cases of noncustodial interrogation of a probationer by a probation officer.

MIRANDA V. ARIZONA, 384 U.S. 436 (1966) Evidence obtained by the police during custodial interrogation of a suspect cannot be used in court during the trial unless the suspect is first informed of the right not to incriminate oneself and of the right to counsel. The following warnings (wording may vary) must be given prior to interrogation:

1. You have a right to remain silent.
2. Anything you say can be used against you in a court of law.
3. You have a right to the presence of an attorney.
4. If you cannot afford an attorney, one will be appointed for you prior to questioning.

MORAN V. BURBINE, 54 L.W. 4265 (1986) A suspect's waiver of the Fifth Amendment right to remain silent and to have counsel present during custodial interrogation is not nullified either by the failure of police officers to inform the suspect that the attorney retained on his or her behalf by a third party is attempting to reach the suspect or by misleading information given to the attorney by the police regarding their intention to interrogate the suspect at that time.

NEW YORK V. QUARLES, 104 S.Ct. 2626 (1984) When questions asked by police officers are reasonably prompted by concern for public safety, the responses are admissible in court even though the suspect was in police custody and was not given the Miranda warnings.

NORTH CAROLINA V. BUTLER, 441 U.S. 369 (1979) The failure to make an explicit statement regarding the waiver does not determine whether the evidence is admissible or not. Instead, the trial court must look at all the circumstances to determine if a valid waiver has in fact been made. Therefore, an express waiver, although easier to establish in court, is not required.

OREGON V. ELSTAD, 53 L.W. 4244 (1985)   If a confession is made after proper Miranda warnings and a waiver of rights, the self-incrimination clause of the Fifth Amendment does not require its suppression solely because the police have obtained an earlier voluntary but unwarned admission from the suspect.

OREGON V. MATHIASON, 429 U.S. 492 (1977)   The Miranda warnings are necessary only if the suspect is interrogated while in custody or otherwise deprived of freedom in a significant way. In this case, the suspect came to the police station in response to an officer's message that the officer would "like to discuss something with you." It was made clear to the suspect that he was not under arrest. The confession made without the Miranda warnings was admissible.

OROZCO V. TEXAS, 394 U.S. 324 (1969)   The questioning of a suspect in his bedroom by four police officers at four o'clock in the morning needed the Miranda warnings.

PENNSYLVANIA V. BRUDER, 109 S.Ct. 205 (1988)   The curbside stop of a motorist for a traffic violation, although representing a Fourth Amendment seizure of the person, is not sufficiently custodial as to require the Miranda warnings.

PENNSYLVANIA V. MUNIZ, 58 L.W. 4817 (1990)   The police may ask people suspected of driving while intoxicated (DWI) routine questions and may videotape their responses without giving the Miranda warnings.

RHODE ISLAND V. INNIS, 446 U.S. 291 (1980)   Conversation between police officers while in a police car about the danger that one of the handicapped children from the school near the scene of the crime might find the loaded shotgun did not constitute interrogation even though it was within hearing of the suspect. Therefore the information given by the suspect, who interrupted the conversation, was not given in response to an interrogation and hence was admissible in court. However, a practice that the police should know is likely to evoke an incriminating response from the suspect amounts to interrogation. Such was not the case here.

ROGERS V. RICHMOND, 365 U.S. 534 (1961)   A confession obtained as a result of interrogation that continued for more than a day, accompanied by a threat that the suspect's wife was going to be taken into custody if he did not confess, was involuntary and therefore not admissible in court.

SMITH V. ILLINOIS, 36 CrL 4126 (1985)   Once a suspect has clearly invoked his or her right to counsel during questioning, nothing the suspect says in response to further interrogation may be used to cast doubt on that invocation. Moreover, an invocation of rights may be made very early in the process—even during the interrogator's recitation of the suspect's rights. Therefore, the questioning of an in-custody suspect may have to end even before it starts.

SPANO V. NEW YORK, 360 U.S. 315 (1959)   The use of deception as a means of psychological pressure to induce a confession was held violative of a defendant's constitutional rights and therefore the evidence obtained is not admissible in court. The trial court's mistaken admission of a confession leads to an automatic reversal of the conviction.

TAGUE V. LOUISIANA, 444 U.S. 469 (1980)   The trial court cannot presume waiver from the failure of the accused to complain after the giving of warning or from the fact that the accused spoke with the police after the warnings were given.

UNITED STATES V. HENRY, 447 U.S. 264 (1979)   The government violates a defendant's Sixth Amendment right to counsel by intentionally creating a situation likely to induce the accused to make incriminating statements without the presence of a lawyer. The right is violated even if the defendant is not explicitly questioned, as long as the incriminating information is secured in the absence of a lawyer and after the defendant has been indicted.

UNITED STATES V. MANDUJANO, 425 U.S. 564 (1976)   Grand jury investigations do not need the Miranda warnings because the answers given are not statements in response to custodial interrogation.

☐ CASE BRIEF—LEADING CASE ON TYPES OF OFFENSES THAT NEED MIRANDA WARNINGS

BERKEMER V. MCCARTY, 35 CrL 3192 (1984)

FACTS: After observing McCarty's car weaving in and out of a highway lane, Officer Williams of the Ohio State Highway Patrol forced McCarty to stop and get out of the car. Upon noticing that McCarty was having difficulty standing, the officer concluded that McCarty would be charged with a traffic offense and would not be allowed to leave the scene, but McCarty was not told that he would be taken into custody. When McCarty could not perform a field sobriety test without falling, Officer Williams asked if he had been using intoxicants, whereupon McCarty replied that he had consumed two beers and had smoked marijuana a short time before. The officer then formally arrested McCarty and drove him to a county jail, where a blood test failed to detect any alcohol in his blood. Questioning was resumed, and McCarty again made incriminating statements, including an admission that he was "barely" under the influence of alcohol. At no point during this sequence was McCarty given the Miranda warnings. He was subsequently charged with operating a motor vehicle under the influence of alcohol and drugs, a misdemeanor under Ohio law. He pleaded "no contest," but later filed a writ of habeas corpus, alleging that the evidence obtained should not have been admitted in court.

ISSUE: *Was the evidence obtained by the police without giving the suspect the Miranda warnings admissible in a prosecution for a misdemeanor offense? No.*

SUPREME COURT DECISION: The Court decided:

1. A person subjected to custodial interrogation must be given the Miranda warnings regardless of the nature or severity of the offense of which the person is suspected or for which he or she was arrested; but
2. The roadside questioning of a motorist detained pursuant to a routine traffic stop does not constitute "custodial interrogation," so there is no need to give the Miranda warnings.

CASE SIGNIFICANCE: This case settles two legal issues that had long divided lower courts. It is clear now that once a suspect has been placed under arrest for any offense, be it for a felony or a misdemeanor, the Miranda warnings must be given before interrogation. It is a rule that is easier for the police to follow than the requirement of determining if the arrest was for a felony or a misdemeanor before giving the warning. The Court said that the purpose of the Miranda warnings, which is to ensure that the police do not coerce or trick captive suspects into confessing, is applicable equally to misdemeanor or felony cases. The second part of the decision is equally important in that it identifies a particular instance when the warnings need not be given. There is no custodial interrogation in a traffic stop because it is usually brief and the motorist expects that, although he or she may be issued a citation, in the end the motorist will most likely be allowed to continue on his or her way. However, if a motorist who has been detained is thereafter subjected to treatment that renders him "in custody" for practical purposes, then he or she is entitled at that stage to be given the Miranda warnings.

EXCERPTS FROM THE DECISION: It must be acknowledged at the outset that a traffic stop significantly curtails the "freedom of action" of the driver and the passengers, if any, of the detained vehicle. Under the law of most States, it is a crime either to ignore a policeman's signal to stop one's car or, once having stopped, to drive away without permission. E.G., Ohio Rev. Code Ann. Paragraph 4511.02 (1982). Certainly few motorists would feel free either to disobey a directive to pull over or to leave the scene of a traffic stop without being told they might do so. Partly for these reasons, we have long acknowledged that "stopping an automobile and detaining its occupants constitute a 'seizure' within the meaning of [the Fourth] Amendmen[t], even though the purpose of the stop is limited and the resulting detention quite brief." Delaware v. Prouse, 440 U.S. 648, 653 (1979) (citations omitted).

        However, we decline to accord talismanic power to the phrase in the Miranda opinion emphasized by respondent. Fidelity to the doctrine announced in Miranda requires that it be enforced strictly, but only in those types of situations in which the concerns that powered the decision are implicated. Thus, we must decide whether a traffic stop exerts upon a detained person pressures that sufficiently impair his free exercise of his privilege against self-incrimination to require that he be warned of his constitutional rights.

        Two features of an ordinary traffic stop mitigate the danger that a person questioned will be induced "to speak where he would not otherwise do so freely," Miranda v. Arizona, 384 U.S., at 467. First, detention of a motorist pursuant to a traffic stop is presumptively temporary and brief. The vast majority of roadside detentions last only a few minutes. A motorist's expectations, when he sees a policeman's light flashing behind him, are that he will be obliged to spend a short period of time answering questions and waiting while the officer checks his license and registration, that he may then be given a citation, but that in the end he most likely will be allowed to continue on his way. In this respect, questioning incident to an ordinary traffic stop is quite different from stationhouse interrogation, which frequently is prolonged, and in which the detainee often is aware that questioning will continue until he provides his interrogators the answers they seek. . . .

        Second, circumstances associated with the typical traffic stop are not such that the motorist feels completely at the mercy of the police. To be sure, the aura of authority surrounding an armed, uniformed officer and the knowledge that the officer has some discretion in deciding whether to issue a citation, in combination, exert some pressure on the detainee to respond to questions. But other aspects of the situation substantially offset these forces. Perhaps most importantly, the typical traffic stop is public, at least to some degree. Passersby, on foot or in other cars, witness the interaction of officer and motorist. This exposure to public view both reduces the ability of an unscrupulous policeman to use illegitimate means to elicit self-incriminating statements and diminishes the motorist's fear that, if he does not cooperate, he will be subjected to abuse. The fact that the detained motorist typically is confronted by only one or at most two policemen further mutes his sense of vulnerability. In short, the atmosphere surrounding an ordinary traffic stop is substantially less "police dominated" than that surrounding the kinds of interrogation at issue in Miranda itself, see 384 U.S., at 445, 491–498, and in the subsequent cases in which we have applied Miranda.

☐ CASE BRIEF—LEADING CASE ON THE "PUBLIC SAFETY" EXCEPTION TO THE MIRANDA RULE

NEW YORK V. QUARLES, 104 S.Ct. 2626 (1984)

FACTS: Quarles was charged in a New York state court with criminal possession of a weapon. A woman had approached two police officers who were on road patrol, told them that she had just been raped, described her assailant, and said that the man had just entered a nearby supermarket and was carrying a gun. While one of the officers radioed for assistance, Officer Kraft entered the store and spotted Quarles, who matched the description given by the woman. Quarles ran toward the rear of the store, but was finally subdued. The officer noticed that Quarles was wearing an empty shoulder holster. After handcuffing the suspect, the police asked where the gun was. Quarles nodded toward some empty cartons and responded that "the gun is over there." Officer Kraft then retrieved the gun from one of the cartons, formally arrested Quarles, and read him the Miranda warnings. The suspect indicated that he would answer questions without an attorney present and admitted that he owned the gun. The trial court excluded Quarles's initial statement and the gun because he had not yet been given the Miranda warnings and also excluded Quarles's other statements as evidence tainted by the Miranda violation. The case eventually reached the Supreme Court.

ISSUE: *Were suspect's initial statement and the gun admissible in evidence despite the failure of the officer to give him the Miranda warnings prior to asking him questions that led to the discovery of the gun? Yes.*

SUPREME COURT DECISION: Responses to questions asked by police officers, which questions are reasonably prompted by concern for public safety, are admissible in court even though the suspect was in police custody and was not given the Miranda warnings.

CASE SIGNIFICANCE: New York v. Quarles carves out a "public safety" exception to the Miranda rule. The Court said that the case presents a situation in which concern for public safety must be paramount to adherence to the literal language of the prophylactic rules enunciated in Miranda. Here, although Quarles was in police custody and therefore ought to have been given the Miranda warnings, concern for public safety prevails. Miranda therefore does not apply in all its rigor to a situation in which police officers ask questions reasonably prompted by a concern for public safety. In this case, said the Court, the gun was concealed somewhere in the supermarket and therefore posed more than one danger to the public. The Court hinted, however, that the "public safety" exception needs to be interpreted narrowly and added that police officers can and will distinguish almost instinctively between questions necessary to secure their own safety or the safety of the public and questions designed solely to elicit testimony evidence from a suspect. Whether or not the police will be able to do this remains to be seen.

EXCERPTS FROM THE DECISION: In this case we have before us no claim that respondent's statements were actually compelled by police conduct which overcame his will to resist. . . . Thus the only issue before us is whether Officer Kraft was justified in failing to make available to respondent the procedural safeguards associated with the privilege against compulsory self-incrimination since Miranda.

We hold that on these facts there is a "public safety" exception to the requirement that Miranda warnings be given before a suspect's answers may be admitted into evidence, and that the availability of that exception does not depend upon the motivation of the individual officers involved. In a kaleidoscopic situation such as the one confronting these officers, where spontaneity rather than adherence to a police manual is necessarily the order of the day, the application of the exception which we recognize today should not be made to depend on post hoc findings at a suppression hearing concerning the subjective motivation of the arresting officer. Undoubtedly most police officers, if placed in Officer Kraft's position, would act out of a host of different, instinctive, and largely unverifiable motives—their own safety, the safety of others, and perhaps as well the desire to obtain incriminating evidence from the suspect.

Whatever the motivation of individual officers in such a situation, we do not believe that the doctrinal underpinnings of Miranda require that it be applied in all its rigor to a situation in which police officers ask questions reasonably prompted by a concern for the public safety. The Miranda decision was based in large part on this Court's view that the warnings which it required police to give to suspects in custody would reduce the likelihood that the suspects would fall victim to constitutionally impermissible practices of police interrogation in the presumptively coercive environment of the station house.

□ NOTES

1. G. M. Caplan, *Modern Procedures for Police Interrogation* (Washington, DC: Police Executive Research Forum, no date), at 2.
2. Ibid.
3. *Houston Chronicle,* January 23, 1987, at 23.
4. *Newsweek Magazine,* July 18, 1988, at 53.
5. Ibid.
6. Ibid.
7. Ibid.

PART FIVE

CONSTITUTIONAL RIGHTS AND RULES DURING TRIAL

CHAPTER TWELVE

CONSTITUTIONAL RIGHTS AND DEFENSES DURING TRIAL

CHAPTER THIRTEEN

WITNESSES, THE HEARSAY RULE, AND PRIVILEGED COMMUNICATIONS

CONSTITUTIONAL RIGHTS AND DEFENSES DURING TRIAL

I. RIGHT TO A SPEEDY AND PUBLIC TRIAL
- A. Speedy Trial
- B. Public Trial

II. RIGHT TO TRIAL BY JURY
- A. Size of Jury May Vary
- B. Unanimous Verdict Not Required by the Constitution
- C. Serious versus Petty Offenses
- D. Right May Be Waived
- E. Selection of Jurors

III. RIGHT TO A FAIR AND IMPARTIAL TRIAL
- A. Prejudicial Publicity Is Prohibited
- B. Controlling Prejudicial Publicity

IV. RIGHT TO CONFRONTATION OF WITNESSES

V. RIGHT TO COMPULSORY PROCESS TO OBTAIN WITNESSES

VI. PRIVILEGE AGAINST SELF-INCRIMINATION
- A. Scope of the Provision
- B. Two Separate Privileges during Trial
- C. Grant of Immunity
- D. Transactional versus Use-and-Derivative-Use Immunity
- E. When the Privilege Is Waived

VII. RIGHT TO COUNSEL
- A. Underlying Theory
- B. How Counsel Is Obtained
- C. Pretrial Proceedings to Which the Right to Counsel Applies
- D. Pretrial Proceedings to Which the Right to Counsel Does Not Apply
- E. Right to Counsel during Trial
- F. Right to "Effective Assistance of Counsel"
- G. Right to Act as One's Own Lawyer

☐ KEY TERMS

speedy trial
public trial
change of venue
sequestration
testimonial self-incrimination
physical self-incrimination
fair response
transactional immunity
use-and-derivative-use immunity
effective assistance of counsel
reasonable doubt
double jeopardy

same offense
conduct that constitutes an offense for
    which defendant has already
    been prosecuted
lesser included offense
M'Naghten test for insanity
irresistible impulse test for insanity
American Law Institute test (or Model
    Penal Code) for insanity
Durham (or product) test for insanity
subjective test for entrapment
objective test for entrapment

The individual rights guaranteed in the Bill of Rights are most carefully protected during the trial stage of a criminal proceeding. This is when the U.S. adversary proceeding is at its peak. The government is represented by the prosecutor and the accused's rights are championed by the defense counsel, either retained by the accused or appointed by the state. The judge, a neutral party, presides over the trial, setting the rules for the lawyers to follow. In bench trials, the judge also determines the facts; in jury trials, that function is performed by the jury.

The Constitution guarantees an accused a number of rights during trial, the most basic of which are discussed in this chapter; namely, the rights

To a speedy and public trial

To trial by jury

To a fair and impartial trial

To confrontation of witnesses

To compulsory process to obtain witnesses

Not to incriminate oneself

To counsel

To proof of guilt beyond reasonable doubt

To protection against double jeopardy

In addition, law enforcement officers must be familiar with two defenses available to defendants: the insanity defense and the entrapment defense.

Each of the above rights applies in both federal and state criminal proceedings because they have all been incorporated and held applicable nationwide through the Fourteenth Amendment "due process" clause of the Constitution. These rights are of *constitutional origin, meaning that they cannot be limited in any way by federal or state legislation.* The federal or state government may, however, create by statute or court decisions additional rights where otherwise no constitutional rights exist. Therefore, constitutional rights cannot be diminished by statute, but a statute may create or establish other rights not given in the Constitution.

Example 1:   There is no constitutional right to a twelve-member jury trial, but the federal government and most states provide for twelve-member juries by statute or by provision in the state constitution.

Example 2:   Refusal by a suspect to take a blood-alcohol test to determine drunkenness may constitutionally be presented as evidence to prove guilt during the trial. Admission of the evidence does not violate the Fifth Amendment's guarantee against compulsory self-incrimination. State statute, however, may prohibit the admission of such evidence in court; such prohibition is binding.

I. RIGHT TO A SPEEDY AND PUBLIC TRIAL

The Sixth Amendment provides that "in all criminal prosecutions the accused shall enjoy the right to a speedy and public trial. . . ." Two separate rights are guaranteed by this provision: a speedy trial and a public trial.

A. Speedy Trial

Speedy trial means a trial that is free from unnecessary and unwanted delay. As the wording states, the Sixth Amendment applies only after a person becomes an "accused," meaning after the person has been formally charged with a crime or placed under arrest and detained to answer to a criminal charge. Most jurisdictions hold that once arrested a person is deemed an accused and is entitled to a speedy trial, even though later released on bail.

Violation of the constitutional right to a speedy trial is not established by delay alone. Instead, the determination of whether a case must be dismissed for lack of a speedy trial requires a balancing test in which the conduct of both the prosecution and the defense are weighed and the following factors are considered: (1) length of delay, (2) reason for delay, (3) defendant's assertion or nonassertion of rights, and (4) prejudice to the defendant. Any one factor alone is usually not sufficient to justify or condemn the delay in the trial (Barker v. Wingo, 407 U.S. 514 [1972]). If the delay is due to willful delay tactics by the accused, the accused will be deemed to have waived the right to a speedy trial. If the defendant's constitutional right to a speedy trial is violated, the only remedy is dismissal of charges. Dismissal prevents any further prosecution of the accused for the same offense.

In addition to the constitutional provision for a speedy trial, some statutes also provide for dismissal of an action when there have been unjustified delays in filing charges or bringing the defendant to trial. An example is the Federal Speedy Trial Act, whose goal is to bring all federal criminal cases to trial within one hundred days following arrest. The act requires that an information or indictment be filed within thirty days after arrest, arraignment follow within ten days thereafter, and the trial commence within sixty days after arraignment. Similarly, many states require trial within a given number of days after the filing of charges against the accused; otherwise the charges are dismissed. Whether or not the charges can later be refiled in court would depend upon the provision of the state statute.

B. Public Trial

The accused has a right that the trial be seen and heard by persons interested in ensuring that the proceedings are fair and just. The right, however, is not absolute.

The trial judge, at his or her discretion, may exclude some or all spectators during particular parts of the proceedings for good cause; but under almost no circumstances may the friends and relatives of the accused be excluded from the trial. Spectators are frequently excluded if necessary to spare a victim extreme public embarrassment or humiliation, as in certain rape cases. Likewise, a judge may properly exclude certain persons if it is shown that they are likely to threaten witnesses. Criminal defendants also have a constitutional right to have their pretrial hearings conducted in public. The Court has not decided, however, whether the public and press have a right to attend pretrial hearings when the defendant wants them conducted in secret.

There is a split of authority on the issue of who may object to exclusions. Some courts hold that only the accused has the right to object. Others have indicated that the right also belongs to the public; therefore, members of the public, such as the press, may properly object to being excluded.

Juveniles have no constitutional right to a public trial. Many states provide for closed juvenile adjudication proceedings and either limit or prohibit press reports. These practices are justified by the concept of *parens patriae* (a doctrine by which the government supervises children or other persons who suffer from legal disability), which diminishes the constitutional rights of juveniles and protects them from unnecessary public exposure.

II. RIGHT TO TRIAL BY JURY

Article III, Section 2, Clause 3 of the Constitution provides that "The Trial of all Crimes, except in cases of Impeachment, shall be by Jury." The Sixth Amendment also provides: "In all criminal prosecutions, the accused shall enjoy the right to a speedy and public trial, by an impartial jury of the State and district wherein the crime shall have been committed."

A. Size of Jury May Vary

In all federal criminal trials, a jury of twelve is required by federal statute but not required by the Sixth Amendment. Thus, the Supreme Court has upheld a Florida law providing for a six-member jury in all criminal cases except those involving capital offenses (Williams v. Florida, 399 U.S. 78 [1970]). The minimum number of jurors is six. Juries of five or fewer members are unconstitutional because the membership is too small to provide effective group discussion. Juries of fewer than six members would also diminish the chances of drawing from a fair section of the community, thus impairing the accuracy of fact finding (Ballew v. Georgia, 435 U.S. 223 [1978]). Although most juries are composed of either twelve or six members, any number from six to twelve should not run into constitutional difficulties. Whether or not death-penalty cases can be decided by juries of fewer than twelve is an issue that the Court has not addressed. Chances are that the Court, given the severity of the punishment involved, will not approve a jury of fewer than twelve in capital cases.

B. Unanimous Verdict Not Required by the Constitution

In federal criminal cases, a unanimous jury verdict is required, but not in state trials. In Johnson v. Louisiana, 406 U.S. 356 (1972), a nine-out-of-twelve verdict for con-

---

HIGHLIGHT 12.1

Most States Have Speedy Trial Restrictions for Defendants Not in Custody

States that restrict time from arrest to trial	Time limit
California	75 days
Nevada	75
Alaska	120
North Carolina	120
Texas	120
Iowa	135
Arizona	150
Illinois	160
Florida	180
Hawaii	180
New Mexico	180
New York	180
Pennsylvania	180
Ohio	270
Idaho	360
Louisiana	360
Indiana	365
Massachusetts	365
Arkansas	3 terms of court
Oklahoma	4
Utah	4

States that restrict time from indictment to trial	Time limit
Minnesota	60 days
Wisconsin	90
Washington	104
Wyoming	120
Colorado	180
Maryland	180
Montana	180
Nebraska	180
Kansas	190
Missouri	190
Mississippi	270
Virginia	270
Georgia	2 terms of court
West Virginia	3

---

viction was upheld as constitutional. But the Court has not decided whether an eight-out-of-twelve or a seven-out-of-twelve verdict for conviction would be constitutional. What this means is that a state can provide for a less-than-unanimous verdict for conviction (usually by law) and that such procedure is constitutional. The Court has rejected the argument that permitting a nonunanimous verdict violates the "reasonable doubt" standard for conviction in criminal cases, saying that the fact that certain jurors disagree would not in itself establish that there was a reasonable doubt as to

---

HIGHLIGHT 12.1 *(continued)*

Most States Have Speedy Trial Restrictions for Defendants Not in Custody

---

States that restrict "unreasonable delay"

Delaware	Oregon
District of Columbia	Rhode Island
Kentucky	South Dakota
Maine	Tennessee
New Jersey	Vermont
North Dakota	

Note: States without restrictions include Alabama, Connecticut, Michigan, New Hampshire, and South Carolina.

Source: Bureau of Justice Statistics, *Report to the Nation on Crime and Justice,* 2d ed. (Washington, DC: U.S. Government Printing Office, 1988), at 85.

---

the defendant's guilt. Reasonable doubt refers to the thinking of an individual juror, not to a split vote among the jurors. If the jury has only *six members,* the verdict must be *unanimous* for conviction or acquittal, otherwise it results in a hung jury.

C. Serious versus Petty Offenses

Despite the wording of Article III, Section 2, Clause 3 of the Constitution, which states that "the Trial of all Crimes . . . shall be by jury," the Court has stated that the Constitution guarantees a jury trial only when a *serious offense* is charged. One must, therefore, distinguish such offenses from mere "petty" offenses. For purposes of the constitutional right to trial by jury, a serious offense is one for which *more than six months' imprisonment is authorized* (Baldwin v. New York, 399 U.S. 66 [1970]). Courts look at the maximum possible sentence that may be imposed in making this determination. An offense is considered serious if the maximum punishment authorized by statute is imprisonment for more than six months, regardless of the penalty actually imposed; therefore the accused is entitled to jury trial. For example, X is tried for theft, the maximum penalty for which is one year in jail. If X is denied a jury trial, convicted, and sentenced to five months in jail, the conviction must be reversed because it violates X's right to trial by jury, even if the actual penalty imposed is less than six months.

By contrast, an offense whose maximum penalty is six months or less is *"petty"* for purposes of the right to trial by jury (regardless of how that offense is classified by state law). Therefore, no right to jury trial exists. The Court has ruled that when a state treats drunken driving as a petty offense, no jury trial is needed even if other peripheral sanctions (such as a fine and automatic loss of driver's license) may also be imposed (Blanton v. North Las Vegas, 109 S.Ct. 1289 [1989]). Some states classify drunk driving as a serious offense where the penalty involved is more than six months of confinement. In those states, a jury trial is constitutionally required. More than six months is therefore the magic number in right to jury trial cases.

If no punishment is prescribed by statute, the offense is considered "petty" when the actual sentence imposed is six months or less. Juveniles do not have a constitutional right to trial by jury regardless of the length of confinement; however, such right may be given juveniles by state law.

D. Right May Be Waived

The right to a trial by jury may be *waived* by the accused, provided that the waiver is *express* and *intelligent*. In some cases, the prosecution also has the right to demand a jury trial even if the defendant waives it. Criminal defendants have no constitutional right to have their cases tried before a judge alone (Singer v. U.S., 380 U.S. 24 [1965]). Thus, in states where the death penalty may be imposed only by a jury, the prosecutor may insist on a jury trial even if the defendant waives that right.

E. Selection of Jurors

The Supreme Court interpretation of the Sixth Amendment requires that trial juries in both federal and state criminal trials be selected from "a representative cross-section of the community." It also guarantees trial by a "jury of peers." That phrase does not mean that a student facing criminal charges must have a jury of students or that female defendants must have an all-female jury. What it does mean is that *jury service cannot be consciously restricted to a particular group*. For example, excluding women from juries, or giving them automatic exemptions with the result that jury panels are almost totally male, is invalid (Taylor v. Louisiana, 419 U.S. 522 [1975]). Likewise, the exclusion of persons because of race, creed, color, or national origin has been held invalid.

A defendant is not entitled to have all diverse groups in the community represented in the jury. It is enough that the jurors be drawn from a group that represents a fair cross-section of the community. For example, it is unconstitutional to exclude for cause potential jurors who have reservations about the death penalty. This would result in "stacking the deck" in favor of the death penalty, thus violating the defendant's right to due process (Witherspoon v. Illinois, 391 U.S. 510 [1968]). Also, a prosecutor's use of peremptory challenges (challenges for which no reason is stated) to exclude from a jury members of the defendant's race solely on racial grounds violates the "equal protection" rights of both the defendant and the excluded jurors

---

HIGHLIGHT 12.2

**Eighteen States and the District of Columbia Require a
Unanimous Verdict in All Trials**

Currently, 45 States require unanimity in criminal verdicts, but 29 of these States do not require unanimity in civil verdicts. Five States (Louisiana, Montana, Oklahoma, Oregon, and Texas) do not require unanimous verdicts in criminal or civil trials.

The proportion of jury votes needed to convict varies among jurisdictions that do not require unanimity, ranging from two-thirds in Montana to five-sixths in Oregon.

All States require unanimity in capital cases, and the U.S. Supreme Court does not permit a criminal finding of guilt by less than a six-person majority. Thus, a six-person jury must always be unanimous in a criminal finding of guilty.

Source: Bureau of Justice Statistics, *Report to the Nation on Crime and Justice*, 2d ed. (Washington, DC: U.S. Government Printing Office, 1988), at 84.

(Batson v. Kentucky, 39 CrL 3047 [1986]). Interestingly, however, the prosecution's racially motivated use of peremptory challenges to exclude people from the trial jury does not violate the defendant's Sixth Amendment right to trial by an impartial jury (Holland v. Illinois, 46 CrL 2067 [1990]). The Court in this case hinted, however, that such challenge could have been raised as a violation of the constitutional right to equal protection under the Fourteenth Amendment, a challenge that was not raised in this case.

III. RIGHT TO A FAIR AND IMPARTIAL TRIAL

The "due process" clauses of the Fifth and Fourteenth Amendments guarantee the accused a fair trial by an impartial jury. What this guarantee basically means is that the circumstances surrounding the trial must not be such that they unduly influence the jury. Undue influence usually takes the form of publicity so massive that it becomes prejudicial to the accused.

A. Prejudicial Publicity Is Prohibited

Two basic principles of the U.S. system of criminal justice are that a person must be convicted by an impartial tribunal and that a person must be convicted solely on the basis of evidence admitted at the trial. The publicity given to a notorious case before or during trial may bias a jury or create a significant risk that the jury will consider information other than the evidence produced in court.

> Example 1: Headlines announced that D had confessed to six murders and twenty-four burglaries, and reports were widely circulated that D had offered to plead guilty. Ninety percent of the prospective jurors interviewed expressed an opinion that D was guilty, and eight out of twelve jurors finally seated, familiar with the material facts, held such a belief. The Court held that D had been denied due process, stressing that this was a capital-offense case (Irwin v. Dowd, 366 U.S. 717 [1961]).

> Example 2: Police arranged to have D's prior confession shown several times on local television. The Court held that D had in effect been "tried" thereby— and that no actual prejudice need be shown to establish a denial of due process under such circumstances (Rideau v. Louisiana, 373 U.S. 723 [1963]).

HIGHLIGHT 12.3

All States and the Federal Government Pay Trial Jurors

Payments to jurors range from $3 per day in Colorado to $30 per day in New Hampshire, Vermont, the District of Columbia, and the Federal courts. Thirty-eight States pay for travel ranging from 2¢ per mile in New Jersey to 20¢ per mile in Hawaii. Some jurisdictions also require employers to pay the salaries of employees while serving on jury duty.

Source: Bureau of Justice Statistics, *Report to the Nation on Crime and Justice,* 2d ed. (Washington, DC: U.S. Government Printing Office, 1988), at 86.

B. Controlling Prejudicial Publicity

In an effort to control prejudicial publicity, the judge has power to order the following:

1. *Change of venue.* A defendant claiming undue pretrial publicity or other circumstances that would endanger his or her right to a fair and impartial trial locally can move to have the place (venue) of trial changed to another county from which more impartial jurors can be drawn. This is allowable in both felony and misdemeanor cases.

2. *Sequestration.* If there is danger that jurors will be exposed to prejudicial publicity during the trial, some states permit sequestration (keeping jurors together during trial and strictly controlling contact with the outside world) at the judge's discretion immediately following jury selection and continuing for the duration of the trial. A few states automatically sequester the jury throughout the trial; however, most states sequester jurors only for serious cases and then only after the case is given to the jury for decision.

3. *Continuance.* If the prejudice is severe, a continuance (postponement) may be granted to allow the threat to an impartial trial to subside.

4. *Control of participating counsel.* The judge may impose a "gag rule" prohibiting the participating attorneys and other parties in the trial from releasing information to the press or saying anything in public about the trial.

5. *Control of the police.* It is generally agreed that police officers connected with a case ought to observe standards similar to those formulated for attorneys. The "gag rule" for lawyers may also be extended to the police.

6. *Control of the press.* This is a very difficult problem for the judge because of the First Amendment guarantee of freedom of the press. The press has a right to attend a criminal trial; however, the media may be excluded if specific findings are made that closure is necessary for a fair trial. The media do not have a Sixth Amendment right to attend a pretrial hearing in a criminal case.

Generally, attempts to control the kind of news items the news media can report in connection with a criminal case are difficult to justify—even where such items may create a "clear and present danger" of unfair trial for the accused. Courts usually prohibit the taking of photographs or the televising of courtroom proceedings. In a number of states, however, the televising of courtroom proceedings is discretionary with the trial judge. But if the judge allows the televising of court proceedings, he or she must be very careful not to create a "carnival atmosphere" inside the courtroom. The Supreme Court has reversed a conviction because press coverage was too intrusive. The Court found the coverage so distractive to the judge, jurors, witnesses, and counsel that it created a "carnival atmosphere" and denied the defendant a fair trial (Sheppard v. Maxwell, 384 U.S. 333 [1966]).

IV. RIGHT TO CONFRONTATION OF WITNESSES

The Sixth Amendment provides that "in all criminal prosecutions, the accused shall enjoy the right . . . to be confronted with the witnesses against him." The right to confrontation exists in all criminal proceedings—including trials, preliminary hearings, and juvenile proceedings in which the juvenile is suspected of having committed a crime. The right does not apply to purely investigative proceedings, such as grand jury proceedings, coroner's inquests, and legislative investigations. The right to confrontation includes the following:

1. *Right to cross-examine opposing witnesses.* Opportunity to cross-examine all opposing witnesses is an important right of the accused. It is the process whereby any falsehood or inaccuracy in the witness's testimony can be detected and exposed, and through which a skillful lawyer may elicit testimony that can be helpful to his or her client.

2. *Right to be physically present.* The right to confrontation also means that the accused must have the opportunity to be physically present in the courtroom at the time any testimony against him or her is offered. However, the right to be present may be waived by the following:

   a. *Deliberate absence.* If an accused is present at the start of the trial but later voluntarily absents himself or herself, the Court has held that the trial may continue in the absence of the accused, meaning that the accused is considered to have waived his or her right to be present (Taylor v. U.S., 414 U.S. 17 [1973]). Note, however, that if the defendant is not present at the start of the trial, the court cannot proceed even though the absence was deliberate.

   b. *Disruptive conduct in courtroom.* Likewise, an accused who persists in disorderly or disrespectful conduct in the courtroom will be held to have waived his or her right to be present and may be excluded from his or her own trial. The Court has approved the following methods for dealing with a disruptive defendant: (1) holding the defendant in contempt of court, (2) binding and gagging the defendant in the courtroom, and (3) removing the defendant from the courtroom until he or she promises to behave properly (Illinois v. Allen, 397 U.S. 337 [1970]).

3. *Right to physically face witnesses at trial.* The Court has decided that the right to confrontation also includes the right to physically face witnesses at trial, hence a state law that allows testimony via closed-circuit television or behind a screen violates defendant's Sixth Amendment right (Coy v. Iowa, 108 S.Ct. 2798 [1988]). In this case, the court allowed a semitransparent screen to be erected in court between the defendant and two youthful complainants in a child sex abuse trial so the children could not see the defendant when they testified. The Court rejected this method, saying that face-to-face confrontation is the "core" of the constitutional right to confrontation.

Two years later, however, the Court carved out an exception to this rule by stating that face-to-face confrontation may be dispensed with when preventing such confrontation is necessary to further important public policy and the reliability of the testimony is otherwise assured (Maryland v. Craig, 47 CrL 2258 [1990]). In that case, Craig was charged and tried in a Maryland court with sexual abuse of a six-year-old child. In accordance with Maryland law, the judge permitted the child to testify in a different room, saying that courtroom testimony would result in the child's suffering such serious emotional distress that she could not reasonably communicate. This procedure allows the child, prosecutor, and defense counsel to withdraw from the courtroom to another room where the child is examined and cross-examined. The judge, jury, and defendant remain in the courtroom where the testimony is seen and heard via one-way closed-circuit television. Craig challenged the Maryland law as violative of his right to confrontation. The Court rejected the challenge, saying that although face-to-face confrontation forms the "core" of this constitutional right, it is not an indispensable element thereof and may be dispensed with "when preventing such confrontation is necessary to further an important public policy and reliability of the testimony is otherwise assured."

4. *Right to know identity of prosecution witnesses.* Any witness who testifies against the accused must reveal his or her true name and address. Such information may be crucial to the defense in investigating and cross-examining the witness for possible impeachment. The Court has concluded, however, that the admission into evidence of a prior, out-of-court identification of a witness who is unable, due to loss of memory, to explain the basis for the identification, is not a violation of the right to confrontation (U.S. v. Owens, 108 S.Ct. 838 [1988]). The Court added that the confrontation clause is satisfied if the defendant had a full and fair opportunity to bring out the witness's lapse of memory and other facts that consequently tend to discredit the testimony.

V. RIGHT TO COMPULSORY PROCESS TO OBTAIN WITNESSES

The Sixth Amendment expressly provides that the accused in a criminal prosecution shall have the right to compulsory process for obtaining witnesses in his or her favor. The right to obtain witnesses includes (1) the power to require the appearance of witnesses and (2) the right to present a defense, which in turn includes the defendant's right to present his or her own witnesses and his or her own version of the facts. This principle means that the defendant is given the same right as the prosecutor to present witnesses in state and federal proceedings. Thus, if the trial judge makes threatening remarks to the only defense witness, in effect driving the witness from the stand, the accused is deprived of the right to present a defense (Webb v. Texas, 409 U.S. 95 [1972]).

The trial court's exclusion of evidence crucial to the defense and bearing substantial assurances of trustworthiness violates the right to present a defense—even when the evidence is technically not admissible under local rules of evidence. For example, a defendant offered evidence of oral confessions to the crime by another witness. The trial court excluded the evidence because it constituted inadmissible hearsay under the local rules of evidence. This ruling was held to violate the defendant's right to present a defense, since the confessions bore substantial assurances of trustworthiness (Chambers v. Mississippi, 410 U.S. 284 [1973]).

VI. PRIVILEGE AGAINST SELF-INCRIMINATION

The privilege against compulsory self-incrimination springs from the Fifth Amendment provision that "no person . . . shall be compelled in any criminal case to be a witness against himself.'' This guarantee is designed to restrain the government from using force, coercion, or other such methods to obtain any statement, admission, or confession.

A. Scope of the Provision

The privilege against self-incrimination extends only to *testimonial (or communicative) self-incrimination* and does not prohibit *physical self-incrimination.* For example, the accused can be forced to submit to reasonable *physical or psychiatric* examinations; and the police may introduce evidence obtained thereby — such as fingerprints, footprints, blood or urine samples, or voice identifications during the trial. Also, a defendant can be forced to stand up for identification in the courtroom, put on certain items of clothing, or give a handwriting sample (Gilbert v. California, 388 U.S. 263 [1967]). Testimonial or communicative self-incrimination is that which in itself explicitly or implicitly relates a factual assertion or discloses information. It is in the form of verbal or oral communication. For example, a question that asks whether or not the defendant killed the deceased is testimonially self-incriminatory because it relates a factual assertion or discloses information of a nonphysical nature. In a recent case, the Court said that asking routine questions of people suspected of driving while intoxicated and videotaping their responses do not elicit testimonial responses that are protected by the right against self-incrimination (Pennsylvania v. Muniz, 58 L.W. 4817 [1990]).

As stated in the chapter on confessions and admissions (Chapter Eleven), Miranda v. Arizona is a case on the right against self-incrimination. Miranda, however, applies to proceedings before trial. The absence of Miranda warnings means that evidence obtained cannot be admitted in court during trial because the accused's right against self-incrimination has been violated.

The Fifth Amendment's protection extends only to *natural persons,* meaning human beings. Corporations or partnerships (considered persons by law) cannot claim the privilege; therefore the records of such entities cannot be withheld on this ground. For example, a corporation faces charges of violating labor and antimonopoly laws. The corporation may be required to produce its official books and records even if they contain incriminating evidence.

The search and seizure of a person's private papers in accordance with legal process, with or without a warrant, does not violate the right to protection against self-incrimination—at least if information on the papers was written voluntarily and hence was not obtained by testimonial compulsion. This is because the protection given to books and papers under the Fifth Amendment is very limited, inasmuch as although perhaps the products of a mental process (such as a diary), the books or documents themselves constitute physical evidence.

A law that allows the accused to refuse to take a blood-alcohol test and provides that such refusal may be admitted in evidence against him or her is constitutional (South Dakota v. Neville, 459 U.S. 553 [1983]). This case involved a South Dakota law that permits a person suspected of driving while intoxicated to refuse to submit to a blood-alcohol test and authorizes revocation of the driver's license of a person who refuses to take the test. Moreover, the statute permits such refusal to be used against the driver as evidence of guilt during the trial. The Court said that the admission into evidence of a defendant's refusal to submit to a blood-alcohol test does not offend the defendant's Fifth Amendment guarantee against compulsory self-incrimination. A refusal to take the test, after a police officer has lawfully requested it, is not an act coerced by the officer and therefore is not protected by the Fifth Amendment. This case legalizes the practice used in some states of giving DWI suspects a choice to take or refuse a blood-alcohol test, but then using a refusal as evidence of guilt later in court. The Court said that any incrimination resulting from a blood-alcohol test is physical in nature, not testimonial or communicative, and hence is not protected by the Fifth Amendment. (Read the South Dakota v. Neville case brief at the end of this chapter.)

May a parent, the custodian of a child pursuant to a court order, invoke the right against self-incrimination to resist an order of a juvenile court to produce the child? The Court has answered in the negative, saying that even though producing the child could be self-incriminating, a parent who agreed to extensive conditions in assuming custody of a child may be required to produce that child (Baltimore City Department of Social Services v. Bouknight, 46 CrL 2096 [1990]). In that case, the child was originally taken from the mother because of suspected child abuse. The mother regained custody of the child, however, after agreeing to submit to various conditions. Several months later, the social service agency (suspecting further child abuse or murder) obtained an order to produce the child, with which the mother refused to comply. The Court said that the mother could be cited for contempt and rejected her claim against self-incrimination.

B. Two Separate Privileges during Trial

The privilege against compulsory self-incrimination during trial guarantees two separate privileges; namely, the *privilege of the accused* and the *privilege of a witness.*

1. Privilege of the Accused

The accused in a criminal case has a privilege *not to take the stand* and *not to testify.* The Court has ruled that the accused "may stand mute, clothed in the presumption of innocence." Moreover, prosecutors cannot comment on a defendant's assertion of the right not to testify. No conclusion of guilt may be drawn from the failure of the accused

---

HIGHLIGHT 12.4

**Distinctions between the Privilege against Self-Incrimination
of an Accused and of a Witness**

Accused	*Witness*
1. An accused need not answer questions or take the witness stand. Such refusal cannot be commented upon by the prosecutor.	1. A witness must testify or risk contempt citation.
2. An accused who takes the witness stand can no longer refuse to answer incriminating questions. The privilege is waived.	2. A witness retains the privilege on the witness stand.

to testify during the trial. Therefore, the prosecutor is not permitted to make any comment or argument to the jury suggesting that the defendant is guilty because he or she refused to testify (Griffin v. California, 380 U.S. 609 [1965]). This rule has been modified, however, by the concept of *"fair response,"* which provides that a prosecutor's statement to the jury, during closing argument, that the defendant could have taken the witness stand but refused to do so, is proper as long as it is in response to defense counsel's argument that the government had not allowed the defendant to explain his or her side of the story (U.S. v. Robinson, 42 CrL 3063 [1988]). Unless it is in the context of a "fair response," the comments of a prosecutor suggesting that the defendant must be guilty because he or she refused to take the stand will lead to a reversal of the conviction.

The privilege to remain silent and not to take the stand applies in all stages of a criminal proceeding, starting with when the suspect is first placed in custody. It applies in criminal prosecutions or contempt proceedings but does not apply when there is no prosecution and no accused, as in grand jury investigations or legislative or administrative hearings.

Once an accused takes the witness stand in his or her own defense, he or she waives the accused's privilege not to be compelled to testify. Therefore, the accused must answer all relevant inquiries about the charge for which he or she is on trial. This is one reason defense lawyers may not want the accused to take the witness stand, particularly if the accused has a bad record or a background that is better kept undisclosed.

2. Privilege of a Witness

Any witness other than an accused on the witness stand has the privilege to *refuse to disclose any matter that may "tend to incriminate" him or her.* The witness is not on trial and is in court merely to shed light on the proceeding. A question tends to incriminate a witness if the answer would directly or indirectly implicate that witness in the commission of a crime. The privilege therefore does not extend to any form of civil liability. But if the facts involved would make the witness subject to both civil and criminal liability, the privilege can be claimed. The privilege cannot be claimed merely because the answer would hold the witness up to shame, disgrace, or embarrassment, as long as no crime is involved. The answer to the question need not prove guilt in order to give rise to the privilege. All that is needed is a reasonable possibility that the answer would "furnish a link in the chain of evidence needed to prosecute."

The witness's privilege protects only against the possibility of prosecution; therefore, if a witness could not be or can no longer be prosecuted, he or she can be compelled to testify.

Example 1: If the statute of limitations (law providing that a crime must be prosecuted within a certain period of time) has run out on the crime, the privilege does not apply.

Example 2: If the accused has been acquitted and therefore cannot be reprosecuted, his or her testimony can be compelled.

Example 3: If the witness is assured of immunity, he or she may not be able to claim the privilege.

The decision about whether or not the witness's answer tends to incriminate the witness is made by the hearing officer or judge. The decision is appealable only after the trial; therefore the witness must testify, if so ordered, or face contempt proceedings.

C. Grant of Immunity

There are many situations in which the government grants *immunity* to a witness or a coaccused in return for his or her testimony. Immunity is usually given when the testimony of the witness is crucial in proving the government's case or when the government needs further information for investigative purposes, particularly in cases involving organized crime. A witness who is granted immunity from prosecution may be forced to testify because the reason for the privilege no longer exists. Once immunity is granted, a witness who still refuses to testify can be held in contempt of court.

1. Immunity Granted by Law, Judge, or Prosecutor

Immunity is granted either by law (which usually refers to a category of witnesses), by the judge, or by prosecutors. In a growing number of cases, such as gambling or drug possession, the same act may constitute a crime under both federal and state laws. The question then arises of whether a grant of immunity from prosecution under one jurisdiction, state or federal, is sufficient to prevent the witness from claiming the privilege. The rules governing the grant of immunity are as follows:

a. If a state has granted the witness valid immunity, the federal government is not permitted to make use of the testimony (or any of its "fruits") in a federal prosecution against the witness (Murphy v. Waterfront Commission, 378 U.S. 52 [1964]). Therefore, the witness may be forced to testify in the state proceedings.

b. The Supreme Court has not decided whether a state would be allowed to use compelled testimony given in federal court under a grant of federal immunity. However, its use would probably be prohibited under the reasoning of the Murphy case.

c. Similarly, testimony given by virtue of immunity in a state court could also not be used as evidence against the witness in the court of another state.

2. Immunity Granted by Congress—The Oliver North Case

Immunity to a witness or suspect may also be granted by the U.S. Congress. Would immunity given by Congress affect the judiciary in a subsequent criminal proceeding? The answer is yes; that was what happened in the Oliver North trial. In that case, the prosecutor also had the burden of proving that none of the evidence used came out of North's congressional testimony.

Oliver North was convicted on three counts of a twelve-count indictment in connection with the Iran-Contra proceedings. Prior to that criminal trial, however, he gave a widely publicized testimony to a congressional committee under a grant of use-and-derivative-use immunity. After conviction in the criminal trial, North appealed, alleging, among other errors, that some of the evidence used by the special prosecutor and witnesses stemmed from his testimony before the congressional committee and therefore ought to have been suppressed. In a 2-to-1 decision, a three-judge panel of the U.S. Court of Appeals agreed, ruling that the presiding trial judge must determine "witness-by-witness; if necessary, line-by-line and item-by-item" if the special prosecutor or the witnesses in North's trial were influenced by the testimony that North gave in the 1987 congressional hearings under a grant of immunity.[1] If they were, the evidence could not be used against North and his conviction would have to be overturned. This decision might be reversed on appeal, but if it holds and becomes precedent, it will be difficult for the government to secure convictions in high-profile cases where immunity has been given by Congress.

D. Transactional versus Use-and-Derivative-Use Immunity

Does the grant of immunity to a witness automatically exempt the witness from any further criminal prosecution? Not necessarily. There are two types of immunity: *transactional immunity* and *use-and-derivative-use immunity.* Transactional immunity means that the witness can no longer be prosecuted for any offense whatsoever arising out of that act or transaction. In contrast, use-and-derivative-use immunity merely means that the witness is assured that his or her testimony and evidence derived from it will not be used against him or her in a subsequent prosecution. The witness can be prosecuted on the basis of evidence other than his or her testimony, if the prosecutor has such independent evidence. The type of immunity given to Oliver North by Congress in the Iran-Contra hearings was use-and-derivative-use immunity.

The Court has decided that prosecutors need only grant use-and-derivative-use immunity to compel an unwilling witness to testify. The witness is not constitutionally entitled to transactional immunity before he or she can be compelled to testify (Kastigar v. U.S., 406 U.S. 441 [1972]). In the Kastigar case, the witness refused to testify under a use-and-derivative-use grant of immunity, saying that the Fifth Amendment guarantee against compulsory self-incrimination requires that transactional immunity must be given before a witness can be required to testify. The Court disagreed, saying that use-and-derivative-use immunity is sufficient for purposes of Fifth Amendment protection; the granting of transactional immunity is not required.

E. When the Privilege Is Waived

The witness's privilege may be waived through the following actions.

1. *Failure to assert.* The witness is the holder of the privilege, and only the witness (or his or her lawyer) can assert it. If the witness fails to assert the privilege at the time an incriminating question is asked, the privilege is waived.
2. *Partial disclosure.* When the witness discloses a fact that he or she knows to be self-incriminating, the witness also waives his or her privilege with respect to all further facts related to the same transaction.
3. *Accused's taking the witness stand.* When the witness is also the accused who voluntarily decides to take the stand, he or she must answer all relevant inquiries about the charge for which he or she is on trial. The accused is therefore "fair game" on all such matters during the cross-examination.

VII. RIGHT TO COUNSEL

The Sixth Amendment of the Constitution provides that "in all criminal prosecutions, the accused shall enjoy the right . . . to have the Assistance of Counsel for his defence." This right has been held applicable to the states since 1963 (Gideon v. Wainwright, 372 U.S. 335 [1963]). A defendant has the right to be represented by counsel at "every critical stage" of the criminal proceeding. The meaning of the term *critical stage* has been determined by the Court on a case-by-case basis.

A. Underlying Theory

The Supreme Court stated the justification for the right to counsel in criminal proceedings in the case of Powell v. Alabama, 287 U.S. 45 (1932). The Powell case was one of the two famous "Scottsboro Cases," in which nine black youths were charged with the rape of two white girls (the other was Norris v. Alabama, 295 U.S. 587, 1935). Justice Sutherland wrote the following often-quoted statement on why an accused needs counsel during the trial:

> Even the intelligent and educated layman has small and sometimes no skill in the science of the law. Left without aid of counsel, he may be put on trial without a proper charge, and convicted upon incompetent evidence irrelevant to the issue or otherwise inadmissible against him. Without counsel, though he may not be guilty, he faces the danger of conviction because he does not know how to establish his innocence.

B. How Counsel Is Obtained

The term *right to counsel* refers to either (1) retained counsel or (2) court-appointed counsel. The discussion here is limited to the right to court-appointed counsel because most cases deal only with that issue.

1. Retained Counsel

Retained counsel is an attorney chosen and paid by the accused him- or herself. With few exceptions, such as in making appearances before a grand jury or in certain identification proceedings, a person who can afford to retain his or her own counsel has a right to have that counsel present at every stage of the criminal proceedings.

A defendant's right to hire an attorney of his or her own choosing is not absolute and may be overridden by the trial court if necessary to avoid conflicts of interest (Wheat v. U.S. 43 CrL 3037 [1988]). In this case, the defendant and others were charged with conspiracy to distribute drugs. Two days before trial, defendant asked to replace his counsel with an attorney who represented two of the other alleged coconspirators. These coconspirators had either already pleaded guilty to or were getting ready to plead guilty to the charges. Prosecution objected to defendant's move to change counsel, alleging conflict of interest if the defense lawyer represented all three defendants. The trial court refused to allow such change of counsel, a decision affirmed by the Court on grounds of conflict of interest.

2. Court-Appointed Counsel

Court-appointed counsel means an attorney appointed by the judge and paid by the county or state to represent an "indigent" accused at a "critical stage" in the criminal proceeding. There is no uniform rule to determine indigency. Some standards used by judges are unemployment, not having a car, not having posted bail, and not having a house. The judge enjoys wide discretion in making this determination and his or her decision is rarely reversed on appeal. The standards for indigency therefore vary from one jurisdiction or judge to another. Nevertheless, more than half of all defendants charged with felonies are classified as indigents.

The method of appointing counsel for an indigent also varies. Most judges use a list containing the names of available and willing attorneys, who are then assigned to cases on a rotation basis. Other judges make assignments at random, assigning any lawyer who may be available in the courtroom at the time the appointment is made. Still other jurisdictions employ full-time public defenders to handle indigent cases. The decision to create a public defender's office usually depends on cost-effectiveness. From an economic perspective, the bigger the city or county, the more attractive the public defender model becomes.

An indigent defendant has no right to designate an attorney of his or her choice to represent him. Selection of a defense lawyer is made purely at the discretion of the court, although the judge may allow the accused some input in the process. Some states provide counsel to defendants but specify as a condition of probation or parole that the defendant reimburse the state or county for the fees of the appointed lawyer. Such laws are valid as long as they exempt indigents who cannot afford to pay (Fuller v. Oregon, 417 U.S. 40 [1974]).

C. Pretrial Proceedings to Which the Right to Counsel Applies

The right to counsel applies only in certain pretrial proceedings that have been considered by the Court to be *"critical stages"* in the criminal process. By implication, therefore, counsel is not required when the proceeding is not deemed by the Court to be in the "critical stage" category. These are considered to be critical pretrial stages:

1. *Custodial interrogations* before or after charges have been filed (Miranda v. Arizona, 384 U.S. 436 [1966]).

2. *Noncustodial interrogations* after the accused has been formally charged. For example, a defendant made incriminating statements to a codefendant whom federal agents had "wired for sound." Wiring the codefendant was held to violate the defendant's Sixth Amendment right to counsel because the defendant at that time was out on bail after having been formally charged with the crime (Massiah v. U.S., 377 U.S. 201 [1964]).

3. *Postindictment line-ups* in which witnesses seek to identify the accused (U.S. v. Wade, 388 U.S. 218 [1967]).

4. *Preliminary hearings* to determine whether there is sufficient evidence against the accused to go to a grand jury (Coleman v. Alabama, 399 U.S. 1 [1970]).

5. *Meetings* in which the defendant's defense strategy is discussed and that the police knew or should have known would produce incriminating statements. In Maine v. Moulton, 54 L.W. 4039 (1985), the police arranged to record conversations between the defendant and his codefendant, who was a government informer, at a meeting in which both defendants, in the absence of a lawyer, planned to discuss defense strategy concerning charges on which the defendant then stood indicted. The Court held that

HIGHLIGHT 12.5

Who Defends Indigents?

Public defender programs are public or private nonprofit organizations with full- or part-time salaried staff. Within the public defender classification, there are two categories—statewide and local. Under statewide systems, one person, designated by statutes of the State as the public defender, is charged with developing and maintaining a system of representation for each county in the State. Often a governing board shares responsibility for program operation. By contrast, most local public defenders operate autonomously and do not have a central administrator.

Local public defenders operate autonomously in 32 States and the District of Columbia, and 15 States have a State-administered system. Public defender systems are the dominant form in 43 of the 50 largest counties and, overall, serve 68% of the Nation's population.

Assigned counsel systems involve the appointment by the courts of private attorneys as needed from a list of available attorneys. There are two main types of assigned counsel systems: *Ad hoc assigned counsel systems* in which individual private attorneys are appointed by individual judges and provide representation on a case-by-case basis. *Coordinated systems* have an administrator who oversees the appointment of counsel and develops a set of standards and guidelines for program administration; coordinated systems are sometimes indistinguishable from public defender programs.

Ad hoc systems represent about 75% of all assigned counsel programs. The others are part of a coordinated system of indigent defense. Though such counsel systems operate in almost two-thirds of the counties, they predominate in small counties with fewer than 50,000 residents.

Contract systems involve government contracting with individual attorneys, bar associations, or private law firms to provide services for a specified dollar amount. County agencies are usually responsible for the award of defender services contracts, and they are now frequently awarded to individual practitioners as opposed to law firms or other organized groups.

Contract systems are a relatively new way to provide defense services. They are found in small counties (less than 50,000) and very large ones. They vary considerably in organization, funding, and size. In about a fourth of the counties reporting them, they serve as an overflow for public defender offices and also represent codefendants in cases of conflict of interest.

Source: Bureau of Justice Statistics, *Report to the Nation on Crime and Justice,* 2d ed. (Washington, DC: U.S. Government Printing Office, 1988), at 74.

the Sixth Amendment right to the assistance of counsel was violated by the admission at trial of the incriminating statements that had been recorded. The statements so recorded had to be suppressed at the defendant's trial on the original charges even though the police conduct was aimed at investigating other crimes on which the defendant had not been indicted.

D. Pretrial Proceedings to Which the Right to Counsel Does Not Apply

1. *Grand jury proceedings.* A witness called to appear before a grand jury is not entitled to have counsel present. The theory is that such proceedings are only investigative in nature. However, to protect the witness's privilege against self-incrimination, a witness who is in doubt about whether his or her answer may be self-incriminating generally may consult his or her attorney outside the jury room to obtain advice.

2. *Purely investigative proceedings.* There is no right to counsel at purely investigative hearings. For example, counsel is not required at a hearing by the state fire marshal to determine if a particular fire was the result of arson. Likewise, there is no right to counsel if a police officer is under administrative investigation, except if counsel is otherwise allowed or provided under administrative or departmental policy.

3. *Police line-ups prior to filing of charges.* There is generally no right to counsel before criminal charges are filed against a suspect. After charges are filed, then the suspect has a constitutional right to counsel.

E. Right to Counsel during Trial

Although the Sixth Amendment extends to "all criminal prosecutions," the Court has held that the right to counsel applies only in the following instances:

1. The crime charged is a felony (Gideon v. Wainwright, 372 U.S. 335 [1963]).
2. The crime charged is a misdemeanor for which the defendant faces a possible jail sentence and actual imprisonment is imposed (Argersinger v. Hamlin, 407 U.S. 25 [1972]; Scott v. Illinois, 440 U.S. 367 [1979]).

To illustrate the above rules, suppose that Y is charged with robbery, a felony in his jurisdiction. Y is entitled to counsel during the trial, even if the actual sentence later imposed is merely a fine. If no counsel was given and the defendant is indigent, then the trial is invalid even if the actual sentence is only a fine. Suppose, however, that Y is charged with theft, a misdemeanor in his jurisdiction. Y is entitled to counsel during the misdemeanor trial only if by law he faces a possible jail sentence and imprisonment is, in fact, imposed. If the sentence imposed is merely a fine, then Y is not entitled to a lawyer during the trial. What this means is that if the judge goes ahead with the trial without giving the defendant in a misdemeanor case a lawyer, then if the defendant is convicted the court may impose a sentence on the defendant, but not an imprisonment. The trial without a lawyer is not invalid per se, but the sentence imposed cannot include imprisonment.

During the trial itself, a judge may not prevent the defendant from talking with counsel during an overnight recess, because otherwise his or her right to counsel is violated (Geders v. U.S., 425 U.S. 80 [1976]). In that case, the trial judge directed the defendant not to talk with his attorney during an overnight recess because the defendant was going to continue his testimony the following day. In a subsequent case, the Court ruled, however, that a defendant who takes the witness stand has no Sixth Amendment right to consult with his lawyer during a brief recess while testifying (Perry v. Leeke, 109 S.Ct. 594 [1989]). In this case, the trial judge declared a 15-minute recess and ordered the witness-defendant not to talk to anyone, including counsel. The different Court rulings are explained by the fact that the Geders case involved an overnight recess where it would be natural for defendant to confer with counsel about the whole case, whereas Perry involved a 15-minute recess where "it is appropriate to presume that nothing but the defendant's testimony will be discussed."

Although juvenile proceedings are not criminal in nature, a juvenile is nonetheless entitled to appointed counsel if the proceeding can lead to commitment in an institution in which the juvenile's freedom is restricted (In Re Gault, 387 U.S. 1 [1967]).

F. Right to "Effective Assistance of Counsel"

As a matter of constitutional law, the defendant may challenge his or her conviction on the ground that his or her lawyer at the trial was so incompetent as to deprive the defendant of the *effective assistance of counsel*. However, although this claim is frequently raised, it is seldom upheld by the courts.

The meaning of "effective assistance of counsel" bothered lower courts for years because of the absence of a clear standard. In two recent cases, however, the Court clarified the issue by specifying the following criteria:

1. A claim of ineffective assistance of counsel can be made only by *pointing out specific errors of trial counsel*. It cannot be based on an inference drawn from defense counsel's inexperience or lack of time to prepare, gravity of the charges, complexity of defense, or accessibility of witness to counsel (U.S. v. Cronic, 104 S.Ct. 2039 [1984]).

2. The Court assumes that effective assistance of counsel is present unless the *adversarial process is so undermined by counsel's conduct that the trial cannot be relied upon to have produced a just result.* An accused who claims ineffective counsel must show the following: (a) deficient performance by counsel and (b) a reasonable probability that but for such deficiency the result of the proceeding would have been different (Strickland v. Washington, 104 S.Ct. 2052 [1984]).

Under the above standards, mere generalizations about the quality of the lawyer or the inadequacy of his or her efforts will not suffice. *Specificity* is required, and the burden is on the convicted defendant to prove that there is a reasonable probability that if the lawyer's performance had not been deficient, the results would have been different. In most cases, these points are difficult for the defendant to prove.

A mere error of law in advising a defendant to enter a guilty plea does not in itself constitute the denial of effective counsel. The test is whether the mistake was "within the range of competency" of most criminal defense lawyers. On the other hand, failure on the part of the lawyer to follow state appellate procedural rule, resulting in the dismissal of the appeal, represents ineffective assistance of counsel.

A *guilty plea* waives all defenses and most objections. Therefore, the effectiveness of counsel's advice to enter such a plea may be more carefully examined. Lower courts have held that if counsel unqualifiedly and falsely represents that the state has accepted a plea bargain, and the representation appeared to be supported by acts or statements of state officers, and the defendant justifiably relied on counsel's misrepresentation in entering his or her guilty plea, the defendant has been denied the effective assistance of counsel and the plea should be set aside.

G. Right to Act as One's Own Lawyer

Under certain conditions an accused has a constitutional right to waive counsel and represent himself or herself in a criminal proceeding (Faretta v. California, 422 U.S. 806 [1975]). In Faretta, the defendant had a high school education, had represented himself before, and had not wanted a public defender to represent him because of the public defender's heavy caseload. The right to self-representation does not require legal skills, but in cases in which the defendant is ignorant or too inexperienced, the request to act as his or her own counsel would probably be denied by the court. An accused who elects to represent himself or herself cannot later claim ineffective counsel.

Before an accused can be permitted to waive counsel and represent himself or herself, the following constitutional requirements must be met:

1. *Awareness of right to counsel.* The court must fully advise the accused of his or her right to be represented by counsel.

2. *Express waiver.* The accused's waiver of counsel cannot be inferred from his or her silence or from his or her failure to request the appointment of counsel.

3. *Competency of the accused.* The trial judge has the duty to determine whether the accused (a) is competent to waive the right to counsel and (b) is competent to make an intelligent choice in the case. In determining the defendant's competency to make an intelligent choice, the court must make the defendant aware of the dangers and disadvantages of self-representation.

VIII. RIGHT TO PROOF OF GUILT BEYOND REASONABLE DOUBT

The "due process" provision of the Fifth and Fourteenth Amendments requires proof beyond a reasonable doubt of every fact necessary to establish the case against the defendant.

A. Scope of the Provision

The prosecution must prove the following beyond a reasonable doubt:

1. The question of guilt
2. Every element of the crime

For example, in a crime of theft the element of intent and the fact that the property belongs to another person must be proved beyond reasonable doubt. However, only elements of the crime that have to do with the defendant's guilt must be established beyond reasonable doubt. Other issues are decided on a lower quantum of proof. Questions relating to the admissibility of evidence, such as whether evidence was obtained by lawful search or whether the defendant's confession was voluntary, need only be proved by a preponderance of the evidence.

B. What Constitutes "Reasonable Doubt"

"Reasonable doubt" is difficult to define. One court, however, has defined "reasonable doubt" as follows:

> It is such a doubt as would cause a juror, after careful and candid and impartial consideration of all the evidence, to be so undecided that he cannot say that he has an abiding conviction of the defendant's guilt. It is such a doubt as would cause a reasonable person to hesitate or pause in the graver or more important transactions of life. However, it is not a fanciful doubt nor a whimsical doubt, nor a doubt based on conjecture (Moore v. U.S., 345 F.2d 97 [DC Cir. 1965]).

In practice, despite instructions from the judge, an individual juror really determines for himself or herself what is meant by "reasonable doubt." Definitions like the above are too legalistic and difficult to apply. They merely provide a general framework for decision making, but fail to supply clear guidelines. No wonder jurors ultimately define the term subjectively. I think that to quantify the term (such as to define reasonable doubt as 95 percent certainty of guilt) removes a lot of confusion, but such a proposal, for various reasons, will not be favorably considered by the legal community.

IX. RIGHT TO PROTECTION AGAINST DOUBLE JEOPARDY

The Fifth Amendment of the U.S. Constitution provides that "no person shall be . . . subject for the same offense to be twice put in jeopardy of life or limb." *"Double jeopardy"* is defined as the successive prosecution of a defendant for the same offense by the same jurisdiction. Like most other constitutional rights, the protection against double jeopardy has been extended to state criminal proceedings.

A. Scope of Provision

A person who has committed a criminal act can be subjected to only one prosecution or punishment for the same offense. Accordingly, when a defendant has been prosecuted for a criminal offense and the prosecution has resulted in either a conviction or an acquittal, or the proceeding has reached a point at which dismissal would be equivalent to an acquittal, any further prosecution or punishment for the same offense is prohibited.

Double jeopardy attaches (meaning the defendant cannot be retried for the same offense) when the trial has reached the following stage:

1. In jury trials, when a competent jury has been sworn
2. In a nonjury (bench) trial, when the first witness has been called and sworn

If the charge is dismissed before either stage is reached, the defendant may be charged and tried again.

B. When Double Jeopardy Is Deemed Waived

Even though double jeopardy attaches under the above conditions, it may be waived in the following instances:

1. *In mistrials.* When a new trial is ordered before verdict on a motion of the defendant or otherwise with the defendant's consent, the defendant waives protection against double jeopardy. Thus if in the course of a trial the defendant moves for a mistrial because of what a prosecutor or a witness has done, and the motion is granted by the judge, the case can be tried again.

2. *When verdict of conviction is set aside on defendant's motion or appeal.* The general view is that a defendant asking for a new trial or appealing a guilty verdict waives his or her protection against double jeopardy; hence the defendant can be tried again for the same offense for which he or she was convicted in the first trial. If the convicted defendant is serving time, he or she will be released from prison and free on bail or be detained in jail pending another trial for the same or related offense. The prosecutor may choose not to reprosecute, but there is no double jeopardy if the same or similar charge is again filed.

In the celebrated Miranda case (discussed earlier in connection with custodial interrogation of suspects), defendant Miranda appealed his original conviction for rape on the ground that his confession was obtained in violation of the guarantee against compulsory self-incrimination. His conviction was reversed by the Supreme Court, but he was tried again, under an assumed name, for the same offense in Arizona and was reconvicted on the basis of other evidence. There was no double jeopardy because his appeal of the first conviction waived his right against a retrial on the same offense.

Despite the above, at a second trial for the same offense following a successful appeal, a defendant cannot be tried on or convicted of charges that are more serious than the ones for which he was originally tried and convicted. For example, a defendant is charged with second-degree murder but is convicted of negligent homicide (a lower offense). If the defendant appeals the conviction and obtains a new trial, he or she cannot be charged with first-degree murder in the second trial (Green v. U.S., 355 U.S. 184 [1957]). Also, a defendant whose conviction is reversed because the evidence is insufficient as a matter of law to sustain the conviction cannot be retried; the reversal amounts to an acquittal (Burks v. U.S., 437 U.S.1 [1978]).

If the jury cannot agree on conviction or acquittal, the judge can declare a "hung" jury and the defendant may be tried again before another jury. How soon this is declared is a matter of the judge's discretion. Some courts will declare a "hung" jury after several days of deadlocked deliberation; others require a longer period of stalemate.

C. What "Same Offense" Means

Double jeopardy applies only to prosecution for the *"same offense"*: once double jeopardy attaches, the defendant cannot be prosecuted a second time for the same offense involved in the first trial or for any other offense included in the act charged in the first trial; nor can the defendant receive more than one punishment for the same offense.

Courts vary in their definition of what constitutes the *"same or an included" offense*. However, the usual test is whether the offense charged in the second trial is the same in law and in fact as the offense charged in the first trial. If so, double jeopardy attaches. On the other hand, if one offense requires proof of some fact in addition to what the other requires, there are two separate offenses—and double jeopardy does not attach. For example, D sets fire to V's house, seeking to kill her, but V escapes. D may be tried for both arson and attempted murder, and an acquittal on one charge will not bar prosecution on the other, because attempted murder requires proof of an additional fact—namely, intent to kill.

D. Conduct That Constitutes an Offense for Which the Defendant Has Already Been Prosecuted

This is a variation of the "same offense" concept. The Court has ruled that the double jeopardy clause bars a subsequent prosecution if, to establish an essential element of an offense charged in that prosecution, the government will have to prove *conduct that constitutes an offense for which the defendant has already been prosecuted* (Grady v. Corbin, 58 L.W. 4599 [1990]). In that case, Corbin's car struck two oncoming vehicles on a New York highway, causing the death of one person and injury to another. Corbin was issued two traffic tickets and charged with the misdemeanor of driving while intoxicated and with failing to keep the right of the median. Corbin pleaded guilty to the traffic tickets in the Town Justice Court. At the time of the guilty plea, the presiding judge did not know of an impending negligent homicide charge or investigation stemming out of the same incidents. Subsequently, Corbin was indicted by a grand jury with reckless manslaughter, criminally negligent homicide, and third-degree reckless assault. To prove these charges, the prosecution would have to establish that the defendant had been (1) operating a motor vehicle on a public highway in an intoxicated condition; (2) failing to keep right of the median; and (3) driving at a speed too fast for the weather and road conditions. Corbin claimed double jeopardy. On appeal, the Court upheld Corbin's contention, ruling that to prove the subsequent offenses the prosecution "would have to prove conduct that constituted offenses to which Corbin had already pleaded guilty." The Court said that "by its own pleadings, the State has admitted that it will prove the entirety of the conduct for which Corbin was convicted—driving while intoxicated and failing to keep right of the median—to establish essential elements of the homicide and assault offenses." Double jeopardy therefore attached, and Corbin could no longer be prosecuted for the second set of charges stemming from the same incident.

This decision, handed down by the Court on May 29, 1990, has caused concern and confusion in many police departments and prosecutors' offices. It is, however, basically a reiteration of a much earlier decision where the Court said that a second prosecution is barred if the two prosecutions reveal that the offenses have identical statutory elements or that one is a lesser included offense of the other (Blackbuster v. U.S., 284 U.S. 299 [1932]). The Corbin decision has two policy implications for police agencies and prosecutors. The first is to adopt policies that avoid situations such as in Corbin wherein an offender was allowed to plead guilty to misdemeanor traffic offenses when more serious ones were still being investigated or were pending. In the Corbin case, there was serious lack of information dissemination. The second police implication is that in offenses of this nature it may be best to completely forgo a lower charge and wait for the more serious charge to develop, if that is a distinct possibility. The problem is that this is easier said than done in jurisdictions that handle thousands of cases and employ hundreds of personnel and where careful monitoring of cases may be difficult.

E. What "Lesser Included Offense" Means

Double jeopardy attaches when the second prosecution is for a *lesser included offense.* For example, X is charged with murder and acquitted. He cannot be prosecuted again for criminally negligent homicide arising out of the same act. Note that if X is charged with murder, in most states he can be convicted of criminally negligent homicide in the same proceeding. Consequently prosecutors usually charge an accused with the highest possible offense warranted by the facts. If the highest charge fails, the accused may still be convicted of a lesser offense. In contrast, an accused can never be convicted of an offense higher than that with which he or she was charged; that would be a violation of an accused's constitutional rights.

F. Prosecution for the Same Offense by Two States—Valid

In a 1985 case, the Court decided that under the dual sovereignty doctrine, successive prosecutions by two states for the same conduct do not violate the "double jeopardy" clause of the Fifth Amendment (Heath v. Alabama, 54 L.W. 4016 [1985]). In the Heath case, the defendant had hired two men to kill his wife. In accordance with the defendant's plan, the hired men kidnapped his wife from their home in Alabama. Her body was later found on the side of a road in Georgia. The defendant pleaded guilty to murder with "malice" in a Georgia court in exchange for a sentence of life imprisonment. Subsequently, he was tried and convicted of murder during a kidnapping (arising out of the same act) by an Alabama trial court and was sentenced to death. His claim of double jeopardy was rejected by the Alabama court, so he appealed his conviction to the U.S. Supreme Court. In rejecting the double jeopardy claim, the Court said that the dual sovereignty doctrine provides that when a defendant in a single act violates the "peace and dignity" of two sovereigns by breaking the laws of each, the defendant has committed two distinct offenses for double jeopardy purposes. The crucial question is whether the two entities that seek to prosecute a defendant successively for the same course of conduct can be termed separate sovereigns. If they are, no double jeopardy occurs. The states of Georgia and Alabama are separate from the federal government and each other; hence there is no double jeopardy. For purposes of criminal law and criminal procedure, therefore, there are in effect fifty-one different sovereigns in the United States, referring to the fifty states and the federal government.

X. THE INSANITY DEFENSE

The *insanity defense* frees a defendant from criminal liability because intent (mens rea) is one of the elements of a criminal act. An accused who was insane at the time of the crime lacks this required intent and therefore should not be punished like other criminals. In the words of Judge David Bazelon, "Our collective conscience does not allow punishment where it cannot impose blame."[2] Insanity, though often used in homicide or murder cases, is a defense in all crimes. It is used in federal and state criminal cases in all but the two states where the insanity defense has been abolished (Montana in 1979 and Idaho in 1982).

A. The Four Insanity Tests

There are four tests used by various jurisdictions to determine whether or not the accused was insane when committing the criminal act.

1. The M'Naghten Test

One who commits a criminal act will be excused from criminal liability if, as a result of a mental disease, the *"accused did not know the nature or quality of his act; or if he did not know that what he did was wrong."* This is the second most popular test; the American Law Institute test is first.

2. The "Irresistible Impulse" Test

One who commits a criminal act will be excused from criminal liability if, "as a result of a mental disease, the accused *did not know the nature or quality of his act; or he did not know that what he was doing was wrong; or if he did not have the ability to control his conduct even if he knew that what he was doing was wrong."* The loss of control must be the result of a mental disease and not just anger, jealousy, or voluntary intoxication. This is known in some legal circles as the "policeman at the elbow" test, meaning that the offender's impulse to commit the act was so irresistible that he would have done it even if a police officer had been at his elbow. The test is used in a number of states, in some cases as a supplement to the M'Naghten test.

3. The American Law Institute (or Model Penal Code) Test

One who commits a criminal act will be excused from criminal liability if it is proved that as a result of suffering from a mental disease or defect, the accused *"lacked substantial capacity either to appreciate the wrongfulness of his or her conduct or to conform his or her conduct to the requirements of the law."* This test does not require the accused's complete lack of knowledge that what he or she did was wrong. All that is needed is proof that the accused lacked the substantial capacity (less strict than complete lack of knowledge) to know right from wrong or to conform his or her conduct to the requirement of the law. This test combines the M'Naghten and the "irresistible impulse" tests and is used in all federal courts and in twenty-five states.

4. The Durham (or Product) Test

One who commits a criminal act will be excused from criminal liability if *"his action was the product of a mental disease or defect."* This means that the accused would not have committed the act "but for" some mental disease. This test is now seldom used.

B. Comparison of the Four Tests

How do the four tests differ from each other? The *M'Naghten test* requires the accused's complete lack of knowledge of the wrongness of what he or she did (or the nature or quality of the act), the lack of knowledge being caused by a mental disease. The *"irresistible impulse" test* says that the accused may or may not know right from wrong, but the crucial element is that he or she cannot control the impulse to commit the act. The *"substantial capacity" test* does not require complete lack of knowledge on the part of the accused that what he or she did was wrong. All that is needed is proof that the accused lacked the substantial capacity to know right from wrong or to conform his or her conduct to the requirement of the law. The *Durham test* requires only that what the accused did was a "product" (although not totally) of a mental disease. The term "product" can mean that the act was 40 percent, 30 percent, or perhaps 20 percent caused by a mental disease—depending upon the standard set by the judge or jury. Whatever that degree of proof may be, it is certainly lower than that required under the other three tests.

The insanity test used in a state is a matter of legislative or, in the absence thereof, judicial choice. In general, prosecutors prefer the M'Naghten test because that test makes it difficult for the defendant to establish insanity. Conversely, defense lawyers prefer the Durham test because it is easier for the defendant to prove that the criminal act was in some way the product of a mental disease or defect and that "but for" the mental disease the act would not have been committed.

C. Incompetency to Stand Trial versus Insanity

Questioning a defendant's competency to stand trial is distinguished from the insanity defense in that in competency cases the accused may have been sane or insane during the commission of the offense. What is under question is the accused's mental condition at the time of the trial. If an accused is incompetent to stand trial, then the trial is simply postponed until such time as the incompetency is cured or removed and competency has been established. The insanity defense looks at the mental condition of the accused at the time the act was committed. It has nothing to do with the accused's condition at the time of the trial. Incompetency to stand trial is not a defense; it merely postpones the trial.

D. Burden of Proof

The success of the insanity defense oftentimes hinges on who bears the *burden of proof*. In about half of the states, a defendant is presumed sane when committing the criminal act. The burden is therefore on the defendant to prove, by a preponderance of the evidence (meaning more than 50 percent certainty), that he or she was insane at the time of the crime. This may be difficult for the defendant to establish; thus the insanity defense is likely to fail. Other jurisdictions provide that once the issue of insanity has been raised by the defense, the prosecution has the burden of proving that the defendant was in fact sane beyond a reasonable doubt (although some jurisdictions require only a preponderance of the evidence). In these jurisdictions, it is very difficult for the prosecution to prove that the defendant in fact was sane, and so the insanity defense succeeds.

At the time of John W. Hinckley's attempt to assassinate President Reagan, federal law provided that once the issue of insanity had been raised by the defense, the prosecution had the burden of proving beyond reasonable doubt that the defendant was sane at the time the act was committed. In the Hinckley case, there was no way the prosecution could have proved beyond reasonable doubt that John Hinckley was sane at the time he shot President Reagan. The act itself and the reasons given were so irrational that they constituted strong evidence that there was something terribly wrong psychologically with Hinckley. The results would perhaps have been different if Hinckley's defense lawyers had been required by law to prove, even by mere preponderance of the evidence, that he was insane at the time of the shooting. At least the prosecutors could have countered by saying that Hinckley knew what he was doing.

As a result of the Hinckley case, the insanity defense in federal courts was changed in 1984 (the Comprehensive Crime Control Act), placing the burden on the defendant to establish insanity by clear and convincing evidence.

E. The Insanity Defense Issue Summarized

In an article titled, "Insanity Defense," written for the National Institute of Justice *Crime File Study Guide,* Norval Morris summarizes the insanity defense standards just discussed and the present federal law on the insanity defense, as shown in Table 12.1.[3]

TABLE 12.1

Test	Legal standard because of mental illness	Final burden of proof	Who bears burden of proof
M'Naghten	"Didn't know what he was doing or didn't know it was wrong"	Varies from proof by a balance of probabilities on the defense to proof beyond a reasonable doubt on the prosecutor	
Irresistible impulse	"Could not control his conduct"		
Durham	"The criminal act was caused by his mental illness"	Beyond reasonable doubt	Prosecutor
American Law Institute (model penal code)	"Lacks substantial capacity to appreciate the wrongfulness of his conduct or to control it"	Beyond reasonable doubt	Prosecutor
Present federal law	"Lacks capacity to appreciate the wrongfulness of his conduct"	Clear and convincing evidence	Defense

XI. THE ENTRAPMENT DEFENSE

Entrapment is defined as the act of government officers or agents in inducing a person to commit a crime that is not contemplated by the person, for the purpose of instituting a criminal prosecution against him or her. There is a difference, however, between entrapment and merely providing an opportunity for a person to commit a crime. For example, it is not entrapment for a female police officer to act as a decoy and walk through a high-crime part of downtown at night as a possible target for robbers, muggers, or rapists. The officer is merely providing an opportunity for the commission of a crime.

A. Basis

The entrapment defense is not based on any provision of the Constitution, but rather on the presumed intent of the legislators when enacting criminal laws. The Court has found it difficult to believe that legislators (federal or state) allow government officials to lure otherwise innocent persons into committing crimes so that these persons can be punished (Sorrells v. U.S., 287 U.S. 435 [1932]).

B. Entrapment Tests

There are two basic tests used by states to determine if entrapment by government officers did in fact take place: the *subjective* test and the *objective* test.

1. The Subjective Test

The federal government and most states use this test, which focuses on the *predisposition of the defendant* to commit the offense with which he or she is charged. Under this test, entrapment exists only if the accused had no predisposition to commit the offense, but did so because of inducement by the government agent. If the accused was predisposed to commit the offense, then there is no entrapment—regardless of the government agent's conduct—because the accused is then an "unwary criminal," not an "unwary innocent."

> Example: A police detective propositions a known prostitute in a bar. The officer mentions the price, location, time, and type of service expected. Despite initiation of negotiation and inducement by the officer, the prostitute cannot claim entrapment because she was predisposed to commit the offense. Under this test, therefore, the defendant's character and prior record become relevant issues and thus may be admitted as evidence in court during trial.

2. The Objective Test

This test, used in some states, rejects the predisposition test as too harsh and focuses instead on an analysis of the *conduct of the government agent.* The test asks whether the activities of the government agent were so instigative in nature that they might well have induced an otherwise innocent person to commit the crime. This means that the accused's past criminal activity is irrelevant and therefore evidence to prove prior similar conduct is not admissible.

> Given the preceding example of the detective and the prostitute, entrapment will be a valid defense by the objective test because the agent's activities might be so instigative in nature as to induce an otherwise innocent person at that specific time (though admittedly a prostitute) to commit the crime. The determination as to when an agent's conduct is so instigative as to constitute entrapment is a question of fact to be determined by a judge or jury.

State law or court decision determines which test (or what modification of the test) is to be used in a particular jurisdiction. The U.S. Supreme Court has not mandated any specific test to be used by the courts.

A leading case on the entrapment defense is United States v. Russell, 411 U.S. 423 (1973). In the Russell case, the defendant and two others were indicted and convicted of illegally manufacturing and selling methamphetamine, a prohibited drug. A government agent had earlier met with the three accused and offered to supply them with phenyl-2-propanone, a chemical required to manufacture methamphetamine. In return, the agent wanted to receive one-half of the drug made. The agent later received his share and also bought some of the remainder from Russell. Russell was charged, tried, and convicted. On appeal, Russell conceded that the jury could have found him predisposed to commit the offenses with which he was charged, but argued that there had been entrapment. The Court held that the act by a government agent of supplying one of the necessary ingredients for the manufacture of a prohibited drug did not constitute an entrapment. The Court said that the agent's conduct had stopped far short of a violation of "fundamental fairness." This statement implies that certain types of governmental conduct may be so outrageous that the entrapment defense prevails even if the defendant was predisposed to commit the offense. The Court added that this was a case of an accused who was an "unwary criminal" and not an "unwary innocent," for whom the entrapment defense would have been available. (Read the U.S. v. Russell case brief at the end of this chapter.)

C. Defendant May Deny Elements of Offense Charged and Still Claim Entrapment

The issue of whether or not the defendant must admit all elements of the offense charged to be able to claim entrapment had divided federal courts of appeals for a long time.[4] That split has now been resolved. The Court has decided that a defendant (in this case a federal court defendant) need not admit all the elements of the offense charged so as to obtain a jury instruction on entrapment (Mathews v. U.S. 42 CrL 3069 [1988]). In that case, Mathews, a federal employee, was accused of asking for loans from a company he was supposed to be helping. At his trial he claimed entrapment, but at the same time refused to admit that he had the requisite intent to accept an unlawful gratuity. The trial court ruled such a claim to be inconsistent with denial of intent, a ruling affirmed by the Seventh Circuit. On appeal, the Court said that even if the defendant denied an element of the crime he was entitled to an entrapment instruction as long as there was sufficient evidence from which a reasonable jury could find entrapment.

☐ SUMMARY

The Bill of Rights in the U.S. Constitution is the main source of rights for an accused during trial. These rights were originally applied only in federal criminal proceedings; however, the U.S. Supreme Court has decided that most of these rights should also be applied in state criminal cases. Except for the right to grand jury indictment and the right against excessive bail, all the protections in the Bill of Rights now apply in state as well as federal criminal proceedings.

An accused is entitled to a fair and impartial trial. This means that a person must be convicted by an impartial tribunal and that the conviction must be based solely on the evidence admitted at the trial—not on other sources, such as newspaper or television. The right to confrontation of witnesses means the right to cross-examine the witnesses for the opposing side.

The right to a speedy and public trial has not received as much attention from the Court as other rights, but federal and some state statutes now set a time limit within which cases must be disposed of or dismissed. Trial by jury is required in all "serious" criminal cases—meaning cases in which the possible penalty is imprisonment for more than six months. Federal cases need twelve-member juries and a unanimous conviction; but the Court has decided that states are not constitutionally required to have a jury of twelve (even in felony cases) or a unanimous verdict for conviction.

The accused is also given the right to compulsory process to obtain witnesses. This includes the right to present a defense: The defendant must be given the opportunity to present his or her own witnesses and his or her own version of the facts.

The privilege against self-incrimination protects an accused from being forced to testify at all in court and protects any witness from being compelled to answer a question that would "tend to incriminate" him or her. The privilege applies only to testimonial evidence, not physical evidence. The right to counsel refers to retained or court-appointed counsel. It applies at every "critical stage" of the criminal proceeding, not just during the trial itself.

In all criminal proceedings, the accused may be convicted only upon proof of guilt beyond a reasonable doubt. Although difficult to define, this requirement ensures that flimsy evidence cannot be the basis of conviction.

The guarantee against double jeopardy ensures that once a person has been tried for an offense, the person cannot be tried again for the same offense unless he or she appeals his conviction—in which case the person is considered to have waived this right. There are other instances when double jeopardy is deemed waived, such as in mistrials or when the verdict of conviction is set aside on defendant's motion or appeal.

Insanity and entrapment are two defenses defendants often use in criminal trials. The insanity defense is undergoing review in many states, both to reconsider the test used to determine insanity and to determine whether the burden of proving sanity or insanity lies with the prosecution or the defense. Entrapment takes place when the act of government officers or agents induces a person to commit a crime. Providing an opportunity, however, for the commission of an offense does not constitute entrapment.

☐ REVIEW QUESTIONS

    1. Suppose California passes a law providing that all crimes are to be tried by six-member juries; will such a law be constitutional? Suppose the same law provides that a 5-to-1 vote for conviction results in conviction; will the law be valid? Explain your answer.

2. Give four ways whereby a trial judge may be able to control the impact of prejudicial trial publicity. Briefly discuss each.
3. Is a defendant entitled to a lawyer in all judicial trials regardless of the offense charged? Discuss your answer.
4. Discuss the standard currently used by the Court to determine ineffective counsel.
5. Compare and contrast the privilege against self-incrimination of an accused and a witness.
6. A witness has been given immunity to testify in a state court proceeding. May that witness refuse to testify on the ground that whatever he or she says in a state court proceeding may be used against him or her later in a federal criminal trial? Discuss.
7. What is meant by "effective assistance of counsel"?
8. Give two instances in which double jeopardy is deemed waived. Discuss each.
9. What does the term "same offense" mean in criminal prosecutions? How about "lesser included offenses"?
10. Distinguish and discuss the four tests used in insanity cases.
11. Distinguish between the subjective test and the objective test used in the entrapment defense.
12. What did the Court hold in United States v. Russell? What entrapment test was used in the Russell case?

☐ DEFINITIONS

American Law Institute (or Model Penal Code) Test for Insanity: One who commits a criminal act will be excused from criminal liability if it is proved that as a result of suffering from a mental disease or defect, the accused lacked substantial capacity either to appreciate the wrongfulness of his or her conduct or to conform his or her conduct to the requirements of the law.

Double Jeopardy: The successive prosecution of a defendant for the same offense by the same jurisdiction.

Durham (or Product) Test for Insanity: One who commits a criminal act will be excused from criminal liability if his or her action was the product of a mental disease or defect.

Entrapment: The act of government officers or agents in inducing a person to commit a crime that is not contemplated by him or her, for the purpose of instituting a criminal prosecution against the person.

Fair Response: A concept providing that a prosecutor's statement to the jury during closing argument that the defendant could have taken the witness stand, but refused to do so, is proper as long as it is in response to defense counsel's argument that the government had not allowed the defendant to explain his or her side of the story.

Federal Speedy Trial Act of 1974:   A law that specifies time standards for each stage in the federal court process. Thirty days are allowed from arrest to the filing of an indictment or an information; seventy days are allowed between information or indictment and trial.

Immunity: Exemption from prosecution granted to a witness in exchange for testimony against a suspect or an accused.

"Irresistible Impulse" Test for Insanity: One who commits a criminal act will be excused from liability if, as a result of a mental disease, the accused did not know the nature or quality of his or her act; or did not know that what he or she was doing was wrong; or did not have the ability to control his or her conduct even if the accused knew that what he or she was doing was wrong.

M'Naghten Test for Insanity: One who commits a criminal act will be excused from criminal liability if, as a result of a mental disease, the accused did not know the nature or quality of his or her act, or did not know that what he or she did was wrong.

Nonunanimous Verdict: Verdict for conviction that is not the product of a unanimous vote by jury members. A 9-to-3 vote for conviction has been declared constitutional by the Court.

Objective Test for Entrapment: There is entrapment if the activities of the government agent were so instigative in nature that they might well have induced an otherwise innocent person to commit the crime. This is the minority view.

Physical Self-Incrimination: A form of self-incrimination, not protected under the Fifth Amendment, that stems from real or physical evidence. Examples are footprints, fingerprints, blood, or urine samples.

Public Trial: A trial open to persons interested in ensuring that the proceedings are fair and just.

Reasonable Doubt: Such a doubt as would cause a juror, after careful and candid and impartial consideration of all the evidence, to be so undecided that he or she cannot say that he or she has an abiding conviction of the defendant's guilt.

Sequestration: The practice of keeping jurors together during the trial and strictly controlling their contact with the outside world.

Speedy Trial: A trial that is free from unnecessary and unwanted delay.

Statute of Limitations: Law providing that a crime must be prosecuted within a certain period of time, otherwise it lapses and can no longer be prosecuted.

Subjective Test for Entrapment: Entrapment exists only if the accused has no predisposition to commit the offense, but did so because of inducement by the government agent. This is the majority view.

Testimonial Self-Incrimination: A form of self-incrimination, protected under the Fifth Amendment, that in itself explicitly or implicitly relates a factual assertion or discloses information. It is in the form of verbal or oral communication.

Transactional Immunity: A type of immunity that exempts the witness from prosecution for any offense arising out of an act or transaction.

Use-and-Derivative-Use Immunity: A type of immunity that assures the witness that his or her testimony and evidence derived from it will not be used against him or her in a subsequent prosecution; however, the witness can be prosecuted on the basis of evidence other than his or her own testimony, if the prosecutor has such independent evidence.

☐ PRINCIPLES OF CASES

ARGERSINGER V. HAMLIN, 407 U.S. 25 (1972)   The right to counsel applies even in misdemeanor cases if the accused faces the possibility of imprisonment, however short.

BALDWIN V. NEW YORK, 399 U.S. 66 (1970)   An offense is considered serious if the maximum punishment authorized by statute is imprisonment for more than six months, regardless of the actual penalty imposed. Therefore, the accused is entitled to a jury trial.

BALLEW V. GEORGIA, 435 U.S. 223 (1978)   The minimum number of jurors is six. Juries of five or fewer members are unconstitutional because the membership is too small to provide effective group discussion. Juries of less than six members would also diminish the chances of drawing from a fair section of the community, thus impairing the accuracy of fact finding.

BALTIMORE CITY DEPARTMENT OF SOCIAL SERVICES V. BOUKNIGHT, 46 CrL 2096 (1990)   Even though requiring the custodial parent to produce the child could be self-incriminating, a parent who agreed to extensive conditions in assuming custody of such child may be required to produce that child in court or otherwise face contempt citation.

BARKER V. WINGO, 407 U.S. 514 (1972)   Violation of the right to a speedy trial is not established by delay alone. Rather, the determination requires a balancing test in which the conduct of both the prosecution and the defense are weighed and the following factors are considered: (1) length of delay, (2) reason for delay, (3) defendant's assertion or nonassertion of rights, and (4) prejudice to the defendant. Usually, any one factor alone is not sufficient to justify or condemn the delay in the trial.

BATSON V. KENTUCKY, 39 CrL 3047 (1986)   A prosecutor's use of peremptory challenges to exclude from a jury members of the defendant's race solely on racial grounds violates the "equal protection" rights of both the defendant and the excluded jurors.

BLANTON V. NORTH LAS VEGAS, 109 S.Ct. 1289 (1989)   When a state treats drunken driving as a petty offense, no jury trial is needed even if other peripheral sanctions (such as a fine and automatic loss of driver's license) may also be imposed.

BURKS V. UNITED STATES, 437 U.S. 1 (1978)   A defendant whose conviction is reversed because the evidence is insufficient as a matter of law to sustain the conviction cannot be retried; such a reversal amounts to an acquittal.

CHAMBERS V. MISSISSIPPI, 410 U.S. 284 (1973)   The defendant offered evidence of oral confession to the crime by another witness. The trial court excluded the evidence because it constituted inadmissible hearsay under the local rules of evidence. This ruling was held to violate the defendant's right to present a defense, since the confessions bore substantial assurances of trustworthiness.

COLEMAN V. ALABAMA, 399 U.S. 1 (1970)   A lawyer is required in a preliminary hearing to determine whether there is sufficient evidence against the accused to go to a grand jury.

COY V. IOWA, 108 S.Ct. 2798 (1988)   The right to confrontation includes the right to physically face witnesses at trial, hence a state law that allows testimony via closed-circuit television or behind a screen violates defendant's Sixth Amendment right.

FARETTA V. CALIFORNIA, 422 U.S. 806 (1975)   An accused has a constitutional right to waive counsel and represent himself or herself in a criminal proceeding.

FULLER V. OREGON, 417 U.S. 40 (1974)   A system that provides counsel to defendants, but specifies as a condition of probation or parole that the defendant reimburse the state or county for the fees of the appointed lawyer, is valid as long as it exempts indigents who cannot afford to pay.

GAULT, IN RE, 387 U.S. 1 (1967)   Although juvenile proceedings are not criminal in nature, a juvenile is nonetheless entitled to appointed counsel if the proceeding can lead to commitment in an institution in which the juvenile's freedom is restricted.

GEDERS V. UNITED STATES, 425 U.S. 80 (1976)   During the trial itself, a judge may not prevent the defendant from talking with counsel during an overnight recess, otherwise his or her right to counsel is violated.

GIDEON V. WAINWRIGHT, 372 U.S. 335 (1963)   The Sixth Amendment right to counsel was held applicable to state proceedings via the "due process" clause of the Fourteenth Amendment. The right to counsel applies every time an accused is charged with a felony offense.

GILBERT V. CALIFORNIA, 388 U.S. 263 (1967)   A defendant can be forced to stand up for identification in the courtroom, put on certain items of clothing, or give a handwriting sample.

GRADY V. CORBIN, 58 L.W. 4599 (1990)   The double jeopardy clause bars a subsequent prosecution if, to establish an essential element of an offense charged in that prosecution, the government will have to prove conduct that constitutes an offense for which the defendant has already been prosecuted.

GREEN V. UNITED STATES, 355 U.S. 184 (1957)   A defendant who appeals a conviction and obtains a new trial cannot be charged with an offense that is higher than that for which he or she was originally convicted.

GRIFFIN V. CALIFORNIA, 380 U.S. 609 (1965)   The prosecutor is not permitted to make any comment or argument to the jury suggesting that the defendant is guilty because he or she refused to testify; making such comments leads to a reversal on appeal of the conviction.

HEATH V. ALABAMA, 54 L.W. 4016 (1985)   Under the dual sovereignty doctrine, successive prosecutions by two states for the same conduct do not violate the "double jeopardy" clause of the Fifth Amendment.

HOLLAND V. ILLINOIS, 46 CrL 2067 (1990)   The prosecution's racially motivated use of peremptory challenges to exclude people from the trial jury does not violate the defendant's Sixth Amendment right to trial by an impartial jury. The Court hinted, however, that such challenge could have been raised as a violation of the constitutional right to equal protection.

ILLINOIS V. ALLEN, 397 U.S. 337 (1970)   The following methods for dealing with a disruptive defendant are approved: (1) holding the defendant in contempt of court, (2) binding and gagging the defendant in the courtroom, and (3) removing the defendant from the courtroom until he or she promises to behave properly.

IRWIN V. DOWD, 366 U.S. 717 (1961)   Headlines announced that the defendant had confessed to six murders and twenty-four burglaries, and reports were widely circulated that the defendant had offered to plead guilty. Ninety percent of the prospective jurors interviewed expressed an opinion that the defendant was guilty, and eight out of twelve jurors finally seated held such a belief. All these circumstances denied the defendant his "due process" right, particularly because this was a capital-punishment case.

JOHNSON V. LOUISIANA, 406 U.S. 356 (1972)   A nine-out-of-twelve jury verdict for conviction is constitutional.

MAINE V. MOULTON, 54 L.W. 4039 (1985)   The right to counsel applies at a meeting in which the defendant's defense strategy is discussed and which the police knew or should have known would produce incriminating statements. Therefore, conversations recorded during this meeting between the defendant and his codefendant, who was a government informer, in the absence of a lawyer, cannot be admitted in court.

MARYLAND V. CRAIG, 47 CrL 2258 (1990)   Despite defendant's Sixth Amendment right, face-to-face confrontation may be dispensed with when preventing such confrontation is necessary to further important public policy and the reliability of the testimony is otherwise assured.

MASSIAH V. UNITED STATES, 377 U.S. 201 (1964)   Noncustodial interrogations made after the accused has been formally charged are not admissible in evidence if made in the absence of a lawyer and using a federal agent who has been "wired for sound."

MOORE V. UNITED STATES, 345 F.2d 97 (DC Cir. 1965)   This case defines "reasonable doubt" as follows: "It is such a doubt as would cause a juror, after careful and candid and impartial consideration of all the evidence, to be so undecided that he cannot say that he has an abiding conviction of the defendant's guilt."

MURPHY V. WATERFRONT COMMISSION, 378 U.S. 52 (1964)   If a state has granted the witness valid immunity from prosecution, the federal government is not permitted to make use of the testimony (or any of its "fruits") in a federal prosecution against the witness.

PENNSYLVANIA V. MUNIZ, 58 L.W. 4817 (1990)   Asking people suspected of driving while intoxicated routine questions and videotaping their responses do not elicit testimonial responses that are protected by the right against self-incrimination.

PERRY V. LEEKE, 109 S.Ct. 594 (1989)   A defendant who takes the witness stand has no Sixth Amendment right to consult with his or her lawyer during a brief 15-minute recess while testifying.

POWELL V. ALABAMA, 287 U.S. 45 (1932)   The trial in state court of nine youths for a capital offense without a defense lawyer violated their right to due process.

RIDEAU V. LOUISIANA, 373 U.S. 723 (1963)   Police arranged to have the defendant's prior confession shown several times on local television. The Court held that the defendant had in effect been "tried" thereby and that no actual prejudice need be shown to establish a denial of due process under such circumstances.

SCOTT V. ILLINOIS, 440 U.S. 367 (1979)   An accused charged with a misdemeanor offense does not have to be provided a lawyer if the sentence imposed does not involve any prison or jail term.

SHEPPARD V. MAXWELL, 384 U.S. 333 (1966)   A courtroom television process that is so distractive to the judge, jurors, witnesses, and counsel that it creates a "carnival atmosphere" denies the defendant a fair trial.

SINGER V. UNITED STATES, 380 U.S. 24 (1965)   The prosecution has the right to demand a trial by jury even if the defendant waives it. Criminal defendants have no constitutional right to have their cases tried before a judge alone.

SORRELLS V. UNITED STATES, 287 U.S. 435 (1932)   The Court said it is difficult to believe that legislators permit government officials to lure otherwise innocent persons into committing crimes so that the government can punish them; hence the entrapment defense is available.

SOUTH DAKOTA V. NEVILLE, 459 U.S. 553 (1983)   A law that allows the accused to refuse to take a blood-alcohol test and provides that such refusal may be admitted in evidence against him or her is constitutional.

STRICKLAND V. WASHINGTON, 104 S.Ct. 2052 (1984)   The Court assumes that effective assistance of counsel is present unless the adversarial process is so undermined by counsel's conduct that the trial cannot be relied upon to have produced a just result. An accused who claims ineffective counsel must show the following: (1) deficient performance by counsel and (2) a reasonable probability that but for such deficiency the result of the proceedings would have been different.

TAYLOR V. LOUISIANA, 419 U.S. 522 (1975)   Excluding women from juries, or giving them automatic exemptions with the result that jury panels are almost totally male, is invalid.

TAYLOR V. UNITED STATES, 414 U.S. 17 (1973)   If an accused is present at the start of the trial but later voluntarily absents himself or herself, the Court has held that the trial may continue in the absence of the accused, meaning that the accused is considered to have waived his or her right to be present.

UNITED STATES V. CRONIC, 104 S.Ct. 2039 (1984)   A claim of ineffective assistance of counsel can be made only by pointing out specific errors of trial counsel. It cannot be based on an inference drawn from defense counsel's inexperience or lack to time to prepare, gravity of the charges, complexity of defense, or accessibility of witness to counsel.

UNITED STATES V. ROBINSON, 42 CrL 3063 (1988)   A prosecutor's statement to the jury during closing argument that the defendant could have taken the witness stand, but refused to do that, is proper as long as it is in response to defense counsel's argument that the government had not allowed the defendant to explain his or her side of the story.

UNITED STATES V. RUSSELL, 411 U.S. 423 (1973)   The act of a government agent of supplying one of the necessary ingredients for the manufacture of a prohibited drug does not constitute entrapment.

UNITED STATES V. WADE, 388 U.S. 218 (1967)   A postindictment line-up in which witnesses seek to identify the accused requires the presence of a lawyer.

WEBB V. TEXAS, 409 U.S. 95 (1972)   If the trial judge makes threatening remarks to the only defense witness, in effect driving the witness from the stand, the accused is deprived of the right to present a defense.

WHEAT V. UNITED STATES, 43 CrL 3037 (1988)   A defendant's right to hire an attorney of his or her own choosing is not absolute and may be overriden by the trial court if necessary to avoid conflicts of interest.

WILLIAMS V. FLORIDA, 399 U.S. 78 (1970)   A Florida law providing for a six-member jury in all criminal cases except those involving capital offenses is constitutional.

WITHERSPOON V. ILLINOIS, 391 U.S. 510 (1968)   It is unconstitutional to exclude for cause potential jurors who have reservations about the death penalty.

☐ CASE BRIEF—LEADING CASE ON SELF-INCRIMINATION

SOUTH DAKOTA V. NEVILLE, 459 U.S. 553 (1983)

FACTS: South Dakota law permits a person suspected of driving while intoxicated to submit to a blood-alcohol test and authorizes revocation of the driver's license of any person who refuses to take the test. The statute permits such refusal to be used against the driver as evidence of guilt during the trial. Defendant Neville was arrested by the police in South Dakota for driving while intoxicated. He was asked to submit to a blood-alcohol test and warned that he could lose his license if he refused to take the test. He was not warned, however, that the refusal could be used against him during trial. Neville refused to take the test. During trial, Neville sought to exclude the evidence obtained, claiming that it violated his right to protection against compulsory self-incrimination. The trial court granted the motion to suppress, a ruling affirmed by the South Dakota Supreme Court. The state appealed to the U.S. Supreme Court.

ISSUE: *Does a state law that allows the admission into evidence of a suspect's refusal to submit to a blood-alcohol test violate a suspect's Fifth Amendment right not to incriminate oneself? No.*

SUPREME COURT DECISION: The admission into evidence of a defendant's refusal to submit to a blood-alcohol test does not offend the suspect's Fifth Amendment right to avoid compulsory self-incrimination. A refusal to take such a test, after a police officer has lawfully requested it, is not an act coerced by the officer, and thus is not protected by the Fifth Amendment.

CASE SIGNIFICANCE: This case legitimizes the practice, established by law in many states, of giving suspected DWI offenders a choice to take or refuse blood-alcohol tests but then using a refusal as evidence of guilt later in court. The defendant in this case argued that introducing such evidence in court in effect coerces the suspect to waive constitutional protection against self-incrimination because of the consequence. The Court rejected this contention, saying that any incrimination resulting from a blood-alcohol test is physical in nature, not testimonial or communicative, and hence is not protected by the Fifth Amendment. Therefore, a suspect has no constitutional right to refuse to take the test. The Court said that the offer to the suspect to take the test is clearly legitimate and becomes no less legitimate when the state offers the option of refusing the test but prescribes consequences for making that choice. The Court added that the failure by the police to warn Neville that his refusal to take the test could be used as evidence against him during trial was not so fundamentally unfair as to deprive him of "due process" rights. Therefore, the evidence obtained could be admissible during trial. The case was remanded to the lower court for further proceedings. Note that in this case, the appeal from the lower court ruling was made by the prosecution, not the accused. Was the accused's right to protection against double jeopardy violated? There was no violation because the appeal involved the trial court's ruling to suppress the evidence on the ground that the constitutional rights of the accused were violated by the state law. The prosecution can appeal on questions of law without violating questions of fact. Besides, there had been no dismissal of the case against the accused prior to the appeal.

EXCERPTS FROM THE DECISION: Here, the state did not directly compel respondent to refuse the test, for it gave him the choice of submitting to the test or refusing. Of course, the fact the government gives a defendant or suspect a "choice" does not always resolve the compulsion inquiry. The classic Fifth Amendment violation—telling a defendant at trial to testify—does not, under an extreme view, compel the defendant to incriminate himself. He could submit to self-accusation, or testify falsely (risking perjury) or decline to testify (risking contempt). But the Court has long recognized that the Fifth Amendment prevents the state from forcing the choice of this "cruel trilemma" on the defendant. Similarly, Schmerber cautioned that the Fifth Amendment may bar the use of testimony obtained when the proffered alternative was to submit to a test so painful, dangerous, or severe, or so violative of religious beliefs, that almost inevitably a person would prefer "confession."

In contrast to these prohibited choices, the values behind the Fifth Amendment are not hindered when the state offers a suspect a choice of submitting to the blood-alcohol test or having his refusal used against him. The simple blood-alcohol test is so safe, painless, and commonplace that respondent concedes, as he must, that the state could legitimately compel the suspect, against his will, to accede to the test. Given, then, that the offer of taking a blood-alcohol test is clearly legitimate, the action becomes no less legitimate when the State offers a second option of refusing the test, with the attendant penalties for making that choice. Nor is this a case where the State has subtly coerced respondent into choosing the option it had no right to compel, rather than offering a true choice. To the contrary, the State wants respondent to choose to take the test, for the inference of intoxication arising from a positive blood-alcohol test is far stronger than that arising from a refusal to take the test. . . .

The judgment of the South Dakota Supreme Court is reversed, and the case is remanded for further proceedings not inconsistent with this opinion.

❏ CASE BRIEF—LEADING CASE ON ENTRAPMENT

UNITED STATES V. RUSSELL, 411 U.S. 423 (1973)

FACTS: Russell and two others were indicted and convicted of illegally manufacturing and selling methamphetamine ("speed"), a prohibited drug. Shapiro, an agent of the Federal Bureau of Narcotics and Dangerous Drugs, had earlier met with the three accused and told them that he represented a group desiring to obtain control of the manufacture and distribution of the drug. Shapiro offered to supply them with phenyl-2-propanone, a chemical required to manufacture methamphetamine. In return, Shapiro wanted to receive one-half of the speed made with the ingredient he supplied. Shapiro later received his share and also bought some of the remainder from Russell. There was testimony at the trial that phenyl-2-propanone was generally difficult to obtain. At the request of the Bureau of Narcotics and Dangerous Drugs, some chemical supply firms had voluntarily ceased to sell the chemical. On appeal, Russell conceded that the jury could have found him predisposed to commit the offenses with which he was charged, but argued that on the facts presented there was entrapment as a matter of law. The trial court rejected Russell's contention, but the Court of Appeals reversed, saying that the conduct of Shapiro in supplying a scarce ingredient essential for the manufacture of the controlled substance constituted entrapment. The case went to the Supreme Court.

ISSUE: *Did the act by the government undercover agent of providing an essential chemical for the manufacture of a prohibited drug constitute an entrapment of the defendant? No.*

SUPREME COURT DECISION: The act by a government agent of supplying one of the necessary ingredients for the manufacture of a prohibited drug does not constitute an entrapment. That conduct stops short of being a violation of "fundamental fairness" that would shock "the universal sense of justice." This is a case of an accused who was an "unwary criminal" and not an "unwary innocent," for whom the entrapment defense would have been available.

CASE SIGNIFICANCE: The Russell case exemplifies the majority view on the entrapment defense. This view focuses on the predisposition of the defendant to commit the alleged act rather than on an analysis of the conduct of the government agent. Under this view, the entrapment defense applies only if the accused has no predisposition to commit the crime, but did so because of inducement by a government agent. The Court minimized the importance of Shapiro's giving the accused an essential ingredient for the manufacture of the prohibited drug, saying that the chemical was a harmless substance and its possession legal. Besides, although it was difficult to obtain the chemical, the evidence showed that it was nonetheless obtainable; therefore the conduct of the government agent here stopped far short of violating that "fundamental fairness" mandated by the "due process" clause of the Fifth Amendment. In using this language, the Court strongly implies that even under the majority test, there may be conduct by the government agent that may entrap even a person who is predisposed to commit the crime. The court, however, did not give any example of that type of prohibited government conduct. Note that had the Court here used the minority (objective) test the accused would most probably have been acquitted.

EXCERPTS FROM THE DECISION: The record discloses that although the propanone was difficult to obtain it was by no means impossible. The defendants admitted making the drug both before and after those batches made with the propanone supplied by Shapiro. Shapiro testified that he saw an empty bottle labeled phenyl-2-propanone on his first visit to the laboratory on December 7, 1969. And when the laboratory was searched pursuant to a search warrant on January 10, 1970, two additional bottles labeled phenyl-2-propanone were seized. Thus, the facts in the record amply demonstrate that the propanone used in the illicit manufacture of methamphetamine not only could have been obtained without the intervention of Shapiro but was in fact obtained by these defendants.

While we may some day be presented with a situation in which the conduct of law enforcement agents is so outrageous that due process principles would absolutely bar the government from invoking judicial processes to obtain a conviction, the instant case is distinctly not of that breed. Shapiro's contribution of propanone to the criminal enterprise already in process was scarcely objectionable. The chemical is by itself a harmless substance and its possession is legal. While the government may have been seeking to make it more difficult for drug rings, such as that of which respondent was a member, to obtain the chemical, the evidence described above shows that it nonetheless was obtainable. The law enforcement conduct here stops far short of violating that "fundamental fairness, shocking to the universal sense of justice," mandated by the Due Process Clause of the Fifth Amendment.

□ NOTES

1. *Houston Chronicle,* July 21, 1990, at 1.
2. As quoted in Norval Morris, "Insanity Defense," *Crime File Study Guide* (Washington, DC: National Institute of Justice), at 1.
3. Ibid.
4. See 43 CrL 4123 (1988).

CHAPTER THIRTEEN

WITNESSES, THE HEARSAY RULE, AND PRIVILEGED COMMUNICATIONS

❑ KEY TERMS

direct examination	inference
repetitive questions	impeachment of witness
narrative questioning	Hearsay Rule
present recollection revived	confession
misleading question	admission
compound question	dying declaration
argumentative question	spontaneous declaration
conclusionary question	res gestae
cross-examination	past recollection recorded
redirect examination	business records
recross-examination	official records
opinion	privileged communication

Three of the topics with which law enforcement officers must be familiar are closely related to a criminal trial. Officers need to obtain basic knowledge about *witnesses* because in the course of police work an officer will doubtless be required to testify in court a number of times. Giving testimony is a necessary and important part of police work. The officer must be familiar with the method and scope of examining witnesses, the types of admissible testimony, and the basic ways whereby witnesses are impeached. Police officers are often the main source of witnesses for the prosecution, and therefore the officer must know who is competent to testify. Often, the officer initiates contact with the witnesses and obtains their statements in writing. An understanding of the *Hearsay Rule* is essential so that the officer knows what types of statements or writings might be admissible in court. For example, dying declarations are sometimes made in the presence of police officers. The admissibility of such evidence may make or break the case for the prosecution. As the term implies, *privileged communications* are protected from disclosure in court or anywhere else. The officer needs to know what types of communication by and from suspects are protected and whether the identity of his or her own informers need be disclosed in court.

I. WITNESSES

A. Competency to Testify

Under old English law, a person could be disqualified from giving testimony on a number of grounds, including having a financial interest in the outcome of the suit, being married to one of the parties, lack of religious belief, conviction of a felony, race, infancy, or mental derangement. The trend in modern law is to abolish all such grounds for disqualification. For example, the federal rule provides that in federal trials, "every person is competent to be a witness, except as otherwise provided by these rules." Most states have followed this trend.

Age is not a decisive factor in determining competency of witnesses. A child of any age may be permitted to testify as long as the trial judge is satisfied that the child possesses the ability to observe, recollect, and communicate. Similarly, a person with a mental impairment may testify as long as the trial judge is satisfied of his or her capacity to communicate and understand the duty to tell the truth. A convicted felon may also be competent to testify; however, the fact of conviction may be used to impeach his or her testimony.

Despite the trend in modern law to abolish common-law grounds for disqualification, a person still needs certain basic qualifications in order to be a witness:

a. *Ability to communicate.* The witness must be capable of expressing himself or herself so as to be understood by the jury—either directly or through an interpreter.

b. *Understanding of duty to tell the truth.* The judge must determine that the witness understands his or her duty to tell the truth. Witnesses always take an oath to "tell the truth, the whole truth, and nothing but the truth" before taking the witness stand.

c. *Personal knowledge of the facts.* A witness possessing personal knowledge is one who has a present recollection of an impression derived through any of his or her five senses. An expert witness is the exception to this rule.

B. Method and Scope of Examining Witnesses

The order of examination in a court trial is as follows:

Direct examination. The first questioning of a witness by the party who called him or her to the stand.

Cross-examination. Examination of the witness by the opposing lawyer following the direct examination.

Redirect examination. The further questioning of the witness by the party who called him or her to the stand.

Recross-examination. Examination of the witness by the cross-examiner following the redirect examination.

1. Direct Examination

Testimony from witnesses on direct examination is presented by placing the witness on the stand, having him or her sworn, and then asking the witness a series of questions. On direct examination, the lawyer is usually limited to questions calling for specific responses by the witness, such as questions preceded by "who," "where," "when," or "how." Certain forms of questioning are considered objectionable on direct examination. These include:

a. *Questions calling for conclusions.* "Did the defendant in this case see the injured person on the sidewalk?" calls for the witness's opinion on what the defendant did or did not see. Likewise, "Why did the defendant shoot the deceased?" calls for a conclusion about the defendant's state of mind.

b. *Repetitive questions.* These are questions designed to bolster or emphasize what has already been established; for example, "Tell us again, did you see the accused beat up the victim or not?"

c. *Narrative questioning.* Questions that alow the witness to tell a narrative are not permitted in many courts; for example, "Can you tell this court everything that happened on the evening of the accident?"

The use of *leading questions* on direct examination is also prohibited. A leading question is one that suggests to the witness the answer that the examining lawyer desires. For example, a lawyer asks, "The accused had a pistol in his hand when you saw him, did he not?" or "Is it not true that the argument was followed by a violent fight?" In both cases, the lawyer has suggested to the witness the answer he or she wants and all the witness need do is say yes. In some instances, leading questions are permitted in direct examination, either because there is little danger of improper suggestion or because such questions are necessary to obtain relevant evidence. These are the instances:

a. Establishment of preliminary or collateral matters that are not in issue, such as name, address, occupation, or date. "You are a detective in the Police Department, are you not?"
b. Reviving or refreshing a witness's memory. "To refresh your memory, Officer Jones, you in fact arrested the accused on December 15, did you not?"
c. Examination of handicapped, timid, or confused witnesses.
d. Examination of expert witnesses.
e. Examination of hostile witnesses.

If the witness on direct examination has absolutely no recollection regarding the matter at issue, he or she obviously is not competent to testify.

More often, however, the witness's memory is merely incomplete, meaning that the witness remembers the event in general, but not the essential details. In such cases, the direct examiner may seek to aid the witness's memory by using two different concepts—"present recollection revived" and "past recollection recorded."

The expression *present recollection revived* means that a testifying witness may refer to a writing or something else to refresh or revive his or her memory, so that he or she will thereafter be able to testify from memory. In contrast, *past recollection recorded* refers to instances when the witness has no independent recollection whatsoever of the contents of a document even after being shown the document. The witness will not be permitted to testify by relying on the writing, since he or she does not recollect anything. However, the contents of the writing itself might be admissible in evidence and are then usually read to the jury.

For example, a retired police captain is called to testify in court concerning an official report that he wrote from personal knowledge and submitted to his superior

---

HIGHLIGHT 13.1

Qualification of a Witness

"There is no rule which excludes an insane person as such, or a child of any specified age, from testifying, but in each case the traditional test is whether the witness has intelligence enough to make it worthwhile to hear him at all and whether he feels a duty to tell the truth. Is his capacity to observe, remember, and recount, such that he can probably bring added knowledge of the facts? The test is sometimes phrased in language as a requirement that the witness must have intelligence enough to 'understand the nature and obligation of an oath.'"[1]

years ago concerning the involvement of the accused in a crime. His memory of the report is incomplete, and he is shown the report in court (reviving his recollection), after which he proceeds to testify on the basis of his recollection. This is an instance of "present recollection revived." If the captain were shown the report but had no recollection of what had been recorded, he could not testify about the report. But the report itself might be read into the record as evidence of what the witness had once known, producing an instance of "past recollection recorded."

TABLE 13.1   Comparison of Concepts Involving Witnesses' Recollections

Present recollection revived	*Past recollection recorded*
1. Something is shown to revive witness's memory and witness recollects.	1. Something is shown to revive witness's memory but witness does not recollect.
2. After memory is revived, witness testifies on the matter.	2. Witness does not testify on the matter because memory is not revived.
3. Material used to revive memory is not admitted in evidence, but other party has right to inspect it.	3. Contents of material used to revive memory may be read into the record.

2. Cross-Examination

On *cross-examination,* a lawyer is permitted to use any type of question that would be allowed on direct examination—plus certain types that are not allowed on direct examination. A cross-examiner may use leading questions that suggest an answer; for examples, "Isn't it true that the accused and you have had fights in the past?" or "You did not actually see the accused stab the deceased, did you?"

Despite the wide leeway given lawyers on cross-examination, certain types of questions are not permitted, such as the following:

a. *Misleading question.* A question that cannot be answered without making an unintended admission is not permitted. The classic example is, "Have you stopped beating your wife?" Any yes or no answer to that question is damaging and may be inaccurate.

b. *Compound question.* A question that requires a single answer to more than one question is not allowed; for example, "Did you see and hear the explosion?" The witness may have seen but not heard.

c. *Argumentative question.* A leading question that also reflects the examiner's interpretation of the facts is impermissible; for example, "Why were you driving so carelessly?" Use of the word *carelessly* is subjective.

d. *Question that assumes facts not in evidence.* A question that assumes that a disputed fact is true although it has not yet been established in the case is not permitted; for example, "Since the wound inflicted by the accused was the cause of death in this case, why did you . . . ?" It assumes that the wound caused the death.

e. *Conclusionary question.* A question calling for an opinion or conclusion that the witness is not qualified or permitted to make may not be asked; for example, "Did your wife understand what was going on?" The witness may not know whether the wife understood what was going on.

A majority of states restrict the scope of cross-examination to matters put in issue on direct examination. However, a minority of states retain the old English rule that a witness may be cross-examined on all relevant matters, whether or not they were covered in direct examination.

3. Redirect Examination

Redirect examination is used to explain or rebut adverse testimony or inferences developed by opposing counsel on cross-examination and to rehabilitate the witness if his or her credibility has been damaged on cross-examination. Those states that follow the restricted view on cross-examination usually also limit the redirect to matters covered on cross-examination. Similarly, those that follow the minority view allow any matter to be inquired into on redirect—subject only to the court's power to limit the scope of questioning.

4. Recross-Examination

After the redirect examination, the trial judge may allow *recross-examination* of the witness for the purpose of overcoming the other party's attempts to rehabilitate a witness or to rebut damaging evidence brought out on cross-examination. Such examination is generally with the trial court's discretion, although some states allow it as a matter of right.

The method and scope of witness testimony is controlled by the judge, who rules on the admissibility of the testimony during the trial. A ruling is made when a lawyer from the opposing side *"objects"* to the question asked, specifying the grounds. If the objection is *"sustained,"* the evidence is excluded and therefore the witness does not have to answer the question. If the objection is *"overruled,"* the evidence is received and so the witness must answer the question. An objection by the opposing lawyer during the trial serves a dual purpose: if sustained, it excludes the evidence from the trial; if overruled, it establishes the basis for an appeal. Some jurisdictions require that the lawyer state in court that he or she "excepts" to an adverse judicial ruling so as to establish the basis for an appeal. Failure to "except" may mean a waiver of the right to challenge that ruling on appeal.

C. Opinion Testimony

An *opinion* is defined as an inference derived from facts observed. An *inference,* in turn, is a rational connection deduced from facts proved. The general rule is that witnesses must testify only to facts within their personal knowledge. It is the function of the jury to draw conclusions from the facts brought out by the witnesses. Therefore, testimony that expresses the opinion or conclusion of the witness generally is not admissible because it usurps this jury function. There are two general kinds of opinion testimony, corresponding to the two basic kinds of witnesses: opinion testimony by lay witnesses (persons with personal knowledge of the facts of the case) and opinion testimony by expert witnesses (persons who have special knowledge, skill, or other qualification beyond that of the average person in the subject on which he or she is testifying).

Opinion testimony by lay witnesses is generally not admissible. Most states, however, recognize a number of exceptions in which lay opinions are admissible, including these:

a. *Physical condition.* A witness may give an opinion in describing the appearance or apparent condition of another person. Thus, descriptions such as "drunken," "angry," or "sad" are admissible.

b. *Physical description.* If the opinion concerns the matter upon which normal persons consistently form reasonably reliable opinions, the opinion likewise is generally admissible. Opinions about the speed of a car, size and weight of a person, color, sound, smell, and distance fall into this category.

c. *Identity of a person.* The identity of a person is generally established through opinion testimony. The witness can testify that he or she recognized a person's face or voice; or the witness may base identification upon a person's physical characteristics or marks.

d. *Sanity.* In most jurisdictions, a lay witness may state an opinion about the sanity of a person who is a close acquaintance.

e. *Handwriting.* The opinion of a lay witness is admissible to identify handwriting if the witness has personal knowledge of the alleged writer's handwriting.

Opinions by an expert are generally admissible, as long as they are limited to matters within his or her expertise. The qualifications of a proposed expert witness must be established before the witness is allowed to testify. This determination is made by the judge and is binding on the jury. The party seeking to use the expert has the burden of establishing the expert's qualifications. The factors considered in determining whether a witness is an expert include special skill and knowledge, training and education, experience, familiarity with standard references and authorities in the field, and membership in professional organizations and societies. Technical expertise and high education are not always required. Any special experience may qualify a person to give an expert opinion. In effect, an expert is one who is believed to be such by the judge, as long as the judge's decision has some basis in fact.

There is a trend toward liberalizing the rules governing qualification of expert witnesses. Thus, the determinative issue is whether the witness has sufficient skill or experience in a particular field so that his or her testimony would be likely to assist the jury in its search for the truth.

The general rule is that the jury is not bound to accept an expert's opinion—even if uncontradicted—as long as there are grounds for objecting to it. The theory

---

HIGHLIGHT 13.2

Expert Testimony

"To warrant the use of expert testimony, then, two elements are required. First, the subject of the inference must be so distinctively related to some science, profession, business or occupation as to be beyond the ken of the average layman. . . . Second, the witness must have sufficient skill, knowledge, or experience in that field or calling as to make it appear that his opinion or inference will probably aid the trier in his search for truth."[2]

is that an expert's opinion is no better than the reasons and factual data upon which it is based; and the trier of fact may choose to disagree or disbelieve such supporting reasons or data. Jurors, however, may not arbitrarily disregard uncontradicted expert opinion on matters in which lay witnesses are not qualified to render valid opinions. If they do so, their verdict may be set aside as unsupported by the evidence.

D. Impeachment of Witnesses

Impeachment is defined as discrediting the witness. The fact that a witness has been impeached does not mean that his or her testimony will be stricken from the record or disregarded. The jury may still choose to believe the witness—since the weight and credibility of the evidence is for the jury, not the judge, to decide. There are six basic grounds for impeachment:

a. *Bias and interest.* Evidence that a witness is biased or has an interest in the outcome of the case tends to discredit his or her testimony. Bias or interest would enter the question if the witness were being paid to testify or if the witness had been promised immunity to punishment for testifying.

b. *Lack of character for honesty or truthfulness.* A witness may be impeached by showing that his or her character is such that he or she is likely to lie. The following evidence is admissible for this purpose: conviction for a felony; misconduct that is not the subject of criminal conviction (such as lying, cheating at poker games, or defrauding others); and poor reputation for truthfulness.

c. *Prior inconsistent statements.* Proof that a witness previously made statements inconsistent with his or her present testimony casts doubt upon his or her truthfulness or accuracy. Before extrinsic evidence can be introduced to prove a prior inconsistent statement, the witness usually must be given an opportunity to say whether or not he or she made the statement and to explain it if possible. The witness is usually asked whether he or she in fact made the statement (identified by its substance and the time, place, and person to whom it was made). This step is known as "laying a foundation" (for contradicting the witness).

d. *Defects in capacity.* A witness may be impeached by showing that his or her perception and recollection are or were so impaired as to make it doubtful that the witness could have perceived the facts to which he or she testifies. For example, a witness can be impeached by showing that he or she has a poor memory of the events about which he or she testifies. A poor memory of related matters suggests that the witness's recollection of the events to which he or she is testifying is likewise doubtful.

e. *Lack of knowledge.* A witness may be impeached by showing that he or she has an insufficient knowledge of the facts to which he or she testifies. This can be done by using either lay or expert witnesses.

f. *Contradiction.* The testimony of a witness may be impeached by introducing rebuttal evidence to disprove the facts to which the witness has testified.

II. THE HEARSAY RULE

Hearsay is defined as a statement, other than one made by a witness while testifying at the trial or hearing, that is being offered to prove the truth of the matter asserted. The *Hearsay Rule* provides that hearsay statements must be excluded from the trial upon appropriate objection, unless they come under one of the exceptions. The justification usually given for excluding hearsay is that in cases of oral declarations, there is danger of inaccurate reporting by the witness who is repeating what he or she heard. The real reason, however, is that the opposing party is denied the opportunity to cross-examine the person who originally made the statement since that person is not on the witness stand.

A. Forms of Hearsay

The term *hearsay* is not limited to spoken words. There are three basic forms of hearsay:

a. *Oral statements.* Example: On the witness stand a witness testifies, "Y told me that he saw the accused at the scene of the crime."

b. *Writings.* A written document offered in evidence may also be hearsay. Example: In court a witness introduces a letter or telegram from Y wherein Y writes: "I saw the accused at the scene of the crime."

c. *Assertive conduct.* This is a type of conduct intended by the actor to be a substitute for words. Example: During an investigation of an attempted murder case, the victim, Y, nodded his head when the officer asked if Z, the accused, had threatened to kill Y. The officer is now on the witness stand saying that the nod of Y's head meant yes.

The test of oral hearsay is this: *If the statement being repeated by the witness is offered to prove the truth of what somebody else has said or other out-of-court statements, the statement is hearsay.* For example, a witness says, "My neighbor told me that he beat up his wife that morning." If the statement is offered to prove that the neighbor did in fact beat up his wife that morning, the statement is hearsay and therefore not admissible. If that same statement is offered to prove that the neighbor talked to the witness that morning or that the witness can hear, the statement is not hearsay and is therefore admissible.

B. Exceptions to the Hearsay Rule

Certain kinds of hearsay have elements of special reliability that make up for the absence of cross-examination. Therefore, exceptions to the Hearsay Rule have been recognized. Hearsay evidence is admissible if the trial judge determines that it falls within one of the exceptions. These are the seven exceptions often used in criminal trials:

1. confessions and admissions
2. dying declarations
3. spontaneous declarations
4. previously recorded testimony
5. past recollection recorded
6. business records
7. official records

1. Confessions and Admissions

A *confession* is a direct acknowledgment of criminal guilt by a suspect. The acknowledgment may be oral or written. *Admissions* are acknowledgments of the existence of facts that are usually favorable to the opposite party. Most courts regard out-of-court confessions as hearsay if offered to prove the truth of the matter confessed. The reason for the exception is that people do not ordinarily admit to a criminal act. Thus if they do so, their statements would most likely be reliable.

Confessions are presented in court through testimony by the person to whom the confession was made, usually a police officer. It is hearsay because the person who allegedly confessed is not testifying on the witness stand. To be admissible, the confession must be voluntary and there must be no violation of the defendant's rights.

2. Dying Declarations

A *dying declaration* is defined as a statement made by a dying person concerning the cause and circumstances of his or her impending death. It is admissible in evidence as an exception to the Hearsay Rule because of the presumption that a person who knows he or she is about to die would probably not want to do so with a lie on his or her lips. Therefore, chances are high that the declaration is trustworthy. Dying declarations may be testified to by any witness who heard or witnessed the declaration. In many cases, this means a police officer. No particular form of declaration is required. Although most dying declarations are oral, they can also be written or given by a sign of the hand or a nod of the head. The general rule is that dying declarations are admissible only in homicide cases; however, several states now admit dying declarations in all civil and criminal cases.

There are four requirements for the admissibility of dying declarations:

a. *Victim must have given up hope of surviving.*   The declaration must have been made by the victim while he or she believed that his or her death was imminent and therefore had given up hope. It is not necessary, however, that the victim die immediately after making the dying declaration. For example, P was seriously wounded. En route to the hospital in an ambulance, he told the police officer, "X shot me"; but he also told the ambulance driver, "Get me to the nearest hospital immediately." P's statement, "X shot me," is not admissible as a dying declaration because his statement to the ambulance driver indicated that he had not given up hope of surviving.

b. *Declaration must concern the cause of death.*   "W stabbed me" is admissible. However, declarations by the victim about previous quarrels or statements about the character of the alleged assailant would not be admissible.

c. *Victim's personal knowledge.*   The statement must concern facts within the personal knowledge of the victim; thus statements of opinion are not admissible. "I think D tried to poison me" is not admissible.

d. *Victim must be dead.*   Most courts require that the victim must be dead when the evidence is ultimately offered. If alive, the victim can testify himself or herself; hence there is no need for admitting the dying declaration.

The above requirements for admissibility need strict compliance. However, statements of the victim that do not comply with all the above requirements may still be admissible, not as a dying declaration but as a spontaneous statement.

3. Spontaneous Declarations

Spontaneous declarations are defined as statements made under the stress of some shocking or exciting event, concerning something related to that event. The term implies that the statement is not in response to a question but was instead uttered spontaneously. Other terms used in various jurisdictions are *excited utterances, spontaneous statements,* and *res gestae statements.* These statements are hearsay because the person who uttered them is not on the witness stand. The spontaneity of such statements, and the lack of opportunity for reflection and deliberate fabrication, guarantee trustworthiness. Spontaneous declarations are testified to *by the person who heard the declaration,* not by the declarant himself. For example, right after the accident, M heard O say, "That sports car ran the red light." That statement can be testified to by M. O may also testify in court as to what he said, but not under the category of spontaneous declarations.

There are three requirements for the admissibility of spontaneous declarations:

a. *Startling event.*   There must have been an occurrence startling enough to produce shock and excitement in the observer, such as a car crash, a shooting, a stabbing, a sudden explosion, the beating up of a person, or the snatching of a handbag.

b. *Declaration made contemporaneously.*   The statement must have been made while the declarant was under the stress of the event and before he or she had time to reflect upon it. The time element is very important. There is no mechanical test, but courts usually limit admissibility to statements made contemporaneously with (meaning while the event is taking place) or immediately after the exciting event. But courts differ as to whether "immediately after" means seconds, minutes, or even hours after the event.

c. *Personal knowledge of the facts observed.*   The statement must relate to the circumstances of the event and must represent the declarant's personal observations of the facts. For example, right after an accident, the declarant was heard by the witness to say, "That sports car ran a red light." This statement is admissible. However, "That guy must have been driving fast" would not be admissible because this statement is not a fact but a conclusion.

The person who makes the spontaneous declaration need not be competent as a witness, as long as he or she had personal knowledge of the facts and powers of perception and recollection. This is because the declarant himself or herself is not a witness. The one who heard him or her is the one testifying. The declarant need not always be identified—as long as his or her existence can be established by inference from the circumstances. For example, a witness testifies that she heard somebody yell, "That man in a white shirt fired the shot." This statement is admissible even though the witness cannot identify who said it.

Although spontaneous declarations are often referred to as "part of the res gestae" (literally, the "thing done"), they are really only a small portion of the whole res gestae concept. *Res gestae* is a much broader concept, which includes

1. statements made by a witness (spontaneous declarations);
2. statements made by the victim;
3. statements made by the suspect or persons involved in the offense;
4. physical objects that can be considered an integral part of a crime or event (such as the gun used in the shooting).

All the above are admissible in evidence under the res gestae rule.

4. Previously Recorded Testimony

"Previously recorded testimony" refers to depositions or transcripts of testimony given under oath by a witness at some former hearing or trial in the same case or another case. Such testimony is considered hearsay in most jurisdictions because it was not given at the present trial or hearing, but is admissible as an exception to the Hearsay Rule. For example, X was convicted of rape, but given a new trial. Before the new trial starts, one of the state's main witnesses dies. The witness's former testimony may be admissible in evidence.

Former testimony is admissible because of the presence of certain elements ensuring reliability—such as the oath, the solemnity of the occasion, and, most important, the opportunity for cross-examination at the former hearing. The usual method of proving the prior testimony is by introducing a certified transcript of the prior proceedings. The court reporter can be called to the witness stand to read the entire testimony of the dead or unavailable witness—including the direct, cross-, redirect, and recross-examinations.

Previously recorded testimony can be used in criminal proceedings as long as the following requirements are met:

a. *Opportunity to cross-examine.* The accused or his or her attorney must have been present and had the opportunity to cross-examine at the time the testimony was given (whether in a preliminary examination, former trial for the same offense, or other setting).

b. *Witness must be unavailable.* The witness whose reported testimony is involved must now be unavailable. The term "unavailable" may mean that the witness is dead or that the witness is insane, is out of the court's jurisdiction, or cannot be found despite sincere efforts to produce him or her. Temporary physical disability or illness is not sufficient to establish unavailability. A mere showing that the witness is incarcerated in a prison outside the state is insufficient if there is no showing that he or she could not be produced (Barber v. Page, 390 U.S. 719 [1968]).

5. Past Recollection Recorded

"Past recollection recorded" refers to the contents of writings made at or near the time of event; the writings may be introduced in evidence if a witness's recollection is not revived even after having been shown the writing on the witness stand. Use of the contents of the writing to prove the facts contained therein raises a hearsay problem. But if a proper foundation can be laid, the contents of the writing may be introduced into evidence under an exception to the Hearsay Rule. Example: A parole officer is called to the witness stand by the prosecution to testify on a report she had submitted to her superiors years earlier, recommending that the parole of X, who is

now on trial for attempted murder, be revoked because X repeatedly displayed violent tendencies while out on parole. If the parole officer has no recollection of the facts contained in the report, even after having been shown the document while on the witness stand, the contents of the document may be read into the record. The reason for admitting past recollection recorded is that a writing made by an observer when the facts were still fresh in his or her mind is probably more reliable than his or her testimony on the witness stand—even though there was no opportunity to cross-examine the witness on that document.

The general view is that the document itself is not admissible; rather, its contents must be read to the jury if it is to become a part of the court's record. The justification for this practice is that juries tend to overvalue documents.

There are five requirements for admissibility:

a. *No present recollection.*   The witness must have no present recollection of the facts recorded in the document.

b. *Recording made when events were fresh in mind.*   The document must have been made at a time when the facts recorded therein were actually occurring or when they were still fresh in the witness's memory. What this means in each particular case is determined by the judge.

c. *Recording made by or under direction of witness.*   In general, the writing must have been made (1) by the witness himself or herself or under his or her direction, or (2) by some other person for the purpose of recording the witness's statement at the time it was made.

d. *Verification.*   The witness must testify that the recording was a true statement of the facts when it was made.

e. *Authentication.*   The document must be authenticated as an accurate record of the statement.

6. Business Records

Business records are defined as official records kept by a person or an organization in the regular course of business. They are considered hearsay but are admissible as one of the exceptions to the Hearsay Rule because they tend to be trustworthy.

Business records are introduced through a witness who is acquainted with the record and business procedure in the particular organization or company whose records are to be introduced. For example, the head accountant of a corporation can testify concerning the business records of the company, or the head physician in a hospital as to medical entries.

There are five requirements for the admissibility of business records:

a. *Satisfying the definition of a business.*   Most statutes define "business" very broadly to include every association, profession, occupation, and calling, whether conducted for profit or not. Thus, the definition of business records would include records made by churches, hospitals, or schools.

b. *Entry made in the regular course of business.*   It must appear that the record was made in the course of a regularly conducted business activity. For example, entries in hospital records, such as records of the kinds of medicine administered or notes of the attending physician, are admissible.

c. *Personal knowledge.* The business record must consist of matters within the personal knowledge of the entrant or within the personal knowledge of someone with a business duty to transmit such matters to the entrant. Police reports based on the personal knowledge of the reporting officer are admissible. But those based on statements of bystanders would not be admissible—because the bystanders had no business duty to report the facts to the officer.

d. *Entry made at or near time of event.* The entry must have been made at or near the time of the transaction, while the entrant's knowledge of the fact was still fresh.

e. *Authentication.* The authenticity of the records must be established. The usual method of authentication is to have the custodian of the records or some other qualified witness (not necessarily the person who made the entry) testify at the trial to the identity of the record, the mode of preparation, and the manner of its safekeeping.

7. Official Records

Official records are defined as statements and documents prepared by a public officer in the performance of his or her official duties. Records of birth, death, marriages, and court judgments are official records. The exception for official records is necessary in order to avoid having public officers leave their jobs constantly to appear in court and testify to acts done in their official capacity. Also, such records are presumed to be trustworthy because public officials are under a duty to properly record what they do.

The exception for official records can be considered a part of, and is in fact usually covered by the provisions of, the exception for business records. The only major difference is that the judge may admit an official record without requiring anybody to testify in court as to its identity and mode of preparation. Official records must be presented in court through the use of a certified copy. However, the keeper of the record need not appear.

Over the years, many exceptions to the Hearsay Rule have developed by statute or judicial decisions. These exceptions can be added to or eliminated at any time. Among the exceptions not discussed in this text are admissions, declaration against interest, declarations re state of mind or physical condition, prior identification, judgment of previous conviction, family history, ancient writings, family records, vital statistics, and reputation as to character.

III. PRIVILEGED COMMUNICATIONS

"Privileged communication" refers to a rule of law that allows a witness to refuse to give testimony that he or she might otherwise be compelled to give, or to prevent someone else from testifying, concerning certain types of communication. The purpose of "privileged communication" is to protect particular relationships or interests that society considers to be more important than the testimony that the witness might otherwise give. For example, the effect on our adversary system of justice would be devastating if lawyers could be compelled to disclose what their clients have told them about the case. The effect on family life would be adverse if either spouse could be compelled to reveal confidential information given by one to the other during the

marriage. The philosophy is that the truth may be sacrificed to protect important relationships.

Of the eight areas of privileged communication, some are highly protected, while others hardly enjoy any protection at all. These are the areas:

1. lawyer–client privilege
2. privilege not to testify against spouse
3. privilege for confidential marital communications
4. physician–patient privilege
5. psychotherapist–patient privilege
6. cleric–penitent privilege
7. identity-of-informer privilege
8. journalist–source privilege

A. Lawyer–Client Privilege

The basic rule is that a client may refuse to disclose, and may prevent another person (usually the attorney) from disclosing, any confidential communication made for the purpose of helping the attorney give proper legal services to the client. The *attorney–client privilege* is designed to encourage full disclosure by the client to his or her attorney of all matters pertinent to his or her case so as to further the administration of justice and the giving of legal advice.

The holder of the privilege is the client, or the client's authorized representative if the client is incompetent or deceased. The privilege cannot be waived unless the waiver is made by the client. The lawyer is not a holder of the privilege and cannot claim it on his or her own behalf. However, an attorney is required to claim the privilege for the client—unless otherwise instructed by the client or his or her authorized representative.

There are four requirements for exercising the lawyer–client privilege:

a. *Client.*   The client must be a person who consults a lawyer for the purpose of retaining the lawyer or securing legal advice.

b. *Lawyer.*   The lawyer must be a person authorized (or reasonably believed by the client to be authorized) to practice law. The rules of several states require that the attorney be a member of the bar of that state.

c. *Communication.*   The communication must be made in the course of the lawyer–client relationship. The client need not actually employ the attorney. The

---

HIGHLIGHT 13.3

Lawyer–Client Privilege

"The notion that the loyalty owed by the lawyer to his client disables him from being a witness in his client's case is deep-rooted in Roman law. . . . [C]laims and disputes which may lead to litigation can most justly and expeditiously be handled by practised experts, namely lawyers, and . . . such experts can act effectively only if they are fully advised of the facts by the parties whom they represent. Such full disclosure will be promoted if the client knows that what he tells his lawyer cannot, over his objection, be extorted in court from the lawyer's lips."[3]

privilege attaches to any communication made while consulting the attorney—even though the attorney declines the case or the client decides not to hire the attorney. For example, X goes to L, a lawyer, and asks L to represent him because he has just been charged with robbery. L listens to X and then declines to represent X because the alleged robbery victim is L's friend. Whatever X told L can never be revealed in court unless there is a waiver by X.

"Communications" include written documents intended to provide information to the attorney; but a suspected murder weapon is not a communication and thus is not protected by the privilege.

d. *Confidentiality.* The client's communication to the attorney must be confidential. If the communication was not made in confidence, then there is no lawyer–client privilege. For example, X meets L at a Christmas party and, upon learning that L is a lawyer, tells L her version of a criminal charge she is facing and asks L to represent her. Any information given by X to L in the presence of other people does not come under the lawyer–client privilege because it is not given in confidence. A communication made in the presence of another person will still be confidential, however, if that person is present to further the interest of the client in the consultation (such as a business associate or consultant of the client). The privilege also applies to communications made by the client to those who confidentially aid the lawyer in performing his or her work—including secretaries, interpreters, clerks, and accountants. Such persons may also be prohibited from testifying.

The lawyer–client privilege cannot be claimed in the following instances:

1. If the aid of the lawyer is sought to perpetrate a crime or a fraud; for example, X goes to a lawyer to seek legal advice on how she might be able to kill her husband and make it appear to be self-defense.
2. In lawsuits involving breach of duty arising out of a lawyer–client relationship—as when a client sues a lawyer for malpractice, or the lawyer sues the client for fees.

B. Privilege against Adverse Spousal Testimony

Under the privilege against *adverse spousal testimony,* a married person whose spouse is the defendant in a criminal case may not be called as a witness or be compelled to testify against the spouse in any criminal proceeding. Note, however, that this privilege has lost much significance because in twenty-six states the holder of the privilege is the witness spouse, meaning that the accused spouse can no longer prohibit the witness spouse from testifying.

The privilege against adverse spousal testimony is designed to protect the marital relationship from the disruption that follows when one spouse is allowed to testify against the other. In contrast, note that one spouse may testify in favor of the other spouse at any time. What is covered in this privilege is adverse marital testimony, not testimony that is favorable to the accused spouse.

The holder of the privilege is determined by state law or judicial decisions. In twenty-four states (as of 1980), the privilege belongs to the accused spouse. He or she can therefore prevent the witness spouse from testifying. In the other twenty-six states the privilege belongs to the witness spouse: If the witness spouse wants to testify, the accused spouse cannot prohibit the testimony. This approach is also now used in federal courts, as decided in Trammel v. United States, 26 CrL 3091 (1980). In Trammel, the defendant was convicted on two counts of federal drug charges on the basis of testimony given in court by his wife. During the trial in the Federal District Court, Trammel objected to the use of his wife's testimony, claiming the privilege against adverse marital testimony. On appeal, the Court held that in federal criminal proceedings, the witness spouse alone can invoke the privilege not to testify adversely against the accused spouse, as long as the testimony does not involve confidential marital information. The accused spouse, therefore, cannot prevent the witness spouse (in federal jurisdictions) from testifying, if the witness spouse so desires.

In the twenty-four states in which the privilege still belongs to the accused spouse, the requirements for the use of the privilege are two:

1. There must be a valid marriage.
2. The privilege lasts only during the marriage and terminates upon divorce or annulment.

If a marriage exists, many states allow the privilege to be asserted even with respect to matters that took place before the marriage. Thus, an accused could effectively seal a witness's lips by marrying the witness.

C. Privilege for Confidential Marital Communications

Under the privilege for *confidential marital communications,* either spouse has a privilege to refuse to disclose, and to prevent the other from disclosing, any confidential communication made between the spouses while they were husband and wife. The rule is designed to protect confidential communications between spouses and to encourage open communication and trust between spouses during the marriage. There must be some assurance that any confidential communication between the spouses cannot be testified to by the other spouse even after the marriage is dissolved. This is particularly important in a society with a high divorce rate. Both spouses jointly hold this privilege. Thus, either can prevent the other from disclosing confidential marital communications, even after the marriage has terminated.

There are three requirements for the use of the privilege:

a. *Communication must have been made when the parties were husband and wife.*   For example, H and W are husband and wife. During the marriage, H confides to W that he is a narcotics addict and has robbed several stores to support his habit.

HIGHLIGHT 13.4

Privilege against Adverse Spousal Testimony Eroded

"The ancient foundations for so sweeping a privilege [referring to the privilege against adverse spousal testimony] have long since disappeared. Nowhere in the common-law world—indeed in any modern society—is a woman regarded as chattel or demeaned by denial of a separate legal identity and the dignity associated with recognition as a whole human being. Chip by chip, over the years those archaic notions have been cast aside so that 'no longer is the female destined solely for the home and the rearing of the family, and only the male for the marketplace and the world of ideas' " (Trammel v. U.S., 26 CrL 3091 [1980]).

Such communication cannot be testified to by W during the marriage or even after the marriage breaks up.

b. *Communication must have been made confidential.* Most states presume that communications between spouses are confidential; therefore the party objecting to the claim of privilege has the burden of showing that it was not privileged.

c. *Only "communications" are privileged.* Thus, for example, opinions by one spouse as to the actions or conditions of the other spouse are not privileged. Some states hold that nonverbal conduct that is private or confidential is also privileged. Thus, if a wife sees her husband hide a gun in their bedroom, the husband's conduct may be treated as a form of communication—on the theory that if the husband did not trust his wife, he would not have hidden the gun while she could see him do it.

The two privileges associated with marriage can be confusing unless the following distinctions are made.

Privilege against adverse spousal testimony	*Privilege for confidential marital information*
1. One spouse can be prevented by the other spouse from testifying on any matter.	1. Witness spouse testifies but not about confidential information given during the marriage.
2. Now used in only twenty-four states. In the other twenty-six states, the holder of the privilege is the witness spouse, meaning that the accused cannot prevent his or her spouse from testifying.	2. Used in practically all states, including the twenty-six states in which the privilege against adverse spousal testimony is held by the witness spouse.
3. Privilege ceases to exist once marriage is dissolved, as by divorce. Former spouses can testify against each other in all states.	3. Exists even after the marriage is dissolved, meaning that a divorced spouse who testifies against the former husband or wife cannot testify concerning confidential marital information given during the marriage.

D. Physician–Patient Privilege

A *patient* has a privilege to refuse to disclose, and to prevent anyone else from disclosing, any confidential communication between himself or herself and his or her *physician.* In many jurisdictions, however, the exceptions to this privilege are so broad as to make the rule almost meaningless.

The holder of the privilege is the patient or the patient's authorized representative. The privilege does not belong to the physician and cannot be claimed by him or her independently. However, as in the attorney–client privilege, the physician is required to assert the privilege on behalf of his or her patient unless the privilege has been waived.

There are three requirements for the exercise of the privilege:

a. *Communication.* In most jurisdictions, the privilege applies only to confidential communications to a physician in the course of consultation for treatment.

Thus, communications made to a physician who examines the patient in order to testify at trial—such as when an accused is sent by the prosecutor to a physician for examination—are not privileged. If the doctor, however, is employed by the patient's attorney, such communications may be privileged.

    b. *Physician.* The physician must be a person authorized (or reasonably believed by the patient to be authorized) to practice medicine.

    c. *Confidentiality.* Confidential communications include any information obtained by a physician in the course of a physician–patient relationship that would be normally regarded as confidential. Therefore the results of physical examinations, blood or urine tests, and so on would be privileged.

The physician–patient privilege cannot be claimed in the following cases:

    1. If the evidence obtained is to be used in criminal proceedings (such as when X goes to a physician for treatment after a shootout with the police and X is later accused of that crime). This exception often makes the physician–patient privilege virtually meaningless in criminal cases. In fact, some states require physicians to report to the authorities any treatment made for a gunshot wound.

    2. Any proceedings in which the condition of the patient has been put in issue by the patient. If P sues Y for damages based on Y's recklessness, P is placing the extent of his or her injury in issue, and thus P has no physician–patient privilege.

    3. Cases in which the services of the physician were sought or obtained to assist anyone to commit a crime or civil damage to another person.

    4. Communications concerning breach of duty arising out of a physician–patient relationship. This is like the exception for the attorney–client privilege; it refers to malpractice cases brought by patients against physicians.

E. Psychotherapist–Patient Privilege

The physician–patient privilege has been extended in a few states to patients of psychotherapists (referring to psychiatrists and psychologists), on the ground that full disclosure between doctor and patient is even more necessary for the treatment of mental and emotional illnesses. It is still uncertain how many other jurisdictions will adopt this privilege. Some states grant the privilege only to some forms of communications, such as the communication between a drug counselor and a drug addict who has sought treatment voluntarily. The rationale is to encourage addicts to seek treatment on their own without fear of disclosure. Other states and the model statute of the American Psychiatric Association provide that even where there is psychotherapist–patient privilege, such should not extend to cases where there is explicit threat on the part of the patient to kill or seriously injure somebody.

F. Cleric–Penitent Privilege

A person may refuse to disclose, and may prevent the *cleric* from disclosing, any confidential communication made to a cleric who was acting in his or her professional capacity as a spiritual adviser. The holder of the privilege is the *penitent,* but most states also allow a cleric independently to refuse to disclose such information—even if disclosure has the penitent's consent. This exception is granted because the cleric's religious beliefs may require him or her to maintain secrecy regardless of the penitent's wishes.

There are three requirements for the exercise of the privilege:

1. The cleric must be a practitioner or functionary of a church or religious organization who is authorized or accustomed to hearing penitential communications and who is under a duty to his or her church to keep such communications secret. Some states limit this privilege to confessions.

2. Only communications are privileged. Therefore, observations and conclusions by the cleric are not.

3. The communication must be made in confidence.

G. Identity-of-Informer Privilege

The state has the privilege of refusing to disclose or of preventing another from disclosing the *identity of an informer.* The only exception is when the informer's identity is material to the issue of guilt or innocence. Refusal by the state to reveal the identity of the informer in this situation requires dismissal of the case. The circumstances in which identity is material to the issue of guilt or innocence are a matter to be determined by the judge. When the identity of the informer relates to a narrower issue, such as determining probable cause for the search or arrest, the state is not required to reveal the identity of the informer in order to establish the legality of the search or arrest.

H. Journalist–Source Privilege

The First Amendment right to freedom of the press has not been interpreted by the courts to protect *journalists* from being required to reveal their sources of information. Over the years, however, more than half of the states have enacted shield laws protecting the confidentiality of journalists' sources. The provisions of these laws vary, some offering broad protection and others being severely limited. Some courts have also ruled that news sources can be revealed, but only as a last resort.

☐ SUMMARY

Under old English law, there were a number of grounds upon which a person could be disqualified from giving testimony. However, the modern trend is to abolish these disqualifications and allow every person to be a witness as long as he or she possesses certain basic qualifications: the ability to communicate, an understanding of the duty to tell the truth, and personal knowledge of the facts in the case.

The obligation of the witness is to tell the facts to the jury, letting the jury draw any conclusions from them. Therefore, the opinions or conclusions of witnesses are generally not admissible. There are two kinds of witnesses—lay and expert. A lay witness is any person who has personal knowledge of the facts of the case; an expert witness is one who has special knowledge, skill, experience, training, or education on the subject on which he or she is testifying. Opinions of expert witnesses may be permitted on subjects within their area of expertise.

Hearsay is a statement, other than one made by the witness while testifying at the trial or hearing, that is being offered to prove the truth of the matter asserted. The Hearsay Rule provides that hearsay evidence must be excluded unless it comes under one of the many exceptions to the rule. The real reason for excluding hearsay is that the opposing party is denied the opportunity to cross-examine the person who originally made the statement. Hearsay evidence not only takes the form of oral statements but also includes writings and assertive conduct.

There are numerous exceptions to the Hearsay Rule, justified on the ground that they have elements of special reliability that make up for the absence of cross-examination. The basic exceptions for purposes of a criminal trial are confessions, dying declarations, spontaneous declarations, previously recorded testimony, past recollection recorded, business records, and official records. Each exception has its own specific requirements for admissibility.

The "privileged communication" rule allows a witness to refuse to give testimony that he or she might otherwise be compelled to give, or to prevent someone else from testifying, concerning certain types of communication. The purpose of the privilege is to protect particular relationships or interests that society considers to be more important than the testimony that the witness might otherwise give. The truth is therefore sacrificed so that certain important relationships may be protected. Among the communications considered privileged are those between lawyer and client, between spouses, and between physician and client.

☐ REVIEW QUESTIONS

1. Under modern law, what are the three basic qualifications to be a witness? How does the modern law differ from the old English law on the qualification of witnesses?
2. What is a leading question? Give an example of a leading question.
3. The words "objection sustained" and "objection overruled" are often heard from the judge during a trial. What do those words mean?
4. Define opinion testimony. Is opinion testimony admissible at all in evidence?
5. There are many grounds for impeaching a witness. Identify four of those grounds.
6. What is the Hearsay Rule? Give an example of a hearsay testimony that is not admissible in court.
7. What is the "dying declaration" exception to the Hearsay Rule? What are its requirements?
8. Give the similarities and then the differences between the business records exception and the official records exception to the Hearsay Rule.
9. What are privileged communications? What is the justification for the "privileged communications" rule?
10. Give three types of privileged communications and discuss each briefly.

☐ DEFINITIONS

Argumentative Question: A leading question that also reflects the examiner's interpretation of the facts.

Business Records: Official records kept by a person or an organization in the regular course of business.

Compound Question: A question that requires a single answer to more than one question.

Confession: A direct acknowledgment of criminal guilt by a suspect or an accused.

Cross-Examination: Examination of the witness by the opposing lawyer following the direct examination.

Direct Examination: The first questioning of a witness by the party who called him or her to the stand.

Dying Declaration: A statement made by a dying person concerning the cause and circumstances of his or her impending death.

Hearsay: A statement, other than one made by a witness while testifying at the trial or hearing, that is being offered to prove the truth of the matter asserted.

Hearsay Rule: A rule of evidence stating that hearsay statements must be excluded from trial upon appropriate objection, unless they come under one of the exceptions.

Impeachment of Witness: Discrediting a witness.

Inference: A rational connection deduced from facts proved.

Leading Question: A question that suggests to the witness the answer the examining lawyer desires.

Misleading Question: A question that cannot be answered without making an unintended admission.

Narrative Questioning: Question that allows the witness to tell a narrative.

Official Records: Statements and documents prepared by a public officer in the performance of his or her official duties.

Opinion: An inference derived from facts observed.

Past Recollection Recorded: The witness has no independent recollection whatsoever of the contents of a document. He or she will not be permitted to testify by relying on the writing; however, the contents of the writing itself might be admissible in evidence, provided that certain requirements are met.

Present Recollection Revived: A testifying witness may refer to a writing or something else to refresh or revive his or her memory, enabling the witness thereafter to testify from memory.

Privileged Communication: Communication concerning which a witness may refuse to give testimony that he or she might otherwise be compelled to give, or may prevent someone else from testifying.

Recross-Examination: Examination of the witness by the cross-examiner following the redirect examination.

Redirect Examination: The further questioning of the witness, after the cross-examination, by the lawyer who called him or her to the stand.

Repetitive Questions: Questions designed to bolster or emphasize what has already been established.

Res Gestae: Literally, the "thing done." A rule of evidence that provides that spontaneous declarations, statements made by the victim, statements made by the suspect, or physical objects that can be considered an integral part of a crime or event are admissible in court.

Spontaneous Declaration:　Statement made under the stress of some shocking or exciting event, concerning something related to that event.

☐　PRINCIPLES OF CASES

BARBER V. PAGE, 390 U.S. 719 (1968)　Temporary physical disability or illness is not sufficient to establish unavailability of a witness. A mere showing that the witness is incarcerated in a prison outside the state is insufficient if there is no showing that he or she could not be produced.

TRAMMEL V. UNITED STATES, 26 CrL 3091 (1980)　In federal criminal proceedings, the witness spouse alone can invoke the privilege not to testify adversely against the accused spouse, as long as the testimony does not involve confidential marital information. The accused spouse therefore cannot prevent the witness spouse from testifying, if the witness spouse so desires.

☐　CASE BRIEF—LEADING CASE ON PRIVILEGE AGAINST ADVERSE SPOUSAL TESTIMONY

TRAMMEL V. UNITED STATES, 26 CrL 3091 (1980)

FACTS:　Trammel was convicted on two counts of federal drug charges on the basis of testimony given in court by his wife. Trammel's wife had been named in the indictment as an unindicted coconspirator. During the trial in the Federal District Court, Trammel objected to the use of his wife's testimony, claiming marital privilege. The District Court held that confidential communications between Trammel and his wife were privileged and therefore inadmissible, but the wife was permitted to testify to any act she observed before and during the marriage and to any communication made in the presence of a third person. The Court of Appeals affirmed the District Court's decision, citing Hawkins v. United States, an earlier ruling, which held that the testimony of one spouse against the other is barred unless both spouses consent to the giving of the testimony. The case was appealed to the Supreme Court.

ISSUE:　*May an accused invoke the privilege against adverse spousal testimony to exclude the voluntary testimony of a spouse, when such testimony does not involve confidential marital communication? No.*

SUPREME COURT DECISION:　In federal criminal proceedings, the witness spouse alone can invoke the privilege not to testify adversely against the accused spouse, as long as the testimony does not involve confidential marital information. The accused spouse, therefore, cannot prevent the witness spouse from testifying, if the witness spouse so desires.

CASE SIGNIFICANCE:　This case changed the rule in federal courts on the issue of adverse spousal testimony. In an earlier case (Hawkins v. U.S., 358 U.S. 74, 1958), the Court said that the accused spouse was the holder of the privilege and hence could prevent the witness spouse from testifying. The Court said that the Hawkins rule had to be discarded in view of recent trends. At the time Trammel was decided, only twenty-four states allowed the accused spouse to prevent the adverse testimony of the witness spouse, the justification being that in cases where one spouse voluntarily wanted to testify against the other spouse, the marriage had already reached a stage anyway at which there was nothing to save. The old rationale that spouses could not testify against each other in order to preserve the marriage was based on a false premise—that the marriage could be saved. To place the Trammel case in proper perspective, note the following:

1. The Trammel ruling applies only to federal criminal cases and cases in twenty-six of the states. In the other twenty-four states, the accused spouse still holds the privilege, meaning that the witness spouse can be prohibited by the accused spouse from testifying.
2. The Trammel case says that in federal cases, the witness spouse can now testify if he or she wants. That does not mean that he or she can be forced by the prosecutor to testify if he or she refuses to be a witness.
3. The Trammel case applies only to cases in which the issue is whether or not one spouse can testify against the other. It does not apply to cases involving confidential marital information; the accused spouse still holds that privilege.

EXCERPTS FROM THE DECISION: The modern justification for this privilege against adverse spousal testimony is its perceived role in fostering the harmony and sanctity of the marriage relationship. Notwithstanding this benign purpose, the rule was sharply criticized. Professor Wigmore termed it "the merest anachronism in legal theory and an indefensible obstruction to truth in practice." The Committee on the Improvement of the Law of Evidence of the American Bar Association called for its abolition. In its place, Wigmore and others suggested a privilege protecting only private marital communications, modeled on the privilege between priest and penitent, attorney and client, and physician and patient.

   In Hawkins v. United States, 358 U.S. 74 (1958), this Court considered the continued vitality of the privilege against adverse spousal testimony in the federal courts. There the District Court had permitted petitioner's wife, over his objection, to testify against him. With one questioning concurring opinion, the Court held the wife's testimony inadmissible; it took note of the critical comments that the common-law rule had engendered, but chose not to abandon it. Also rejected was the Government's suggestion that the Court modify the privilege by vesting it in the witness spouse, with freedom to testify or not independent of the defendant's control. The Court viewed this proposed modification as antithetical to the widespread belief, evidenced in the rules then in effect in a majority of the States and in England, "that the law should not force or encourage testimony which might alienate husband and wife, or further inflame existing domestic differences."

   Hawkins, then, left the federal privilege of adverse spousal testimony where it found it, continuing "a rule which bars the testimony of one spouse against the other unless both consent." However, in so doing, the Court made clear that its decision was not meant to "foreclose whatever changes in the rule may eventually be dictated by 'reason and experience.' "

☐ NOTES

1. E. Cleary et al., *McCormick on Evidence* (St. Paul, MN: West, 1972), at 140.
2. Ibid., at 29–30.
3. Ibid., at 175.

PART SIX

CONCERNS RELATED TO LAW ENFORCEMENT

SENTENCING, APPEAL, AND HABEAS CORPUS

❑ KEY TERMS

sentencing	shock probation
bifurcated trial	intermediate punishments
proportionality review	community service program
death-qualified juries	restitution
concurrent sentences	electronic monitoring
consecutive sentences	RICO
fine	Rule of Four
probation	per curiam decision
intensive supervision probation	habeas corpus

I. SENTENCING

Sentencing is defined as the formal pronouncement of judgment and punishment on the defendant following his or her conviction in a criminal prosecution. Sentences are usually imposed by a judge, but a few states provide an option for jury sentencing. Death sentences, however, are decided or recommended by juries in all states that impose the death penalty.

The vice and vagaries of sentencing are highlighted in a magazine article that says:[1]

> There are signs posted on the counters of branches in the Chemical Bank in New York which read, in large capital letters: BANK ROBBERY PUNISHABLE BY 20 YEARS IN FEDERAL PRISON.

The article then continues:

> The signs are a deception. The sign could more accurately have read: "The symbolic penalty for bank robbery is 20 years in prison." The actual penalty for bank robbery is difficult to determine in that it can be anything from probation up to 20 years, depending on the nature of the plea bargain, the personal policy of the judge toward bank robbery, the severity of overcrowding in federal prisons, and the opinion of parole hearing officers on the extent of the rehabilitation and/or dangerousness of the criminal.

Sentencing authorities usually enjoy wide discretion in determining the sentence to be imposed. This vast discretion is implied in state penal codes, which usually provide for a wide range between the minimum and maximum penalties for an offense. The practice of giving vast discretion to sentencing authorities reflects the philosophy of the *positive school of criminology,* which advocates that the penalty should *"fit the offender"* instead of the offense. In practice, wide discretion in sentencing results in sentencing disparity—different sentences are given for similar crimes committed under similar circumstances. For example, the Texas Penal Code provides for imprisonment of five to ninety-nine years for first-degree felonies. Therefore, D can get five years and E can get thirty years for the same type of crime committed under similar circumstances. It is difficult to remedy disparity of sentencing in individual cases since the appellate court generally will not reverse or modify a sentence imposed by the trial court if it is within the allowable statutory limit, as it is in the example just given.

In jury sentences, the presentation of evidence for the sentencing phase follows immediately after the pronouncement of guilt, at least in states where the trial is bifurcated. A *bifurcated trial* is defined as one divided into two stages: the *guilt–innocence stage* and the *sentencing stage*. In jurisdictions that do not use bifurcated trials, the jury decides the sentence to be imposed at the same time it decides guilt or innocence. Even in these jurisdictions, however, a bifurcated trial is usually required in capital offenses. In bifurcated trials the jury announces the verdict first and, if the defendant is found guilty, deliberates again on the proper punishment.

Lawyers for the government and the defendant present evidence during the sentencing stage seeking a heavier or lighter sentence. If the sentence is to be imposed by a judge (as it usually is in most states), the sentencing phase is usually postponed until from two to four weeks later. This delay enables the judge to order a presentence investigation (PSI) report, which is prepared by a probation officer. The report includes details regarding the accused's background, prior criminal record, family circumstances, and other relevant facts that may affect the penalty to be imposed. The PSI report usually also includes a recommendation concerning the grant or denial of probation and the amount of time to be served, if imprisonment is to be imposed. Such reports are required in some states for felony convictions but are optional with the judge in others. The defendant does not have a constitutional right to see the PSI report, but many judges make it available to the lawyer for the defendant prior to the sentencing hearing so that the defendant may contest any factual inaccuracies it contains. Some states provide by law that the defendant be allowed to see the PSI report.

The accused does not have many constitutional rights during sentencing. Even the rules of evidence are relaxed so that the judge during the sentencing phase may take into account inadmissible hearsay or unsworn reports. The accused does not have a right to cross-examine witnesses. The accused does, however, have the following rights:

HIGHLIGHT 14.1

Sentencing Goals

The sentencing of criminals often reflects conflicting social goals

These objectives are—

Retribution—giving offenders their "just deserts" and expressing society's disapproval of criminal behavior

Incapacitation—separating offenders from the community to reduce the opportunity for further crime while they are incarcerated

Deterrence—demonstrating the certainty and severity of punishment to discourage future crime by the offender (specific deterrence) and by others (general deterrence)

Rehabilitation—providing psychological or educational assistance or job training to offenders to make them less likely to engage in future criminality

Restitution—having the offender repay the victim or the community in money or services.

Source: Bureau of Justice Statistics, *Report to the Nation on Crime and Justice,* 2d ed. (Washington, DC: U.S. Government Printing Office, 1988), at 90.

HIGHLIGHT 14.2

Current Sentencing Alternatives Reflect Multiple Objectives

What types of sentences usually are given to offenders?

Death penalty—In most States for the most serious crimes such as murder, the courts may sentence an offender to death by lethal injection, electrocution, exposure to lethal gas, hanging, or other method specified by State law.

• As of 1985, 37 States had laws providing for the death penalty.
• Virtually all death penalty sentences are for murder.
• As of yearend 1985, 50 persons had been executed since 1976, and 1,591 inmates in 32 States were under a sentence of death.

Incarceration—The confinement of a convicted criminal in a Federal or State prison or a local jail to serve a court-imposed sentence. Confinement is usually in a jail, administered locally, or a prison, operated by the State or Federal Government. In many States offenders sentenced to 1 year or less are held in a jail; those sentenced to longer terms are committed to a State prison.

• More than 4,200 correctional facilities are maintained by Federal, State, and local governments. They include 47 Federal facilities, 922 State-operated adult confinement and community-based correctional facilities, and 3,300 local jails, which usually are county-operated.
• On any given day in 1985 about 503,000 persons were confined in State and Federal prisons. About 254,000 were confined in local jails on June 30, 1985.

Probation—The sentencing of an offender to community supervision by a probation agency, often as a result of suspending a sentence to confinement. Such supervision normally entails specific rules of conduct while in the community. If the rules are violated a sentence to confinement may be imposed. Probation is the most widely used correctional disposition in the United States.

• State or local governments operate more than 2,000 probation agencies.
• At yearend 1985, nearly 1.9 million adults were on probation, or about 1 of every 95 adults in the Nation.

Split sentences, shock probation, and intermittent confinement—A penalty that explicitly requires the convicted person to serve a brief period of confinement in a local, State, or Federal facility (the "shock") followed by a period of probation. This penalty attempts to combine the use of community supervision with a short incarceration experience. Some sentences are periodic rather than continuous; for example, an offender may be required to spend a certain number of weekends in jail.

• In 1984 nearly a third of those receiving probation sentences in Idaho, New Jersey, Tennessee, Utah, and Vermont also were sentenced to brief periods of confinement.

HIGHLIGHT 14.2 *(continued)*

Restitution and victim compensation—The offender is required to provide financial repayment or, in some jurisdictions, services in lieu of monetary restitution, for the losses incurred by the victim.

Community service—The offender is required to perform a specified amount of public service work, such as collecting trash in parks or other public facilities.

Fines—An economic penalty that requires the offender to pay a specified sum of money within limits set by law. Fines often are imposed in addition to probation or as alternatives to incarceration.

• Nearly all States have statutory provisions for the collection and disbursement of restitution funds. A restitution law was enacted at the Federal level in 1982.

• Many States authorize community service work orders. Community service often is imposed as a specific condition of probation.

• The Victims of Crime Act of 1984 authorizes the distribution of fines and forfeited criminal profits to support State victim-assistance programs, with priority given to programs that aid victims of sexual assault, spousal abuse, and child abuse. These programs, in turn, provide assistance and compensation to crime victims.

• Many laws that govern the imposition of fines are being revised. The revisions often provide for more flexible means of ensuring equity in the imposition of fines, flexible fine schedules, "day fines" geared to the offender's daily wage, installment payment of fines, and the imposition of confinement only when there is an intentional refusal to pay.

• A 1984 study estimated that more than three-fourths of criminal courts use fines extensively and that fines levied each year exceed one billion dollars.

Source: Bureau of Justice Statistics, *Report to the Nation on Crime and Justice,* 2d ed. (Washington, DC: U.S. Government Printing Office, 1988), at 96.

1. *Right to counsel.*   The accused has a right to counsel because sentencing is considered a "critical stage" of the criminal proceeding. If the accused is indigent, a lawyer must be appointed for him or her by the state. This is a constitutional right under the Sixth Amendment.
2. *Right of allocution.*   Most courts provide that the defendant is entitled to make a statement on his or her own behalf as to why the sentence should not be imposed. This is not a constitutional right, but it is usually provided by state law.

A defendant has no constitutional right to be present in court during sentencing. Most states do provide for such right by law, but it is subject to exceptions. Exception is usually made (1) if the defendant has escaped the court's jurisdiction during the trial and can no longer be found or (2) if the offense involved is minor, in which case the defendant may be sentenced in his or her absence or be represented by his or her lawyer.

The sentences imposed by the court or jury usually fall into five general categories:

- death
- imprisonment
- payment of a fine or restitution
- probation
- intermediate punishments

More than one type of punishment may be imposed for a crime. For example, the death penalty may carry with it the payment of a huge fine or restitution; similarly, probation may involve having to perform a special service for the community. Each of these penalties raises constitutional issues. The issues raised are the focus of the discussion of each sanction in this chapter, starting with the death penalty.

A. The Death Penalty

The most severe penalty for crime is death. This sanction had traditionally been used in the United States with apparent public acceptance and without much legal controversy. It was not until the early seventies that the constitutionality of the death penalty drew greater attention from the Court. Prior to that, the death-penalty cases that reached the Court dealt more with the procedure for execution than with the constitutionality of the penalty itself. For example, in 1878, the Court found that execution by firing squad was not cruel and unusual (Wilkerson v. Utah, 99 U.S. 130 [1878]). In 1890, electrocution was found not to be cruel and unusual punishment (In re Kemmler, 136 U.S. 436 [1890]).

One of the interesting death-penalty cases decided by the Court before the seventies was State of Louisiana ex rel. Francis v. Resweber, 67 S.Ct. 374 (1947). In that case, the accused had gone through the difficult preparation for execution and had once received through his body a current of electricity intended to cause death. For some reason, the condemned man did not die, so Louisiana subsequently scheduled him again for execution. He objected, claiming a violation of his constitutional rights against double jeopardy and cruel and unusual punishment. On appeal, the

Court disagreed, saying that carrying out the execution of a convicted murderer, after the first attempt at execution had failed because of mechanical defect in the electric chair, was constitutional. In effect, the Court gave approval to the adage that "if at first you don't succeed, try again"—even in death-penalty cases.

In the seventies, two cases emerged as the authoritative decisions on the death-penalty issue, each case enunciating different but reconcilable principles. The cases are *Furman v. Georgia* and *Gregg v. Georgia*.

1. Furman v. Georgia: Death Penalty Unconstitutional

In this case, 408 U.S. 238 (1972), three defendants were convicted by a jury in state court and were sentenced to death. Two of the defendants were convicted of rape and the other of murder. On appeal, the Court held that the imposition and carrying out of the death penalty in these cases constituted a violation of the Constitution. Of the five justices who voted for unconstitutionality, three based their vote on the "equal protection" clause of the Fourteenth Amendment, while the other two justices (Brennan and Marshall) voted on the basis of the death penalty's being per se cruel and unusual punishment. The justices who based their opposition on the *"equal protection"* clause said that the penalty was applied in such a *"freakish and wanton"* manner as to be unconstitutional. Too much discretion was vested in the sentencing authority, and hence the penalty could be applied selectively and capriciously. Unless these infirmities were removed from the statute, the penalty could not be imposed because it violated the "equal protection" clause.

After the Furman decision, thirty-five states and the federal government revised their capital punishment statutes in an effort to eliminate the equal protection problems. The revised statutes fell into two categories: those that made the death penalty mandatory for certain crimes and those that allowed the judge or jury to decide, under legislative guidelines, whether to impose the death penalty. Each state statute that carried the death penalty had to undergo review by the U.S. Supreme Court in a proper case to determine if the revision had removed equal protection infirmities. The stage was therefore set in 1976 for Gregg v. Georgia (decided with four other cases from the states of Texas, Florida, Louisiana, and North Carolina).

2. Gregg v. Georgia: Death Penalty Constitutional

Four years after Furman, the Court decided Gregg v. Georgia, 428 U.S. 153 (1976). In Gregg, the Court said that the *death penalty is not per se cruel and unusual punishment* and may be imposed if the sentencing authority, usually a jury, is given guidance by law sufficient to remove arbitrariness and capriciousness from the sentencing process. In this case, defendant Gregg was charged with two counts of first-degree murder and two counts of robbery. The evidence showed that Gregg and a traveling companion were picked up by two motorists while hitchhiking in Florida. The next morning the bodies of the two motorists were discovered in a ditch near Atlanta. Gregg was tried, convicted, and sentenced to death. In accordance with Georgia law in capital cases, the trial was bifurcated. In addition to a bifurcated trial, Georgia law also provided the following: it required that the jury consider aggravating and mitigating circumstances, imposed the death penalty only in a very limited number of cases, and provided for automatic appeal to the Georgia Supreme Court. In a 7-to-

2 vote, the Court held that the death penalty is not per se cruel and unusual punishment; however, any arbitrary or capricious imposition of it is unconstitutional. The Georgia law was declared constitutional because it has sufficient provisions to preclude arbitrary or capricious imposition.

Gregg is important because for the first time a majority of the Court said that the death penalty is not in itself cruel and unusual punishment and can therefore be imposed. This judgment did not mean, however, that the statutes in the various states were automatically declared constitutional. What it meant was that the Court could now look at each state statute to determine whether or not its provisions were in accord with the "equal protection" clause. If they were, then executions could take place in that state. By a slow process, the Court has had to review the death-penalty statute of each state, in appropriate cases, before any execution could take place. In the case of Gary Gilmore (executed in Utah in 1977), the defendant did not bother to challenge the constitutionality of the Utah law; hence his speedy execution. (Read the Gregg v. Georgia case brief at the end of this chapter.)

The Furman and Gregg cases tell us that the death penalty does not constitute cruel and unusual punishment per se, but that it could run into equal protection problems if the law does not contain enough provisions to guard against capricious and arbitrary implementation. Over the years since Gregg, the Court has decided a number of cases upholding the constitutionality of specific state statutes. As a result, executions have resumed in many states. Despite the burgeoning population in prison death rows, executions in great numbers have not ensued. As of 1984, the total number of death row inmates had gone up to 1,540. Twenty-one were executed in 1984, but the number of death row convicts went up by 16 percent.[2] The explanation for this comparatively low number of executions may be twofold. First, there is an apparent hesitation by the public to carry out the death penalty despite its availability. It is the most severe of sanctions and society wants to use it very sparingly. It is easy to leave that ultimate sanction in our penal codes; it is difficult to actually carry it out. Second, numerous appeals are available to capital offenders in the United States. Various allegations of violation of constitutional rights can be raised on appeal, ranging from disproportionality of punishment to the way jury members were chosen. Hints and traces of impropriety are usually viewed seriously; courts are reluctant to dismiss the allegations as unfounded, perhaps because the ultimate irreversible penalty is involved. The benefit of the doubt is often resolved in favor of the defendant; hence executions are postponed repeatedly. This process frustrates the public, which feels that justice is not served by repeated delays. There is no simple solution to the problem, except to realize that the wheels of justice usually grind very slowly in a civilized and constitutional society. The higher the penalty, the more slowly the wheels of justice move.

3. Important Decisions after Gregg v. Georgia

The Gregg decision settled the issue of constitutionality of the death penalty; however, since then the Court has continued to accept cases in an effort to address other issues of law that were left unanswered in the Furman and Gregg cases. We are therefore in a stage of rights refinement. The more significant decisions of the Court since 1976 are the following.

HIGHLIGHT 14.3

The Death Penalty in the United States

Methods of execution used by the various states

Lethal injection	Electrocution	Lethal gas	Hanging	Firing squad
Arkansas[a]	Alabama	Arizona	Delaware	Idaho[a]
Idaho[a]	Arkansas[a]	California	Montana[a]	Utah[a]
Illinois	Connecticut	Colorado	New Hampshire	
Mississippi[a,b]	Florida	Maryland	Washington[a]	
Montana[a]	Georgia	Mississippi[a,b]		
Nevada	Indiana	Missouri		
New Jersey	Kentucky	North Caro-		
New Mexico	Louisiana	lina[a]		
North Carolina[a]	Nebraska	Wyoming[a]		
Oklahoma[c]	Ohio			
Oregon	Pennsylvania			
South Dakota	South Carolina			
Texas	Tennessee			
Utah[a]	Vermont			
Washington[a]	Virginia			
Wyoming[a]				

[a]Authorizes two methods of execution.
[b]Mississippi authorizes lethal injection for persons convicted after 7/1/84; executions of persons convicted before that date are to be carried out with lethal gas.
[c]Should lethal injection be found to be unconstitutional, Oklahoma authorizes use of electrocution or firing squad.

Minimum age authorized for capital punishment

10 years	13 years	14 years	15 years	16 years	17 years	18 years
Indiana	Georgia	Missouri	Arkansas	Connecticut	New Hampshire	California
Vermont	Mississippi	North Carolina	Louisiana	Montana	Texas	Colorado
			Virginia	Nevada		Illinois
						Nebraska
						New Jersey
						New Mexico
						Ohio
						Oregon
						Washington

No minimum age specified

Federal	Oklahoma
Alabama	Pennsylvania
Arizona	South Carolina
Delaware	South Dakota
Florida	Tennessee
Idaho	Utah
Kentucky	Wyoming
Maryland	

Source: Bureau of Justice Statistics, *Report to the Nation on Crime and Justice,* 2d ed. (Washington, DC: U.S. Government Printing Office, 1988), at 99.

a. *Invalid if disproportionate to the offense.* It is unconstitutional to impose the death penalty for the crime of raping an adult woman because the penalty is so *disproportionate* to the offense as to constitute cruel and unusual punishment (Coker v. Georgia, 433 U.S. 584 [1977]). The Court has also decided that it is unconstitutional to impose the death penalty on a defendant convicted of a felony murder as an accomplice when the defendant did not kill, or intend that a killing occur or that deadly force be used (Enmund v. Florida, 102 S.Ct. 3368 [1982]). Implicit in these decisions is the assumption that the death penalty must be commensurate with the severity of the offense. The court did not (as it probably could not) prescribe a severity-of-punishment scale; what it did say was that the death penalty in these offenses was too severe.

In a subsequent case, however, the Court said that a defendant who took part in a felony-murder but did not himself intend to kill or commit the specific act leading to that result, may nonetheless be sentenced to death as long as his participation in the felony was major and his mental state was one of reckless indifference to the value of human life (Tison v. Arizona, 41 CrL 3023 [1987]).

b. *Mandatory penalty unconstitutional.* The death penalty is cruel and unusual when it is made *mandatory* for a broad category of homicides and the law does not provide a meaningful opportunity for considering the presence of mitigating factors (Woodson v. North Carolina, 428 U.S. 280 [1980]). This decision underscores the need for the law to provide for mitigating and aggravating circumstances and for sentencing juries to consider them when imposing the sentence.

c. *Need for flexibility.* *Flexibility* must be afforded the jury in reaching its verdict in death-penalty cases. Therefore, the imposition of the death penalty is unconstitutional when the jury is not allowed to reach a verdict on a lesser included offense (Beck v. Alabama, 447 U.S. 625 [1980]). And yet in Furman v. Georgia the Court frowned on excessive discretion, which facilitated the imposition of the death penalty in a "freakish and wanton" manner. The Court has failed to give adequate guidance on where the line should be drawn between excessive discretion and flexibility. It merely says that laws that permit broad discretion and under which the penalty may be selectively and capriciously applied are unconstitutional. For example, a state law authorized the imposition of the death penalty for a killing that was "outrageously or wantonly vile, horrible or inhuman in that it involved torture, depravity of mind, or an aggravated battery to the victim." The law is unconstitutional because it is vague and could therefore be applied by the jury capriciously (Godfrey v. Georgia, 446 U.S. 420 [1980]).

In a subsequent case, the Court declared unconstitutional because of vagueness a portion of Oklahoma's death-penalty law that made it an aggravating circumstance for a murder to be "especially heinous, atrocious, or cruel," saying that those words had not been given a sufficiently narrow interpretation by state courts to comply with constitutional standards (Maynard v. Cartwright, 43 CrL 3053 [1988]).

d. *Proportionality review not needed.* State appellate courts are not constitutionally required to provide, upon request by the defendant, a *"proportionality* *review"* of death sentences in which the court would have to compare the sentence in the case before it with the penalties imposed in similar cases in that state (Pulley v. Harris, 34 CrL 3027 [1984]). In this case, the accused was convicted of murder and, after a separate sentencing hearing in which the jury found several aggravating factors, received the death penalty. On automatic appeal, the California Supreme Court affirmed the sentence without conducting a proportionality review of other cases in California in which the death penalty had been imposed. On appeal, the Court said that proportionality review even in death-penalty cases is not required by the Eighth Amendment prohibition against cruel and unusual punishment. The Court added that "the Eighth Amendment does not require, as an invariable rule in every case, that a state appellate court, before it affirms a death sentence, compare the sentence in the case before it with the penalties imposed in similar cases if requested to do so by the prisoner." It noted that the outcome in Gregg v. Georgia (upholding Georgia's statute under which the appellate court performed proportionality review despite the absence of a statutory requirement) did not hinge on the proportionality review. Proportionality reviews are constitutional and are provided for by law or judicial practice in some states, but that does not mean that such review is required by the Constitution. For example, the Court had earlier upheld the constitutionality of the Texas death-penalty law even though neither the law nor judicial practice provided for any form of proportionality review.

e. *Judge may override jury recommendation.* The trial judge may impose a death sentence even though an advisory jury has recommended a sentence of life imprisonment (Spaziano v. Florida, 35 CrL 3199 [1984]). In this case, following a sentencing hearing at which evidence was presented on mitigating and aggravating circumstances, a majority of the jury recommended life imprisonment. The trial judge disregarded the recommendation and instead imposed the death penalty after concluding that mitigating factors were insufficient to outweigh the two aggravating factors. The judge acted in accordance with state law. The Court, on appeal, decided that what the judge did was not violative of the guarantee against cruel and unusual punishment.

f. *Death-qualified jurors are valid.* In 1968, the Court held that states *could not exclude for cause in capital cases potential jurors who are merely opposed to the death penalty.* Such exclusion results in a jury that is not fairly representative of the community. Significantly, however, the Court also said that in choosing juries to *sentence* defendants in capital cases, prosecutors may exclude for cause potential jurors who say they are unwilling to vote for a death sentence under any circumstance (Witherspoon v. Illinois, 391 U.S. 510 [1968]). The Witherspoon ruling led to *"death-qualified" juries.* These juries were later challenged as being more "conviction-prone" than "non–death-qualified" juries. In subsequent cases, opponents of "death-qualified juries" argued that although persons who are unwilling to vote for the death sentence under any circumstance may be disqualified from the sentencing stage, a different jury should pass on guilt or innocence of the defendant, a jury that is not "death-qualified." This, in effect, would have required two juries in capital cases— a "non–death-qualified" jury to determine guilt or innocence and a "death-qualified jury" to determine the sentence to be imposed.

In 1986, the Court resolved that issue, deciding that prospective jurors whose opposition to the death penalty is so strong as to prevent or impair the performance of their duties as jurors at the sentencing phase of the trial may also be removed for cause from jury membership in capital cases (Lockhart v. McCree, 39 CrL 3085 [1986]). *These two decisions mean that prospective jurors whose opposition to capital punishment is so strong as to lead them to say at the outset that they would never vote for imposing death as a penalty for a crime may now be excluded both from the stage of determining guilt or innocence and from the stage of sentencing.* Note, however, that prospective jurors in capital cases still *cannot be rejected from either stage* merely because they are opposed to the death penalty. To be disqualified, these jurors must indicate that they would *automatically vote* against the death penalty irrespective of the facts of the case.

The preceding discussion of "death-qualified" juries may be summarized as shown in Figure 14.1.

g. Cannot execute the insane.   In 1986, the Court ruled in a 5–4 vote that the Eighth Amendment provision against cruel and unusual punishment prohibits the state from executing a prisoner who is *insane* at the time of the scheduled execution (Ford v. Wainwright, 39 CrL 3197 [1986]). The prisoner in this case was convicted of murder in a Florida state court and sentenced to death. He was sane at the time of the offense, at the trial, and at sentencing. But subsequently he began to show changes in behavior, indicating a mental disorder. The governor appointed three psychiatrists to evaluate the prisoner's mental competence. The psychiatrists reached conflicting diagnoses concerning the nature of the mental disorder, but were agreed that the prisoner was insane. Speaking for the majority, Justice Marshall said: "For centuries, no jurisdiction has countenanced the execution of the insane, yet this court has never decided whether the Constitution forbids the practice. Today we keep faith with that common law heritage in holding that it does."

h. May execute the mentally retarded.   The Court has held, in a 5–4 vote, that the Eighth Amendment provision against cruel and unusual punishment does not categorically prohibit the execution of mentally retarded capital murderers (Penry v. Lynaugh, 45 CrL 3188 [1989]). In this case, defendant Penry was sentenced by a Texas court to death for rape-murder. Although he was around 30 years old when the offense was committed, psychological testimony during trial showed that Penry had the mental age of a 6½-year-old, the social maturity of a 9- or 10-year-old, and an IQ of between 50 and 63. Testimony also showed that he suffered from organic brain damage and moderate retardation, which resulted in poor impulse control and an inability to learn from experience. The Court rejected the defense of cruel and unusual punishment, saying that there was no constitutional prohibition against the execution of mentally retarded capital murderers of Penry's reasoning ability. Specifically, the Court took into account the fact that (1) Penry was found by the jury competent to stand trial, that (2) he had the ability to consult with his lawyer with a reasonable degree of rational understanding, and that (3) the jury had rejected his insanity defense, reflecting their conclusion that Penry knew that his conduct was wrong. (The case

1. What opponents of "death - qualified" juries wanted:

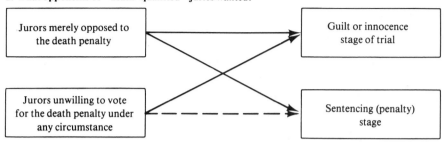

2. What the Court decided in the Witherspoon v. Illinois (1968) and later affirmed in Lockhart v. McCree (1986) cases:

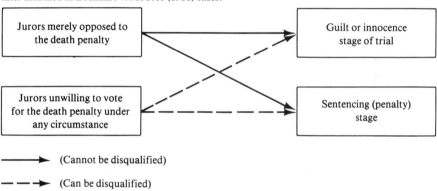

FIGURE 14.1

was remanded for new trial anyway because of defects in the judge's instruction to the jury on the mitigating circumstance of mental retardation.)

i. Cannot execute a 15-year-old, but can execute a 16-year-old. A state cannot execute a defendant who committed first-degree murder when he was only 15 years old (Thompson v. Oklahoma, 43 CrL 3197 [1988]). Such execution constitutes cruel and unusual punishment. The Court failed to state, however, the exact age when juveniles could be given the death penalty. This was resolved one year later when the Court ruled that the imposition of the death penalty for a crime committed at 16 or 17 years of age does not constitute cruel and unusual punishment (Stanford v. Kentucky, 109 S.Ct. 2969 [1989]). Therefore, the magic age for juveniles in death penalty cases is 16 at the time of the commission of the offense. If the crime was committed at that age, the death penalty may be imposed; if committed before that age, the death penalty cannot be imposed. The age of the offender at the time of trial is unimportant.

j. Use of victim impact statements is unconstitutional. Victim impact statements, which typically describe a victim's characteristics and the effect of the crime on the victim's family, are not admissible in death-penalty cases (Booth v. Maryland, 41 CrL 3282 [1987]). This is because the death sentence must relate to the moral culpability of the defendant and not to the impact of the crime on the victim's family. The Court therefore invalidated a Maryland law that required the inclusion of victim impact statements in presentence reports on capital offenses. The Court added that such statements introduce irrelevant and prejudicial matters that may create a risk that the death penalty will be imposed arbitrarily and capriciously.

k. Psychological examination without a lawyer is a violation of the right to counsel.   The admission at trial of testimony by a psychologist about his or her examination of a capital offense defendant without defense lawyer's knowledge violates defendant's right to counsel (Satterwhite v. Texas, 108 S.Ct. 1793 [1988]). In that case, Satterwhite was charged with capital murder. Before being represented by a lawyer, he was subjected to a court-ordered psychological examination. After defendant's conviction, the psychologist testified during the penalty phase of the trial that the defendant "had a severe antisocial personality disorder and is extremely dangerous and will commit future acts of violence." On appeal, the Court said that such testimony should not have been admitted into evidence because it violated the right to counsel. Moreover, its admission into evidence was not harmless.

l. Statistically proven disparity in capital offenses does not prohibit the imposition of the death penalty.   The existence of statistical disparity in the imposition of capital sentences, reflecting systematic bias of death-sentencing outcomes against black defendants and those whose victims are white, does not bar the imposition of the death penalty (McCleskey v. Kemp, 41 CrL 3047 [1987]). This case featured the so-called Baldus study of death-penalty cases in Georgia, indicating that the death penalty tends to be imposed more often when the victim is white and the defendant is black. Such study showed that defendants charged with killing whites were 4.3 times more likely to receive a death sentence than those charged with killing blacks. Also, blacks accused of murder were 1.1 times more likely than other races to be sentenced to die. In this case, the defendant was black; the victim, a police officer, was white. The Court decided that even if the study were statistically valid, it did not establish a violation of either the "equal protection" clause or the prohibition against cruel and unusual punishment. What is needed is proof by the defendant that there was discrimination in his or her particular case, and not merely an allegation of general discrimination against a particular race.

m. "Friends" cannot appeal death-penalty decision.   Third parties who consider themselves friends of death row inmates lack standing to challenge a death sentence imposed on a defendant who has waived his or her right to a direct appeal of his or her conviction and death sentence (Whitmore v. Arkansas, 58 L.W. 4495 [1990]). In that case, defendant Simmons waived his right to direct appeal of his conviction after he was sentenced to death on multiple murder charges. Such waiver is allowed by Arkansas law as long as the defendant is found competent to waive further proceedings. Another death row inmate, Whitmore, sought to intervene on behalf of his "next friend" Simmons, and alleged that he had standing to do that; further alleging that it was a violation of the ban against cruel and unusual punishment and equal protection for the state to carry out a death sentence without first conducting a mandatory appellate review of the conviction and sentence. The Court rejected the challenge, saying that Whitmore lacked standing, either in his personal capacity or as "next friend," to seek review by the U.S. Supreme Court of the death sentence imposed on a fellow inmate who had "knowingly, intelligently, and voluntarily" waived his right to an appeal. The Court did not address the issue of whether or not a defendant can waive his or her right to appellate review of a death sentence or whether such review is mandatory.

4. Prospects

It is obvious from the preceding cases that death-penalty issues are far from resolved and that the U.S. Supreme Court continues to fine-tune its 1976 ruling in the Gregg case. Gregg settled the substantive phase of the death-penalty issue (whether the death penalty is per se cruel and unusual punishment) but it failed to address the many procedural phases of the question. These are the issues now being addressed by the Court on a continuing basis. It is conceivable that the Court at some future time might change its mind and ban the death penalty altogether. The chances of that happening in the next decade with a conservative Court appear remote.

In the meantime, about 300 prisoners are condemned to death every year, but fewer than 20 are actually executed. The death row population now exceeds 2,300 in the thirty-six states that impose capital punishment.[3] In the past thirteen years, 121 executions have been carried out in the United States, most of them being in Texas, Florida, Louisiana, and Georgia. Of those executed, 40 percent were black, 52 percent white, and 8 percent were of other races.[4]

B. Imprisonment

Imprisonment means keeping a detainee or convicted criminal in jail or prison. A *detainee* is a person who has been charged with a crime but who has not been found guilty. The detainee is incarcerated either because he or she cannot raise bail or because his or her offense is so serious that bail is denied. Jails are places of confinement that are usually reserved for detainees and minor offenders. They are operated by cities or counties and are usually under the supervision and control of a sheriff. In contrast, prisons are managed, funded, and controlled by either the state or the federal government. Most prisons do not hold detainees, although many include persons whose cases are on appeal. Jails and prisons may be distinguished as follows:

Jails	*Prisons*
1. Usually for minor offenders (misdemeanants)	1. Usually for serious offenders (felons)
2. Hold detainees and convicts	2. Hold only those who have been convicted or whose cases are pending appeal
3. Established and funded by local governments	3. Established and funded by state or federal governments
4. Administered by the sheriff or chief of police	4. Administered by a state or federal correctional officer

The use of jails and prisons has been a part of the American corrections practice for centuries and its constitutionality has seldom been challenged. The Thirteenth Amendment of the Constitution provides that "neither slavery nor involuntary servitude, except as a punishment for crime whereof the party shall have been duly convicted, shall exist within the United States, or any place subject to their jurisdiction." Admittedly, imprisonment constitutes involuntary servitude, but it is of the kind that is permitted by the Constitution.

1. Cruel and Unusual Punishment

The more plausible challenge to the constitutionality of imprisonment comes from allegations of cruel and unusual punishment. What constitutes cruel and unusual punishment, prohibited by the Eighth Amendment, has not been made clear by the Court. One standard often used, however, is *whether the punishment fits the crime.* For example, Rummel was sentenced by the state of Texas to life imprisonment under a habitual offender law. The sentence was mandatory after conviction of a third felony. Rummel contended that the punishment violated his right to protection against cruel and unusual punishment because his nonviolent crimes, committed over several years, dealt with property valued only at $80, $28, and $121, respectively. The Court held the law constitutional, noting that even with mandatory life sentence, there was strong possibility of parole under Texas law after twelve years (Rummel v. Estelle, 445 U.S. 263 [1980]). In contrast, the Court has ruled that a South Dakota law that imposed a life sentence without possibility of parole upon a habitual offender convicted of seven nonviolent felonies, totaling a small amount, violated the defendant's constitutional guarantee against cruel and unusual punishment as *grossly disproportionate* to the offense (Solem v. Helm, 33 CrL 3220 [1983]). The difference between Rummel and Solem is that in Rummel there was a strong possibility of parole under Texas law and practice, whereas that possibility was almost nil in South Dakota.

2. Concurrent versus Consecutive Sentences

If the defendant has been convicted of two or more crimes, or is already serving a sentence on some other offense, it is necessary to determine whether the new sentence

---

HIGHLIGHT 14.4

Only 46 Percent of Convicted State Felons Incarcerated

"State courts throughout the United States convicted an estimated 583,000 felons during 1986 and sent about 46 percent of them to a state prison, the U.S. Justice Department's Bureau of Justice Statistics (BJS) said on February 5 [1989].

"An estimated 110,000 people were convicted of a violent felony (a murder, rape, robbery or aggravated assault), 103,000 were convicted of a burglary and 76,000 were convicted of trafficking in drugs, accounting for one-half of the 1986 total, the Bureau said. . . .

"About two-thirds of the convicted felons were sentenced to incarceration—46 percent to a state prison and 21 percent to a local jail (usually to serve a term of a year or less). An estimated 31 percent were given straight probation with no prison or jail time and 2 percent were given other sentences that did not include incarceration."

Source: Crime Control Digest, February 13, 1989, p. 4. Reprinted with permission.

imposed will run *concurrently* (at the same time) or *consecutively* (one after the other, or "stacked"). The decision usually lies within the discretion of the judge who imposes the sentence. In the absence of any specific indication, the sentences are to be served concurrently. For example, X is tried and convicted of two robberies. He is sentenced to five years in prison for each conviction. If the sentences are imposed concurrently, X will serve a total of five years. If served consecutively, X stays in prison for 10 years. If nothing is noted in the sentence, the penalties are to be served concurrently, meaning that X serves five years.

3. Prohibition against Double Jeopardy

There are jurisdictions that by law allow judges to increase the penalty imposed within a certain period of time after the defendant starts serving a prison sentence. The Supreme Court has not ruled on the issue, but lower courts have held it to be a violation of the "double jeopardy" clause for the trial court to increase its original sentence while the defendant is serving that sentence. Whether the "double jeopardy" provision applies if there is a specified time limit remains to be seen.

The Constitution does not prohibit the imposition of a longer sentence upon reconviction for the same offense, provided that the longer sentence is imposed for a valid reason and not out of judicial vindictiveness, meaning punishing the defendant for a successful appeal (North Carolina v. Pearce, 395 U.S. 711 [1969]). For example, X is serving five years in prison for murder. He succeeds in a habeas corpus case and obtains a new trial. If reconvicted in the second trial, X may be given a sentence of more than five years as long as there is new information to justify the harsher sentence (such as the defendant's case history, which was unavailable during the first trial). The reason for the increased sentence must be stated by the judge, otherwise the *presumption of judicial vindictiveness* applies. The requirement of new information applies only if the sentence is determined by the judge. If determined by a jury, the requirement does not apply; therefore the second jury can impose a harsher sentence even in the absence of new information. The presumption of judicial vindictiveness does not apply, however, if the first sentence was based on a guilty plea and the second, harsher sentence follows a trial (Alabama v. Smith, 57 L.W. 4626 [1989]).

The prohibition against double jeopardy also requires that a person reconvicted after a new trial be given full credit against the new sentence for the time served (or fine paid) under his or her original conviction. For example, Y is convicted of robbery and sentenced to ten years in the state penitentiary. After serving two years, Y is given a new trial on the ground that the evidence used against her was obtained without the Miranda warnings. If Y is retried, reconvicted, and given a six-year sentence, she must be given credit for the two years she has already served. She must therefore be released after four more years, subject to the provisions of the state parole and good-time laws.

C. Fine

A *fine* is defined as a pecuniary punishment imposed by lawful tribunal upon a person convicted of a crime.[5] The amount imposed may be fixed by state or left to the discretion of the Court. The term *fine* is to be distinguished from *civil penalty,* which means a sum of money exacted for the doing of or failure to perform some act. A civil penalty is usually imposed by an administrative agency, whereas a fine is imposed by the Court. Payment of a penalty of $50 by a tavern owner for failure to obtain a liquor license is different from paying a fine of $100 for driving while intoxicated.

The "equal protection" clause prohibits the imposition of a greater punishment on a poor person than on a rich person. Thus, if nonindigents can pay a fine and avoid imprisonment, then indigent defendants cannot be sent to jail because they are unable to pay the fine. The Court has said that "there can be no equal justice where the kind of trial a man gets depends on the amount of money he has." This can be paraphrased to say that there can be no equal justice if the punishment imposed depends on a defendant's ability to pay.

> Example 1:   A state law imposes imprisonment plus a fine and provides that if the fine is not paid the prisoner must remain in jail longer than the prescribed maximum sentence to "work off" the unpaid fine. This law is unconstitutional because it violates the "equal protection" clause (Williams v. Illinois, 399 U.S. 235 [1970]). In this case, Williams was convicted of a misdemeanor in an Illinois court. He was sentenced to one year of imprisonment, a $500 fine, and court costs of $5. Illinois law provided that if a defendant failed to pay the fine and court costs by the end of the prison term, the prisoner was required to remain in jail to "work off" the fine at the rate of $5 a day. Williams did not have any money to pay the fine and court costs, so he was held in jail for 101 days beyond the maximum term. The Court held that when the aggregate imprisonment exceeds the maximum period fixed by the statute and results directly from an involuntary nonpayment of a fine or court costs, the additional "work-off" imprisonment time violates the "equal protection" guarantee of the Constitution. (Read the Williams v. Illinois case brief at the end of this chapter.)
>
> Example 2:   Texas law provided only for fine in traffic offenses. An indigent was convicted of traffic offenses and fined a total of $425. Texas law also provided that persons unable to pay the fine must be incarcerated at the rate of $5 per day until the fine was "worked off." In this case, the defendant would have had to serve an 85-day term. The Court said that it is a denial of equal protection to limit punishment to payment of a fine for those who are able to pay it but to convert the fine to imprisonment for those who are unable to pay (Tate v. Short, 401 U.S. 395 [1971]).

The Williams and Tate cases must be understood in the context of the state statutes involved. In the Williams case, the defendant would have served 101 days over the maximum imprisonment of one year allowed by law if the "work-off" provision were valid. In the Tate case, the defendant would have served 85 days in jail because he could not pay the fines. In both cases, the defendants would not have suffered extra incarceration if they had had money. The crucial consideration in the Williams case was that the time spent in jail would have gone beyond the usually allowable maximum. In the Tate case, the statute itself did not provide imprisonment for those who could pay, but converted the fine to imprisonment if the defendant could not pay. These cases are different from a sentence requiring the defendant to "work off" the unpaid fine but keeping the extra time within the maximum allowed by law. For example, Z is guilty of a traffic offense for which the maximum sentence is one year in jail and a $200 fine. In addition to giving Z six months' incarceration, the judge asks Z if he has $200 to pay the fine. Z says that he does not have the money. The judge sentences Z to a total of six months and twenty days in jail (the twenty days are for the unpaid fine, at a rate of $10 a day). The sentence is valid because the extra twenty days are still within the maximum allowed by law for that offense. It is important to remember, therefore, that in the Williams case the "work-off" time went beyond the maximum allowed by law, whereas in the Tate case the law authorized only a fine for traffic offenses, but automatically converted it into incarceration if the defendant could not pay.

D. Probation

Probation is defined as a type of sentence under which a convicted offender is allowed to remain free in the community, subject to court-imposed conditions and under the supervision of a probation officer. If the imposed conditions are violated, the probation may be revoked and the probationer imprisoned. According to 1981 figures of the Bureau of Justice Statistics, 63 percent of all adults under correctional supervision were on probation.[6] That figure has remained constant over the years. Probation is a widely used form of punishment, primarily because it is cost-effective and humanitarian. It is usually given to first-time or minor nonviolent offenders.

1. Probation Is a Priviiege, Not a Right

This means that in most jurisdictions probation is available only at the discretion of the judge or jury. A defendant cannot demand that the judge or jury grant probation, unless such is the penalty provided by law. In most cases, probation is authorized as an alternative to incarceration, at the option of the judge or jury. Probation differs from a *suspended sentence* in that probation involves some type of supervision (minimum, medium, maximum, or intensive) by a probation officer, whereas a suspended sentence does not. "Suspended sentence" means that the defendant is given a prison sentence, the sentence is suspended, and the defendant remains free. If the defendant runs afoul of the law again, that sentence is revived and the defendant goes to jail or prison. In most states, probation is a sentence and may therefore be appealed; in a few states, however, the appeal can be made only if the probation is revoked.

Probation is granted for a specified number of years, usually to coincide with the prison term imposed. For example, X is sentenced to seven years, but instead of serving time in prison, X is placed on probation. X will be on probation for seven years. Some states, however, provide that the probationer be discharged after having been on probation for a minimum number of years. For example, Y is sentenced to seven years' probation. The law may provide that Y may be discharged from probation and the court record dismissed after two years if during that time Y does not violate any condition of probation.

2. Intensive Supervision Probation

Intensive supervision probation (ISP) is a form of supervision in probation where the caseload is low and the probationer is supervised more closely. Considered a more effective type of probation, it usually applies to offenders who otherwise would have been in prison or jail. Regular probation caseload may vary from 100–250 probationers; by contrast, the ideal intensive supervision caseload is 25. One or more probation officers are assigned to monitor a group, depending on how the system is structured. Intensive supervision probation differs from regular probation mainly in the intensity of the supervision and the clientele involved. Regular probationers are usually those who commit minor offenses, while those in intensive supervision are those who in the absence of such program would have been sent to prison, hence the higher-risk offenders.

The legal problems raised in intensive supervision are usually twofold: the equal protection problem associated with the selection process and the cruel and unusual punishment argument. Both objections have been rejected by the courts primarily based on the concept of diminished constitutional rights for offenders and the fact that the offenders on intensive supervision are those who otherwise deserve to be sent to prison anyway. Intensive supervision is therefore viewed as a more humane approach, to which offenders and their lawyers readily give consent, the alternative being institutionalization.

3. Shock Probation

A variation of regular probation, *shock probation* provides that an offender serve a fixed minimum time in prison, after which he or she is discharged and placed on probation. (Some jurisdictions call this a split sentence.) The idea is to expose the offender to the harsh realities of prison life so as to deter him or her from further criminality. It is called "shock probation" because the defendant is not supposed to know that he or she will be placed on probation after serving only a fraction of the prison term. More often, however, the defendant knows through his or her lawyer that he or she will soon be free; hence if anybody is shocked, it will most likely be the public.

4. Terms of Probation

The authority granting probation has broad discretion in setting terms and conditions for offenders to follow. Courts have held that a probationer may be subject to these restrictions as a condition of receiving the privilege of probation. The Court may surround probationers with restrictions and requirements that a defendant must follow to retain his or her probationary status.

Decided cases show that there are four general requirements for the validity of a probation condition:

    a. The condition must be reasonably related to the protection of society and/or the rehabilitation of the probationer.

    b. The condition must be clear.

    c. The condition must be reasonable.

    d. The condition must be constitutional.

The condition attached to the probation must be accepted by the probationer, otherwise probation may be withheld. Probation conditions are usually listed in state statute, but the conditions specified are usually merely suggestive, meaning that they may be imposed at the option of the judge, who may impose some, all, or none of the

IN THE SUPERIOR COURT OF

Deputy Clerk

VS

COUNTY, GEORGIA   FINAL DISPOSITION

CRIMINAL ACTION NO. _____

OFFENSE(S) _____

_____

_____

_____ **TERM, 19____**

☐ **PLEA:**		☐ **VERDICT:**	☐ **OTHER DISPOSITION**
☐ NEGOTIATED	☐ JURY	☐ GUILTY ON	☐ NOLLE PROSEQUI ORDER ON
☐ GUILTY ON COUNT(S) _____	☐ NON-JURY	COUNT (S) _____	COUNT(S) _____
☐ NOLO CONTENDERE ON		☐ NOT GUILTY ON	☐ DEAD DOCKET ORDER ON
COUNT(S) _____		COUNT(S) _____	COUNT(S) _____
☐ TO LESSER INCLUDED		☐ GUILTY OF INCLUDED	
OFFENSE(S) _____		OFFENSE(S) OF _____	
		ON COUNT(S) _____	(SEE SEPARATE ORDER)
ON COUNT(S) _____			

☐ DEFENDANT WAS ADVISED OF HIS/HER RIGHT TO HAVE THIS SENTENCE REVIEWED BY THE SUPERIOR COURTS SENTENCE REVIEW PANEL.

☐ **FIRST OFFENDER TREATMENT**

WHEREAS, the above-named defendant has been found guilty of the above-stated offense, and; WHEREAS, said defendant has not previously been convicted of a felony nor availed himself of the provision of the First Offender Act (Ga. Laws 1968, p. 324),

NOW, THEREFORE, the defendant consenting hereto, it is the judgment of the Court that no judgment of guilt be imposed at this time, but that further proceedings are deferred and defendant is hereby sentenced to confinement for the period of _____ and/or placed on probation for the period of _____ from this date provided that said defendant complies with the following general and special conditions herein imposed by the Court as part of this sentence; PROVIDED, further, that upon violation of the terms of probation, the Court may enter an adjudication of guilt and proceed to sentence defendant to the maximum sentence provided by law. Upon fulfillment of the terms of probation, or upon release of the defendant by the Court prior to the termination of the period thereof, the defendant shall stand discharged of said offense charged and shall be completely exonerated of guilt of said offense charged.

Let a copy of this Order be forwarded to the Office of the State Probation System of Georgia, and the Identification Division of the Federal Bureau of Investigation.

☐ **GENERAL CONDITIONS OF PROBATION**

The defendant, having been granted the privilege of serving all or part of the above-stated sentence on probation, hereby is sentenced to the following general conditions of probation:

☐ 1) Do not violate the criminal laws of any governmental unit.

☐ 2) Avoid injurious and vicious habits — especially alcoholic intoxication and narcotics and other dangerous drugs unless prescribed lawfully.

☐ 3) Avoid persons or places of disreputable or harmful character.

☐ 4) Report to the Probation Officer as directed and permit such Officer to visit him (her) at home or elsewhere.

☐ 5) Work faithfully at suitable employment insofar as may be possible.

☐ 6) Do not change his (her) present place of abode, move outside the jurisdiction of the Court, or leave the State for any period of time without prior permission of the Probation Supervisor.

☐ 7) Support his (her) legal dependants to the best of his (her) ability.

☐ **OTHER CONDITIONS OF PROBATION**

IT IS FURTHER ORDERED that the defendant pay a fine in the amount of _____ plus $50 or 10%, whichever is less pursuant to O.C.G.A. § 15-21-70, and pay restitution in the amount of _____ ; Probation Fee _____ ; Court Costs _____ ; Attorney's Fees _____

Payments are: _____

_____

_____

IT IS THE FURTHER ORDER of the Court, and the defendant is hereby advised that the Court may, at any time, revoke any conditions of this probation and/or discharge the defendant from probation. The probationer shall be subject to arrest for violation of any condition of probation herein granted. If such probation is revoked, the Court may order the execution of the sentence which was originally imposed or any portion thereof in the manner provided by law after deducting therefrom the amount of time the defendant has served on probation.

The defendant was represented by the Honorable _____ , Attorney at Law, _____ County, by (Employment) (Appointment).

By the Court _____ , 19 ___

So ordered this _____ day of _____ , 19 ___   _____

Judge,   Superior Court

Certificate of Service — This is to certify and acknowledge that a true and correct copy of this Final Disposition has been delivered in person and the defendant has been duly instructed regarding the conditions as set forth.

This _____ day of _____ , 19 ___ .

_____   _____

Probation Officer   Defendant

SC-6.1 Rev. 85   P-9 Rev. 10/85

Filed in Open Court, this _____ day of _____ , 19 ___

Original - Clerk
Duplicate - District Attorney
Triplicate - Probation Office

---

conditions suggested by law. Moreover, the judge may impose "special conditions," meaning conditions that are not listed by law but that may nonetheless be imposed to meet the special rehabilitative needs of a probationer. For example, Z is placed on probation for use of drugs. In addition to the conditions specified by law, the judge may require Z to submit to a urine test every week.

E. Intermediate Punishments

The term *"intermediate punishments"* has different meanings in various states. An operational definition that embodies the term's modern concept is that it "means all punishments lying between imprisonment and 'ordinary' probation"[7] This includes such sanctions as participation in community service programs, restitution, intensive supervision probation, electronic monitoring, and forfeiture of proceeds of criminal activity.

1. Community Service Programs

A *community service program* is defined as a program that places a convicted offender in unpaid positions with nonprofit or tax-supported agencies to perform a specified number of hours of work or service within a given time limit as a sentencing option or condition. Community service programs operate under a variety of official titles, among them court referral, volunteer work, service restitution, and symbolic restitution programs. There are as many types of programs as there are opportunities for service in the community, among which are hospital work, helping the elderly, counseling drug offenders, and providing manual labor in public service jobs.

Probation is a form of community-based corrections program, but there are forms other than probation. For example, X is guilty of DWI and is sentenced to 200 hours of community service in the form of free hospital work. X will likely not be under the supervision of a probation officer, but supervision may be provided by other volunteers or the hospital staff. It must be noted, however, that judges may impose some form of community service as a condition of probation. For example, as a condition for placing a person guilty of littering on probation, the judge may require that the person help clean up the streets during weekends.

The legal issues involved in community service programs are essentially similar to those in probation. Judges or juries have wide leeway in choosing the conditions to be imposed, subject only to the same four requirements for the validity of the terms of probation conditions: reasonable relatedness to the protection of society or the rehabilitation of the individual, clarity, reasonableness, and constitutionality.

2. Restitution

Restitution is defined as the restoring of property or of a right to a person who has been unjustly deprived of it.[8] It differs from a fine in that the money paid in a fine does not go to the victim, but instead goes to the state. Victim restitution also differs from victim compensation in that the money in victim restitution is given by the offender, whereas the money given to the victim in victim compensation programs comes from the state. Restitution may be imposed together with other forms of punishment. For example, Z is found guilty of driving while intoxicated, in the process of which he injures a pedestrian. Z may be placed on probation, ordered to perform community service, and pay restitution to the injured party. Restitution money is usually paid through the court or the probation officer.

Restitution has become a more popular form of criminal sanction because the money goes to the victim of crime instead of to the state. Moreover, it is an act of atonement for the criminal because the money taken from him or her helps rehabilitate the victim financially. Restitution is statutorily authorized in many states as a form of criminal sanction, but even in states where it is not specifically provided for by statute, courts usually consider it a valid sanction because of its restorative and rehabilitative effects.

The two legal problems associated with restitution are indigency of the defendant and the setting of the restitution amount. If the defendant is indigent and cannot pay, courts cannot cite the defendant for contempt or send the defendant to prison; if, however, the defendant refuses to pay, then incarceration is valid. The restitution amount must be set by the judge and cannot be delegated unless specifically authorized by statute. In some jurisdictions, the judge delegates the setting of the amount to the probation officer as a part of the probation conditions. This is invalid; however, the judge can ask the probation officer to recommend the restitution amount and, having imposed the amount, leave the mode of payment to the probation officer. For example, X is sentenced by the judge to pay restitution to a robbery victim. The judge must set the amount even though the restitution is a part of the probation condition. Assume that the judge sets the amount at $500. How that amount is to be paid can be determined by the probation officer. The officer can, for example, require that the amount be paid in monthly installments of $50 for ten months. What the judge cannot validly do, unless specifically authorized by statute, is set as a condition of probation that the offender "shall pay restitution in an amount to be set by the probation officer." This is an improper delegation of the judicial sentencing authority.

3. Electronic Monitoring

Electronic monitoring is a recent criminal sanction that is a form of an electronically monitored curfew. It may be used as a separate sanction in the nature of a house arrest, or as a condition of probation, parole, or release without bail before trial. The monitoring system is usually composed of a control computer located at the controlling agency, a receiver unit located in the offender's home, and a transmitter device worn by the offender. The style of the transmitter varies from those that are worn on the ankle to those that are worn on the wrist or around the neck. It monitors the presence of an offender in a vicinity during times when he or she is supposed to be there. Although the offender conceivably can remove the device by cutting the strap or stretching it and taking it off, an electronic circuit within the device detects such tampering and sends an alarm to the receiving unit. The device has been continually improved over the years and is now accepted by the scientific community as reliable and difficult for the offender to manipulate.

Legal and constitutional issues have been raised about electronic monitoring, but the courts have consistently rejected them. Issues such as that it constitutes an unconstitutional search and seizure or that it violates the offender's right to privacy have not made much headway. "Equal protection" and "due process" arguments have also been raised without success. In sum, electronic monitoring has passed constitutional muster and has become an often-used alternative sanction to prisons, primarily because it is cost-effective and keeps the offender in the community.

4. Forfeiture of Proceeds of Criminal Activity

Forfeiture is a sanction that requires the defendant to give up various property rights and interests related to a criminal act.[9] The United States has long had criminal forfeiture statutes, but it enjoyed a revival in 1970 when the federal government passed the Racketeer Influenced and Corrupt Organization (*RICO*) statute and the Comprehensive Drug Prevention and Control Act. It has since been included in various crime control legislations, the common element in these statutes being the confiscation by the government of goods or items connected with criminal activity. This form of criminal sanction has become a convenient and popular tool for prosecutors in drug-related cases.

Many states have passed their own version of RICO laws. Some provide for forfeiture of property connection with the commission of any felony, but most state statutes allow for civil rather than criminal forfeiture. The federal RICO statute renders criminally and civilly liable "any person" who conducts the affairs of an enterprise engaged in interstate commerce through a "pattern of racketeering activity." Although RICO was originally intended as a weapon to fight organized crime, portions of the statute have been used more frequently in recent years to recover damages for business fraud. Moreover, the Court has also upheld a state racketeering law (similar to the provisions of RICO) to fight obscenity, but limited its application in these cases by prohibiting prosecutors from padlocking adult bookstores without first proving that their contents are obscene (Fort Wayne Books, Inc. v. Indiana, 44 CrL 3093 [1989]). It is clear that this form of sanction has found favor with prosecutors and judges and will be used even more extensively in the future, unless curtailed by law.

II. APPEAL

The right to appeal is not guaranteed anywhere in the U.S. Constitution. State laws in all fifty states, however, provide for the right to appeal in criminal cases. The right to appeal is so pervasive in the United States that appellate courts are virtually awash in cases, resulting in lengthy delays in appealed decisions.

State courts have their own appellate procedures, which must be followed before any case can be taken to the U.S. Supreme Court. Most states have intermediate courts of appeals; others provide for convictions to be appealed directly to the State Supreme Court. In some states there is a two-level system of appellate review, with automatic review at the first level and discretionary review at the second level. Automatic appeals are given to defendants upon request, meaning that if the defendant asks the appellate court to review the case, the court must do so. In discretionary appeals, the defendant asks the appellate court for review but that court has the option to accept or reject the appeal. In all states that impose the death penalty, any death-penalty conviction is automatically elevated to the State Supreme Court and, if further appealed (on the basis of a federal or constitutional question), from there to the U.S. Supreme Court.

In theory, any criminal conviction may reach the U.S. Supreme Court on appeal. In reality, the Court has the option to accept only those cases that any four (out of the nine) justices consider sufficiently important to warrant inclusion in the Court docket. Known as the *"Rule of Four,"* this is the main method by which the Supreme Court determines which of the thousands of cases the Court will decide on its merits. It applies whether a case is brought on a writ of *certiorari* (a Latin term meaning "made more certain") or on a writ of appeal—the two ways by which appealed cases are brought to the Court. The Court hears constitutional issues only when dealing with cases tried in state courts. The cases not accepted by the Court are dismissed *per curiam,* a Latin phrase meaning "by the court." This dismissal consists of a brief unsigned statement that the Court does not consider the case to be of sufficient merit to warrant full consideration. A *per curiam decision* does not mean that the Court agrees with the decision of the immediate lower court. What it means is simply that the Court does not consider the appeal to be of such significance as to warrant full deliberation by the Court.

As in the case of sentencing, defendants have minimal rights during appeal. Among their constitutional rights are these:

1. If the appeal requires a transcript of the trial proceeding, the transcript must be given to an indigent free of charge (Mayer v. City of Chicago, 404 U.S. 189 [1971]).
2. If a state provides for an appeal as a matter of right, counsel must be appointed for indigent defendants. The Court has said that equal protection is violated if the state makes appellate review less accessible to the poor than to the rich (Griffin v. Illinois, 351 U.S. 12 [1956]).

State statutes provide for a specified period of time after sentence is pronounced during which a defendant may file an appeal. If the defendant is sentenced to jail or prison, there is no constitutional right to bail while the case is on appeal. Many states give the judge discretion to release or imprison the accused pending resolution of the appeal, at least in cases in which the actual imprisonment imposed is not so high as to induce the defendant to flee the jurisdiction. In serious cases, however, imprisonment pending appeal is required in most states. If life imprisonment or the death penalty is imposed, imprisonment upon conviction and pending appeal is usually automatic. But if imprisonment is five years or less, bail may be optional with the judge.

Whether a defendant stays in a *local jail* (where he or she stayed as a detainee) or in a *state prison* pending the appeal (if the judge refuses bail) is governed by state law. Some states provide that an accused may stay in jail for certain offenses but must be transferred to the state prison for others.

The general rule is that a defendant can be retried if the appeal succeeds, particularly if it succeeds because of errors committed during the trial (Burks v. U.S.,

---

HIGHLIGHT 14.5

Both Convictions and Sentences May Be Appealed

"Defendants have as many as three possible avenues of appeal; the *direct appeal, postconviction remedy,* and *federal habeas corpus.* Defendants appeal their convictions alleging that their rights were violated during the criminal justice process. Reversal of a conviction on appeal sets aside only the prior conviction. Defendants may be retried. In many States criminal appeals are a matter of right and most States provide for an automatic appeal of death sentences. A sentence may be appealed on grounds it violates the Constitutional prohibition against cruel and unusual punishment" [Italics added].

Source: Bureau of Justice Statistics, *Report to the Nation on Crime and Justice,* 2d ed. (Washington, DC: U.S. Government Printing Office, 1988), at 88.

437 U.S. 1 [1978]). For example, Y is convicted in state court of possession of cocaine. On appeal, Y alleges that the trial court erred in ruling that the evidence used against him was admissible. The appellate court agrees with Y and reverses the conviction. The conviction is set aside, but Y may be tried again without using the illegally obtained evidence, if the prosecutor so desires. There is no double jeopardy because by appealing Y is deemed to have waived protection against double jeopardy.

The usual appeal route is from the trial court to the state appellate court (or courts, if there is more than one level), and from there to the U.S. Supreme Court (in cases involving federal questions or basic constitutional issues). The only exception to this sequence is a habeas corpus case filed by a state prisoner. If a habeas corpus petition fails in the State Supreme Court, the case goes down to the Federal District Court and works its way up to the Federal Court of Appeals, and then to the U.S. Supreme Court. The reason for this unusual procedure is that there are two kinds of habeas corpus proceedings—state and federal. The state proceeding must be exhausted first before the federal procedure can be used by state prisoners. Federal prisoners, of course, may go straight to the Federal District Court.

III. HABEAS CORPUS—POSTCONVICTION REMEDY

Habeas corpus (a Latin term that literally means "you have the body," the body being that of the suspect or criminal) is defined as a writ directed to a sheriff or other person detaining another, commanding him or her to produce the body of the prisoner at a certain time and place and to report the day and cause of the prisoner's taking and detention to the judge awarding the writ.[10] Upon proper hearing, the court will continue the imprisonment or discharge the prisoner from custody, as seems just and legal. Habeas corpus is the remedy against any type of illegal restraint by a government official and has frequently been called the Great Writ of Liberty.

Habeas corpus proceedings have their basis in Article I, Section 9, of the Constitution, which provides that "the Writ of Habeas Corpus shall not be suspended, unless when in Cases of Rebellion or Invasion the public Safety may require it." The First Judiciary Act in 1789 empowered federal judges to grant the writ of habeas corpus to federal prisoners. In 1867, Congress extended the writ to all those restrained of their liberty, including state prisoners.[11]

A writ of habeas corpus is distinguished from an appeal in that a writ is usually filed to secure a person's release from imprisonment, after appeals on the conviction have been exhausted and usually after the defendant has started serving time. It is therefore a separate proceeding from the criminal case that led to the conviction. In contrast, an appeal is filed after a person has been convicted, usually alleging that there was something wrong with the trial and thus that the conviction should be reversed. Appeals are a part of the criminal proceeding and therefore the parties remain the same. For example, X is charged with, tried, and convicted of murder in California. The murder case is titled State of California v. X. X may appeal her conviction through the California courts and up to the U.S. Supreme Court (if a federal or constitutional question is involved). Assume that X has exhausted her appeals and that her conviction has been affirmed. X must now serve time in a California prison.

While serving time, X obtains evidence that the jury in her trial was in fact tampered with by the prosecution. X cannot now file an appeal; she may, however, file a habeas corpus case seeking her release. The title of the case will be X v. Y, Y being the director of the California prison system. If X succeeds and is released, she may be tried again for the same case (if the prosecutor so desires). The differences between a habeas corpus and an appeal may be summarized as follows:

Appeal	*Writ of habeas corpus*
1. A direct attack upon the conviction	1. A collateral attack, meaning a separate case from the criminal conviction
2. Part of the criminal proceeding	2. A civil proceeding
3. Purpose is to reverse conviction	3. Purpose is to secure release from prison
4. Filed only after conviction	4. May be filed any time a person is deprived of freedom illegally by a public officer, before or after conviction
5. Accused has been convicted, but may be free on bail	5. Person is serving time or is detained illegally; cannot be filed if person is free
6. Based on any type of error made during the trial	6. Based on a violation of a constitutional right, usually during the trial
7. Must be undertaken within a certain period of time after conviction, otherwise the right of action lapses	7. Right of action does not lapse; may be filed even while person is serving time in prison
8. All issues must be raised from the trial record	8. New testimony may be presented

A writ of habeas corpus may be filed any time a prisoner establishes (or thinks he or she can establish) that his or her constitutional rights have been violated. The rights prisoners usually invoke in habeas corpus proceedings are the guarantee against unreasonable searches and seizures, the exclusionary rule, the right not to incriminate oneself, the right to counsel, the right to effective counsel, the guarantee against double jeopardy, and the right to due process.

A legal wit has said that the success rate of habeas corpus cases is similar to the chances of finding snow in June in Texas. This is obviously an exaggeration, but not by much. The reason habeas corpus cases seldom succeed is that although new issues may be raised, prisoners may also raise the same issues adjudicated during the trial. For example, a prisoner may allege on habeas corpus that her counsel was ineffective, a claim she must also have raised on appeal when represented by a different lawyer. Or the prisoner might claim that the judge erred in admitting as evidence the pound of cocaine used against him during the trial. Chances are that he raised the same issue during the trial and on appeal, but lost.

Why would a prisoner raise the same issue in a writ of habeas corpus as he or she did during trial and on appeal? The answer is that a prisoner may feel that he or she has new evidence to support the allegation. For example, a retired police officer, who arrested X and gathered the evidence against him, now admits that in fact he threatened to kill X unless X confessed. The time for appeal is past; therefore X may file for a writ of habeas corpus, based on a violation of his Fifth Amendment right. In this type of case, the writ will succeed if the prisoner establishes his or her new allegation.

Law enforcement officers need to be familiar with habeas corpus proceedings because they may be filed by anybody who has been arrested and is awaiting trial or by a prisoner who has been sentenced to serve time in jail. It focuses on the *lawfulness of the detention;* therefore the respondent is usually the sheriff (in jail cases) or the warden (in prison cases). If filed prior to trial, the allegation would be that the detention is unconstitutional as violative of the detainee's rights; for example, if an arrest has been made without probable cause or if a detainee is charged and held for a crime for which he or she has already been tried and acquitted. In these cases, the officer must be ready to prove that there was no such violation and that the incarceration is valid.

Habeas corpus cases must also be distinguished from civil rights (otherwise known as Section 1983) cases. The primary distinction is that habeas corpus cases seek release, whereas civil rights cases seek improvement of prison conditions and/ or a damage award from the officer. Habeas corpus may also be used to improve conditions of confinement, but it is a remedy seldom used by prisoners because of the advantages in taking the civil rights route. Moreover, habeas corpus cases must have exhausted state judicial remedies, whereas civil rights cases are filed directly with the federal district court. The distinction between these two proceedings may be summarized as follows:

State habeas corpus case	*Civil rights case (Section 1983)*
1. Heard in state court	1. Usually heard in federal court, although may also be heard in state court
2. Need to exhaust state judicial remedies before going to federal court	2. Filed directly in federal court
3. Purpose is to seek release	3. Purpose is to improve conditions of confinement and/or obtain damages
4. Affects only petitioner if it succeeds	4. Affects all prisoners if it succeeds
5. Filed by or for person seeking release	5. May be filed as a class action suit

❑ SUMMARY

Sentencing is defined as the formal pronouncement of judgment and punishment upon the defendant following his or her conviction in a criminal prosecution. Sentences are usually imposed by a judge, but some jurisdictions provide an option for jury sentencing. Defendants have few rights during sentencing. One is the right to counsel and the other is the right of allocution.

Courts or juries usually impose five categories of sentences: death, imprisonment, payment of a fine or restitution, probation, and community service programs. Each category of penalty raises constitutional issues, particularly the death penalty.

In 1972, the Court said that the death penalty was unconstitutional, primarily because it was administered in such a freakish and wanton manner as to violate the "equal protection" clause of the Constitution. After that decision, the states and the federal government revised their death-penalty statutes to eliminate equal protection problems. In 1976, the Court concluded that the death penalty is not per se cruel and unusual punishment; however, any arbitrary or capricious imposition of it is unconstitutional. Since 1976, the Court has decided a number of death-penalty cases raising various issues, such as whether or not the death penalty can be imposed for the crime of raping an adult woman and whether a state appellate court is constitutionally required to provide a "proportionality review" of death sentences in that state, if so requested by the defendant. The Court is still engaged in the process of fine-tuning the issues in death-penalty cases, particularly those relating to procedural matters.

Imprisonment is a legitimate form of punishment, except when it constitutes cruel and unusual punishment because of excessiveness. Fine is constitutional, but a defendant cannot be sent to jail because of inability to pay a fine; therefore, "work-off" arrangements are unconstitutional if they exceed the maximum time allowed by law or if they result in automatic conversion of a fine into jail time.

Probation is defined as a sentence under which a convicted offender is allowed to remain free in the community, subject to court-imposed conditions and under the supervision of a probation officer. It is a privilege that may be granted or withheld. Probation conditions are valid as long as they are reasonably related to the protection of society or the rehabilitation of the probationer and if they are clear, reasonable, and constitutional. Intermediate sanctions means all punishments lying between imprisonment and ordinary probation. It includes such sanctions as participation in community service programs, restitution, intensive supervision probation, electronic monitoring, and forfeiture of proceeds of criminal activity.

Appeal is not a constitutional right, but it is granted in every jurisdiction by law or practice. Defendants have very few rights on appeal. If an appeal succeeds, the defendant may be tried again because he or she is considered to have waived protection against double jeopardy by instituting the appeal. In theory, an appeal in a criminal case can go all the way to the U.S. Supreme Court; in reality very few criminal cases are ever decided by the Court on their merits. The rest are dismissed "per curiam."

Habeas corpus may be used any time a person feels he or she is being held in jail or prison unconstitutionally. It is distinguished from an appeal in that an appeal is filed after a person has been convicted, usually alleging that there was something wrong with the trial and that the conviction should thus be reversed. In contrast, habeas corpus is usually filed to secure a person's release from imprisonment. A writ of habeas corpus, for various reasons, seldom succeeds; however, it provides prisoners with a ray of hope after the appellate process has lapsed.

❑ REVIEW QUESTIONS

1. What rights do defendants have during sentencing?
2. What is a presentence investigation report? Does the defendant have a constitutional right to see the PSI report?
3. The two leading death-penalty cases are Furman v. Georgia and Gregg v. Georgia. What did the Court say in each case?
4. The death penalty constitutes cruel and unusual punishment if it is disproportionate to the offense committed. What does that mean? Give an example.
5. May juveniles be given the death penalty? Discuss.
6. May prospective jurors who are morally opposed to capital punishment be disqualified from the guilt–innocence stage of a death-penalty trial? May they be disqualified from the sentencing stage of the trial? Discuss your answers.
7. X has been convicted of two murders by the same court in the same trial. He is sentenced to ten years in prison for the first murder and five years for the second murder. How much time, in all, will X serve in prison (disregarding that state's parole and good-time laws)?
8. Discuss whether or not a defendant may be sent to jail or prison for failure to pay a fine or restitution.
9. There are four general requirements for the validity of a probation condition. What are they?
10. What is the "Rule of Four" on appeal?
11. Give five distinctions between an appeal and a writ of habeas corpus.
12. Distinguish between state habeas corpus and civil rights (Section 1983) cases.

❑ DEFINITIONS

Bifurcated Trial: A trial that is divided into two stages: the guilt–innocence stage and the sentencing stage.

Community Service Program: A type of sentence that places a convicted offender in unpaid positions with nonprofit or tax-supported agencies to perform a specified number of hours of work or service within a given time limit as a sentencing option or condition.

Concurrent Sentences: Sentences that are to be served at the same time by the convict.

Consecutive Sentences: Sentences that are to be served one after the other by the convict.

Death-Qualified Juries: Juries from which prospective jurors have been disqualified because they oppose the death penalty.

Electronic Monitoring: A criminal sanction in the form of an electronically monitored curfew.

Fine: A pecuniary punishment imposed by lawful tribunal upon a person convicted of a crime.

Habeas Corpus: A writ directed to a sheriff or other person detaining another, commanding him or her to produce the body of the prisoner at a certain time and place and to report the day and cause of the prisoner's taking and detention to the judge awarding the writ.

Intensive Supervision Probation (ISP):   A form of supervision in probation where the caseload is low and the probation is supervised more closely.

Intermediate Punishments: All punishments between imprisonment and ordinary probation; includes such sanctions as participation in community service programs, restitution, intensive supervision probation, electronic monitoring, and forfeiture of proceeds of criminal activity.

Penalty: A sum of money exacted for the doing of or failure to perform some act.

Per Curiam: A Latin phrase meaning "by the court." This is a brief unsigned statement that the Court does not consider a case to be of sufficient merit to warrant full consideration and inclusion in the docket.

Presentence Investigation Report: A report, usually prepared by the probation officer, that contains details regarding the accused's background, prior criminal record, family circumstances, and other relevant facts that may affect the sentence to be imposed by the judge.

Probation: A type of sentence allowing a convicted offender to remain free in the community, subject to court-imposed conditions and under the supervision of a probation officer.

Proportionality Review: A request by the defendant for the court to compare the sentence in the case before it with the penalties imposed in similar cases in that state to determine whether it is proportionate; usually invoked in death-penalty cases.

Restitution: The restoring of property or a right to a person who has been unjustly deprived of it.

RICO: Stands for Racketeer Influenced and Corrupt Organization. This law is aimed at this type of criminality and provides for the confiscation by the government of goods or items connected with criminal activity.

Right of Allocution: The defendant is entitled to make a statement on his or her own behalf as to why the sentence should not be imposed.

Rule of Four: At least four members of the U.S. Supreme Court must vote to include an appealed case in the Court's agenda in order for the case to be considered on its merits; otherwise the case is dismissed "per curiam."

Sentencing: The formal pronouncement of judgment and punishment upon the defendant following his or her conviction in a criminal prosecution.

Shock Probation: A form of probation in which an offender serves a fixed minimum time in jail or prison, after which he or she is discharged and placed on probation.

Work-off: An arrangement whereby a defendant who cannot pay a fine must remain in jail or prison to "work off" the unpaid fine at a specified rate per day.

□   PRINCIPLES OF CASES

ALABAMA V. SMITH, 57 L.W. 4626 (1989)   The presumption of judicial vindictiveness when a defendant is given a harsher sentence in a second trial does not apply if the first sentence was based on a guilty plea and the second, harsher sentence follows a trial.

BECK V. ALABAMA, 447 U.S. 625 (1980)   Flexibility must be afforded the jury in reaching its verdict in death-penalty cases; hence the imposition of the death penalty is unconstitutional when the jury is not allowed to reach a verdict on a lesser included offense.

BOOTH V. MARYLAND, 41 CrL 3282 (1987)   Victim impact statements, which typically describe a victim's characteristics and the effect of the crime on the victim's family, are not admissible in death-penalty cases.

COKER V. GEORGIA, 433 U.S. 584 (1977)   It is unconstitutional to impose the death penalty for the crime of raping an adult woman because the penalty is so disproportionate to the offense as to constitute cruel and unusual punishment.

ENMUND V. FLORIDA, 102 S.Ct. 3368 (1982)   It is unconstitutional to impose the death penalty on a defendant convicted of a felony murder as an accomplice when the defendant did not kill, or intend that a killing occur or that deadly force be used.

FORD V. WAINWRIGHT, 39 CrL 3197 (1986)   The Eighth Amendment provision against cruel and unusual punishment prohibits the state from executing a prisoner who is insane at the time of the scheduled execution.

FURMAN V. GEORGIA, 408 U.S. 238 (1972)   The imposition and carrying out of the death penalty was declared unconstitutional. Three of the five justices who voted for unconstitutionality based their votes on the "equal protection" clause, saying that the death penalty was applied in such a "freakish and wanton" manner as to violate the Fourteenth Amendment, while the other two justices said that the death penalty was cruel and unusual punishment per se.

GODFREY V. GEORGIA, 446 U.S. 420 (1980)   A state law authorizing the death penalty for a killing that is "outrageously or wantonly vile, horrible or inhuman in that it involved torture, depravity of mind, or an aggravated battery to the victim" is unconstitutional because of vagueness.

GREGG V. GEORGIA, 428 U.S. 153 (1976)   The death penalty is not per se cruel and unusual punishment; however, any arbitrary or capricious imposition of it is unconstitutional.

GRIFFIN V. ILLINOIS, 351 U.S. 12 (1956)   If a state provides for an appeal as a matter of right, counsel must be appointed for indigent defendants. Equal protection is violated if the state makes appellate review less accessible to the poor than to the rich.

KEMMLER, IN RE, 136 U.S. 436 (1890)   Death by electrocution is not cruel or unusual.

LOCKHART V. MCCREE, 39 CrL 3085 (1986)   Prospective jurors whose opposition to the death penalty is so strong as to prevent or impair the performance of their duties as jurors at the sentencing phase of the trial may also be removed for cause from jury membership in capital cases.

MAGGIO V. WILLIAMS, 34 CrL 4075 (1984)   The execution of an inmate who challenged the "proportionality review" conducted by the state courts did not have to await the pronouncement on this subject that the Court was expected to give and did give later that year. The execution could go on even though that same issue was pending court decision in another case.

MAYER V. CITY OF CHICAGO, 404 U.S. 189 (1971)   If the appeal requires a transcript of the trial proceedings, the transcript must be given to an indigent free of charge.

MAYNARD V. CARTWRIGHT, 43 CrL 3053 (1988)   Declared as unconstitutional because of vagueness a portion of Oklahoma's death-penalty law that made it an aggravating circumstance for a murder to be "especially heinous, atrocious, or cruel."

MCCLESKEY V. KEMP, 41 CrL 3047 (1987)   The existence of statistical disparity in the imposition of capital sentences, reflecting systematic bias of death-sentencing outcomes against black defendants and those whose victims are white, does not bar the imposition of the death penalty.

NORTH CAROLINA V. PEARCE, 395 U.S. 711 (1969)   The Constitution does not prohibit the imposition of a longer sentence upon reconviction for the same offense, provided that the longer sentence is imposed for a valid reason and not out of judicial vindictiveness, meaning punishing the defendant for a successful appeal.

PENRY V. LYNAUGH, 45 CrL 3188 (1989)   The Eighth Amendment provision against cruel and unusual punishment does not categorically prohibit the execution of mentally retarded capital murderers.

PULLEY V. HARRIS, 34 CrL 3027 (1984)   State appellate courts are not constitutionally required to provide, upon request by the defendant, a "proportionality review" of death sentences in which the court would have to compare the sentence in the case before it with penalties imposed in similar cases in the state to determine whether it is proportionate.

RUMMEL V. ESTELLE, 445 U.S. 263 (1980)   The mandatory sentence of life imprisonment under a habitual offender law after conviction for a third felony did not violate the "cruel and unusual punishments" clause because there was possibility of parole under state law after twelve years of imprisonment.

SATTERWHITE V. TEXAS, 108 S.Ct. 1793 (1988)   The admission at trial of testimony by a psychologist about his or her examination of a capital offense defendant without defense lawyer's knowledge violates defendant's right to counsel.

SOLEM V. HELM, 33 CrL 3220 (1983)   A state law that imposed a life sentence without possibility of parole upon a habitual offender convicted of seven nonviolent felonies violated the defendant's constitutional guarantee against cruel and unusual punishment as grossly disproportionate to the offenses committed.

SPAZIANO V. FLORIDA, 35 CrL 3199 (1984)   A trial judge may impose a death sentence even though an advisory jury has recommended life imprisonment, as long as the judge acted in accordance with state law authorizing him or her to do that.

STANFORD V. KENTUCKY, 109 S.Ct. 2969 (1989)   The imposition of the death penalty for a crime committed at sixteen or seventeen years of age does not constitute cruel and unusual punishment.

STATE OF LOUISIANA EX REL. FRANCIS V. RESWEBER, 67 S.Ct. 374 (1947)   Carrying out the execution of a convicted murderer, after the first attempt at execution had failed because of mechanical defect in the electric chair, was constitutional.

TATE V. SHORT, 401 U.S. 395 (1971)   A law providing only for a fine for traffic offenses, but adding that the offender must "work off" the fine in jail at $5 a day if the offender cannot pay, is unconstitutional because it violates the "equal protection" clause.

THOMPSON V. OKLAHOMA, 43 CrL 3197 (1988)   A state cannot execute a defendant who committed first-degree murder when he or she was only fifteen years old.

TISON V. ARIZONA, 41 CrL 3023 (1987)   A defendant who took part in a felony-murder but did not himself or herself intend to kill or commit the specific act leading to that result, may nonetheless be sentenced to death as long as his or her participation in the felony was major and his or her mental state was one of reckless indifference.

WHITMORE V. ARKANSAS, 58 L.W. 4495 (1990)   Third parties who consider themselves friends of death row inmates lack standing to challenge a death sentence imposed on a defendant who has waived the right to a direct appeal of his or her conviction and death sentence, as long as the waiver was knowing, intelligent, and voluntary.

WILKERSON V. UTAH, 99 U.S. 130 (1878)   Execution by firing squad is not cruel and unusual.

WILLIAMS V. ILLINOIS, 399 U.S. 235 (1970)   A state law imposing imprisonment plus a fine and providing that if the fine is not paid the prisoner must remain in jail longer than the prescribed maximum sentence to "work off" the unpaid fine is unconstitutional because it violates the "equal protection" clause of the Constitution.

WITHERSPOON V. ILLINOIS, 391 U.S. 510 (1968)   States may not exclude for cause in capital cases prospective jurors who are merely opposed to the death penalty. To do that results in a jury that is biased and unrepresentative of the community. But states may exclude for cause prospective jurors who say they are unwilling to vote for a death sentence under any circumstance.

WOODSON V. NORTH CAROLINA, 428 U.S. 280 (1980)   The death penalty is cruel and unusual when it is made mandatory for a broad category of homicides and the law does not provide a meaningful opportunity for considering the presence of mitigating factors.

☐ CASE BRIEF—LEADING CASE ON THE CONSTITUTIONALITY OF THE DEATH PENALTY

GREGG V. GEORGIA, 428 U.S. 153 (1976)

FACTS: Gregg was charged with two counts of first-degree murder and two counts of robbery. The evidence showed that Gregg and a traveling companion were picked up by two motorists while hitchhiking in Florida. The next morning the bodies of the two motorists were discovered in a ditch near Atlanta. The following day, Gregg and his companion were arrested in the motorists' car and a .25-caliber pistol, later proved to be the murder weapon, was found in Gregg's possession. Gregg confessed to the shooting and robbery but claimed self-defense. In accordance with Georgia law in capital cases, the trial was bifurcated (meaning that the determination of guilt and the sentencing were separate). The law also provided for automatic review by the Georgia Supreme Court and a weighing by the jury of mitigating and aggravating circumstances. Gregg was found guilty by a jury, which then recommended that the sentence of death be imposed on each count.

ISSUE: *Is the death penalty per se cruel and unusual punishment and therefore violative of the Eighth Amendment of the Constitution, as incorporated by the Fourteenth Amendment? No.*

SUPREME COURT DECISION: By a 7-to-2 vote (Justices Brennan and Marshall dissenting), the Court held that the death penalty is not in itself cruel and unusual punishment. However, any arbitrary or capricious imposition of it (such as when the sentencing authority is not given sufficient statutory guidance on what aggravating or mitigating circumstances must be considered when imposing the penalty) is unconstitutional.

CASE SIGNIFICANCE: In 1972, the Court in Furman v. Georgia, 408 U.S. 238, decided by a 5-to-4 vote that the death penalty could not be carried out because it was imposed in such a "freakish and wanton" manner as to violate the "cruel and unusual punishments" prohibition of the Constitution. Four years later, in Gregg, the Court gave the go-ahead signal for the death penalty to be carried out, as long as state law is so worded, as the Georgia law was, as to avoid arbitrary and capricious imposition. As of 1985, thirty-four states had death-penalty statutes.

EXCERPTS FROM THE DECISION: We address initially the basic contention that the punishment of death for the crime of murder is, under all circumstances, "cruel and unusual" in violation of the Eighth and Fourteenth Amendments of the Constitution. In Part IV of this opinion, we will consider the sentence of death imposed under the Georgia statutes at issue in this case.

The Court on a number of occasions has both assumed and asserted the constitutionality of capital punishment. In several cases that assumption provided a necessary foundation for the decision, as the Court was asked to decide whether a particular method of carrying out a capital sentence would be allowed to stand under the Eighth Amendment. But until Furman v. Georgia, 408 U.S. 238 (1972), the Court never confronted squarely the fundamental claim that the punishment of death always, regardless of the enormity of the offense or the procedure followed in imposing the sentence, is cruel and unusual punishment in violation of the Constitution. Although this issue was presented and addressed in Furman, it was not resolved by the Court. Four Justices would have held that capital punishment is not unconstitutional per se; two Justices would have reached the opposite conclusion; and three Justices, while agreeing that the statutes then before the Court were invalid as applied, left open the question whether such punishment may ever be imposed. We now hold that the punishment of death does not invariably violate the Constitution. . . .

The most marked indication of society's endorsement of the death penalty for murder is the legislative response to Furman. The legislatures of at least 35 States have enacted new statutes that provide for the death penalty for at least some crimes that result in the death of another person. And the Congress of the United States, in 1974, enacted a statute providing the death penalty for aircraft piracy that results in death. These recently adopted statutes have attempted to address the concerns expressed by the Court in Furman primarily (i) by specifying the factors to be weighed and the procedures to be followed in deciding when to impose a capital sentence, or (ii) by making the death penalty mandatory for specified crimes. But all of the post-Furman statutes make clear that capital punishment itself has not been rejected by the elected representatives of the people. . . .

We hold that the death penalty is not a form of punishment that may never be imposed, regardless of the circumstances of the offense, regardless of the character of the offender, and regardless of the procedure followed in reaching the decision to impose it.

☐   CASE BRIEF—LEADING CASE ON IMPRISONMENT FOR FAILURE TO PAY A FINE AND COURT COSTS

WILLIAMS V. ILLINOIS, 399 U.S. 235 (1970)

FACTS: Williams was convicted in an Illinois court of petty theft and received the maximum sentence allowed by state law—one year of imprisonment and a fine of $500. Williams was also assessed $5 in court costs. The judgment provided, as permitted by state statute, that if the defendant was in default of the payment of the fine and court costs at the expiration of the maximum one-year sentence, he should remain in jail and "work off" the monetary obligation at the rate of $5 a day. The result was that whereas the maximum term of imprisonment for petty theft was one year, the effect of the sentence imposed required Williams to be confined for 101 days beyond the maximum period of confinement fixed by the statute because he could not pay the fine and costs of $505.

ISSUE: *Is a state law constitutional that imposes imprisonment plus a fine and provides that if the fine is not paid the prisoner must remain in jail longer than the prescribed maximum sentence to "work off" the unpaid fine? No.*

SUPREME COURT DECISION: A state law that imposes imprisonment plus a fine and provides that if the fine is not paid the prisoner must remain in jail longer than the prescribed maximum sentence to "work off" the unpaid fine is unconstitutional because it violates the "equal protection" clause of the Fourteenth Amendment.

CASE SIGNIFICANCE: The Williams case was the precedent for a similar case (Tate v. Short), decided a year later, wherein the Court said that the Texas law that provided only for a fine for traffic offenses, but converted the fine to imprisonment if the defendant was unable to pay the fine, was also violative of the "equal protection" clause. Together, these cases stand for the proposition that there can be no equal justice where the poor go to prison primarily because they do not have the money to pay the fine. It must be stressed, however, that the Court itself said that the holding in Williams "does not deal with a judgment of confinement for nonpayment of a fine in the familiar pattern of alternative sentence of $30 or 30 days." This distinction means that a defendant in court who does not have $30 to pay his or her fine may instead be validly sent by the judge to jail for thirty days. The key to understanding the Williams case is to realize that the "work-off" arrangement exceeded the maximum allowed by law for the offense. Note that a distinction must be made between inability to pay a fine because of indigency and refusal to pay a fine. A defendant may be sent to prison any time if, being able to do so, he or she refuses to pay the fine for any reason.

EXCERPTS FROM THE DECISION: The custom of imprisoning a convicted defendant for nonpayment of fines dates back to medieval England and has long been practiced in this country. At the present time almost all States and the Federal Government have statutes authorizing incarceration under such circumstances. Most States permit imprisonment beyond the maximum term allowed by law, and in some there is no limit on the length of time one may serve for nonpayment. While neither the antiquity of a practice nor the fact of steadfast legislative and judicial adherence to it through the centuries insulates it from constitutional attack, these factors should be weighed in the balance. Indeed, in prior cases this Court seems to have tacitly approved incarceration to "work off" unpaid fines.

The need to be open to reassessment of ancient practices other than those explicitly mandated by the Constitution is illustrated by the present case since the greatly increased use of fines as a criminal sanction has made nonpayment a major cause of incarceration in this country. Default imprisonment has traditionally been justified on the ground that it is a coercive device to ensure obedience to the judgment of the court. Thus, commitment for failure to pay has not been viewed as a part of the punishment or as an increase in the penalty; rather, it has been viewed as a means of enabling the court to enforce collection of money that a convicted defendant was obligated by the sentence to pay. The additional imprisonment, it has been said, may always be avoided by payment of the fine.

We conclude that when the aggregate imprisonment exceeds the maximum period fixed by the statute and results directly from an involuntary nonpayment of a fine or court costs we are confronted with an impermissible discrimination that rests on ability to pay, and accordingly, we vacate the judgment below.

☐   NOTES

1. "Determinate Sentencing: The History, the Theory, the Debate," *Corrections Magazine*, September 1977, at 3.
2. *U.S. News & World Report,* March 26, 1990, at 24.
3. Ibid.
4. *Time Magazine,* April 2, 1990, at 19.
5. H. C. Black, *Black's Law Dictionary,* 4th ed. (St. Paul: West Publishing Company, 1968), at 759.
6. *Probation and Parole 1981,* Bureau of Justice Statistics Bulletin, U.S. Department of Justice, at 1.
7. N. Morris and M. Tonry, "Between Prison and Probation—Intermediate Punishments in a Rational Sentencing System," *NIJ Reports,* January/February 1990, at 8.
8. W. Gilmer, *Cochran's Law Dictionary: Police Edition* (Cincinnati: Anderson, 1973), at 261.

  9. Bureau of Justice Statistics, *Report to the Nation on Crime and Justice,* 2d ed. (Washington, DC: U.S. Government Printing Office, 1988), at 93.
 10. S. Kling, *The Legal Encyclopedia and Dictionary* (New York: Pocket Books, 1970), at 262.
 11. M.D. Forkosch, *Constitutional Law,* 2d ed. (Mineola, NH: The Foundation Press, Inc., 1969), at 307.

CHAPTER FIFTEEN

LEGAL LIABILITIES OF LAW ENFORCEMENT PERSONNEL

☐ KEY TERMS

tort	"public duty" doctrine
intentional tort	special relationship
false arrest	Section 1983
assault	acting under color of law
battery	"good faith" defense
wrongful death	"acting within the scope of
infliction of mental or emotional	employment" defense
distress	"probable cause" defense
negligence tort	municipal policy or custom

I. INTRODUCTION

Liability lawsuits have become a major concern in criminal justice, particularly in law enforcement where the number of lawsuits has steadily escalated over the years. Recent headlines such as the following have become common:

- SUPREME COURT LEAVES INTACT $425,000 LIABILITY AWARD FOR D.C. POLICE SHOOTING[1]
- TWO BROOKLYN MEN AWARDED $76 MILLION IN BRUTALITY CASE[2]
- FEDERAL JUDGE UPHOLDS $170,014 AWARD AGAINST [L.A. CHIEF] GATES[3]
- COURT AFFIRMS $4.5 MILLION JURY VERDICT AGAINST DRUG ENFORCEMENT OFFICERS, SUPERVISORS AND DEPARTMENT HEADS[4]
- HONOLULU PAYS $100,000 TO SETTLE POLICE BRUTALITY SUIT[5]
- HOUSTON SHOOTING VICTIM'S SURVIVORS FILE WRONGFUL DEATH SUIT AGAINST POLICE[6]

Most lawsuits are eventually settled for a lower amount than those featured in the preceding headlines because plaintiffs may be unwilling to go through the delay and uncertainty of the appellate process. In a survey of jury awards in South Carolina, the Bar Association of that state found that between 1976 and 1986, in roughly half of the cases where the award was $100,000 or more, the parties settled for a lower amount. Another study showed that between 1982 and 1984, in some California and Illinois counties, jury awards to plaintiffs were reduced in about 25 percent of all verdicts won by the plaintiffs. On the average, the awards were cut in half, the larger verdicts getting the biggest cuts. A third study found that of 198 verdicts (including nonpolice cases) totaling $700 million, the amount actually paid to victims was $339 million, a reduction of more than 55 percent. Despite these figures, damage awards can be high in many cases and the time and effort required can be a drain on the agency's limited resources.[7]

Although it is true that the number of lawsuits is high, cases decided in favor of the police are more numerous than those where liability is imposed. Headlines such as the following are more common than those heralding liability:

- NO MUNICIPAL LIABILITY FOR INJURY CAUSED BY STUN GUNS WHEN OFFICERS USE THEM IN MANNER INCONSISTENT WITH EXPRESS POLICY[8]
- KNOWLEDGE OF SPECIAL DANGER TO WOMAN SHOT BY FORMER BOYFRIEND WAS INSUFFICIENT TO IMPOSE LIABILITY ON OFFICERS AND CITY[9]
- CITY NOT LIABLE TO MOTORIST INJURED BY FLEEING SUSPECT'S AUTO: OFFICERS EXERCISED DUE CARE DURING HIGH-SPEED PURSUIT[10]
- INVESTIGATING AND RESPONDING TO 911 CALL CREATES NO DUTY TO GIVE PROTECTION; NO LIABILITY FOR WOMAN'S ASSAULT AFTER POLICE LEFT HER OUT OF GAS[11]

Civil liability lawsuits are not limited to police work. They are brought with increased frequency against private people, business enterprises, and public officials. Liability awards have also increased dramatically. In 1970, there were only seven multimillion-dollar damage awards involving private and public persons. In 1984, that figure went up to 401.[12] These figures do not include the number of damage awards of less than a million dollars and the unknown number of cases that are settled out of court without trial.

II. OVERVIEW OF LEGAL LIABILITIES

Police legal liabilities come from varied sources. They range from state to federal laws that carry civil, criminal, and administrative sanctions. For the purpose of an overview, legal liabilities may be categorized as Table 15.1 shows.

The differences among these categories of liability are summarized as follows: *civil liabilities* result in monetary award for damages; *criminal liabilities* mean imprisonment, fine, or other forms of criminal sanction; *administrative liability* results in dismissal, demotion, transfer, reprimand, or other forms of sanction authorized by agency rules or guidelines.

Two points must be stressed. First, the above liabilities apply to all public officers, not just to law enforcement personnel. Probation and parole officers, jailers, prison officials, and other personnel in the criminal justice system are liable under the above provisions. Second, an officer may be liable under any or all of the above on account of what essentially may be a single act, if all elements are present. The provision against double jeopardy of the Fifth Amendment does not apply; double jeopardy applies only in criminal cases when both prosecutions are for the same offense and by the same jurisdiction.

Although various legal remedies are available to the public, as the above categorization indicates, plaintiffs are strongly inclined to use two remedies against police officers. The discussion in this chapter will therefore focus on those two sources of liability to the exclusion of others. These sources are

- civil liability under *state tort law,* and
- civil liability under *federal law* (under 42 U.S. Code, Section 1983—also known as civil rights cases).

III. CIVIL LIABILITY UNDER STATE TORT LAW

Tort is defined as a civil wrong in which the action of one person causes injury to the person or property of another, in violation of a legal duty imposed by law. Tort law is primarily a product of judicial decisions; hence it may not be as clear or precise as a legislatively established remedy. Moreover, legislatures in some states by law add to the category of tortious acts, thus further expanding the scope of tort law. Tortious acts vary in name and scope from one state to another. Nonetheless, certain categorizations, such as the following, are identifiable. State tort actions are the second most popular form of remedy (Section 1983 cases being the remedy most often used), but more plaintiffs may be using the tort route in the future if the Court continues to further circumscribe the use of Section 1983 cases as a remedy for violations of rights.

There are three general categories of state tort, based on the officer's conduct: (1) intentional tort, (2) negligence tort, and (3) strict liability tort. Of the three, only intentional and negligence torts are often used in police cases. Strict liability torts are applicable in activities that are so abnormally dangerous that they cannot be carried out safely even with reasonable care. (An example is the use of nuclear power to generate electricity.) Police work does not fall under strict liability tort, and therefore that category will not be discussed.

A. Intentional Tort

Intentional tort occurs when there is an intention on the part of the officer to bring some physical harm or mental effect upon another person. Intent is mental and thus difficult to establish; however, courts and juries are generally allowed to infer the existence of intent from the facts of the case. For example, an officer takes a person to the police station in handcuffs for questioning. When charged with false arrest the officer denies that he intended to place the person under arrest. Chances are that the judge or jury will decide otherwise.

In police work, several kinds of intentional tort are often brought against police officers.

1. False Arrest and False Imprisonment

In a tort case for *false arrest,* the plaintiff alleges that the officer made an illegal arrest, usually an arrest without probable cause. A claim of false arrest also arises if the officer fails to arrest the "right" person named in the warrant. An officer who makes a warrantless arrest bears the burden of proving that the arrest was in fact based on probable cause and that an arrest warrant was not necessary because the arrest came under one of the exceptions to the warrant rule. If the arrest is made with a warrant, the presumption is that probable cause exists, except if the officer obtained the warrant with malice, knowing that there was no probable cause (Malley v. Briggs, 54 L.W. 4342 [1986]). Civil liability for false arrest in arrests with warrant is, therefore, unlikely unless the officer serves a warrant that he or she knows to be illegal or unconstitutional. For example, if Officer M serves an unsigned warrant or a warrant that is issued for the wrong person, M will be liable for false arrest despite the issuance of a warrant.

False arrest is a separate tort from *false imprisonment,* but in police tort cases the two are virtually identical in that arrest necessarily means confinement, which is in itself an element of imprisonment.[13] In both cases, the individual is restrained or deprived of freedom without legal justification. The cases do differ, however, in that although false arrest leads to false imprisonment, false imprisonment is not necessarily the result of a false arrest. For example, a suspect is arrested with probable cause (it is therefore a valid arrest) but is detained in jail for days without the filing of charges (false imprisonment). If an officer makes an arrest based on probable cause, but later finds out that the person is innocent, then continued imprisonment is false imprisonment even though the arrest was valid.

The best defense in false arrest and false imprisonment cases is that the arrest or detention was justified and valid. An officer who arrests someone with probable cause is not liable for false arrest simply because the suspect is later proved innocent. Neither does liability exist if the arrest is made by virtue of a law that is later declared unconstitutional. In the words of the Court: "We agree that a police officer is not charged with predicting the future course of constitutional law" (Pierson v. Ray, 386 U.S. 555 [1967]). In these cases, however, the officer must have believed in good faith that the law was constitutional. Also, the fact that the arrested person is not prosecuted or that he or she is prosecuted for a different crime does not make the arrest illegal. What is important is that there be a valid justification for the arrest and detention at the time those took place.

TABLE 15.1 Sources of Police Liabilities

	State law	Federal law
Civil liabilities	State tort law	1. Title 42 of U.S. Code, Section 1983—Civil Action for Deprivation of Civil Rights 2. Title 42 of U.S. Code, Section 1985—Conspiracy to Interfere with Civil Rights 3. Title 42 of U.S. Code, Section 1981—Equal Rights under the Law

Criminal liabilities	1. State penal code provisions specifically aimed at public officers for such crimes as
	   a. official oppression,
	   b. official misconduct, and
	   c. violation of the civil rights of prisoners.
	2. Regular penal code provisions punishing such criminal acts as assault, battery, false arrest, serious bodily injury, homicide, etc.
		1. Title 18 of U.S. Code, Section 242—Criminal Liability for Deprivation of Civil Rights
		2. Title 18 of U.S. Code, Section 241—Criminal Liability for Conspiracy to Deprive a Person of Rights
		3. Title 18 of U.S. Code, Section 245—Violation of Federally Protected Activities

Administrative liabilities	Agency rules or guidelines on the state or local level—vary from one agency to another.	Federal agency rules or guidelines—vary from one agency to another.

2. Assault and Battery

Although sometimes used as one term, "assault" and "battery" represent two separate acts. *Assault* is usually defined as the intentional causing of an apprehension of harmful or offensive conduct; it is the attempt or threat, accompanied by the ability to inflict bodily harm on another person. An assault is committed if the officer causes another person to think that he or she will be subjected to harmful or offensive contact. For example, for no justifiable reason, Officer X draws his gun and points it at another person. In many jurisdictions, words alone will not constitute assault. There must be an act to accompany the threatening words.

 Battery is the intentional infliction of harmful or offensive body contact. Given this broad definition, the potential for battery exists every time an officer uses force on a suspect or arrestee. The main difference between assault and battery is that assault is generally menacing conduct that results in a person's fear of imminently receiving battery, whereas battery involves unlawful, unwarranted, or hostile touching—however slight. In some jurisdictions, assault is attempted battery.

3. Excessive Use of Force

The police are often charged with "brutality" or using "excessive force." The general rule is that nondeadly force may be used by the police in various situations as long as such force is *reasonable*. Reasonable force, in turn, is force that a prudent and cautious person would use if exposed to similar circumstances and is limited to the amount of force that is necessary to achieve valid and proper results. Any force beyond what is necessary to achieve valid and proper results is punitive, meaning that it punishes rather than controls. In one case, the court found that the police had used excessive force on a family when responding to a call to settle a neighborhood dispute, and they were made to pay $10,000. The court said that excessive force was used on the father, who was not of great physical strength and who was already being subdued by his brother when the police kicked him in the groin and struck him on the head with a nightstick. It was alleged that the officers kicked the mother on the back and buttocks after she was handcuffed and lying face down in the mud. The son was also injured during the arrest process (Lewis v. Downs, 774 F.2d 711 [6th Cir. 1985]).

 The defense in "excessive use of force" cases is that the force used by the

---

HIGHLIGHT 15.1

Reasonableness of Use of Force

"The 'reasonableness' of a particular use of force must be judged from the perspective of a reasonable officer on the scene, rather than with the 20/20 vision of hindsight. . . . With respect to a claim of excessive force, the same reasonableness of the moment applies: 'Not every push or shove, even if it may later seem unnecessary in the peace of a judge's chamber,' violates the Fourth Amendment. The calculus of reasonableness must embody allowance for the fact that police officers are often forced to make split-second judgements in circumstances that are tense, uncertain, and rapidly evolving—about the amount of force that is necessary in a particular situation" (Graham v. Connor, 109 S.Ct. 1865 [1989]).

police was reasonable under the circumstances. What standard is to be used to determine reasonableness—the perspective of a judge or jury sitting in a courtroom or the perspective of an officer on the scene? The Court has answered this question saying that the reasonableness of a particular use of deadly or nondeadly force by the police "must be judged from the perspective of a reasonable officer on the scene, rather than with the 20/20 vision of hindsight" (Graham v. Connor, 109 S.Ct. 1865 [1989]). The Court added that whether the conduct of an officer is reasonable in an "excessive use of force" case is determined by asking the following question: Are the officers' actions "objectively reasonable" in light of the facts and circumstances confronting them, without regard to their underlying intent or motivation? Under this test, therefore, the officer's motivation becomes unimportant. Said the Court in Graham: "An officer's evil intentions will not make a Fourth Amendment violation out of an objectively reasonable use of force; nor will an officer's good intentions make an objectively unreasonable use of force constitutional." In short, good motives will not justify the use of unreasonable force; conversely, bad motives do not lead to liability as long as the use of force is objectively reasonable, judged from the perspective of an officer on the scene.

4. Wrongful Death

This tort, usually established by law, arises whenever death occurs as a result of an officer's action or inaction. It is brought by the surviving family, relatives, or legal guardian of the estate of the deceased for pain, suffering, and actual expenses (such as expenses for the funeral) and for the loss of life to the family or relatives. Instances include shooting and killing a fleeing suspect, firing shots at a suspect in a shopping center that result in the death of an innocent bystander, and negligently operating a motor vehicle, resulting in the death of an innocent party. In some states, a death resulting from the police's use of deadly force comes under the tort of misuse of weapons. An officer has a duty to use not merely ordinary care but a high degree of care in handling a weapon, otherwise he or she becomes liable for wrongful death.[14]

Sometimes an officer is held liable because of failure to follow good police procedure. In one case, a police officer was liable for $202,295.80 in a wrongful death action for shooting and killing a man suspected of buying marijuana. The officer was liable even though he thought he was shooting in self-defense. This was because the district judge, relying on the testimony of an expert witness on police procedures, found that the police officer had acted negligently and contrary to good police procedure in the following respects:

1. failure to use his radio;
2. failure to utilize a back-up unit;
3. dangerous placement of his patrol car in a "cut off" maneuver;
4. ordering the two men to exit their car rather than issuing an immobilization command to remain in the car with their hands in plain view;
5. increasing the risk of an incident by having two suspects getting out of a car; and
6. abandoning a covered position and advancing into the open, where the odds of overreacting would be greater.

The judge concluded that the officer's fault in not following good police procedure not only placed the officer in a position of greater danger but also imperiled the deceased suspect by creating a situation in which a fatal error was likely (Young v. City of Killeen, 775 F.2d 1349 [1985]).

The use of *deadly force* is governed by specific departmental rules or, in their absence, by state rules that must be strictly followed. The safest rule is that deadly force may be used only in self-defense or in protecting the life of another endangered person, when the use of deadly force is immediately necessary to protect that life. Agency rules or state law, however, may give the officer more leeway in the use of deadly force. These rules are to be followed as long as they are constitutional.

5. Infliction of Mental or Emotional Distress

Tort liability rises when an officer inflicts severe emotional distress on a person through intentional or reckless extreme and outrageous conduct. Physical harm need not follow. For example, a plaintiff who is illegally arrested suffers psychological dysfunction and trauma because the officer pointed a loaded gun at her during the arrest. The nature of this tort is such that it may be alleged any time an officer's conduct is so extreme and outrageous as to cause severe emotional distress. What is extreme and outrageous is difficult to determine; moreover, the effect of an act may vary according to the plaintiff's disposition or state of mind. Somebody has said, with a grain of truth, that this tort is limited only by the plaintiff's creativity and imagination. Most state appellate courts that have addressed the issue have held, however, that more than rudeness or isolated incidents are required. The plaintiff must allege and prove some kind of pattern or practice over a period of time rather than just isolated incidents. The case law on this tort is still developing, but it has already found acceptance in nearly every state.

B. Negligence Tort

For tort liability, *negligence* may be defined as the breach of a common law or statutory duty to act reasonably toward those who may foreseeably be harmed by one's conduct. This general definition may be modified or superseded by specific state law that provides for a different type of conduct in terms usually more restrictive than this definition.

Negligence tort applies in many aspects of police work, but only four will be discussed here: liability for failure to protect, liability for negligent use by police of

---

HIGHLIGHT 15.2

A Firearms Policy Is Needed

"Probably the most volatile issue that creates friction between the police and the minority community today is that of police use of deadly force. To correct this problem, police departments must develop firearms policies that restrict the use of deadly force and place a high value on human life."

Source: L. Brown and H. Locke, "The Police and the Community," in R. Staufenberger, ed., *Progress in Policing: Essays on Change* (Cambridge, MA: Ballinger, 1980), at 101.

motor vehicles, liability for injury caused by a fleeing motorist-suspect, and liability for failure to respond to calls.[15]

1. Liability for Failure to Protect

The general rule is that there is no liability on the part of police officers for failure to protect. This is because of the *"public duty" doctrine,* which holds that government functions are owed to the general public, but not to specific individuals; therefore, police officers who fail to prevent crime while acting within the scope of their official capacity are not liable to specific individuals for injury or harm that may have been caused by a third party. For example, the police are not liable if X is sexually assaulted, Y is murdered, or Z is robbed.

The public duty doctrine, however, admits of one major and multifaceted exception: "special relationship." This exception holds that if a duty is owed to a particular person rather than to the general public, then a police officer or agency that breaches that duty can be held liable for damages. The problem is that the term *"special relationship"* admits of various meanings depending on state law, court decisions, or agency regulations. Based on decided cases, a "special relationship" will most likely arise in the following situations:

a. When the police deprive an individual of liberty by taking him or her into custody. For example, in a Florida case, a person was arrested for possession of a lottery ticket. He was handcuffed by the police but then was stabbed by another person. The court ruled that once the suspect was handcuffed and taken into custody, a special relationship was created that made the city responsible for his safety as though he had been incarcerated in the city jail. In this case, however, the court did not find the officers liable because there was no negligence in the officers' handling of the suspect—they were just as surprised as was the arrested person when a woman ran by and stabbed him (Sanders v. City of Belle Glade, 510 So. 2d 962 [Fla. App. 1987]).

b. When the police assume an obligation that goes beyond police duty to protect the general public. For example, a young man provided New York City police officers with information that led to the arrest of a fugitive. The incident received considerable media attention, exposing Schuster as the individual who assisted in the fugitive's capture. When Schuster received life-threatening phone calls, he notified the police. Several weeks later, Schuster was shot and killed. Schuster's family brought suit alleging that the city police failed to provide Schuster with adequate protection and that New York City breached its special duty owed to individuals who provide the police with information about a crime. A New York court imposed liability, saying that "in our view the police owe a special duty to use reasonable care to protect persons who have collaborated with them in the arrest or prosecution of criminals" (Schuster v. City of New York, 154 N.E. 2d 534 [NY 1958]).

c. When protection is mandated by law. Some states enact laws expressly protecting special groups or individuals. In other states, judicial decisions consider certain laws as protecting special groups or individuals although they are not specifically protected by law. For example, in a case in Maine, the police were liable for failing to arrest a drunk driver who subsequently caused injury to the plaintiff. Special relationship was considered created by the legislature in a state statute that prohibited drunken driving. The court reasoned that "statutes which establish police responsibility in such circumstances evidence a legislative intent to protect both the intoxicated persons and users of the highway" (Irwin v. Town of Ware, 467 N.E. 2d 1292 [MA 1984]). This case does not necessarily mean that an automatic "special relationship" exists every time there is a drunk-driving statute. What it means is that the Maine statute was interpreted by the Maine court to have established a special relationship sufficient to hold the police liable.

d. When protection is ordered by the court.   This is illustrated in the case of Sorichetti v. City of New York, 482 N.E. 2d 70 (1985), a much-publicized case wherein the New York Court of Appeals upheld a judgment for $2 million against the New York police for failure to protect a child who was under an order of protection issued by the court. In that case, a mother had obtained an order for protection curtailing her husband's access to their child because of the husband's violent tendencies. One weekend, the mother agreed to permit the husband to keep the child if he met her at the police station. At the station, the husband yelled to the wife that he was going to kill her, and then pointed to the daughter and said, "You better do the sign of the cross before this weekend is up." The wife immediately asked the police to arrest her husband; the police replied that there was nothing they could do. The wife went again to the police the next day and demanded that they return her daughter and arrest her husband, but the police denied her request. That same weekend, the child was attacked by the father and suffered severe wounds. The appellate court upheld the huge damage award, saying that the court-issued protective order created a "special relationship" that required the police to take extra steps to protect the daughter from harm from a known source.[16]

e. In some domestic abuse cases.   The general rule is that the police do not have any liability in domestic abuse situations. This is because the duty to protect an abused spouse comes under the "public duty" doctrine—the same duty an officer owes to the general public. There are instances, however, when a special relationship has been established and so failure to protect would lead to liability. Foremost among these are cases when the state has passed legislation authorizing courts to issue protective orders to spouses in domestic abuse situations. In these cases, the existence of a statute and the issuance of a judicial order to protect a particular spouse creates a special duty on the part of the police to extend protection. Failure to give the necessary level of protection in the face of a judicial order may create liability.

2. Liability for Negligent Use by Police of Motor Vehicles

As in other negligence cases, the general rule is that there is no liability for police use of motor vehicles because of the "public duty" doctrine. There are exceptions, however, created by law, court decisions, or departmental policy. In the absence of specific law governing the conduct of the police in the use of motor vehicles during emergencies, courts have set standards by which "special relationship" will be considered to have existed. The standards are what is the justification for the chase, the actual physical operation of the vehicle, and the circumstances surrounding the operation, and whether there was a violation of departmental policy. Negligence that leads to liability will be determined on the basis of the above factors.

3. Liability for Injury Caused by Fleeing Motorist-Suspect

Some cases have been filed by third parties against police officers and departments seeking damages for injuries caused by a fleeing motorist-suspect who, in the course of the pursuit, hits and injures a pedestrian. In these cases, liability usually hinges on whether or not the police conduct in breaching a duty owed to the public was the proximate cause of the injury to the third party. Most states hold that the police are not liable for injuries or harm caused by a fleeing violator because the proximate cause of the injury was not the conduct of the police in making the chase, but the negligent behavior of the fleeing violator. Although the police caused the violator to flee, the subsequent negligent conduct by the violator in the course of that flight should not be directly attributed to the chase by the police.

4. Liability for Failure to Respond to Calls

Numerous cases have been filed against the police based on alleged negligent failure to respond to calls for police help, including 911 calls. Most police departments encourage the public to call 911 in cases of emergency, and some have assured the public that such calls will be given priority and responded to promptly, sometimes stating the number of minutes it takes the police to respond. The general rule, based on court decisions, is that the police cannot be held liable for either slow or improper response to calls for police help, including 911 calls, except when a "special relationship" exists between the police and the caller. It is not a good policy for police departments to assure the public that they will respond within five, ten, or fifteen minutes after a 911 call. Such a policy exposes the department to liability in case the police are unable to live up to that promise.

IV. CIVIL LIABILITY UNDER FEDERAL LAW (CIVIL RIGHTS OR SECTION 1983 CASES)

A. The Law

Liability under federal law is based primarily on Title 42 of the U.S. Code, Section 1983, titled Civil Action for Deprivation of Rights. The law provides the following:

> Every person who, under color of any statute, ordinance, regulation, custom, or usage, of any State or Territory, subjects, or causes to be subjected, any citizen of the United States or other persons within the jurisdiction thereof to the deprivation of any rights, privileges, or immunities secured by the Constitution and laws, shall be liable to the party injured in an action at law, suit in equity, or other proper proceeding for redress.

This law, usually referred to as the *civil rights law* or *Section 1983,* is the most frequently used remedy in the arsenal of legal liability statutes available to plaintiffs.

The law, originally passed by Congress in 1871, was then known as the Ku Klux Klan law because it sought to control the activities of state officials who were also members of that organization. For a long time, however, the law was given a limited interpretation by the courts and was seldom used. In 1961, the Court adopted a much broader interpretation, thus opening wide the door for liability action in federal courts. Among the reasons for the popularity of this statute are that Section 1983 cases are usually filed in federal court, where discovery procedures are more liberal and the recovery of attorney's fees by the "prevailing" plaintiff in accordance with the Attorney's Fees Act of 1976.

In many cases the same act by the police may be the basis of a Section 1983 lawsuit as well as an action under state tort law. For example, arrest without probable cause may constitute false arrest under state tort law and a violation of the arrestee's Fourth Amendment right against unreasonable search and seizure, compensable under Section 1983. In such cases, a plaintiff may combine his or her claims and sue under multiple legal theories in federal court. Civil rights claims under federal law may usually be brought in state courts as well, but there is no agreement on whether or not state courts must entertain such claims. Note, however, that the acts of police officers are actionable as civil rights violations only if the act constitutes a violation of a constitutional or of a federally guaranteed right. Not all acts fall under this category. The Fifth Circuit Court of Appeals has held that slapping an arrestee is not actionable under Section 1983 because it does not amount to a violation of a constitutional right (Mark v. Caldwell, 754 F.2d 1260 [5th Cir. 1985]). What this means is that a civil rights case against the officer will not succeed but the officer may be liable under state tort.

B. Basic Elements of a Section 1983 Lawsuit

As interpreted by the courts, there are two basic elements in a Section 1983 lawsuit: (1) the defendant must be acting under color of law, and (2) there must be a violation of a constitutional or a federally protected right.

1. Acting under Color of Law

This means the use of power possessed by virtue of law and made possible only because the officer is clothed with the authority of the state. The problem is that although it is usually easy to identify acts that are wholly within the term *color of law* (as when an officer makes a search or an arrest while on duty), there are some acts that are not as easy to categorize. For example, P, a police officer, works during off hours as a private security agent in a shopping center. While in that capacity, P shoots and kills a fleeing shoplifter. Is P acting under color of law? Or suppose an officer arrests a felon during off hours and when not in uniform. Is the officer acting under color of law? The answer usually depends upon job expectation. Many police departments (by state law, judicial decision, or agency regulation) consider officers to respond as officers twenty-four hours a day. In these jurisdictions any arrest made on or off duty comes under the designation of color of law. In the case of police officers who "moonlight," courts have held that their being in police uniform while acting as private security agents, the use of a gun issued by the department, and the knowledge of department authorities that the officer has a second job, all indicate that the officer is acting under color of law.

The courts have interpreted the term *color of law* broadly to include local laws, ordinances, and agency regulations. The phrase does not mean that the act was in fact authorized by law. It suffices that the act appeared to be lawful even if it was not in fact authorized; hence an officer acts under color of law even if he or she exceeds lawful authority. Moreover, the concept includes clearly illegal acts committed by the officer by reason of position or opportunity. For example, an officer arrests a suspect without probable cause or brutalizes a suspect in the course of an arrest. These acts are clearly illegal, but come under the term *color of law.*

2. Violation of Right

There must be a violation of a constitutional or a federally protected right. The right violated must be given by the Constitution or by federal law. Rights given only by state law are not protected under Section 1983. For example, the right to a lawyer during police line-up prior to being charged with an offense is not given by the Constitution or by federal law; therefore, if an officer forces a suspect to appear in a line-up without a lawyer, the officer is not liable under Section 1983. If the right is given by state law, its violation may be actionable under state law or agency regulation, not under Section 1983.

Listed below are the basic constitutional rights guaranteed in the Bill of Rights that are of importance to law enforcement. Any violation of these rights exposes the police officer to a Section 1983 lawsuit:

FIRST AMENDMENT: Freedom of religion, freedom of speech, and freedom of assembly. There are five freedoms guaranteed under the First Amendment, but these three are the freedoms the police are likely to be charged with violating. For example, is it constitutional for police officers to prohibit religious groups (such as the Hare Krishna) from soliciting religious contributions at airports or other public places? Can the police prohibit picketeers from blocking entry to a manufacturing plant that is on strike? May a person who advocates the overthrow of the U.S. government be prevented from giving a speech in a shopping mall? These are questions to which the answers may not be very clear to the police officers. General advice is that officers should be guided by state law or departmental rules and guidelines. If state law or guidelines do not address these issues, advice must be sought from legal counsel.

FOURTH AMENDMENT: Prohibition against unreasonable arrest and unreasonable search and seizure. The discussions in Chapters Four to Nine of this text should help determine what a police officer can or cannot do under the Fourth Amendment.

FIFTH AMENDMENT: The right not to incriminate oneself and the right to due process. The discussions in Chapters Ten and Eleven of this text should help answer questions about what police officers can or cannot do.

SIXTH AMENDMENT: Right to have the assistance of counsel. The discussions in Chapter Twelve of this text should help answer questions about what police officers can or cannot do.

EIGHTH AMENDMENT: Prohibition against cruel and unusual punishment. This amendment is used by sentenced inmates; pretrial detainees, on the other hand, use the Fourteenth Amendment right to due process. Allegations of violation usually come from a jail prisoner or detainee who maintains that conditions in jail are so bad as to amount to cruel and unusual punishment. Law enforcement officers do not run prisons, but they usually take care of jails and temporary detention centers. The Court has decided a number of cases saying that conditions in some jails or prisons can in fact violate this constitutional right. When do conditions in jails amount to cruel and unusual punishment? The answer is complex and is determined on a case-by-case basis since conditions in no two jails are exactly alike. In general, courts look at the "totality of conditions," meaning that the court will not focus on one condition alone, but will inquire into all phases of the jail situation and operation to determine if their totality amounts to cruel and unusual punishment. Obviously, the judgment tends to be subjective, depending upon the perceptions of the trier of fact, usually a judge. Another source of an Eighth Amendment violation is the denial by the police of medical attention in jail or prison cases. The Court has decided that any denial of medical attention that amounts to "deliberate indifference" violates a prisoner's or detainee's right to protection against cruel and unusual punishment (Estelle v. Gamble, 429 U.S. 97 [1976]).

FOURTEENTH AMENDMENT: There are two basic rights under this Amendment—the *right to due process* and the *right to equal protection* of the laws. "Due process" basically means fundamental fairness; therefore an allegation by a plaintiff that an officer violated his or her "due process" right means that the officer was being fundamentally unfair. For example, charges of excessive use of force usually come under violation of due process, meaning that the officer was being fundamentally unfair in administering punishment to a suspect without proper court proceeding. It can also come under the Fourth Amendment, however, because the Court has said that the use of deadly force by an officer is the ultimate form of "seizure."

By contrast, "equal protection" means that people should be treated alike, unless there is sufficient legal justification for treating them differently. For example, Officer X violates equal protection by arresting only black drug dealers and prostitutes and not bothering drug dealers or prostitutes who are white. So does a sheriff managing a jail who isolates inmates according to race or gives work assignments based on race.

V. DEFENSES IN CIVIL LIABILITY CASES

Various legal defenses are available in state tort and Section 1983 cases, three of which will be discussed here: (1) good faith, (2) acting within the scope of employment, and (3) probable cause. These defenses are not exclusive and may apply only to certain types of lawsuits. There are other defenses available, but they are not discussed here because they are too technical and are of use only to lawyers defending civil liability cases.

A. The "Good Faith" Defense—The Harlow v. Fitzgerald Case

1. Definition

The good faith defense holds that the officer should not be held civilly liable if he or she "did not violate a clearly established statutory or constitutional right of which a reasonable person would have known." The "good faith" test therefore is: Did the official, at the time the act was committed, violate a clearly established statutory or constitutional right of which a reasonable person would have known? If the answer is yes, liability ensues; conversely, if the answer is no, liability does not ensue. This test was enunciated by the Court in Harlow v. Fitzgerald, 457 U.S. 800 (1982), when the Court said:[17]

> We therefore hold that government officials performing discretionary functions generally are shielded from liability for civil damages insofar as their conduct does not violate a clearly established statutory or constitutional right of which a reasonable person would have known.... The judge appropriately may determine, not only the currently applicable law, but whether that law was clearly established at the time an action occurred. If the law at that time was not clearly established, an official could not reasonably be expected to anticipate subsequent legal developments, nor could he fairly be said to "know" that the law forbade conduct not previously identified as unlawful.

2. How It Applies in Police Cases

Although the *Harlow* case involved the actions of two White House aides under former President Nixon, the Court has said that the Harlow standard, which affords immunity from acts that the official could have reasonably believed were lawful, also applies to police officers who are performing their responsibilities (Anderson v. Creighton, 483 U.S. 635 [1987]). In the Anderson case, a federal agent and other law enforcement officers made a search without warrant of a home, believing that a bank robber was hiding there. The family that occupied the home then sued for violation of the Fourth Amendment right against unreasonable search and seizure, alleging that the agents' act was unreasonable. On appeal, the Court said that the lower court should have considered not only the general rule about home entries, but also the facts known to the agents at the time of entry. According to the Court, the proper inquiry was whether a reasonable law enforcement officer could have concluded that the circumstances surrounding that case added up to probable cause and exigent circumstances that could then justify a warrantless search. If such conclusion is possible, then the "good faith" defense applies.

The Harlow rule may be illustrated as follows: X, a police officer, arrests a suspect, takes her to the police station, and keeps her in jail for two days without filing charges. Assume that this is an accepted practice in the department and that Officer X did not know it was illegal. The suspect challenges the constitutionality of such practice as violative of due process and the court declares the practice to be unconstitutional. If a Section 1983 case is filed, chances are that X will have a "good faith" defense because what he did was not violative of a "clearly established statutory or constitutional right of which a reasonable person would have known." If liability exists at all, it will probably be with the agency. By contrast, suppose Officer X knows (as officers are supposed to know) that an arrest cannot be based on a mere hunch, but makes an arrest anyway; then Officer X does not have a "good faith" defense because the right not to be arrested except on probable cause is a "clearly established constitutional right of which a reasonable person would have known."

3. Implications of the "Good Faith" Defense

The "good faith" defense has two important implications for police officers and agencies. First, the requirement that liability ensues if there is a violation of a statutory or a constitutional right of which a reasonable person would have known requires that police officers know the basic constitutional and statutory rights of their constituents. While officers are familiar with these rights from college courses and police academy training, such knowledge needs constant updating in the form of new court decisions in criminal procedure and constitutional law. For example, in 1985, the U.S. Supreme Court decided Tennessee v. Garner, 471 U.S. 1 (1985), an important case on the use of deadly force. That case says that deadly force may be used to apprehend a fleeing suspect only if (1) the suspect threatens the officer with a weapon or (2) there is probable cause to believe that the suspect has committed a crime involving the infliction or threatened infliction of serious physical harm, and that (3) in addition the suspect must first be warned, when feasible. The case is clearly important in that any police behavior or departmental policy that goes beyond the limitations prescribed by the Court exposes the officer and the department to civil liability. Any police officer who is not familiar with that case and acts outside its limitations exposes himself or herself to possible liability.

The second important implication of the Harlow test is that it places an obligation on police agencies to update their officers' knowledge of new cases and developments that have civil liability implications. This can be done through continuing education programs or an occasional memorandum. Moreover, agencies must update their manuals or guidelines to reflect developing case law. It is in the agency's best interest to do this because chances are that the agency will be included in a lawsuit that alleges failure to train, direct, or supervise. Updating can be done in a number of ways depending on agency size and resources. What is important is for the agency to realize that this is a responsibility it cannot ignore if it is to minimize the incidence of liability lawsuits.

Courts have said that good faith is an affirmative defense, meaning that it must be raised by the defendant claiming it, otherwise it is deemed waived (Satchell v. Dilworth, 745 F.2d 781 [2d Cir. 1984]). Under the affirmative defense concept, plaintiff has no specific obligation to prove bad faith on the part of the officer. It is enough that plaintiff proves that the injury resulted from an unconstitutional or illegal act. Once that is established, the officer then has the obligation to prove that the act was done in good faith.

B. The "Acting within the Scope of Employment" Defense

This defense is available to the police officer and supervisors, but not to the agency. In raising this defense, the officer is saying that the act was authorized by agency rules or regulations and therefore the officer should not be held liable. The fault, if any, lies with the supervisors or the agency. An Oregon case sets the following standard for determining whether or not the act was "within the scope of employment." Said the court:

> In order to determine whether defendant's actions fall within the scope of his employment, we consider whether the act in question is of a kind he was hired to perform, whether the act occurred within the authorized time and space and whether the employee was motivated, at least in part, by a purpose to serve the employer. (Stanfield v. Laccoarce, 284 Or. 651 [1978])

Courts and juries vary in their perception of what "acting within the scope of employment" means, but chances are that the defense will succeed in the following instances:

1. *If the officer acted in accordance with agency rules and regulations.* This is because agency rules and regulations are law as far as the officer is concerned, unless declared otherwise by the courts. In one case the court said that "good faith" reliance on departmental regulation precludes liability for improper detention (Moore v. Zarra, 700 F.2d 329 [6th Cir. 1983]).

2. *If the officer acted pursuant to a statute that is reasonably believed to be valid but is later declared unconstitutional.* The Court has noted that a police officer is not charged with predicting the course of constitutional law. For example, Officer P arrests D for disorderly conduct. During trial, D challenges the constitutionality of the law because of vagueness. The law is declared unconstitutional by the court. D subsequently brings a tort or Section 1983 lawsuit against Officer P for false arrest. There is no liability because Officer P had good reasons to assume at the time of the arrest that the law was constitutional.

3. *If the officer acts in accordance with orders from a superior that are reasonably believed to be valid.* The reason for this is that the officer is under orders from a superior who supposedly knows what he or she is doing. Conversely, if the officer acts in compliance with a patently invalid order, the officer may be held liable.

4. *If the officer acts in accordance with advice from a legal counsel, as long as the advice is reasonably believed to be valid.* The presumption is that the legal counsel knows what he or she is doing and therefore the officer needs to follow that advice.

In the preceding instances, the officer would have good reasons to believe that he or she acted within the scope of employment because the act is in accordance with agency rules, state law, orders from a superior, or advice from a legal counsel. It is therefore reasonable to assume that at the time the act was committed, the officer could not reasonably have known that the act was unconstitutional or violative of somebody's rights. The only exception would be if the rules of the agency, orders of a superior, or advice of a legal counsel are so gross or blatant as to be clearly illegal or unconstitutional.

C. The "Probable Cause" Defense

This defense is limited in that it applies only in cases of false arrest, false imprisonment, and illegal searches and seizures, either under state tort law or Section 1983. One court has said that for the purpose of a legal defense in Section 1983 cases, probable cause simply means "a reasonable good faith belief in the legality of the action taken" (Rodriguez v. Jones, 473 F.2d 599 [5th Cir. 1973]). That expectation is lower than the Fourth Amendment concept of probable cause, which is usually defined as "more than bare suspicion; it exists when the facts and circumstances within the officers' knowledge and of which they had reasonably trustworthy information are sufficient in themselves to warrant a man of reasonable caution in the belief that an offense has been or is being committed" (Brinegar v. United States, 338 U.S. 160 [1949]). For example, an officer makes an arrest, which is later determined to be without probable cause. According to the preceding decision, the officer may be exempt from liability if he or she reasonably and in good faith believed at the time of the arrest that it was legal. Conversely, liability will likely be imposed if the officer either did not honestly believe that there was cause or if such belief was unreasonable.

Although not an absolute defense, an arrest or search by an officer based on a warrant issued by a magistrate falls under the "probable cause" defense. In these cases, the presence of probable cause has already been determined by the magistrate; the duty of the officer is merely to execute the warrant. Should the warrant turn out to be invalid, the officer would not be liable because he or she is entitled to presume that the warrant is valid. The only exception to this rule is if the warrant is clearly defective or unjustified.

VI. DEFENDANTS IN CIVIL LIABILITY CASES: LEGAL REPRESENTATION AND INDEMNIFICATION

Plaintiffs generally use the *"shotgun approach"* in liability lawsuits. This means that plaintiffs will include as parties-defendant everyone who may have any possible connection with the case. For example, a police officer, while on patrol, shoots and kills a suspect. The victim's family will probably sue under Section 1983 or state tort law and include as defendants the officer, his or her immediate supervisor, the police chief, and the city or county. The allegation may be that the officer is liable because he or she pulled the trigger; the supervisor, police chief, and the city are also liable because of failure to properly train, direct, supervise, or assign, or because of an unconstitutional policy or practice. The legal theory is that some or all of the defendants had something to do with the killing, and hence liability attaches. It is for the court during the trial to determine who is liable and who is not.

A. Individual Officer as Defendant

The officer is an obvious liability target because he or she allegedly committed the violation. The officer will be a party-defendant whether he or she acted within or outside the scope of authority. Most state agencies, by law or official policy, provide representation to state law enforcement officers in civil actions. Such representation is usually undertaken by the state attorney general, who is the legal counsel of the state.

The situation is different in local law enforcement agencies. In most counties, cities, towns, or villages, there is no policy that requires the agency to defend public officials in liability lawsuits. Legal representation by the agency is usually decided on a case-by-case basis. This means that the local agency is under no obligation to provide a lawyer should an officer be sued. If the agency provides a lawyer, it will probably be the district attorney, the county attorney, or another lawyer working in some capacity with the government. In some cases, the officer is allowed to choose a lawyer, but the lawyer's fees are paid by the agency. This is an ideal arrangement, but it is unpopular with agencies because of the cost.

If the agency refuses to defend, then the officer must provide his or her own lawyer at his or her own expense. This worsens the officer's problem and concerns. A suggested approach is to make legal representation an obligation of the agency, except when the officer acts in gross excess of his or her authority. This policy may be provided for in the agency guidelines or manual or specifically granted as a benefit of employment.

If an officer is held liable in a lawsuit, who pays for the plaintiff's attorney's fees and the assessed damages? A majority of states provide some form of indemnification for state employees. (Indemnification is the reimbursement of the amount paid by the officer.) The amount varies considerably; some states set no limit, but most states do. If the court awards the plaintiff an amount larger than the maximum allowed by the agency, the employee pays the difference. Although most state agencies provide some form of indemnification, it does not follow that the agency will automatically indemnify every time liability is imposed. Most agencies will pay if the officer acted "within the scope of employment." This means that the agency will not indemnify if the officer's act is gross, blatant, or outrageously violative of individual rights or of agency regulations, as determined by the court. In contrast, local agencies vary in practice from full indemnification to no indemnification whatsoever. Many state and local agencies will not pay punitive damages (as opposed to token or actual damages) against a public employee because the imposition of punitive damages means that the employee acted outside the scope and course of employment in such a way that the payment by the agency of punitive damages would be against public policy.

B. Supervisor as Defendant

Although lawsuits against law enforcement officers are usually brought against field officers, a recent trend among plaintiffs is to include supervisory officials, cities, and counties as defendants. Supervisors may be held liable under the following theories of supervisory liability: negligent failure to train, negligent failure to direct, negligent failure to supervise, negligent hiring, negligent retention, negligent assignment, and negligent entrustment. Liability might arise if plaintiff can prove that the injury caused by a subordinate can be linked or traced to any failure on the part of the supervisor to do his or her job in the preceding areas.

There are definite advantages for the plaintiff in including supervisors and departments in a liability lawsuit. First, lower-level officers may not have the financial resources to satisfy a judgment; neither are they in a position to prevent similar future violations by other officers. Second, chances of financial recovery are enhanced if supervisory personnel are included in the lawsuit. The higher the position of the employee, the closer the plaintiff gets to the *"deep pockets"* of the county or state agency. Third, inclusion of the supervisor and agency may create inconsistencies in the legal strategy of the defense, hence strengthening the plaintiff's claim against one or some of the defendants. For example, P, an officer, is sued for the wrongful death of a suspect. The lawsuit includes P's immediate supervisor (the police captain), the police chief, and the city. P's act that resulted in the wrongful death may be so outrageous that her supervisors and the city may not want to defend her, hence depriving P of agency resources and perhaps biasing the case against the officer.

What happens if the supervisor does not want to defend the officer? A conflict of interest ensues. In these cases, the agency makes a choice and that choice will most probably be to defend the supervisor. There is nothing the officer can do about that, unless formal policy requires the agency to undertake the officer's defense even in these cases.

In 1985, the Ninth Circuit Court of Appeals judged an action brought against police supervisors for promulgating a policy that allegedly gave rise to police misconduct in using excessive force during an arrest. The court ruled that it is improper to substitute the names of new employees for those who have left their positions. The court added that the proper defendants, who may be personally liable for actions taken in their official capacity, are those who were in office at the time of the incident and who may have had a hand in the plan (Heller v. Bushey, 759 F.2d 1371 [9th Cir. 1985]). What this means is that a supervisor may still be a defendant even after he or she is out of office.

C. Governmental Agency as Defendant

Most courts have decided that when supervisory liability extends to the highest ranking individual in the department, municipality or agency liability follows.[18] The inclusion of the governmental agency (specifically the city or county) as defendant is anchored on the "deep pockets" theory: whereas officers and supervisors may have a "shallow pocket," agencies have a deep pocket because they have a deeper financial base and can always raise revenue through taxation.

States and state agencies generally cannot be sued under Section 1983 in either a federal or state court because they enjoy sovereign immunity under the Eleventh Amendment to the Constitution. This does not mean that state officials are immune to liability. Sovereign immunity extends only to the state itself and its agencies; state officials may be sued and held liable just like local officials. It must be noted that although states are generally immune to liability in Section 1983 cases because of the Eleventh Amendment, that protection has largely been terminated for liability purposes in state courts.[19] Accordingly, states may generally be sued under state tort for what their officers do.

Local agencies (agencies below the state level) enjoyed sovereign immunity until 1978 in Section 1983 cases. That year the Court decided that local agencies could be held liable under Section 1983 for what their employees do, depriving local governments of the "sovereign immunity" defense (Monnell v. Department of Social Services, 436 U.S. 658 [1978]). This change may be partly responsible for the increase in the number of liability cases because now plaintiffs know that if the officer is too poor to pay, the agency may be held liable, if proper circumstances are present. The Court held in Monnell that the municipality will be liable if the unconstitutional action taken by the employee is caused by a *municipal policy or custom*, whether such be written or unwritten. The Fifth Circuit Court of Appeals defines "policy or custom" as

1. a policy statement, ordinance, regulation, or decision that is officially adopted and promulgated by the municipality's lawmaking officers or by an official to whom the lawmakers have delegated policy-making authority; or
2. a persistent widespread practice of city officials or employees that, although not authorized by officially adopted and promulgated policy, is so common and well settled as to constitute a custom that fairly represents municipal policy (Webster v. City of Houston, 735 F.2d 838 [5th Cir. 1984]).

(*Note:* The above standard caused the majority of the court to vacate the judgment awarding damages against the City of Houston for the actions of police officers who killed an unarmed youth and then placed a "throw-down" weapon next to his body so they could claim self-defense.)

There are instances in which an officer or a supervisor will not be held liable for damages, but the agency or municipality may be. In Owen v. City of Independence, 445 U.S. 622 (1980), the Court said that a municipality sued under Section 1983 cannot invoke the "good faith" defense, which is available to its officers and employees, if its policies are violative of constitutional rights. In that case, a police chief was dismissed by the city manager and city council for certain misdoings while in office. The police chief was not given any type of hearing or "due process" rights because the city charter under which the city manager and city council acted did not give him any rights prior to dismissal. The Court held that the city manager and members of the city council acted in good faith because they were authorized by the provisions of the city charter, but that the city itself could not invoke the "good faith" defense.

In a 1985 decision, the Court ruled that a monetary judgment against a public officer "in his official capacity" imposes liability upon the agency that employs him or her, regardless of whether or not the agency was named as a defendant in the suit (Brandon v. Holt, 105 S.Ct. 873 [1985]). In this case, the plaintiff alleged that although the director of the police department had no actual notice of the police officer's violent behavior, administrative policies were such that he should have known. The Court added that although the director could be shielded by qualified immunity, the city could be held liable.

HIGHLIGHT 15.3

Good Faith Defense Available

"The innocent individual who is harmed by an abuse of governmental authority is assured that he will be compensated for his injury. The offending official, so long as he conducts himself in good faith, may go about his business secure in the knowledge that a qualified immunity will protect him from personal liability for damages that are more appropriately chargeable to the populace as a whole. And the public will be forced to bear only the costs of injury inflicted by the 'execution of a government's policy or custom, whether made by its lawmakers or by those whose edicts or acts may fairly be said to represent official policy' " (Owen v. City of Independence, Missouri, 445 U.S. 622 [1980]).

In a 1986 case, the Court decided that municipalities could be held liable in a civil rights case for violating constitutional rights on the basis of a *single decision* (therefore there is no need for a "pattern of decisions") made by an authorized municipal policymaker (Pembauer v. City of Cincinnati, 54 L.W. 4289 [1986]). In this case, the county prosecutor made official policy, and thereby exposed his municipal employer to liability, by instructing law enforcement officers to make a forcible entry, without search warrant, of an office in order to serve capiases (a form of warrant issued by the judge) on persons thought to be there. The case was brought by a Cincinnati, Ohio, physician on the basis of an incident in which law enforcement officers, under advice from the county prosecutor, broke down the door in his office with an ax. The officers were trying to arrest two of the doctor's employees, who had failed to appear before a grand jury. The Court decided that this action violated the Fourth Amendment rights of the office owners and concluded that the city of Cincinnati could be held liable.

In a recent case, the Court held that inadequate police training may serve as the basis for municipal liability under Section 1983, but only if the failure to train amounts to "deliberate indifference" to the rights of people with whom the police come into contact and if the deficiency in the training program is closely related to the injury suffered (City of Canton v. Harris, 109 S.Ct. 1197 [1989]). This case settles an issue that has long bothered lower courts: Can a municipality be held liable for failure to train? The Court in Harris answered yes, but subject to strict requirements: (1) the failure to adequately train must reflect a "deliberate" or "conscious" choice by the municipality; (2) such inadequate training must represent city policy, and (3) the identified deficiency in the training program must be closely related to the injury. What this means is that not every injury caused by police officers leads to municipal liability for failure to train. Only when the three requirements just given are met does municipality liability ensue.

In sum, it is advantageous for the plaintiff to include the agency in a liability lawsuit and avoid suing a police officer in his or her individual capacity. The plaintiff has nothing to lose and a lot to gain when suing the officer in his or her official capacity and including supervisors and the governmental employer as parties-defendant. This approach enables the plaintiff to dip into the "deep pockets" of the supervisor and agency for damages and attorney's fees, should the plaintiff prevail.

VII. CAN THE POLICE SUE BACK?—YES, BUT . . .

Can the police strike back by suing those who sue them? The answer is yes, and some departments are in fact striking back. Illustrative is this newspaper headline: "Grand Jurors Face $1.7 Million Suit for Criticism of Police."[20] The Fifth Circuit Court of Appeals has held that a city can criminally prosecute individuals for knowingly filing false complaints against the police (Gates v. City of Dallas, 729 F.2d 343 [5th Cir. 1984]). In a policy change, New York City has adopted a policy of countersuing some people who have brought civil suits in which they accuse police officers of brutality. In these cases, the City of New York will countersue by asserting that it was the complainant who attacked the police.[21] Nonetheless, the number of civil cases actually brought by the police against the public has remained comparatively small.

The reality is that although police officers may file tort lawsuits against arrestees or suspects, there are disadvantages in doing that. The first is that in a tort case the officer will have to hire his or her own lawyer, necessitating financial expense that the officer cannot recover from the defendant. Should the officer file a tort case, chances of meaningful success may not be good because most of those who run afoul of the law and have encounters with the police may be too poor to pay damages. Moreover, officers oftentimes refrain from filing civil cases for damages because it is less expensive and more convenient to get back at the suspect in a criminal case. Almost every state has provisions penalizing such offenses as deadly assault of a peace officer, false report to a police officer, resisting arrest or search, hindering apprehension or prosecution and aggravated assault. These offenses can be added to the regular criminal offense charged against the arrested person, thereby increasing the penalty or facilitating prosecution. Moreover, many officers feel that the harsh treatment they sometimes get from the public is part of police work, to be accepted without retaliation. Whatever the attitude, the police do have legal remedies available should they wish to exercise them.

VIII. LEGALITY OF "WE WILL RELEASE IF YOU WILL NOT SUE" ARRANGEMENT

Some jurisdictions unofficially practice a *quid pro quo* (something for something) arrangement whereby a criminal case against an arrested person is dismissed in exchange for a promise not to file a civil liability lawsuit against the officer or department. Is this practice legal? The Court has said that such an agreement is not per se invalid (Town of Newton v. Rumery, 40 CrL 3335 [1987]). In that case, Rumery was arrested by the police for making telephone calls to the complaining witness in connection with a sex charge filed against Rumery's friend. He was charged with witness tampering. Subsequently, the prosecutor and Rumery's lawyer struck a deal that provided that the charges would be dropped by the police if Rumery agreed not to sue for damages caused by his arrest.

Three days after his release, Rumery sued anyway, alleging that the agreement not to file charges was invalid because it violated public policy. The Court, in a 5-to-4 decision, said that the agreement was valid and that it was not inherently coercive to present a defendant with a choice between facing criminal charges and waiving the right to bring a Section 1983 lawsuit, as in this case. A major reason why these types of agreement are carefully reviewed by the courts is that the waiver might be coerced by the police. In the present case, however, Rumery was characterized by the Court as a "sophisticated businessman" whose lawyer fully explained the release-dismissal agreement. Moreover, the prosecutor had a valid reason for agreeing to the deal—his wish to spare the victim the embarrassment she would have had to face had either the criminal case or the civil rights suit been pursued. Given these circumstances, the Court upheld the agreement as valid.

The Rumery case was decided based on the peculiar facts of that case and therefore should not be used as precedent for similar police conduct. Were the circumstances different, the Court would have decided otherwise. An example of an invalid arrangement is Hal v. Ochs, 817 F.2d 920 (1st Cir. 1987). In that case, the police illegally arrested a suspect and held him in detention until he signed a release agreement. Detention was continued even after the police had determined that the charges were unfounded. The First Circuit Court of Appeals held that since the plaintiff was detained without probable cause and knew he could not be released until he signed the papers relinquishing his right to a civil lawsuit, such release was coerced and therefore invalid under the Rumery principle.

IX. WAYS TO MINIMIZE LEGAL LIABILITIES

Liability lawsuits may be filed by anybody against an officer at any time. One of the fundamental rights in U.S. society is the right of access to court. Whether or not the lawsuit will succeed is an entirely different matter. Figures show that most cases filed against public officers fail for various reasons. Nonetheless, it is unrealistic in modern-day policing to expect that no lawsuit will ever be filed against an officer during his or her years of police work. There are ways, however, whereby lawsuits may be minimized. In no particular order of importance, they are:

1. Know and follow your department's manual or guidelines. If you do, you will have a strong claim to a "good faith" defense.
2. Act within the scope of your duties.
3. Act in a professional and responsible manner at all times. When faced with a difficult situation, use reason instead of emotion.
4. Know the constitutional rights of your constituents and respect them.
5. Consult your legal counsel or supervisor if you have doubts about what you are doing. Be able to document the advice given.
6. In sensitive cases, document your activities. Keep good written records.
7. Establish and maintain good relations with your community.
8. Keep yourself well informed on current issues and trends in civil and criminal liability cases.

HIGHLIGHT 15.4

Police Officer Suing Lottery Winner for Harassment

"West Bridgewater, Mass., Police Officer Raymond Rogers was happy to see the man he arrested win part of the Massachusetts megabucks jackpot the day before he went on trial, because now he's going to sue him for damages.

Charles C. Babicz, 23, of West Bridgewater, won $289,763 the day before he was convicted of firing three shotgun blasts at Rogers' home, apparently because the patrolman had given him a traffic ticket.

Babicz was one of six winners sharing in the April 30 megabucks jackpot and will get $10,866 a year after taxes annually for 20 years.

Now the officer plans to sue Babicz for peppering his house with .28-gauge shotgun shells.

'Things like this happen to cops a lot,' Rogers said. 'But usually the guy who does it to you doesn't have any money, so you can't pursue him with a civil suit. This guy now has some money.' "

Source: Crime Control Digest, May 12, 1986, p. 6. Reproduced with permission.

Departmental manuals or guidelines play an important part in police work. The advantages are twofold: Manuals tell police officers what is expected of them and how their tasks can be performed properly, and manuals constitute a good defense for police officers and the agency in liability cases. Manual provisions have the force and effect of law for the officers. If the provisions of the manual are illegal, then the agency or supervisor might be held liable, not the officer. For example, an agency manual provides that the officer may "shoot to kill" a fleeing misdemeanant. If Officer Z does that, is sued, and the statute is declared unconstitutional, the department might be liable because of the violation of a constitutional right. Chances are that Z would have a "good faith" defense. The only possible exception is if Z should have known that the provisions of the manual were clearly illegal.

The list just given is by no means exhaustive. There is no substitute for the specific advice of a competent lawyer when an officer is faced with a difficult situation that carries potential legal consequences. Liability sources and defenses vary from state to state, or even from one jurisdiction to another within a state. When a lawsuit is filed, it is important for the officer to obtain the services of a good lawyer, either on his or her own or through the department. Liability lawsuits must be taken seriously, even if the allegations appear to be groundless or trivial; otherwise, undesirable consequences can follow.

□ SUMMARY

Liability lawsuits have become common in policing, so law enforcement officers should be familiar with them. Lawsuits against officers may be filed under state and federal laws, and the sanctions can be civil, criminal, or administrative. Most plaintiffs, however, prefer to sue under the provisions of state tort laws and the Federal Civil Rights Act, otherwise referred to as Section 1983.

State tort is a civil wrong in which the action of one person causes injury to the person or property of another, in violation of a legal duty imposed by law. Liability under state tort law may come under intentional tort or negligence tort. There are also other, related torts to which officers may be liable, such as misuse of legal procedure, invasion of privacy, illegal electronic surveillance, and defamation.

By far the most popular form of redress against public officials is a Section 1983 lawsuit. The elements of a Section 1983 case are that the officer must have been acting under color of law and that there must be a violation of the plaintiff's constitutional or federally guaranteed right.

There are a number of available defenses in civil liability cases, among them the "good faith" defense, the "acting within the scope of employment" defense, and the "probable cause" defense. The "good faith" defense holds that the officer should not be held civilly liable if he or she "did not violate a clearly established statutory or constitutional right of which a reasonable person would have known." The "acting within the scope of employment" defense holds that the officer should not be held liable if what he or she does is within the scope of employment. In these cases, however, the agency itself that promulgated the rules might be liable. The "probable cause" defense holds that there is no liability if what the officer does is supported by probable cause. This defense is limited, in that it applies only in cases of false arrest, false imprisonment, and illegal searches and seizures where probable cause is required.

In addition to the police officer, plaintiffs usually include the supervisor and governmental agency as defendants. This approach enables the plaintiff to dip into the "deep pockets" of the supervisor or local agency in case the officer-defendant cannot pay. Legal representation and indemnification is usually undertaken by the agency unless what the officer did was grossly and clearly outside the scope of authority. Indemnification is also usually undertaken by the agency under the same standard of "acting within the scope of authority."

A police officer can sue back if the case brought against him or her is utterly without merit. This may, however, be difficult to establish. Moreover, an officer will most likely have to provide his or her own lawyer and that discourages further lawsuits because of the expense involved. Civil liabilities may be minimized in a number of ways. Police officers need to be familiar with those ways if they are to spare themselves the trouble and expense of a civil liability lawsuit.

☐   REVIEW QUESTIONS

1. What is a tort? Distinguish between intentional tort and negligence tort.
2. What standard is used by courts to determine whether or not there is use of excessive force by the police?
3. What is the "public duty" doctrine? What is its exception?
4. Are the police liable for failure to protect? Discuss fully.
5. What is a Section 1983 case? Give its two basic elements.
6. What is the "good faith" defense? Give two instances in which the "good faith" defense will likely succeed.
7. What is the "probable cause" defense? Does it apply to all civil liability lawsuits?
8. What are some advantages to the plaintiff in including the supervisor and agency as defendants in a lawsuit?
9. If an officer is sued, will the agency provide a lawyer to defend him or her? If the officer is held liable, will the agency pay? Discuss.
10. What is meant by a "policy or custom" for which a municipality may be held liable in a Section 1983 lawsuit?
11. What are some reasons why police officers do not sue back even if there are legal remedies available to them?
12. State five ways whereby police officers can minimize legal liabilities.

☐   DEFINITIONS

Acting under Color of Law: The use of power possessed by virtue of law and made possible only because the officer is clothed with the authority of the state.

Assault: An intentional tort wherein an officer causes apprehension of a harmful or offensive conduct; it is the attempt or threat, accompanied by the ability to inflict bodily harm on another person.

Battery: An intentional tort caused by the infliction of harmful or offensive body contact by an officer on another person. It usually involves unlawful, unwarranted, or hostile touching—however slight.

"Deep Pockets" Theory: A theory in liability lawsuits that suggests that it is best to include the agency-employer in liability lawsuits because whereas public officers may have "shallow pockets," agencies have "deep pockets" in that the government has a deep financial base and can always tax its constituents to raise revenue.

False Arrest: An intentional tort that results when an officer makes an illegal arrest, usually arrests without probable cause.

False Imprisonment: An intentional tort that results when an officer places a person in confinement or deprives him or her of freedom without legal justification.

"Good Faith" Defense: A defense in civil liability cases that holds that the officer should not be held civilly liable if he or she did not violate a clearly established constitutional right of which a reasonable person would have known.

Infliction of Mental or Emotional Distress: A form of intentional tort that takes place when an officer inflicts severe emotional distress on a person through intentional or reckless extreme and outrageous conduct.

Intentional Tort: Type of tort that occurs when an officer intends to bring some physical harm or mental effect upon another person.

Municipal Policy or Custom: A policy statement, ordinance, regulation, or decision that is officially adopted and promulgated by the municipality's lawmaking officers or by an official to whom the lawmakers have delegated policymaking authority; or a persistent widespread practice of city officials or employees that, although not authorized by officially adopted and promulgated policy, is so common and well settled as to constitute a custom that fairly represents municipal policy.

Negligence Tort: The breach of a common law or statutory duty to act reasonably toward those who may foreseeably be harmed by one's conduct.

Probable Cause Defense: In Section 1983 cases, the reasonable good faith belief of the officer in the legality of the action taken.

"Public Duty" Doctrine: A doctrine that holds that government functions are owed to the general public, but not to specific individuals; therefore, police officers who fail to prevent crime while acting within the scope of their official capacity are not liable to specific individuals for injury or harm that may have been caused by a third party.

Section 1983 Cases (also known as civil rights cases): Civil liability lawsuits seeking damages and/or improvement of confinement conditions, brought against a public officer under Title 42, U.S. Code, Section 1983, when an officer, acting under color of law, violates a person's constitutional or federally protected right. This is the most popular form of legal redress used by plaintiffs against public officers.

Special Relationship: An exception to the "public duty" doctrine (which exempts the police from liability for failure to protect), meaning that the police will be held civilly liable if a special relationship with a particular individual has been created.

Tort: A civil wrong in which the action of one person causes injury to the person or property of another, in violation of a legal duty imposed by law.

Wrongful Death: A tort action in which the surviving family, relatives, or legal guardian of the estate of the deceased bring a lawsuit against an officer on account of death caused by the officer's conduct.

□ PRINCIPLES OF CASES

ANDERSON V. CREIGHTON, 483 U.S. 635 (1987)   The Harlow standard, which affords immunity from acts that the official could have reasonably believed were lawful, applies to police officers in the performance of responsibilities.

BRANDON V. HOLT, 105 S.Ct. 873 (1985)   A monetary judgment against a public officer in his or her official capacity imposes liability upon the agency that employs him or her, regardless of whether or not the agency was named as a defendant in the suit.

BRINEGAR V. UNITED STATES, 338 U.S. 160 (1949)   *Probable* means more than mere suspicion; it exists when the facts and circumstances within the officers' knowledge and of which they had reasonably trustworthy information are sufficient in themselves to warrant a man of reasonable caution in the belief that an offense has been or is being committed.

CITY OF CANTON V. HARRIS, 109 S.Ct. 1197 (1989)   Inadequate police training may serve as the basis for municipal liability under Section 1983 if the failure to train amounts to "deliberate indifference" to the rights of people with whom the police come into contact and the deficiency in the training program is closely related to the injury suffered.

GATES V. CITY OF DALLAS, 729 F.2d 343 (5th Cir. 1984)   A city can criminally prosecute individuals for knowingly filing false complaints against the police.

GRAHAM V. CONNOR, 109 S.Ct. 1865 (1989)   The use of deadly or nondeadly force by the police must be judged from the perspective of a reasonable officer on the scene, rather than with the 20/20 vision of hindsight. The officer's action must be tested based on the "objective reasonableness" standard in light of surrounding circumstances.

HARLOW V. FITZGERALD, 457 U.S. 800 (1982)   Government officials performing discretionary functions generally are shielded from liability for civil damages insofar as their conduct does not violate clearly established statutory or constitutional rights of which a reasonable person would have known.

HELLER V. BUSHEY, 759 F.2d 1371 (9th Cir. 1985)   In an action against police supervisors for promulgating a policy that allegedly gave rise to police misconduct in using excessive force during an arrest, it is improper to substitute the names of new employees for those who have left their positions. The proper defendants, who may be personally liable for actions taken in their official capacity, are those who were in office at the time of the incident and who may have had a hand in the plan.

IRWIN V. TOWN OF WARE, 467 N.E. 2d 1292 (MA 1984)   Statutes that establish police responsibility in DWI cases show a legislative intent to protect both the intoxicated people and the users of the highway and therefore create a special relationship that can lead to police liability.

LEWIS V. DOWNS, 774 F.2d 711 (6th Cir. 1985)   The court found that the police had used excessive force on a family when responding to a call to settle a neighborhood dispute; the police were made to pay $10,000. The court said that excessive force was used on the father, who was not of great physical strength and who was already being subdued by his brother when the police kicked him in the groin and struck him on the head with a nightstick. It was alleged that the officers kicked the mother on the back and buttocks after she was handcuffed and lying face down in the mud. The son was also injured during the arrest process.

MALLEY V. BRIGGS, 54 L.W. 4342 (1986)   A police officer, when applying for an arrest warrant, is entitled only to qualified immunity, not absolute immunity, in Section 1983 cases. This means that even if a warrant is issued by a magistrate as a result of the officer's complaint, the officer could be liable if it is established that the complaint was made maliciously and without probable cause.

MARK V. CALDWELL, 754 F.2d 1260 (5th Cir. 1985)   Slapping an arrestee is not actionable under Section 1983 because it does not amount to a violation of a constitutional right.

MONNELL V. DEPARTMENT OF SOCIAL SERVICES, 436 U.S. 658 (1978)   Local units of government may be held liable in a civil rights lawsuit if the allegedly unconstitutional action was taken by the officer as a part of an official policy or custom.

MOORE V. ZARRA, 700 F.2d 329 (6th Cir. 1983)   "Good faith" reliance on departmental regulation precludes liability for improper detention.

OWEN V. CITY OF INDEPENDENCE, MISSOURI, 445 U.S. 622 (1980)   A municipality sued under Section 1983 cannot invoke the "good faith" defense, which is available to its officers and employees, if its policies are violative of constitutional rights.

PEMBAUER V. CITY OF CINCINNATI, 54 L.W. 4289 (1986)   Municipalities could be held liable in a civil rights case for violating constitutional rights on the basis of a single decision (therefore there is no need for a "pattern of decisions") made by an authorized municipal policymaker.

PIERSON V. RAY, 386 U.S. 555 (1967)   Liability does not exist if an arrest is made by virtue of a law that is later declared unconstitutional. A police officer is not charged with predicting the future course of constitutional law.

RODRIGUEZ V. JONES, 473 F.2d 599 (5th Cir. 1973)   Probable cause, as a defense in civil rights cases, simply means "a reasonable good faith belief in the legality of the action taken."

SANDERS V. CITY OF BELLE GLADE, 510 So. 2d 962 (Fla. App. 1987)   Once a suspect is handcuffed and taken into custody, a special relationship is created that makes the city responsible for his safety as though he were incarcerated in the city jail.

SATCHELL V. DILWORTH, 745 F.2d 781 (2d Cir. 1984)   The "good faith" defense is an affirmative defense, meaning that it must be raised by the defendant claiming it; otherwise, it is deemed waived.

SCHUSTER V. CITY OF NEW YORK, 154 N.E. 2d 534 (NY 1958)   The police owe a special duty to use reasonable care to protect people who have collaborated with them in the arrest or prosecution of criminals.

SORICHETTI V. CITY OF NEW YORK, 482 N.E. 2d 70 (1985)   The police may be civilly liable for failure to protect if a "special relationship" has been created—such as, if a judicial order has been issued for the police to protect a child but they fail to do so.

STANFIELD V. LACCOARCE, 284 Or. 651 (1978)   To determine whether a police officer's actions are within the scope of employment, the court considers whether the act in question is of a kind he or she was hired to perform, whether the act occurred within the authorized time and space, and whether the employee was motivated, at least in part, by a purpose to serve the employer.

TOWN OF NEWTON V. RUMERY, 40 CrL 3335 (1987)   An arrangement whereby a criminal case against an arrested person is dismissed by the police in exchange for a promise not to file a civil liability lawsuit is not per se invalid; it may be valid if the waiver of rights is not coerced.

WEBSTER V. CITY OF HOUSTON, 735 F.2d 838 (5th Cir. 1984)   "Official policy or custom" means (1) a policy statement, ordinance, regulation, or decision that is officially adopted and promulgated by the municipality's lawmaking officers or by an official to whom the lawmakers have delegated policymaking authority; or (2) a persistent widespread practice of city officials or employees that although not authorized by officially adopted and promulgated policy, is so common and well settled as to constitute a custom that fairly represents municipal policy.

YOUNG V. CITY OF KILLEEN, 775 F.2d 1349 (1985)   The court found a police officer liable for $202,295.80 in a wrongful death action for shooting and killing a man suspected of buying marijuana. The officer was liable even though he thought he was shooting in self-defense because the judge, relying on the testimony of an expert witness on police procedures, found that the officer had acted negligently and contrary to good police procedure. The action of the officer not only placed him in a position of greater danger but also imperiled the deceased suspect by creating a situation in which a fatal error was likely.

☐ CASE BRIEF—LEADING CASE ON THE TYPE OF IMMUNITY POLICE OFFICERS HAVE

MALLEY V. BRIGGS, 54 L.W. 4342 (1986)

FACTS: On the basis of two monitored telephone calls pursuant to a court-authorized wiretap, Rhode Island state trooper Malley prepared felony complaints charging Briggs and others with possession of marijuana. The complaints were given to a state judge together with arrest warrants and supporting affidavits. The judge signed the warrants, and the defendants were arrested. The charges, however, were subsequently dropped when the grand jury refused to return an indictment. The defendants then brought action under Section 1983, alleging that Malley, in applying for the arrest warrants, had violated their rights against unreasonable search and seizure. The case was tried by a jury and the court, while granting a directed verdict in favor of the officers based on other grounds, stated that a police officer who believes that the facts stated in an affidavit are true and submits them to a neutral magistrate may be entitled to absolute immunity. The Court of Appeals reversed that decision.

ISSUE: *What type of immunity is accorded a defendant police officer in Section 1983 actions when it is alleged that the officer caused the plaintiffs to be unconstitutionally arrested by presenting a judge with a complaint and a supporting affidavit that failed to establish probable cause? Qualified immunity.*

SUPREME COURT DECISION: A police officer is not entitled to absolute immunity, but only to qualified immunity to liability for damages in Section 1983 cases. Qualified immunity is not established simply by virtue of the fact that the officer believed the allegations in the affidavit that the magistrate found to be sufficient.

CASE SIGNIFICANCE: Officer Malley in the preceding case argued that he should be given absolute immunity, despite early decisions to the contrary, because his function in seeking an arrest warrant was similar to that of a complaining witness. The Court answered saying that complaining witnesses were not absolutely immune at common law, adding that in fact the generally accepted rule in 1871, when the civil rights law was passed, was that one who procured the issuance of an arrest warrant by submitting a complaint could be held liable if the complaint was made maliciously and without probable cause. If malice and lack of probable cause are proved, the officer enjoys no absolute immunity. The Court also refused to be swayed by the officer's argument that policy considerations require absolute immunity for the officer applying for a warrant, saying that "as the qualified immunity defense has evolved, it provides ample protection to all but the plainly incompetent or those who knowingly violate the law." The Court considered this protection sufficient because, under current standards, the officer is not liable anyway if he or she acted in an objectively reasonable manner. The Malley case therefore makes clear that under no circumstance will the Court extend the "absolute immunity" defense (available to judges, prosecutors, and legislators) to police officers. The only exception occurs when the officer is testifying in a criminal trial. This means that officers enjoy only qualified immunity, but that they will not be liable if they act in an objectively reasonable manner.

EXCERPTS FROM THE DECISION: Although we have previously held that police officers sued under Section 1983 for false arrest are qualifiedly immune, petitioner urges that he should be absolutely immune because his function in seeking an arrest warrant was similar to that of a complaining witness. The difficulty with this submission is that complaining witnesses were not absolutely immune at common law. In 1871, the generally accepted rule was that one who procured the issuance of an arrest warrant by submitting a complaint could be held liable if the complaint was made maliciously and without probable cause. Given malice and the lack of probable cause, the complainant enjoyed no immunity. The common law thus affords no support for petitioner.

Nor are we moved by petitioner's argument that policy considerations require absolute immunity for the officer applying for a warrant. As the qualified immunity defense has evolved, it provides ample protection to all but the plainly incompetent or those who knowingly violate the law. At common law, in cases where probable cause to arrest was lacking, a complaining witness's immunity turned on the issue of malice, which was a jury question. Under the Harlow standard, on the other hand, an allegation of malice is not sufficient to defeat immunity if the defendant acted in an objectively reasonable manner. The Harlow standard is specifically designed to "avoid excessive disruption of government and permit the resolution of many insubstantial claims on summary judgment," and we believe it sufficiently serves this goal. Defendants will not be immune if, on an objective basis, it is obvious that no reasonably competent officer would have concluded that a warrant should issue; but if officers of reasonable competence could disagree on this issue, immunity should be recognized.

☐   CASE BRIEF—LEADING CASE ON POLICE LIABILITY FOR EXCESSIVE USE OF FORCE

GRAHAM V. CONNOR, 109 S.Ct. 1865 (1989)

FACTS: Graham, a diabetic, asked a friend, Berry, to drive him to a convenience store to buy orange juice, which he needed to counteract the onset of an insulin reaction. They went to the store, but Graham saw many people ahead of him in line so he hurried out and asked Berry to drive him, instead, to a friend's house. Officer Connor became suspicious after he saw Graham hastily enter and leave the store. He followed Berry's car, made an investigative stop, and ordered Graham and Berry to wait while he determined what happened at the store. Other officers arrived, handcuffed Graham, and ignored Graham's attempt to explain his condition. An encounter ensued wherein Graham sustained multiple injuries. Graham was later released when officer Connor learned that nothing had happened at the store. Graham brought a Section 1983 lawsuit against the police alleging a violation of his Fourth Amendment constitutional right.

ISSUE: *May police officers be held liable under Section 1983 for using excessive force? Yes. If yes, what should be the standard for liability?*

SUPREME COURT DECISION: Police officers may be held liable under the Constitution for using excessive force. Such liability must be judged under the Fourth Amendment's "objective reasonableness" standard, rather than under a "substantive due process" standard.

CASE SIGNIFICANCE: This case gives police officers a "break" in civil liability cases involving the use of force. The old "substantive due process" test used by many lower courts prior to the Graham case required the courts to consider whether the officer acted in "good faith" or "maliciously and sadistically for the very purpose of causing harm." This meant that the officer's "subjective motivations" were of central importance in deciding whether the force used was unconstitutional. The Graham case requires a new test—that of "objective reasonableness" under the Fourth Amendment. This means that the reasonableness of an officer's use of force must be judged "from the perspective of a reasonable officer on the scene, rather than with the 20/20 vision of hindsight." This makes a big difference in determining whether or not such use of force was reasonable. This new test recognizes that police officers often make split-second judgments in situations that involve their own lives and must, therefore, be judged in the context of "a reasonable officer at the scene." This is a test most police officers welcome.

EXCERPT FROM THE DECISION: The "reasonableness" of a particular use of force must be judged from the perspective of a reasonable officer on the scene, rather than with the 20/20 vision of hindsight. The Fourth Amendment is not violated by an arrest based on probable cause, even though the wrong person is arrested, nor by the mistaken execution of a valid search warrant on the wrong premises. With respect to a claim of excessive force, the same standard of reasonableness at the moment applies: "Not every push or shove, even if it may later seem unnecessary in the peace of a judge's chamber," violates the Fourth Amendment. The calculus of reasonableness must embody allowance for the fact that police officers are often forced to make split-second judgements—in circumstances that are tense, uncertain, and rapidly evolving—about the amount of force that is necessary in a particular situation. [Citations omitted.]

☐ NOTES

1. *Crime Control Digest,* March 13, 1989, at 1.
2. *Crime Control Digest,* March 19, 1990, at 9.
3. *Crime Control Digest,* May 1, 1989, at 9.
4. *Liability Review,* Spring 1990, at 5.
5. *Crime Control Digest,* January 9, 1989, at 9.
6. *Crime Control Digest,* December 11, 1989, at 10.
7. Taken from R. V. del Carmen, *Civil Liabilities in American Policing* (Englewood Cliffs, NJ: Prentice-Hall, in press), Chapter 1.
8. *Liability Reporter,* October 1987, at 9.
9. *Ibid.* at 12.
10. *Liability Reporter,* September 1987, at 11.
11. *Liability Reporter,* July 1987, at 11.
12. "Sky-High Damage Suits," *U.S. News & World Report,* January 27, 1986, at 35.
13. I. Silver, *Police Civil Liability* (New York: Bender, 1986), at 4–3. This is an excellent book (updated yearly) on the subject of police civil liability, particularly for lawyers and judges.
14. *Ibid.* at 5–7.
15. This section on liability for failure to protect is taken, with modification, from R. V. del Carmen, *Civil Liabilities in American Policing* (Englewood Cliffs, NJ: Prentice-Hall, in press), Chapter 11.
16. A good source of cases on "negligent failure to protect" and the "special relationship" doctrine are the various monthly issues of the *Liability Reporter,* published by the Americans for Effective Law Enforcement. This publication has an annual index of cases, classified according to topics. A number of cases discussed in this chapter first came to my attention through this publication.
17. This section on the good faith defense is taken, with modification, from R. V. del Carmen, *Civil Liabilities in American Policing* (Englewood Cliffs, NJ: Prentice-Hall, in press), Chapter 5.
18. See Silver, note 13, at 7–5.
19. *Ibid.,* at 1–17
20. *The Houston Chronicle,* January 29, 1984, at 31.
21. *The New York Times,* February 20, 1985, at B1.

APPENDIX A

GUIDE TO CASE CITATIONS
IN THIS TEXT

For readers unfamiliar with legal citation, the following provides guidance for the citations used in this text:

U.S.   *United States Reports*—The official source of U.S. Supreme Court decisions; published by the U.S. government; reports only Supreme Court cases.

S.Ct.   *Supreme Court Reporter*—Reports U.S. Supreme Court decisions; published by the West Publishing Company, a private publisher.

CrL   *Criminal Law Reporter*—Reports U.S. Supreme Court decisions; published by the Bureau of National Affairs, Inc., a private publisher.

L.W.   *United States Law Week*—Reports U.S. Supreme Court decisions; published by the Bureau of National Affairs, Inc., a private publisher.

F.2d   *Federal Reports,* Second Series. Reports Federal Court of Appeals (13 circuits) decisions; published by West Publishing Company.

P.2d   *Pacific Reporter,* Second Series. Reports state court decisions in the Pacific states. The Pacific Reporter is one of seven "regional reporters" that publish state court cases. The other six reporters are *Atlantic Reporter* (A), *North Eastern Reporter* (N.E.), *North Western Reporter* (N.W.), *South Eastern Reporter* (S.E.), *Southern Reporter* (S), and *South Western Reporter* (S.W.). Published by West Publishing Company.

Cal Rptr   *California Reporter*—Publishes California state court appellate-level cases. The various states have a state reporter series like the *California Reporter.*

Illustrations:

- Miranda v. Arizona, 384 U.S. 436 (1966)—This case is found in volume 384 of *United States Reports,* starting on page 436 (and going on for however many pages) and was decided in 1966.
- Miranda v. Arizona, 86 S.Ct. 1602 (1966)—Miranda v. Arizona is also found in volume 86 of *Supreme Court Reporter,* starting on page 1602.
- Alabama v. White, 58 L.W. 4747 (1990)—This case is found in volume 58 of *United States Law Week,* starting on page 4747, and was decided in 1990.
- United States v. Bok, 188 F.2d 1019 (DC Cir. 1951)—This case is found in

volume 188 of *Federal Reports,* Second Series, starting on page 1019, and
was decided by the District of Columbia Federal Court of Appeals in 1951.

- United States v. Davis, 482 F.2d 893 (9th Cir. 1973)—This case is found in
volume 482 of *Federal Reports,* Second Series, starting on page 893, and
was decided by the Ninth Circuit Court of Appeals in 1973.

- Peterson v. City of Long Beach, 155 Cal Rptr 360 (1979)—This case is found
in volume 155 of *California Reporter,* starting on page 360, and was decided
by a state appeals court in California in 1979.

GUIDE TO CASE BRIEFING

Case briefs help the reader to understand court cases better and are used extensively as a learning tool in law schools and in the practice of law. Students read a case, take it apart into classified segments, and then reassemble it in a more concise and organized form.

In order to familiarize students with the basics of case briefing, a sample case is presented here. It must be stressed that there are various ways to brief cases, usually depending on what the reader or instructor considers important. For example, some instructors discuss only the court's majority opinion (what the majority of the justices said in the case), while others go into concurring opinions (opinions agreeing with the majority's conclusion but using a different legal reasoning) and dissenting opinions (opinions disagreeing with the majority's conclusion). What follows is perhaps the simplest way to brief a case.

The basic elements of a case brief are

1. Name of the case
2. Citation (where the case can be found)
3. Date decided
4. Facts of the case
5. Main issue in the case
6. Decision of the court
7. Principle of law in the case

Example: The Case of MIRANDA V. ARIZONA

1. NAME OF THE CASE: MIRANDA V. ARIZONA

2. CITATION: 384 U.S. 486

3. DATE DECIDED: 1966

   Note: In your brief, the preceding elements go in this order: Miranda v. Arizona, 384 U.S. 486 (1966).

4. FACTS OF THE CASE: Ernesto Miranda was arrested at his home and taken to the police station in Phoenix, Arizona, where he was interrogated by two police officers for two hours. He was not advised of his right to remain silent or of his right to an attorney. Miranda signed a written confession and was later convicted of kidnapping and rape. He appealed his conviction to the U.S. Supreme Court,

stating that the evidence against him was obtained in violation of his constitutional right against self-incrimination and therefore should not have been admitted in court.

Note: The FACTS OF THE CASE can be too detailed or too scanty, both of which are bad. In general, be guided by this question: "What minimum facts must I include in my brief so that a person who has not read the whole case (as I have) will still understand it?" That amount of detail is for you to decide—you must judge what facts are important or unimportant.

5. MAIN ISSUE IN THE CASE: Are statements made by suspects during custodial interrogation—where the suspect has not been advised of his or her right to remain silent or to have an attorney—admissible as evidence in court during the trial?

Note: The ISSUE statement must always be in question form, as here. Be sure that your issue statement is neither too narrow (as to be applicable only to the peculiar facts of that case) or too general (as to apply to every case remotely similar in facts), so that it is useless. Also, some cases have more than one issue.

6. DECISION OF THE COURT: The conviction of the accused, Miranda, was reversed and the case was sent back to trial court for new trial without using the evidence that was illegally obtained.

Note: The DECISION OF THE COURT answers the following questions: Did the Supreme Court affirm, reverse, or modify the decision of the immediate lower court where the case came from, and what happened to the case?

7. PRINCIPLE OF LAW IN THE CASE: When a suspect is taken into custody or otherwise deprived of his or her freedom in a significant way, the suspect must be given the following warnings:

   a. You have the right to remain silent.
   b. Anything you say can be used against you in a court of law.
   c. You have a right to the presence of an attorney.
   d. If you cannot afford an attorney, one will be appointed for you by the state.

If these warnings are not given, any evidence obtained by the police cannot be admitted in court during the trial because it has been obtained in violation of a suspect's constitutional right against self-incrimination.

Note: Most cases do not have a PRINCIPLE OF LAW section as lengthy as this. You must, however, be able to state in brief, exact, clear language what the courts said. In most cases, you can pick the PRINCIPLE out from the decision itself, particularly toward the end of the court decision.

The PRINCIPLE OF LAW (otherwise known as *doctrine* or *ruling*) is the most important part of the case because it states the rule of law as promulgated by the Court, such rule of law being applicable to all similar cases to be decided by state and federal courts in the future. It therefore sets a *precedent* by which similar cases in the future are to be decided.

AMENDMENTS I–XV TO THE CONSTITUTION OF THE UNITED STATES OF AMERICA

AMENDMENT I

Congress shall make no law respecting an establishment of religion, or prohibiting the free exercise thereof; or abridging the freedom of speech, or of the press; or the right of the people peaceably to assemble, and to petition the government for a redress of grievances.

AMENDMENT II

A well-regulated militia, being necessary to the security of a free state, the right of the people to keep and bear arms, shall not be infringed.

AMENDMENT III

No soldier shall, in time of peace be quartered in any house, without the consent of the owner, nor in time of war, but in a manner to be prescribed by law.

AMENDMENT IV

The right of the people to be secure in their persons, houses, papers, and effects, against unreasonable searches and seizures, shall not be violated, and no warrants shall issue, but upon probable cause, supported by oath or affirmation, and particularly describing the place to be searched, and the persons or things to be seized.

AMENDMENT V

No person shall be held to answer for a capital, or otherwise infamous crime, unless on a presentment or indictment of a grand jury, except in cases arising in the land or naval forces, or in the militia, when in actual service in time of war or public danger; nor shall any person be subject for the same offense to be twice put in jeopardy of life or limb; nor shall be compelled in any criminal case to be a witness against himself, nor be deprived of life, liberty, or property, without due process of law; nor shall private property be taken for public use, without just compensation.

AMENDMENT VI

In all criminal prosecutions, the accused shall enjoy the right to a speedy and public trial, by an impartial jury of the state and district wherein the crime shall have been committed, which district shall have been previously ascertained by law, and to be informed of the nature and cause of the accusation; to be confronted with the witness against him; to have compulsory process for obtaining witnesses in his favor, and to have the assistance of counsel for his defense.

AMENDMENT VII

In suits at common law, where the value in controversy shall exceed twenty dollars, the right of trial by jury shall be preserved, and no fact tried by a jury, shall be otherwise reexamined in any court of the United States, than according to the rules of the common law.

AMENDMENT VIII

Excessive bail shall not be required, nor excessive fines imposed, nor cruel and unusual punishments inflicted.

AMENDMENT IX

The enumeration in the Constitution, of certain rights, shall not be construed to deny or disparage others retained by the people.

AMENDMENT X

The powers not delegated to the United States by the Constitution, nor prohibited by it to the states, are reserved to the states respectively, or to the people.

AMENDMENT XI

The judicial power of the United States shall not be construed to extend to any suit in law or equity, commenced or prosecuted against one of the United States by citizens of another state, or by citizens or subjects of any foreign states.

AMENDMENT XII

The electors shall meet in their respective states and vote by ballot for president and vice-president, one of whom, at least, shall not be an inhabitant of the same state with themselves; they shall name in their ballots the person voted for as president, and in distinct ballots the person voted for as vice-president, and they shall make distinct lists of all persons voted for as president, and of all persons voted for as vice-president, and of the number of votes for each, which lists they shall sign and certify, and transmit sealed to the seat of the government of the United States, directed to the president of the Senate;—the president of the Senate shall, in the presence of Senate and House of Representatives, open all the certificates and the votes shall then be counted;—the person having the greatest number of votes for president, shall be the president, if such number be a majority of the whole number of electors appointed;

and if no person have such majority, then from the persons having the highest numbers not exceeding three on the list of those voted for as president, the House of Representatives shall choose immediately, by ballot, the president. But in choosing the president, the votes shall be taken by states, the representation from each state having one vote; a quorum for this purpose shall consist of a member or members from two-thirds of the states, and a majority of all the states shall be necessary to a choice. And if the House of Representatives shall not choose a president whenever the right of choice shall devolve upon them, *before the fourth day of March next following,*[1] then the vice-president shall act as president, as in the case of the death or other constitutional disability of the president. The person having the greatest number of votes as vice-president shall be the vice-president, if such number be a majority of the whole number of electors appointed, and if no person have a majority, then from the two highest numbers on the list, the Senate shall choose the vice-president; a quorum for the purpose shall consist of two-thirds of the whole number of senators, and a majority of the whole number shall be necessary to a choice. But no person constitutionally ineligible to the office of president shall be eligible to that of vice-president of the United States.

AMENDMENT XIII

Section 1. Neither slavery nor involuntary servitude, except as a punishment for crime whereof the party shall have been duly convicted, shall exist within the United States, or any place subject to their jurisdiction.

Section 2. Congress shall have the power to enforce this article by appropriate legislation.

AMENDMENT XIV

Section 1. All persons born or naturalized in the United States, and subject to the jurisdiction thereof, are citizens of the United States and the state wherein they reside. No state shall make or enforce any law which shall abridge the privileges or immunities of citizens of the United States; nor shall any state deprive any person of life, liberty, or property, without due process of law; nor deny to any person within its jurisdiction the equal protection of the laws.

Section 2. Representatives shall be apportioned among the several states according to their respective numbers, counting the whole number of persons in each state, excluding Indians not taxed. But when the right to vote at any election for the choice of electors for president and vice-president of the United States, representatives in Congress, the executive and judicial officers of a state, or the members of the legislature thereof, is denied to any of the male inhabitants of such state, being twenty-one years of age, and citizens of the United States, or in any way abridged, except for participation in rebellion, or other crime, the basis of representation therein shall be

---

[1]Altered by the Twentieth Amendment.

reduced in the proportion which the number of such male citizens shall bear to the whole number of male citizens twenty-one years of age in such state.

Section 3.   No person shall be a senator or representative in Congress, or elector of president and vice-president, or hold any office, civil or military, under the United States, or under any state, who, having previously taken an oath, as a member of Congress, or as an officer of the United States, or as a member of any state legislature, or as an executive or judicial officer of any state, to support the Constitution of the United States, shall have engaged in insurrection or rebellion against the same, or given aid or comfort to the enemies thereof. But Congress may by a vote of two-thirds of each house, remove such disability.

Section 4.   The validity of the public debt of the United States, authorized by law, including debts incurred for payment of pensions and bounties for services in suppressing insurrection or rebellion, shall be questioned. But neither the United States nor any state shall assume or pay any debt or obligation incurred in aid of insurrection or rebellion against the United States, or any claim for the loss or emancipation of any slave; but all such debts, obligations, and claims shall be held illegal and void.

Section 5.   The Congress shall have power to enforce, by appropriate legislation, the provisions of this article.

AMENDMENT XV

Section 1.   The right of citizens of the United States to vote shall not be denied or abridged by the United States or by any state on account of race, color, or previous condition of servitude.

Section 2.   The Congress shall have power to enforce this article by appropriate legislation.

INDEX

Abandonment:
  defined, 135
  factors determining, 235–236
  intent and, 136
  plain view doctrine compared, 137
  search of abandoned vehicles, 214
  where property is left, 236
Absolute certainty, 89
Accusatory pleadings, 32
Acquittal:
  conviction rates versus, 44
  motion for, 41
Actual seizure, 127–128
Adams v. Williams, 407 U.S. 143, 147 (1972), 95, 105, 115
Ad hoc assigned counsel systems, 340
Administrative searches, 182
Admissions:
  confession distinguished, 281
  hearsay exception for, 373
  voluntary admission, 281–284
Adverse spousal testimony, 379–380
Affirmations, 164–166
Aguilar v. Texas, 378 U.S. 108 (1964), 85–86, 92
Airport searches, 178
Alabama v. Smith, 57 L.W. 4626 (1989), 407, 422
Alabama v. White, 58 L.W. 4747 (1990), 104, 105, 115
Alimentary canal smuggling, 111
Allocution, right to, 396
Amendments to Constitution, 11–13, 466–469
American Law Institute Test for insanity, 348–349
Anderson v. Creighton, 483 U.S. 635 (1987), 443, 456
Announcement:
  of arrest, 132
  and search warrants, 169
Anticipatory search warrants, 170–171
Apartment houses, open fields doctrine and, 232
Apodaca v. Oregon, 406 U.S. 404 (1972), 43, 49, 51–52
Appeals, 45, 414–416
  appellate courts, 5
  death penalty appeals, 404–405
  double jeopardy waived by, 345
  habeas corpus distinguished, 417
  Rule of Four, 414–415
Appearance:
  after arrest, 26–27
  before magistrate, 141
Appellate courts, 5
Argersinger v. Hamlin, 407 U.S. 25 (1972), 341, 356
Argumentative questions to witnesses, 368
Arizona v. Hicks, 480 U.S. 321 (1987), 227, 247
Arizona v. Mauro, 481 U.S. 520 (1987), 297, 311
Arizona v. Roberson, 108 S.CT. 2093 (1988), 302, 311
Arraignment, 34–35
  right to counsel invoked at, 303
  on warrant, 26
Arrest, 121–159 (*see also* Arrest warrants; Search and seizure; Warrantless arrests)
  actual seizure, 127–128
  announcement requirement, 132
  appearance after, 26–27
  authority for, 127
  bench warrants for, 133
  capias for, 133
  citation for, 26, 133

Arrest *(continued)*
  citizen's arrest, 136
  constructive seizure, 128
  crimes cleared by, 124
  defined, 123–124
  disposition of prisoner after, 140–141
  elements of, 124–128
  exclusionary rule where illegal arrest, 66
  false arrest, 432–433
  force during, 141–149
  handcuffs, use of, 138–139
  immediate control of arrested person, search of area in, 137–138
  intention to arrest, 124–127
  invalid arrest, 9, 11
  list of offenses and, 125
  monitoring arrested person, 139
  place of detention, search of arrestee at, 140
  postarrest procedure, 136–140
  probable cause requirements, 83
  searches incident to lawful arrest exception, 171–172
  search of detainees, 177
  stop and frisk distinguished, 108–109
  summons for, 133
  types of, 128–136
  understanding of individual, 128
  after vehicle stops and searches, 205
  Vermont arrest/custody report, 130
Arrest warrants, 25–26
  contents of, 131
  defined, 128
  example of, 129
  issuance of, 128–131
  probable cause with, 83–84
  service of, 131–132
  Vermont arrest/custody report, 130
Ashcraft v. Tennessee, 322 U.S. 143 (1944), 282, 311
Assault and battery liability, 434
Assembly, freedom of, 11–12
Assigned counsel systems, 340
Associate Justices, 4
Assumptions in questions to witnesses, 368
Attorney–client privilege, 378–379
Attorney's Fees Act of 1976, 440
Attorneys (*see also* Right to counsel):
  attorney–client privilege, 378–379
  line-ups, role during, 263–264
  pretrial publicity and, 330
Atwell v. United States, 414 F.2d 136 (1969), 232, 247
Au Yi Lau v. United States INS. 445 F.2d 217 at 223 (9th Cir.), 110, 115
Automobile exception, 198–199
Automobiles, *see* Motor vehicles; Vehicle stops and searches

Bail, 13
  defined, 27
  financial bond options, 30
Baldus study, 404
Baldwin v. New York, 399 U.S. 66 (1970), 21, 327, 356
Ballew v. Georgia, 435 U.S. 223 (1978), 44, 49, 325, 356
Balloon swallowing smuggling, 111
Baltimore City Department of Social Services v. Bouknight, 46 CrL 2096 (1990), 334, 356
Barber v. Page, 390 U.S. 719 (1968), 375, 386